# *The Press Speaks . . .*



Direct mail is the source of foreclosure wizard's power. ***— San Francisco Examiner***

He buys the properties fast and cheap, often 20 to 30 percent below their market value. Then he quickly resells them at wholesale prices. It works this way: He buys a piece of property appraised at $150,000 for $110,000. He then turns around and resells it for $120,000. He gets $10,000 profit, and the buyer gets $30,000 worth of equity. ***— Chicago Tribune***

In less than three years, he has become one of California's largest buyers of foreclosure properties. ***— Bucks County Courier Times, Pennsylvania***

Few people know how to buy foreclosure properties and fewer still are successful at it. Ted Thomas is one of the few who knows how and has succeeded. ***— Inland Valley Daily Bulletin, Upland, California***

His vehicle has been shrewd use of a direct mail system that lets him buy before a formal foreclosure takes place on the county courthouse steps. ***— Naples Daily News, Naples, Florida***

If I get a house this afternoon, I'll try and get it sold wholesale in the next two weeks. (The buyers) have an instant profit the day they buy it. ***— St. Louis Post-Dispatch, St. Louis, Missouri***

Although Thomas' written format doesn't allow him to answer questions, the book does allow him to explore the material in depth, and readers can absorb its information at their own pace. ***— The Inter-City Express, Oakland, California***

Ted Thomas is one of the few who knows how and has succeeded. ***— Marietta Daily Journal, Marietta, Georgia***

System is a win, win, win situation, because everybody involved benefits. ***— Seattle Daily Journal of Commerce***

This is one of the BEST business opportunities books I have seen in a DECADE! ***— Business Opportunities Digest***

It is a system where a person willing to work dilligently could earn himself from $10,000 to $30,000 each month on a regular basis. ***— The Real Estate Digest***

# *The Experts Agree . . .*

The Thomas System is absolutely THE ideal real estate program for our times becauseit doesn't depend on tax shelter benefits, inflation, appreciation, income, or management skills, and it's ideal during a recession. It's a unique opportunity and what's more, it meets a growing demand. **— Howard J. Ruff**
**Publisher, *The Ruff Times***

Foreclosures are on the rise. However, there is a silver lining. Real estate investors are in perhaps the best position to help people avoid foreclosure and make good money at the same time. It's a true win/win.
**— Mark O. Haroldsen**
**Publisher, *Financial Freedom Report***

When it comes to real estate foreclosures, Ted Thomas has developed the best low-risk, high-potential investment techniques available anywhere. His book is absolutely indispensable. **— Albert Lowry**
**Best Selling Author**

Ted's book is packed with hundreds of tips, techniques, and strategies that can help you make the most of foreclosure buying. Anyone who begins a real estate career should read this book.
**— Melvin Powers, Author**
***How To Get Rich in Mail Order***

Ted Thomas has perfected a truly ingenious cash-flow system. A proof positive, I tested this out myself and I pulled in $22,735 on my first deal. Highly recommended. **— Mark Nolan, President and Founder**
**The Financial Freedom Foundation**

Still today, real estate is the arena of the greatest opportunity for entrepreneurs. Ted Thomas' book is full of profitable hands-on information as only a real world practitioner could provide.
**— Joe Mancuso, Founder**
**Center for Entrepreneurial Management**

With this book you can quickly learn and master the secrets to "Foreclosure Profits." This is the bsst money-making information ever published on this profitable subject. **— Russ von Hoelscher**
**Marketing and Small Business Expert**

# *Read What Others Are Saying . . .*

Whole chapters explore every major problem, and every chapter is jam packed with useful and practical assistance coupled with Ted's phenomenal success and extremely professional approach to purchasing foreclosure properties. I am confident that this book will pay for itself a hundred times over.
— **Barry A. Adams**, Owner, Editor & Publisher, L & A Real Estate Publications, Inc.

A great guide to show how to create that "win-win" situation for all in the foreclosure market. An absolute necessity for your library.
**— Sally C. Aldrich**

This is *the book* on distressed property! Ted Thomas gives a comprehensive, well-tested sytem that can help you save time and make more money.
**— James B. Anderson, Ph.D.**

*Foreclosure Profits* is must reading for anyone in real estate — or anyone wanting to get into real estate.
— **Francis L. Bitney,** Author, How to Buy Recreational Land for Profit

It would be hard not to succeed in this field if you do what Ted Thomas says in *Your Complete Guide to Foreclosure Profits.*
— **Gordon Burgett,** Author, *Empire Building by Writing and Speaking*

A basic clear and thorough explanatioin of the steps required to succeed. "HOT TIPS" sample materials and case studies for further help.
— **Don Camp,** President, World Entertainment Photo

Ted Thomas' *Foreclosure Profits* is an excellent road map for those who wish to work in the foreclosure arena. Ted's methodical approach to the subject is not onlyrealistic but quite complete. I would highhly recommend this book to professionals who wish to be knowledgeable in the acquisition of distressed properties.
— **Philip Deutscher,** Real Estate Broker

Ted Thomas is one lean mean investing machine. His easy-to-follow easy-to-succeed system lays it all on the line so virtually ANYONE can prosper. This book is PROFIT-PACKED. The Thomas System works...to the tune of $7,500 and more in profits almost every single deal.
— **Richard E. Dewberry,** Publisher, *The Real Estate Digest*

If you want to earn a lot of money in real estate and you need an easy-to-follow map toward your goal, it's in your hands. Read this step-by-step guide and you will have an answer to how real dollars are made in foreclosure real estate.
— **Thomas T. Gardner,** "Thomas System" Graduate

Ted Thomas' book is fantastic. Very practical.
**— Julie Hayes**

The Ted Thomas' system works! I have watched and listened as Ted has experimented and developed his system since 1987. He has incurred the expensive "learning curve" mistakes for you.
**— John L. Herrick**

Ted, your new book is brilliant! It's a clear, step-by-step explanation of how anyone can succeed in the foreclosure field. I am a novice when it comes to real estate. After reading your book, I'm convinced and I could make a million (or much, much more) using your system.
**— Ken Kerr**

You can make the seller smile when you go the second mile for him. You can count on Ted Thomas when he makes a promise.
**— Don Joss, Investor**

# Foreclosure Gold Mining

## Your Illustrated Guide

## High Profit, Low Risk Real Estate for the 90's

Ted Thomas
New Growth Financial
Danville, California

**Ted Thomas, New Growth Financial**
**P. O. Box 490**
**Danville, California 94526-0490**



Cover and book design by
Robert Howard Graphic Design

Edited by Frances P. Bowles

Third Printing 1994.

Printed in the United States of America

10 9 8 7 6 5 4

ISBN 0-9623701-7-7

***This book is dedicated to my wife Pamela,***
***whose world was crushed by fate.***
***She bravely fought the battle with cancer and won.***
***Although her own body was ravaged by cancer, she always had***
***a little extra encouragement to pass on to me.***
***This book would never have reached your hands without***
***her encouragement, faith, and everlasting love.***

# CONTENTS

# PREFACE

**H**ow did I get into publishing this book? Several years ago, while I was going through a messy business failure (bankruptcy), I realized that I needed a business that did not require thousands of start-up dollars, lots of employees, huge, expensive office facilities, or lots of wheeling and dealing. I searched for years and investigated franchising, multilevel marketing, real estate brokerage, restaurants, stock brokerage, employment as a commercial pilot, import/export ventures, and finally the fast food industry. This searching taught me a great deal. First and foremost, in order to be successful, I obviously needed a proven system. That makes sense, but I found out these systems really cost. Whether it is a haircare franchise or a fast food concession, you pay for the privilege. For example, in 1991, Subway Sandwich shops are the fastest growing franchise and the cost of entry is $45,000 — just for the franchise agreement. Then you must add money for the shop equipment and furnishings, marketing, advertising, and training. Wow! Big bucks! A guy could have a bundle invested very quickly and no guarantee that he has picked the right corner to do business in.

In 1988 and 1989 the real estate market went into a frenzy. Prices did not just sky rocket, they went into the stratosphere. Unbelievable! The Boston market went up by 20 percent, San Francisco by 25 percent. It was a nationwide phenomenon. Everyone was trying to get on the bandwagon. It looked as if it would never end and, if you were not part of it, you felt left out.

Sometimes when things are going in one direction, it pays to be aware of the other direction. While the real estate market, according to the news media, was taking off, the *hidden market,* although completely different, was also taking off.

The *hidden market?* Hidden only because no one was looking. In almost every small or large county in the United States, government officials were posting record numbers of foreclosures, the results of defaulted mortgages, Sheriff's Sales, judicial actions between mortgagees and mortgagors, Trustee's Sales, and lawsuits between homeowners and banks. Foreclosure had reached unprecedented levels. I suddenly realized that right under my nose was a legal, profitable, and very exciting business that did not require big bucks to begin with.

The business could be learned on paper, tested, and even practiced before I invested my hard-earned dollars. Then I could settle down and begin systematically making money. I started by doing the things you will learn about by reading this book; making mistakes at first and ultimately developing a system. What I did was carefully and honestly study my own experiences, analyzing what had contributed to my failures and what had contributed to my successes. Then I pieced together an overall strategy and system based on those successes and undertakings that had generated positive results. Although over time I have made some minor changes, the basic strategies are the same and you will find them easily learned.

This is a recession-proof business. In the best and in the worst real estate markets, you will see Sheriff's Sale and Trustee's Sale properties sell at public auction; sometimes for as low as 50 percent of market value. Not all of them, of course, but enough to make it very interesting for those who learn how to take advantage of the system.

Wouldn't it be nice if you could buy the property *before* the Sheriff's or Trustee's sale? That would give you a head-start so you could beat the competition. It would allow you to inspect the property for damage caused by termites or roof leaks or maybe reveal a possible deteriorating foundation. When you buy before the auction you can bargain with the owner for a lower price. Prices usually come down rapidly as the public auction date approaches. After a number of experiments, I have figured out how to work in this *hidden market*.

This book gives the basic rules of how to buy and sell all types of foreclosure properties. Your path to success has been carefully outlined. This volume should be viewed as a guide, however, not as the ultimate authority. It is impossible to cover all the contingencies, conditions, and circumstances for every situation that one might encounter. My intent is provide a practical and easy-to-use guide that introduces the subject and contains enough information to enable you to succeed.

I hope you enjoy this book and look forward to hearing from you about your experiences. If you purchase this book from someone other than myself, send me a note with your address and I will keep you apprised of new developments.

### *Disclaimer*

Information contained in *Foreclosure Goldmining* has been carefully compiled from sources believed reliable, but the accuracy of the information is not guaranteed. If you need legal or accounting advice, please consult a professional in that field.

Chapter 1

# The Street-Smart Way to Buy Real Estate Foreclosures

## *Three Universal Steps Revealed*

**S**uccess in the business of purchasing distressed property is often a matter of how good you are at helping others out of trouble. This means that you must understand the homeowner's needs and wants. In this chapter you will learn:

- About the three stages of the foreclosure property markets.
- What a foreclosure is.
- Advantages and disadvantages of buying before the Trustee's/Sheriff's Sale.
- The secret of getting a postponement for that desperate seller who calls hours before the Trustee's Sale.
- The millionaire's three-letter word for success.

Distressed property sales fall into three markets, depending on the particular stage of the foreclosure process: pre-foreclosure, Trustee's/Sheriff's Sales, and Real Estate Owned (REOs). You can make money in all three markets.

You can buy from the property owner before the foreclosure auction, while the owner is in default. You can buy from the Trustee or Sheriff at the Trustee's/Sheriff's Sale, which is an auction. You can buy from the lender who has foreclosed and now has the property, the REOs, in his inventory. This book deals chiefly with the purchase of property during the time that the loan is in default, but before it has been foreclosed/auctioned. The procedures involved in buying at Trustee's/Sheriff's Sales are considered in Chapter 13, and the requirements for buying REOs are discussed in Chapter 12.

## REASONS FOR FORECLOSURE

Foreclosure properties have always been available in large numbers. Foreclosures take place all over the country in good economic times as well as in bad, in wealthy areas as well as in poor areas. Economic change does not restrict itself to just the poor: wealthy people, too, get divorced and run up debts. However, only those few individuals who have the free time, energy, and commitment to research Notices of Default (NODs) and Trustee's/Sheriff's Sale notices filed at the county recorder's office will know where to find the foreclosed properties, when the Trustee's/Sheriff's Sales are scheduled, and how to follow up and whom to contact.

### Divorce

Divorce is the most common reason for foreclosure. According to government statistics, approximately 50% of all married women work full-time. This extra income is significant, especially if both incomes were needed to purchase the house in which the couple lived. With half of all marriages ending in divorce, you can easily see that we will continue to have foreclosure problems in the future. With a divorce reducing the household income to that of one person, there is usually insufficient income to support the same life-style and make payments on the house.

The divorce may be clean or it may be messy but often creates resentment and vindictiveness. If cool heads prevail, the home can be sold without too big a loss. But if the partners begin to fight, no one makes the house payment. Maybe they are only trying to get even, but getting even probably means foreclosure and lost equity.

### Unemployment

We all have friends, or neighbors, or relatives who have lost their jobs. Unemployment is no fun, not just because of the loss of income but also because of the loss of self-esteem. As the country changes from a labor/manufacturing economy to a service economy and computers change the ways in which we work, jobs will disappear; many more people will be displaced and require retraining.

The oil business is a good example of this change. Cities such as Houston and Denver in the mid-eighties saw dramatic changes in the work force. These changes in turn led to widespread foreclosures throughout the area. It is not uncommon to see half-page advertisements in the *Wall Street Journal* for 100 homes for sale, all foreclosures. Small towns that provide the work force for major factories often see numerous foreclosures immediately after a layoff or slowdown in the local industry. When major industries such as automobiles, oil, and aerospace go through changes in policy, direction, or normal business cycles you'll find the number of foreclosures rising soon after.

### Medical Problems

Medical bills must be paid or the treatment stops. Hospital and doctor's bills compete with the house payments. When you are sick and you have no insurance, the situation can get out of control very quickly. Sickness or disability usually precedes the loss of work. Medical problems are thus another of the prime reasons for foreclosure. The homeowner confronted with loss of income and large bills from doctors and hospitals is in deep trouble.

### Death

From time to time foreclosures will be a result of death. Without the breadwinner, who will pay the bills? If insurance is not forthcoming and friends and relatives cannot or will not make the payments, foreclosure is inevitable.

### Balloon Payments

Balloon payments can trigger a foreclosure when they come due if the owner is unable to refinance the property or pay off the debt. The value of the property may have fallen; interest rates may be too high for the owner to qualify for another loan; or the owner may simply not be able to afford it. If the property has not appreciated as expected, the owner must sell or face foreclosure. Most prospective sellers wait until the last possible date and then find themselves in foreclosure. They're always hoping that a miracle will come along and save them.

## MAKING MONEY WHILE HELPING OTHERS OUT OF TROUBLE

### Some Basic Questions and Answers for First-Time Foreclosure Buyers

*Do you live in a mortgage or trust deed state?*

If you are located in a state that uses the mortgage as a loan/security instrument, a judicial foreclosure is the legal action that takes place. Simple stated, the party borrowing the money is named the mortgagor, and the party lending the money is the mortgagee. If the borrowing party (mortgagor) fails to make payments as promised, the lender (mortgagee) must file a complaint (lawsuit) with a court to recover the property. The property is normally pledged as security for the loan, an action called hypothecation. The action the lender/mortgagee takes to recover the security (home) is a judicial/legal action and is usually initiated by an attorney or some other qualified party.

Most foreclosure sales are actually auctions, formally called Trustee's/Sheriff's Sales. In a trust deed state, when a property owner has not honored his mortgage commitment or agreement the lender can order the Trustee (a third and neutral party between the lender and borrower) to sell the property at a public auction. In a mortgage state, the court orders the Sheriff to auction the property. If you bid at the auction for more than the sum owed on the property, the Sheriff or Trustee will usually accept your bid. Keep in mind that mortgage lenders are in the finance business, not the real estate business. They would sooner recover their financial commitment (get the money back so that they can lend it out again) than hold out for a profit on the real estate.

*Who are the winners and the losers at foreclosure sales? Isn't the foreclosure buyer taking advantage of someone else?*

If you buy from the owner before the sale or auction, you can offer the owner some money. Although this sum will probably be less than the full market value of the property, it will be more than he or she would get at the auction because the lender will accept whatever bid will give him (the lender) the most money. In order to dispose of the property, the lender may accept a bid that does not cover the entire amount outstanding on the loan, having decided that he can write off at least part as a bad debt. Your pre-auction offer benefits the owner directly. Keep in mind that you didn't create the problems of the troubled property seller. Because the seller stands to gain little or nothing from the Trustee's/Sheriff's Sale, you are not taking advantage of him or her.

*Is it possible to save money at the foreclosure sale?*

Yes, foreclosure sales (Trustee's/Sheriff's Sales) can save you money. A knowledge of property values is especially important. Properties at these sales are sold at discounts from the retail market. But the properties are also sold on an "as is" basis. Pay close attention, because the 30% to 50% you may have saved could easily be spent on repairing a deteriorating roof, crumbling foundation, or termite damage before you can re-sell the property.

*What price should I bid?*

That is easy! Bid just enough to buy the property but no more than it is worth. Keep in mind you will have holding costs, fix-up and rehabilitation costs, and selling costs before you can recover your investment.

*Should I buy from the owner before the sale or would it be less complicated to buy after the foreclosure sale?*

Both methods have their advantages. The properties and the circumstances will be different for every sale. If you are buying before the Trustee's/Sheriff's Sale, you will be able to visit, inspect, and evaluate the property first. If you are buying at an auction, you will not become involved with the emotions of the sellers, you will need few or no negotiation skills, and there will be very little legal hassle.

*Don't banks and savings and loans sell properties?*

Yes, these bank-owned properties are called REOs or Real Estate Owned. The banks will sell these properties to a qualified buyer; however, you should plan to pay very close attention to market price. The banks rarely feel obligated to just dump the properties at low prices. See Chapter 12 for more information on REOs.

*Do the auction sales require cash?*

Depending on the state, most Trustee's/Sheriff's Sales will require that the bidders qualify before the sale. To qualify, you must show your cash or the equivalent up to the amount you intend to bid, usually in the form of a cashier's check. Each state is different, so visit the auction sale in your county, watch how it works, and ask questions. The County Recorder or Sheriff will provide you with a rule or procedure book or qualification standards (see Appendix C).

*Will all the properties at the Trustee's / Sheriff's Sale be sold "as is"?*

Yes. Some banks and savings and loans associations will allow you to visit the properties before the sale. Take advantage of this opportunity. Ask professional structural engineers, termite contractors, and roofing experts to accompany you on such tours.

*What are the "outstanding loans and judgments"?*

Such debts constitute your biggest risk when buying before the Trustee's/Sheriff's Sale. All liens, loans, and judgments against the property will be recorded at the County Recorder's Office of the county in which the property is located. You can research the county records yourself. In addition, most title companies maintain copies of the county records. If you have a close relationship with a title company, it is possible the company will allow you to use its records to research the title and any possible liens or encumbrances.

*Is it possible to get rich buying foreclosures?*

It is up to you! Like most of the other ways to make a great deal of money, it takes work and talent, lots of education (failures), and a little luck. Mostly you need knowledge and dedication or perseverance. The disappointments will exceed the rewards during the learning (failure) period. The profitability is up to you. You can control your destiny through your own efforts.

*How soon can I start making money?*

It depends on your own motivation and desire. Many people make money after less than one month. However, I'd suggest you be prepared to wait ninety days for your first check.

*Can I begin part-time?*

It is probably the best way. While you go through the learning process, you can keep your regular job and build up a reserve of funds to use as fixer-upper funds or purchase money.

*How much money will I need?*

None if you want to borrow from partners, or very little if you are willing to start out small.

## WHAT'S DIFFERENT ABOUT THE FORECLOSURE MARKET?

The Sunday newspaper is a good measure of the real estate market. Literally thousands of homes and properties are listed for sale each week. These advertisements are so lucrative for the newspaper that editors are assigned just to write articles about how great the market is for the developer, the real estate agents and, of course, the buyers. However, they are talking about buyers at retail.

### Different

Foreclosure buyers are different. First of all, you won't get wealthy buying homes or properties at retail prices. A general rule of thumb is that property advertised and listed for sale is priced at 110% of its real value. Keep this rule in mind when you read any real estate advertisement. Foreclosure buying is not part of the regular real estate market. You must also understand that only a small percentage of all the properties nationwide will end up in foreclosure. Unless the country is in a deep recession or depression, it is likely that less than 1% of the homes will be in foreclosure. Most buyers check the newspapers and MLS (the broker Multiple Listing Service), which shows the majority of homes that the brokerage currently has for sale county by county) to find properties for sale. Foreclosure buyers check the county records or commercial default listing services (see Chapter 2) to find bargain properties for sale.

### Not the Normal Market

Foreclosure sales are outside of the normal marketplace, and the market for them is dominated by investors who are, or should be, knowledgeable about property values and understand what they are purchasing. Most savvy investors require substantial profits from the sale of foreclosures, and, because they know values and retail sales prices, they don't bid too much at auctions. This is very important to understand. Brokers intentionally whip up a competitive atmosphere around properties — as recently evidenced, for example, in hot retail markets such as San Francisco, Boston, and Seattle — to create a near frenzy of escalating prices that benefits sellers and brokers. Many buyers stop negotiating for their purchases much too early and so pay more than the market values for properties because they are afraid that they will miss the boat. Experienced foreclosure buyers are careful not to bid the prices up: This market is not emotional. Typically, foreclosure buyers will start at 70% and will usually stop bidding and let the amateur take the property if the bidding goes above 80% of market value.

### Profit 25% to 30%

Remember, you're looking for a profit of between 25 and 50%. Time, research, and lots of diligent effort are required to buy successfully at a Trustee's/Sheriff's Sale. Once you have attended a few sales and understand how the process works, much of the mystery and glamor will be gone. As an intelligent investor, you can reduce the risks by doing your homework. Knowing values, understanding the market, estimating repair costs, and confirming your figures will make you a tough competitor in the foreclosure market.

To gain the knowledge you need, be prepared to take the time to understand the foreclosure marketplace. This is not as simple as calling a broker, but it is also not as expensive. Think about buying properties for between 25 and 50% less than the retail asking price. Believe me, it only takes one and you'll be a real estate bargain hunter for a long, long time. Foreclosure properties are worth the effort. First of all, most people would be afraid even to consider buying such properties. After all, it is doing something different and who wants to be different? Don't you dress the same as everyone else at the office? Is your car the same? Do you live in the same model of tract house?

### Unique Market

The foreclosure buyer is unique in many ways. First, he or she must research many properties to find that one profit-maker or ideal candidate. Second, foreclosure purchases require thorough investigation of the County Recorder's records to seek out any undisclosed liens or encumbrances. Third, negotiations with the seller take place in an atmosphere that is much different from normal market sales in terms of the motivation of the seller and the buyer. Traditional real estate sellers have very little motivation, if any, but an owner facing foreclosure is under pressure to make a deal.

The average person wants a bargain property. However, the searching, investigation, and negotiation with the seller might prove to be too much work for the average person. The foreclosure property could well be in a state of disrepair and thus require extra diligence on the part of the foreclosure buyer.

### Equity Purchase

Readers who use an equity purchase contract similar to the one I use will require the seller to make many of the repairs. (Have your attorney read your contract to make sure it complies with the law in your state.) The termite and roof repairs will become the buyer's responsibility after the purchase of the foreclosure. Using professional inspectors and "due diligence" TRAIT reports (refer to Chapter 6) before completing the purchase is of utmost importance. In summary, foreclosure buyers move rapidly but cautiously because they understand the risks and work to manage those risks.

## THE FORECLOSURE MARKET: STAGES IN A PROCESS

The foreclosure market in the USA has three separate submarkets, corresponding to the time when the distressed property is for sale. Each has its advantages and disadvantages for the foreclosure buyer. Some buyers specialize in purchasing during one stage in the foreclosure process, while others will consider purchases during any of the stages, depending on the conditions applicable to the particular property.

### First Stage

The first stage, called pre-foreclosure, lasts from the time a lender begins foreclosure proceedings until the property goes on the block at a Trustee's/Sheriff's Sale.

### Second Stage

The second stage is the Trustee's/Sheriff's Sale itself.

### Third Stage

The third stage begins after the Trustee's/Sheriff's Sale, when the property, having received no bids, reverts to the lender and is then referred to as Real Estate Owned. At each stage you will be buying from a different seller, so you must tailor your approach accordingly. During pre-foreclosure, you are buying from the property owner who is unable to pay the loan; at the Trustee's/Sheriff's Sale you are buying from the Trustee or Sheriff (who is acting on behalf of the lender); you buy REOs from the bank or savings and loan association that made the original loan on the property. This book will help you understand all the steps in the process, but you'll have to decide for yourself which submarket you prefer. I like to work in all three because each offers different advantages.

**PRE-FORECLOSURE: BUYING BEFORE THE TRUSTEE'S/SHERIFF'S SALE**

The principal advantage in buying before foreclosure/auction is the seller's motivation. Usually the property owner would rather sell than be foreclosed upon. However, although owners are motivated to sell, they must be contacted and at times this can prove difficult. Most property owners have been delinquent (in default) for a period of time, so they have received numerous telephone calls from the lender and, in many cases, from collection agencies as well. So don't expect one telephone call to work. You will have to knock on the door.

If you can reach the owner before the foreclosure sale and help solve his or her difficulties, you'll find a motivated seller. Do remember that sellers are under severe stress, so don't expect them to welcome your first call. Persistence will, however, build a small amount of trust that will open the door to negotiation.

### Pre-Foreclosure

Pre-foreclosure buying can be especially lucrative, and the author has had continual success with properties bought before the Trustee's/Sheriff's Sale. To be able to take advantage of these opportunities, you must adhere to the *Foreclosure Consultants Law* in your state without fail. (See pages 14–19 for the text of the California foreclosure law.) Simple and straightforward, the California law appears to be one of the toughest in the country. Such laws specify in detail what you can and cannot do, and violators may be prosecuted and penalized. The penalties for violators appear to be excessive from the standpoint of someone who really is helping the troubled homeowner, who, without the foreclosure buyer, will lose both his home and his equity in the property. The Foreclosure Consultants Law was written to protect the homeowner and is, nevertheless, a good law. It's advantageous to understand the law because, once you learn it and use the proper legal contracts, as this book will teach you, you will have an advantage over your competition. (This, like any other body of law, is rapidly changing, and you should consult an attorney who is versed in this segment of real estate law as it applies to your particular state or area.)

You gain a number of advantages by buying before the sale. You are helping the owner, and your help will be appreciated by the motivated seller who is wise enough to sell and save some dollars to take care of his family. The testimonial on page 74 of Chapter 3 is proof that owners would prefer some money before the sale to having nothing after the Trustee's/Sheriff's Sale.

### Key Advantage

A key advantage of buying before the actual sale is that you get to view the inside of the home and are able to observe and discuss any damage that might require repair before you resell the property. This is an advantage that the buyer at a Trustee's/Sheriff's Sale doesn't enjoy.

An additional advantage in purchasing before the Trustee's/Sheriff's Sale is that you will have time to review the market and appraise the property. Real estate brokers use the Multiple Listing Service almost exclusively to find and evaluate property. The MLS is an excellent tool for comparing local values and prices and comparing neighborhoods and various sections of cities and towns. However, the foreclosure market has no multiple listing service. Foreclosure notices are listed in the legal newspaper, posted at the county courthouse, or published by one of the services that lists Trustee's/Sheriff's Sales, defaults, and REOs. If you follow the contract provisions and appraisal techniques explained in this book, you will not buy a bad property.

### Sheriff's/Trustee's Sale

For example, when you buy before the Trustee's/Sheriff's Sale, you have time to hire a professional to perform a termite inspection. If the home has termite damage, you can further negotiate with the owner for a lower purchase price, and if the owner refuses, you have the right to cancel the contract. You have only wasted time and not spent your money.

You also need less cash to buy from the owner during pre-foreclosure than you would to buy at a Trustee's/Sheriff's Sale. Following is an example of the cash outlay for a typical purchase.

| | |
|---|---|
| House value | $100,000 |
| Loan in default | 60,000 |
| Past-due payments | 4,000 |
| Foreclosure trustee's fees | 1,000 |
| | $ 65,000 |

Let's assume that you negotiate and sign an equity purchase agreement to pay the owner $5,000 in cash. You then pay the back payments of $4,000 plus the foreclosure fees of $1,000 and take over the loan. For a cash outlay of $10,000, you have assumed $60,000 of debt and have a house with a market value of $100,000, that is, you have bought the house for 70% of its value — an excellent purchase.

This should also be a profitable purchase. Even if you had paid more and owned the house for $80,000, you would have made a deal better than any you might have made at the Trustee's/Sheriff's Sale because you didn't have any competitive bidders. And you have used only $10,000 of your cash. If you had purchased the property at the Trustee's/Sheriff's Sale, you would have spent a minimum of $65,000 (the amount of the loan and fees and back payments), in cash. Having to put down so little cash, you can purchase many more distressed properties during pre-foreclosure than you could have if you had been obliged to put the full $65,000 down to buy at the Trustee's Sale. Don't lose sight of your objective: to gain wealth as soon as possible. The ability to purchase numerous properties accelerates your chance of making big profits.

## UNDERSTANDING THE LOAN DOCUMENTS

Pre-foreclosure property may be characterized as one of two types, depending on the type of legal instrument by which the loan was granted. The loan document will be either a deed of trust (trust deed) or a mortgage. The legal requirements for foreclosing on delinquent loans differ, depending on which document is used in your state.

### The Deed of Trust

A deed of trust is a contract by which title to a property is conveyed to a Trustee as security for the repayment of a loan. This contract involves three parties. The *trustor* is the owner who borrows from the lender, or creditor, who is called the *beneficiary*. In order to control the property during the period of the obligation, "bare legal" title is held by the *Trustee* designated in the deed of trust.

If the borrower does not meet the obligations of the promissory note, the lender may initiate foreclosure. If the security document is a deed of trust, foreclosure may be sought through a

Trustee's Sale. If the security document is a mortgage, foreclosure becomes a judicial action and the property will be disposed of at a Sheriff's Sale.

If foreclosure is sought as a trust deed, the beneficiary (the lender) sends a Declaration of Default to the Trustee, who is then instructed to record a Notice of Default in the county in which the property is located. The foreclosure clock starts running when the Notice is recorded: the owner then has three months in which to make the loan current. This is called the *reinstatement period.* At the end of this period, the Notice of Sale is recorded and published once a week for the following three weeks. At the end of this publication period, the Trustee's Sale is held at a location set by the Trustee. The successful bidder or the beneficiary receiving the property at the Trustee's Sale receives a Trustee's deed. Foreclosure using a trust deed normally takes about four months or 111 days in California. An example of this is noted on page 20.

### The Mortgage

A mortgage is a contract by which property in the form of real estate is *hypothecated* (pledged without delivery of title) for the repayment of a loan. This means that the mortgage could very well qualify as the security document for the promissory note offered by the borrower. The mortgage, however, has a number of features that affect the usefulness of the document as a security device should the borrower fail to meet the obligations of the promissory note. In order to understand those features, we must examine the mortgage in some detail.

### Mortgagor/Mortgagee

A mortgage requires interaction between two parties, the borrower (the mortgagor) and the lender (the mortgagee). When the mortgagor borrows money using a mortgage, he does not relinquish title to the property even temporarily, although not all of the obligations of the promissory note have been met. When the borrower defaults, the lender who expects payment must foreclose through a court action. Judicial foreclosure is instituted by the mortgagee's filing of a lawsuit to foreclose. The mortgagor retains the right to reinstate the obligation up to the point of the court decree. This procedure could easily take the mortgagee a year or more. Further complicating the situation in many states is the mortgagor's right of redemption. (Different states have different laws regarding mortgage and trust deed foreclosures. Review your state's legal requirements for foreclosure with your attorney and title company.) Even when the mortgagee has successfully foreclosed on the property by a judicial action, the property owner in many states retains a legal right of redemption. This right may last a very short time, for example, one month, or it may be as long as one year. Under such right-of-redemption rules, the homeowner who lost the home at the foreclosure action is allowed to redeem the property by paying the auction sale price plus interest to the new buyer and then retaking control of the property.

## THE DIFFERENCE BETWEEN THE FORECLOSURE OF A MORTGAGE AND A TRUST DEED

It is important to recognize several differences in the foreclosure processes for deeds of trust and for mortgages. First of all, the original owner of a trust deed retains no rights after the Trustee's Sale, that is, there is no equity right of redemption, as there is with foreclosure of a mortgage. Conversely, the original borrower does not have any further obligations to the lender, who may not pursue the borrower for any deficiency between the amount of money obtained at the Trustee's Sale and the amount owing to the lender if the loan was a purchase money trust deed.

However, if the property is foreclosed as a trust deed and the debt is not a purchase money installment, the beneficiary may pursue the borrower for the difference between the amount owed and the amount collected.

## THE BASIC STEPS OF PRE-FORECLOSURE BUYING

Let's briefly review the methods by which you can help defaulting homeowners solve their problems and receive a substantial reward for doing so. After you have located a potential seller, you must make contact by telephone, by direct mail, or by knocking on the door. Your success rate will improve dramatically if you pursue all three approaches simultaneously. Then you must investigate the seller's problems. When you have found out what he needs, negotiate a purchase of his equity and, finally, sign an equity purchase agreement. Remember: All the parties who signed the original deed, called the grant deed, warrantee deed, or quitclaim deed must sign the equity purchase agreement, unless an original interest has been disposed of.

On pages 21 through 23 of this chapter, you will find a sample of the contract that the author has used successfully to purchase properties prior to the Trustee's Sale. The contract is simple to read and understand and complies with the foreclosure statutes and pertinent sections of the California Civil Code.

### Caution

You must be cautious and especially alert when dealing with the owners, some of whom will waste your time by acting as though they are willing to sell to you. They will invite other foreclosure buyers to bid on your contract. When a person is in default, he or she receives mail from other foreclosure buyers and from lenders who want to lend out even more money. You should therefore expect the owners to be pursuing several alternatives. If they are not happy with your proposal, they will keep looking until the final hour. Plan on this and keep on trying to solve their problems, or you may lose your prospective bargain purchase.

Buying before the sale is easier for you if the owner is running out of time. As you recall from the review of the foreclosure period (graphically shown on page 20), the homeowner has (in California) three months to reinstate the default (bring the payments current) before the start of the twenty-one-day publication period and final Trustee's Sale. If you contact the owner immediately after the default notice is issued, he or she probably won't be motivated to sell. After all, ninety days plus twenty-one days is almost four months, and the miracle the homeowner has been waiting for will certainly arrive in that time.

### Motivated

The really motivated sellers will answer your telephone inquiries, letters, and house calls about four to six weeks before the Trustee's Sale, when they realize that the foreclosure clock is running down. Think about the problems of the owner at this point: no money, no place to go, and no alternatives.

But don't believe that, in purchasing the equity, you have solved the owner's problems. Even if you have made a deal with the owner, he or she has nowhere to go and very little money, so their problems will soon become yours. The owner will not move. Plan ahead for this contingency. Be sure the sellers understand that you will pay them only when they have left the premises and removed all of their personal possessions. And, even with such an understanding, don't expect each of the homeowners that you deal with to give you the keys and then walk away with your check. Remember, you must be a problem-solver. People pay for solutions. The homeowner will need help with moving, organizing garage sales, transferring the utilities, and lots of TLC and understanding. If you intend to succeed again and again you'll need to establish a positive attitude and handle the homeowner's problems.

If you do otherwise, you will be making a costly mistake. Possession of the property might require you to evict the former owner. If the owner is not receiving enough money to move and get re-established, I'd suggest you pay for the move and the initial costs of renting an apartment. This cost is insignificant when compared to the time and effort involved in an eviction. The dollar costs will add up rapidly in the eviction process, including attorney's fees, mortgage payments, property taxes, filing fees, and insurance. In addition, the owner may become hostile and could damage the property as a result.

### Irrational

If the owner does show signs of behaving irrationally, you should probably walk away from the deal. The foreclosure marketplace is full of opportunities that make sense. Owners who try to take advantage of your good intentions will use up your time and money. Forget them and keep moving.

## AUTOMATIC POSTPONEMENT

There is another type of transaction you may be inclined to walk away from, even though the seller is motivated to the point of desperation. What, you may ask, will I do if the seller contacts me one day before the sale? If you normally purchase property in California and use a home equity purchase agreement, Section 1695 of the Civil Code (page 14) requires that you allow the owner a five-day right of rescission. But in this case you don't have five days. The Civil Code in California also allows the home equity purchaser to buy the property just before it goes on the auction block. For example, even if a property is scheduled to be sold at 10:00 A.M., the law allows you to buy it at 8:00 A.M. Running through your mind will be the regularly recurring theme of this book: Do your homework.

### Before the Trustee's or Sheriff's Sale

If you purchase before the Trustee's Sale, you must know what you are purchasing. You have very little time to do a thorough title search, and you *must* find out about the existence of any encumbrances or liens on the property. But you don't have to simply shrug your shoulders and tell the owner that you can't help him. Get a postponement. Section 2924g (6)(1) of the Civil Code in California (see page 24) allows the trustor (the owner) to be granted a twenty-four-hour postponement of the sale. Check the rules that apply in your state. First, have a home equity purchase agreement signed and agreed to by all parties. Then have the seller sign the request for automatic postponement. Do not simply give the automatic postponement document to the seller and then expect him or her to show up to sign the contract. Many sellers won't. They will get the postponement and then go shop for a better deal. This is desperation!

You need the one-day postponement to review the records at the County Recorder's Office. Then you will be knowledgeable enough to purchase the property with its known liens and encumbrances. Don't let the seller hurry you into paying out any cash until you are sure of the condition of his or her title.

Your state may not have a code provision protecting foreclosure sellers. Do your homework and find out.

## THIS THREE-LETTER WORD WILL MAKE YOU A BUNDLE

This three-letter word will make you rich! This three-letter word will make you respected in your community. You'll be loved by your fellows if you use this three-letter word. Life will become a smooth road for you if you will use this three-letter word. Worry will not be part of your life if you will use this three-letter word. You won't be embarrassed by mistakes if you'll use this three-letter word. It is possible to become a hard-nosed millionaire if you will acknowledge and use this three-letter word.

You will make more money, save time and earn praise if you'll use this three-letter word. You'll be in style and avoid criticism if you just use this three-letter word.

### What is the Word?

Do you want to be healthier? Wouldn't it be nice to avoid physical pain and be more comfortable? Then you must use the three-letter word. Yes. The word is **ASK!!**

- **Ask** your friends
- **Ask** your doctor
- **Ask** your attorney
- **Ask** the real estate brokers
- **Ask** the sellers
- **Ask** other buyers
- **Ask** the neighbors
- **Ask** the shop-keepers
- **Ask** the County Clerk
- **Ask** trustees
- **Ask** bankers
- **Ask** loan officers
- **Ask** your spouse

Ask and keep on asking: that is the road to riches. Everyone will help if you just ask.

## *CIVIL CODES*

# CALIFORNIA CIVIL CODE

***Home Equity Sales Contracts***

**STATE LAWS DIFFER**

**Check the civil code in your own state and double-check with an attorney**

# CIVIL CODES



## CHAPTER 2.5. HOME EQUITY SALES CONTRACTS



### § 1695. Legislative findings and declarations

(a) The Legislature finds and declares that homeowners whose residences are in foreclosure have been subjected to fraud, deception, and unfair dealing by home equity purchasers. The recent rapid escalation of home values, particularly in the urban areas, has resulted in a significant increase in home equities which are usually the greatest financial asset held by the homeowners of this state. During the time period between the commencement of foreclosure proceedings and the scheduled foreclosure sale date, homeowners in financial distress, especially the poor, elderly, and financially unsophisticated, are vulnerable to the importunities of equity purchasers who induce homeowners to sell their homes for a small fraction of their fair market values through the use of schemes which often involve oral and written misrepresentations, deceit, intimidation, and other unreasonable commercial practices.

(b) The Legislature declares that it is the express policy of the state to preserve and guard the precious asset of home equity, and the social as well as the economic value of homeownership.

(c) The Legislature further finds that equity purchasers have a significant impact upon the economy and well-being of this state and its local communities, and therefore the provisions of this chapter are necessary to promote the public welfare.

(d) The intent and purposes of this chapter are the following:

(1) To provide each homeowner with information necessary to make an informed and intelligent decision regarding the sale of his or her home to an equity purchaser; to require that the sales agreement be expressed in writing; to safeguard the public against deceit and financial hardship; to insure, foster, and encourage fair dealing in the sale and purchase of homes in foreclosure; to prohibit representations that tend to mislead; to prohibit or restrict unfair contract terms; to afford homeowners a reasonable and meaningful opportunity to rescind sales to equity purchasers; and to preserve and protect home equities for the homeowners of this state.

(2) This chapter shall be liberally construed to effectuate this intent and to achieve these purposes. *(Added by Stats.1979, c. 1029, § 1.)*

### § 1695.1. Definitions

The following definitions apply to this chapter:

(a) "Equity purchaser" means any person who acquires title to any residence in foreclosure, except a person who acquires such title as follows:

(1) For the purpose of using such property as a personal residence.

(2) By a deed in lieu of foreclosure of any voluntary lien or encumbrance of record.

(3) By a deed from a trustee acting under the power of sale contained in a deed of trust or mortgage at a foreclosure sale conducted pursuant to Article 1 (commencing with Section 2920) of Chapter 2 of Title 14 of Part 4 of Division 3.

(4) At any sale of property authorized by statute.

(5) By order or judgment of any court.

(6) From a spouse, blood relative, or blood relative of a spouse.

(b) "Residence in foreclosure" and "residential real property in foreclosure" means residential real property consisting of one- to four-family dwelling units, one of which the owner occupies as his or her principal place of residence, and against which there is an outstanding notice of default, recorded pursuant to Article 1 (commencing with Section 2920) of Chapter 2 of Title 14 of Part 4 of Division 3.

(c) "Equity seller" means any seller of a residence in foreclosure.

(d) "Business day" means any calendar day except Sunday, or the following business holidays: New Year's Day, Washington's Birthday, Memorial Day, Independence Day, Labor Day, Columbus Day, Veterans' Day, Thanksgiving Day, and Christmas Day.

(e) "Contract" means any offer or any contract, agreement, or arrangement, or any term thereof, between an equity purchaser and equity seller incident to the sale of a residence in foreclosure.

# CIVIL CODES

(f) "Property owner" means the record title owner of the residential real property in foreclosure at the time the notice of default was recorded. *(Added by Stats.1979, c. 1029, § 1. Amended by Stats.1980, c. 423, § 4.)*

**§ 1695.2. Written contract; size of type; language; signature and date**

Every contract shall be written in letters of a size equal to 10-point bold type, in the same language principally used by the equity purchaser and equity seller to negotiate the sale of the residence in foreclosure and shall be fully completed and signed and dated by the equity seller and equity purchaser prior to the execution of any instrument of conveyance of the residence in foreclosure. *(Added by Stats.1979, c. 1029, § 1.)*

**Cross References**

Failure to comply with this section, right of cancellation, see § 1695.5.
Requirements of this section to be provided by equity purchaser, see § 1695.6.

**§ 1695.3. Contents; survival of contract**

Every contract shall contain the entire agreement of the parties and shall include the following terms:

(a) The name, business address, and the telephone number of the equity purchaser.

(b) The address of the residence in foreclosure.

(c) The total consideration to be given by the equity purchaser in connection with or incident to the sale.

(d) A complete description of the terms of payment or other consideration including, but not limited to, any services of any nature which the equity purchaser represents he will perform for the equity seller before or after the sale.

(e) The time at which possession is to be transferred to the equity purchaser.

(f) The terms of any rental agreement.

(g) A notice of cancellation as provided in subdivision (b) of Section 1695.5.

(h) The following notice in at least 14-point boldface type, if the contract is printed or in capital letters if the contract is typed, and completed with the name of the equity purchaser, immediately above the statement required by Section 1695.5(a):

"NOTICE REQUIRED BY CALIFORNIA LAW

Until your right to cancel this contract has ended,

______________________________
(Name)

or anyone working for______________________
(Name)

CANNOT ask you to sign or have you sign any deed or any other document."

The contract required by this section shall survive delivery of any instrument of conveyance of the residence in foreclosure, and shall have no effect on persons other than the parties to the contract. *(Added by Stats.1979, c. 1029, § 1. Amended by Stats.1980, c. 423, § 5.)*

**Cross References**

Failure to comply with this section, right of cancellation, see § 1695.5.
Requirements of this section to be provided by equity purchaser, see § 1695.6.

**§ 1695.4. Right of cancellation; time and manner of exercise**

(a) In addition to any other right of rescission, the equity seller has the right to cancel any contract with an equity purchaser until midnight of the fifth business day following the day on which the equity seller signs any contract or until 8 a.m. on the day scheduled for the sale of the property pursuant to a power of sale conferred in a deed of trust, whichever occurs first.

(b) Cancellation occurs when the equity seller personally delivers written notice of cancellation to the address specified in the contract or sends a telegram indicating cancellation to that address.

(c) A notice of cancellation given by the equity seller need not take the particular form as provided with the contract and, however expressed, is effective if it indicates the intention of the equity seller not to be bound by the contract. *(Added by Stats.1979, c. 1029, § 1.)*

**Cross References**

Return of original contract and other documents upon cancellation, see § 1695.6.

**§ 1695.5. Right of cancellation; notice of right; form**

(a) The contract shall contain in immediate proximity to the space reserved for the equity seller's signature a conspicuous statement in a size equal to at least 12-point bold type, if the contract is printed or in capital letters if the contract is typed as follows: "You may cancel this contract for the sale of your house without any penalty or obligation at any time before ______________.
(Date and time of day)

See the attached notice of cancellation form for an explanation of this right." The equity purchaser shall accurately enter the date and time of day on which the rescission right ends.

(b) The contract shall be accompanied by a completed form in duplicate, captioned "notice of cancellation" in a size equal to 12-point bold type, if the contract is printed or in capital letters if the contract is typed, followed by a space in which the equity purchaser shall enter the date on which the equity seller executes any contract. This form shall be attached to the contract, shall be easily detachable, and shall contain in type of at least 10-point, if the contract is printed or in capital letters if the contract is typed, the following statement written in the same language as used in the contract:

"NOTICE OF CANCELLATION

______________________________
(Enter date contract signed)

You may cancel this contract for the sale of your house, without any penalty or obligation, at any time before ______________________.
(Enter date and time of day)

# CIVIL CODES

To cancel this transaction, personally deliver a signed and dated copy of this cancellation notice, or send a telegram ______________________________,
(Name of purchaser)

at ______________________________________
(Street address of purchaser's place of business)

NOT LATER THAN ______________________.
(Enter date and time of day)

I hereby cancel this transaction ______________.
(Date)

______________"
(Seller's signature)

(c) The equity purchaser shall provide the equity seller with a copy of the contract and the attached notice of cancellation. *(Added by Stats.1979, c. 1029, § 1. Amended by Stats.1980, c. 423, § 6.)*

**Cross References**

Mortgage foreclosure consultants, owner's right to cancel contract with consultant until midnight of "third business day" as defined by provision of this section, see § 2945.2.
Requirements of this section to be provided by equity purchaser, see § 1695.6.
Return of original contract and other documents upon cancellation, see § 1695.6.

**§ 1695.6. Contract requirements; responsibility of equity purchaser; prohibited transactions; bona fide purchasers and encumbrancers; cancellation; return of original documents; untrue or misleading statements; encumbrances**

(a) The contract as required by Sections 1695.2, 1695.3, and 1695.5, shall be provided and completed in conformity with those sections by the equity purchaser.

(b) Until the time within which the equity seller may cancel the transaction has fully elapsed, the equity purchaser shall not do any of the following:

(1) Accept from any equity seller an execution of, or induce any equity seller to execute, any instrument of conveyance of any interest in the residence in foreclosure.

(2) Record with the county recorder any document, including, but not limited to, any instrument of conveyance, signed by the equity seller.

(3) Transfer or encumber or purport to transfer or encumber any interest in the residence in foreclosure to any third party, provided no grant of any interest or encumbrance shall be defeated or affected as against a bona fide purchaser or encumbrancer for value and without notice of a violation of this chapter, and knowledge on the part of any such person or entity that the property was "residential real property in foreclosure" shall not constitute notice of a violation of this chapter. This section shall not be deemed to abrogate any duty of inquiry which exists as to rights or interests of persons in possession of the residential real property in foreclosure.

(4) Pay the equity seller any consideration.

(c) Within 10 days following receipt of a notice of cancellation given in accordance with Sections 1695.4 and 1695.5, the equity purchaser shall return without condition any original contract and any other documents signed by the equity seller.

(d) An equity purchaser shall make no untrue or misleading statements regarding the value of the residence in foreclosure, the amount of proceeds the equity seller will receive after a foreclosure sale, any contract term, the equity seller's rights or obligations incident to or arising out of the sale transaction, the nature of any document which the equity purchaser induces the equity seller to sign, or any other untrue or misleading statement concerning the sale of the residence in foreclosure to the equity purchaser.

(e) Whenever any equity purchaser purports to hold title as a result of any transaction in which the equity seller grants the residence in foreclosure by any instrument which purports to be an absolute conveyance and reserves or is given by the equity purchaser an option to repurchase such residence, the equity purchaser shall not cause any encumbrance or encumbrances to be placed on such property or grant any interest in such property to any other person without the written consent of the equity seller. *(Added by Stats.1979, c. 1029, § 1. Amended by Stats.1980, c. 423, § 7.)*

**Cross References**

Transfer or encumbrance of interest to third party by equity purchaser, treble damages, see § 1695.7.
Violations of this section or practice of fraud or deceit by equity purchaser, civil and criminal sanctions, see §§ 1695.7, 1695.8.

**§ 1695.7. Violations by equity purchaser; civil actions; actual damages; equitable relief; attorneys' fees and costs; exemplary damages**

An equity seller may bring an action for the recovery of damages or other equitable relief against an equity purchaser for a violation of any subdivision of Section 1695.6 or Section 1695.13. The equity seller shall recover actual damages plus reasonable attorneys' fees and costs. In addition, the court shall award exemplary damages or equitable relief, or both, if the court deems such award proper, but in any event shall award exemplary damages in an amount not less than three times the equity seller's actual damages for any violation of paragraph (3) of subdivision (b) of Section 1695.6 or Section 1695.13. Any action brought pursuant to this section shall be commenced within four years after the date of the alleged violation. *(Added by Stats.1979, c. 1029, § 1. Amended by Stats.1980, c. 423, § 8.)*

**§ 1695.8. Violations by equity purchaser; criminal penalties**

Any equity purchaser who violates any subdivision of Section 1695.6 or who engages in any practice which would operate as a fraud or deceit upon an equity seller shall, upon conviction, be punished by a fine of not more

## CIVIL CODES

than ten thousand dollars ($10,000), by imprisonment in the county jail for not more than one year, or in the state prison, or by both that fine and imprisonment for each violation. *(Added by Stats.1979, c. 1029, § 1. Amended by Stats. 1985, c. 270 § 1.)*

§ **1695.9. Nonexclusivity of chapter**

The provisions of this chapter are not exclusive and are in addition to any other requirements, rights, remedies, and penalties provided by law. *(Added by Stats.1979, c. 1029, § 1.)*

§ **1695.10. Waiver**

Any waiver of the provisions of this chapter shall be void and unenforceable as contrary to the public policy. *(Added by Stats.1979, c. 1029, § 1.)*

§ **1695.11. Severability**

If any provision of this chapter, or if any application thereof to any person or circumstance is held unconstitutional, the remainder of this chapter and the application of its provisions to other persons and circumstances shall not be affected thereby. *(Added by Stats.1979, c. 1029, § 1.)*

§ **1695.12. Absolute conveyance with repurchase option deemed loan transaction; rights of bona fide purchasers or encumbrancers**

In any transaction in which an equity seller purports to grant a residence in foreclosure to an equity purchaser by any instrument which appears to be an absolute conveyance and reserves to himself or herself or is given by the equity purchaser an option to repurchase, such transaction shall create a presumption affecting the burden of proof, which may be overcome by clear and convincing evidence to the contrary that the transaction is a loan transaction, and the purported absolute conveyance is a mortgage; however, such presumption shall not apply to a bona fide purchaser or encumbrancer for value without notice of a violation of this chapter, and knowledge on the part of any such person or entity that the property was "residential real property in foreclosure" shall not constitute notice of a violation of this chapter. This section shall not be deemed to abrogate any duty of inquiry which exists as to rights or interests of persons in possession of the residential real property in foreclosure. *(Added by Stats.1979, c. 1029, § 1. Amended by Stats.1980, c. 423, § 9.)*

§ **1695.13. Prohibited acts**

It is unlawful for any person to initiate, enter into, negotiate, or consummate any transaction involving residential real property in foreclosure, as defined in Section 1695.1, if such person, by the terms of such transaction, takes unconscionable advantage of the property owner in foreclosure. *(Added by Stats.1980, c. 423, § 10.)*

**Cross References**

Exempt persons and firms, see Business and Professions Code § 10133.1.

§ **1695.14. Rescission**

(a) In any transaction involving residential real property in foreclosure, as defined in Section 1695.1, which is in violation of Section 1695.13 is voidable and the transaction may be rescinded by the property owner within two years of the date of the recordation of the conveyance of the residential real property in foreclosure.

(b) Such rescission shall be effected by giving written notice as provided in Section 1691 to the equity purchaser and his successor in interest, if the successor is not a bona fide purchaser or encumbrancer for value as set forth in subdivision (c), and by recording such notice with the county recorder of the county in which the property is located, within two years of the date of the recordation of the conveyance to the equity purchaser. The notice of rescission shall contain the names of the property owner and the name of the equity purchaser in addition to any successor in interest holding record title to the real property and shall particularly describe such real property. The equity purchaser and his successor in interest if the successor is not a bona fide purchaser or encumbrancer for value as set forth in subdivision (c), shall have 20 days after the delivery of the notice in which to reconvey title to the property free and clear of encumbrances created subsequent to the rescinded transaction. Upon failure to reconvey title within such time, the rescinding party may bring an action to enforce the rescission and for cancellation of the deed.

(c) The provisions of this section shall not affect the interest of a bona fide purchaser or encumbrancer for value if such purchase or encumbrance occurred prior to the recordation of the notice of rescission pursuant to subdivision (b). Knowledge that the property was residential real property in foreclosure shall not impair the status of such persons or entities as bona fide purchasers or encumbrancers for value. This subdivision shall not be deemed to abrogate any duty of inquiry which exists as to rights or interests of persons in possession of the residential real property in foreclosure.

(d) In any action brought to enforce a rescission pursuant to this section, the prevailing party shall be entitled to costs and reasonable attorneys fees.

(e) The remedies provided by this section shall be in addition to any other remedies provided by law. *(Added by Stats.1980, c. 423, § 11.)*

§ **1695.15. Liability of equity purchaser for statements or acts committed by representative**

(a) An equity purchaser is liable for all damages resulting from any statement made or act committed by the equity purchaser's representative in any manner connected with the equity purchaser's acquisition of a

## CIVIL CODES

residence in foreclosure, receipt of any consideration or property from or on behalf of the equity seller, or the performance of any act prohibited by this chapter.

(b) "Representative" for the purposes of this section means a person who in any manner solicits, induces, or causes any property owner to transfer title or solicits any member of the property owner's family or household to induce or cause any property owner to transfer title to the residence in foreclosure to the equity purchaser. *(Added by Stats.1990, c. 1537 (S.B.2641), § 1.)*

**§ 1695.16. Limitation of liability under section 1695.-15; voiding provision or contract; arbitration**

(a) Any provision of a contract which attempts or purports to limit the liability of the equity purchaser under Section 1695.15 shall be void and shall at the option of the equity seller render the equity purchase contract void. The equity purchaser shall be liable to the equity seller for all damages proximately caused by that provision. Any provision in a contract which attempts or purports to require arbitration of any dispute arising under this chapter shall be void at the option of the equity seller only upon grounds as exist for the revocation of any contract.

(b) This section shall apply to any contract entered into on or after January 1, 1991. *(Added by Stats.1990, c. 1537 (S.B.2641), § 2.)*

**§ 1695.17. Representative of equity purchaser; statements to be provided to seller; remedies**

(a) Any representative, as defined in subdivision (b) of Section 1695.15, deemed to be the agent or employee, or both the agent and the employee of the equity purchaser shall be required to provide both of the following:

(1) Written proof to the equity seller that the representative has a valid current California Real Estate Sales License and that the representative is bonded by an admitted surety insurer in an amount equal to twice the fair market value of the real property which is the subject of the contract.

(2) A statement in writing, under penalty of perjury, that the representative has a valid current California Real Estate Sales License, is bonded by an admitted surety insurer in an amount equal to at least twice the value of the real property which is the subject of the contract and has complied with paragraph (1). The written statement required by this paragraph shall be provided to all parties to the contract prior to the transfer of any interest in the real property which is the subject of the contract.

(b) The failure to comply with subdivision (a) shall at the option of the equity seller render the equity purchase contract void and the equity purchaser shall be liable to the equity seller for all damages proximately caused by the failure to comply. *(Added by Stats.1990, c. 1537 (S.B.2641), § 3.)*

# TRUSTEE/TRUSTOR RELATIONSHIP

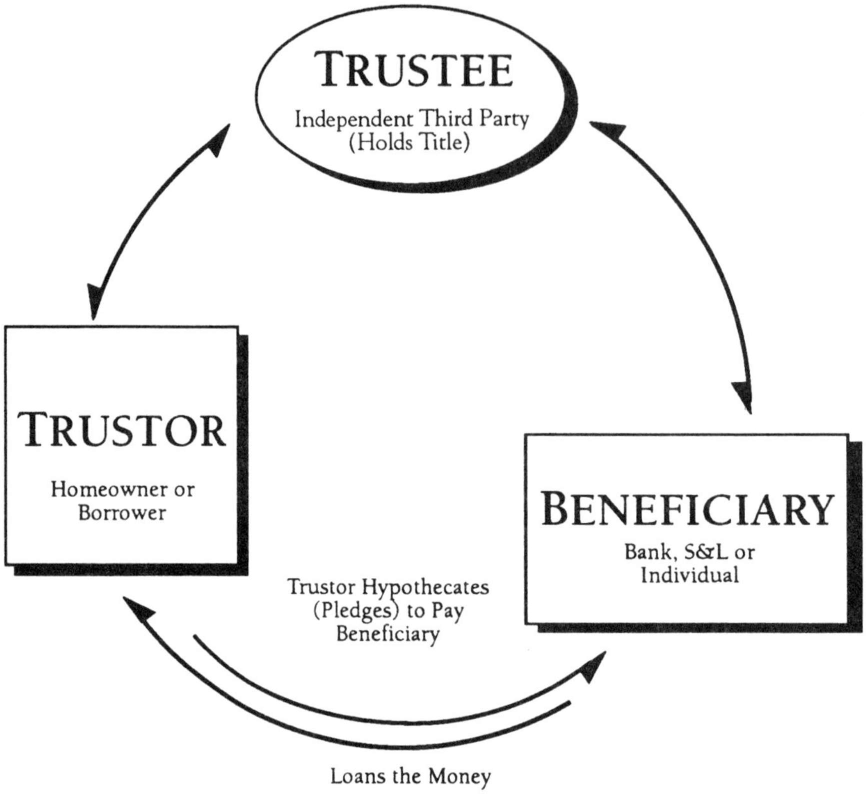

## Default Time Period in California

| Notice of Default Issued | 1/1 | ◀ 3 Months ▶ Loan Reinstatement Period | 4/1 | 21 DAY Advertising Period "Full Balance Due" | Trustee's Sale Auction |
|---|---|---|---|---|---|

# *NEW GROWTH FINANCIAL*

## EQUITY PURCHASE AGREEMENT

*Page 1 of 3*

THIS AGREEMENT, made this__________day of__________________, 19__________
between New Growth Financial and/or assignees (hereinafter "Buyer"); in consideration of the covenants and agreements hereinafter contained, Seller agrees to sell and convey to Buyer and Buyer agrees to purchase from Seller, the following real property located in (city) ______________
County___________,California (street address)______________________________________
Assessor's parcel no.) ______________________Tract_______Lot_______Block _____________________
Page(s)__________(Attach legal description as Exhibit "A"). The following personal property is also included in this purchase:____________________________________________________________

Said real and personal property is collectively known as the "Property".

1. In consideration for said property, [illegible] agrees to pay to Seller, as Seller's equity in the Property, the total sum ($ [illegible] at the time Seller delivers to Buyer both (1) A properly prepared, notarized and va[illegible]erty (and bill of sale for any personal property included in the s[illegible] hereof, the transfer of possession of the Property to Buye[illegible] in good repair. All documents to be execu[illegible]gning the grant deed. No payment will be m[illegible] and approved. IN NO EVENT SHALL [illegible]NSFERRED TO SELLER BY BUYER AT ANY T[illegible]GHT TO CANCEL THIS CONTRACT. PROVIDED FO[illegible]S PROHIBITED BY CALIFORNIA LAW.



2. (a) Seller represents that the following are the deeds of trusts, liens, [illegible]ces, judgments, bonds assessments (hereinafter "Encumbrances")

1st TD $__________________payable $___________per month___________% Int. Incl. T & I

2nd TD $__________________payable $___________per month_______%_______due date

3rd TD $__________________payable $___________per month_______%_______due date

(b) Seller represents that said Encumbrances each have the following amounts which are now due or past due: ____________________________________________________________________
From the NET amount due Seller may be deducted all payments on existing encumbrances through the payments due______________________, 19_______. Also, any taxes, judgments, assessment bonds, prepayment penalties, and other liens if any. Impounds, if any, are to be assigned without charge to the Buyer, in any amount satisfactory to the lending institution. Any impound shortage will be deducted from the funds due Seller. Insurance Fire Casualty Policy will be assigned to the Buyer without charge.

(c) Buyer shall take title to the property subject to all of said Encumbrances and amounts due or past due, except ____________________________________________________________________
Buyer shall further take title subject to all easements, zoning and land-use restrictions, and covenants, conditions and restrictions of record, so long as the same do not adversely affect the continued use of the Property for its present use.

(d) Buyer shall have the right to rescind this agreement and to receive a refund of all consideration paid to Seller if within (5) days after receiving a Grant Deed to the Property Buyer notifies Seller in writing that the principal amounts of, and/or the amounts due or past due on, one or more of the Encumbrances are greater than as represented hereinabove, or that there are one or more easements, zoning or land use restrictions, or covenants, conditions and restrictions concerning the Property which adversely affect the continued use of the Property for its present use. Said notice shall demand rescission and shall specify the Encumbrance(s) which are not in compliance with the representations made by Seller or the easements, etc. which interfere with the continued use of the Property for its present use. Upon receipt of said notice Seller shall immediately cooperate with Buyer to execute all documents and do all things necessary to fully rescind the sale and return the full amount of money and/or other property transferred to Seller in connection with this sale. If Seller shall fail or refuse to so cooperate, Seller shall be liable for all loss or harm caused by said failure or refusal.

## NEW GROWTH FINANCIAL

### EQUITY PURCHASE AGREEMENT

*Page 2 of 3*

(e) Buyer shall pay all the following, if any: escrow fees, title insurance fees, transfer taxes, recording fees, notary fees. Seller agrees to pay for any damages and/or repairs found by termite and roof inspections.

(f) Possession of the Property shall be transferred to Buyer on _______________, 19______. Any and all risk of loss of the Property or any part thereof shall be born by Seller until possession of the Property has passed to Buyer. Any possession, occupancy or tenancy by the Seller at any time after the Grant Deed has been delivered to Buyer shall be on the following terms: Rent to be paid by Seller to Buyer: ($____________) per day__________, month_________ year_________. Seller to vacate Property on or before:__________________. Other terms of rental: Seller agrees to pay for any damage done to the Property that is caused by Seller or tenants after the date this contract is signed. Balance of funds due Seller are to be paid after the premises are vacated and all documentation has been executed and approved. ________ ________

3. ATTORNEY'S FEES.

In the event that any legal or equitable action is brought to enforce the terms of this agreement, including but not limited to [illegible]ific performance, or rescission of contract, the prevailing party in such action shall be [illegible]llect reasonable attorney's fees, expert witness fees and cost of suit, as detern[illegible]

4. EFFECT OF PARTIAL INVALIDITY.

The provisions of this Agreement a[illegible] invalidity or partial invalidity of one or more p[illegible]aining provisions invalid or unenforceable.



5. AGREEMENT BINDING UPON HEIRS, ASSIGNS.

This Agreement, and all terms hereof, shall be binding on the he[illegible]tors, personal representative, conservators, successors, and assigns of the undersigned [illegible] Seller.

6. WARRANTY OF TITLE; WARRANTIES TO SURVIVE DELIVERY OF DEED.

Seller hereby warrants, jointly and severally, that each of the undersigned, as Seller, is the lawful owner of any ownership interest in the Property, and that collectively the Property and Seller has the right and authority to convey said ownership to Buyer. This warranty, and all warranties, terms and conditions hereof, shall survive the delivery and recordation of any deed to buyer, and the close of any escrow.

(a) Seller is not entitled to receive any other consideration or thing of value or services from Buyer, in connection with or incident to the sale of the Property to Buyer, except as stated hereinabove and except the following: ______________________________________
______________________________________________________________________

Ted Thomas is an employee of New Growth Financial and holds a valid Broker's License issued by the State of California.

7. PHYSICAL CONDITION OF PROPERTY

The Property is free of all defects in its structure and its operating systems such as plumbing, electrical, roof and metal work, gas and sewer, except for the following: ____________________ ______________________________Seller agrees to pay for all damages and repairs found by termite and roof inspectors. Buyer takes the property subject to the above disclosed defects. Seller hereby warrants that the property is free of other defects, as of the date of delivery of a Grant Deed to the Property to Buyer.

8. COMMISSIONS

Seller hereby represents that there is no licensed real estate salesperson or broker representing Seller in any way in connection with this purchase and sale, and Seller agrees to hold Buyer harmless and defend Buyer from any claim to commission in connection with this purchase and sale.

9. UNCONSCIONABILITY

Seller hereby represents that all negotiations and dealings with Buyer have been and are at arm's length, and that no duress or undue influence has been exerted by Buyer over Seller or Seller's family in connection with this purchase and sale. Seller is aware that the Buyer may be purchasing property for immediate resale.



*(Page 2 of 3)*

# *NEW GROWTH FINANCIAL*

## EQUITY PURCHASE AGREEMENT

*Page 3 of 3*

10. Property MUST appraise at $____________. Less than that amount will be DEDUCTED from net to seller.

(c) Seller is aware and understands that the present fair market value of the Property probably is higher than the purchase price set forth herein. Seller hereby expressly waives any and all claim to any potential or actual income, profits or other sums in excess of the above mentioned purchase price, which may be realized by Buyer or others as a result of any transaction involving the Property. Seller acknowledges that the purchase price stated herein is fair and equitable and is in Seller's best interests, and that Seller's decision to sell was based on Seller, and that Seller has not relied on any representations of Buyer which are not contained expressly herein.

11. POOL/SPA, POOL EQUIPMENT AND SOLAR EQUIPMENT

Seller agrees to pay any damages or repairs found by pool inspector. ________

12. EXISTING LOANS

(a) Buyer and Seller acknowledge th[illegible] the property may contain an "Acceleration" or "Due on Sale Claus[illegible] require payment in full on the balance of the loans as a resu[illegible] Seller are advised to seek independent legal advice re[illegible] satisfy themselves as to these issues. ________

(b) Seller acknowledges that Buye[illegible] the property subject to the existing loans. ________



**NOTICE REQUIRED BY CALIFORNIA L[illegible]HT TO CANCEL THIS CONTRACT HAS ENDED NEW G[illegible]CIAL AND OR ASSIGNEES OR ANYONE WORKING FOR NEW GR[illegible]FINANCIAL CANNOT ASK YOU TO SIGN OR HAVE YOU SIGN ANY DEED OR ANY OTHER DOCUMENT.**

**YOU MAY CANCEL THIS CONTRACT FOR THE SALE OF YOUR HOUSE WITHOUT ANY PENALTY OR OBLIGATION AT ANY TIME BEFORE ____________________ (DATE AND TIME OF DAY). SEE THE ATTACHED NOTICE OF CANCELLATION FORM FOR AN EXPLANATION OF THIS RIGHT**

**Signed:**

________________________ ______________

**Seller** **Date**

**Signed:**

________________________ ______________

**Seller** **Date**

BUYERS NAME, BUSINESS ADDRESS AND TELEPHONE NUMBER

New Growth Financial
P.O. Box 5000, Suite 412
Danville, CA 94526
(415) 837-2106

Offices Located at:
185 Front Street, #207
Danville, CA 94526

(Seller's time for cancellation ends at midnight on the fifth business day following the day the Seller signs this Agreement, or until 8:00 a.m. on the day scheduled for sale of the Property under power of sale conferred by deed of trust, whichever comes first.)



*(Page 3 of 3)*

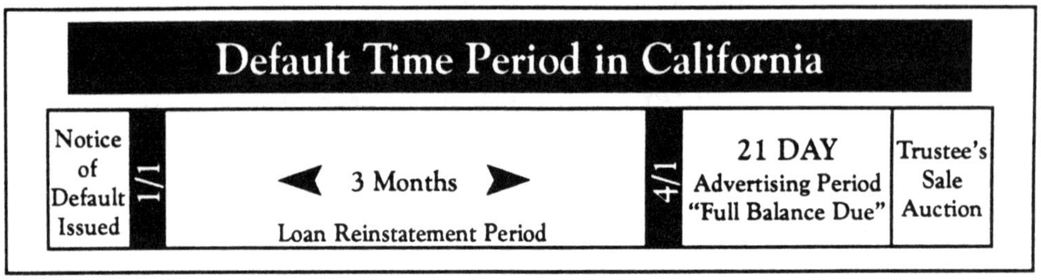


**Request for Automatic Postponement by Trustor**
**Pursuant to California Civil Code Section 2924g(c)(1)**

I/we, ______________________________, being the trustor(s) under that deed of trust having as security property located at ______________________________, City of ____________________, State of California hereby request the one-time, one business day postponement of the trustee's sale currently scheduled for __________ A.M/P.M., ________________, 198___, pursuant to California Civil Code Section 2924g(c)(1) to obtain cash sufficient to satisfy the obligation secured by said deed of trust and/or bid at the sale of said property. The source from which the funds are being obtained is as follows: ________________________________________________________________
________________________________________________________________.

Date: ____________________, 197____

______________________________
**Trustor**

______________________________
**Trustor**

# JUDICIAL PROCESS - COURT ACTION

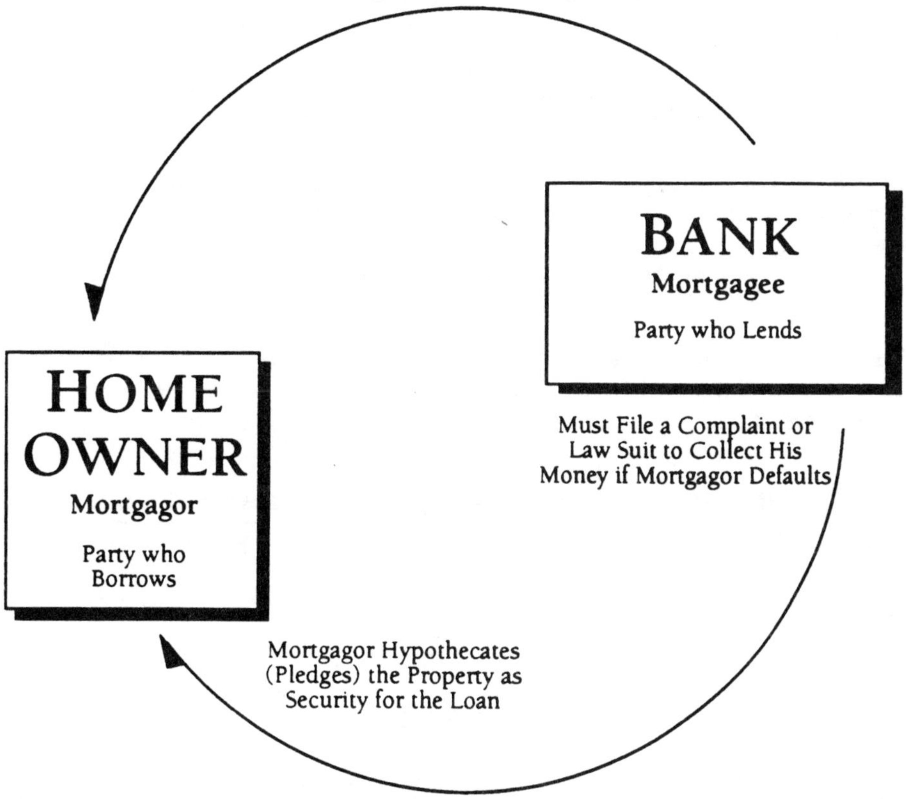

## FILE SUIT & GO TO JUDGE

# *NEW GROWTH FINANCIAL*

## NOTICE OF CANCELLATION

________________________
(Enter Date Contract Signed)

You May Cancel This Contract For The Sale Of Your House Without Penalty Or Obligation At Any Time
Before ________________________________________
(Enter Date and Time Of Day)

To Cancel This Transaction, Personally Deliver A Signed and Dated Copy Of This Cancellation Notice or Send a Telegram To:

New Growth Financial 185 Front St. #207 Danville, Ca 94526
(Name of Purchaser) Street Address of Purchaser

Not Later Than __________________________________
(Enter Date and Time of Day)

I HEREBY CANCEL THIS TRANSACTION

____________________
(DATE)

____________________
SELLER SIGNATURE

____________________
SELLER SIGNATURE

I have received notice to cancel.

Seller ____________________________ Date________________

Seller ____________________________ Date________________

Chapter 2

# Finding the Defaulting Owner's Name and Address

*Here's How*

**COMMERCIAL DEFAULT-REPORTING SERVICES**

Commercial default-reporting services list hundreds of properties being foreclosed upon weekly. One such service, provided by Daily Default Infoservice of Antioch, California, is shown on page 48.

In addition to reporting services such as Daily Default Infoservice, most areas have a legal newspaper that publishes virtually everything that is recorded: sales tax permits, bankruptcies, divorces, probates, liquor licenses, and so on. On page 34 we show a page of the *Mecklenburg Times,* published in Charlotte, North Carolina, in which legal notices of sale are printed. Pages 35 through 39 show a summary of similar information. *The Daily Commerce*, the legal newspaper of Los Angeles County, California (see page 50), displays the notices according to the stage of foreclosure. Generally, legal newspapers are very inexpensive.

**All Day**

You could thus easily spend all day, every day, driving from property to property trying to find that nugget that will turn into a gold mine. But you don't have that time. The volume of defaults, Trustee's/Sheriff's Sales, and REOs in most counties will overwhelm you unless you quickly eliminate the properties that do not have a high income potential. To do this screening, the more data you have available the better. It is instructive to compare listings in legal newspapers with the commercial daily default listings. You can easily see how the extra data provided by the commercial infoservice will save hundreds of hours of wasted time. It is also interesting to compare the Daily Default Infoservice and its competitor, REDLOC Publications (see page 51). Here again you can see that the more information you get, the better your chances of eliminating the timewasters before you leave your home or office.

If you can't find a reporting service for default and foreclosure information, go to the County Recorder's Office and get the desired information. While you're there, ask the clerks and other people using the records if there is a reporting service for your county. Some buyers of distressed property spend one day a week researching the records and the remaining time contacting the property owners or following the Trustee's/Sheriff's Sales.

## FINDING PROPERTIES: DEVELOPING YOUR OWN SYSTEM

Your system for finding properties may include reviewing lawsuits filed for nonpayment of mortgages and tracking notices of default, notices of impending Trustee's/Sheriff's Sales, and notices of real estate owned by the banks. Many buyers of distressed property also follow the county tax sale auctions and the Small Business Administration's foreclosure sales and auctions. Foreclosure on Housing & Urban Development (HUD) and Veterans Administration (VA) properties is a business in itself. Ask a broker to take you to one of the HUD auctions or a VA property sales seminar. You'll find hundreds of brokers at those meetings. Yes, hundreds, because the VA and HUD have thousands of these properties for sale.

Segmenting your market is probably the best way to start. After you review the defaults and Trustee's/Sheriff's Sale listings thoroughly you may decide to start with the defaults. Before doing anything else, review the foreclosure consultants law in your state. The specific statute in the State of California is in sections 1695.1 to 1695.14 of the Civil Code (reproduced in Chapter 1, beginning on page 15).

The appropriate foreclosure laws may have a different name or reference in your state. A visit to the local library should answer your questions. If the public library does not have the codes or statutes, check with a business school, university, or law school library, or as a last resort contact a real estate attorney.

## KNOW YOUR LOCAL MARKET

The more you know about your local market, the easier it is to control it. Study your territory as precisely as possible. This work should be done methodically on a regular basis.

The county records are available to the public. This is a vast source of information, and you can only benefit by the knowledge you'll gain through the records. I suggest that you search the county records to determine if the property you plan to purchase has any liens or encumbrances upon it, whether or not it is in foreclosure. This is especially important if you buy at the Trustee's/Sheriff's Sale, where all the property is sold "as is." At such sales, you get whatever is owned. That means you get not only the house, but also all of the liens and encumbrances that are on file against the property.

## USING THE PUBLIC RECORDS TO RESEARCH A TITLE, COMPLAINT, DEFAULTS, AND LAWSUITS

One of your first steps to finding your way around the courthouse is to ask for help. Begin with a title search on your own home and perhaps your neighbors. Depending on the state, information on foreclosure properties can be obtained through the following: A review of the daily docket, or sheriff's notices of sale, or the commissioner's sales notices. You are searching for foreclosure notices, Sheriff's Sale, or Notices of Equity cases. In trust deed states, you are looking for the Notice of Defaults or Notices of Trustee's Sale.

In mortgage/judicial states, it is your objective to look for separate divisions or locations within the county offices, where they store case files which house the foreclosures and the proceedings against the homeowner/defendants.

First, obtain the case number and then use this number to locate the specific cases. This process is not complicated and once you grasp the foreclosure process and figured out the system in your state, you will soon become an expert. In many eastern states you can expect the procedures and proceedings to differ from county to county even within the state.

It is advisable to research the courthouse county records for the actual foreclosure laws pertaining to your particular state. The local county employees at the records office will have a working knowledge, viewpoints, and opinions as to how the foreclosure law works and is administered; however, a detailed analysis and review with your attorney is certainly advisable.

In your search for information, whether you obtain the case numbers from the dockets, sheriff's office, or the newspaper, it is always appropriate to review the case with an attorney who is listed as the responsible representative of the plaintiff. In trust deed states, a telephone check with the Trustee will provide you with the loan amounts and minimum bid estimates.

### The Public Records Are Public

To review, the courthouse/public records maintain several different files which you may check to discover the total debt on a property. Mortgages, judgments, trust deeds, taxes, abstracts or liens, IRS and state tax liens, options, and lis pendens are there for your review.

At first this range of records may seem overwhelming, but in a short time you will become proficient at finding the properties and reading and researching the documents. The description of the system should be helpful. Keep in mind that your county office may use a slightly different system, but the following description will give you a general knowledge of the process and the records.

### General Index

Start with what is called the General Index. The General Index could be on microfiche cards, microfilm cassettes, or on computerized printouts. Look in the General Index under the name of the trustor/mortgagor or owner of the property that is being foreclosed upon. All of the documents that relate to that person will be filed here. Expect the General Index to be divided into different time periods. If you have a question, simply ask one of the Recorder's staff. In Alameda County (Oakland, California), for example, the Recorder's staff includes two people whose job it is to help members of the public find the various records.

Claims are filed according to an overall system called a Book and Page System or a Reel and Image System. If you live in a populous county you could expect the Reel and Image System to be in use. Less populous counties may still use the Book and Page System. If you live in a section of the country that has many older properties, expect to become familiar with an even older system by which claims are filed in Grantee and Grantor books.

### Book and Page System

In the Book and Page System, you look for property information that is to be found in a particular book, on a particular page, the number of which you find in the General Index. Then you simply pull the book, go to the correct page, and find the information you need. The more progressive counties use a simpler, modern system called the Reel and Image System. These counties have taken the time to put the property information on microfilm or large cassettes (reels), the contents of which have been indexed. Viewers are provided for the public. This system is easy to learn, and you can thoroughly research many properties in a short time.

In your records research you will soon learn that each document is given an identifying number that indicates the order in which it was received by the Recorder's Office. This is important, as are the dates. Remember, a first trust deed or first mortgage is first only because it was recorded first. Expect to find the document numbers and dates on both the microfilm (Reel and Image) and the Book and Page systems.

With this knowledge of the records and how to find them, you are now prepared to look for documents that pertain to your proposed purchase. Remember, you will rarely see a deed of trust/mortgage that says: "This is the first deed of trust." The second loan will rarely say: "This is the second deed of trust." You will know whether a deed of trust or mortgage is a first or second loan only by the date upon which it was filed and recorded. (First in filing date means first in priority.)

### Deed of Trust/Mortgage

Once you have found the trust deed/mortgage, read it. It will show the specific date on which it was filed and recorded, and it will probably have the name of the party who requested the recording. Make a note of these items because you may need them later. Check thoroughly until you've found all the trust deeds/mortgages recorded against the property. Also, be sure to find documents showing any judgments and tax liens filed against the property.

If you are buying at the Trustee's/Sheriff's Sale, you may be purchasing a second deed of trust/mortgage or junior loan. This is fine if you are aware that is what you are buying. Even then, you should obtain as much information about the first trust deed/mortgage, or senior loan, as possible. If it has a high interest rate or an imminent maturity date, you may not want to bid at the sale. The opposite could also apply. For example, the first lender may want to refinance at favorable rates after you purchase the property. The lesson is, make yourself knowledgeable. Don't just buy and hope for the best.

### Know What You Own and Know What You Are Buying: Liens and Encumbrances That Will Be Yours

What happens to the other liens and judgments if you buy a first trust deed/mortgage at the Trustee's/Sheriff's Sale? At some Trustee's/Sheriff's Sales, the owners of the second trust deed/

mortgage and those who have other liens will not show up to bid. If that is the case and you purchase a first trust deed/mortgage from the Trustee/Sheriff you will own the house for what you pay the auctioneer, and the other lenders or judgment holders will have their liens or judgments extinguished by the sale. (The status of tax liens is different and is explained below.)

If this were always the situation, the Trustee's/Sheriff's Sales would be mobbed with interested buyers. In the real world the holders of the second trust deeds/mortgages will show up at the sale to bid. Many holders of junior trust deeds/mortgages understand the situation and will attempt to bid more than you bid in order to salvage the loan they have already made on the property. Keep in mind that loans recorded later than the foreclosing loan are extinguished by the foreclosing loan at the Trustee's/Sheriff's Sale, so the holders of the junior loan could be your competition.

### Second Lienholder

Some foreclosure buyers approach the second lienholder and buy his or her interest at a discount, or less than its face value. They then cure, or reinstate, the defaulting first loan by paying what is in arrears. This procedure will take the property out of the foreclosure process temporarily.

If you then foreclose under the second trust deed/mortgage and no one shows up at the Trustee's/Sheriff's Sale to outbid you, you will own the property for the price of the discounted second trust deed/mortgage plus whatever it took to cure the default on the first trust deed/ mortgage. If someone outbids you and is prepared to pay more than your note value plus penalties, costs, and back payments, you'll still profit, because you purchased the note at a discounted value and will be receiving the face value of the note.

Whether you buy real estate at the Trustee's/Sheriff's Sale or from the owner, you get exactly what is owned by the seller. You will own all liens and encumbrances that are senior or recorded prior to the date the trust deed/mortgage that you are purchasing was recorded. Keep in mind that any liens or abstracts of judgment recorded before the foreclosing loan will still apply to the property after the Trustee's/Sheriff's Sale. Most liens and abstracts of judgments recorded after the foreclosing loan will be extinguished by the Trustee's/Sheriff's Sale.

The worst mistake you can make will be made in ignorance. If you don't know what is owed against the property and cannot get that information from a title company or your own records, search some more — but don't bid.

### Lis Pendens

From time to time, you find a property with a *lis pendens* filed against it. This is simply a notice that some form of legal action has been filed against the property. This could be a lawsuit filed to obtain money from the owner. If the *lis pendens* was filed after the foreclosing trust deed/mortgage, it will be extinguished; if it was filed before, it will have seniority.

### Quitclaim Deeds

In researching the records you may come across a document called a *quitclaim deed* (see page 56). Like a grant deed/warrantee deed, this document shows a transfer of ownership, but its use is limited. It is considered legally binding in California only when the property is being transferred between spouses. Check your state for its escape. The following statement should be included on the quitclaim deed: "It is the intention of the Grantor herein to relinquish all of his/her rights, title and interest whether community property or otherwise in and to the herein above described property and to vest said property in the above Grantee as his/her sole and separate property." Because of the quitclaim deed's limitations, most title companies prefer to have grant deeds as evidence of the transfer of ownership.

### Tax Liens

Tax liens are more complicated. They may be filed by municipal, state, or federal authorities. Any tax lien filed before the foreclosing trust deed/mortgage was recorded will be senior in priority and (you guessed it) you will be assuming those liens if you buy from the owner or at the Trustee's/Sheriff's Sale. Keep in mind that all liens junior to the foreclosing lien are eliminated at the Trustee's/Sheriff's Sale, except those of the IRS.

### Municipal and County

Municipal and county liens will be extinguished by the foreclosure (Trustee's/Sheriff's Sale). These liens are eliminated from the property but will remain in force against the individual. Likewise, state tax liens recorded after the foreclosing loan will be extinguished by the foreclosure. Extinguished, that is, with regard to the property you have just bought but still payable by the previous owner.

### Federal Tax Liens

Federal tax liens are different. The buyer at a Trustee's/Sheriff's Sale is required to wait 120 days for the federal government to exercise its right of redemption. If the federal government does not exercise its right within 120 days, you will own the property clear of liens that were junior to your purchase. Title insurance is not usually available until the federal government releases the lien after 120 days. At that time a purchaser will be cleared by the title insurance company to purchase title insurance, and all other liens including state tax liens, trust deed, mortgages, mechanic's liens, abstracts of judgment, and everything junior are extinguished by the Trustee's/Sheriff's Sale.

By researching the County Recorder's files, the purchaser-investor who plans to buy at the foreclosure sale can determine if a federal lien (filed by the IRS) is still in effect. If a lien is found, contact the party handling the sale and ask if the federal government has been notified of the approaching sale. The law requires the government be given a 25-day notice of the sale. If the government is not notified, the lien will not be extinguished with the expiration of the 120-day right of redemption.

### Is the Seller Motivated? If So, Why? Find Out!

Ten Reasons Why Sellers Want Out:

1. Management problems, possibly a rental with poor cash flow.
2. Divorce: they need the money.
3. Purchase of another property.

4. Transfer out of state.
5. Illness/health: money required for doctor bills.
6. Behind in payments.
7. Investor sees no upside profit potential.
8. Tax problems: IRS breathing down their necks.
9. Deferred maintenance: property is now a fixer-upper.
10. Doesn't want zero coupon bonds or a promissory note — just cold hard cash.

## NOTICE OF SHERIFF'S SALE

Ted Thomas
PO Box 5000 #412
Danville CA 94526

Don't Miss business focus
See Pages 3 and 6

# THE Mecklenburg TIMES

Legal,
Real Estate
& General News

Established 1924

**Price: 50¢**

VOL. 67, NO. 1 | CHARLOTTE, N.C. | TUESDAY, JANUARY 1.

## PUBLIC NOTICES

### NOTICE OF SALE

IN THE GENERAL COURT OF JUSTICE
OF NORTH CAROLINA
SUPERIOR COURT DIVISION
MECKLENBURG COUNTY
90 SP 1993
Before the Clerk

IN THE MATTER OF THE FORECLOSURE of the lands of Russell W. Haskin & Beth B. Haskin, under Deed of Trust, Dated June 2, 1989. Recorded in Book 6010, at Page 0414 and rerecorded at Book 6040, Page 0552 in the Mecklenburg County Registry.

Pursuant to an order of the Clerk of Superior Court and under and by virtue of the power and authority contained in the above-referenced deed of trust and because of default in the payment of the indebtedness thereby secured and failure to carry out and perform the stipulation and agreements therein contained and, pursuant to demand of the owner and holder of the indebtedness secured by said deed of trust, the undersigned substitute trustee will expose for sale at public auction to the highest bidder for cash at the usual place of sale at the county courthouse of said county at 12:00 Noon on January 14, 1991 the following described real estate and any other improvements which may be situated thereon, situated in Mecklenburg County, North Carolina, and being more particularly described as follows:

BEING all of Lot 26 as shown upon a map of FORESTBROOK SUBDIVISION recorded in the Mecklenburg Public Registry in Map Book 22, at Page 703, to which map reference is hereby made for a more particular description.

The record owners of the property, as reflected on the records of the Register of Deeds, are Russell W. Haskin & Beth B. Haskin.

This sale is made subject to all prior liens and encumbrances, and unpaid taxes and assessments for paying, if any. A deposit of 10% of the amount of the bid is required and must be tendered in the form of certified funds at the time of the sale. This sale will be held open ten days for upset bids as required by law. Following the expiration of the statutory upset period, all remaining amounts are immediately due and owing.

The date of this Notice is December 17, 1990.

J. Elizabeth Bagwell and/or Cheryl Samons
Substitute Trustee
301 S. McDowell Street
Suite 408
Charlotte, North Carolina 28204
(704) 333-8107

# FORECLOSURE INFORMATION

## MORTGAGEE'S FORECLOSURE SALE

**Tuesday, January 29, 1991 at 9:00 A.M.**
**Lot A-15, Kennedy Drive, Huntington, MA**

A newly constructed home located on Lot A-15 Kennedy Drive, Huntington, MA, in a residential area.

**TERMS: $10,000.00 on day of sale. Cash, Bank Treasurer's Check of Certified Check.**

**BALANCE DUE 10 DAYS AFTER APPROVAL OF SALE BY LAND COURT.**

For further information call:
**SCHAROFF, SMITH, MURRAY AND NANNINI,**
**9 Chapel Street, Westfield, MA**
**Tel: (413) 562-9607**

---

FIRST MORTGAGEE'S SALE OF REAL ESTATE

## AT PUBLIC AUCTION

**JANUARY 30, 1991 at 11:00 A.M.**
**ON THE PREMISES**
**71 THOMPSON STREET, SPRINGFIELD, MA**

Two-family house located in Residence B Historic District, presently used as a single family with five (5) rental rooms.

$5,000.00 deposit in cash, cashier's or certified check required at the time of sale, the balance to be paid in full within 14 days. Other terms to be announced at the sale.

**David W. Young, Esq.**
**62 Suffield Street**
**Agawam, MA 01001**
**(413) 786-1360**
**WARREN N. SCHREIBER, Auctioneer**
**License No. 101**

---

## MORTGAGEE'S SALE OF REAL ESTATE AT PUBLIC AUCTION

**16 HALL AVENUE**
**GREENFIELD, MASS.**
**TUESDAY, JANUARY 29, 1991, AT 2:00 P.M.**
**ON THE PREMISES**

Single family, two-story colonial with wood clapboard siding and detached garage located close to all amenities. House has three bedrooms, one bath in 1344 square feet of living space. Two porches, one open and one enclosed.

All of the above has been taken from an independent appraisal. The mortgagee does not warrant the information contained therein.

TERMS OF SALE: Five Thousand Dollars ($5,000) of the purchase price must be paid in cash, certified check, or bank check at the time and place of the sale by the purchaser, and the balance of the purchase price shall be paid in chas, certified check, or bank check within thirty (30) days after the date of sale. Other terms to be announced at the sale.

**Suzanne S. Davis, Esquire**
**Attorney for the Mortgage**
**BBO 545927**
**LEVY WINER P.C.**
**277 Main Street**
**Greenfield, MA 01301**

---

MORTGAGEE'S SALE OF REAL ESTATE BY

## PUBLIC AUCTION

**SPRINGFIELD, MA**

Commercial dwelling present use restaurant/ offices, with paved parking for approximately 40 vehicles. Situated on approximately 20,132 sq. ft. of land. Many amenities too numerous to mention. Please call for fact sheet.

**TO BE SOLD ON: JANUARY 25, 1991 at 11:00 A.M.**

**ON THE PREMISES: 456 SUMNER AVENUE, SPRINGFIELD, MA**

**MORTGAGE RECORDED IN HAMPDEN COUNTY REGISTRY OF DEEDS AT BOOK 5734, PAGE 454.**

TERMS OF SALE: SEVENTEEN THOUSAND AND 00/100 ($17,000.00) DOLLARS must be paid in cash, certified check, bank treasurer's check or cashier's check at the time and place of sale. Other terms and conditions to be announced at the sale.

**Sale By Order of Attorney for Mortgagee**
**James H. Fierberg, Esq.**
**GOLDMAN, ALBANO, CARUSO AND FIERBERG, P.C.**
**95 State Street, Suite 600**
**Springfield, MA 01103**

SALE CONDUCTED BY AND FOR FURTHER INFORMATION CONTACT:

**IRVING SHECHTMAN & CO.**
**PROFESSIONAL AUCTIONEERS & APPRAISERS**
**M.C. Ponte Jr.**
**RI Lic. #11000, MA Lic. #658; NH Lic. #2484**
**1006 Reservoir Avenue, Cranston, RI**
**(401) 944-4600**

## SHERIFF'S REAL ESTATE

BULK RATE
U.S. Postage Paid
Permit #742
New Orleans, LA 70113

$1.00

JEFFERSON PARISH

# TIMES & DEMOCRAT

Vol. 49, No. 5 January 31, 1991

### Sheriff's Real Estate

**JUDICIAL ADVERTISEMENT**

**24TH JUDICIAL DISTRICT COURT
PARISH OF JEFFERSON
STATE OF LOUISIANA**

**NO. 333-364**

**DRYADES SAVINGS AND LOAN ASSOCIATION
versus
MICHELLE JILEK, WIFE OF, AND EARL E. WEBER, JR. AND SUSAN SMITH, WIFE OF, AND JOHN A. MAHNKE**

By virtue of and in obedience to a writ of FIERI FACIAS from the 24th Judicial District Court, Parish of Jefferson, State of Louisiana in the above numbered and entitled cause, dated December 3, 1990, I have seized and will proceed to sell to the highest bidder at public auction, at the front door of the New Courthouse Building, Derbigny Street, between Second and Third streets, Gretna, Louisiana, on Wednesday, March 6, 1991, at 10 o'clock a.m., the following described property to wit:

TWO CERTAIN LOTS OF GROUND, together with all the buildings and improvements thereon, and all the rights, ways, privileges, servitudes, appurtenances and advantages thereunto belonging or in anywise appertaining, situated in the TOWN OF KENNER, PARISH OF JEFFERSON, STATE OF LOUISIANA, designated according to plan on file in the office of the Clerk of Court and Recorder for the Parish of Jefferson as LOTS 5 and 6, in SQUARE NO. 292, Highway Park (WESTLAKE SUBDIVISION), bounded by MAIN (formerly Massachusetts Avenue) and MARYLAND (formerly Michigan) AVENUES, INTERSTATE HIGHWAY 10 (formerly West Canal), and 30th (formerly 12th) STREET, which said lots adjoin each other and measure each 25 feet front on Main Street, the same width in the rear, by a depth of 127.5 feet between equal and parallel lines; said lots were originally 120 feet in depth but were increased 7.5 feet in the rear by Kenner Ordinance No. 1575 revoking the dedication of the alleys; Lot 5 lying nearer to and commences at a distance of 100 feet from the corner of Maine Avenue and 30th Street. All in accordance with the survey of Walker & Avery, Inc., C.E. & S., dated October 18, 1976, recertified correct on June 13, 1977 to show said property as Highway Park (West Lake).

Improvements thereon bear Municipal No. 2912 Maine Avenue.

The above description is also in accordance with a survey by Gilbert, Kelly & Couturie, Surveyors, dated July 2nd, 1983, a copy of which is annexed to an act passed before David J. Halpern, Notary Public, dated July 8th, 1983.

Being the same property acquired by Michele Jilek, wife of/and Earl E. Weber, Jr. and Susan Smith wife of/and John Alan Mahnke from Suk Hi Kil, wife of/and Iain McLaren by act passed before David J. Halpern, Notary Public, dated July 8th, 1983, registered in COB 1052, folio 545.

## FORECLOSURE INFORMATION

INVESTOR'S EDGE

THE GUIDE TO FORECLOSED PROPERTIES IN KING COUNTY/P.O. BOX 698, BELLEVUE, WA 98009 827-4545

January 21, 1991

Mr. Ted Thomas
Box 5000, Suite 412
Danville, CA 94526

Dear Ted

I ran some numbers on foreclosure volume this year versus last year. Through January 15, the volume is up about 15 percent in the Puget Sound Region (King, Snohomish, Pierce Counties).

We have been in a much slower "buyers" market for the past 6 months. This slower market will have a direct effect on foreclosure volume. In fact, I would predict the level of foreclosures in 1991 to be 25 to 30 percent higher than 1990.

If I can be of any further assistance, please call me at 206-827-4545.

Sincerely

Douglas L. Hallauer
Publisher

## FORECLOSURE INFORMATION

01/14/91

PIERCE COUNTY

# INVESTOR'S EDGE

THE GUIDE TO FORECLOSED PROPERTIES IN KING COUNTY/P.O. BOX 698, BELLEVUE, WA 98009/827-4545

### TRUSTEE SALES

| | | | |
|---|---|---|---|
| CITY: Gig Harbor | AUDITOR #: 8803040441 | OWNER: John T. Punchak | TRUSTEE: Timothy Carpenter |
| ADD: 14007 14th Ave. NW | BENEFICIARY: Retirement | | TRUSTEES PHONE: 676-1000 |
| ZIP: 98335 | Accounts, Inc. | ADD: 3839 6th Ave. | SALE DATE: 10:00 04/19/91 |
| ASSESSED VALUE: 130,200 | ASSIGNED TO: | CITY: Tacoma, WA 98406 | LOCATION: PCC |
| USE: 1103 | | DOCUMENT #: 9101140075 | |
| AMOUNT O-DUE: 5,320 | TAX #: 022221-5-009 | LOT 1.22 BLDG: 3341 | |
| PRINCIPAL BAL: 5,288 | NOTES: Taxes due: 1,947. Purchased in 1982 for 130,000. | | |
| PAYMENT: | | | |

| | | | |
|---|---|---|---|
| CITY: Gig Harbor | AUDITOR #: 2889788 | OWNER: Robert A. Grant | TRUSTEE: Sharon Rheinschild |
| ADD: 8814 Danforth St. NW | BENEFICIARY: Tacoma S & L | | TRUSTEES PHONE: 572-4161 |
| ZIP: 98335 | Assn. | ADD: Same | SALE DATE: 10:00 04/26/91 |
| ASSESSED VALUE: 94,700 | ASSIGNED TO: | CITY: Same | LOCATION: PCC |
| USE: 1101 | | DOCUMENT #: 9101140225 | |
| AMOUNT O-DUE: 3,291 | TAX #: 012222-8-049 | LOT 1.92 BLDG: 2008 | |
| PRINCIPAL BAL: 50,713 | NOTES: Notices also sent to: Security Pacific Financial Corp., Rainier Industrial Loan Co. | | |
| PAYMENT: 615 | | | |

| | | | |
|---|---|---|---|
| CITY: Gig Harbor | AUDITOR #: 8310250295 | OWNER: Peter B. Sorgenfrei | TRUSTEE: Edwin Emerick, Jr. |
| ADD: 5314 Viewpoint Dr. NW | BENEFICIARY: University | Emily P. Sorgenfrei | TRUSTEES PHONE: 632-0575 |
| ZIP: 98335 | Savings Bank | ADD: Same | SALE DATE: 10:00 04/19/91 |
| ASSESSED VALUE: 77,300 | ASSIGNED TO: | CITY: Same | LOCATION: PCC |
| USE: 1101 | | DOCUMENT #: 9101100372 | |
| AMOUNT O-DUE: 1,080 | TAX #: 976540-020-0 | LOT .76 BLDG: 1492 | |
| PRINCIPAL BAL: 11,585 | NOTES: Underlying on property in favor of Tacoma S & L. Approximate Balance: 28,446. Purchased in 1975 for 39,500. | | |
| PAYMENT: 194 | | | |

| | | | |
|---|---|---|---|
| CITY: Graham | AUDITOR #: 8903200384 | OWNER: Joseph E. Humiston | TRUSTEE: James Christnacht |
| ADD: 32518 Lk Whitman Dr. E. | BENEFICIARY: Frank Skipton | | TRUSTEES PHONE: 564-2111 |
| ZIP: 98338 | | ADD: 32326 Lk Whitman Dr. E. | SALE DATE: 09:30 01/18/91 |
| ASSESSED VALUE: 9,900 | ASSIGNED TO: | CITY: Graham, WA 98338 | LOCATION: PCC |
| USE: 1100 | | DOCUMENT #: 9101080486 | |
| AMOUNT O-DUE: 3,500 | TAX #: 510000-207-3 | LOT .62 BLDG: | |
| PRINCIPAL BAL: 19,000 | NOTES: Purchased in 1989 for 20,000. Notices also sent to: State of Washington. Amended Notice. | | |
| PAYMENT: 200 | | | |



Reprinted by permission of Investor's Edge

## FORECLOSURE INFORMATION

# ATLANTA FORECLOSURE REPORT

P.O. Box 440474
Kennesaw, Georgia 30144
(404) 924-6755

### FULTON COUNTY RESIDENTIAL

| FULTON COUNTY | CURRENT OWNER | LL/D/Z | VAL/YR BLT | MTG INFO | MORTGAGOR/MORTGAGEE | DB/Pg # | ATTORNEY/PH # | SUBJECT TO |
|---|---|---|---|---|---|---|---|---|
| Lot 46F | B R K Inc | 147/14 | | 7,412 | Owner | 13313 | City & State | |
| Ezra Church Heights | | R | | 4 mo/90 | City & State Factors Inc | 36 | 522-3388 | |
| 2801 Tee Rd | B R K Inc | 212/14 | | 3,310 | Owner | 13313 | City & State | |
| Atlanta, GA | | R | | 3 mo/90 | City & State Factors Inc | 40 | 522-3388 | |
| 1809 Monroe Dr NE | Balard, Hilda F | 56/17 | 81,500-6/85 | 69,000 | Owner | 9560 | Prior & Buser | |
| Atlanta, GA 30324 | | R | 1930 | ARM/85 | Home Savings of America | 127 | 876-7541 | |
| 4810 N Bridges Dr | Barton, Ronald O | 190/1/1 | 74,515-2/86 | 74,700 | Owner | 9954 | S H McCalla | |
| Alpharetta, GA 30201 | | R | 1986 | FHA/86/11 | BancPlus Mortgage Corp | 53 | 804-0400 | |
| 957 Piedmont Ave (C) | Batson, Buren W Jr | 106/17 | 110,000-12/88 | 88,000 | Owner | 12186 | S Andrew Shuping | |
| Atlanta, GA 30309 | | R | | Cnv/88 | FNMA (Home Federal) | 112 | 991-0000 | |
| 3931 Land O'Lakes Dr NE | Bazan, Nicholas G & | 63/17 | 99,060-TV | 455,000 | Owner | 11089 | S H McCalla | |
| Atlanta, GA 30342 | Jeani B | R | 1967 | ARM/87/9.875 | The North Atlantic Life Ins Co | 404 | 804-0400 | |
| 4110 East Brookhaven Dr* | Bebeau, E Leo | 11/17 | | 206,200 | Owner | 10955 | Raymond S Martin | *Property is divided by |
| Atlanta, GA 30319 | | R | | Cnv/87 | Southeast Bank NA | 124 | 392-0041 | Fulton/Dekalb Co Line |
| 1705 Brandon Hall Dr | Beggs, Daniel C & | 359/6 | 170,060-TV | 60,600 | Owner | 9985 | Lewis N Jones | 1st/C&S Bnk/DB 9302/321 |
| Dunwoody, GA 30338 | Victoria A (A) | R | 1986 | 3rd/85 | First Union National Bank of Ga | 382 | 658-1670 | 2nd/Cal Fed/DB 9958/341 |
| 1705 Brandon Hall Dr | Beggs, Daniel C & | 359/6 | 496,700-2/86 | 50,000 | Owner | 12652 | Andrew C Shovers | 3 senior deeds & |
| Dunwoody, GA 30338 | Victoria A (A) | R | 1987 | 4th/89 | Enterprise Financial Corp | 83 | 656-1800 | 3 Federal Tax Liens |
| 844 Woods Dr NW | Belt, Gregory | 208/14 | 6,280-TV | 28,700 | Owner | 11747 | Bradley M Hoyt | |
| Atlanta, GA 30318 | | R | 1966 | Cnv/88 | Associates Financial Services | 96 | 457-1850 | |
| 1650 Derry Ave SW | Bennett, Deborah D (A) | 149/14 | 35,000-8/87 | 35,200 | Owner | 11072 | S H McCalla | |
| Atlanta, GA 30310 | | R | 1948 | FHA/87/10.5 | Altus Bank | 63 | 804-0400 | |
| 255 Fairway Ridge Dr | Blackmon, Larry | 888/1/2 | 407,100-3/87 | 325,650 | Owner | 10698 | J Michael Campbell | |
| Alpharetta, GA 30201 | | R | 1986 | ARM/87/8.25 | The Dime Savings Bank of NY | 466 | 392-0041 | |
| 880 Glendale Terr #6 (C) | Bond, Kenneth R | 48/14 | 16,740-TV | 44,000 | Thomas R & Wendy L Pulling | 9650 | Donald Jones | |
| Atlanta, GA 30308 | | R | | Cnv/85 | Wells Fargo Credit Corp | 50 | #Not in Legal Ad | |
| 2878 Blossom Lane | Booker, Kenneth F & | 222/14 | 24,220-TV | 63,006 | Owner | 10354 | S H McCalla | |
| East Point, GA 30344 | Theresa S | R | 1962 | FHA/86/9.5 | McCaughan Mortgage Co Inc | 368 | 804-0400 | |

ISSUE DATE: DECEMBER 11, 1990  AUCTION DATE: JANUARY 2, 1991 PAGE 1

# FORECLOSURE UPDATE

INFORMATION SHEET

<u>Areas We Cover:</u>

Volusia County
Seminole County
Orange County
Pasco County
Pinellas County
Hillsborough County
Polk County
Dade County
Broward County
Palm Beach County
Lee County
Sarasota County
Duval County

**Foreclosure Service Bureau**
7154 N UNIVERSITY DR, #324
TAMARAC, FL 33321
305-720-0526

Reprinted by permission of Foreclosure Service Bureau

## Foreclosure Service Bureau

DADE COUNTY January 4, 1991 Page 7

.OAN STREET ADDRESS DEFENDANT PLAINTIFF
CONV SEE BELOW WILLIAM MARKETS CORP SECURED REALTY INVES
PL. ATTY. STEVEN JACOBSON
CASE NO. 90-61171-24 PHONE NO. (407) 241-5551
LEGAL DESC'N L 5-8 B 1 NORTH SILVER CREST 40/24
INT. BALANCE OWING MTHLY. PMT. ORIG. LOAN DATE/AMT. LAST PMT
.5% $180,284.00 2639 05/13/88 $188,500.00 09/01/90
LIENS FIRST MIAMI INVESTMENTS MTG B 13678 P 1350; LITTLE HAITI FOOD MARKET LEASE
ITG. RECORD B 13678 P1338 A/V $0.00 FOLIO #:
ADDT'L INFO: 1152 NW 103 ST A/V $9076; 1166 NW 103 $13770;1186 NW 103

.OAN STREET ADDRESS DEFENDANT PLAINTIFF
CONV 4416 SW 132 PLACE WESTBROOKE POINT INC CORAL GABLES FED
MIAMI 33175 PL. ATTY. THOMAS DAVISON IV
CASE NO. 90-61187-03 PHONE NO. (305) 441-8864
LEGAL DESC'N L 9 B 27 SAN SEBAASTIAN UNIT 5 111/9
INT. BALANCE OWING MTHLY. PMT. ORIG. LOAN DATE/AMT. LAST PMT
11.25% $51,328.00 538 08/01/79 $55,300.00 09/01/90
LIENS SEARS FJ B 11442 P 199; MM GASCUE MTG B 13385 P 4125; MERRILL-STEVENS DRY DOCK FJ B 13681 P 921 MORE
MTG. RECORD B 10470 P1769 A/V $93,199.00 FOLIO #: 30 4923 032 0910
ADDT'L INFO: 3/2/2109 POOL 10-79 $68900

LOAN STREET ADDRESS DEFENDANT PLAINTIFF
FHA 10743 SW 144 STREET EMMA REED LOMAS MTG USA
MIAMI 33176 PL. ATTY. BARRY YARCHIN
CASE NO. 90-61188-09 PHONE NO. (305) 374-6600
LEGAL DESC'N L 2 B 49 RICHMOND HEIGHTS 92/77
INT. BALANCE OWING MTHLY. PMT. ORIG. LOAN DATE/AMT. LAST PMT
7% $13,882.00 140 10/30/72 $21,000.00 07/01/90
LIENS HH REALTY MTG B 13869 P 1840; LIS PENDIS B 14751 P 206
ITG. RECORD B 7959 P 713 A/V $62,488.00 FOLIO #: 30 5019 011 0540
ADDT'L INFO: 4/2/2204 10-72 $21500 TENANTS

.OAN STREET ADDRESS DEFENDANT PLAINTIFF
FHA 2550 NW 26 STREET EDWINA CLARKE LEADER FEDERAL
MIAMI 33142 ANDREW PL. ATTY. BARRY YARCHIN
CASE NO. 90-61189-03 PHONE NO. (305) 374-6600
LEGAL DESC'N L 6 B 1 CLAYTON HEIGHTS 21/10
INT. BALANCE OWING MTHLY. PMT. ORIG. LOAN DATE/AMT. LAST PMT
10.5% $53,197.00 501 04/23/86 $54,700.00 07/01/90
LIENS GLENDALE MTG B 14286 P 2327; MIAMI HERALD CREDIT UNION FJ B 12578 P 753; FIDELITY CASUALTY FJ B 11174 P 459
MTG. RECORD B 12866 P1556 A/V $54,323.00 FOLIO #: 01 3127 004 0060
ADDT'L INFO: 4/3/2319 12-85 $62000 DUPLEX TENANTS

LOAN STREET ADDRESS DEFENDANT PLAINTIFF
PVT 1041 NW 38 STREET FRANCES PENNELL HARDERICK TUCKER
MIAMI 33127 PL. ATTY. JAMES SILAFIAN
CASE NO. 90-61205-28 PHONE NO. (305) 385-0144
LEGAL DESC'N L 17 B 3 LEROI SUBD 12/9
INT. BALANCE OWING MTHLY. PMT. ORIG. LOAN DATE/AMT. LAST PMT
10% $28,453.00 290 05/19/81 $31,900.00 05/01/90
LIENS DEPT OF HRS MTG B 12973 P 654
MTG. RECORD B 11437 P 410 A/V $18,014.00 FOLIO #: 01 3123 021 0560
DDT'L INFO: 2/1/987 5-81 $33900

.OAN STREET ADDRESS DEFENDANT PLAINTIFF
ND 14035 NE 6 AVENUE ANTONIA ROSEMOND MICHAEL CHASE
MIAMI PL. ATTY. MICHAEL CHASE
CASE NO. 90-61216-30 PHONE NO. (305) 945-4155
LEGAL DESC'N L 1 B 9 RUCKS PARK 44/97
NT. BALANCE OWING MTHLY. PMT. ORIG. LOAN DATE/AMT. LAST PMT
3% $19,421.00 250 05/10/89 $20,000.00 10/01/90
LIENS TA: 92 NE 90 STREET EL PORTAL, FLA
TG. RECORD B 14101 P1224 A/V $39,298.00 FOLIO #: 06 2219 011 1210
DDT'L INFO: 3/3/1524 5 UNITS APTS 5-89 $67700 TENANTS

Reprinted by permission of Foreclosure Service Bureau

FORECLOSURE UPDATE NEWSLETTER
*Researchers and Publishers Since 1979*

2701 East Camelback Road, Suite 341 • The Quadrangle • Phoenix, Arizona 85016 • 602/381-0725

January 28, 1991

Ted Thomas
P. O. Box 5000 Suite 412
Danville, CA 94526

Dear Ted:

In Arizona about 125 residential foreclosures occur each business day. In Maricopa county (Phoenix and the Valley of the Sun) we average 75 foreclosures per day or 1484 per month. This is not significantly less than the 1486 we averaged last year.

In Maricopa county there are approximately 550,000 single family homes. In the last four years one out of every ten homeowners has received a foreclosure notice!

I have provided seminars for homeowners facing foreclosure. Based on surveys from over 1,000 attendees, the average homeowner facing foreclosure is over 45 years of age and 29% had more than 30% equity they were going to lose in their home.

The opportunity to help homeowners avoid possible lender lawsuits, trashing of their credit and reporting of relief of debt to the IRS via 1099-A is available to foreclosure investors.

Arizona is at the bottom of the economic cycle and is one of the best buyer's markets in America. As the average resale is about $75,000 for a 1500 square foot home, it is a lot like investing in Sunnyvale California in 1975. The likelihood that the Sunnyvale home will grow to $550,000 from its current $275,000 is far less than the likelihood that the Phoenix home will be worth $275,000 over the same time frame.

Cordially,

Ralph Shattuck, Publisher
Foreclosure Update Newsletter

## FORECLOSURES

**FORECLOSURE UPDATE NEWSLETTER**

*2701 E. Camelback Road, Suite 341 - Phoenix, Arizona 85016 - (602-381-0725)*

RESIDENTIAL NOTICE OF TRUSTEE'S SALE RECORDED ON: 10-02-90 PAGE 5
PUBLISHED ON: 10-04-90

| | | | | |
|---|---|---|---|---|
| FILE NUMBER | REFILE=R | | | |
| ORIGINAL TRUSTOR | PARCEL # | | BENEFICIARY | TRUSTEE |
| LEGAL DESCRIPTION | PLAT/MAP # | | DOCKET/PAGE | DATE/TIME/LOC |
| STREET ADDRESS | CITY | ZIP TD | AMOUNT/DATE | TRUSTEE # |
| [1] SUCCESSOR OWNER LAND USE | CODE | | LAST SALE/DATE | SQ.FT. POOL=P |

### *MARICOPA RESIDENTIAL FORECLOSURES*

| | | | | |
|---|---|---|---|---|
| R 445408 | | | | |
| LANDRITH, JANET M | 137-21-148 | | Standard Fed | Specialized |
| Lt110 Northwood Park | 230/09 | | 83-436732 | 1-08/11:00/OC |
| 222 W. Brown U110 | Mesa | 85201 | $60,700/FHA/10-83 | 90-1444AZ |
| | 07-36 | | $60,900 /10-83 | 1152/ |
| R 445727 | | | | |
| STARKS, JAMES A | 134-22-439A | | Anchor Svngs | T.D. Svc |
| U359 Circle Tree | 231/32 | | 87-474391 | 1-03/11:00/CH |
| 461 W. Holmes Ave #359 | Mesa | 85202 | $30,000/FHA/ 7-87 | A1-4429 |
| | 07-35 | | $29,974 /11-89 | 582/ |
| R 445357 | | | | |
| MITCHELL, JAY R | 140-24-299 | | Independence One | C. Sutton |
| Lt221 Eastbrook | 269/29 | | 86-334440 | 1-10/10:30/TO |
| 2301 E. University Dr #221 | Mesa | 85203 | $62,072/FHA/ 7-86 | 05-01591OM |
| Eampire Investments | 07-36 | | $61,066 /11-89 | 1118/ |
| R 445996 | | | | |
| PEEL, RICHARD W | 137-33-033 | | Chemical Fin | Peelle |
| Lt3 Hillview Acres | 091/41 | | 89-527037 | 1-04/ 3:30/CH |
| 1725 E. Brown Rd | Mesa | 85203 | $300,000//11-89 | 9077726 |
| same | 01-51 | | $400,000 /11-89 | 4056/P |
| R 445363 | | | | |
| BRINKERHOFF, RANDOLPH D | 139-02-137 | | Banner Banc | C. Sutton |
| Lt124 Villa Park U3 | 152/18 | | 83-524032 | 1-10/10:30/TO |
| 1541 E. Diamond | Mesa | 85204 | $55,740/FHA/12-83 | 01-0363BBJ |
| Velasquez, Victoriano | 01-31 | | $57,419 / 1-75TFV | 1446/ |
| R 446068 | | | | |
| BLANTON, DOLORES F | 139-13-246 | | T. Guleserian | Statewide |
| Lt2 Sunset Mesa | 167/43 | | 89-111291 | 1-03/11:00/TO |
| 1217 S. Hobson | Mesa | 85204 | $30,000// 3-89 | 010399 |
| | 01-31 | | $40,450 / 7-76 | 1747/ |
| R 445362 | | | | |
| REUTING, RONALD E | 141-65-158R | | Independence One | C. Sutton |
| Lt37 Golden West 2 | 199/11 | | 86-711184 | 1-10/10:30/TO |
| 1508 N. 62nd Pl | Mesa | 85205 | $83,600/FHA/12-86 | 08-0862IOM |
| same | 01-41 | | $83,000 /12-86 | 1638/ |

*SORTED BY ZIP CODE*

## *FORECLOSURES*

# RESIDENTIAL FORECLOSURES FIVE YEAR TREND DECEMBER 1990

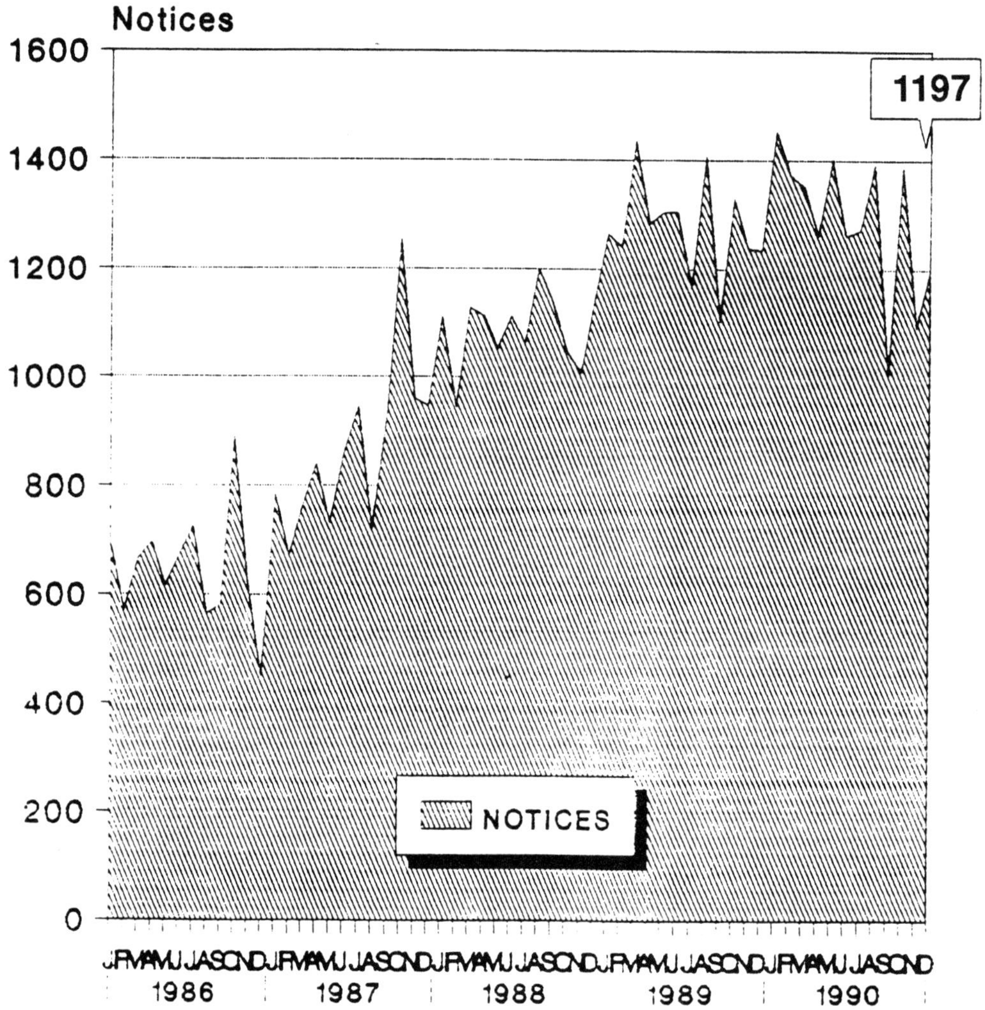


Published by Foreclosure Update Newsletter (602-381-0725).
Not for resale, reproduction, duplication or distribution without the written permission of the publisher.

Reprinted by permission of Foreclosure Update Newsletter

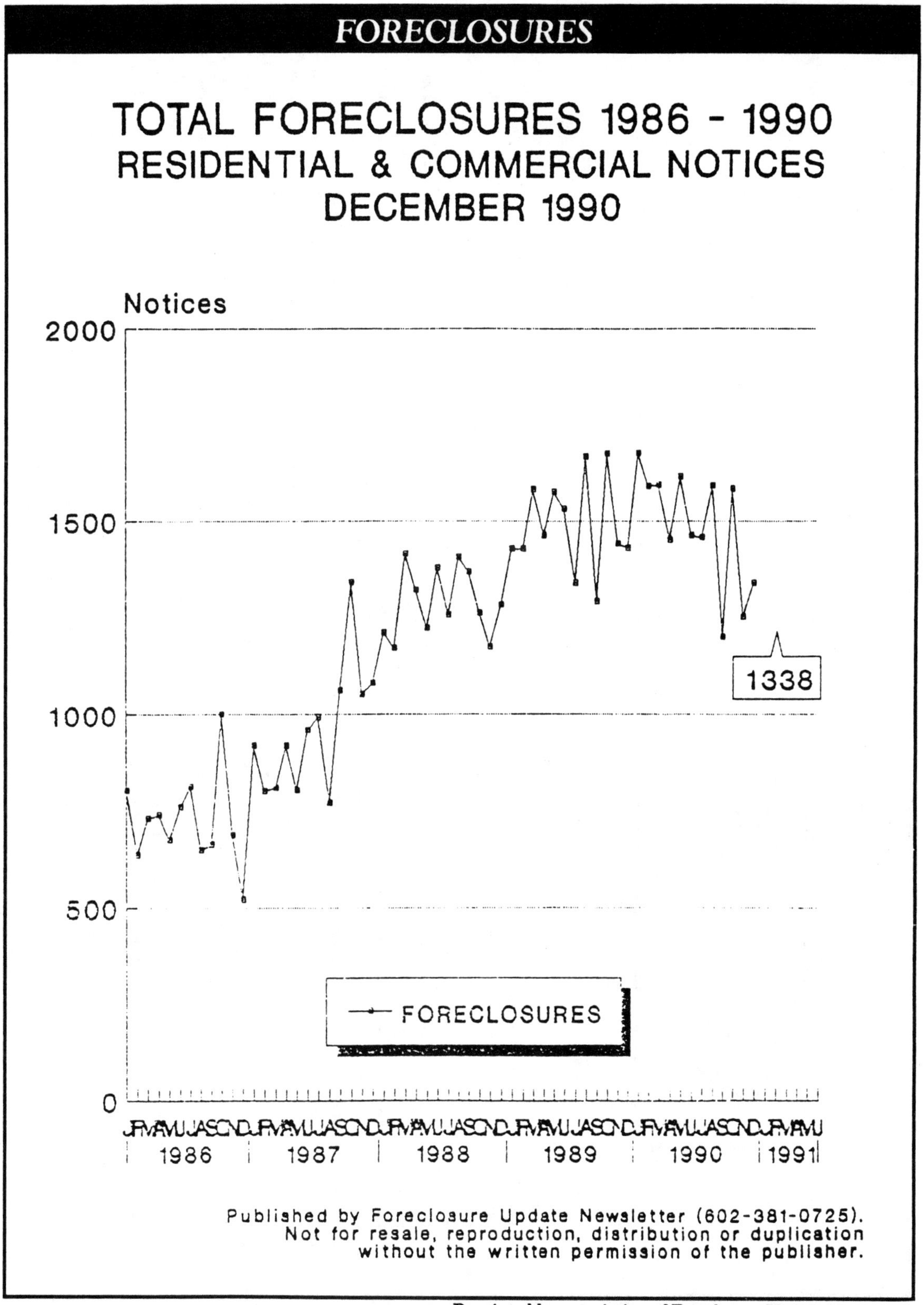


Reprinted by permission of Foreclosure Update Newsletter

# FORECLOSURE INFORMATION

FLS **FORECLOSURE LISTING SERVICE, INC.**
P.O. BOX 1011
CARROLLTON, TEXAS 75011-1011

(214) 242-6163
(214) 245-9022

OWNERS
Ginger Canfield
Patricia Buckley

Serving the Dallas Financial, Real Estate and Investment Sector Since **1963**

| No. | MAPCO | CLASS | TYPE | ADDRESS | ZIP | LEGAL DESCRIPTION | MORTGAGOR ORIGINAL/(CURRENT) | MORTGAGEE (LENDER) | TRUSTEE | TIME | VOL/PAGE | DATE | ORIG AMT | NO PMT | INTRT | EXP DATE |
|---|---|---|---|---|---|---|---|---|---|---|---|---|---|---|---|---|
| S.E. DALLAS PROPER | | | | | | | | | | | | | | | | |
| 61 | 65A | 4PLEX | CV | 1821+ EWING AVE S | 75216 | L-6.7/3679 TRINITY HTS #3 | WYATT, HELEN | FIRST CITY BANK DALLAS | DANNA, RICHARD A | 10-1 | 84221/1673 | 11/84 | $36,640 | --- | --- | --- |
| 62 | 65D | RES | VA | 1242 EXETER | 75216 | L-18.C/6007 GLENDALE HGTS | WILKERSONA, SWENDALL/NAOMI | M P CRUM COMPANY | SPEIDEL/HUDSON, | 11-2 | 72246/1832 | 12/72 | $21,000 | 139 | 7. | 12/2002 |
| 63 | 55Z | RES | CV | 2523 EXETER DR | 75216 | L-17.1/5852 LISBON HGTS | MUHAMMAD, ELIJAH/BRIDGETTE | TAYLOR, MARY M | THOMAS, CATHERINE | 10-1 | 87030/1134 | 02/87 | $5,900 | --- | --- | --- |
| 64 | 25E | RES | CV | 9744 FAIRCLOUD DR | 75217 | L-11.2/6714 ST AUGUSTINE PK #3 | ANDREWS, JUANELL | BRIGGS, HELEN RUTH ALVORD | BUGBEE, MELANIE H | 10-1 | 89123/1270 | 06/89 | $34,500 | --- | --- | --- |
| 65 | 47H | RES | VA | 8016 FALL RIVER DR | 75228 | L-3.1/7060 CLAREMONT | WRIGHT, NEIL/PATRICIA | NORWEST MTG INC | BAUM, CHARLES F | 10-1 | 83147/1370 | 07/83 | $78,000 | 832 | 12.50 | 08/2013 |
| 66 | 47C | DUP | CV | 8235 FERGUSON RD | 75228 | L-2.21 SOMERSET HTS | DARDICK ET AL, MICHAEL | MCNB TEXAS NATL BK | FIELDS JR, EDWARD J | 10-1 | 86123/0145 | 06/86 | $112,000 | --- | --- | --- |
| 67 | 55S | RES | FHA | 2735 FERNWOOD | 75216 | L-21.35/4224 BROADMOOR ADDN | PAUL, ETHEL MARION | F & L MTG BANKERS | SPEIDEL/HUDSON/CAGLE, | 11-2 | 86244/0988 | 12/86 | $49,400 | 415 | 9.5 | 01/2017 |
| 68 | 65B | RES | CV | 3914 FERNWOOD AVE | 75216 | L-4 J E KINNARD'S SUB | CAMPBELL, DWAYNE | SEARS FEDERAL CREDIT UNION | GOODALE, DRUE | 10-1 | 88039/2118 | 02/88 | $7,921 | --- | --- | --- |
| 69 | 56W | RES | FHA | 2634 FORDHAM RD | 75216 | L-9.2/5852 LISBON HTS ADDN | BRYER, ADRIENNE GRIER | COUNTRYWIDE FUNDING CORP | DRAPER, J D | 1-4 | 88215/2516 | 11/88 | $36,050 | 329 | 10.5 | 11/2018 |
| 70 | 56W | RES | FHA | 2651 FORDHAM RD | 75216 | L-12.18/5855 FORDHAM HGTS | PHILLIPS, JAMES/LETHA | UNITED S/A OF TEXAS | WEBB, D PAUL | 10-1 | 69087/1894 | 04/69 | $7,600 | 53 | 7.5 | 05/1999 |
| 71 | 48P | RES | CV | 7704 FORNEY RD | 75227 | L-6A.5827 DAVIS FIN SER SUB | DAVIS FIN SER INC | COMMERCIAL NATL BK | ULMER, MICHAEL | 1-4 | 86093/2102 | 04/86 | --- | --- | 11. | 04/1989 |
| 72 | 65E | RES | FHA | 3909 FORTUNE LN | 75216 | L-19.8/6003 MARSALIS PK | HODGE, CARL & HODGE, WILLIE | CITY FEDERAL S/L ASSN | LEDBETTER, DON W | 1-4 | 85130/4639 | 06/85 | $51,300 | --- | - - | --- |
| 73 | 65F | RES | FHA | 4025 FORTUNE LN | 75216 | L-37.F MARSALIS PK | ANDERSON, ALVIN/FRANCIS | EXCHANGE MTG CO | BROOKS, SUSAN | 11-2 | 73066/2222 | 03/73 | $18,600 | 123 | 7. | 4/2003 |
| 74 | 59W | RES | CV | 9036 FOSTORIA DR | 75217 | L-7.K/7876 CRAWFORD PK | JONES, MILDRED | SIEGEL, SARAH | POE, A C | 11-2 | 75163/1492 | 08/75 | $17,500 | --- | --- | --- |
| 75 | 59H | RES | VA | 1532 FOX RUN DR | 75217 | L-15.10/6720 HERITAGE PK II | SHAMSID-DEEN, ASADI/HALIMAH | ADMIN VETERANS AFFAIRS | JONES/HAMILTON, | 10-1 | 88182/1947 | 09/88 | $42,750 | 375 | 10. | 9/2018 |
| 76 | 58H | RES | FHA | 8312 FOXWOOD | 75217 | L-2.11/6317 TANGLEWOOD | MONEY, GREG/LAURIE | THE MURRAY INV CO | SCHROEDER, MICHAEL J | 10-1 | 83239/4744 | 11/83 | $56,412 | 602 | 12.50 | 12/2013 |
| 77 | 66T | RES | FHA | 3448 FROSTY TRAIL | 75241 | L-16.10/8294 HIGHLAND HILLS #9 | CARR JR, GEORGE/MARY | FEDERAL NATL MTG ASSN | DRAPER, J D | 1-4 | 69194/0530 | 09/69 | $14,900 | 104 | 7.5 | 10/1999 |
| 78 | 76E | RES | C/F | 2643 GADBERRY ST | 75241 | TR-13 CLOVER BLOSSOM FARMS | CRUMP, ROBERT W | MBANK PRESTON | LEDBETTER, DON W | 1-4 | 86007/1774 | 09/85 | $74,000 | --- | --- | 10/2015 |
| 79 | 69A-H | RES | FHA | 13809 GARDEN GROVE DR | 75253 | PT L-6.A BERRY & RUTHERFORD | DYE, JOHN ROBERT/DONNA SUE | SOUTHLAND MTG | CHAMBERS, MARILYN R | 1-4 | 86136/0221 | 06/86 | --- | 328 | 9.5 | 07/2016 |
| 80 | 45M | VAC-C | CV | 3008 GASTON AVE | 75226 | L-3,24.B/491 NUSSBAUMR 4,875SF | CBD PROPERTIES | BANCTEXAS DALLAS | ROBERTS, KENT H | 1-4 | 84182/4257 | 09/84 | $150,000 | --- | --- | --- |
| 81 | 46B | APT-B | CV | 4915 GASTON AVE | 752146 | PT L-4 PT L-3.C/681 MUNGER PL | FALVO, JAMES L & DICKEY JR, W | MERCHANTS STATE BANK | PARKER, TERRY R | 10=1 | 85068/5204 | 03/85 | $735,000 | --- | --- | --- |
| 82 | 58J | RES | VA | 1621 GILLETTE RD | 75217 | L-10.4/6236 PIEDMONT PK #1 | ROSE, ALVIN C & POWERS, WILLIA | ADMIN VETERANS AFFAIRS | JONES/HAMILTON, | 10-1 | 85058/3075 | 03/85 | $48,800 | 520 | 12.5 | 04/2015 |

Reprinted by permission of Foreclosure Listing Service, Inc.

**DAILY DEFAULT**
**INFOSERVICE**

*Complete default, trustee sale, and REO information sent to you daily!*
P.O. BOX 456, ANTIOCH, CALIFORNIA 94509 ■ 415/754-7039

March 25, 1991

Ted Thomas
New Growth Enterprises
P. O. Box 5000 Ste 412
Danville, Ca. 94526

Dear Ted,

This is in response to your inquiry regarding the recent upsurge in foreclosures in Northern California. As you correctly surmised there has been a solid increase in the number of default notices filed on real estate properties in the 3 counties we service: Contra Costa County, Alameda County and Sacramento County.

To be specific, we're seeing between 385 - 440 defaults a month in Alameda County. This represents about a 30% increase over 6 months ago. In Contra Costa County and Sacramento County we're averaging between 275 -330 defaults a month in each county on real estate secured loans. This represents close to a 40% increase over 6 months ago.

From my various contacts in the industry I understand this is about the average increase being seen in California. I know Marin and Napa Counties are seeing over 100% increases, San Mateo, San Francisco and Solano Counties are seeing over 50% increases.

In my view, although people losing their homes is a very sobering and sad situation, it does represent a unique "window of opportunity" for the vary preforeclosure purchaser. More leads to pursue, means more chances for success for Daily Default Infoservice customers.

I personally feel the "window of opportunity" will be "open" for a limited time, then the extreme buyers market we're in will gradually come to an end.

I hope this information is of benefit.

Sincerely Yours,

Russ

Russell E. Olson, Sr.
Owner/Publisher
Daily Default Infoservice
415/754-7039; 916/371-7747

RO/rh

*"A dynamic tool you can't afford to be without — on your road to financial independence through Real Estate."*

```
DAILY DEFAULT INFOSERVICE ** P.O. BOX 456, ANTIOCH, CA 9452[illegible]
        415/754-7039   ****   916/371-7747                          03SM111
INSTRUMENT NO.: DFL[illegible]-[illegible]38 | RECORD DATE: 03/06/91     AP#: 206-1[illegible]-5      TAX ASSESSED VALUE: $97,000.00 : 1988
     LOAN DATE: 12/08/86  |     TRUSTOR: GRACE HILL                           SINCE SOLD TO: MARY A. TARFIN - 1988
     BOOK-PAGE: 1874 -    | TRUSTOR ADD: 6811 5TH AVE., RIO LINDA,95673
ORIG. LN. AMT.: $75,000.00 |    TRUSTEE: OAKLEY R. WHALEN                     PHONE: 916/991-7331   TS#: 9103-40
  DELINQ. DATE:  / /       |    ADDRESS: PO BOX 310, ELVERTA, CA 95626
DELINQUENT AMT: $ N/A      |     LENDER: OAKLEY R. WHALEN                     PHONE: 916/991-7334   LN#:
         AS OF: 03/06/91   |    ADDRESS: 300 CHARLES AVE., ELVERTA, CA 95626
   ADD'L INFO: MAILING ADD. - PO OBX 114, RIO LINDA, CA 95673; APARTMENTS; 5-UNITS; PAVED PARKING; 1960 SUBDIVIDED; 1-STORY;
INSTRUMENT NO.: DFLT-1214 | RECORD DATE: 03/06/91       AP#: 25-2[illegible]-27      TAX ASSESSED VALUE: $64,000.00 : 1987
     LOAN DATE: 11/06/87  |     TRUSTOR: ARITO KOMURE , ET AL                 SINCE SOLD TO:
     BOOK-PAGE: 2234 -    | TRUSTOR ADD: 1429 CLAUDIA DR., SAC,95822
ORIG. LN. AMT.: $38,000.00 |    TRUSTEE: STANDARD TITLE                       PHONE: 415/685-5680   TS#: 5036011595
  DELINQ. DATE: 02/01/91   |    ADDRESS: 1355 WILLOW WAY #245, CONCORD, CA 94520
DELINQUENT AMT: $1,604.00  |     LENDER: BENEFICIAL CALIRORNIA                PHONE: 916/726-1393   LN#: 74751592
         AS OF: 03/06/91   |    ADDRESS: 6201 GREENBACK LN, #F, CH, CA 95621
   ADD'L INFO: MAILING ADD. - 19 WESTLAKE CT., SAC, CA 95831; SFR; 1508 SQFT; 3/2; DEEDED 7-87 TO CURRENT OWNER; PHONE 916-424-5829; .
INSTRUMENT NO.: DFLT-1288 | RECORD DATE: 03/06/91       AP#: 229-410-24      TAX ASSESSED VALUE: $35,000.00 : 1990
     LOAN DATE: 01/26/90  |     TRUSTOR: JERRY HYATT                          SINCE SOLD TO: JERRY C. HYATT, ET AL -1990
     BOOK-PAGE: 1558 -    | TRUSTOR ADD: 6329 WEXFORD CIR., CH,95621
ORIG. LN. AMT.: $24,750.00 |    TRUSTEE: FIRST INDEPENDANT                    PHONE: 818/783-4500   TS#: 91-3126
  DELINQ. DATE: 02/15/91   |    ADDRESS: 17609 VENTURA BLVD., #305, EUNCINO, CA 91316
DELINQUENT AMT: $27,351.00 |     LENDER: REPUBLIC CAPITOL CORP                PHONE:                LN#:
         AS OF: 03/06/91   |    ADDRESS: C/O TRUSTEE
   ADD'L INFO: SFR; 1323 SQFT; 3/1.5; DEEDED 3-90 TO CURRENT OWNER; 2-CAR CARPORT; CENTRAL AIR/HEAT; 2-STORIES; 1973 SUBDIVIDED; .
INSTRUMENT NO.: DFLT-1290 | RECORD DATE: 03/06/91       AP#: 262-284-15      TAX ASSESSED VALUE: $N/A
     LOAN DATE: 09/18/90  |     TRUSTOR: JACK C. HALL , ET AL                 SINCE SOLD TO:
     BOOK-PAGE: 1108 -    | TRUSTOR ADD: 2831 NORMINGTON DR., SAC,95833
ORIG. LN. AMT.: $59,270.42 |    TRUSTEE: ATTORNEYS EQUITY CORP                PHONE: 714/364-4414   TS#: 6230 CA
  DELINQ. DATE: 01/18/91   |    ADDRESS: 27882 FORBES RD.#206, LAGUNA NIGUEL, CA 92677
DELINQUENT AMT: $2,607.00  |     LENDER: ITT FINANCE SERVICES                 PHONE: 800/827-8268   LN#: 5747850
         AS OF: 03/06/91   |    ADDRESS: 4 CENTERPOINTE DR., #210, LA PALMA, CA 90623
   ADD'L INFO: SFR; 1206 SQFT; 3/2; DEEDED 9-80 TO CURRENT OWNER; 2-CAR GARAGE; CENTRAL AIR/HEAT; 1971 SUBDIVIDED .
INSTRUMENT NO.: DFLT-0032 | RECORD DATE: 03/01/91       AP#: 14-122-9        TAX ASSESSED VALUE: $58,000.00 : 1983
     LOAN DATE: 10/29/82  |     TRUSTOR: PHYLLIS A. BRADLEY BAKER             SINCE SOLD TO:
     BOOK-PAGE: 431 -     | TRUSTOR ADD: 2774 43RD ST., SAC,95817
ORIG. LN. AMT.: $47,500.00 |    TRUSTEE: CHURCHILL SERVICE CORP               PHONE: 619/292-2000   TS#: F-35680-KB
  DELINQ. DATE: 09/01/90   |    ADDRESS: 9330 SKY PARK CT., SAN DIGEO, CA 92123
DELINQUENT AMT: $3,197.00  |     LENDER: IMPERIAL CORP                        PHONE: 619/292-2000   LN#:
         AS OF: 02/01/91   |    ADDRESS: 9330 SKY PARK CT., SAN DIEGO, CA 92112
   ADD'L INFO: SFR; 1342 SQFT; 3/1; DEEDED 10-82 TO CURRENT OWNER; CENTRAL AIR/HEAT; 2-STORIES; COMP.ROOF; SLAB FLOOR; .
INSTRUMENT NO.: DFLT-0051 | RECORD DATE: 03/01/91       AP#: 117-234-19      TAX ASSESSED VALUE: $54,000.00 : 1984
     LOAN DATE: 07/29/77  |     TRUSTOR: JOHN D. DANKOFF JR. , ET AL          SINCE SOLD TO: DONNA C. WONG - 1984
     BOOK-PAGE: 2375 -    | TRUSTOR ADD: 6300 HESBY WAY, SAC,95823
ORIG. LN. AMT.: $39,700.00 |    TRUSTEE: WESTWOOD ASSOC.                      PHONE: 818/712-4027   TS#: 4265
  DELINQ. DATE: 11/01/90   |    ADDRESS: PO BOX 54089, LOS ANGELES, CA 90054
DELINQUENT AMT: $2,261.00  |     LENDER: WEYERHAUSER MTG.                     PHONE: 818/704-8822   LN#: D06086
         AS OF: 02/01/91   |    ADDRESS: PO BOX 54089, LOS ANGELES, CA 90045
   ADD'L INFO: SFR; 1399 SQFT; 4/2; DEEDED 12-84 TO CURRENT OWNER; 2-CAR GARAGE; CENTRAL AIR/HEAT; COMP.ROOF; FIREPLACE; FHA LOAN; .
INSTRUMENT NO.: DFLT-0205 | RECORD DATE: 03/01/91       AP#: 220-401-6       TAX ASSESSED VALUE: $103,000.00 : 1989
     LOAN DATE: 11/16/79  |     TRUSTOR: DORIS L. DOTSON                      SINCE SOLD TO: A.J. SAULSBURY, ET AL - 1989
     BOOK-PAGE: 514 -     | TRUSTOR ADD: 6625 SILVERTHORN CIR., SAC,95842
ORIG. LN. AMT.: $45,000.00 |    TRUSTEE: GRAMERCY MTG. CO                     PHONE: 415/692-9010   TS#: 911950-4
  DELINQ. DATE: 11/01/90   |    ADDRESS: 979 BROADWAY, MILLBRAE, CA 94030
DELINQUENT AMT: $3,039.00  |     LENDER: HOMESTEAD S&L                        PHONE: 415/692-9010   LN#:
         AS OF: 02/01/91   |    ADDRESS: PO BOX 6008, MILLBRAE, CA 94030
   ADD'L INFO: SFR; 1441 SQFT; 3/2; 2-CAR CENTRAL AIR/HEAT; FIREPLACE; POOL; WOOD SHINGLE ROOF; 1-STORY; 1962 SUBDIVIDED .
INSTRUMENT NO.: DFLT-0235 | RECORD DATE: 03/01/91       AP#: 115-580-27      TAX ASSESSED VALUE: $112,000.00 : 1987
     LOAN DATE: 12/27/89  |     TRUSTOR: THOMAS O. VELEZ , ET AL              SINCE SOLD TO:
     BOOK-PAGE: 1797 -    | TRUSTOR ADD: 8571 CORD WAY, SAC,95828
ORIG. LN. AMT.: $10,000.00 |    TRUSTEE: PLACER FORECLOSURE INC               PHONE:                TS#:
  DELINQ. DATE: 12/15/90   |    ADDRESS: 12150 HERDAL DR., AUBURN ,CA 95603
DELINQUENT AMT: $1,569.00  |     LENDER: JULIAM R. LIDBERG                    PHONE: 916/989-8616   LN#:
         AS OF: 02/01/91   |    ADDRESS: 547 SOUTHWOOD DR., FOLSOM, CA 95630
   ADD'L INFO: SFR; 1644 SQFT; 3/2; DEEDED 1-87 TO CURRENT OWNER; 2-CAR GARAGE; CENTRAL AIR/HEAT; FIREPLACE; SHAKE ROOF; SLAB FLOOR; .
INSTRUMENT NO.: DFLT-0238 | RECORD DATE: 03/01/91       AP#: 224-730-37,38   TAX ASSESSED VALUE: $N/A
     LOAN DATE: 08/29/89  |     TRUSTOR: JRH CAPITAL INVESTMENT INC           SINCE SOLD TO:
     BOOK-PAGE: 447 -     | TRUSTOR ADD: 8186 & 8188 BUTCH CASSIDY PL., CH,95610
ORIG. LN. AMT.: $275,000.00 |   TRUSTEE: PLACER FORECLOSURE INC               PHONE:                TS#:
  DELINQ. DATE: 10/01/90   |    ADDRESS: 12150 HERDAL DR., AUBURN, CA 95603
DELINQUENT AMT: $22,498.00 |     LENDER: ROBERT L. RONNE                      PHONE: 916/482-1518   LN#:
         AS OF: 02/01/91   |    ADDRESS: 3160 WATT AVE., SAC, CA 95821
   ADD'L INFO: MAILING ADD. - 1733 WOODSIDE RD., #210, REDWOOD CITY, CA 94061; DEEDED 6-86 TO CURRENT OWNER; SFR; .
INSTRUMENT NO.: DFLT-0912 | RECORD DATE: 03/01/91       AP#: 252-172-10      TAX ASSESSED VALUE: $19,000.00 : 1981
     LOAN DATE: 12/23/75  |     TRUSTOR: RAYMOND DILLARD , ET AL              SINCE SOLD TO: MAGDALENA R. MARLER - 1981
     BOOK-PAGE: 168 -     | TRUSTOR ADD: 3608 MAHOGANY ST., SAC,95838
ORIG. LN. AMT.: $14,050.00 |    TRUSTEE: CHURCHILL SERVICE CORP               PHONE: 619/292-2000   TS#: F-33473-BH
  DELINQ. DATE: 05/01/90   |    ADDRESS: 9330 SKY PARK CT., SAN DIEGO, CA 92123
DELINQUENT AMT: $4,294.00  |     LENDER: IMPERIAL CORP                        PHONE: 619/292-2000   LN#:
         AS OF: 02/01/91   |    ADDRESS: 9330 SKY PARK CT., SAN DIEGO, CA 92112
   ADD'L INFO: SFR; 1138 SQFT; 2/1; GARAGE; COMP.ROOF; 1-STORY; 1947 SUBDIVIDED; FHA LOAN; .

THIS IS NOT A BONAFIDE TITLE REPORT, VALIDITY NOT GUARANTEED ** ABOVE INFO IS AVAILABLE TWICE A MONTH ON FLOPPY DISK - CALL FOR DETAILS
```

**Reprinted by permission of Daily Default Infoservice**

Daily Journal Corporation

The Los Angeles
Daily Journal
915 East First Street
Los Angeles, CA 90012
(213) 625-2141

San Francisco
Daily Journal
1390 Market Street
Suite 910
San Francisco, CA 94102
(415) 558-9888

Southern California
Real Estate Journal
915 East First Street
Los Angeles, CA 90012
(213) 625-2141

Northern California
Real Estate Journal
1390 Market Street
Suite 910
San Francisco, CA 94102
(415) 558-9888

Daily Commerce
915 East First Street
Los Angeles, CA 90012
(213) 625-2141

The Inter-City Express
125 12th Street
Oakland, CA 94607
(415) 465-3121

Orange County
Reporter
817 North Broadway
Suite A
Santa Ana, CA 92701
(714) 543-2027

Marin County
Court Reporter
4380 Redwood Highway
Suite B-10
San Rafael, CA 94903
(415) 479-4311

San Jose Post-Record
90 North First Street
San Jose, CA 95113
(408) 287-4866

Sonoma County
Daily Herald-Recorder
1818 Fourth Street
Santa Rosa, CA 95402
(707) 545-1166

The Daily Recorder
1115 H Street
Sacramento, CA 95814
(916) 444-2355

Back Country Trader
6150 Mission Gorge Road
Suite 205
San Diego, CA 92120
(619) 584-0588

California Lawyer
1390 Market Street
Suite 1016
San Francisco, CA 94102
(415) 558-9888

April 10, 1991

Ted Thomas
New Growth Financial
P.O. Box 5000 #412
Daneville, CA 94526

Ted:

Enclosed is the information for your new book, as requested by Linda Wright, regarding Notices of Default counts in the Daily Commerce.

Beginning in November 1990, defaults filed numbered 2,798. In December the number increased to 4,191. Then in January 1991 the number escalated to 5,281, followed by a further increase in February to 5,382.

Please keep in mind that these numbers are collective for Los Angeles, Orange, Riverside, San Bernardino and Ventura counties.

For Los Angeles County alone, defaults numbered 1.645 for the month of February 1991, and in Orange County the number was 343 for that same month.

By way of comparison, in April 1990, Los Angeles County had 1,169 defaults. In May there were 1,886 defaults, in June 1,929 and July had 1,479 defaults recorded.

I hope this information helps in your fact gathering endeavor for the new book. Let me know if I can be of further assistance. I look forward to seeing the book when published.

Sincerely,

Joel Cone
Staff Reporter

NOTICE OF DEFAULT

# DAILY COMMERCE

Vol. 75, No. 58 • Los Angeles Calif • SERVING THE SOUTHERN CALIFORNIA REAL ESTATE INVESTOR • 50c • Tuesday, March 26, 1991

## PROPERTY LISTINGS AND SALES LEADS

## LA - LOS ANGELES NOTICES OF DEFAULT

### LOS ANGELES ( 51-E3 )

**1318 W 55TH ST 90037**

T: B: L: U:
APN:5002-009-025 LAST SOLD: 08/23/89
BUILT: 1915 ZONING: R2-1 LAND $: 12835
BR: 2 USE CODE: 0100 BLDG $: 10165
BA: 2 BLDG SIZE: 1461 ASSD $: 23000
UNITS: LOT SIZE: 5100
T/DEED#: 89-1756423 DEFAULT#: 91-235157
LOAN DATE: 10/31/89 DEF REC: 02/19/91
LOAN AMT: 34000 DEL AMT: 37360
OTH LOAN: AS OF: 02/14/91

LEE,PATRICIA
1318 W 55TH ST
LOS ANGELES 90037
TRUSTEE NO:
LOAN NO:
RAINBOW TRUST DEED SERVICES
P.O. BOX 148
TOPANGA 90290
BENEFICIARY: 213-455-1864
RAINBOW TRUST DEED SERVICES
P.O. BOX 148
TOPANGA 90290

### LOS ANGELES ( 51-E4 )

**1536 W 59TH ST 90047**

T:4342 B: L:64 U:
APN:6002-010-027 LAST SOLD: 08/02/78
BUILT: 1924 ZONING: R3-1 LAND $: 26923
BR: 3 USE CODE: 0100 BLDG $: 19077
BA: 1 BLDG SIZE: 980 ASSD $: 46000
UNITS: LOT SIZE: 3400
T/DEED#: 90-645432 DEFAULT#: 91-247107
LOAN DATE: 04/04/90 DEF REC: 02/20/91
LOAN AMT: 5000 DEL AMT: 1758
OTH LOAN: AS OF: 02/14/91

PETERS,RAY
1536 W 59TH ST
LOS ANGELES 90047
TRUSTEE NO: 91-106
LOAN NO:
GATEWAY TITLE CO
534 N A ST
OXNARD 93030
805-647-7777
BENEFICIARY: 805-647-7777
LUIS C PEREZ
534 N A ST
OXNARD 93030

### LOS ANGELES ( 52-E6 )

**7927 ALIX AVE 90001**

T:NADEAU PARK TR 5/79 B:5 L:15-16 U:
APN:6026-005-008 LAST SOLD: 03/01/90
BUILT: 1953 ZONING: LCR2 LAND $: 14117
BR: 3 USE CODE: 0100 BLDG $: 7056
BA: 2 BLDG SIZE: 1209 ASSD $: 21173
UNITS: LOT SIZE: 6000
T/DEED#: 90-337877 DEFAULT#: 91-246889
LOAN DATE: 03/01/90 DEF REC: 02/20/91
LOAN AMT: 105000 DEL AMT: 4817
OTH LOAN: AS OF: 02/20/91

GONZALEZ, MARGARITA M.
7927 ALIX AVE.
LOS ANGELES 90001
TRUSTEE NO:
LOAN NO: 0136937
AMERICAN NATIONAL FINCL. CORP
800 S. BROADWAY, STE 410
WALNUT CREEK 94596
BENEFICIARY: 415-597-5630
HAMILTON SAVINGS BANK, F.S.B.
525 MARKET ST
SAN FRANCISCO 94105

### LOS ANGELES ( 57-D1 )

**2147 W 78TH ST 90047**

T:5107 B:21 L:15 U:
APN:6017-021-015 LAST SOLD: 06/14/77
BUILT: 1927 ZONING: R1-1 LAND $: 14348
BR: 2 USE CODE: 0100 BLDG $: 14652
BA: 1 BLDG SIZE: 1504 ASSD $: 29000
UNITS: LOT SIZE: 6700
T/DEED#: 90-263308 DEFAULT#: 91-247114
LOAN DATE: 02/15/90 DEF REC: 02/20/91
LOAN AMT: DEL AMT: 9630
OTH LOAN: AS OF: 02/14/91

DIXON,RICHARD E
2147 W 78TH ST
LOS ANGELES 90047
TRUSTEE NO: TH1062
LOAN NO:
TAYOLR HALL, INC.
11101 WASHINGTON BLVD., #208
CULVER CITY 90232
BENEFICIARY: 213-204-6100
UNITED INTERSTATE FIN'L SERVS
11101 WASHINGTON BLVD., #200
CULVER CITY 90232

### LOS ANGELES ( 57-F4 )

**1023 W 110TH ST 90044**

T:1248 B: L:4-5 U:
APN:6076-012-012 LAST SOLD: 09/19/84
BUILT: 1954 ZONING: R320U* LAND $: 52287
BR: 9 USE CODE: BLDG $: 79713
BA: 11 BLDG SIZE: 4770 ASSD $: 132000
UNITS: 11 LOT SIZE: 8100
T/DEED#: 90-209657 DEFAULT#: 91-253168
LOAN DATE: 02/07/90 DEF REC: 02/21/91
LOAN AMT: 27000 DEL AMT: 1160
OTH LOAN: AS OF: 02/20/91

MONTEZ,ALBERT JR
1117 STONEMAN AVE
ALHAMBRA 91081
TRUSTEE NO: 21713-G
LOAN NO: PS6858
CONSOLIDATED RECONVEYANCE CO.
21031 VENTURA BLVD. # 202
WOODLAND HILLS 91364
818-340-4010
BENEFICIARY: 818-340-4010
ARTHUR W. WEISS
21031 VENTURA BLVD. 2ND FL.
WOODLAND HILLS 91364

### LOS ANGELES 37 ( 52-A3 )

**706 W 50TH ST 90037**

T: B: L:24 U:
APN:5018-020-007 LAST SOLD: 04/21/88

MACIAS,VICENTE & TERESA
706 W 50TH ST
LOS ANGELES 37 90037
TRUSTEE NO: 91-3057
LOAN NO: MACIAS

Reprinted by permission of Daily Commerce

**REDLOC**
INFOSYSTEMS, INC.

*The Professional's Choice*

April 10, 1991

Mr. Ted Thomas
NEW GROWTH FINANCIAL
185 Front Street, Suite 207
Danville, CA 94526

Dear Ted,

It was very nice chatting with you the other day as always, and here is the information you requested showing the numbers of Notice of Defaults and Notice of Trustee Sales that we've published for the first quarter of 1991.

**Defaults For 1991 (1/1 to 3/31)**

| County | Year | Month | Week | Day |
|---|---|---|---|---|
| Los Angeles | 6,637 | 2,212 | 511 | 102 |
| Orange County | 1,853 | 617 | 143 | 29 |
| Riverside | 1,672 | 557 | 129 | 26 |
| San Bernardino | 1,692 | 564 | 130 | 26 |
| San Diego | 1,676 | 559 | 129 | 26 |

**Trustee Sales For 1991 (1/1 to 3/31)**

| County | Year | Month | Week | Day |
|---|---|---|---|---|
| Los Angeles | 3,035 | 1,012 | 233 | 47 |
| Orange County | 649 | 216 | 50 | 10 |
| Riverside | 831 | 277 | 64 | 13 |
| San Bernardino | 845 | 282 | 65 | 13 |
| San Diego | 738 | 246 | 57 | 11 |

Ted, I hope this information is helpful to you and is what you wanted. If you have any further questions on this, please let me know.

Very truly yours,

Ronald M. Frumkin
Chief Executive Officer

```
R E D L O C (c) 1990  *  Default Listing  *  THIS IS NOT A BONAFIDE TITLE REPORT  *  VALIDITY OF THIS LISTING IS NOT GUARANTEED

City.: ANAHEIM        TMG: 12-A4   AP:253-353-04      Trustor: NOE, MARILYN D                  REDLOC Listing #:     1
Situs: 2635 E AMES CIR ANAHEIM, CA 92806                       2635 E AMES CIR                  Default Rec Date: 10/05/90
Tract: 4597 Lot: 6 Book: 162 Page: 012                         ANAHEIM CA 92806                 Instrument #....:   534644

__________PROPERTY INFORMATION___________   __________VALUES__________   _____EXISTING LOANS_____   ____LOAN IN DEFAULT____
Built: 1963  BR.: 4   Rooms: 7                 Assessed 1989.:   $251,544   1st:*  $165,200  5/13/88   Document #.:       224611
Age..: 27    BA.: 3.0 Units:                   Land Value....:   $155,275   2nd:    $20,000 11/22/88   Loan Date..:      5/13/88
Flrs.: 1     A/C:     Bldg Size:   1,629       Bldg Value....:    $96,269   3rd:    $45,000 10/05/89   Loan Amount:     $165,200
Use..: RES   P&S: Y   Lot  Size:   9,000                                    -----                      Delinq Date:      5/01/90
                                                                            TOTAL  $230,200            Delinq Amt.:       $8,587
Trustee#: 90-10369 LN #763705-1      Beneficiary:                                                      As Of......:     10/04/90
THE SMCA CO                          FUNDAMENTAL MORTGAGE CORP                                         Last Sold..:     10/05/89
221 WEST ALAMEDA AVE #102            P.O. BOX 353
BURBANK CA                           LOUISVILLE KY 40201 (800)333-3204                                 REDLOC File #:     248441
--------------------------------------------------------------------------------------------------------------------------
City.: BUENA PARK     TMG: 9-E2    AP:263-202-25      Trustor: GRAFF, GLENN D                   REDLOC Listing #:     2
Situs: 7556 MEXICO WY BUENA PARK, CA 90620                     7556 MEXICO WY                   Default Rec Date: 10/05/90
Tract: 3317 Lot: 4 Book: 104 Page: 009                         BUENA PARK CA 90620              Instrument #....:   533672

__________PROPERTY INFORMATION___________   __________VALUES__________   _____EXISTING LOANS_____   ____LOAN IN DEFAULT____
Built: 1958  BR.: 3   Rooms: 6                 Assessed 1975.:    $29,731   1st:    $68,000 11/23/88   Document #.:       655114
Age..: 32    BA.: 1.0 Units:                   Land Value....:    $16,941   2nd:*   $14,500 12/04/89   Loan Date..:     12/04/89
Flrs.: 1     A/C:     Bldg Size:     980       Bldg Value....:    $12,790   3rd:    $10,950  6/27/90   Loan Amount:      $14,500
Use..: RES   P&S:     Lot  Size:   6,600                                    -----                      Delinq Date:      8/15/90
                                                                            TOTAL   $93,450            Delinq Amt.:         $477
Trustee#: 908185                     Beneficiary:                                                      As Of......:     10/01/90
WINDSOR MANAGEMENT CO                SANDRA WELLS %AAMES HOME LOAN                                     Last Sold..:
3731 WILSHIRE BLVD-10TH FLR          3731 WILSHIRE BLVD #10-FLR
LOS ANGELES CA                       LOS ANGELES CA 90010 (213)351-6100                                REDLOC File #:     248440
--------------------------------------------------------------------------------------------------------------------------
City.: BUENA PARK     TMG: 9-E2    AP:263-202-25      Trustor: GRAFF, GLENN D                   REDLOC Listing #:     3
Situs: 7556 MEXICO WY BUENA PARK, CA 90620                     7556 MEXICO WY                   Default Rec Date: 10/05/90
Tract: 3317 Lot: 4 Book: 104 Page: 009                         BUENA PARK CA 90620              Instrument #....:   533671

__________PROPERTY INFORMATION___________   __________VALUES__________   _____EXISTING LOANS_____   ____LOAN IN DEFAULT____
Built: 1958  BR.: 3   Rooms: 6                 Assessed 1975.:    $29,731   1st:    $68,000 11/23/88   Document #.:       338845
Age..: 32    BA.: 1.0 Units:                   Land Value....:    $16,941   2nd:    $14,500 12/04/89   Loan Date..:      6/27/90
Flrs.: 1     A/C:     Bldg Size:     980       Bldg Value....:    $12,790   3rd:*   $10,950  6/27/90   Loan Amount:      $10,950
Use..: RES   P&S:     Lot  Size:   6,600                                    -----                      Delinq Date:      8/27/90
                                                                            TOTAL   $93,450            Delinq Amt.:         $470
Trustee#: 908190                     Beneficiary:                                                      As Of......:     10/01/90
WINDSOR MANAGEMENT CO                LOUISE M MCMILLAN %AAMES HOME LOAN                                Last Sold..:      9/18/74
3731 WILSHIRE BLVD-10TH FLR          3731 WILSHIRE BLVD #10-FLR
LOS ANGELES CA                       LOS ANGELES CA 90010 (213)351-6100                                REDLOC File #:     248439
--------------------------------------------------------------------------------------------------------------------------
City.: FOUNTAIN VALLEY TMG: 27-A1  AP:169-251-09      Trustor: GONZALES, DANIEL R               REDLOC Listing #:     4
Situs: 10432 LA TORTOLA CIR FOUNTAIN VALLEY, CA 92708          10432 LA TORTOLA CIR             Default Rec Date: 10/05/90
Tract: 6879 Lot: 22 Book: 256 Page: 027                        FOUNTAIN VALL CA 92708           Instrument #....:   532504

__________PROPERTY INFORMATION___________   __________VALUES__________   _____EXISTING LOANS_____   ____LOAN IN DEFAULT____
Built: 1969  BR.: 4   Rooms: 7                 Assessed 1987.:   $124,899   1st:*   $64,500  4/20/79   Document #.:        25529
Age..: 21    BA.: 2.0 Units:                   Land Value....:    $61,675                              Loan Date..:      4/20/79
Flrs.: 1     A/C:     Bldg Size:   1,599       Bldg Value....:    $63,224                              Loan Amount:      $64,500
Use..: RES   P&S:     Lot  Size:   8,100                                                               Delinq Date:
                                                                                                       Delinq Amt.:       $3,092
Trustee#: 14940 LN #196313-9         Beneficiary:                                                      As Of......:     10/05/90
SHEARSON LEHMAN TD SERVICES          BEVERLY HILLS SAVINGS %SHEARSON LEHMAN M                          Last Sold..:     12/30/86
1201 EAST HIGHLAND AVE #D            1201 E HIGHLAND AV #D
SAN BERNARDIN CA (714)886-7811       SAN BERNARDIN CA 92404 (714)886-7811                              REDLOC File #:     248430
--------------------------------------------------------------------------------------------------------------------------
```

```
R E D L O C (c) 1990  *  Trustee Sale Listing  *  THIS IS NOT A BONAFIDE TITLE REPORT  *  VALIDITY OF THIS LISTING IS NOT GUARANTEED

City.: ANAHEIM        TMG: 10-D5   AP:126-152-07       Trustor: MOORE, PATRICK J                                 REDLOC Listing #:     1
Situs: 2854 W ORANGE AV ANAHEIM, CA 92804                       2854 W ORANGE AV                                 Sale Rec Date...: 10/09/90
Tract: 2797 Lot: 40 Book: 107 Page: 010                         ANAHEIM CA 92804                                 Instrument #....:   536486
__________PROPERTY INFORMATION___________      __________VALUES___________     ______EXISTING LOANS_____       _____LOAN IN DEFAULT_____
Built: 1958  BR.: 4   Rooms: 8                 Assessed 1987.:       $136,291   1st:     $80,000  1/09/87   Document #.:            76959
Age..: 32    BA.: 3.0 Units:                   Land Value....:        $82,420   2nd:*    $11,000  2/13/90   Loan Date..:          2/13/90
Flrs.: 1     A/C:     Bldg Size:    1,741      Bldg Value....:        $53,871   3rd:     $68,000  3/09/90   Loan Amount:          $11,000
Use..: RES   P&S:     Lot  Size:    7,949      Transfer Value:       $131,000 F -----                       Minimum Bid:           $6,828
                                                                                TOTAL    $159,000           Sale Date..:         10/26/90
Trustee#: 90-060                     Beneficiary:                                                           Sale Time..:           9:45AM
ORANGE COAST FINANCIAL CORP          FOUNDERS TRUST & LOAN INC %ORANGE COAST                                Last Sold..:          1/09/87
640 NORTH TUSTIN AVE #204            640 N TUSTIN AV #204
SANTA ANA CA (714)836-7973           SANTA ANA CA 92705 (714)836-7973                                       REDLOC File #:         232412
Sale Location: CT HSE, 700 CIVIC CENTER DR WEST, SANTA ANA
----------------------------------------------------------------------------------------------------------------------------------------
City.: ANAHEIM        TMG: 15-F1   AP:128-581-05       Trustor: LE COMPTE, PHILLIP                               REDLOC Listing #:     2
Situs: 2032 W MIDWOOD LN ANAHEIM, CA 92804                      2032 W MIDWOOD LN                                Sale Rec Date...: 10/09/90
Tract: 2689 Lot: 37 Book: 76 Page: 015                          ANAHEIM CA 92804                                 Instrument #....:   537021
__________PROPERTY INFORMATION___________      __________VALUES___________     ______EXISTING LOANS_____       _____LOAN IN DEFAULT_____
Built: 1955  BR.: 3   Rooms: 6                 Assessed 1984.:       $107,091   1st:*    $92,100  3/27/84   Document #.:           125049
Age..: 35    BA.: 1.5 Units:                   Land Value....:        $67,877   2nd:      $3,000  4/03/84   Loan Date..:          3/27/84
Flrs.: 1     A/C:     Bldg Size:    1,126      Bldg Value....:        $39,214   3rd:     $22,550  3/15/89   Loan Amount:          $92,100
Use..: RES   P&S:     Lot  Size:    7,230                                       -----                       Minimum Bid:          $99,035
                                                                                TOTAL    $117,650           Sale Date..:         11/05/90
Trustee#: B112295 LN #1-929830-6     Beneficiary:                                                           Sale Time..:           1:30PM
TD SERVICE CO                        QUAKER CITY FEDERAL SAVINGS %MICHELLE DE                               Last Sold..:          2/18/86
601 SOUTH LEWIS STREET               7021 S GREENLEAF AV
ORANGE CA (714)385-4837              WHITTIER CA 90608 (213)698-151                                         REDLOC File #:         232712
Sale Location: TD SERVICE, 601 SOUTH LEWIS STREET, ORANGE
----------------------------------------------------------------------------------------------------------------------------------------
City.: COSTA MESA     TMG: 31-A2   AP:422-013-18       Trustor: BURTON, ROBERT L                                 REDLOC Listing #:     3
Situs: 1091 SEA TERRACE LN COSTA MESA, CA 92627                 1091 SEA TERRACE LN                              Sale Rec Date...: 10/09/90
Tract: 10018 Lot: 35 Book: 425 Page: 031                        COSTA MESA CA 92627                              Instrument #....:   538115
__________PROPERTY INFORMATION___________      __________VALUES___________     ______EXISTING LOANS_____       _____LOAN IN DEFAULT_____
Built: 1978  BR.: 2   Rooms: 5                 Assessed 1987.:       $150,596   1st:*   $112,000  1/27/87   Document #.:            46873
Age..: 12    BA.: 1.5 Units:                   Land Value....:        $78,320   2nd:     $39,500 12/13/88   Loan Date..:          1/27/87
Flrs.: 2     A/C:     Bldg Size:    1,241      Bldg Value....:        $72,276   3rd:     $28,863  1/16/90   Loan Amount:         $112,000
Use..: RES   P&S:     Lot  Size:    1,890      Transfer Value:       $145,000 F -----                       Minimum Bid:         $117,622
                                                                                TOTAL    $180,363           Sale Date..:         11/02/90
Trustee#: 6-90-13172 LN #20161485    Beneficiary:                                                           Sale Time..:           9:45AM
INTERSTATE TRUST DEED SERVICE        DOWNEY SAVINGS & LOAN %NANCY CHEN                                      Last Sold..:          1/27/87
3002 DOW AVE #318                    3501 JAMBOREE RD
TUSTIN CA (714)730-5561              NEWPORT BEACH CA 92660 (714)854-3100                                   REDLOC File #:         233238
Sale Location: CT HSE, 700 CIVIC CENTER DR WEST, SANTA ANA
----------------------------------------------------------------------------------------------------------------------------------------
City.: FULLERTON      TMG: 6-D2    AP:293-176-19       Trustor: GUERTIN, JEANNE M                                REDLOC Listing #:     4
Situs: 1017 E ARROUES DR FULLERTON, CA 92635                    1017 E ARROUES DR                                Sale Rec Date...: 10/09/90
Tract: 4312 Lot: 26 Book: 156 Page: 006                         FULLERTON CA 92635                               Instrument #....:   538114
__________PROPERTY INFORMATION___________      __________VALUES___________     ______EXISTING LOANS_____       _____LOAN IN DEFAULT_____
Built: 1963  BR.: 3   Rooms: 7                 Assessed 1975.:        $74,385   1st:    $150,000  1/15/88   Document #.:           562230
Age..: 27    BA.: 2.0 Units:                   Land Value....:        $20,369   2nd:*    $72,000 10/18/89   Loan Date..:         10/18/89
Flrs.: 1     A/C:     Bldg Size:    1,668      Bldg Value....:        $54,016   3rd:     $25,000 12/05/89   Loan Amount:          $72,000
Use..: RES   P&S: Y   Lot  Size:   13,200                                       -----                       Minimum Bid:          $78,717
                                                                                TOTAL    $247,000           Sale Date..:         10/26/90
Trustee#: 6-90-13118 LN #90560712    Beneficiary:                                                           Sale Time..:           9:45AM
INTERSTATE TRUST DEED SERVICE        BENEFICIAL MORTGAGE CO                                                 Last Sold..:
3002 DOW AVE #318                    1440 N HARBOR BLVD #100
TUSTIN CA (714)730-5561              FULLERTON CA 92635 (714)870-8851                                       REDLOC File #:         231744
Sale Location: CT HSE, 700 CIVIC CENTER DR WEST, SANTA ANA
----------------------------------------------------------------------------------------------------------------------------------------
```

REDLOC (c) 1990 * 4175 E La Palma Ave #270, Anaheim CA 92807 (714)996-4000 * NOT A BONAFIDE TITLE REPORT - VALIDITY NOT GUARANTEED *

Orange County Default Listings for
Publication Date Of............: October-18-1990 T A B L E O F C O N T E N T S S A M P L E

| No. | City | Thomas Map | Age | Beds | Baths | A/C | Pool Spa | Land Use | Bldg Size | Lot Size | Loan Amount | Loan Date | Assessed Value | Delinquent Date | Delinquent Amount |
|---|---|---|---|---|---|---|---|---|---|---|---|---|---|---|---|
| 1 | ANAHEIM | 12-A4 | 27 | 4 | 3.0 | | Y | RES | 1,629 | 9,000 | $165,200 | 5/13/88 | $251,544 | 5/01/90 | $8,587 |
| 2 | BUENA PARK | 9-E2 | 32 | 3 | 1.0 | | | RES | 980 | 6,600 | $14,500 | 12/04/89 | $29,731 | 8/15/90 | $477 |
| 3 | BUENA PARK | 9-E2 | 32 | 3 | 1.0 | | | RES | 980 | 6,600 | $10,950 | 6/27/90 | $29,731 | 8/27/90 | $470 |
| 4 | FOUNTAIN VALLEY | 27-A1 | 21 | 4 | 2.0 | | | RES | 1,599 | 8,100 | $64,500 | 4/20/79 | $124,899 | | $3,092 |
| 5 | FULLERTON | 2-C6 | 24 | 5 | 2.5 | | | RES | 2,692 | 7,171 | $120,000 | 11/29/83 | $178,658 | 7/01/90 | $7,068 |
| 6 | GARDEN GROVE | 16-C3 | 36 | 4 | 2.0 | | Y | RES | 2,123 | 7,541 | $127,500 | 2/27/89 | $47,302 | 7/01/90 | $4,989 |
| 7 | IRVINE | - | | | .0 | | | RES | | | $35,000 | 11/21/89 | $255,000 | 9/01/90 | $1,597 |
| 8 | LA HABRA | 6-A1 | 11 | 2 | 1.5 | | | RES | 1,080 | | $68,000 | 7/08/88 | $85,000 | 4/15/90 | $4,207 |
| 9 | LAGUNA BEACH | 34-C2 | | | .0 | | | APT | | | $15,210 | 6/06/89 | | 1/15/89 | $6,360 |
| 10 | LAGUNA BEACH | 34-C2 | | | .0 | | | APT | | | $8,700 | 4/28/87 | $7,352 | 5/01/90 | $5,427 |
| 11 | LAGUNA BEACH | 34-C2 | | | .0 | | | APT | | | $6,400 | 9/21/84 | $6,417 | 2/01/88 | $4,392 |
| 12 | LAGUNA BEACH | 34-C2 | | | .0 | | | APT | | | $11,200 | 9/01/84 | $12,148 | 3/01/88 | $7,451 |
| 13 | MISSION VIEJO | 29-BB | 21 | 3 | 2.0 | | | RES | 1,360 | 8,400 | $201,600 | 5/10/89 | $145,422 | 6/01/90 | $11,055 |
| 14 | SANTA ANA | 17-D6 | 26 | 3 | 2.5 | | | RES | 1,834 | 8,420 | $12,500 | 8/24/89 | $46,241 | 9/24/90 | $21,935 |
| 15 | SANTA ANA | 18-B4 | 61 | 3 | 2.5 | | | RES | 3,064 | 15,050 | $504,000 | 6/28/90 | $202,980 | 9/01/90 | $10,336 |
| 16 | SANTA ANA | 21-A3 | 44 | 2 | 1.0 | | | RES | 730 | 25,480 | $94,250 | 9/25/89 | $37,452 | 6/01/90 | $5,975 |
| 17 | TRABUCO CANYON | 56- | 11 | 3 | 2.5 | Y | | RES | 1,995 | 25,000 | $230,100 | 1/24/90 | $159,179 | 6/01/90 | $13,837 |
| 18 | YORBA LINDA | 7-E4 | 27 | 4 | 2.0 | | | RES | 1,590 | 7,313 | $173,142 | 2/03/89 | $129,347 | 7/03/90 | $8,322 |
| 19 | YORBA LINDA | 8-C4 | 7 | 4 | 3.0 | Y | | RES | 2,554 | 8,300 | $588,000 | 7/31/90 | $249,683 | 8/24/90 | $588,000 |

THE FOLLOWING EXPANDED LISTINGS ONLY
REPRESENT THE FIRST 4 LISTINGS ON THIS PAGE!

REDLOC (c) 1990 * 4175 E La Palma Ave #270, Anaheim CA 92807 (714)996-4000 * NOT A BONAFIDE TITLE REPORT - VALIDITY NOT GUARANTEED *

Orange County Trustee Sale Listings for
Publication Date Of............: October-18-1990

T A B L E  O F  C O N T E N T S

S A M P L E

| No. | City | Thomas Map | Age | Beds | Baths | A/C | Pool Spa | Land Use | Bldg Size | Lot Size | Loan Amount | Loan Date | Assessed Value-Yr | Sale Date | Unpaid Balance |
|---|---|---|---|---|---|---|---|---|---|---|---|---|---|---|---|
| 1 | ANAHEIM | 10-D5 | 32 | 4 | 3.00 | | | RES | 1,741 | 7,949 | $11,000 | 2/13/90 | $136,291-87 | 10/26/90 | $6,828 |
| 2 | ANAHEIM | 15-F1 | 35 | 3 | 1.50 | | | RES | 1,126 | 7,230 | $92,100 | 3/27/84 | $107,091-84 | 11/05/90 | $99,035 |
| 3 | COSTA MESA | 31-A2 | 12 | 2 | 1.50 | | | RES | 1,241 | 1,890 | $112,000 | 1/27/87 | $150,596-87 | 11/02/90 | $117,622 |
| 4 | FULLERTON | 6-D2 | 27 | 3 | 2.00 | | Y | RES | 1,668 | 13,200 | $72,000 | 10/18/89 | $74,385-75 | 10/26/90 | $78,717 |
| 5 | GARDEN GROVE | 14-F3 | 30 | 3 | 2.00 | | | RES | 1,293 | 6,700 | $48,000 | 12/08/89 | $36,922-75 | 11/02/90 | $60,137 |
| 6 | LAGUNA NIGUEL | 37-C1 | 14 | 3 | 2.50 | | Y | RES | 2,660 | 11,200 | $68,000 | 11/02/88 | $196,784-78 | 11/02/90 | $96,143 |
| 7 | LAGUNA NIGUEL | 39-A2 | | | | | | RES | | | $277,000 | 10/13/88 | $380,100-89 | 11/02/90 | $310,157 |
| 8 | NEWPORT BEACH | 31-A4 | 30 | 3 | 2.00 | | | RES | 1,001 | 2,635 | | 4/17/90 | $162,361-85 | 10/30/90 | $12,000 |
| 9 | YORBA LINDA | 8-A3 | 17 | 4 | 2.00 | | | RES | 1,864 | 10,038 | $65,811 | 3/28/89 | $155,954-87 | 11/02/90 | $72,687 |

THE FOLLOWING EXPANDED LISTINGS ONLY
REPRESENT THE FIRST 4 LISTINGS ON THIS PAGE!

RECORDING REQUESTED BY

86 96207

SAN JOAQUIN COUNTY RECORDER'S OFFICE
JAMES M. JOHNSTONE

1986 NOV 17 PM 3:08

RECORDED AT REQUEST OF Alebyne Bishop
FEE 4-1

AND WHEN RECORDED MAIL TO

Name DEBORA A. Bishop
Street Address 3440 Sunny Rd.
City & State Stockton, Calif. 95205

MAIL TAX STATEMENTS TO

Name
Street Address
City & State

SPACE ABOVE THIS LINE FOR RECORDER'S USE

CAT. NO. NN00580
TO 1922 CA (2-83)

## Individual Quitclaim Deed

THIS FORM FURNISHED BY TICOR TITLE INSURERS

ALL | PTN.

The undersigned grantor(s) declare(s):
Documentary transfer tax is $ Ø
( ) computed on full value of property conveyed, or
( ) computed on full value less value of liens and encumbrances remaining at time of sale.
( ) Unincorporated area: ( ) City of ________, and

36

FOR A VALUABLE CONSIDERATION, receipt of which is hereby acknowledged,

MARION LEO BISHOP AND REGINA JEAN BISHOP, HUSBAND AND WIFE

130

hereby REMISES, RELEASES AND QUITCLAIMS to
DEBORA A. BISHOP, a single woman

181

the following described real property in the
County of San Joaquin, State of California:

The North 240 Feet of the East 69.5 feet of the following described property:

The East one-half (E ½) of Lot Twenty-four (24) of Map entitled, Tract No. 227 of SUNNY ACRES, filed for record August 19, 1949, in Book 13 of Maps and Plats, page 45, San Joaquin County Records.

Dated: July 29, 1986.

Marion Leo Bishop
MARION LEO BISHOP

Regina Jean Bishop
REGINA JEAN BISHOP

STATE OF CALIFORNIA
COUNTY OF San Joaquin } ss.

On July 29 1986, before me, the undersigned, a Notary Public in and for said State, personally appeared Marion Leo Bishop and Regina Jean Bishop, his wife personally known to me or proved to me on the basis of satisfactory evidence to be the person s whose name s are subscribed to the within instrument and acknowledged that they executed the same.

WITNESS my hand and official seal.

Signature John O. Fugazi
John O. Fugazi, Notary Public

OFFICIAL SEAL
JOHN O. FUGAZI
NOTARY PUBLIC-CALIFORNIA
SAN JOAQUIN COUNTY
MY COMMISSION EXPIRES DEC. 1, 1986

(This area for official notarial seal)

Title Order No. ________ Escrow or Loan No. ________

MAIL TAX STATEMENTS AS DIRECTED ABOVE

Chapter 3

# Direct Mail That Works!

## *The Amazing Direct Mail Secret that Makes Foreclosures Easy Money*

### DIRECT MAIL IS DIFFERENT

The commercial default information services described thus far will identify a lot of local foreclosed properties for you to pursue. But to make the system really work for you, you need access to a wider marketplace. That is where direct mail advertising of your services comes in. Direct mail is different. The whole city, the whole state, and perhaps the whole country is your marketplace. And you get all those free employees (the mail carriers) helping you deliver your message to hundreds of people every day.

### APPEAL TO THE RIGHT PERSON

Once you have targeted your prospects, people who are interested in your services, you know to whom you will be addressing your appeals. Having researched the county records or the default listing services, you'll not waste your time with people who have no motivation to use your service. Only homeowners in default are motivated to read your letters; the others will trash your letters, no matter how appealing.

Foreclosure sellers may not be interested in your first letters because they may believe they'll solve the problem before it becomes critical. About 80% of the defaulting homeowners do cure (make healthy) their loans.

It's that small percentage who can't get a loan from their Uncle Charlie that you are targeting with your letters. Expect to see this pattern. Send numerous letters to the homeowner. The results will improve as the homeowner gets to know your name and company (recognition) as the foreclosure clock slowly ticks its way down to the Trustee's/Sheriff's Sale.

### Most Important Contact

The mail may thus be your most important means of contacting your prospects on a regular basis. But let's face it, with everybody and his uncle getting tons of mail daily, effective use of the mail can be a real challenge. We've all seen mailboxes in apartment houses with giant garbage cans next to them. What makes your mail different? The name of the game is to make sure that what you send gets opened and kept. The objective of direct mail is to get the seller to telephone you.

My mail gets opened and read. Why? I don't send mail that can easily be identified as advertising mail and consequently thrown away without being opened. I send between five and ten mailing pieces to each prospective client during the default period. Every one of these pieces is in a different colored and shaped envelope. No business name appears on the outside, and therefore it looks like mail from a friend or relative. You must make it appear like *real mail* — the kind you want to receive, the kind that makes you curious about the contents.

### Third Class — Routine

If you're going to send out the routine stuff with third class postage, your materials will look like all the other mail that mostly gets thrown away. Of course, some of that mail does get read; however, the odds are not in your favor. The secret is to make your mailing as creative and interesting as you can. With a little use of your imagination you can think of a dozen things to do that will get your letter past the wastebasket.

### Success

One of the keys to success is understanding how the concept of return on investment applies in direct marketing. You must reach enough people by whatever method you use to make your presentation and get a response. If you send out 100 letters offering to purchase houses in default and you get only 1 response, that is a response rate of 1%. If you purchase that house, fix it up, and sell it at a profit of, say, $5,000, that is a great return. So whether you get a 1% or 10% response rate is less important than the amount you make in net profit from each sale. The critical question is not *rate of response* but *return on investment*. Judge your results by how much profit you make on each purchase and subsequent sale, and not on how many telephone responses you receive.

### Get in the Door

Personal visits can be productive, but they are also time-consuming, especially if you travel any distance. And you may not get in the door. (Women are sometimes more able than men at convincing homeowners to let them in.) Homeowners in default have been called on by process servers, bill collectors, and disgruntled people in general. Their answer to the doorbell is usually hostile and aggressive. In many cases they will not answer the doorbell even though you can hear the television playing and people talking. Direct mail allows you to tell your customers, inexpensively, about what you can do to help them. Telephone calls are effective, but homeowners are usually available only before and after normal business hours. Again, bill collectors and other creditors attempt to contact homeowners by telephone. If you are planning to use the telephone to contact defaulting homeowners, expect them to hang up frequently and to offer considerable resistance. Keep in mind that the foreclosure process makes defaulting homeowners street-wise. Plan your telephone presentation and try to establish a rapport that will give you time to convince the homeowner that you are trying to solve their foreclosure problem.

## ASK YOURSELF, WHAT DOES THE CUSTOMER WANT?

What does the customer (in this case the homeowner whose loan is in default) want to know? The same things you want to know each time you buy something. In one sentence you could sum it up: *What's in it for me?* That's a realistic question to ask yourself, because the customer will. The customer will want to know what you can do for him. So tell him — more than once. Give him a good answer, or your letter will go in the trash. What do you want him or her to do? Telephone? Write? Wait? Do nothing? You must tell him what you want him to do, exactly, specifically, and repeatedly. Will you pay cash? Or will the customer expect deferred payments? What about a guarantee? Do you offer a free consultation? Should you? In other words, you must make an offer your customer can't refuse.

## LETTERS THAT BRING RESULTS

I use a series of letters, coupons, fliers, and seminars to inform prospects of my services and clarify for them the procedures of a foreclosure action. But mere information is not enough. Repetition is important. First of all, recognize that buying and selling decisions are emotional decisions, not necessarily logical decisions. This means that you'll need to be in the prospect's mind when he or she makes the decision to sell the defaulted property. Persistence/perseverance is therefore what counts. According to Walter Hailey, "In selling a product or a service the typical sales person must call on a prospect 4 times before 20% of the buyers will say 'Yes'. After 8 times 50% will buy, and after a dozen calls 70% will have become customers. After 15 calls 90% of all those called will buy." According to Hailey, the number 15 is at the apex; it never gets better. That is to say, you can keep on calling and make 20 or 25 calls, and the number who buy will still be the same 90%. The message is simple. We never sell them all. But — and it's a big "BUT" — the problem is that 80% of all sales people quit after the first, second, and third call — right when the odds are very few that sales will be made. Remember, 80% of all sales are made after the fifth call.

### Mail, Mail, Mail

The point of all this is that you must continuously mail, mail, mail to the homeowner who is in the foreclosure process. Repetition is the answer. Experience has shown me that when I ask foreclosure sellers why they called, they tell me that they received more letters from me than from any other buyer. It would be nice to believe that my letters were the best, but rarely will my client tell me that. They always say, "Your letter arrived when I knew enough to help me make up my mind."

I recommend that you ask your homeowners in foreclosure to give you the letters they receive from your competitors. This will be a real education. Not only will you find letters that are better than yours, but you will learn who your competitors are. Read through letters from your competitors and use the information if it's appropriate to improve your letters. BUT DON'T COPY. The not-so-successful people are the only ones who copy. Take the time to digest and understand the appeal's wording and the intent of your competitors. Then figure out how to improve their letters and finally incorporate those improvements into your own letter.

## SOME TECHNICAL GUIDELINES FOR GOOD LETTERS

It is important to keep in mind that direct mail is a personal medium. You are approaching your reader on a person-to person basis.

One of the most important guidelines for publishing successful mail pieces is to make them look and read like personal messages. On a volume basis it's difficult, but you must keep moving toward documents that have that personal touch along with a down-to-earth message. Typewritten letters are better than typeset. Copies of letters are taboo.

If we could all dictate and have a secretary write our letters that would certainly improve our response. However, it's not cost-effective to individually type and sign all the hundreds of letters sent out monthly. The next best alternative is to concentrate on the message and make it as clear and understandable as possible.

### Long Letters — Short Letters

How long should the letters be? To answer that question, I'll use a quote from Richard S. Hodgson in his book, *Direct Mail Sales Letters:* "There's no such thing as a letter that is too long—just one that is too boring." The Howard Ruff organization traditionally uses mail pieces of ten or more pages that are loaded with information, quotes, graphics, and well-researched information.

My suggestion is to watch the big boys in direct mail. They spend a lot of time testing their mailings to see what works and what doesn't. Based on the successful newsletter editors' tactics, I'd suggest that more narrative is best. I don't recall who said it, but it's probably valid for all of us. "The more you tell, the more you sell." I'm not advocating a lot of worthless copy, but including a lot of facts, benefits, and reasons will never hurt your letters.

### Reading Patterns: Headlines, Subheads, and Getting Started

Spend some time analyzing successful mailings. Try to get a feel for what worked and what didn't. Try to see if you can spot the real difference between successful mail and mail that failed.

Have someone read your letters *to* you. Don't write your letter and then read it to someone for approval. Of course they will approve; they don't want to hurt your feelings. Rather than read to an audience, ask an individual to read your letter to you and listen to where he or she puts the emphasis and listen to see if that's what you intended. Someone who doesn't know anything about your market is a much better critic than a friend or someone you work with.

You should expect that you'll be doing a lot of rewriting on the first few letters. It's difficult to write clearly and even more difficult to get your points across to people in distress.

### Special Effort

Don't overestimate the knowledge of your audience. But don't underestimate their intelligence. Make a special effort to remember that the reader probably has very little previous knowledge of foreclosure or Trustee's/Sheriff's Sales.

Ask yourself: Does my letter meet this ABC formula?

A. Attract the reader's attention.

B. Arouse the reader's interest in the proposition.

C. Stimulate the reader's desire to take the desired action.

Or maybe you'd like to test your letter against Jack Kacy's five-point guideline for sales letters:

1. What will you do for me if I listen to your story?
2. How are you going to do this?
3. Who is responsible for the promises you make?
4. For whom have you done this?
5. What will it cost me?

Victor Schwartz has suggested this formula:

G. Get attention.

S. Show people the advantage.

P. Prove it.

P. Persuade people to grasp this advantage.

A. Ask for action.

### Formulas

There are many formulas, but the key is to write letters that are loaded with benefits. The customer/distressed property owner is saying to himself, "What's in it for me?" You must answer that question in your letter and keep answering it all the way to the final sale.

The direct mail experts test headlines until they find the one test headline that brings results. You screen out the people who have little or no interest with your headlines or openings. Now your job is to convince the reader you have enough benefits.

Once the opening has done its job, you end up with readers who want to know more about your propositions or proposals. They are not ready to make a decision but are willing to read further for more information.

Most people don't read the letters from beginning to end on a word-for-word basis. They skim the letter looking for answers to their problems. The body of your letter should have the answers to these problems. It should be organized for the easy location of answers to the prospect's problems.

Eye-catching devices like the Johnson Box, a box that is highlighted or has a dark line around a section of copy, will gain the prospect's attention and are a good place to highlight your guarantee or maybe your unique selling proposition. When you have completed the letter be sure to sign it. Letters from the executives of companies are better read than those from the manager.

And be sure to add a postscript below the signature. According to surveys, this is the most-read part of a sales letter.

## WHAT MAKES THE CUSTOMER RESPOND?

People usually buy benefits or whatever it is that a product will do for them. Remember, the customer is saying over and over again in his or her mind: *What's in it for me?* The benefit of doing business with you must be stated clearly and expressed repeatedly. Revlon products provide a good analogy. Revlon doesn't sell products, it sells benefits, such as hope and beauty, self-esteem, attractiveness.

In your letters to customers you must appeal to such fundamental human needs. You experience these needs every day of your life, but it is sometimes difficult to reduce them to written form. One of the strongest human needs is for love and affection. This is a difficult need to appeal to if you are buying foreclosure properties, but you can make use of motivations that are relatively easy to appeal to: fear and greed.

### Fear and Greed

In your day-to-day business you may notice many appeals targeted to fear and greed. Burglar alarms, life insurance, health insurance are all sold by using these negative appeals. The fear of loss is a tremendous motivator, and when the defaulting homeowner finally realizes that his house will be sold at auction and all of the funds will go to others, he will become motivated. Your letters should arrive at this stage of the foreclosure process to tap this motivation.

The question the recipient of your letter is asking himself is: *What is in it for me?* Your letter must answer this question by offering a clear, easy-to-understand solution to the homeowner's problem. Continue to describe all of your other benefits within the body of the letter. If possible, make your prospect visualize himself enjoying the benefits. Show him how easily he can get the benefits.

Your customer will buy results and benefits from you, not things or services. Don't offer things; offer proven or guaranteed results. Tell the customers about the wonderful things that will happen as a result of doing business with you; have them envision no more bill collectors, no more tax payments, no more judgments on the public record. Sell them on fast relief, just as the cold remedies or painkillers do on television: fast, easy relief.

Once the prospect knows what he gains by doing what you suggest, then tell him what he will lose by not taking action. Tell him what to do and how to do it. Then repeat the information. Tell him again what he stands to lose by not acting immediately.

### Credibility

Why, you ask, will the customer respond to my letter? He will not, unless you have credibility. If you send postcards and letters that are poorly drafted, misspelled, and not professionally reproduced, you will lose them to the trash can. Upon receiving your letter the customer will require proof; show him. He will want proof, or at least some evidence, that you can perform as your letter says you will. It is not enough to make a promise. You must back it up with proof, such as a copy of a testimonial from a satisfied customer or an unconditional, written guarantee. In short, you must make your claims creditable.

### Why Your Mail Is Always Effective

Your letter may be rejected by defaulting homeowners for many reasons. The least important is fear. Think about the fear you have sometimes felt when you went to purchase something. Then you'll begin to understand what is going on in the customer's head when you meet him or when you write to him. Think of how people look for a friend when they are scared, and then be that friend; make yourself a friend that your customer can trust and believe in.

Let's take a look at the way we perceive customers and what they are really like. First off, they are people, human beings with the same kinds of feelings and needs that we have, even though we tend to think of them as a different breed. Remember, the customer is scared of what will happen to him/her in the foreclosure — and scared of you, too, because he knows or thinks he knows that you are out to take advantage of him. And, in addition to being scared of you, he is scared of what he is about to do. The customer is therefore at *war* with you, and whether you think so or not, that means you are at war with him. This is a fact that you must deal with and turn to everyone's advantage.

If you understand what is going through the defaulting homeowner's mind, you can win the war and turn it into a valuable experience for both you and the defaulting homeowner. Try to sort out your own feelings about the defaulting homeowner. He'll run away from you if he is scared, so you must get him on your side by understanding and appealing to his needs and desires.

## FOLLOW UP — FOLLOW UP — FOLLOW UP

You will need to repeat your prospecting letters again and again. (See pages 67 through 72 for examples and page 73 for an example of an insert that can be used in follow-up letters.) Most people are very slow to react. They delay and hope a miracle will save them from foreclosure. The first three or four letters probably go in the wastebasket. You must try to build their confidence so that they believe that you are a reliable source of money and can solve their problems. Don't take it for granted that they know who you are or understand what you can do.

### Persistence

In the subsequent sales letters you must be persistent. Otherwise you'll soon be forgotten and the procrastinating, slow-moving client will end up at the Trustee's/Sheriff's Sale or in bankruptcy, and you'll need lots of cash to buy that same property at those sales. So in your succession of letters you must tell your prospect that you are offering specific benefits that he needs or wants. Again, try to put yourself in the prospect's place. Analyze the situation that the prospective seller is in. Ask the hard questions. Demonstrate that you are the one who can solve the problems of the world for him. Show proof, in your letters, that you are superior to the competition. The customer doesn't care how good you might be at buying and selling real estate. He wants benefits and solutions; cash today; no more collection agencies. If you don't show why you are superior, your prospects will go to your competition, and you'll suffer the financial costs of wasted letters and time. Demonstrate to the defaulting homeowners that you will pay more money for the home. Substantiate your superiority by having a guarantee that is better than those offered by your competitors — for example, "if you can beat our price we will cancel this contract."

### Helping Hand

The overall theme of your letter-writing campaign should be to extend a helping hand and offer assistance to the homeowner in foreclosure. However, the need for action, for the homeowner in foreclosure to "act now," is the primary emphasis of each piece of correspondence. It is wise to stress in your letter what will take place when the homeowner telephones you. It is also sensible to explain exactly what will take place if the homeowner takes no action.

Your letters should cover the following concepts. The homeowner has a large problem hanging over his head. The foreclosure clock is running. Isn't it time to save face? Do you need money? You only have a limited number of days left till the Trustee's/Sheriff's Sale. We care. Here is what we will do for you. You can't lose. This is a sure thing. This is your last chance; after this letter I give up. The bank only wants its money and nothing else.

### Remind Sellers of the Risks of Waiting

Your letters should be planned with an objective, convincing argument that moves the prospect to call you and makes him eager to sell to you. You've got to help your prospect make up his mind. Prove that this is the right time to sell. Point out that the prospective seller will begin to enjoy the benefit he or she wants as soon as the sale is completed. Also point out the risks of loss if he does not sell to you. Keep in mind that your prospective seller is continually searching for ways to find money. Foreclosure actions don't spring up out of nowhere. Your prospective clients have had difficulties with money for a while. By the time the foreclosure notice comes, they know that they are at the end of the line. Your letter can be a lifesaver. If you want to be a great success, you'll help them find ways to solve their problems. Study their needs for your service and you'll gain them as your clients. Show them how they will get more of what they need when they sell to you.

Ask questions, questions that push the customers to admit their problem and allow you to solve it for them. Be specific when you tell them you can save money for them or help them avoid losses, then spell out the specific terms and make sure that they understand each benefit you offer. Learn enough about your potential clients so that you can anticipate and answer their questions. Determine exactly when and how you will ask them to sell to you. Ask for the order in the letter; otherwise you miss your objective.

## MAP OUT YOUR TERRITORY

When you have responses to your letter-writing campaign, don't run around haphazardly from one place to another. Get a clear picture of the location of your prospects. Get a map of your territory or territories. Plot your calls and know exactly where you are going so that you don't criss-cross the territory and waste time.

Become the best-known buyer in your territory. We have all heard the old saying, "Out of sight, out of mind." It's also true in the foreclosure business. After all, your prospect is living through a time of great stress and tension. More than likely he is not thinking as practically and rationally as a normal person would. You need to keep your name in front of him as a problem-solver.

## Checklist for Letters

1. First, target your audience. The right letter to the wrong person will net you zero results.
2. Second, send the letter or letters more than once. Your timing is critical; possibly the seller is thinking he can save his home with a new loan when your first letter arrives. After trying to get a second or third loan and being refused, your second or subsequent letters will get more results. Clients don't worry about Christmas in July.
3. Maybe the seller doesn't believe your first letter and needs additional reinforcement. More letters — testimonials — repetition.
4. What is the context of your letter? Does it offer benefits to the client? Why should he call you? Why are you better?
5. Why are you better than your competition? You are, aren't you?
6. Are your letters professional, or do you copy them from others and then use a local printshop to copy a few hundred? The customer knows the difference between a copy and an original.
7. Are you solving a problem in your letters, or are you just getting yourself in a position to profit?
8. Will the client be convinced by reading your letter that your company is the best one to do business with? Why?
9. Will the client trust you? Why? Did others receive benefits from your services? Who? When?
10. If you mail only once, you are wasting your time and money. A series of three to ten letters is a must. Single-shot offers will not work.
11. What makes you different from others in the same business? What benefits do you offer that others don't? Prove it!
12. Why should I trust you? If you want them to take action and telephone, you better get them to trust you.
13. Don't expect the customer to act immediately. If you persist again and again and the client perceives the benefits you offer clearly, your telephone will ring.
14. Provide a solution to the client's problem. Don't expect immediate results, and continuously demonstrate that you understand the client's difficulties.

15. Remember, people buy because they have problems to solve and anxieties to resolve. Your job is to find the solution to their anxieties.
16. Tell them how you will solve their problems and then show them how you have done it with others.
17. Tell them in clear, understandable English what to do next: call you — write you. Make it easy for them to do so.
18. End by telling them what will happen if they do not take action.

# *New Growth Financial*

*"The Distressed Property Experts"*

*(415) 837-2106 Fax #743-0926*

**Example of a letter sent out to a foreclosing homeowner. Be sure to change the wording of the letter to best suit you and your approach to the homeowner.**

Dear Homeowner,

SURVIVAL IS THE BOTTOM LINE!! Don't end up looking like a fool by losing your home at PUBLIC AUCTION (trustee sale).

ARE YOU DROWNING IN A SEA OF DEBT??

Be honest with yourself for a minute. Do you really think that the lender cares what happens to you? Many people in your situation fall victim to their fears and anxieties and simply decide to do nothing. They can't believe that their home will be taken away from them by a bank or lending institution. They can't believe the law allows this. And they hope some legal angle will rescue them.

Don't be embarrassed to ask a professional how to save your equity. This is the opportunity you have been waiting for.

You'll suffer a tremendous loss of pride and prestige if you don't stop the foreclosure process.

In San Joaquin County, over one hundred homes go into default each month. We know, because we have corresponded with each of them. We can help you.

If you do nothing . . . hoping for a miracle — the law will take its course and you will lose your house at Public Auction.

By the time the lender forces the Public Auction, they are only interested in getting their money back. The fact that you want to save your equity isn't of much interest to them. We pay cash for houses and do so in 10 days.

Are you hiding inside your home — hoping the problem will simply go away — taking no action; meanwhile, you are running out of time and options.

It's time to make a decision. Time is running out. Your family deserves a fresh start. You need cash and you need it fast. We pay cash for houses and do so in 10 days. Don't turn your back on a sure thing. This is the opportunity you have been waiting for.

(Please turn to reverse side)

*Our mailing address is: P.O. Box 5000, #412, Danville, Ca. 94526*
*Our offices are located at 185 Front Street, Suite 207 in Danville, California just behind the First Interstate Bank and only steps from Father Nature's Famous Restaurant.* ©

**************************************************************************************

**OUR GUARANTEE TO YOU**: Let's be perfectly frank. You are afraid someone will take advantage of you. Let's relieve you of that anxiety. If you get a better written offer (and we know you won't) that is more beneficial than our proposal, we will cancel our contract. Yes! That is correct! We will release you from this contract if you get a better deal. You be the judge. Is that fair treatment? How can you lose? Stop procrastinating; indecision could cost you thousands of dollars if your property is sold at public auction (trustee sale).

**************************************************************************************

WE CARE!! We have taken the time to write you a letter which could save you a dreadful experience. This isn't another one of those xerox copies of some bland letter. Of course, you are skeptical. That just proves you are a responsible person.

Let's face it. Your life would be better if you had some cash to deal with the present difficult circumstances. We will buy your house for cash.

Don't turn your back on a sure thing. Take action right away.

Make this the turning point in your life. Reach for the telephone and dial (415) 837-2106. Ask for Ted or Diane.

P.S.

You need cash to solve your problem!!

We have the cash you need!!!

Just pick up the telephone and dial 837-2106.

The CASH you need will be in your hands in TEN (10) DAYS.

Remember: If you take no action, your home will be sold at public auction and you will be evicted. That is the law. Make sure this doesn't happen to you.

Warmly,

Ted Thomas
Vice President

# *New Growth Financial*

*"The Distressed Property Experts"*
*(415) 837-2106 Fax #743-0926*

**Example of a letter sent out to a foreclosing homeowner. Be sure to change the wording of the letter to best suit you and your approach to the homeowner.**

Dear Homeowner,

Be honest with yourself for a minute. Do you really think the lender cares what happens to you? Aren't they really only interested in getting their money back?

Many people panic when they receive a Notice of Default. This is a moment of careful planning, not procrastination, not self-defeating panic.

If you do nothing — hoping for a miracle — the law will take its course and you will lose your house at Public Auction. Not only will you lose your house but also your equity in your home, because houses sold at Public Auction usually sell for twenty-five percent (25%) to fifty percent (50%) less than houses sold on the open market. This isn't surprising when you think about it.

We will buy your house and pay you cash.

By the time the lender forces the public auction, he is really only interested getting his money back. The fact that you want to get your money out of the house isn't of much interest to him.

You can save the equity in your house and stop the legal hassle.

If you sit back and do nothing you will lose not only your house, but you will lose the equity you have earned.

Many people in your situation who fall victim to their fears and anxieties simply decide to do nothing. They can't believe that their home will be taken away from them by a bank or lending institution. They can't believe the law allows this and they hope that some legal angle will rescue them. They therefore hide inside their homes hoping the problem will simply go away, procrastinating about taking no action; meanwhile, they are running out of time and options.

Let's review. The moment you were sent the NOTICE OF DEAULT notifying you that you weren't making your mortgage payments, the law took over. If you take no action your home can and will be sold right out from under you. The company that loaned you the money to buy your home has the power to do this. And if you don't pay them what you owe them, they will.

(Please turn to reverse side)

*Our mailing address is: P.O. Box 5000, #412, Danville, Ca. 94526*
*Our offices are located at 185 Front Street, Suite 207 in Danville, California just behind the First Interstate Bank and only steps from Father Nature's Famous Restaurant.* 

We know you are in a difficult situation. We have helped many others through it. I'm including a notarized testimonial from one of our recent clients so you can see for yourself.

We pay cash for houses in 10 days. You owe it to your family to seek a money solution!! We do the work for you; we guide you every step of the way. You can turn to us with confidence. Make this the turning point in your life. Reach for the telephone and dial (415) 837-2106. Ask for Ted or Diane.

P.S.

You need cash to solve your problem!!

We have the cash you need!!

Just pick up the telephone and dial (415) 837-2106.

The CASH you need will be in your hands in TEN (10) DAYS.

Remember: If you take no action, your home will be sold at public auction. And you will be evicted. That is the law.

Make sure this doesn't happen to you.

Warmly,

Ted Thomas

Ted Thomas
Vice President

# *New Growth Financial*

*"The Distressed Property Experts"*

*(415) 837-2106 Fax #743-0926*

**Example of a letter sent out to a foreclosing homeowner. Be sure to change the wording of the letter to best suit you and your approach to the homeowner.**

Dear Homeowner,

This may well be the most important letter you will ever receive. It is so important, in fact, that I'm ready to pay you $20 just for reading it. Because this letter repeats the offer I made to you a few weeks ago:

I will buy your house
now in foreclosure, for a fair market value
in cash — so you can walk away free and clear

You now have less than one month before the sheriff posts an auction notice on your front door telling the whole world, including your friends and neighbors, that your house is in foreclosure.

You'll suffer tremendous loss of pride and prestige if you don't stop the foreclosure process now. What's worse, you'll lose your house and probably lose all the cash (equity) you have in it. And still worse, you'll <u>lose your chance to walk away clean, with the cash to make a new start.</u>

Because in today's hot real estate market, the fair market value for your house is probably a lot more than you paid for it. If your house is sold on the auction block, it will probably go for <u>20% to 50% less</u> than the fair market value. So the bank will get its money back. But <u>you may get absolutely nothing.</u>

And make no mistake — time is running out on the foreclosure action on your house. The moment you received your notice of default, the law took over. The law is not on your side. But I am. I'll bring you cash instead of grief. Because once the public auction happens, you'll lose more than your home and all your equity. Consider your credit rating: ruined. Your family: shamed. Your employer: shocked and concerned about your judgment. Think about the mental, emotional and physical stress on you and your family that can affect you negatively for years to come!

BUT IF YOU ACT RIGHT NOW, THERE'S STILL TIME TO SAVE YOUR EQUITY, SOLVE YOUR FORECLOSURE PROBLEM AND WALK AWAY WITH CASH IN YOUR POCKET. I told you before, and I will tell you again: I will buy your house, for cash, for a fair market price in ten days or less so you can walk away free and clear to make a new start. Sounds like a pretty good deal but there's still more.

(Please turn to reverse side)

*Our mailing address is: P.O. Box 5000, #412, Danville, Ca. 94526*
*Our offices are located at 185 Front Street, Suite 207 in Danville, California just behind the First Interstate Bank and only steps from Father Nature's Famous Restaurant.* ©

I WILL GIVE YOU A CHANCE TO TURN YOUR RUN OF BAD LUCK INTO A STROKE OF GOOD FORTUNE!

Because along with this letter I am sending you a special certificate that will entitle you to TWENTY CHANCES TO WIN THE CALIFORNIA LOTTERY — ABSOLUTELY FREE.

This certificate is to show my good faith and sincere interest in helping you. When I come over to explain the details of my offer to buy your home for cash at a fair market value, not at the depressed foreclosure price, I will bring twenty lottery tickets with me as a gift to you.

You might hit the jackpot with one of those free lottery tickets — but even if you don't it will put a little fun back into your life which right now looks so bleak.

Remember, you're under no obligation. If you don't like what you see and hear, we'll shake hands and walk away, friends. And if you decide to take me up on my written offer to buy your home and then get a better offer from somebody else, I'll let you off the hook with no hard feelings.

You deserve that chance to start again but I can only give it to you if you PICK UP THE PHONE AND CALL ME at once. Call me, Ted Thomas, at (415) 837-2106. Take me up on it. But do it now.

Your time is running out.

Warmly,

Ted Thomas
Vice President

## INSERTS TO LETTERS

# INSIDE FACTS!

### How to Avoid Foreclosure Without Leaving Home

Foreclosure Hot Line 24 Hours. 5 Minute RECORDED message explains how to save your home. Procedures, laws, penalties. No salesman will answer or call. No obligation.

**24 Hours**
**PREVENT FORECLOSURE HOT LINE**
**415-837-0170**

**New Growth Financial**

**FREE ★ FREE ★ FREE ★ FREE ★ FREE ★ FREE ★ FREE ★ FREE ★ FREE** ©

### MAIL THIS NO RISK COUPON TODAY!

*(SAVE YOUR HOME EQUITY RESPONSE COUPON)*

☐ Yes, Ted, I want to save the equity in my home. I don't want my home to be sold at public auction and lose the money I've got in it. Please help. I understand you will give me a free, no obligation consultation to examine my options at this point. If I decide to sell my home at this time, you will give me a bank check within ten days. I understand you will also deal with the lenders so they'll stop bugging me and that you'll help me move and find a new place. All without cost. This sounds good to me. Please call me.

Name ______

Address ______

City ______ State______ Zip______

Daytime Telephone ( ) ______

Nighttime Telephone ( ) ______

Best time to reach me: ______

Return this coupon in the enclosed envelope to: Ted Thomas
New Growth Financial
P.O. Box 5000, Suite 412
Danville, CA 94526

For faster service, call us at **(415) 837-2106.** ©

**Examples of inserts sent out to foreclosing homeowners. Be sure to change the wording of the inserts to best suit you and your approach to the homeowner.**

### OUR GUARANTEE TO YOU!!

Let's be perfectly frank. If you are afraid someone will take advantage of you, let me relieve you of that anxiety. If you get a better written offer that is more beneficial than our proposal, I will cancel our contract. Yes! That is correct! We will release you from the contract if you get a better deal. You are the judge. Is that fair treatment? How can you lose? Stop procrastinating; indecision could cost you thousands of dollars if your property is sold at public auction (trustee sale). ©

To Whom It May Concern:

Selling ones home under duress of foreclosure can never be a pleasant experience. It touches ones sense of dignity and is territly destabilizing to ones family.

Having endured such an experience, I would like to recommend that anyone else finding himself in similar circumstances contact Ted Thomas of New Growth Enterprises.

Mr. Thomas not only correctly advised me of my options, but outlined a plan that helped me in resettling my family and regaining a measure of stability in our lives.

Mr. Thomas and his staff performed efficiently and with sensitivity to our problems at a time which that kind of professionalism and attitude was essential to me and my family.

**IF YOU WANT HELP . . .**
**READ THIS TESTIMONIAL**
**IT'S NOTARIZED PROOF.**

Jane and Jim Jacks

**STATE OF CALIFORNIA**

**COUNTY OF** CONTRA COSTA ss.

On this 11 day of November in the year 1990 before me, NANCY M PATTERSON, a Notary Public, State of California, duly commissioned and sworn, personally appeared Thomas Webb Johnson personally known to me (or proved to me on the basis of satisfactory evidence) to be the person whose name is subscribed to this instrument, and acknowledged that he executed it.

IN WITNESS WHEREOF I have hereunto set my hand and affixed my official seal in the STATE OF CALIFORNIA County of CONTRA COSTA on the date set forth above in this certificate.

OFFICIAL SEAL
NANCY M PATTERSON
NOTARY PUBLIC - CALIFORNIA
CONTRA COSTA COUNTY
My Comm. Expires March 27, 1990

*Notary Public, State of California*

*My commission expires* March 27, 1991

This document is only a general form which may be proper for use in simple transactions and in no way acts, or is intended to act, as a substitute for the advice of an attorney. The printer does not make any warranty either express or implied as to the legal validity of any provision or the suitability of these forms in any specific transaction.

© **Cowdery's Form No. 32 — Acknowledgement to Notary Public — Individuals — (C.C. Sec. 1189) — (Rev. 1/83)**

## WHAT OTHERS SAY ABOUT OUR SERVICE

Mr. Ted Thomas
New Growth Financial
185 Front Street, Suite 207
Danville, CA 94526

Dear Ted:

I want to thank you for coming to our rescue and buying our house from us.

It will be so nice being reunited with my husband again. Even though three months may not seem like a long time - it was. The waiting and uncertainty of how many more months we'd be trying to sell. For us buying another home and keeping this home on the market was financially impossible. In a short time, our equity would have been gobbled up. You have done what no other realtor was able to do. The best thing about the whole process was the speed and knowing everything would be acomplished with no contingencies or waiting.

I really feel that more and more people will be using your service in the future.

Thank you again and good luck with your book.

Sincerely,

Karen Karlyle

Karen Karlvle

# *New Growth Financial*

*"The Distressed Property Experts"*

*(415) 837-2106 Fax #743-0926*

April 23, 1991

McKaley Harris
PO Box 85
Likely, CA 96116

Dear McKaley,

As you can see, I've attached a nice, crisp one dollar bill to the top of this letter.

Why have I done this? Actually, there are two reasons.

1. I have something very important to say to you and I needed some way to make sure this letter catches your attention.

2. And secondly, I wanted you to experience, as you opened this letter, the total unique thrill of receiving money from a completely unexpected source!

We realize you have a problem. We have helped many people in your situation by buying their property. We pay cash.

According to county records, your property will be sold at public auction on 4/24/91 at 2:pm.

This problem can be solved! We will give you a fair price.

Call today - (415) 837-2106

**WE PAY CASH**

TT/cs

*Our mailing address is: P.O. Box 5000, #412, Danville, Ca. 94526*
*Our offices are located at 185 Front Street, Suite 207 in Danville, California just behind the First Interstate Bank and only steps from Father Nature's Famous Restaurant.* ©

## FOR YOUR SAKE BE SURE TO READ THIS TESTIMONIAL

Mr. Ted Thomas
New Growth Financial
185 Front Street, Suite 207
Danville, CA 94526

Dear Ted:

Recently, my family and I found ourselves in the terrible, uncomfortable and frightening experience of foreclosure totally without a plan or any idea of what we should do.

Shortly after we received our Notice of Foreclosure, we started getting alot of mail telling us that we might possibly have some alternatives that we hadn't considered. So I started calling a few of them and, as it turned out, each one of them told us that we didn't have enough equity in our house for them to get involved or loan us money. So, when we saw the mailer from New Growth Financial it basically was ignored. However, by the time the third one came, we were desperate so my wife filled it out and sent it in. Within a week, we got a call from New Growth Financial and an appointment was made that afternoon. We signed a contract then and in less than two weeks we were able to leave our house with enough money to rent another house and our credit rating wasn't adversely affected.

I can honestly say that New Growth Finacial helped us more than we ever imagined. We were treated with respect rather than comtempt like so many others had. We really appreciate the help we received.

Sincerely.

Sally and Sid Snow

**EQUITY RESOURCE FINANCIAL**
(214) 231-8777

MICHAEL HAYNES
*Distressed Property Expert*

9794 Forest Lane
Suite 578
Dallas, Texas 75243

Member National Society
Of Foreclosure Professionals

December 20, 1990

Ted Thomas
New Growth Financial
P.O. Box 5000, #412
Danville, CA 94526

Dear Ted:

Congratulations in advance on the completion of your second book. I'm anxious to see how you have improved your first book,which has guided me every step of the way.

I bought my first property last month. I'm having the repairs done now and expect to have it sold by February or March.

I do have several questions I need to ask,so I will be calling you next month.

Enclosed are two letters which I have been using the past two months. I've had good responses from them so far, hope you find them useful too.

Ted do you plan on having another seminar and do you plan on coming to Texas anytime soon?

Best wishes for success with your second book. Happy Holidays to you, your family, and everyone at New Growth Financial.

All the best,

Michael Haynes

EQUITY RESOURCE FINANCIAL

Distressed Property Experts

9794 Forest Lane, Ste. 578
Dallas, Texas 75243

(214) 231-8777

**Dear Friends,**

Listen to experience. Your troubles won't end when your home is sold at Public Auction--they'll only multiply. I know first hand, having been through it myself, and can testify that your credit rating will be seriously damaged. You'll have trouble borrowing even the smallest amounts of money.

Save yourself from this future humiliation and pain.

Let me give you **CASH** for the equity in your home. You can use this MONEY to find a new home, take care of your family, and make a fresh start.

As a result of my own misfortune, it has been my desire to learn all I can about foreclosures in order to help others avoid this needless and painful experience. I am a graduate of the Thomas Foreclosure System Boot Camp, and I am currently a member of the National Society of Foreclosure Professionals.

Give me the opportunity to use my specialized knowledge to help you, and I'll show you how to solve your money problem. Call 553-9558 today, and ask for Michael.

You can have cash for your home equity in 7 days or less!

This straightforward option is yours, but remember, if you do nothing, you'll lose your home at Public Auction. It's the law.

Please, don't wait too long! I'm here to help you -- **BEFORE** the Auction takes place.

Don't feel alone! You aren't.

Warmest Regards,

Michael Haynes

Michael Haynes

P.S. **Texas foreclosure laws are swift and final. Time is running. Get help before it's too late. Call Today 553-9558. There is no obligation.**

Reprinted by permission of Michael Haynes

EQUITY RESOURCE FINANCIAL
Distressed Property Experts

9794 Forest Lane, Ste. 578
Dallas, Texas 75243

(214) 231-8777

**Dear Friends,**

Although your home is now posted for sale at public auction, there is still time to stop this from happening.

I can show you how to get **CASH** for your home equity in a week or less. It's really very simple. My business is helping people **Avoid Foreclosure**. I want to help you.

If your home goes to foreclosure, you'll lose everything. First, you'll receive an eviction notice, then a visit from the sheriff. He has authority to remove you and your family from your home. You'll not only lose your home but also the **EQUITY** in your home.

Houses sold at Public Auction usually sell for 25% to 50% less than houses sold on the open market. This doesn't have to happen to you. I can help you **Stop the Foreclosure** and put some money in your pocket, as well.

Call 553-9558 and ask for Michael. Time is running out. Please call today.

Sincerely,

Michael Haynes

P.S. Let me give you **CASH** for the equity in your home! Call 553-9558. There is no obligation.

Reprinted by permission of Michael Haynes

MAILER EDUCATION CENTER™

U.S. POSTAL SERVICE
P.O. BOX 836
WINDSOR, CT 06006-0836
TELEPHONE (203) 285-7030
TOLL-FREE (800) 877-7843

UNITED STATES POSTAL SERVICE
We Deliver.

April 10, 1991

Ms Linda Wright
New Growth Financial
PO Box 5000, Suite 412
Danville CA 94526-1061

Dear Ms Wright:

Thank you for your interest in the U.S. Postal Service Mailer Education Center™ seminars.

As requested, please find a copy of our promotional literature and press releases.

If you need additional information, please don't hesitate to call me on (203) 285-7034.

Very truly yours,

Stephen A. Medaglia
Merchandising Programs Coordinator
Marketing & Communications

Attachments

SAM:df
C:M194

- Increase productivity and eliminate waste
- Save time and money

MAILER EDUCATION CENTER

# Marketing with Direct Mail

No area of marketing is growing as rapidly today as direct mail. . . for both reaching your prospects and having them respond to you. It is a multi-billion dollar a year industry with an extremely healthy annual growth rate. Marketers can no longer compete today without mastering the effective use of this often misunderstood communication vehicle in the marketing plan.

Direct response fits right in with the needs of today's cost-conscious marketer because it is specifically targeted to reach only predefined prospects in specific market niches. It eliminates the waste sometimes found with broad, widely focused media, and gives marketers an exact accounting of their results.

## Participation is a Must if You. . .

- Are an administrator in a sales, marketing, advertising, public relations, promotion, or service group of small companies, entrepreneurs, copywriters, artists and advertising. Public relations agency personnel will also find it especially useful.

## Learn About These Key Topics and More. . .

- Why direct response has become so popular as marketers become increasingly cost conscious, demanding more and more accountable results from the mailings they do. . . direct mail provides this accountability, allowing marketers to test and measure their results.
- How and when to use direct mail. . . how to integrate direct mail strategy into your marketing mix and how to minimize your mailing costs.
- What makes an effective direct mail piece, including planning, formats, response devices, and other creative considerations such as headline elements, copy flow, layouts, and personalized effects.

Bring samples of your mailing pieces and get a FREE evaluation.

---

*"Information was well presented and in a language all could understand. . . I truly felt that the seminar gave a terrific 'outline' on the subject."*

**Frances Lowe**
***Marketing Manager***
***Baracuda International***

---

- The heart of any effective direct response campaign is of course proper list selection. . . learn how to determine which mailing list will work best for you, and where to get or rent these lists.
- Techniques for improving responses and what to do with those responses. . . data base marketing, fulfillment and analysis.
- Determining costs and benefits.
- The proper use of the mail system to reach your target audience. . . use of the mail system to get back your responses. . . business reply considerations, bulk sorting, metered indicia, bonded mail houses and more.
- How ZIP + 4 can be used to best target your audience. . . addressing for automation. . .common problems.

***Instructor:*** **Adrienne Wax, Wunderman Worldwide**
**New York, NY**
***Instructor:*** **Pat Scully, Marketing & Communications**
**US Postal Service - Manchester, NH**
***Instructor:*** **Charlie Messina, Marketing & Communications**
**US Postal Service - New York, NY**

**February 20, 1991 — Oklahoma City, OK**
**March 14, 1991 — New York, NY**
**March 19, 1991 — Atlanta, GA**
**March 26, 1991 — Phoenix, AZ**
**April 2, 1991 — Grand Rapids, MI**
**April 4, 1991 — Altoona, IA**
**April 9, 1991 — Modesto, CA**
**April 10, 1991 — Sacramento, CA**
**April 12, 1991 — Reno, NV**
**April 17, 1991 — Lubbock, TX**
**April 18, 1991 — Amarillo, TX**
**May 7, 1991 — New York, NY**
**May 22, 1991 — Arlington, TX**
**June 11, 1991 — Marlborough, MA**
**June 13, 1991 — Hindsdale/Oakbrook, IL**
**July 16, 1991 — Medford, OR**
**July 18, 1991 — Portland, OR**
**July 23, 1991 — New Brunswick, NJ**
**July 26, 1991 — Nashville, TN**

***Registration at 8:30 am***
***Seminar 9:00 am - 4:00 pm***

1 DAY SEMINAR

# Mailing Procedures For Administrative Personnel

This course was developed for administrative personnel. If you are a one-person operation in charge of the incoming and/or outgoing mails for your company, you must attend this seminar. Learn how to reduce postal costs, improve mail service, and master all the basic postal services.

Some of the topics covered include:

- Addressing requirements
- Using ZIP Codes
- Postage rates
- Ancillary services
- Special services
- Choosing the right envelope
- Overnight services
- Packaging procedures
- International mail
- Postage payment methods
- Selecting mailing equipment

## Participation is a must if you. . .

- Are an employee in a mail center - small or large
- Secretary who handles important correspondence
- Department administrator
- Administration supervisor responsible for a secretarial group

*Instructor:* **Charlie Messina, Marketing & Communications**
**US Postal Service - New York, NY**

*Instructor:* **John Baslie, Marketing & Communications**
**US Postal Service - Springfield, MA**

**March 6, 1991 — New York, NY**
**March 12, 1991 — Nashville, TN**
**March 27, 1991 — Phoenix, AZ**
**May 2, 1991 — New York, NY**
**June 14, 1991 — Naperville, IL**
**July 10, 1991 — Minneapolis, MN**
**July 11, 1991 — Grand Rapids, MI**
**July 31, 1991 — Falls Church, VA**

***Registration at 8:30 am***
***Seminar 9:00 am - 1:00 pm***

½ DAY SEMINAR

**Note:**
The material covered in this ½ day seminar is completely covered in the full day Professional Mail Center Management Seminar. There is no need to take both seminars.

# DIRECT MAIL

THE READER'S DIGEST ASSOCIATION, INC. PLEASANTVILLE, N.Y. 10570 CB2751-P

021182109 NOT OVER D 25 CENTS 75-1131/919

| MO | DAY | YEAR |
|---|---|---|
| 12 | 20 | 90 |

PAY TO
BEARER OR

MR. TED THOMAS
-P. O. -BOX 5000 -STE 412
DANVILLE, CA 94526-1061

| DLRS | CTS |
|---|---|
| XXX | 25 |

FIRST STATE BANK
LAKE LILLIAN
MINNESOTA 56253

CB2751

CHECK NO. CB2751

0 15863 62731 15453 369

THE READER'S DIGEST ASSOCIATION, INC.

THIS CHECK NOT VALID AFTER
6 MONTHS FROM DATE SHOWN ABOVE

AUTHORIZED SIGNATURE

⑆091911315⑆ 160⑈000⑈

**Typical mass mailer. Your mail must be a step or two above the competition mail or yours won't get opened.**

THEODORE E. THOMAS

Here is your exclusive entry number valid for all prizes:

C84103X7

All prizes are guaranteed to be awarded but you must enter to win! Mail your official Entry Certificate today!

15863 62731 78683

SWEEPSTAKES PRIZE
SELECTION DEPARTMENT

PLEASANTVILLE NEW YORK 00401

TOTAL SWEEPSTAKES VALUE

D 10,250,000.00

**The Reader's Digest Association, Inc.**

THE SOONER YOU ENTER—THE MORE YOU COULD WIN...MAIL ALL 4 TICKETS BY STATED DEADLINE DATE

MAIL BACK ALL FOUR SELECTION TICKETS BY DEADLINE STATED FOR IMMEDIATE PRIZE ELIGIBILITY (POSTMARK DETERMINES DATE OF ENTRY)

SWEEPSTAKES TT STAR

DOCUMENTATION OF PRIZE AWARD ENTRY CONFIRMED: T E D (FIRST) T H O M A S (LAST)

IN THE EVENT MR. TED THOMAS is chosen as Grand Prize Winner, you will be notified by MAIL OR SPECIAL COURIER. Follow our instructions and within 14 days from notification your first $167,000.00 Prize Check will arrive. Act now and you could win FIVE MILLION DOLLARS total.

| | | | | | |
|---|---|---|---|---|---|
| 1 PRIZE OF | $100,000 | 4 PRIZES OF | $25,000 | 30 PRIZES OF | $500 |
| 1 PRIZE OF | $50,000 | 6 PRIZES OF | $5,000 | 400 PRIZES OF | $125 |

55313 PRIZES OF $89 WRISTWATCHES

1 GRAND PRIZE AND BONUS PRIZE OF UP TO $5,100,000.00

VALID A TOTAL OF $10,250,000.00 IN PRIZES VALID

## DIRECT MAIL

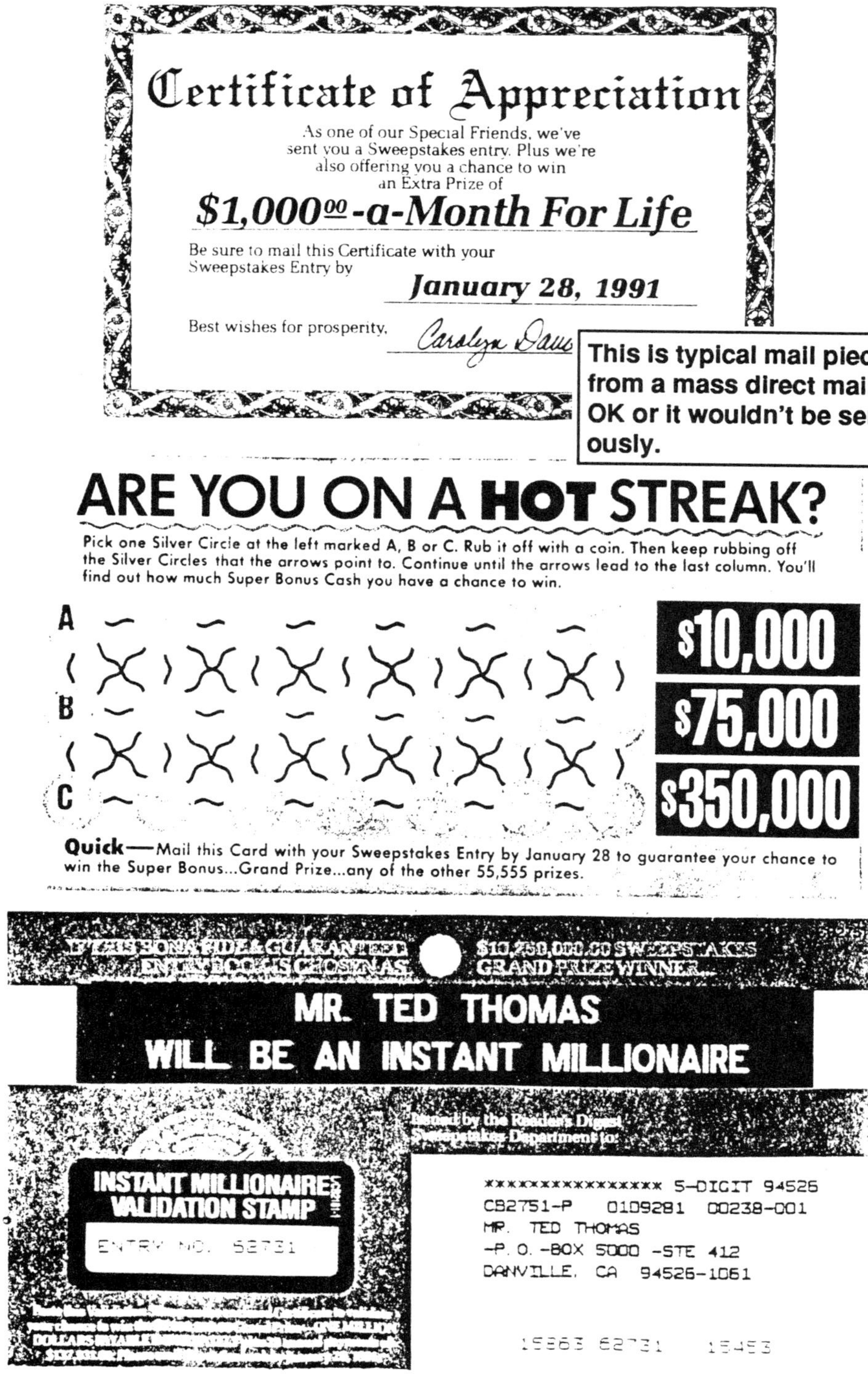


**This is typical mail piece received from a mass direct mailer. It works OK or it wouldn't be sent continuously.**

Western Union
49 Geary Street
San Francisco, CA 94108

**western union Priority Letter**

9110900050512 108116A

***BUSINESS REPLY***

NEW GROWTH FINANCIAL
ATTN: MANAGER, MKTG SERVICES
PO BOX 5000 #412
DANVILLE CA 94526

Western Union can be your resource for quick, cost effective, communications to your customers and distribution channels.

We can help you with last minute mailings, time sensitive or important communications like;

- Price Change Notifications
- Announcing new sales programs
- Seminar/conference communications
- Policy changes
- New product announcements

For more information call Western Union at 415/956-1112 to get your messages delivered as overnight Mailgrams, two-day Priority Letters or high-impact, first class Custom Letters. (Or, fax page two of this letter to us at; 415/956-5130).

Sincerely,

Rick Pucci
Regional Manager
Western Union Priority Services

P.S. If you are using overnight courier services for single letters, Western Union can cut your overnight mail and labor costs by more than half!

NEW GROWTH FINANCIAL
P.O. BOX 5000, NO. 412
DANVILLE, CA 94526

western union **Priority Letter**

9007200016412 072110A

Example of a letter sent out to a foreclosing homeowner. Be sure to change the wording of the letter to best suit you and your approach to the homeowner.

MEW GROWTH FINANCIAL
ATTN: DIANE SWENSON
P.O. BOX 5000, NO. 412
DANVILLE CA 94526

HI,

I'M TED THOMAS AND I CAN'T OFFER YOU A MAGIC SOLUTION OR A MIRACLE, BUT I CAN GIVE YOU PRACTICAL ADVICE ABOUT THE FORECLOSURE PROCESS YOU ARE INVOLVED IN. PLEASE READ ON TO MY WIN-WIN PROPOSAL FOR YOU.

BEFORE I GET TO THAT PROPOSAL, I WANT YOU TO KNOW THAT I'VE BEEN THROUGH THE FORECLOSURE PROCESS MYSELF. YES, I LOST MY HOME. I WISH SOMEBODY HAD GIVEN ME THE FACTS.

JUST LIKE YOU, I LEARNED THE ROPES THE HARD WAY. WHEN I DESPERATELY NEEDED HELP, ALL I GOT WAS A LOT OF TALK AND NO HELP.

MY TECHNIQUES WILL HELP YOU GET THE MOST MONEY QUICKLY WITHOUT A LOT OF RED TAPE. MY METHODS ARE REALLY DIFFERENT COMPARED TO MOST PEOPLE IN THE REAL ESTATE BUSINESS. SMALL PROFITS AND LOTS OF VOLUME, THAT'S HOW I DO IT.

YES, I HAVE A SELFISH INTEREST! SINCE I'VE ALREADY BEEN THROUGH FORECLOSURE AND LOST MY HOME, I FIGURED OUT A WAY TO SELL HOUSES QUICKLY WITH A VERY SMALL PROFIT AND I DO THAT THREE OR FOUR TIMES A MONTH. I MAKE A SMALL PROFIT EACH TIME I SELL A PROPERTY BUT MORE IMPORTANTLY THE PERSON SUFFERING WITH FORECLOSURE, BACK PAYMENTS AND SCREAMING, RUDE BILL COLLECTORS, GETS T O P D O L L A R FOR THEIR PROPERTY. JUST ASK ABOUT MY IRON-CLAD GUARANTEE.

I'M SURE THIS METHOD MAKES SENSE TO YOU. THIS IS A WIN-WIN SITUATION.

FINALLY, I'M NOT OVERWHELMINGLY GREEDY! THIS IS IMPORTANT. MANY PEOPLE IN THE REAL ESTATE BUSINESS ARE ONLY IN IT FOR THE MONEY. THEY ONLY SELL ONE OR TWO HOUSES PER YEAR AND TRY TO MAKE HUGE PROFITS ON EACH; NOT SO WITH ME. I SELL OVER 40 HOUSES PER YEAR AND MAKE A SMALL PROFIT ON EACH. FURTHERMORE, I KNOW YOU ARE ANXIOUS AND VERY NERVOUS RIGHT NOW AND MORE THAN LIKELY YOU'VE HAD A BAD TIME FOR MONTHS. I HAVE THE ANSWERS TO YOUR PROBLEM AND CAN GIVE YOU RELIEF FROM WORRY.

western union Priority Letter

9007200016422 072110A (CONT) PAGE: 0002
IF YOU ARE LIKE MOST PEOPLE, THE PROBLEM IS YOU ARE WORRYING THAT SOMEONE WILL TAKE ADVANTAGE OF YOU. LET ME RELIEVE YOU OF THAT STRESS. YOU CAN RELY ON MY OFFER.

IT'S EASY FOR YOU TO CHECK US OUT! WE ARE MEMBERS OF THE CHAMBER OF COMMERCE IN DANVILLE, ALAMEDA/CONTRA COSTA COUNTY BETTER BUSINESS BUREAU AND FINALLY, WE ARE MEMBERS OF THE CONTRA COSTA BOARD OF REALTORS. ALL OF THESE ORGANIZATIONS HAVE TELEPHONES; WHY NOT GIVE THEM A CALL.

TIME IS RUNNING OUT FOR YOU. IF YOU DON'T ACT QUICKLY, YOUR HOME WILL BE SOLD AT TRUSTEE'S SALE. REACH FOR THE TELEPHONE AND DIAL (415) 837-2106 AND ASK FOR TED. YOU'LL BE GLAD YOU DID.

WARMLY,

TED THOMAS

P.S. THIS IS YOUR LAST CHANCE.

Chapter 4

# Property Evaluation Questionnaire

## *You Can Laugh at Money Worries if You Use this Questionnaire*

### WHAT TO DO WHEN THEY TELEPHONE

Your direct mail success will be almost instantaneous if you are using the methods explained in the previous chapter. The defaulting sellers who need help will start making telephone calls to your home or office within days of receiving your letter. Don't expect every defaulting seller to call, but do expect a percentage of those who are scheduled for auction to call in desperation.

My experience has been that approximately 80% of the defaulting homeowners will cure the loan and make it healthy. But many of those who do cure their loans will do so by placing additional debt on their property. Expect to see many of these cured loans back on the default list in the near future. After all, if these owners couldn't make the payment on one loan, how will they make payments on two — especially at the higher interest rates usually charged for secondary loans?

When the telephone rings, you must be prepared to handle the situation. This chapter explains how you should get the buy/no buy information that you need from the homeowners.

This information is critically important. The purpose of your direct mailing was to get the defaulting homeowner to telephone you. The purpose of the telephone call is to gather information and then get an appointment to see the property. If the homeowner telephoned you, then he or she is interested in your services — so go after the appointment. The negotiation dynamics are in favor of the buyer at this point. The homeowner's call is your cue to take advantage of this opportunity: Treat the homeowner with respect and get the all-important information about the property.

## THE APPRAISAL PROCESS

Before returning a seller's telephone call, I start the appraisal process. Assume that the property is located in Manteca, California, which is in San Joaquin County, a rural, agricultural area. Therefore the sophisticated DAMAR database is not available to help find the value of comparable homes. More than likely the real estate brokerage community will have appraisal or comparable data recorded in a Multiple Listing Service Book or on-line retrieval system. If you don't subscribe to either the printed MLS book or have the computer access to the information, you can use the good old reliable telephone. In just minutes the information operator gives us the telephone numbers of four real estate offices in the area.

I telephone the brokers and explain who I am. You should be open with brokers; do not try to hide what you are doing. It isn't necessary to tell the exact address of your prospective purchase, just the neighborhood it is in. Then have your pencil and your questions ready. The following list will help you get started.

- What's that neighborhood like? Good or bad?
- Is it desirable? Why?
- Is it improving? Why?
- Is it deteriorating? Why?
- Who likes to live there: commuters, families, singles?
- Are the houses all the same or custom built?
- Is it exclusive?
- Will a house priced correctly sell quickly? Why?
- Is the market good? Why?
- Is the appreciation up or down? Why? How much?

Familiarize yourself with the property and market values:

- Ask neighbors about values and selling prices
- Check the local newspapers to review asking prices
- Ask FSBOs (For Sale By Owners) to determine asking prices

A property profile from the title company will give you data on comparable houses in the area.

## OBTAIN FINANCIAL/PROPERTY INFORMATION

When a defaulting homeowner calls, complete a Property Evaluation Questionnaire (pages 103 and 104). If you follow the form as a checklist, ask all the questions, and then think the situation through. You'll be able to save yourself hundreds of hours of time spent driving and looking around. Each of the questions is important, so I suggest you get all the answers to your questions on the telephone before you visit the property. With these parameters in mind, let's work our way through the Property Evaluation Questionnaire.

*Where is the property located?*

Have you restricted your purchases to certain towns or locations? Do you know the street or neighborhood? Is it desirable? If so, why is it desirable?

*What kind of property is it?*

Is it a single-family home, a duplex, an apartment, a farm, a trailer in a trailer park? Each is an opportunity for the knowledgeable buyer.

*Description, age, size, and improvements?*

You will need these details in order to compare the property with others in the neighborhood to decide if you can make a profit on the deal. If the house is too old, it might not meet current building codes. If it is too new, the owner may not have enough equity to make it worth your while.

*What condition is the property in?*

This estimate is subjective. Everyone has a different opinion of condition. It's probably wise to ask how old the carpets are and when the drapes were installed. In that way you can compare your experience of their probable condition with what you are being told.

*How old is the roof?*

Shake roofs will deteriorate rapidly after ten years, so you should take that into account in your appraisal. In any case, you must pay professionals to look at the roof and evaluate it. Don't guess; this is a fatal mistake, and it will prove costly. Sellers will generally assure you that the roof is in excellent condition. When you see spots on the ceilings, you'll be convinced otherwise.

*Have you had a recent termite inspection?*

Most termite reports are valid for only 90 days. Unless the homeowner has tried to sell the house he probably does not have a recent report. Professional termite reports are as important as roof reports. Remember the three-letter word: Ask. You'll save yourself a considerable amount of money if you ask a professional how to handle the termite work.

*How long have you had the property? What did you pay for it?*

The answers to these questions will tell you how much equity the owner is likely to have and will also give you some idea of whether or not values in the neighborhood are appreciating.

*How much do you owe on it?*

Many homeowners do not know what they owe. Before leaving your home or office, you must determine what they owe. Ask the caller to read the default notice to you (for an example, see page 188). You need to know what is owed and what the selling prices are in the neighborhood so that you can decide if it is profitable to visit the property and make a deal with the owner.

*Is the loan that is foreclosing a first, second, or third loan?*

This is an important question. You will find that owners will, from time to time, forget about one loan or another. When you buy from the owner, you buy what he owes and that includes all his loans on that property. The biggest mistake new buyers of distressed property make is to buy from the owner and then discover the existence of an additional trust deed/mortgage that is senior to the one they bought. You must find out about all the loans and distinguish the senior loans from the junior loans. (See Chapter 8 for procedures to research these loans.)

*Are the loans assumable?*

This consideration could be a deal breaker. If the loan is not assumable and the lender is hostile to your taking the loan, you may find that after you cure the default the lender takes foreclosure action against *you*. The suggested method is for you to take the loan "subject to," which simply means that you will pay the deficit and make the loan healthy and thereafter make the future payments as they come due. This is not a formal assumption and you are not taking on the responsibility or the liability for the payment of the loan.

*How much will it take to cure the default?*

The lenders will generally welcome your payment to cure the loan. However, they have the right, specified in the contract (trust deed/mortgage), to accelerate the loan if the title is "alienated," that is, transferred. It is rare for the lenders to accelerate the loan, but they do have the contractual right to do so and they have federal law to back them up. You will quickly find that most lenders will just accept payments. The few who even trouble to communicate with you will simply request that you assume the existing loan and pay them a fee for doing so. If they don't suggest an assumption, you should offer a small fee to do so. By small fee, I mean 1/2 to 1% of the principal amount of the loan. Expect some brief negotiation, as 1% is normal.

*Are you behind in any payment?*

Of course they are, or they wouldn't be calling you. But this is not a silly question. The *number* of payments in areas is critical. If the owner has a Veterans Administration or Federal Housing Administration loan, all of the equity could easily have been used up or have disappeared by the time you ask the question. Homes bought with HUD or VA loans are difficult to deal with because the VA and HUD react slowly when it comes to foreclosure. In many cases, the agencies do not start foreclosure proceedings until a year or more has elapsed since the first default notice. If the homeowner has only a small amount of equity, the late payments and interest on the loan together with late charges and foreclosure fees will have used it all up. In other words, the loan and the penalties and fees will exceed the retail value of the house.

*Are you only in default or is the date of the Trustee's / Sheriff's Sale set?*

Remember that the seller has three months to cure a default. Therefore, he might just be shopping around for a good deal. The motivated sellers are the homeowners who have been issued a Notice of Default (NOD). Under California law, you will recall, the NOD is the first notice that the trustor (homeowner) receives, and it signals the start of the three-month reinstatement period during which, if the loan is made current, the foreclosure is cancelled. If the homeowner does not cure the loan, the lender will, at the end of the three months, publish in a newspaper of general circulation a Notice of Trustee's Sale. This notice is a powerful motivator for defaulting homeowners. If the homeowner doesn't sell his property before the auction sale, he will lose it all on the twenty-second day.

*When is your property going up for sale?*

Don't be surprised if the property is going on the block at the Trustee's/Sheriff's Sale tomorrow morning. It's not unusual for some people to wait until the last minute. (See Chapter 1 for details on how to get a twenty-four-the hour postponement.)

*How much is the property worth?*

The homeowner will either have no idea or will have an inflated idea of the value. For example, you can expect to be told that the house three doors away just sold for $XYZ. You will probably not be told that it was the best house on the block, that the seller financed it with a low-interest loan, and that the house you are discussing has two fewer bedrooms, no pool, and has never been painted, cleaned, or cared for.

*Is that what homes in the neighborhood are selling for?*

Having heard what the owner thinks his house is worth, you must ask this question. Most sellers will guess! So, as part of your homework before you go out to look at the property, *ask* brokers who know the area, *ask* for Multiple Listing Service (MLS) reports, *ask* appraisers, *ask* neighbors, *ask* the mailman, *ask* the merchants. Keep asking, and you'll get rich.

*Do you have a recent appraisal?*

This is another way of asking, "What is the value of your home?" This is a difficult question for most homeowners, for the same reason: They usually have an inflated idea of value. An appraisal to them could easily be a comment Uncle Milton made last Christmas. Uncle Milton lives in Hawaii and has only visited the property, located in Kansas City, once.

Appraisals from brokers are fairly useful, but I'd advise caution here. Most brokers appraise properties at about 10% above market value. If the seller does not have a professional appraisal provided by a Member of the Appraisers Institute (MAI), you can be assured that it is your job to determine the value.

*Have you had the property for sale?*

Don't be surprised if they tell you it hasn't been for sale at all. (These are the people who are waiting for a miracle to come along and make their house payments.) If it has been for sale, ask why it did not sell. Ask what the people who had looked at it had said about it. Find out what price the owners had been asking for it. Ask them what the realtor had told them.

*How much will you take for the property?*

After all the other questions, this one will be easy to answer. Don't be surprised when you are immediately challenged with "What will you give me?" or, "As much as I can get." Be prepared for that kind of answer. Don't offend the caller. Just tell him that it is too early to evaluate the dollars and cents without visiting the property. This will lead you into the next question.

*How do I get there?*

Make sure that you have the:

- Name
- Address (always get the nearest cross street)
- Telephone number (day and night)

Then make an appointment to visit the property and remember to note the date and time on your form. When you have hung up the telephone, check the address on the Thomas Brothers Map and make a note of the relevant page. Remember: When you make an appointment, also remember to ask the owner to have all the loan documentation available for your inspection. Your time is too valuable to waste waiting while the seller turns his attic upside down looking for pieces of paper. And I can't stress enough how important it is to get the name, address, and telephone number. This information will be of value over and over again, and without it you'll waste more time than you can afford.

The record-keeping is very simple in this business, but you'll be surprised how many times you'll refer to this Property Evaluation Questionnaire. You'll also be surprised how many people call but do not set an appointment and then call again a few weeks later (as their time is running out) and don't realize they have already talked to you. It is always interesting to see if the information and motivation are the same on the subsequent call.

## AFTER THE TELEPHONE INTERVIEW

Here are the key questions to ask yourself after you have completed the telephone interview. Make sure you can answer *every* question.

- Do you want property in this area?
- Will it meet building code or the requirements for building permits?
- Does the owner the owe banks too much?
- Is it insurable?
- Is financing available?
- Are you wasting your time?

- Are the comparables easy to verify?
- Do you have different options, for instance, a better property, or one in a better neighborhood?
- Does the house have dry rot?
- Can you buy it and sell it for a profit?

**Quote**

*"It is not doing things right that counts, it is doing the right thing."*
*—Peter Drucker*

## TRIPLE YOUR DOLLARS WITH A PLANNED PRESENTATION

Planning is the key to making an effective presentation to the homeowner — and effective planning. A number of sources will provide information, including the Multiple Listing Service provided by real estate brokers, the Real Estate Data, Inc. (REDI), and databanks such as DAMAR and CMDC.

### Before You Leave the Office, Get the Following Reports of Evaluation

***Multiple Listing Service:*** A listing is an authorization given by a homeowner to a broker to advertise and sell a house. The written listing agreement is taken by a member of a group of brokers organized so that each member of the group shares his listings with fellow members. The listings are usually circulated in a printed book subscribed to by each of the members. The book is called the MLS or Multiple Listing Service Book.

Before meeting the property owner, it is wise to check with local brokers and on homes for sale by owners to establish the values in a particular neighborhood. However, a quick review of values with your local broker will reveal the houses listed in the MLS Book.

***REDI:*** The Real Estate Data, Inc., provides assessors' information—plot maps, property characteristic information, the name and address of the current owner, and a list of other information pertaining to the property.

***DAMAR:*** This computer databank provides current information taken from the assessor's roll and characteristics of the property. The computer read-out shows a name, address, property description, and comparable sales data. Such information saves buyers of distressed property hours of driving through neighborhoods looking for comparable properties. An example of the information provided by DAMAR is shown on page 105.

County assessors are required by state law to keep a list of all properties within the county and establish values for the properties so that the board of supervisors has accurate data on how much the tax receipts (revenue) will be for the coming years. With this knowledge, the supervisors direct the county administrators to budget expenditures. The list of real estate properties is generally referred to as the assessor's roll and it is updated regularly as property is bought and sold. Recently sold properties are very easy to assess, as the assessment is a matter of reviewing the sales contract or simply having the seller and buyer advise the county of the sale price as part of the escrow procedures. DAMAR purchases the county records data and then inputs the data into a mainframe computer. Subscribers can then access the data.

In attempting to analyze a property, the investor is always concerned with paying too much. By using the DAMAR or similar databank system as well as a Thomas Brothers Map Book, the investor simply selects the page and grid number of the applicable map and the DAMAR system responds with an Area Sales Analysis Profile. These data can then be compared with the price the investor expects to spend or negotiate.

This information is extremely valuable, since it is detailed and can be restricted to a very small area. The data are excellent for any foreclosure buyer who is purchasing in a metropolitan area. The same data and maps are available, with even more detail, for other regions and cities. All types of properties are included: office buildings, industrial sites, single-family homes, apartment buildings, and condominiums. Sales information and purchase dates are shown, so it is clearly specific to the property you are researching. DAMAR makes it easy to get complete sales information and market value data on your home computer with a modem.

The DAMAR or similar computer information is extensive, but it is essential, whether you are researching a prospective purchase and performing an in-house appraisal prior to purchase or just becoming familiar with the neighborhood. Buyers at Trustee's Sales should be especially alert to the Assessor's Parcel Number (or a tax number in your state), which DAMAR will supply. This and the legal description, which is provided on the Notice of Trustee's Sale, will define the property to be sold; the street address is not used.

***CMDC:*** The California Market Data Cooperative is a databank or clearinghouse of appraisal data for the State of California. The data are obtained from public records, independent appraisers, lenders, and government appraisers. The data are available to any individual or investor who is willing to pay the annual fee of approximately $100 plus a monthly fee.

### Establish the Loan Amounts and Payments That Are in Arrears

It is especially important to establish the extent of the default, since you will be the one to make payments and so stop the foreclosure process. Know what you are buying. Property owners, under stressful conditions such as foreclosure, have a tendency to forget loans other than those being foreclosed. It might be the second trust deed or mortgage that is foreclosing and the owner forgot to tell you about the first loan.

You certainly don't want to buy a property until you understand the lien situation. If you buy a pre-foreclosure property, you buy exactly what the owner owns. If you find that the owner has not told you about all the encumbrances, you could inadvertently buy an extra trust/mortgage deed that would make the purchase *unprofitable*. So it is important to determine the encumbrances of all types, including taxes, bonds, judgment liens, assessments, and trust deeds/mortgages (first, second, and third). Remember: You purchase what the owner has committed to ownership. The wise foreclosure buyer reviews the loan documents, specifically seeking information about prepayment penalties, assumptions, and/or alienation clauses.

**Meet the Owner**

Establish rapport with the owner. Tour the house and observe its good and bad points. Will it be marketable?

- Confirm the information you have already received and recorded on the Property Evaluation Questionnaire.
- Is the information the same as you received over the telephone? For example, the owner might have said that the roof does not leak, but you notice stains on the bedroom ceiling.
- Determine if the owner really does own the property. (Review the grant deed/warranty deed.)
- Before leaving the office, remind the owner to have the grant deed available for review when you visit the property. Otherwise the search could take hours, while you sit and watch papers — everything from high-school pictures to love notes from old friends — being dredged up out of shoe boxes and metal containers. The grant deed, along with the Notice of Default and the promissory note, mortgage, or trust deed, will usually be sufficient proof of ownership. Once your contract is effective, you will order a preliminary title report from the title company to confirm the information.

Once you meet your prospective seller, get him to focus his attention on you. To do this you need a planned presentation.

At times you will have the feeling that the people you are talking to aren't listening; their minds are on other things instead. Even as they are talking to you, they are searching for the miracle that will rescue them. And they are still asking themselves, "What is in it for me?" You must focus the prospective seller's attention on what you have to say.

Demonstrate your interest in the seller's predicament. Give him a booklet or information about seminars on the ways in which your business can help; something that will show him a way out. If you are solving the seller's problems and talking about the benefits he will gain, you will have his attention.

Remember, too, that you must demonstrate that the benefits you can offer are superior. Why are your services more valuable than those of your competition? Think this over and be prepared to demonstrate your superiority. When your prospect is convinced that you can deliver the benefits you promise and that you can do so better than the competition, he will sell his distressed property to you. If you want to succeed in this business, you must be good at solving problems. Think about what makes you different. If your services *are* different, you will be successful. In summary, analyze your prospect, try to visualize the individual and understand what motivates him, and then tailor your presentation to suit him.

The testimonials reproduced on pages 74 and 75 are an example of the type of proof that helps convince sellers.

## Caution: Some Do's and Don't's

To emphasize the necessity of doing your homework and to give you some pointers for the all-important planned, individually tailored presentation, here are some do's and don't's.

- Don't argue with the homeowner, even if he or she is wrong. Remember: Time is on your side.
- Do keep in contact. Sellers will rarely make up their minds the first time they receive your letter, or even the first time you meet them.
- Do ask questions. Estimate the repair costs before you make a money commitment.
- Don't get discouraged if the homeowner brings his payments current. Keep an eye on the default list. Many of these owners — a surprising number — will be back in default within the next six months. By then they will have more debts to pay.
- Do caution the homeowner that, if he or she signs an exclusive "right to sell" agreement with a real estate broker, a commission will be due and deducted from the proceeds of the sale.
- Do appraise the property. Does it need paint, carpet, wallpaper, linoleum, repairs? The seller, in most cases, knows whether the home has serious structural problems. If you are not careful, these sellers will take advantage of your ignorance. Keep in mind that the prospective seller is obligated to take care of himself and his family. He is not interested in making you wealthy. Your contract should include various cancellation or escape clauses to allow you to reject the purchase if you do discover serious structural problems.
- Do expect a no to your first offer.
- Do leave the door open for new talks with the owner if you get an initial rejection.
- Do tell the owners that time is of the essence and that you have limited capital that must be put to work.
- Do tell the homeowner that foreclosure causes other credit problems if the bank or savings and loan association reports the action to the credit bureaus.
- Do remind the homeowner that each day the situation gets worse: payments are further behind, late charges are accruing, and property taxes and penalties are adding up.
- Do get all the owners to sign the purchase contract. Review the grant deed to make sure you know who owns the property and what the legal description consists of.
- Do be Mr. Good Guy, the man in the white hat. Yes, you're saving them from foreclosure and embarrassment.

- Do think about the financing for the new buyer before you put the house up for sale. Financing is the most important part of the sale.
- Do review the default list daily.
- Do establish an attitude that tells the world: "I know it can be done."

Once again, remember the millionaire's secret of success: prepare — prepare — prepare; do your homework — do your homework — do your homework.

**Review the Equity Purchase Contract with the Seller**

Use the grant deed to determine the Assessor's Parcel Number or tax number and obtain an accurate property description. Later you will compare this information with the preliminary title report to confirm that you are buying what you have contracted for and what you think you are buying.

List the loan balances you are buying. Determine the price you will pay the owner.

**Avoid the Pitfalls That Many Foreclosure Buyers Ignore**

Ask the owner about termite reports that might have been recently completed. If no report has been completed, ask the owner about known termite damage. In most circumstances the owner will respond as if you accused him of living in a dirty house. Expect the owner to be very protective of his property, and be aware that your questions may seem offensive. Use a tone of voice that is pleasant, not accusatory. It is your objective at this point to prepare the owner for the costs of repairing the termite damage if there is any. The contract that I have used successfully specifically states that the seller will pay for repairing damage found by termite and roof inspectors. Readers who use this or a similar clause in their equity purchase contracts will find that it saves thousands of dollars in unforeseen repair costs.

**The Dreaded Due-on-Sale Clause**

Loan documents should be reviewed in detail. Many loans are due on sale. If you are buying from the owner before the foreclosure sale, you should review the loan documents and determine if the loan has an alienation or acceleration clause. These are options that the lender may have written into the contract made with the owner from whom you are purchasing. Either of these clauses will allow the lenders to begin a foreclosure action against you if they become aware that you have purchased the property.

As a wise buyer, you should give this some thought prior to the purchase and determine alternatives. If, for example, the lenders are not getting paid and have started a foreclosure action, you could advise them that you will buy the property from the seller and then bring the payments up-to-date, provided that they agree, in writing, not to exercise their right to accelerate the loan.

Or you could simply pay the back payments on the loan that is in arrears. The lender will then remove the property from the defaulted list or problem property list. This action will give you time to plan a strategy or even buy the property, fix it up, and resell it before the lender becomes aware that the property has been sold to you. When the seller transfers the property to you by grant deed or warrantee deed and your escrow office records the deed to establish your right of ownership in the property, the act of recording the deed will make it part of the public records. Some lenders subscribe to a service that investigates the records at the Recorder's Office and so may become aware that title has been transferred from the defaulting owner to you. What action the lender takes at this point varies. Lenders certainly have rights under the loan contract to take action. Some take action, some don't. If interest rates are rising rapidly and the loan you are curing and hoping to take (subject to) is a low-interest instrument, you should expect the lender to make some changes.

### On-Time Payment

In the day-to-day world of hurry, hurry, most lenders are happy to receive payment on time, and in my experience loans are rarely accelerated. This is not a rule, but it certainly is a win-win situation. The defaulting property owner is saving his credit rating; the lender is getting paid, which is what he contracted for in the first place; and you are benefiting by buying a property with very little actual cash.

In practice you will find that although lenders will allow you to bring delinquent loans current, they will rarely allow you to pay off the loan when you sell the property without a prepayment penalty. Prepayment penalties vary in amounts and terms with each lender. It is not unusual to find prepayment penalties amounting to six months' interest. Private lenders, mortgage companies, and personal property lenders are especially severe in the written terms of their prepayment penalty clauses. In reviewing the updated contracts shown in this text you will notice that a prepayment penalty is included in the seller's cost of sale.

### Summarize the Ways to Evaluate (Appraise) the Real Estate Property

1. Drive by and notice For Sale By Owners (FSBOs), as well as real estate signs. Telephone these owners, sellers, and brokers.
2. Talk to owners in the neighborhood and tell them you are interested in purchasing a property in the neighborhood and would like information as to prices, schools, shopping, rising values, etc.
3. Ask broker/agents about their experience in the neighborhood and if they will give you comparable data, perhaps even the MLS data.
4. Check the county records. Tax Assessments and recent sales are reported to the assessor as a matter of policy by the title and escrow companies, as part of the settlement.
5. Use DAMAR, DATAQUICK, or other compatible computer system to gather data about the neighborhoods.
6. Use a service similar to the CMDC book. California Market DATA Cooperative produces books of the different regions of the state which show the sale as reported by appraisers. Different states have different services and anyone can buy the service or, as they say, be a member and subscribe to the appraisal data. It is all very useful and will save you countless hours of research.

# *PROPERTY EVALUATION QUESTIONNAIRE*

Date ______________________

ThBr ______________________

1. Name of Owner ______________________
2. Property Address ______________________
3. City ______________ County ______________
4. Phone # (Day) ______________ (Evenings) ______________

   Best time to call ______________________
5. What kind of property is it? Age ____________ Sq. Ft. __________
6. # Bedrooms ______ # Baths ______ Other ______________

   Pool (Yes / No) Garage ( 1 2 3 )
7. General Condition of the Property (Drapes - Carpets - Paint)

   ______________________________________________

   ______________________________________________
8. How Old is the Roof? ______________________
9. Have You Had a Recent Termite Inspection? Yes / No Year__________
10. How Long Have You Owned the Property? ______________________
11. What Did You Pay for the Property? ______________________
12. How Much do You Owe on it? ______________________

    1st__________ 2nd__________ 3rd__________ Other__________
13. Are These Loans Assumable? (1st) Yes / No (2nd) Yes / No (3rd) Yes / No
14. How Many Payments Are You Behind______ Total $ Amount __________
15. Amount to Cure ______________________
16. Are You in Default or Foreclosure? Yes No
17. Do You Have a Trustee Sale Date? ______________________

## PROPERTY EVALUATION QUESTIONNAIRE

18. How Much is the Property Worth? ______________________

19. How Do You Know This? ______________________

20. Is That What Homes in the Neighborhood Are Selling For? Yes No

21. Do You Have a Recent Appraisal? Yes No

22. Have You Had the Property For Sale? Yes No How Long? __________

    If Yes, Do You Know Why it Hasn't Sold? ______________________

23. How Much Will You Take For the Property? ______________________

24. Do You Have the Grant Deed / Warrantee Deed Available? ______________________

25. Do You Have the Notice of Default or Complaint Filed With the Court? __________

______________________

Appointment: Date __________ Time __________

Notes / Comments ______________________

A S A P Report
Area Sales Analysis Profile

County: LOS ANGELES CA  Page/Grid: 51-A5

**DAMAR**

| | |
|---|---|
| Sample Size (for 10 year period) | 314 |
| New Home Sales (sold within one year of construction) | 1 |
| Average Living Area Size | 1076 |
| Average Year Built | 1931 |
| Average Lot Area | 6482 |
| Average Number of Rooms | 5.08 |
| Average Number of Bedrooms | 2.25 |
| Average Number of Baths | 1.29 |

Pool= 2%  View=  Central Air=  Waterfront=  Floodzone=33%

Price Range 1989-1990* $90,000 to $240,000  Predominant Value $163,000
Age Range (entire sample) 2 yrs to 71 yrs  Predominant Age 68 yrs

% Distribution of Sales (in Thousands of $) for 1989-1990*

| 21- 30 | 31- 40 | 41- 50 | 51- 60 | 61- 70 | 71- 80 | 81-100 | 101-125 | 126-150 |
|---|---|---|---|---|---|---|---|---|
| | | | | | | 8.6% | 8.6% | 27.6% |
| 151-175 | 176-200 | 201-225 | 226-250 | 251-275 | 276-300 | 301-350 | 351-400 | 401-450 |
| 20.7% | 20.7% | 8.6% | 5.2% | | | | | |
| 451-500 | 501-600 | 601-700 | 701-800 | 801-900 | 901-1000 | >1000 | | |

Type Loan for 1989-1990*

| Conventional | FHA | VA | Assumable | Variable | Other |
|---|---|---|---|---|---|
| | 3.4% | | 3.4% | 44.8% | |

Living Area in Square Feet (entire sample):

| 200- 400 | 401- 600 | 601- 800 | 801-1000 | 1001-1200 | 1201-1500 | 1501-1750 |
|---|---|---|---|---|---|---|
| | 3.8% | 15.3% | 29.9% | 22.6% | 17.2% | 6.4% |
| 1751-2000 | 2001-2500 | 2501-3000 | 3001-3500 | 3501-4000 | 4001-5000 | over 5000 |
| 1.9% | 2.5% | 0.3% | | | | |

| Year built: | Pre-1900 | 01-20 | 21-30 | 31-40 | 41-50 | 51-60 | 61-70 | 71-80 | 81-90 |
|---|---|---|---|---|---|---|---|---|---|
| | | 0.6% | 61.7% | 19.5% | 10.9% | 4.2% | 1.6% | 0.6% | 1.0% |

A V E R A G E  S A L E S  D A T A  ( B y  Y e a r )

| Year | Total Sales | Average Price | Average Loan | Living Area | $ Per Sq Ft | Median Price |
|---|---|---|---|---|---|---|
| 1990* | 26 | $170,767 | $141,861 | 991 | $172.22 | $175,000 |
| 1989 | 32 | $150,224 | $121,203 | 1,042 | $144.13 | $146,000 |
| 1988 | 45 | $125,867 | $106,565 | 1,084 | $116.08 | $124,000 |
| 1987 | 54 | $113,232 | $96,325 | 1,172 | $96.54 | $107,000 |
| 1986 | 39 | $98,096 | $83,746 | 1,010 | $97.05 | $86,000 |
| 1985 | 40 | $94,350 | $86,851 | 1,175 | $80.24 | $90,000 |
| 1984 | 39 | $83,410 | $78,235 | 1,041 | $80.10 | $81,000 |
| 1983 | 23 | $78,521 | $62,647 | 981 | $79.97 | $73,000 |
| 1982 | 5 | $75,300 | $62,116 | 962 | $78.24 | $70,000 |
| 1981 | 11 | $74,672 | $40,000 | 1,117 | $66.80 | $69,950 |

* 1990 data current through DECEMBER

DAMAR (c)1991 Real Estate Information Service  213/380-7105, 800/873-2627

# SALES DATA

**CMDC** CALIFORNIA MARKET DATA COOPERATIVE

## SINGLE FAMILY RESIDENTIAL / PUD SALES DATA

SCEN: FRESNO

| Map Code or City Name or Census Tract | Source | Property Address / Lot/Tract | Assessor's Parcel Number | Recording Number | Clsd Sale | Sales Price (Committed / Closed) | Sales Date | Loan Type / MRTG % | Price per SqFt | Year Blt / Style, Stories | Tot Rooms, Bedrooms / Baths | Sq Feet Liv Area | Oth Rms / Kitchen Equipment | Heat / Air Cond | Fuel / Fireplace | Utils / Zoning | Site, Topo, View / Prkg (Spaces, Type, Constr) | Property Codes | Lot Size or Area | Flood Zone | Other Improvements / Comments | HOA Dues; Tot Units; Amenities | Pool/Spa | Phys / Upd |
|---|---|---|---|---|---|---|---|---|---|---|---|---|---|---|---|---|---|---|---|---|---|---|---|---|
| 55 01 | F | 9448 N WOODMONT DR, FRESNO / 50/3904 | 401-354-04-0 | | N | 290,000 | 031191 | C | 108 | 1991 / M 1 | 7 4 / 2 50 | 2685 | DLY / BMC | A / C | G / 2 | P P P P / R-1 SFR | N D G / 3 G A | G G T C C | 85X116 | N | EE ITM: GLZD WIN, B/I CHINA CAB, CEIL FAN, TONGUE & GROOVE CATH | $11; 1; D | | F / I |
| 55 02 | F | 566 W BEDFORD AVE, CLOVIS / 43/4058 | | | N | 202,250 | 040491 | C | 82 | 1991 / N 1 | 7 4 / 2 50 | 2455 | DY / BM | A / C | G / 1 | P P P P / SFR | D G / 3 G A | G G C C V | 80X110 | N | CVRPAT, FEN / EE ITM GLZD WIN, WT BAR, COV FR PCH, LNDSCP | 1; S | | F / I |
| | F | 943 N CHAPEL HILL AVE, CLOVIS / 78/4014 | | | N | 132,700 | 060190 | | 68 | 1991 / L 1 | 6 3 / 2 00 | 1962 | ANL / RDMS | A / C | G / 1 | P P P P / SFR | V D A / 2 G A | A G C C V | 63X118 | N | CVRPAT, FEN / EE ITM GLZD WIN, | 1; S | | F / I |
| | H | 955 N CHAPEL HILL DR, CLOVIS / 77/4014 | 304-543-04-0 | 21718 | Y | 111,000 | 022291 | C F / 80% | 74 | 1990 / N 1 | 6 3 / 2 00 | 1500 | ANLY / BM | A / C | G / 1 | P P P P / R-1 | N D A / 2 G A | A G W C C | 63X118 | N | EE ITM GLZD WIN; VAUL CEIL, RECESS KIT LT, TILE KIT | 1; S | | F / I |
| | F | 765 N CLAREMONT, CLOVIS / 49/4161 | | | N | 117,950 | 030191 | F / 93% | 70 | 1991 / N 1 | 7 3 / 2 00 | 1676 | DFLY / B | A / C | G / 1 | P P P P / SFR | V D A / 2 G A | A G C C C | 60X100 | N | EE ITM GLZD WIN; BIRCH CAB, TILE CNTRS | 1; S | | F / I |
| | F | 786 N EZIE AVE, CLOVIS / 72/4161 | | | N | 124,598 | 050190 | C | 70 | 1991 / N 1 | 6 4 / 2 00 | 1781 | FLY / B | A / C | G / 1 | P P P P / R16000 | N D A / 2 G A | A G T C C | 85X106 | N | FEN | 1; S | | F / I |
| | F | 1410 FIR AVE, CLOVIS / 42/4161 | | | N | 116,900 | 020191 | C | 66 | 1991 / N 1 | 6 3 / 2 00 | 1781 | ANY / B | A / C | G / 1 | P P P P / R1 SFR | N D G / 2 G | G G A C C | 7500 | N | COV PCH, OAK CAB, TILE CNTR, VAUL CEIL | 1; S | | F / I |
| | F | 1420 FIR AVE, CLOVIS / 41/4161 | | | N | 142,000 | 070190 | C | 61 | 1991 / N 1 | 8 5 / 2 50 | 2312 | FL / BM | A / C | G / 1 | P P P P / R16000 | N D A / 3 G A | A G C C C | 59X102 | N | FEN | 1; S | | F / I |
| | F | 1426 FIR AVE, CLOVIS / 51/4161 | | | N | 117,950 | 030191 | F / 94% | 70 | 1991 / N 1 | 7 3 / 2 00 | 1676 | DFLY / B | A / C | G / 1 | P P P P / SFR | V D A / 2 G A | A G C C C | 60X100 | N | EE ITM GLZD WIN; BIRCH CABS, TILE CNTRS | 1; S | | F / I |
| | F | 1445 FIR AVE, CLOVIS / 53/4161 | | | N | 101,430 | 030191 | C | 76 | 1991 / N 1 | 5 3 / 2 00 | 1342 | AL / B | A / C | G / 1 | P P P P / R-1 | N D G / 2 G A | A G C C C | 60X100 | N | FEN / EE ITM GLZD WIN; VAUL CEIL, AUTO SPRNK | 1; S | | F / I |
| | F | 1465 FIR AVE, CLOVIS / 55/4161 | | | N | 110,190 | 070190 | C | 66 | 1991 / N 1 | 6 3 / 2 00 | 1678 | FLY / B | A / C | G / 1 | P P P P / R16000 | N D A / 2 G A | A G C C C | 60X100 | N | FEN | 1; S | | F / I |
| | F | 1475 FIR ST, CLOVIS / 56/4161 | 304-600-27-0 | 36424 | Y | 125,355 / 125,500 | 022291 / 032991 | C / 75% | 66 | 1991 / N 2 | 6 3 / 2 50 | 1897 | DL / B | A / C | G / 1 | P P P P / R-1 SFR | D A / 2 G A | A G C C C | 70X100 | N | FEN / EE ITM GLZD WIN; SPRNK SYS | 1; S | | F / I |
| | F | 1600 FIR AVE, CLOVIS / 29/26 | | | N | 116,005 | 030191 | | 69 | 1991 / N 1 | 6 3 / 2 00 | 1678 | AF / B | A / C | G / 1 | P P P P / R1 | N D A / 2 G A | A G C C C | 60X100 | N | FEN | 1; S | | F / I |
| | F | 783 N FORDHAM AVE, CLOVIS / 59/4161 | | | N | 142,000 | 100190 | C | 66 | 1991 / N 1 | 6 4 / 2 50 | 2164 | FL / BM | A / C | G / 1 | P P P P / R16000 | N D A / 2 G A | A G C C C | 60X103 | N | FEN | 1; S | | F / I |
| | F | 9723 N FOWLER, CLOVIS | 304-401-30 | | N | 176,000 | 020191 | C | 81 | 1979 / R 1 | 7 3 / 3 00 | 2183 | DFLY / BMC | A / C | G / 1 | P P P P / AL | N D A / 2 G A | G G A C C | 2 25 | Y | CVRPAT / TILE KT CNTR, VAUL CEIL, AUTOMATIC SPRNK SYS | 1; S | | F / I |
| | F | 1470 FU AVE, CLOVIS / /4161 | | | N | 113,025 | 032091 | F / 78% | 74 | 1991 / N 1 | 7 3 / 2 00 | 1532 | DNRL / B | A / C | G / 1 | P P P P / SFR | V D A / 2 G A | A G C C C | 60X100 | N | TILE CNTRS, SPLASH, BIRCH CABS | 1; S | | F / I |
| | F | 5605 E INTERNATIONAL, CLOVIS / 68 | 301-151-30-S | | N | 145,000 | 022591 | C | 66 | 1975 / N 1 | 6 4 / 2 00 | 2212 | ARL / BMC | A / C | G / 1 | P P X / SFR | N D G / 2 G A | A F A T C | 2 42 | N | BRN | 1; S | BOTH | F / I |
| | F | 681 N STANFORD, CLOVIS / 66/4161 | | | N | 104,025 | 030191 | C / 90% | 78 | 1991 / N 1 | 5 3 / 2 00 | 1335 | AL / B | A / C | G / 1 | P P P P / R1 | N D A / 2 G A | A G C C C | 6000 | N | FEN | 1; S | | F / I |
| | F | 771 N STANFORD AVE, CLOVIS / 6715/4161 | | | N | 100,940 | 060190 | C | 76 | 1991 / N 1 | 5 3 / 2 00 | 1324 | FLY / B | A / C | G / 1 | P P P P / R16000 | N D A / 2 G A | A G C C C | 60X105 | N | FEN | 1; S | | F / I |
| 56 01 | C | 657 W BEVERLY, CLOVIS / /1804 | 420-123-24 | 23926 | Y | 91,000 / 91,000 | 020491 / 022891 | C / 75% | 64 | 1960 / N 1 | 6 3 / 2 00 | 1428 | F / B | A / C | G / 1 | P P P P / SFR | N D A / 2 G A | A G C C C | 7955 | N | | 1; S | POOL | F / I |
| | F | 1205 KAREN, CLOVIS / 40/1804 | 420-112-20 | | N | 75,000 | 010191 | F | 60 | 1965 / N 1 | 6 3 / 1 50 | 1248 | AFL / RH | A / C | G | P P P P / R-1 | N D A / 2 G A | A A C C X | 65X104 | N | CVRPAT, FEN / CEIL FAN, TILE CNTR, AUTO SPRNK | 1; S | | F / I |
| | F | 6820 N LAUREEN, FRESNO / /2836 | 410-333-02 | 31228 | Y | 123,900 / 124,000 | 020191 / 031891 | C F / 90% | 62 | 1978 / N 1 | 7 3 / 2 00 | 1996 | AFLY / B | A / C | G / 1 | P P P P / R-1 | N D A / 2 G A | A A A C X | 67X118 | N | CVRPAT / ALARM SYS, AUTO SPRNK, TILE KIT/BATH CNTR, CAB | 1; S | | F / I |
| | C | 3334 E LOS ALTOS, FRESNO / 14/2786 | 410-302-08 | 25544 | Y | 118,000 / 118,000 | 010191 / 030491 | C F / 68% | 69 | 1978 / N 1 | 7 3 / 2 00 | 1702 | DFLY / B | A / C | G / 1 | P P P P / SFR | N D A / 2 G A | A A A C C | 82X112 | N | CVRPAT, FEN | 1; S | | F / I |
| 56 02 | C | 105 BEVERLY, CLOVIS | 497-173-20 | 26659 | Y | 60,000 / 60,000 | 010191 / 030691 | | 40 | 1961 / N 1 | 6 3 / 1 50 | 1485 | DF | W | G | P P P P / R1 | N D A / 2 G D | A A C C C | 6572 | N | FEN | 1; S | | F / I |
| | F | 1711 OXFORD, CLOVIS / /1921 | 497-193-31 | 31698 | Y | 91,000 / 91,000 | 012691 / 031991 | F F / 99% | 68 | 1963 / N 1 | 5 3 / 2 00 | 1329 | A / B | A / C | G / 1 | P P P P / RES | V D A / 2 G A | A A C C C | 65X100 | N | CVRPAT, DEC, FEN | 1; S | POOL | F / I |
| 56 03 | F | 3314 E TENAYA, FRESNO / 12/2658 | 410-202-06 | 36891 | Y | 107,000 / 107,000 | 030191 / 032991 | F F | 63 | 1976 / R 1 | 6 3 / 2 00 | 1687 | AFLY / B | A / C | G / 1 | P P P P / R-1 | N D A / 2 G A | A A A C C | 67X110 | N | CVRPAT, FEN / TILE ENT, SPRNK | 1; S | | F / I |

THE ABOVE DATA IS BELIEVED TO BE RELIABLE BUT ACCURACY IS NOT GUARANTEED

APR 1991 — 16 —

MAP / CITY / CENSUS: 55.01 THRU 56.03

**SINGLE FAMILY / PUD FRESNO**

Reprinted by permission of California Market Data Cooperative

DATAQUICK
INFORMATION NETWORK

**1):**

| | | | | |
|---|---|---|---|---|
| | 350-530-01 | SITE: 1422 WINTON DRIVE*SAN DIEGO CA | | 92037 |
| OWNR: | BLAKELY, NICOLE T | MAIL: 1422 WINTON DRIVE*LA JOLLA CA | | 92037 |
| USE: | SINGLE RESIDENCE | XMPT: HO TFR: $407,500F DATE: | 12/30/86 | |
| LOANS: | $262,500 | DOC NUM: 0229996 ASD:$415,650 IMP: 26% | #UN: | 1 |
| PH: 954-6195 | YR BT: 66 | SQ FT: 1435 BDRMS: 4 BTHS:4.5 | LOTSZ: | 8712 |

**2):**

| | | | | |
|---|---|---|---|---|
| | 350-530-02 | SITE: 1423 WINTON DRIVE*SAN DIEGO CA | | 92037 |
| OWNR: | AUSTIN, KENT B | MAIL: 1423 WINTON DRIVE*LA JOLLA CA | | 92037 |
| USE: | SINGLE RESIDENCE | XMPT: HO TFR: $164,500F DATE: | 11/30/86 | |
| LOANS: | $156,500 | DOC NUM: 0234567 ASD:$125,900 IMP: 46% | #UN: | 1 |
| PH: 989-2222 | YR BT: 68 | SQ FT: 1535 BDRMS: 3 BTHS:2.5 | LOTSZ: | 5090 |

**3):**

| | | | | |
|---|---|---|---|---|
| | 350-530-03 | SITE: 1424 WINTON DRIVE*SAN DIEGO CA | | 92037 |
| OWNR: | MORRISEY ALFRED I | MAIL: 1424 WINTON DRIVE*LA JOLLA CA | | 92037 |
| USE: | SINGLE RESIDENCE | XMPT: NO TFR: $167,500F DATE: | 06/07/90 | |
| LOANS: | $150,000 | DOC NUM: 0234568 ASD:$168,300 IMP: 76% | #UN: | 1 |
| PH: | YR BT: 78 | SQ FT: 1568 BDRMS: 4 BTHS:2.5 | LOTSZ: | 5000 |

**4):**

| | | | | |
|---|---|---|---|---|
| | 350-530-04 | SITE: 1560 ABBEY DRIVE*SAN DIEGO CA | | 92037 |
| OWNR: | HARTE DEXTER HO | MAIL: 1560 ABBEY DRIVE*LA JOLLA CA | | 92037 |
| USE: | SINGLE RESIDENCE | XMPT: NO TFR: $142,500F DATE: | 02/12/91 | |
| LOANS: | $135,500 | DOC NUM: 0234569 ASD:$108,465 IMP: 70% | #UN: | 1 |
| PH: 555-2222 | YR BT: 87 | SQ FT: 1098 BDRMS: 3 BTHS:2.0 | LOTSZ: | 5000 |

**5):**

| | | | | |
|---|---|---|---|---|
| | 350-530-05 | SITE: 1590 ABBEY DRIVE*SAN DIEGO CA | | 92037 |
| OWNR: | CASTILLE TERRI J | MAIL: 1590 ABBEY DRIVE*LA JOLLA CA | | 92037 |
| USE: | SINGLE RESIDENCE | XMPT: NO TFR: $145,500F DATE: | 05/09/90 | |
| LOANS: | $116,000 | DOC NUM: 0234575 ASD:$111,743 IMP: 69% | #UN: | 1 |
| PH: | YR BT: 87 | SQ FT: 1146 BDRMS: 3 BTHS:2.0 | LOTSZ: | 4790 |

**6):**

| | | | | |
|---|---|---|---|---|
| | 350-530-06 | SITE: 1234 VALETA LANE*SAN DIEGO CA | | 92037 |
| OWNR: | TIBERIO MARTIN A | MAIL: 1234 VALETA LANE*LA JOLLA CA | | 92037 |
| USE: | SINGLE RESIDENCE | XMPT: HO TFR: $345,000 DATE: | 06/15/90 | |
| LOANS: | | DOC NUM: 0234780 ASD:$214,223 IMP: 73% | #UN: | 1 |
| PH: | YR BT: 80 | SQ FT: 2457 BDRMS: 4 BTHS:2.0 | LOTSZ: | 4980 |

**7):**

| | | | | |
|---|---|---|---|---|
| | 350-530-07 | SITE: 1255 VALETA LANE*SAN DIEGO CA | | 92037 |
| OWNR: | SPENCER JON F & | MAIL: 1255 VALETA LANE*LA JOLLA CA | | 92037 |
| USE: | SINGLE RESIDENCE | XMPT: NO TFR: $162,000F DATE: | 08/29/90 | |
| LOANS: | $140,000 | DOC NUM: 0234885 ASD:$135,541 IMP: 76% | #UN: | 1 |
| PH: 555-9043 | YR BT: 82 | SQ FT: 2116 BDRMS: 4 BTHS:2.0 | LOTSZ: | 9450 |

**8):**

| | | | | |
|---|---|---|---|---|
| | 350-550-08 | SITE: 1282 VALETA LANE*SAN DIEGO CA | | 92037 |
| OWNR: | KAMMERER FRED & | MAIL: 1282 VALETA LANE*LA JOLLA CA | | 92037 |
| USE: | SINGLE RESIDENCE | XMPT: NO TFR: $12,000F DATE: | 11/06/90 | |
| LOANS: | $141,000 | DOC NUM: 0234890 ASD:$130,613 IMP: 75% | #UN: | 1 |
| PH: 555-4439 | YR BT: 85 | SQ FT: 1440 BDRMS: 3 BTHS:2.0 | LOTSZ: | 9650 |

**9):**

| | | | | |
|---|---|---|---|---|
| | 350-550-09 | SITE: 1295 VALETA LANE*SAN DIEGO CA | | 92037 |
| OWNR: | HENRI BAXTER E | MAIL: 1295 VALETA LANE*LA JOLLA CA | | 92037 |
| USE: | SINGLE RESIDENCE | XMPT: NO TFR: $162,000 DATE: | 08/29/90 | |
| LOANS: | | DOC NUM: 0234891 ASD:$119,231 IMP: 74% | #UN: | 1 |
| PH: 555-1112 | YR BT: 84 | SQ FT: 1440 BDRMS: 3 BTHS:2.0 | LOTSZ: | 6500 |

**10):**

| | | | | |
|---|---|---|---|---|
| | 350-570-01 | SITE: 1347 VALETA COURT*SAN DIEGO CA | | 92037 |
| OWNR: | BLAKE MANDY C | MAIL: 1347 VALETA COURT*LA JOLLA CA | | 92037 |
| USE: | SINGLE RESIDENCE | XMPT: NO TFR: $160,500F DATE: | 03/12/91 | |
| LOANS: | $72,000 | DOC NUM: 0234893 ASD:$123,598 IMP: 77% | #UN: | 1 |
| PH: 555-0077 | YR BT: 84 | SQ FT: 1392 BDRMS: 3 BTHS:2.0 | LOTSZ: | 4900 |

DATAQUICK®
INFORMATION NETWORK

| | | | |
|---|---|---|---|
| PARCEL NUMBER | : 555-032-001 | | |
| OWNER 1ST | : CRISCOLA ANTHONY | | |
| 2ND | : NONE | | |
| SITE ADDRESS | : 2302 AVENIDA DEL VERDE | | |
| | : CORONA CA 91720 | | |
| MAIL ADDRESS | : 2302 AVENIDA DEL VERDE | | |
| | : CORONA CA 91720 | | |
| PHONE NUMBER | : 555-1462 | | |
| OWNERSHIP DESC | : SINGLE MAN | | |
| LEGAL DESCRIPT | : LOT 133 MB 056/050 TR 3368 | | |
| | : | | |

PROPERTY CHARACTERISTICS

| | | | |
|---|---|---|---|
| USE DESC | : SINGLE FAMILY RESIDENCE | | |
| LOT SIZE | : 7840 SQ FT | SQUARE FEET | : 1532 |
| YEAR BUILT | : 68 | BEDROOMS | : 3 |
| SECURED PRCL | : | BATHROOMS | : 2.0 |
| | | GARAGES | : Y |
| | | POOL | : Y |

SALE/LOAN INFORMATION

| | | | |
|---|---|---|---|
| LAST SALE DATE | : 01/88 | | |
| AMOUNT | : $126,000 FULL | COST/SQ FT | : $82.57 |
| DOCUMENT NUM | : 3957 | | |
| LENDER | : HOME FED S&L | | |
| LOAN 1ST TD | : $113,850 | LOAN TYPE | : |
| ADDT'L TDS | : | | |

ASSESSMENT/TAX INFORMATION

| | | | |
|---|---|---|---|
| ASSESSED TOTAL | : $131,090 (00) | TAX AMOUNT | : $1,318.00 |
| LAND | : $42,656 | TAX STATUS | : CURRENT |
| IMPROVEMENT | : $88,434 | YEAR DELINQ | : |
| % IMPROVEMENT | : 67 % | TAX RATE AREA | : 04006 |
| EXEMPTION | : HOMEOWNER | (CORONA) | |

*** THE ACCURACY OF THE ABOVE INFORMATION IS ***
*** DEEMED RELIABLE BUT IS NOT GUARANTEED ***

DATAQUICK
INFORMATION NETWORK

DATABASE OPTIONS

A. Real Estate Data - Full Service Counties
B. Statewide Searches - Name, Address, Parcel (CA Only)
C. Map Track - Proposed Residential Developments
D. Verifacts - Property Profile with Sales Comps
E. BusinessLink - California/Arizona
F. COMPS, Inc. - In-Depth Apt, Land, C&I Sales Data
G. New Homes/New Owners - Full Service Counties
H. CMDC Members Only - Enhanced Residential Appraisals

1. Helpful Hints
2. End Session
3. Pricing Info.
4. ATTENTION APPRAISERS!

Connect time charges will not begin until option A, B or H is selected.
The accuracy of our information is deemed reliable, but not guaranteed.

Enter Option >d

SELECT ONE OF THE FOLLOWING OPTIONS:

1. PROPERTY DETAIL
2. PROPERTY DETAIL WITH SALES COMPS
3. STATEWIDE NAME SEARCH
4. RETURN TO DATABASE MENU

ENTER CHOICE > 2
(PRESS RETURN AT ANY PROMPT WHERE INFO IS UNAVAILABLE)
ENTER COUNTY NAME >
ENTER OWNER NAME (LAST,FIRST) >
ENTER HOUSE NUMBER (5 CHARS) >
ENTER STREET NAME (32 CHARS) >
ENTER UNIT NUMBER (8 CHARS) >
ENTER CITY NAME (20 CHARS) >
ENTER MINIMUM TRANSFER AMOUNT>
DO YOU WANT SALES HISTORY (Y/N) ? >y
ENTER 'S' TO SAVE REQUEST OR, TO PRINT CURRENT REQUEST,
PRESS RETURN WHEN PRINTER IS READY

## PROFIT POTENTIAL

### *Before the Trustee's/Sheriff's Sale*

Probable selling price: $___________/Comparables $___________

**Expenses:**

| | |
|---|---|
| Cash to seller | $ ___________ |
| Amount of 1st loan | $ ___________ |
| Amount of 2nd loan | $ ___________ |
| Amount of 3rd loan | $ ___________ |
| Prepayment penalties (if any) | $ ___________ |
| Fire/Casualty policy | $ ___________ |
| Eviction costs | $ ___________ |
| Appraisal fees | $ ___________ |
| Roof inspection fee | $ ___________ |
| Termite repairs | $ ___________ |
| Estimated repairs | $ ___________ |
| Attorney's fees | $ ___________ |
| Property taxes | $ ___________ |
| Delinquencies and back payments | $ ___________ |
| Loan payments during the holding period | $ ___________ |
| Homeowner's Dues/Assessments | $ ___________ |
| Closing/Broker/Title/Escrow | $ ___________ |
| Points | $ ___________ |
| Reserves | $ ___________ |
| TOTAL COSTS | $ ___________ |

| | |
|---|---|
| NET PROFIT | $ ___________ |
| Profit as a percentage of investment | $ ___________ |

## PROPERTY INSPECTION CHECKLIST

### EXTERIOR

#### STRUCTURAL - FOUNDATION

Nature of Foundation: ❑ Full basement ❑ Crawl space ❑ Slab ❑ Pier & post

Condition: ❑ Excellent ❑ Deteriorating mortar ❑ Serious signs of shifting cracking

Dampness & Decay: ❑ None ❑ Moisture, but not noticeable decay ❑ Define dry rot in structural members

Comments: ______________________________________________

______________________________________________

______________________________________________

#### THE ROOF

Roofing Material: ❑ Slate or tile ❑ Wood shingles ❑ Asphalt ❑ Flat roof

Other: ______________________________________________

Condition: ❑ Excellent ❑ Slight signs of wear ❑ Replacement necessary of one portion of roof surface ❑ Entire roof must of replaced

Condition of Flashing: ❑ Excellent ❑ Signs of previous repair ❑ Must be replaced

Chimney Condition: ❑ Excellent ❑ Needs some repair ❑ Needs flu lining ❑ Must be rebuilt ❑ Spark Arrester

Condition of Gutter & Downspouts: ❑ Excellent ❑ Need cleaning ❑ Needs some pieces repaired/replaced ❑ Must be replaced

Comments: ______________________________________________

______________________________________________

______________________________________________

#### EXTERIOR WALLS:

Siding Material: ❑ Masonry Clapboard ❑ Wood Shingles ❑ Other wood surfaces ❑ Aluminum or vinyl siding ❑ Other

Conditions: ❑ Excellent ❑ Needs painting or other superficial work

## PROPERTY INSPECTION CHECKLIST

❑ Needs partial replacement ❑ Must be replaced

Decay: ❑ Excellent ❑ Dry rot in one confined area ❑ Widespread decay

Caulking Conditions: ❑ Excellent ❑ Some re-caulking required ❑ Substantial recaulking needed

Comments: ______________________________

______________________________

______________________________

### WINDOWS AND DOORS:

Nature of Windows: ❑ Double-hung ❑ Sliding ❑ Casement ❑ Awning ❑ Jalousie ❑ Fixed

Glazing: ❑ Single-pane ❑ Double-glazed ❑ Triple-glazed

Storm Windows: ❑ Yes ❑ No

Tight Fit In Frame: ❑ Yes ❑ No

Nature Of Doors: ❑ Flush ❑ Stile & rail

Exterior Door Material: ❑ Wood ❑ Metalclad ❑ Glass

Security: ❑ Bolt locks on all exterior doors ❑ Some ❑ None

Comments: ______________________________

______________________________

### GARAGE AND OTHER OUT-BUILDINGS

Nature of Structure: ❑ Attached garage ❑ Separate garage ❑ Other out-buildings

Conditions of Garage: ❑ Excellent ❑ Requires painting or other superficial work ❑ Needs limited carpentry or other attention ❑ Must be totally reconstructed or replaced

Garage Door Opener: ❑ Yes ❑ No

Other Concerns: ❑ Fire wall missing in attached garage ❑ Garage door problems

Comments: ______________________________

______________________________

## PROPERTY INSPECTION CHECKLIST

Condition of Out-Buildings: ❑ Excellent ❑ Usable but need work ❑ Needs major repairs

❑ Must be torn down or completely rebuilt

Comments: ______________________________

______________________________

______________________________

### THE YARD AND THE NEIGHBORHOOD:

Condition of Lawn & Landscaping: ❑ Excellent ❑ In minor maintenance

❑ Requires extensive attention ❑ Major excavation, planting & landscaping required

❑ Trees & Shrubs: ❑ Healthy & well-trimmed ❑ Minor pruning needed

❑ Additional planting necessary ❑ Safety hazard due to overgrowth

Sprinkler System: ❑ Yes ❑ No

Grading: ❑ Ground slopes away from building ❑ Pitched toward building level

Exterior Lighting: ❑ Ground/wall/ceiling ❑ Loose, missing or damaged

❑ Wall receptacle outlet ❑ U-grounded ❑ GFI

Condition of Fence & Retaining Walls: ❑ Excellent ❑ In need of minor repairs

❑ Replacement of posts or rails required in one section of fencing ❑ Major construction required of all or a major portion of the fence

Condition of Driveway & Other Utility Surfaces: ❑ Excellent ❑ In need of minor filling at sides

❑ Required extensive patching or sealing work ❑ Major excavation & reconstruction required

Swimming Pool/Spa: ❑ Excellent ❑ Needs cleaning & possible minor repairs

❑ Major cracks & leaks appear evident ❑ Fencing ❑ Non-slip pave walks & decks

❑ Pool maintenance equipment ❑ Diving board/ladder/hand rail ❑ Solar blanket or cover

Comments: ______________________________

______________________________

______________________________

______________________________

## PROPERTY INSPECTION CHECKLIST

### INTERIOR

#### LIVING ROOM

Condition: ❑ Excellent ❑ Signs of deterioration ❑ Requires refinishing

Walls: ❑ Painting ❑ Wallpaper ❑ Paint

Ceiling: ❑ Acoustical ❑ Plaster ❑ Sheetrock

Flooring: ❑ Carpeted ❑ Hardwood ❑ Tile ❑ Excellent ❑ Requires refinishing ❑ Signs of curling/cupping/shrinkage & needs considerable work ❑ Floor surface must be replaced

Fireplace: ❑ Brick/rock/other ❑ Free-standing ❑ Firescreen ❑ Mortar in good repair

Comments: ____________________________________________

____________________________________________

____________________________________________

#### DINING ROOM:

Condition: ❑ Excellent ❑ Signs of deterioration ❑ Needs refinishing

Walls: ❑ Paint ❑ Wallpaper ❑ Paneling

Floors: ❑ Hardwood ❑ Carpeted ❑ Tile ❑ Excellent ❑ Required refinishing ❑ Signs of curling/cupping/shrinkage & needs considerable work ❑ Floor surface must be replaced

Comments: ____________________________________________

____________________________________________

____________________________________________

#### KITCHEN:

Kitchen Triangle: ❑ Within specifications ❑ Too small ❑ Too large ❑ Breakfast bar ❑ Dining Area in Kitchen

Comments: ❑ Sufficient ❑ Too little ❑ Tile ❑ Formica ❑ In good condition ❑ Needs minor repair ❑ Needs total replacement

## PROPERTY INSPECTION CHECKLIST

Floor: ❑ Wood ❑ Vinyl tile ❑ Waterproof surface in good condition ❑ Needs repair ❑ Must be replaced

Rangetop/Oven Condition: ❑ Gas ❑ Electric ❑ In need of cleaning but functional ❑ Not working

Disherwasher Condition: ❑ Excellent ❑ In need of cleaning but functional ❑ Not working

Miscellaneous Concerns: ❑ Garbage disposal not working ❑ No hood vent over stove ❑ Water pressure insufficient ❑ Too few outlets ❑ Minor plumbing leaks

Comments: ______________________________

______________________________

______________________________

### FAMILY ROOM:

Condition: ❑ Excellent ❑ Signs of deterioration ❑ Needs refinishing

Walls: ❑ Paint ❑ Paneling ❑ Wallpaper

Floor: ❑ Hardwood ❑ Carpeted ❑ Tile ❑ Excellent ❑ Required refinishing ❑ Signs of curling/cupping/shrinkage & needs considerable work ❑ Floor surface must be replaced

Fireplace: ❑ Brick ❑ Stone/rock ❑ Mortar in good repair ❑ Firescreen ❑ Needs cleaning & repair

Ceiling: ❑ Acoustical ❑ Plaster ❑ Sheetrock

Sliding Glass Door: ❑ Safety tempered glass ❑ Operable ❑ Lock present ❑ Insulated

Comments: ______________________________

______________________________

______________________________

### MASTER BEDROOM:

Condition: ❑ Excellent ❑ Signs of deterioration ❑ Needs considerable attention

Walls: ❑ Paint ❑ Paneling ❑ Wallpaper

## PROPERTY INSPECTION CHECKLIST

Ceiling: ❑ Acoustical ❑ Plaster ❑ Sheetrock

Floor: ❑ Hardwood ❑ Carpeted ❑ Tile ❑ Excellent ❑ Required refinishing

❑ Signs of curling/cupping/shrinkage & needs considerable work ❑ Floor surface must b replaced

Closets: ❑ Sufficient ❑ Insufficient

Comments: ____________________

____________________

____________________

### ADDITIONAL BEDROOMS

Condition: ❑ Excellent ❑ Signs of deterioration ❑ Needs considerable attention

Walls: ❑ Paint ❑ Paneling ❑ Wallpaper

Ceiling: ❑ Acoustical ❑ Plaster ❑ Sheetrock

Floor: ❑ Hardwood ❑ Carpeted ❑ Tile ❑ Excellent ❑ Required refinishing

❑ Signs of curling/cupping/shrinkage & needs considerable work ❑ Floor surface must be replaced

Closets: ❑ Sufficient ❑ Insufficient

Comments: ____________________

____________________

____________________

### HALL:

Walls: ❑ Paint ❑ Paneling ❑ Wallpaper

Ceiling: ❑ Acoustical ❑ Plaster ❑ Sheetrock

Floor: ❑ Hardwood ❑ Carpeted ❑ Tile ❑ Excellent

❑ Required refinishing ❑ Signs of curling/cupping/shrinkage & needs considerable work

❑ Floor surface must be replaced

Closets: ❑ Linen ❑ Coat closet ❑ Extra storage space

Comments: ____________________

____________________

## PROPERTY INSPECTION CHECKLIST

### BATHROOMS:

Walls: ❑ Paint ❑ Wallpaper

Floors: ❑ Hardwood ❑ Carpeted ❑ Tile ❑ Excellent ❑ Required refinishing

❑ Signs of curling/cupping/shrinkage & needs considerable work ❑ Floor surface must be replaced

GFI: ❑ Yes ❑ No

Tub Shower: ❑ Curtain rod ❑ Tub enclosure ❑ Excellent ❑ Showing signs of deterioration & needs minor repairs ❑ Need to be completely replaced

Ceiling Ventilation: ❑ Yes ❑ No

Plumbing Condition: ❑ Excellent ❑ No leakage now, but water stains present ❑ Leaking

Water Pressure Test: ❑ Ample pressure ❑ Some decrease with three or more faucets running

❑ Significant decrease when second faucet turned on

Miscellaneous Concerns: ❑ No shut-off valves for each fixture ❑ No electrical outlets

❑ Improper traps hard water (Indication: soap difficult to lather)

Comments: ______________________________

______________________________

______________________________

______________________________

### THE ATTIC

Nature of Attic: ❑ Finished ❑ Full unfinished ❑ Crawl

Dampness & Decay: ❑ None ❑ Moisture but not noticeable decay

❑ Decay in structural members

Ventilation: ❑ Adequate ❑ Marginal ❑ Insufficient

Miscellaneous Concerns: ❑ Attic fan ❑ Exposed wiring

Comments: ______________________________

______________________________

______________________________

## PROPERTY INSPECTION CHECKLIST

### WATER, PLUMBING AND HOT WATER HEATERS:

Source Of Water: ❑ Municipal ❑ Shallow well ❑ Deep well

Shut-Off Valves: ❑ Main ❑ For each fixture

Hot Water Heater: ❑ Independent ❑ Attached to heating system burner ______Age

Hot Water Circulation: ❑ Adequate ❑ Marginal ❑ Insufficient

Pipes: ❑ Copper ❑ Galvanized ❑ Brass ❑ Plastic

Condition of Pipes: ❑ Excellent ❑ No leakage, but water stains present ❑ Leaking

Drainage & Sewage Problems: ❑ Improper traps ❑ Inadequate pitch on drainage pipes ❑ Slow flow from drains

Comments: ______________________________

______________________________

______________________________

### HEATING AND AIR CONDITIONING SYSTEM:

Nature of System: ❑ Wall furnace ❑ Floor furnace ❑ Gas ❑ Electric

Condition: ❑ Clean ❑ Adequate combustion air ❑ Noisy ❑ Quiet

❑ Recently service ❑ Meets minimum heat requirements ❑ Exhaust to exterior

Comments: ______________________________

______________________________

______________________________

### UTILITY ROOM:

Location: ❑ Area in garage ❑ Area inside house ❑ Separate room inside house

Dryer Hook-Up: ❑ Gas ❑ Electric

Laundry Tub: ❑ Yes ❑ No

Comments: ______________________________

______________________________

______________________________

TYPICAL BROKER FLYER

# NOW SHOWING TO CONDO BUYERS!

## GREAT SACRAMENTO AREA BUYS FOR INVESTORS OR FIRST TIME HOMEOWNERS!

**Hot On Market!**

**$65,000**

Priced $$ Below other Bridgeport units...and it's simply about the nicest unit available. Your clients will love the updated decor! Very Motivated to Close Quickly.. It's an upper 2 bedroom, 1 bath in quiet part of Bridgeport complex. Refrigerator, too! Real Quality at a Super Price. Drive by.....

**8244 Center Parkway #66**

MLS #S105173 Zn: 5-11 TB: 338A6

**$49,000...**

Buys cute just like new one bedroom condo. Woodburning fireplace, private patio, ceramic tile counter top, microwave and refrigerator, too! Just redone with new carpets, etc. Walk to Florin Mall from...

**7283 Florin Mall Dr #9**

MLS:: S105168 TB: 338A2

Also Available!

**#12 $46,000!**

**VACANT ...TOUR TODAY!**

**EXCEPTIONALLY MOTIVATED...EXCEPTIONAL VALUE!**

**A GREAT TOWNHOME AT 8276 CENTER PARKWAY #127 IN BRIDGEPORT**

Super in and out , a 2 Bedroom, 1.5 Bath 2-Story end unit near Swimming Pool and Spa. Formal living room with fireplace, dining room, private patio. Carport is enclosed and includes steel roll-up door. Priced Thousand$ below similar units...well below last 2 closed sales!

Below Market at **$69,500** MLS #109171 TB: 338A6 Zn: 5-11

**GORDON ATCHLEY at...RE/MAX Fair Oaks**

Office: 863-0300 Digital Pager: 551-9191 Home: 686-7002

Information provided from sources deemed reliable, but not guaranteed by broker.

Reprinted by permission of Gordon Atchley, Remax Fair Oaks

## BROKER ESTIMATES OF CLOSING COSTS

**2660 PORTOLA WAY**
**SACRAMENTO, CALIF., 95818**

REALTOR: **MICHAEL BERRINGER**
CENTURY 21 424-3334

SALES PRICE:$224,000.00

| | | | |
|---|---|---|---|
| INTEREST RATE (30 YRS) | 10.50% | 9.75% | 9.75% |
| DOWN PAYMENT % | 10% | 20% | 25% |
| DOWN PAYMENT AMOUNT | $22,400.00 | $44,800.00 | $56,000.00 |
| LOAN AMOUNT | $201,600.00 | $179,200.00 | $168,000.00 |
| PAYMENT (P&I) | $1844.11 | $1539.60 | $1443.38 |
| PAYMENT (PITI) | $2144.64 | $1840.13 | $1743.71 |

**ESTIMATED CLOSING COSTS**

| | | | |
|---|---|---|---|
| POINTS @ 2.00 | $4032.00 | $3584.00 | $3360.00 |
| LOAN FEE | 300.00 | 300.00 | 300.00 |
| TITLE INSURANCE (ALTA) | 345.00 | 345.00 | 345.00 |
| ESCROW FEE | 425.00 | 425.00 | 425.00 |
| APPRAISAL (EST) | 300.00 | 300.00 | 300.00 |
| CREDIT REPORT | 48.00 | 48.00 | 48.00 |
| DOCUMENT FEE | 75.00 | 75.00 | 75.00 |
| TAX SERVICE | 62.00 | 62.00 | 62.00 |
| RECORDING/NOTARY FE | 40.00 | 40.00 | 40.00 |
| PREPAID INTEREST | 922.00 | 769.00 | 721.00 |
| TOTAL EST CLOSING COST | $6549.00 | $5948.00 | $5676.00 |

*****************************************************************

**SPECIAL NOTES**

***ZERO POINT LOAN OPTION AVAILABLE**
*NO PMI REQUIRED ON 20% DOWN
*PREQUALIFICATIONS DONE AT HOME OR IN OFFICE AT NO CHARGE
*ADJUSTABLE RATE MORTGAGES AVAILABLE

FOR COMPLETE DETAILS CALL:
**MITCH DRILLER** AT UNION BANK
OFFICE:969-5040
VOICE MAIL:325-2754

*ALL FIGURES ARE WITHOUT APR, AND NO IMPOUNDS CALCULATED*

## FOR SALE BY OWNER

**★ BY OWNER ★**
1800 square foot 4 bedroom 1¾ bath, pool with fence, many extras, 938-9395.

**3br, living rm, fam rm w/ frpl, formal dining rm, new carpet, custom kitchen, 938-2704.**

**★ BY OWNER ★**
3BR 2BA, pool, 2 gar, new cpt pnt, 14842 N 36th Dr. $81,500. Open 11-4. Jeff 995-9284

**NO QUALIFYING**
**GORGEOUS MINI ESTATE**
**OPEN SUN 12-5**
EASY TO OWN w/$15K dn, carry $20K (OBO) bal, & wrap $228K loan. MOVE IN BY MAY! Cust. newer 3-4 br, 2½ ba, 2 frplc, on lovely ½ac. Guest house & pool. **NO RE AGENTS!** Owner. 938-0416

**No Qualify assume $847 PITI 3br 2ba pool lrg corner lot R.V. parking 83rd Ave T-bird $10,000 CTM OWC w/$5000 down 979-9797**

**NO qualifying, $7000 ctm (owc portion), $846/mo, 3 or 4 Br, frplc, vaulted ceilings, pond, malibu lites, on huge cul de sac lot 43Av/Union 978-8379**

**MUST SEE! 3br, 2ba 1660sf, Lrg lot, quiet Cul-de-sac. Beautifully landscaped. Great neighborhood. By Owner, Low CTM, 878-2014**

**MUST SELL: 35th Av/ Beardsley. 3/2. Built 1988. No qual. $65K. FHA 10%, $663 PITI, $7900 equity, OWC..will deal! Call now! 789-1810, 581-6646**

**★ BY OWNER ★**
**Handyman Special $44,000, No Qual $6000dnOWC 3br,2ba Pool. 4232 N 55Ave 926-4591**

**ASSUME 8½ FHA, $575 PITI, immaculate upgraded 2br 1½ba TH nr 46Av/Maryland. Call owner 953-1528 931-9856**

**By Owner Assume no qual 9½% lo dn, 3br 1½ba 47 Av & Thomas 233-2089 aft 5 wkdys**

N. Canyon Ranch. Lg corner lot. 40Dr/W Mariposa Grande Beaut lg 4BR 2BA FR, formal LR/vlt ceil, din rm, dbl gar, evap cooler/air, 2150sf, $98K. 4010 W Mariposa Grande, Glendale. Owner 492-9343.

**OPEN HOUSE SUN 12-5**
**Assume, no qual, 4br 2ba, 2213 sf, ½ac, fam rm w/frpl, formal liv & din, huge cust pool, dbl gar, reduced $10K. Owner may carry 3001 W Julie Dr $129,000. 582-8292**

**OPEN** HOUSE Sa-Su 12-5pm 4001 W. Voltaire Ave 4Br/2Ba 1950 sf, $90K, owner 486-7316

**OPEN** HOUSE SAT-SUN 12-4 2926 W Glenn Dr. 4BR, 2BA POOL $107,000. 995-8236

**★ BY OWNER ★**
Assume No qual 3Bd 2Ba Blk Hm, pool, frplc, 1800+sf, fans SRP & more. Super family area, 2blks to park & school. Must sell this wknd. $7500 ctm $949 PITI, OWC. SUBMIT ALL OFFERS! 979-8741 own/agt

**ASSUME NO QUALIFYING**
4BR 2BA. Pay trans fees, 1800sf, 200sf workrm. Good schools. $73K. 873-2258

## BEAUTY IS IN THE EYE OF THE BEHOLDER

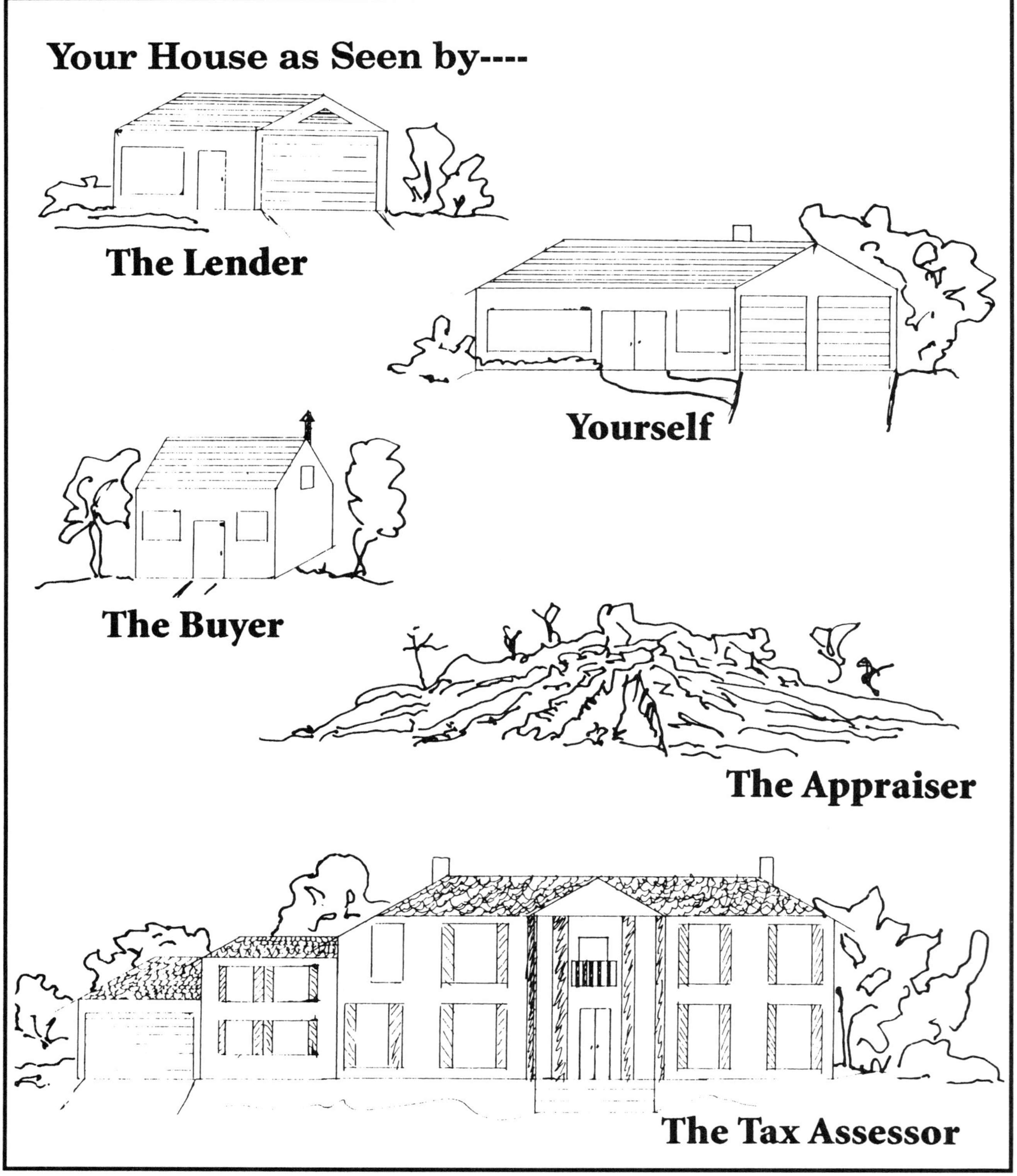

Chapter 5

# Searching for the Profitable Neighborhood

## *Easy Steps to the Appraisal*

### LOCATION — LOCATION — LOCATION

Location is the key to deciding whether a particular foreclosure is right for you. Choosing the right neighborhood is not only a question of value and price but also of resale possibilities. Can the property be resold quickly? Is it too run-down to rehabilitate economically? Is the neighborhood deteriorating, or are property values rising? Will the home appeal to all buyers or only a select few? Is your objective to turn over the property quickly (make a quick sale), or do you plan to rehabilitate and then rent it and wait for appreciation? Is your philosophy that of a long-term holder or a short-term profit maker? If you know your objective, you will be able to select the right foreclosure opportunity.

Choose neighborhoods that produce profits. Most communities have affluent areas. If you plan to work the foreclosure market in these areas you will succeed. However, proportionately fewer foreclosures are available in the country club sections of town. You will have a wider choice in the less prosperous neighborhoods.

Many communities have sections in which only minorities reside and, while they may not be as exclusive as the country club neighborhood, they are clean, the homes are well-kept, and the ghborhood desirable. Foreclosures purchased in these areas are very easy to sell because first-time homebuyers start in these types of neighborhoods.

Middle-class neighborhoods between these two extremes provide most of the foreclosures. These foreclosures are caused by a number of different factors or problems. Divorce, sickness, death, and changes in economic conditions in the area all cause homeowners to miss payments and ultimately to end up in foreclosure.

## REAL ESTATE, THE IMPERFECT MARKET

It's possible to beat the odds of buying real estate on favorable terms because the residential real estate market is not a perfect one. There's no central mechanism, as is the case with a stock exchange or commodity market, to carry out transactions and set prices. As you know, IBM stock sells for the same price in New York as in Honolulu or Tokyo. The perfect market of the stock exchanges thus has its antithesis in the real estate market, where similar properties may sell for very different prices.

In the larger states, such as Illinois, New York, California, and Florida, hundreds of thousands of existing houses are sold each year, and many of these transactions are indeed different from one another. It is rare indeed to find two exactly the same. This imperfect market creates lucrative opportunities for individuals who will take the time and energy to investigate and appraise the situation.

## MARKET STRATEGIES

Think about combining as many strategies as possible to succeed with your bargain purchase.

1. Don't buy until you have enough money. Beware. You don't want to end up in FORECLOSURE!
2. Look in affordable areas of your state and county.
3. Buy less desirable homes than you really want, in order to get started...but GET STARTED!!
4. Buy fixer-uppers at prices you can afford, not what the seller wants to sell them for.
5. Think about small houses on large lots and add on a bedroom and bath.
6. Don't let structural problems scare you away. Investigate. Most people won't, and the structural problem may have been the cause of the foreclosure. Many times these sellers walk away from the problem rather than fix it.
7. Think about living in part of the house and renting rooms in other areas of the home.
8. Watch for duplex units or houses with in-law units.

### Desirable Area/Marginal House

In older residential areas where houses were typically built one-by-one, or in small groups, lot size, house size, construction, and design techniques vary considerably. Within the same four-to-five-block area homes may differ in price by several thousand dollars. So keep your eyes open in upscale neighborhoods in addition to looking in moderately priced neighborhoods. You might just locate a diamond in the rough.

Many houses that seem undesirable can be improved at modest expense. Traffic may be one negative factor that may cause a house to be underpriced. Think about adding a fountain with water flowing to make a pleasant sound, thereby eliminating the traffic noise. Another solution to eliminating street noise is to plant shrubs, or put in walls and fencing. Unsightly homes are always great opportunities. Many foreclosure buyers will just drive by without using their imagination. Don't be one of them. Keep in mind that a simple change can often turn a dull stone into a gem.

Neglected interiors can conceal opportunities. Many foreclosure buyers are only looking for a quick buck and don't want to fix up run-down interiors. If you don't, that's O.K., because there are hundreds of handyman types who will gladly share a joint venture with you. They will do the work in return for a share of the profits. Not everyone will pass up your fixer if you take the time to make it desirable.

If your goal is to maximize your gain over the next few years (and I'm sure it is), look to purchase a good house in a marginal area which will improve quickly after your purchase. Many of these areas are continually upgrading. With the continued trend of high fuel prices and daily gridlock on the highways, many affluent people have elected to return to cities and inner suburbs. Be observant and try to predict what inner-city areas will follow this trend.

### Spotting Neighborhoods on Their Way Up

I doubt if anyone has a sure-fire technique for spotting a marginal area that is about to improve. Avoid the slums and high-crime areas, because they will improve only slowly and this is a cash-flow business. Avoid marginal areas on the immediate periphery of slums; these areas are also unlikely to improve rapidly.

Observe when things change. Railroad yards aren't necessarily areas that people want to live near. However, more and more railroads are abandoning tracks and stations, and old brick warehouses are then turned into condominiums and offices. Suddenly, these areas have romance and people want to reside there, providing you with an opportunity. Watch the handymen and craftspeople who buy and fix up. Their activity can make bad neighborhoods suddenly look good, and then people start moving back. Become a trend-watcher, because such areas can have their ups and downs. Keep up with the local news media.

Avoid areas with many apartment buildings that are old and in disrepair. Many of these units were built in the 1950s or earlier, and until they are torn down they will continue to deteriorate.

Look for areas where transportation is good, especially new public transit systems that have recently been completed or where systems are projected for the near future. The key phrase "near future" indicates a few years, not ten.

Look for areas that are affordable and have excellent school districts. As long as the school district is good to excellent, families with children will consider a so-so neighborhood.

The United States has had a long history of accepting immigrants from various countries. Pay attention to immigration patterns and to the locations these immigrants have settled in. Property values in many depressed areas have moved up substantially as large numbers of hardworking immigrants move in and work hard to improve their life and neighborhood as well.

### Fixer-Uppers

The demand for fixer houses has risen with the inflated housing prices. Not only is this a good opportunity for many to start, but it's also a business. Small contractors search for fixers, are willing to pay high prices, and expect to be confronted with some competition in this area. On a more positive note this is a great way to sell your foreclosure property. When you buy a foreclosure property that falls in this category, inform them.

In your search for property, be sure to consider the moderate to upper end of the market. Many repairable fixer-upper properties are on the moderate to upper side. The type of buyer looking for the upscale property usually does not want to be a fixer.

### Big Lot/Small House

According to Ira Serkes, author of *How to Buy a House in California*, 30 years ago land made up 25% or less of the cost of buying a house. In California it typically represents about 40% of value, and in many desirable areas up to 85%.

Don't expect to find many subdividable lots. The sellers of those lots will probably have already figured out that they have something extra. Look for small houses that will adapt to an additional add-on of a bedroom or bath. Many foreclosure buyers completely overlook the 2-bedroom, 1-bath house because they believe there is little demand for it on the market. Many of these homes are convertible to 3-bedroom, 2-bath homes without much difficulty and expense. Your alternatives are numerous — hire a contractor to do the work, sell to a small contractor, joint venture with either, or just do it yourself.

## COMPARABLE EVALUATION FORM

### Market Value Analysis

**Property Being Considered**

**Part 1**

Date ______________

Address ______________________________________________

City ______________________ State ______________ Zip ______________

Owner ______________________________ Phone ______________________

Agent ______________________________ Phone ______________________

Listing Price $ ______________________________________________

Original Terms ______________________________________________

______________________________________________________________

# of Weeks on Market ______________

**Part II**

**Comparables**

| Address | Date Sold | #Weeks on Mkt. | Listing Price | Selling Price | No. of Bedrooms | No. of Baths |
|---|---|---|---|---|---|---|
| 1) ________ | ____ | ____ | ____ | ____ | ____ | ____ |
| 2) ________ | ____ | ____ | ____ | ____ | ____ | ____ |
| 3) ________ | ____ | ____ | ____ | ____ | ____ | ____ |
| 4) ________ | ____ | ____ | ____ | ____ | ____ | ____ |
| 5) ________ | ____ | ____ | ____ | ____ | ____ | ____ |

Totals $ ________ $ ________

Averages $ ________ $ ________

1) ______________________________________________________________

2) ______________________________________________________________

3) ______________________________________________________________

4) ______________________________________________________________

5) ______________________________________________________________

## PROPERTY PROFILE

COMPARISON SHOPPING MAY SAVE YOU MONEY

THIS TITLE INFORMATION HAS BEEN FURNISHED IN CONFORMANCE WITH THE RULES ESTABLISHED BY THE CALIFORNIA INSURANCE COMMISSIONER, WHO URGES YOU TO SHOP FOR THE BEST SERVICE AVAILABLE AND COMPARE CHARGES AND FEES FOR TITLE INSURANCE, ESCROW, AND OTHER SERVICES ASSOCIATED WITH THE PURCHASE OR SALE OF A HOME.

# Property Profile

Address: 535422 Sterling St.

OAKLAND, CALIFORNIA

Record Owner: Ann Adams

Deed Recording Date: FEB 24,1988 Documentary Transfer Tax: $121.00

Concurrent Trust Deed, If Any: SEE ATTACHED (See Attached)

Legal Description: SEE ATTACHED (See Attached Deed Copy and Plat)

TAX INFORMATION: Assessors Parcel No. 00-112233

| | |
|---|---|
| Assessed Value Land | $ 40,800.00 |
| Assessed Value Improvements | $ 86,700.00 |
| Exemption | $ 7,000.00 |
| Net Assessed Value | $ 120,500.00 |

Installments $ 957.23 $ 957.23

☐ **In lieu of the above, see attached copy of Assessment Roll.**

The information attached, is provided at no cost to you. IT IS NOT AN ABSTRACT OF TITLE, nor a complete representation of the condition of title to the property. While this information is believed to be correct, this Company assumes no liability for any loss occurring by reason of reliance thereon. If it is desired that liability be assumed by this Company, you may request issuance of a policy of title insurance, a binder or a commitment to issue a policy of title insurance.

TRW

REAL ESTATE INFORMATION SERVICES

SALES – PARCEL SEQUENCE    ALAMEDA    1989-07    GRID—F 02    PAGE 517

| ASSESSORS PARCEL NO.<br>LEGAL DESCRIPTION | TRA | | OWNER<br>MAILING ADDRESS<br>LOCATION ADDRESS | SELLER | TRNSFR<br>USE | DATE/NUMBER<br>LENDER<br>TTL CO | TFR AMT<br>LOAN AMT<br>ASSD VAL IMP% |
|---|---|---|---|---|---|---|---|
| 053 1612 025 | 13000 | I | CRUTCHFIELD, CARMELITA<br>1528 ASHBY AVE., BERKELEY CA<br>1528 ASHBY AVE BERKELEY | BELL, EFFIE<br>94703 | 10/31/88<br>11 | 88 276865<br>WORLD S&L<br>N. AM | 135,000 F<br>108,000 D<br>36,894 62% |
| 053 1613 016 | 13000 | T | MACK, ROBERT & IZORA<br>1510 TYLER ST., BERKELEY CA<br>1510 TYLER ST BERKELEY | MACK, ROBERT<br>94703 | 11/23/88<br>11 | 88 300388<br>CALFED S&L | 90,000 D<br>23,697 47% |
| 053 1616 020 01<br>SUBDIV. MAP 9 PG 59<br>BLK C LT 19+ | 13000 | I | WILLIAMS, GARY<br>2508 79TH ST, OAKLAND CA<br>1401 PRINCE ST BERKELEY | WILLIAMS, HE<br>94605 | 7/06/88<br>24 | 88 166660<br>CONT SV AM<br>N. AM | 112,000 F<br>100,800 D<br>58,742 56% |
| 053 1616 020 01<br>SUBDIV. MAP 9 PG 59<br>BLK C LT 19+ | 13000 | I | MUNA, DEANNA<br>PO BOX 21847, SAN JOSE CA<br>1401 PRINCE ST BERKELEY | WILLIAMS, GA<br>95151 | 10/05/88<br>24 | 88 252659<br>WILLIAMS, GA<br>N. AM | 110,000 F<br>100,800 O<br>58,742 56% |
| 053 1616 028 | 13000 | I | PRICE, WILLIAM & EMMA<br>3033 ACTON ST, BERKELEY CA<br>3033 ACTON ST BERKELEY | GIBSON, RODN<br>94702 | 9/15/88<br>11 | 88 233503<br>HM SV AMER<br>CHIGO | 119,000 F<br>107,100 D<br>56,285 46% |
| 053 1618 004 | 13000 | I | JOHNSON, LEROY<br>2344 9TH ST, BERKELEY CA<br>2914 SACRAMENTO ST BERKELEY | LONG, JOHN<br>94710 | 7/01/88<br>31 | 88 157782<br>LONG, JOHN<br>CHIGO | 45,000 F<br>42,000 O<br>16,908 66% |
| 053 1618 011 01<br>*NEW* | 13000 | I | WEST OAKLAND HEALTH COUNCIL<br>700 ADELINE, OAKLAND CA<br>2960 SACRAMENTO ST BERKELEY | RUMFORD, ELS | 5/23/89<br>32 | 89 138123<br>RUMFORD, ELS | 200,000 F<br>170,000 O<br>68,912 79% |
| 053 1618 022<br>SUBDIV. MAP 8 PG 8<br>BLK F LT 11 | 13000 | I | AUSTIN, JAMES & BARBARA<br>PO BOX 1176, BERKELEY CA<br>2925 STANTON ST BERKELEY | JAMES +, VER<br>94701 | 6/28/88<br>24 | 88 153644<br>CITICORP SV<br>N. AM | 150,000 F<br>135,000 D<br>112,680 73% |
| 053 1623 001 01<br>*NEW* | 13000 | T | LIGHTFOOT, CHARLES<br>2910 ACTON ST, BERKELEY CA<br>2910 ACTON ST BERKELEY | LIGHTFOOT, L<br>94702 | 5/23/89<br>11 | 89 137674<br>HOME FED'L S | 80,000 D<br>30,998 50% |
| 053 1623 014 01 | 13000 | T | CHOYCE, GORDON<br>2981 BIRINGHAM DR., RICHMOND CA<br>1327 ASHBY AVE BERKELEY | GORDON W. CH<br>94806 | 10/12/88<br>77 | 88 257138<br>BAYVIEW F SL<br>N. AM | 180,000 D<br>113,175 70% |
| 053 1623 032 01<br>SUBDIV. MAP 8 PG 8<br>BLK C LT 5+ | 13000 | I | KOLMAN +, AMY<br>1330 BURNETT ST, BERKELEY CA<br>1334 BURNETT ST BERKELEY | MUSCARELLA,<br>94702 | 6/02/88<br>26 | 88 131015<br>HSHLD BK FSB<br>FNDRS | 135,000 F<br>108,000 D<br>34,141 29% |
| 053 1624 007<br>SUBDIV. MAP 6 PG 34<br>BLK A LT 17 | 13000 | I | WILEY, PEARL<br>10609 STELLA ST, OAKLAND CA<br>1335 CARRISON ST BERKELEY | CITY FED'L S<br>94605 | 2/24/89<br>11 | 89 052306 | 45,000 F<br>89,000 60% |
| 053 1624 009<br>*NEW* | 13000 | I | BELLAMY, ALAN<br>1331 CARRISON ST, BERKELEY CA<br>1331 CARRISON ST BERKELEY | WILKINS, LUC<br>94702 | 6/07/89<br>11 | 89 151885<br>ANDERSON, HE | 91,500 F<br>90,000 D<br>22,415 41% |
| 053 1624 018<br>SUBDIV. MAP 8 PG 34<br>BLK A LT 25 | 13000 | I | EASTMAN, SAMUEL & EMMA<br>6225 RALSTON AVE, BERKELEY CA<br>1305 CARRISON ST BERKELEY | MANTABE, MUS<br>94702 | 1/26/89<br>26 | 89 021065<br>AETNA FIN<br>N.WST | 82,000 F<br>140,260 D<br>93,207 43% |
| 053 1625 021 | 13000 | I | RUTHERFORD, STEPHEN AND KIM<br>1044 POMONA AVE, ALBANY CA<br>1306 CARRISON ST BERKELEY | STENBORG, MI<br>94706 | 2/28/89<br>11 | 89 055256<br>FIRST NATION | 146,000 F<br>116,800 D<br>98,838 45% |
| 053 1625 027 | 13000 | T | HUYNG +, VO<br>1328 CARRISON ST., BERKELEY CA<br>1328 CARRISON ST BERKELEY | HUYNH, VO &<br>94702 | 6/15/88<br>11 | 88 142665<br>BK AMERICA<br>CONT | 49,500 D<br>63,240 52% |
| 053 1626 020 01<br>SUBDIV. MAP 10 PG 69<br>BLK D LT 9+ | 13000 | I | LAWYERS ASSET MANAGEMENT, INC.<br>449 – 15TH ST., OAKLAND CA<br>1207 HASKELL ST BERKELEY | LEONARD & BE<br>94612 | 1/20/89<br>21 | 89 016348<br>N.WST | 110,000 F<br>121,137 24% |
| 053 1626 020 01<br>SUBDIV. MAP 10 PG 69<br>BLK D LT 9+ | 13000 | I | WILKINSON, DANA & JACKIE<br>1207 HASKELL ST., BERKELEY CA<br>1207 HASKELL ST BERKELEY | LAWYERS ASSE<br>94702 | 1/20/89<br>21 | 89 016349<br>N.WST | 110,000 F<br>121,137 24% |
| 053 1626 020 01<br>SUBDIV. MAP 10 PG 69<br>BLK D LT 9+ | 13000 | I | WILKINSON, DANA & JACKIE<br>1207 HASKELL ST., BERKELEY CA<br>1207 HASKELL ST BERKELEY | WILLIAMS, ET<br>94702 | 1/20/89<br>21 | 89 016350<br>1NATWIDEBKSV<br>N.WST | 55,000 F<br>132,000 D<br>121,137 24% |

Reprinted by permission of TRW, Inc.

REDI 800-3[illegible]-1085 **Real Estate Data, Inc.**



ZIP CODE 94702

NEIGHBORHOOD MARKET PROFILE

ALAMEDA , CA

**HOUSEHOLD STATISTICS**

| | |
|---|---|
| OWNER OCCUPIED DWELLING | 43.0 % |
| OWNER OCCUPIED S F D | 65.0 % |
| RENTER OCCUPIED DWELLING | 57.0 % |
| YEAR ROUND CONDOMINIUMS | .0 % |
| RENTED CONDOMINIUMS | .0 % |
| RURAL RESIDENCE | .0 % |
| OWNER WITH NO MORTGAGE | 38.6 % |
| MARRIED COUPLES | 30.6 % |
| FAMILIES | 50.7 % |
| AVG PERSONS PER HOUSEHOLD | 2.1 |
| 3+ PERSONS PER HOUSEHOLD | 28.0 % |
| 4+ PERSONS PER HOUSEHOLD | 13.7 % |
| 5+ PERSONS PER HOUSEHOLD | 5.8 % |
| CHILDREN PER HOUSEHOLD | .35 |
| 1+ CHILDREN UNDER 18 YRS | 24.7 % |

**EDUCATION**

| | |
|---|---|
| ATTEND PRIVATE SCHOOL | 48.5 % |
| OVER 18 WITH 5+ YRS COLLEGE | 15.1 % |
| AGE 25+ SOME ELEMENTARY | 16.2 % |
| AGE 25+ 1-3 YEARS HIGH SCHOOL | 13.0 % |
| AGE 25+ 4 YEARS HIGH SCHOOL | 21.1 % |
| AGE 25+ 1-3 YEARS COLLEGE | 21.3 % |
| AGE 25+ 4+ YEARS COLLEGE | 28.4 % |
| AGE 25+ MEDIAN YEARS SCHOOL | 13.4 |

**POPULATION - AGE**

| | |
|---|---|
| 4 & UNDER | 4.8 % |
| 5 TO 9 | 4.7 % |
| 10 TO 13 | 4.7 % |
| 14 TO 18 | 6.5 % |
| 19 TO 21 | 4.9 % |
| 22 TO 24 | 6.3 % |
| 25 TO 29 | 11.2 % |
| 30 TO 34 | 10.9 % |
| 35 TO 44 | 11.7 % |
| 45 TO 54 | 8.7 % |
| 55 TO 59 | 5.5 % |
| 60 TO 64 | 5.4 % |
| 65 & OVER | 14.9 % |
| MEDIAN AGE (OVER 25) | 45.4 |

**VALUE - OWNER OCCUPIED UNIT ****

| | |
|---|---|
| 200,000 OR MORE | .2 % |
| 150,000 - 199,999 | .7 % |
| 100,000 - 149,999 | 8.0 % |
| 80,000 - 99,999 | 14.5 % |
| 50,000 - 79,999 | 41.5 % |
| 40,000 - 49,999 | 11.6 % |
| 30,000 - 39,999 | 10.3 % |
| 20,000 - 29,999 | 10.4 % |
| LESS THAN 20,000 | 2.8 % |

HOME VALUE INDEX - 71.8
MEDIAN VALUE - 61.2
(IN THOUSANDS)

**HOUSEHOLD UNITS PER STRUCTURE**

| | |
|---|---|
| 1 UNIT | 62 % |
| 2+ UNITS | 38 % |
| 3+ UNITS | 24 % |
| 10+ UNITS | 10 % |

**YEAR BUILT**

| | |
|---|---|
| 1979-1980 | .2 % |
| 1975-1978 | .7 % |
| 1970-1974 | 2.0 % |
| 1960-1969 | 9.0 % |
| 1950-19[illegible] | 15.4 % |
| 1940-1949 | 25.0 % |
| 1939 OR EARLIER | 47.7 % |

**OUTWARD MOBILITY**

| | |
|---|---|
| TOTAL DWELLING UNITS | 14.18 % |
| SINGLE FAMILY UNITS | 10.06 % |
| MULTI-FAMILY UNITS | 18.84 % |
| NET GROWTH RATE | .00 % |

**INCOME/WEALTH ***

MEDIAN INCOME - 24.5
INCOME INDEX - 64 %
WEALTH RATE QUINTILE - E

*QUINTILE RATE IS A TO E, HIGH TO LOW TO THE STATE MEDIAN

**POPULATION**

| | |
|---|---|
| WHITE | 41.6 % |
| NON-WHITE | 58.4 % |
| BLACK | 47.4 % |
| SPANISH | 4.7 % |

**TRANSPORTATION TO EMPLOYMENT**

| MODE | | TIME | |
|---|---|---|---|
| PRIVATE | 63.2 % | LESS THAN 15 MIN | 24.5 % |
| PUBLIC | 24.6 % | 15-29 MINUTES | 40.8 % |
| | | 30-59 MINUTES | 26.7 % |
| | | 60+ MINUTES | 7.9 % |

** HOME VALUE INDEX IS MEDIAN HOME VALUE OF THE ZIP CODE TO THE STATE MEDIAN

ALL DATA IS BASED UPON 1980 STATISTICS EXCEPT FOR MEDIAN INCOME WHICH IS FOR 1985-86

Reprinted by permission of Real Estate Data, Inc.

## PROFITABLE NEIGHBORHOODS

**Familiarize Yourself with the Property and Market Value**

- Ask neighbors about values and selling prices
- Review the local newspapers - review asking prices
- Ask FSBO's (For Sale By Owners)

**Nine Location Pitfalls You Should Avoid:**

1. Does the area show a lack of pride in ownership?
2. Is there junk in the streets, high crime rate area?
3. Is there lack of appealing shopping close by?
4. Is the neighborhood improving or declining?
5. Is there abandoned buildings and boarded up properties?
6. What about the freeway/expressway system, is it close by - too close by?
7. What type of industrial sites are close by?
8. Clean - computer polluters - refining?
9. Is it a long commute?

**Eight Location Possibilities With Upside Potential:**

1. Clean, older homes
2. Older neighborhood but no trash in streets or uncut lawns and abandoned cars
3. Shopping, churches and schools close by
4. Neighborhood beginning to show signs of age
5. Area appears to be improving. A few homes have already been rehabilitated.
6. Fix-up costs 5-10% of purchase price - cosmetic improvements
7. Little or no structural repair required
8. Buyers attitude is adjusted to the circumstances, fix-up with the objective being making money with sweat equity.

**The Ideal Location**

1. Clean streets, freshly cut lawns and only a few cars on the street, others garaged.
2. Upscale neighborhood - high demand by the young and old.
3. No damaged homes, all well kept and maintained.
4. Not a main or busy street. Think cul-de-sac.
5. Short drive/good access to expressways and public transportation systems.
6. Homes are homogeneous.
7. Recent renovation.
8. Appeals to men and women.
9. Need only carpet, drapes, linoleum and outside paint.
10. Good curb appeal
11. Buyer is excited and willing to complete the project and will be enthusiastic.

# SAMPLE OF "HOMES FOR SALE" ADS

**4072 Homes For Sale — Littleton**

RANCH STYLE with mtn view, Bow Mar South, 3400s.f. main flr., 2800s.f. full fin. bsmt., 3 car gar., great lot. Fantastic rec. area, pool, tennis, lake, beach. Underpriced for great val. $259,900. BY OWNER. 795-0545

(THE Ridge) Fab. 3200 sf, open contemp/traditional. 2 sty., open flr. plan, main flr. master, qual. blt., best $$ in area. $259K.Int'l. Net. 790-4400. Craig Mundt 850-5455

**4078 Homes For Sale — Loveland**

SMALL town living city amenities. 6K sqft 2 story on the golf course. Indoor pool/hottub $229,900 & trade for Denver real estate. The Group Inc. Rick 669-7032

**4080 Homes For Sale — Montbello**

PAYMENT LESS THAN RENT
Newly decor 4 Bed, 2 Bath, Bsmt. [illegible]3351 Randolph, ONLY $45,900 w/$600 DN. Ernie Stone 759-3095 United Prop Brokers, 671-9311

**4082 Homes For Sale — Morrison**

**DEER & THE 14TH TEE**
Along with a great view of red rock formations from new redwood deck, 4 bdrms., 3 baths, over 3000 sq. ft. + 3-car gar., 2 frpls., new carpet, tile & roof. Includes golf membership. 3 min. to C-470 & Quincy. Will trade up. (15WE)
TOM TAMBURELLO, 888-5954
RE/MAX 100 232-4444

GORGEOUS home on .7 A, redrock view & privacy. $153K. Shean, 770-8880, Omnivest Rlty., 722-3300

HORSE PROPERTY 3.5 AC.
5-stall barn, oversized 2 car., 3 bdrm., 3 bath. Call Bob, 973-3408. Foothills of Golden R.E.

**4084 Homes For Sale — Northglenn**

$89,000, $5000 Dn FHA assum. no qual. 2 stv, 4 bdrm, full bsmt, 2 car gar. grt yd & area. Close to shls/shopping. 9970 Clark Dr., Motivated Seller. 457-9361/owner

THIS IS IT
Must sell. $3,995 non-qual. By owner. 3 bdrm., 2 bath, $679/month. Must see. 457-8155 .

**4086 Homes For Sale — Parker**

4 BDRM. 2400 sq.ft. brick ranch style. 5.8 Acres. 2 1/2 baths. 100 mi. view! $153,500. [illegible]-1928

BUY direct from builder. [illegible] ranch or build on new site. [illegible] Pat, builder/agent. 841-28[illegible].

BY OWNER: Price reduced $20k. Located in the town of Parker. Vacant custom 2 sty. 4 bdrm., 2 1/2 bath, 2800 sq. ft., fresh paint. $129,500 or reas. offer. Immed. possession. For appt., 646-0907.

BY OWNER-Cottonwood 3 bdrm., 2 bath, frpl., 2 car, bi-level. FHA assumable. $79,250. 693-0427

NON QUALIFYING
2 beaut. homes in Saddlebrook Farms. Low dn. pymt., hdwd. flrs., ceiling fans, lg. country kit., deck w/mtn. view and many upgrades. $96,900 and $101,000. Call now. Bob Howrey, 841-7519 (21SA and 21SI)
CENTURY 21 Howrey, 841-2121

**4086 Homes For Sale — Parker**

ASSUME immac. 3 bdrm. 1 bath with fncd. yard, backs to greenbelt, spklr. sys., main floor laundry, many extras. Call Stephanie, Miller & Assoc., 841-8878

**BETTER THAN NEW! Under $100K**
**Immac. NON QUAL. ASSUME**
**3-yr old, open, sunny, neutral.**
**Fantastic Deck, Pines/Aspens**
**3 blocks to Elem. & Pool**
**SAVE: No Realtors Fees!**
**No Closing Costs!**
**All Appliances Included!**
**Loaded w/Upgrades**
**OPEN SUN 1-6 841-5115**

CORPORATE OWNED!
Seller says sell! Reduced to $129,900, contemporary 2-story, walk-out bsmt., great Pinery location, well landscaped, mtn. views, light & airy. Drive by 5700 Irish Pat Murphy, then call Karen Kaufman, 779-1955, for your private showing.
PERRY & BUTLER
779-9501

LOW DOWN
Spacious 4-level home, vaulted ceilings, 3 bdrms, 2 baths, comfortable fam. rm. with gas frpl., 2 car gar. 841-8878. Miller & Assoc.

9 1/2% NON-QUAL. loan. $788 PITI, 3 bdrm., 1½ bath 766-1160

**OPEN HOUSE, Sat. & Sun., 12-4. 4 bdrm., 2 bath, 2 car gar., wraparound deck, immac. cond!** DR **Real Estate Brokers, 755-3700**

PINERY 1/3 ac. Mtn. view, deck, 3 bdrm. 3 ba, walk schls. 9% assm. mtg. $116,900. 841-9079/699-2500

PRIDE of ownership plus value-4 bdrm, 2 bath, approx 1745 sq. ft. Immac. cond. Skylts. Wraparound deck + more! DR Real Estate Brokers Ed Hageman 755-3700

OPEN SUNDAY 1:00-5:00PM
IDEAL HORSE PROPERTY
7767 VILLAGE ROAD
Comfortable country living, 3278 sq.ft., 2 lvls., mtn view, 12-stall barn, arena, in Hidden Village off Hilltop Road. Call Lou Frazier, 771-3311 or 936-6540
Moore AND COMPANY/REALTOR

OPEN SUNDAY 1:00 4:00
Parker's finest, super 4 bdrm., 4-level, new condition. Vaulted ceilings, 3-car gar. Located east of Parker in Rowley Downs. $151,900 Stop by 11451 Marlborough Dr. or call Jack McLaughlin, 841-4422.
RE/MAX Services, Inc. 741-1400

UNIQUE NEW ENGLAND SALT-BOX - 3 wooded acres, fin. bsmt., 2 frpl[illegible], 4 bdrm. 3½ bath. By owner. $16[illegible]. 84[illegible]-2478

**4090 Homes For Sale — Southglenn**

MTN. view, pk. in back yd. 3 bdrm., 3 bath, class int., 2000 s.f., creative options, $119,900. 721-1540

FOUND ADS ARE FREE!
CALL 825-2525
POST CLASSIFIED
Works All Day!
EVERY DAY!

**4086 Homes For Sale — Parker**

**4090 Homes For Sale — Southglenn**

OPEN SUNDAY 1:00-4:00
SOUTHGLENN
6731 S. Kit Carson Cr. W. New crpt., hrdwd.flrs.,3-bdrm.,2-1/2 ba., country kitchen. Lg. yrd. $89,900. Call 798-9100. (67KIS)
COLDWELL BANKER
PROFESSIONALS.INC.

OPEN SUNDAY 1:00-4:00
LARGE HOME & LOT
7361 S. Wellington St. 2600 S.F. 2-story, 4 spacious bdrms., decks w/hot tub, screened patio. $137,500. Call 798-9100 (73WES)
COLDWELL BANKER
PROFESSIONALS.INC.

**4092 Homes For Sale — Thornton**

5 BDRM. brick home near Skyview H.S. Fam. rm., lg. corner lot. $67,000. 4 Bdrm. Cottonwood Lake, huge yd., huge bdrm., $92,000. Hamilton Properties, 340-3510 or 452-5233

BILL WALL- 4 bdrm. w/3 ba., din. rm., fam. rm. w/frpl., 2 car, a/c, steel/brick ext. $105K 451-7748

1802 E. 99th Av. 4bd. tri. 1870sf, 1¾ ba, famrm w/frpl., stove, appls, gas ht, A/C, 2 car, cov'd patio, pvt. fence, sprinklers. Priced to sell by owner, $74,500. 450-9738

**8½% NON-QUAL**
**$10K assumes PITI $631. Newer 3 bdrm, 2 bath, 2 car gar., deck, vaulted. Beaut. home; won't last. By owner.** 280-0991 or 252-1613

NON Qual assmptn, low dn., under $4000: 2 car gar., 2 bdrm., 2.5 bath, backs to open space. 451-8650

OPEN 1-5. **GORGEOUS** contemp. 2000 sf. 3 bdrm., 3 bath, 4 lvl. 3 car gar., view. Custom decor. Hunters Glen. 910 E. 130th. $129,900.
**3% ASPEN GOLD WAY 368-8300**

**OPEN Sat., Sun., 11-4. Hunter's Glenn 5 bdrm., 3 & 1/2 bath, mtn. view, skylights. $169,000. 252-4210**

**4094 Homes For Sale — Westminster**

MOVING! Must sell. 1 yr. new. 3 bdrm., 2½ bath + loft, 2½ car gar., terms, by owner. $111,900. 469-1297

MUST SELL THIS MONTH!!!
Beautiful home and pool in move-in cond. 3 bdrm., 3 bath, 3 decks and a huge garage. All this for only $94,500. Must see today! Call Evelyn Sigg, 424-2041 or Faber & Assoc. 422-1915. (10OA)

OPEN HOUSE 2-4 SUNDAY
10589 PIERSON CIRCLE
Loads of room in this flowing 4-level. Under $80,000! Fncd., sprinklered. June Steely, RE/MAX Horizons Group, 465-6412, 469-8821

OPEN 1-5. MUST SELL low dn. assume FHA. Exquisite 2000 sq. ft. 4 bdrm., contemp. 2 story. Upgrades, oak cabinets and trim. 3 baths, $108,900. HURRY! 9532 W. 104th Ct. 469-5956
**3% ASPEN GOLD WAY 368-8300**

SKYLAND VILLAGE
9816 Meade, 2400 sq. ft., 3 car gar., fantastic prices, $130's.

NEW HOMES OPEN 12-4
Stunning contemp. homes on large lot, priced from the low $160's. Some avail. immed. Near 95th & Pierce. See today or call Dick Morehouse, 424-5077.

**4094 Homes For Sale — Westminster**

COUNTRYSIDE tri., non-qual., low assume, $764 PITI. Lynn, Realty Profiles, 425-5322 .

DESPERATE! 3 bdrm., 1 bath. $58,800. After 3 p.m., 428-8383

OPEN & ROOMY
Extra sharp, 4 lvl. home w/open loft. 2300 sq. ft., 4 bdrm., 2.5 bath, lg. corner lot + bsmt. & 2 car gar. $103,900 w/terms. Ask for Jonathan Miller, 423-9464 or 422-5200.
REALTY PROFESSIONAL

OPEN SUNDAY 2-5 SEE IT!
Spacious, sunny family home, 3 bdrm., 2 bath, becomes 4 bdrm. plan easily! 2-car gar. + extra pad, great yard, central air, easy turnpike access. Just reduced! 6301 W. 93rd Ave. Bruce, 239-8922.
PERRY & BUTLER
969-8000

QUIET area/views. 2 bdrm/2 baths, tri-level, 1250 s.f. Soothing redwood hot tub and deck. $82,500. 10% Q/A, 11547 W. 102nd Pl. Near Standley Lake. 469-6753

OPEN SUNDAY 1:00 4:00
DRASTICALLY REDUCED
to $86,000. Seller retiring. Beautiful 4 bdrm., 2 bath, 2-car gar. 6311 Wolff St. Elaine, 888-3602
RE/MAX WEST 232-2244

**4095 Homes For Sale — Wheat Ridge**

3 BDRM. BRICK RANCH: H.W. HT. 1 car att., no bsmt., 82K, 238-1548

BY OWNER., 3 bdrm., 2 bath brick ranch. Gar., bsmt. 2910 Webster St. $87,500. 238-6140 or 429-9184.

BY Owner, 1100 s.f., brick, 2 bdrms, 1 bath. Appls., new kitch. 467-1120

COPPER HARBOR BY OWNER
5 bdrm., 3 bath. Low down or lease OP. Avail. Immed. 423-8995.

JUST LISTED
WHAT A VIEW!
Overlooks Clear Creek and has a panoramic mountain view. Ranch-style home with walk-out basement on approx. 1/2 acre. Nice master bedroom with floor to ceiling windows facing the mtns. Large deck plus covered patio. $199,900. Drive by 4181 Everett Drive and call Jackie Hollenbeck, 877-5107 or 985-4555.
RE/MAX Professionals, Inc.

OPEN SUNDAY 1:00-4:00
COUNTRY ATMOSPHERE
Horse ok. Home occup. income. 10755 W. 46th Ave. Duplex w/potential. 4-bdrm., 2-ba. sharp! $104,900 Call 425-6526 (10W46)
COLDWELL BANKER
PROFESSIONALS, INC

OPEN Sun. 12:00pm 3:00pm
OLD WORLD CHARM UPDATED
4610 Teller St. 4-bdrm., 2-ba. ranch. Updated kitchen, bath & windows. 3-car gar., mtn. view. Must see! $127,000. Call 231-9400. (46TE)
COLDWELL BANKER
PROFESSIONALS, INC.

## SAMPLE OF "HOMES FOR SALE" ADS

SOR
HOMES
MODELS OPEN DAILY
$95,000 - $126,950
STROH RANCH
2-1/2 Miles South of Parker
840-1050

ENUMCLAW

Pinnacle Estates
LONDO-TIBERIO CONST. INC.

New Homes From $106,990
Easy Commute to:
Kent, Auburn, Puyallup, Tacoma, Bellevue, Seattle
FHA, VA TERMS or HELP WITH CLOSING COSTS!
Directions: SR 169 from Renton, SR 516 from Kent, SR 164 from Auburn, SR 410 from Puyallup. Take Griffin Street in Enumclaw east to Blake St. Go south on Blake, follow signs to model.
Call 343-0309 or 735-4414 for details.

**SENSATIONAL ENTRY** **$169,950**
**12333 SE 204th. Kent: Open 1-4.** Gourmet kitchen w/gas range. Large family room and beautiful French doors to large deck. 4 bdrm. 2 bath. Call **852-8110** on Ad #KT489

**ROLLING HILLS RAMBLER** **$162,500**
**1731 Jones Dr. SE: Open 1-5.** Immaculate 3 bdrm. 2.5 baths, in exclusive Renton community, with pool, tennis, and park. View of city, terrace & mtns. Call **228-6739** on RT#055.

**EXTRA LARGE LOT** **$149,950**
**20504 SE 152nd St: Open 12-4.** Walk to community park, pool and tennis. Issaquah schools. Large immaculate 3 bdrm. 3 bath home. RV pkg. Call **228-6730** on RT #983.

**EXCELLENT LOCATION** **$145,750**
**27709 128th Pl. SE. Kent: Open 1-4.** Great family home in Easthill. Big yard, covered patio, excellent landscaping. Master bdrm has fireplace, Mt. Rainier view. 3 bdrm, 2½ bath. Call **852-8110 on Ad. #KT475.**

**CHILDREN'S DELIGHT** **$135,950**
**21733 121st Pl. SE. Kent: Open 12-3.** Well maintained family home with 4 bdrms & 2.5 baths. Home features fenced backyard & children's play area with a sandbox & combination swingset slide. Security system also available. Call **852-8110** on Ad #KT486.

**4 BDRM FAMILY HOME** **$114,500**
**7447 So. 116th Pl: Open 12-4.** Fenced yard, double garage. New paint, carpet and more. Rec room w/fireplace. Call **228-6730** on RT #034.

**AFFORDABLE NEW CONST** **$98,500**
**307 "R" St. NE, Auburn: Open 1-4.** 3 bedroom, 2 bath cutie with gorgeous oak cabinetry. Convenient location! Call **852-8110** on Ad #KT470.

**LYNNWOOD: 778-2101**
**BELLEVUE: 451-8300**
**KIRKLAND-REDMOND: 822-0263**
**WOODINVILLE: 483-0511/622-3730**
**EVERETT: 743-5902/353-9600**

### NORTH SEATTLE

**NORTHSHORE** **$237,500**
**6439 NE 188th. Open 1-5.** Exciting tri-level with spectacular mtn. view. Excellent condition, lots of light, gourmet kitchen, family dining, hot tub, wet bar and much more. See Dick or call **364-4020.** Ad #T-64.

**INCREDIBLE OPPORTUNITY** **$229,950**
**316 NE 167th. Shoreline. Open 1-4.** Price includes extra building & lot, plus extra platting possibilities. 6 year young. Better than new 2 story with main floor master bedroom. Oak kitchen. Spacious family room, garden window. 20x20 Deck. Come by and see today or call **546-4124.**

**NEW CONSTRUCTION!** **$219,500**
**19519 Whitman Ave. N: Open 1-4.** Seller motivated! Huge, new home on quiet street. Features family room off kitchen, formal dining, master suite, large fenced back yard and close to bus and shopping. See May Harper today or call **546-4124.** Ad T-195.

**LAKE FOREST PARK** **$199,900**
**19515-67th NE. Open 1-4.** Custom designed top entry bi-level home, 4 bedrooms, 2½ bath, gourmet kitchen designed for entertaining. Large rooms. Private enchanted garden. Visit Julie or call **364-4020.** Ad #T-195.

**SHERIDAN TERRACE** **$189,500**
**3637 NE 156TH ST: Open 1-4.** View of Lake Washington from the best buy in Sheridan Terrace! 3 bedrooms, 2 baths, remodeled rambler on terraced 17,000 square foot double lot. See Dawn Blumel today or call **783-4900** on Ad T-36.

**SPACIOUS 5 BEDROOMS** **$179,950**
**17043-2ND NW. Richmond Highlands. Open 12-4.** Newly listed. Great family home. 4 bedrooms on main floor. Large rec room plus den. Fully fenced back yard. Safe for children. Located near King County Park. Host: Ron Tarrar. **546-4124.**

**SHERIDAN BEACH** **$169,950**
**3810 NE 155th. Open 1-4.** Panaramic Lake Washington and Mtn. view. Old World charm in tip top condition. 3 spacious bedrooms M-I-L potential down. Rose garden and BBQ patio. See Bruce or call **364-4020.** Ad T3-38.

**NORTH CITY/FIRST OPEN** **$154,950**
**15234 12th Ave. NE. Open 1-4.** Tucked at the end of a private cul-de-sac is this spacious 3 bdrm. 2.5 bth home. Dining room, family room, 2 fireplaces, deck, wet bar, 2 car garage and a wonderful huge back yard too! Don't miss it. Meet Rita Lindle or call **525-6300.**

**YOUR SKILLS FINISH BSMT.** **$135,950**
**1537 NE 170TH ST. Open 12-4.** Large 3 bedroom rambler with country kitchen. Detached garage and workshop plus unfinished basement for your growing needs. TF-88. **778-2101.**

**SHORELINE** **$134,900**
**335 NE 180TH ST: Open 1-4.** 3 Bedroom/1.5 Bath home with 2 car garage. One year new roof, new carpet. Immaculate condition, beautifully manicured yard. Situated on private road. Meet Penny Juttner or call **783-4900** on Ad T-33.

**JACKSON PARK/FIRST OPEN** **$133,500**
**12515 12th AVE NE. Open 1-4.** Peaceful location!! Beautiful tree-lined street near Jackson Golf Course. Convenient access to freeways, Northgate etc. Very comfortable home with hardwood floors and completely remodeled basement. Large yard & deck. 3 bdrm. Meet Ken Kleist or call **525-6300.**

**NORTHEND** **$119,500**
**5406-232nd SW. Open 1-4.** "Diamond in the smooth" Immaculate 3 bdrm main house plus cottage. See Mick or call **364-4020.** Ad #T-54.

**GREAT STARTER HOME** **$105,000**
**16520-3RD NE. Shoreline. Open 1-4.** In great condition, 2 bedroom with fireplace, garage. Economical gas heat and well insulated. Desirable location. Easy access to I-5. See Eva Oak today or call on Ad T-5. **546-4124.**

**SHORELINE** **$[illegible]5,000**
**18054 8th AV NE: Open 1-4.** LOOK AT THIS PRICE! Great starter home, recently updated interior w/designer touches. 2 bedrooms, 1 bath, gas forced air heat. Large lot with fenced yard & dog run. Meet Hal Sipe or call **546-4124** on Ad T-180.

## SAMPLE OF "HOMES FOR SALE" ADS

### WEST SEATTLE

**PRESTIGIOUS NO. ADMIRAL — $259,000**
**5722 Admiral Way S.W. Open 1-4.** Unobstructed sound & mountain view. 3 bdrm plus master suite w/view deck, frpl & full bath w/jacuzzi. Walking distance to Alki Beach. Meet Carol Hoffman or call now on Ad #T-308. 937-9700.

**DREAM HOME — $245,000**
**3551 S.W. Austin St. Open 12-3.** Brand new! 4 bd, 2½ ba, 2 frpl, 2 decks, skylights, wainscotting — truly custom! Meet Russ Bassett or call now on Ad #T-329 **937-9700.**

**MINT CONDITION! — $104,500**
**8644 18th Ave. S.W. Open 12-3.** Sunny 3bd home w/frpl, hardwood floors and patio off the dining room. PLUS a garage! Meet Ed Huet or call now on Ad #T-355 **937-9700.**

### SNOHOMISH COUNTY

**CANYON PARK EXECUTIVE — $279,950**
**23007 49th Ave. SE. Bothell: Open 1-4.** Inviting tri-level home w/3 bd & 4 ba. Shy acre of land. Stop by or call now on Ad. #T334. **937-9700.**

**1.25 ACRES - NEWER RAMBLER — $279,950**
**23420 - 53rd Ave. SE. Bothell: Open 12-4.** Custom detailing in this 3 bed, 2½ bath spacious home. Nearly 2500 sq. ft. of beautiful hardwoods, solid raised-panel doors, brick & cedar exterior, and private estate-type setting. Ad. #TF-90. **778-2101.**

**EDMONDS RAMBLER – 1/3 ACRE — $219,950**
**19409 88th Ave. W: Open 12-4.** Wonderful Seaview setting for this beautifully maintained 3 bedroom, 2½ bath plus family room and sun room with spa! Ad. #TF-89 **778-2101.**

**HORSE ACRE/36x40 SHOP — $198,000**
**By Appointment:** Great Lynnwood location! Four br/2.5 bath home ideal for easy entertaining. Fenced property is beautifully landscaped. For the horse lover or hobbiest, this is a bargain of a lifetime. See today or call on Ad. #T175 **822-0263/622-7406.**

**CASCADE VIEW-ON GREENBELT — $196,500**
**20823 32nd Pl. W. Lynnwood: Open 12-4.** Dramatic and gorgeous almost new multi-level with all the extra amenities - security alarm system, multiple decks & hot tub, huge bonus room plus fam room — a must see! Ad. #TF-93 **778-2101.**

**QUALITY CUSTOM HOME — $185,500**
**4010 116th St. SE: Open 12-4.** Built with beautiful materials and craftsmanship, open beam ceilings, lots of skylights. Huge family room with wet bar and fireplace, beautifully landscaped yard. A combination of warm country appeal and contemporary design. Ad. #266. **353-9600/743-5902.**

**EDMONDS 2-STORY — $158,950**
**7804 194th St. SW: Open 12-4.** Delightful N.W. contemporary set on a great cul-de-sac lot with tall firs. Light & open plan with soaring ceiling, marvelous kitchen and family room. Ad. #TF-91. **778-2101.**

**EDMONDS MEADOWDALE — $152,900**
**15611 52nd Pl. W: Open 12-4.** Immaculate 2 yr. old tri-level, fully fenced in back with deck & patio. Soaring vaulted ceilings and stunning master bath with separate tub & shower. Ad. #TF-92. **778-2101.**

**BRIER - GREENBELT LOT — $139,950**
**3361 224th Pl. SW: Open 12-4.** Family neighborhood setting and a great 3 - bedroom tri-level with 2½ baths, family room and double car garage. Ad. #TF-94. **778-2101.**

**EDMONDS RAMBLER — $119,950**
**8718 220th St. SW: Open 12-4.** Charming 2 bedroom with large 14 x16' master bedroom. Entertaining-size living room and huge, treed lot close to downtown, beaches, and ferry service. Ad. #TF-95. **778-2101.**

### EASTSIDE

**WIN $25.00 TODAY — $275,000**
**19728-192nd Ave. NE. Open 1-4.** This 4 bdrm, 2½ bath, 2 story is in a great Woodinville neighborhood and sits on a horse acre. Well appointed, quality 4 yr old hm with all the extras. Vacant and ready to close now. Ad T-17. **483-0511 or 622-3730.**

**KENNYDALE VIEW — $209,950**
**1116 N. 30th Street. Open 12-4.** Quality 2 story 4 bdrm, 2.5 bath, hardwood floors. Entertainment size kitchen, family room with gas log lighter fireplace. View of Lk Wash. walk to community beach. Call **228-6730** on RT #050.

**RAMBLER-BELLEVUE — $199,900**
**3118 167th Ave NE. Open 12-4.** 4 bedrooms include large master suite with walk-in cedar closet. Beautiful remodeled and marble shower, living and family rooms have window seats & built-in bookcases. And so much more. Meet Bart Borusinski **451-8300.**

**1720 SQ. FT. RAMBLER — $174,940**
**6309 NE 156th. Bothell. Open 1-4.** Custom 3 bdrm, 2½ bath hm on ½ acre. Extensive use of glass, sugar maple frplc, hdwd flrs throughout. Cedar lined closets. Quiet neighborhood. Ad T-90. **483-0511 or 622-3730.**

**GREAT FAMILY HOME — $137,500**
**13833 115th Ave NE. Open 1-4.** Looking to steal a great home? 3 bdrm, 3 bath, new carpet, paint & roof. 1700 sq. ft. Won't last! Ad J-59. **483-0511 or 622-3730.**

**3 BR/2 BATH RAMBLER — $119,900**
**By Appointment: Kirkland.** Large 10,000+ sq. ft. cul-de-sac lot. Detached garage. Certified wood stove, washer, dryer, refrigerator and freezer included. Great value! Great location! Call **882-0263/622-7406** on Ad #T167

**BETTER THAN RENTING — $77,949**
**19230 128th Pl. NE. Space #-1. Open 1-4.** 2 bdrms, 2 bath, 24x52 home in Holly Hills. Fenced yard, carport, extra storage. Clean. Ad. #T-1 **483-0511 or 622-3730.**

### KITSAP PENINSULA

**BREMERTON — $92,500**
BY APPT: New on the market. Beautiful 3 bdrm, 2 bath rambler. Fireplace, garage on .8 of an acre. Skylight in kitchen. It won't last. Bob Searle 282-5340/697-2052.

**KINGSTON — $107,000**
BY APPT: Delightful 3 bdrm farmhouse on 1 acre. Bay window in breakfast nook & utility rm conveniently located off kitchen. House is 3 yrs old and has certified wood stove. Call Colleen Keilbart 842-6241/842-8561.

**KINGSTON/PILOT PT. — $169,500**
BY APPT: Weekend/summer hideaway 3 bed cabin. Large lot w/73 ft no-bank waterfront. Great yard w/custom deck. Wonderful beach. Scott Whaley 367-4720/389-0508.

**SILVERDALE — $349,500**
BY APPT: Puget Sound & Mt. Rainier set the stage for this very special waterfront home. 5 bdrm, 2.5 baths, 3,346 sq ft. Built with pride, this is a home to love. Blaine Highfield 282-5340/692-6742.

### OLYMPIC PENINSULA

**PORT TOWNSEND — $150,000**
BY APPT: On Morgan Hill: The most desirable area of Port Townsend, a five bedroom Victorian on 3 view lots overlooking Port Townsend Bay and the Olympics. Home needs work but the property is outstanding.

**SEQUIM — $169,900**
BY APPT: Stunning 3 bedroom, 2 bath home with a magnificent water view, formal dining room, gourmet kitchen, 2-car garage plus an attached artist studio. Elegance throughout. 1-800-366-6867.

**QUILCENE RIVER — $375,000**
BY APPT: Over 5,000 ft of prime river frontage, and over 120 acres. Mostly pastureland, great development potential, beautiful grounds. 1-800-676-3450.

**HOODSPORT — $315,000**
BY APPT: Private estate on 38 acres featured in Sunset. Magnificent home, quiet meadow, 2 creeks, horse barn, trout pond, walk to canal. Carol Connell 937-7600/726-5830.

## SAMPLE OF "HOMES FOR SALE" ADS

4203 Condo/T'home Sales

**Southeast Denver**

WINDSTREAM townhome, mtn. views, end unit, 3 bdrm., 2 1/2 bath, loaded, $137,000. 752-2232.

WINDSTREAM

Mountain View! Fronts to High-line Canal & Golf Course! Spacious, Open & Bright! 2-story Patio home w/fin. bsmt. & 2-car gar. $123,950. Call CHUCK TRAUTMAN, 478-9590 or 757-7474. RE/MAX Central

WONDERFUL 2 bdrm., 1 1/2 bath, $34,900. Eureka Realty. 321-7807

4209 Condo/T'home Sales

**Southwest Denver**

BEAR VALLEY CLUB
End unit, ground level, pool, tennis, 2 bdrm., 1 bath, MARITA, 798-9000
DAWSON & CO 795-5511

TALL PINES MODEL CONDO
2 bdrm., loft, frplc., 2 bath, all appl., immac., assume FHA loan, no closing costs, broker/owner. 979-0369

4210 Condo/T'home Sales

**South Suburban**

FORECLOSURE SALE
Beautiful Sanford Ranch duplex, 3 fin. garden level bsmt., 2 bdrms., 2 frplcs., 2 car garage, decks, small fenced yard, $107,000. Sue 795-5135 or 798-5888

OPEN SUNDAY 2:00-5:00
GEORGETOWN VILLAGE
New listing! Fabulous contemp. townhome in great area. 2-bdrm., 3-ba., den. Vaults & skylt. 6450 S. Filbert Lane $112,500 Call 773-1820 (64FIS)

COLDWELL BANKER
PROFESSIONALS, INC.

OPEN Sun. 1pm-4pm
1521 E. NICHOLS CIRCLE
Woodridge Terrace Townhome! Fully upgraded 3 bdrm., 2 car gar. South on Clarkson off Dry Creek. JENNIFER KOPINA 797-3187
FIELD Real Estate 571-1313

WILLOW CREEK TOWNHOME
GREAT ASSUMPTION
Luxury 4 bdrm 2 bath, w/loft study, finished basement, 2 car garage, approx 2200 SF, Cherry Creek Schools, assume $90,300 Non Qual. 9.5% loan. $102,500. KENTWOOD-MOORE, Glenn Thomas 773-3399. 759-2480

4211 Condo/T'home Sales

**Southeast Suburban**

2 bdrm., 2½ bath, 1400 + sq. ft., Sanford Sturbridge Sq., CC schools, appl., $86,000. 972-9554

**OPEN SUNDAY**
**11:30 - 2:00**
**0 DOWN!**
Great for professionals. 2 bdrm., new carpet and paint. Carol or Terri Chestnut, call 750-7070. See at 4096 S. Carson #B
RE/MAX Southeast Inc. 750-7070

OPEN SUNDAY 2:00-5:00
HILLCREST AT HOMESTEAD
100% PERFECTION' 2-story, 3-bdrm., plus fam. rm. Worth seeing, worth owning! 7503 S. Ivanhoe Circle $147,500 Call 773-1820 (75NS)

COLDWELL BANKER

4211 Condo/T'home Sales

**Southeast Suburban**

2-3 BDRM. thms. Exc. cond., $40-50K. IMS Inc. 337-9751; 755-7411

GREAT DTC LOCATION
2 bdrm. condo with all the amenities, all appls. incl. Enclosed patio, air cond., storm windows, newer paint, in great condition. For only $45,900. At this price, it won't last! Call Duke Fyffe, 771-9400, 877-4135.
RE/MAX MASTERS 771-9400

OPEN SAT., SUN. 12-5
New ranch end unit. You pick colors. 10% down. 8-1/8% interest. 6304 S. Harrison Way. Call Elizabeth 399-9000 or 689-9000

15 TOWNHOMES, exc. cond., 2 and 3 bdrm., indiv. or package sale. IMS Inc. 337-9751; 755-7411

4212 Condo/T'home Sales

**East Suburban**

FHA Non-qual. assumable loan. Owner/occupant. 1177 sq. ft. Ranch style. 3 bdrm. 2 bath, appls. incl. Pay closing cost and take-over pymt. Contact Dewey Work: 534-8641; Home: 755-5430

4217 Condo/T'home Sales

**Southwest Suburban**

$0 DOWN, NON-QUAL. FHA 4 bdrm., 2 3/4 bath. 972-3720

LUXURY Condo: With club house, tennis courts, park, underground pkng. at the Promontory, I-225 & I-25. A very good condo assn. $150K. Call Todd Bailey, 980-0440.

NO DOWN, Non Qual assume $723. 2 bdrm 2 1/2 bath, skylite, fplc, pool, applcs, 1120+ sf 979-3175

NON-QUAL. assumpt. Low down. 2 bdrm., frplc., fncd. yd., solar, appls., pool, great location! Must see! 797-3494

OPEN SUNDAY 2:00-4:30
SILVER VALLEY
2-story, 2 bdrm., 2 ba., 2-car garage. View over Bear Creek Park. Cream puff condition. Pool, tennis. Quick possession. 8781 W. Cornell Ave. #4. $78,900 Call 988-7630 (87 COW)

COLDWELL BANKER
PROFESSIONALS, INC.

OPEN SUN 1-4PM
WATERFRONT TWNHMS
**$60,000-$83,000**
4202 W. Pondview Dr
Across from Columbine Country Club, ranch and 2-story townhomes, overlooking 3 ponds filled with great fishing. Amenities include indoor pool, 2 raquetball courts, 2 tennis courts. Ranches have 1271 sq. ft. on main level and 1271 sq ft. basements, most with walkouts. 2 & 3 bedroom 2-story styles have over 1200 sq. ft with additional full finished basement.
SUSIE DEWS
388-6861
DISTINCTIVE MOORE PROPERTIES LTD
355-7653

4220 Condo/T'home Sales

**Applewood**

SPACIOUS 3 bdrm., 2 bath, Applewood exec. condo. Small, quiet complex. 12820 Willow Lane. $83,500. Schild & Co., 233-3313

4225 Condo/T'home Sales

**Arvada**

4070 Homes For Sale

**Lakewood**

ASSUMABLE STARTER
1375 Brentwood is a clean, cozy & cheerful updated home with spacious covered patio & many other extras. Save thousands in closing cost by assuming this outstanding FHA loan. Won't last at $69,500.
MONA & MARK, 989-9588
RE/MAX PROFESSIONALS, INC.

4 BDRM. brick home, 2 bath, full bsmt., gar., Meadowlark Hills subdiv. $85,500. 234-0221

**BEST OF HERITAGE WEST!**
Dramatic 2-story, vaulted ceil., spacious kit, sunny walkout bsmt, million $ view, 4 bdrm., 3 bath, lg. yard, $230,000. 1938 S. Robb Wy.

Sunny 2-story, 3 car gar., front court yard, walkout master bdrm to patio & hot tub, sun room & more. $265,000. 1957 S. Queen Dr.

Freshly updated 4-level, walkout to greenbelt, hardwood flooring, new carpet, paint, kitchen, fncd. yard. $204,500. 2133 S. Parfet Dr.

Call John at Semich & Assoc. for showings, 973-1350, 989-6800

★ BY OWNER ★
Open Sat., 12-5, 8060 W. Woodard Dr. Immac. 5 bdrm, 3 bath, frpl, 2700 s.f. Non-qual. 9% loan. Below mkt. $106,500. 989-1767; 238-3316.

**CITY FARMER?**
Spotless ranch style on 1/3 ac. Features 2 bdrm., din. rm., spac. liv. area, 2 car gar., new elec. & furnace. $71,500. Call Dennis at 478-7003, MB Unique Properties.

COUNTRY atmosphere. 1605 saft brick ranch w/2 car det. gar. Fmly rm. w/skylts., lg. priv. bk yd. 2 bath. NICE neighborhood! $99,950. Design Realty 232-7076

IMMAC. brick ranch, 2 bdrm., 1 bath, car, low $60's. Nickie, Corel Rltrs., 428-9850

LIGHT & BRIGHT
Exceptional 4 bedroom, 2 bath brick 4-level in one of the city's best neighborhoods. Close to schools, shopping and park. $89,900. JIM THOMAS, 888-7274
RE/MAX PROFESSIONALS, INC.

**LOWEST PRICE**
In area on this upgraded newer home. Great loc. Won't last. Manny, 898-5776. Omnivest, 722-3300

Main Floor Master Suite
1-1/2 story, 4 bdrm. in Threemoor. Fantastic view from large deck. 3-car gar. Walkout bsmt. Many extras. Price $219,000. Call Pat Kelly, 986-7506.
PERRY & BUTLER 986-4400

BY OWNER. Hutchinson bi-level, 3 bdrm., 2 3/4 bath, fin. lower level w/ brick frpl. Assm. loan, must qual. Upgrades. 969-8830

BY OWNER-3 bdrm. 2 bath, 1,800 sq. ft. Close to schls. Nice yd. $85,500. 987-8708. 917 S. Owens Ct.

HURRY - WON'T LAST!
1406 S. Ward Way. Beautiful 4 bdrm. ranch with fin. walk-out bsmt., view, cov. deck & patio, $117,900. Pat McDonnell, 986-4675.
PERRY & BUTLER 986-4400

NON QUAL ASSUMPTION
56K assumes 3 bdrm., 2 bath 2-sty. w/2 car, loft and full bsmt., vaults. Like new. Call Brian, 888-5520, Basham & Assoc.

OPEN SUN. 1-4
A true '10'. Large bi-level (R) plan, views of the foothills, profess. landscaped, tons of upgrades, extremely clean, 3 bdrms., 3 baths, lg. covered patio & deck. Stop by and see this at 2455 S. Deframe. South of Jewell off of Bear Creek Rd. $117,000. Joe Bilicki 877-6521, Edelweiss Realty.

4064 Homes For Sale

**Highlands Ranch**

AUBURN Park, 5 bdrm., 3 bath, 3 car gar. AC, cul de sac, adj. to Sd. Crk. Elem. 2 yr. old. $189,900. 1761 E. Red Fox. Open 11-6 791-1324

**6 Bdrm., 4 Bath 2-Story!**
BACKS TO GREENBELT
6721 EAGLE PLACE
$239,000
No other home in Highlands Ranch offers this mtn. view! upgraded, meticulous, contemporary 2-story with main flr. master bdrm., 6 bdrms., 4 baths, walk-out bsmt., hdwd. flrs. YOU MUST SEE IT TO BELIEVE IT! Call Kathie Copley for dir. & details. 791-8901
RE/MAX Services, Inc. 741-1400

2 BDRM. + loft, 1 & 1/2 baths + full bsmt., 1206 sq. ft., immac. FHA NQ, at 9.5%. $96,500 by owner, 3% to broker. Open Sun. 1-4pm. 1040 E. Ridgeglen Wy. 791-8037

BEST BUY IN HIGHLANDS RANCH! Immac. 3 bdrm. tri-lvl. Fam. rm. w/frpl. More! Metro Brokers, Milley & Co. 795-9735/797-1700

BRADFORD Hills patio home, dramatic open flr. plan, impeccable cond., easy living lifestyle, low interest, easy qualifying, assumable loan. 791-8833

BY OWNER. Falcon Creek, Parade of Homes design. 4-5 bdrm., 5 baths, frpl., JennAire kit., walkout bsmt., 3 car gar., mtn. view, 9 1/2% assum. $235,000. 470-0403

BY OWNER, 9 1/2% non-qual. VA, Richmond 2 story, 3 bdrms., 2 1/2 baths, lg. lot with view, lg. deck, hot tub. Many upgrades. 470-0254

**1217 E. ASCOT AVE.**
WINDHAM HILLS
NON-QUAL ASSUMPTION
WOW!! High loan balance, low interest rate, great pymts. 2-story open contemporary, central air cond. Kathie Copley, 791-8901
RE/MAX Services, Inc. 741-1400

GORGEOUS EXECUTIVE HOME
4/3/3 study/LR/DR/FR. Upgrades throughout, walk-out bsmt. on greenbelt, fantastic mtn. views. Open Sat. 1-4 9477 S. Chesapeake St. 470-9532, $230,000.

HOT TUB/MTN. VIEW
4 bdrm., 2 1/2 bath, famrm., fin. bsmt., 3 decks, neut. colors, frpl., clean! $133.5K. By owner. 791-2484

**NON QUAL ASSUMPTION!!**
1555 E. HERMOSA DR.
IMPRESSIONS
$129,900
Corner lot, contemporary 3 bdrm., 3 bath, 2-story with neutral colors. Close fast!!! Call KATHIE COPLEY for details, 791-8901.
RE/MAX Services, Inc. 741-1400

NON-QUAL. assumpt. By owner. Immac. 2 bdrm. 4 lvl. Mtn. view, lg. redwd. deck, sprklr. $5K assumes 10% NQ FHA loan. $862 PITI. Great starter! 791-0584

QUIET TRI-LEVEL, Lochwood area, 3 bdrm. Very Good Cond. Assumable. 985-8206. BY OWNER.

4060 Homes For Sale

**Green Valley Ranch**

BY owner, new on mkt. 3 bdrm. tri-lvl., FHA non qual., low assumpt. 9%. 371-8248

0 DOWN - ASSUMPTION
OPEN SUNDAY 1-4
Richmond's Bentley, 3 bdrm., 3 bath, 4-level, former model. Approx. 1700 sq. ft. of perfection. Loaded. Central air, intercom, parquet floors, upgrades galore. Qualifying assumption at 7-7/8% interest rate. PITI $971. APR 7-7/8%. Priced at $105,500. See 4361 Malaya St. Call Liz Carter, 771-9400 or 230-9067, 24-hr. pager
RE/MAX MASTERS 771-9400

## EXAMPLE OF MAPS

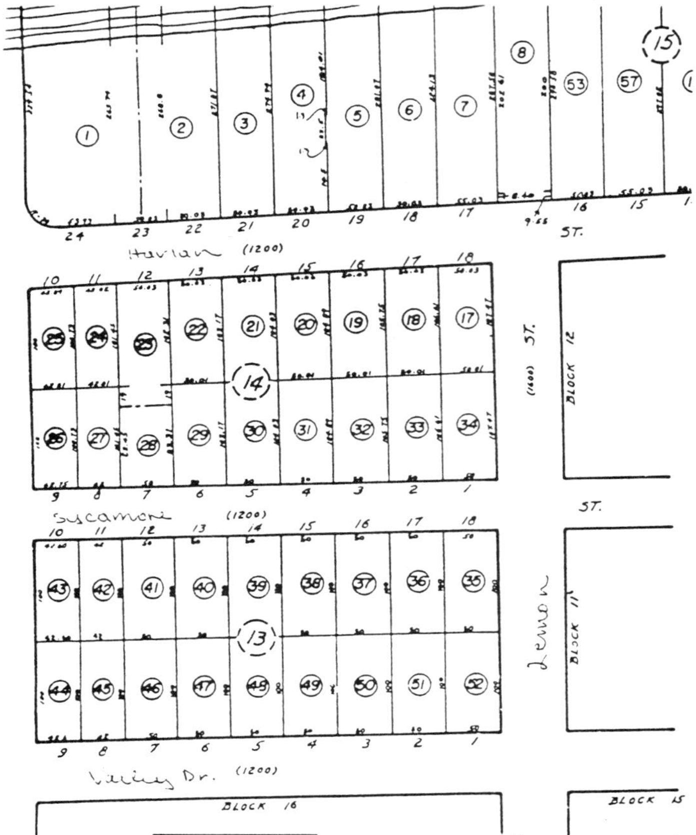

Plat Map

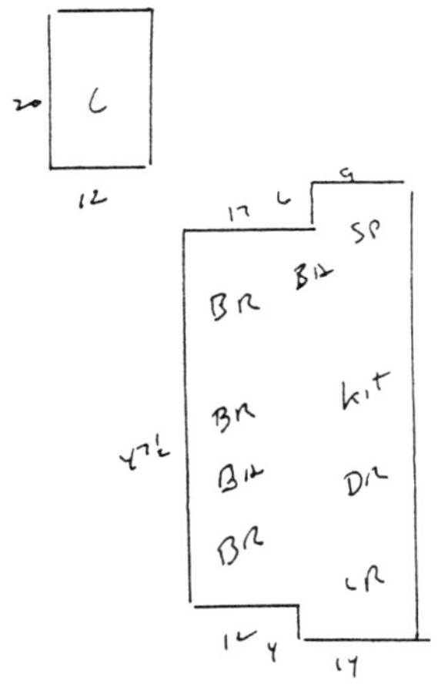

Building Sketch

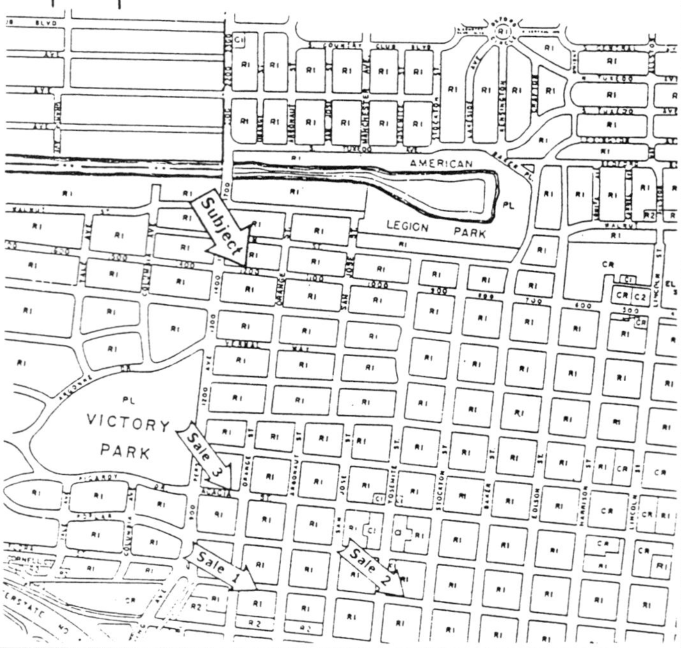

Comparable Sales Map

## MINI-APPRAISAL

Competitive Comparable Market Analysis Questionaire

| For Sale Now | Bedrooms | Bathrooms | Sq. Ft. | Extras | Pool | Market Time | Financing 1, 2, 3, | Motiv. | Terms |
|---|---|---|---|---|---|---|---|---|---|
| 1. | | | | | | | | | |
| 2. | | | | | | | | | |
| 3. | | | | | | | | | |
| 4. | | | | | | | | | |
| Sold This Year | | | | | | | | | |

**CMDC** CALIFORNIA MARKET DATA COOPERATIVE

## SINGLE FAMILY RESIDENTIAL / PUD SALES DATA

SCEN FRESNO

| Map Code or City Name or Census Tract | Source | Property Address / Assessor's Parcel Number | Lot/Tract | Recording Number | Price Code / Clsd Sale | Sales Price (Committed / Closed) | Sales Date (Committed / Closed) | Loan Type, Type Seller / Mrtg % 1st # Oth | Price per SqFt | Year Blt / Style Stories | Tot Rooms Bedrooms / Baths | SqFt Liv Area / Basement SqFt | Oth Rms / Kitchen Equipmnt | Heat / Air Cond | Fuel Type / Fireplace | Utils E G S W / Zoning | Swim Tmpl Floor / Prkg Spaces Type Constr | Qual Cond Ext Roof Floor | Lot Size or Area | Flood Zone | Other Improvements / Comments | HOA Dues | Total Units | Common Amenities | Ownership | Pool /Spa | Prop |
|---|---|---|---|---|---|---|---|---|---|---|---|---|---|---|---|---|---|---|---|---|---|---|---|---|---|---|---|
| 55.01 | F | 9448 N WOODMONT DR, FRESNO | | | | 290,000 | 031191 | C | | 1991 | 7 4 | 2685 | DLY | A | G | P P P P | N D G | G G T C C | 85X116 | N | | $11 | 1 | | D | | F |
| | | 401-354-04-0 | 50/3904 | | N | | | | 108 | M 1 | 2.50 | | BMC | C | 2 | R-1 SFR | 3 G A | | | | EE ITM: GLZD WIN; B/I CHINA CAB, CEIL FAN, TONGUE & GROOVE CATH | | | | | | 1 |
| 55.02 | F | 566 W BEDFORD AVE, CLOVIS | | | | 202,250 | 040491 | C | | 1991 | 7 4 | 2455 | DY | A | G | P P P P | D G | G G C C V | 80X110 | N | CVRPAT, FEN | | 1 | | S | | F |
| | | | 43/4058 | | N | | | | 82 | N 1 | 2.50 | | BM | C | 1 | SFR | 3 G A | | | | EE ITM: GLZD WIN; WT BAR, COV FR PCH, LNDSCP | | | | | | 1 |
| | F | 943 N CHAPEL HILL AVE, CLOVIS | | | | 132,700 | 060190 | | | 1991 | 6 3 | 1962 | ANL | A | G | P P P P | V D A | A G C C V | 63X118 | N | CVRPAT, FEN | | 1 | | S | | F |
| | | | 78/4014 | | N | | | | 68 | L 1 | 2.00 | | RDMS | C | 1 | SFR | 2 G A | | | | EE ITM: GLZD WIN; | | | | | | 1 |
| | H | 955 N CHAPEL HILL DR, CLOVIS | | | | | | C F | | 1990 | 6 3 | 1500 | ANLY | A | G | P P P P | N D A | A G W C C | 63X118 | N | | | 1 | | S | | F |
| | | 304-543-04-0 | 77/4014 | 21718 | Y | 111,000 | 022291 | 80% | 74 | N 1 | 2.00 | | BM | C | 1 | R-1 | 2 G A | | | | EE ITM: GLZD WIN; VAUL CEIL, RECESS KIT LT, TILE KIT | | | | | | 1 |
| | F | 765 N CLAREMONT, CLOVIS | | | | 117,950 | 030191 | F | | 1991 | 7 3 | 1676 | DFLY | A | G | P P P P | V D A | A G C C C | 60X100 | N | | | 1 | | S | | F |
| | | | 49/4161 | | N | | | 93% | 70 | N 1 | 2.00 | | B | C | 1 | SFR | 2 G A | | | | EE ITM: GLZD WIN; BIRCH CAB, TILE CNTRS | | | | | | 1 |
| | F | 786 N EZIE AVE, CLOVIS | | | | 124,598 | 060190 | C | | 1991 | 6 4 | 1781 | FLY | A | G | P P P P | N D A | A G T C C | 85X106 | N | FEN | | 1 | | S | | F |
| | | | 72/4161 | | N | | | | 70 | N 1 | 2.00 | | B | C | 1 | R16000 | 2 G A | | | | | | | | | | 1 |
| | F | 1410 FIR AVE, CLOVIS | | | | 116,900 | 020191 | C | | 1991 | 6 3 | 1781 | ANY | A | G | P P P P | N D G | G G A C C | 7500 | N | | | 1 | | S | | F |
| | | | 42/4161 | | N | | | | 66 | N 1 | 2.00 | | B | C | 1 | RI SFR | 2 G | | | | COV PCH, OAK CAB, TILE CNTR, VAUL CEIL | | | | | | 1 |
| | F | 1420 FIR AVE, CLOVIS | | | | 142,000 | 070190 | C | | 1991 | 8 5 | 2312 | FL | A | G | P P P P | N D A | A G C C C | 59X102 | N | FEN | | 1 | | S | | F |
| | | | 41/4161 | | N | | | | 61 | N 1 | 2.50 | | BM | C | 1 | R16000 | 3 G A | | | | | | | | | | 1 |
| | F | 1426 FIR AVE, CLOVIS | | | | 117,950 | 030191 | F | | 1991 | 7 3 | 1676 | DFLY | A | G | P P P P | V D A | A G C C C | 60X100 | N | | | 1 | | S | | F |
| | | | 51/4161 | | N | | | 94% | 70 | N 1 | 2.00 | | B | C | 1 | SFR | 2 G A | | | | EE ITM: GLZD WIN; BIRCH CABS, TILE CNTRS | | | | | | 1 |
| | F | 1445 FIR AVE, CLOVIS | | | | 101,430 | 030191 | C | | 1991 | 5 3 | 1342 | AL | A | G | P P P P | N D G | A G C C C | 60X100 | N | FEN | | 1 | | S | | F |
| | | | 53/4161 | | N | | | | 76 | N 1 | 2.00 | | B | C | 1 | R-1 | 2 G A | | | | EE ITM: GLZD WIN; VAUL CEIL, AUTO SPRNK | | | | | | 1 |
| | F | 1465 FIR AVE, CLOVIS | | | | 110,190 | 070190 | C | | 1991 | 6 3 | 1678 | FLY | A | G | P P P P | N D A | A G C C C | 60X100 | N | FEN | | 1 | | S | | F |
| | | | 55/4161 | | N | | | | 66 | N 1 | 2.00 | | B | C | 1 | R16000 | 2 G A | | | | | | | | | | 1 |
| | F | 1475 FIR ST, CLOVIS | | | | 125,355 | 022291 | C | | 1991 | 6 3 | 1897 | DL | A | G | P P P P | D A | A G C C C | 70X100 | N | FEN | | 1 | | S | | F |
| | | 304-600-27-0 | 56/4161 | 36424 | Y | 125,500 | 032991 | 75% | 66 | N 2 | 2.50 | | B | C | 1 | R-1 SFR | 2 G A | | | | EE ITM: GLZD WIN; SPRNK SYS | | | | | | 1 |
| | F | 1600 FIR AVE, CLOVIS | | | | 116,005 | 030191 | | | 1991 | 6 3 | 1678 | AF | A | G | P P P P | N D A | A G C C C | 60X100 | N | FEN | | 1 | | S | | F |
| | | | 29/26 | | N | | | | 69 | N 1 | 2.00 | | B | C | 1 | R1 | 2 G A | | | | | | | | | | 1 |
| | F | 783 N FORDHAM AVE, CLOVIS | | | | 142,000 | 100190 | C | | 1991 | 6 4 | 2164 | FL | A | G | P P P P | N D A | A G C C C | 60X103 | N | FEN | | 1 | | S | | F |
| | | | 59/4161 | | N | | | | 66 | N 1 | 2.50 | | BM | C | 1 | R16000 | 2 G A | | | | | | | | | | 1 |
| | F | 9723 N FOWLER, CLOVIS | | | | 176,000 | 020191 | C | | 1979 | 7 3 | 2183 | DFLY | A | G | P P P P | N D A | G G A C C | 2.25 | Y | CVRPAT | | 1 | | S | | F |
| | | 304-401-30 | | | N | | | | 81 | R 1 | 3.00 | | BMC | C | 1 | AL | 2 G A | | | | TILE KT CNTR, VAUL CEIL, AUTOMATIC SPRNK SYS | | | | | | 1 |
| | F | 1470 FU AVE, CLOVIS | | | | 113,025 | 032091 | F | | 1991 | 7 3 | 1532 | DNRL | A | G | P P P P | V D A | A G C C C | 60X100 | N | | | 1 | | S | | F |
| | | | /4161 | | N | | | 78% | 74 | N 1 | 2.00 | | B | C | 1 | SFR | 2 G A | | | | TILE CNTRS, SPLASH, BIRCH CABS | | | | | | 1 |
| | F | 5605 E INTERNATIONAL, CLOVIS | | | | 145,000 | 022591 | C | | 1975 | 6 4 | 2212 | ARL | A | G | P P X | N D G | A F A T C | 2.42 | N | BRN | | 1 | | S | BOTH | F |
| | | 301-151-30-S | 68 | | N | | | | 66 | N 1 | 2.00 | | BMC | C | 1 | SFR | 2 G A | | | | | | | | | | 1 |
| | F | 681 N STANFORD, CLOVIS | | | | 104,025 | 030191 | C | | 1991 | 5 3 | 1335 | AL | A | G | P P P P | N D A | A G C C C | 6000 | N | FEN | | 1 | | S | | F |
| | | | 66/4161 | | N | | | 90% | 78 | N 1 | 2.00 | | B | C | 1 | R1 | 2 G A | | | | | | | | | | 1 |
| | F | 771 N STANFORD AVE, CLOVIS | | | | 100,940 | 060190 | C | | 1991 | 5 3 | 1324 | FLY | A | G | P P P P | N D A | A G C C C | 60X105 | N | FEN | | 1 | | S | | F |
| | | | 6715/4161 | | N | | | | 76 | N 1 | 2.00 | | B | C | 1 | R16000 | 2 G A | | | | | | | | | | 1 |
| 56.01 | C | 657 W BEVERLY, CLOVIS | | | | 91,000 | 020491 | C | | 1960 | 6 3 | 1428 | F | A | G | P P P P | N D A | A G C C C | 7955 | N | | | 1 | | S | | F |
| | | 420-123-24 | /1804 | 23926 | Y | 91,000 | 022891 | 75% | 64 | N 1 | 2.00 | | B | C | 1 | SFR | 2 G A | | | | | | | | | POOL | 1 |
| | F | 1205 KAREN, CLOVIS | | | | 75,000 | 010191 | F | | 1965 | 6 3 | 1248 | AFL | A | G | P P P P | N D A | A A C C X | 65X104 | N | CVRPAT, FEN | | 1 | | S | | F |
| | | 420-112-20 | 40/1804 | | N | | | | 60 | N 1 | 1.50 | | RH | C | | R-1 | 2 G A | | | | CEIL FAN, TILE CNTR, AUTO SPRNK | | | | | | 1 |
| | F | 6820 N LAUREEN, FRESNO | | | | 123,900 | 020191 | C F | | 1978 | 7 3 | 1996 | AFLY | A | G | P P P P | N D A | A A A C X | 67X118 | N | CVRPAT | | 1 | | S | | F |
| | | 410-333-02 | /2836 | 31228 | Y | 124,000 | 031891 | 90% | 62 | N 1 | 2.00 | | B | C | 1 | R-1 | 2 G A | | | | ALARM SYS, AUTO SPRNK, TILE KIT/BATH CNTR, CAB | | | | | | 1 |
| | C | 3334 E LOS ALTOS, FRESNO | | | | 118,000 | 010191 | C F | | 1978 | 7 3 | 1702 | DFLY | A | G | P P P P | N D A | A A A C C | 82X112 | N | CVRPAT, FEN | | 1 | | S | | F |
| | | 410-302-08 | 14/2786 | 25544 | Y | 118,000 | 030491 | 68% | 69 | N 1 | 2.00 | | B | C | 1 | SFR | 2 G A | | | | | | | | | | 1 |
| 56.02 | C | 105 BEVERLY, CLOVIS | | | | 60,000 | 010191 | | | 1961 | 6 3 | 1485 | DF | W | G | P P P P | N D A | A A C C C | 6572 | N | FEN | | 1 | | S | | F |
| | | 497-173-20 | | 26659 | Y | 60,000 | 030691 | | 40 | N 1 | 1.50 | | | | | R1 | 2 G D | | | | | | | | | | 1 |
| | F | 1711 OXFORD, CLOVIS | | | | 91,000 | 012691 | F F | | 1963 | 5 3 | 1329 | A | A | G | P P P P | V D A | A A C C C | 65X100 | N | CVRPAT, DEC, FEN | | 1 | | S | | F |
| | | 497-193-31 | /1921 | 31698 | Y | 91,000 | 031991 | 99% | 68 | N 1 | 2.00 | | B | C | 1 | RES | 2 G A | | | | | | | | | POOL | 1 |
| 56.03 | F | 3314 E TENAYA, FRESNO | | | | 107,000 | 030191 | F F | | 1976 | 6 3 | 1687 | AFLY | A | G | P P P P | N D A | A A A C C | 67X110 | N | CVRPAT, FEN | | 1 | | S | | F |
| | | 410-202-06 | 12/2658 | 36891 | Y | 107,000 | 032991 | | 63 | R 1 | 2.00 | | B | C | 1 | R-1 | 2 G A | | | | TILE ENT, SPRNK | | | | | | 1 |

THE ABOVE DATA IS BELIEVED TO BE RELIABLE BUT ACCURACY IS NOT GUARANTEED. **APR 1991** – 16 –

**MAP / CITY / CENSUS: 55.01 THRU 56.03**

**SINGLE FAMILY / PUD FRESNO**

**PHOTOGRAPH ADDENDUM**

| | | | | | | | |
|---|---|---|---|---|---|---|---|
| Borrower/Client | COLLUM | | | | | | |
| Property Address | 1251 W. HARDING WAY | | | | | | |
| City | STOCKTON | County | SAN JOAQUIN | State | CA. | Zip Code | 95203 |
| Lender | NEW GROWTH FINANCIAL | | | | | | |

FRONT OF SUBJECT PROPERTY

REAR OF SUBJECT PROPERTY

STREET SCENE

## PHOTOGRAPH ADDENDUM

Borrower/Client COLLUM
Property Address 1251 W. HARDING WAY
City STOCKTON County SAN JOAQUIN State CA. Zip Code 95203
Lender NEW GROWTH FINANCIAL

**COMPARABLE #1**

1111 W.
FLORA

| | |
|---|---|
| Price | $78,785 |
| Price/SF | 56.28 |
| Date | 5/12/89 |
| Age | 60 YEARS |
| Room Count | 7-3-2 |
| Living Area | 1,400 |
| Gross Adj. | 31% |
| Net Adj. | 25% |
| Value Indication | $58,785 |

**COMPARABLE #2**

920 W.
FLORA

| | |
|---|---|
| Price | $60,000 |
| Price/SF | 50.00 |
| Date | 12/21/89 |
| Age | 60 YEARS |
| Room Count | 6-3-2 |
| Living Area | 1,200 |
| Gross Adj. | 47% |
| Net Adj. | 14% |
| Value Indication | $51,500 |

**COMPARABLE #3**

1210 W.
ACACIA

| | |
|---|---|
| Price | $65,000 |
| Price/SF | 54.17 |
| Date | 2/21/89 |
| Age | 60 YEARS |
| Room Count | 6-3-1 |
| Living Area | 1,200 |
| Gross Adj. | 34% |
| Net Adj. | 19% |
| Value Indication | $52,500 |

Chapter 6

# Negotiations that Work, and the Magic of TRAIT in Due Diligence

## *The Street-Smart Way to Eliminate Risk*

At every stage in the purchase and resale of property, you will be negotiating something.

People do not make decisions easily. Once a decision is made they have to convince themselves that it is a good one. Having gone through the effort of negotiating, making up their minds, and proving to themselves that the decision is sound, they are reluctant to reopen the matter. In the process of deciding, they have further committed themselves by telling others that the deal is reasonable, so it becomes even harder to resist escalation. The difference between what they thought they were going to get and what they actually get becomes relatively less important.

Make the deal difficult to get! It is a fact of life: People put greater value on things that are hard to get. Sellers and buyers don't appreciate easy victories as much as they should. So, if you really want to make them happy, make them work hard for everything they get. Don't be in a big hurry to make concessions, to offer extra money or service.

### TIME

First, you must understand the key role that time plays in negotiations. The best negotiators use time to their advantage. For example, if you know that the other party to a home sale has a deadline, such as a forthcoming job transfer, a pending foreclosure, or a need to raise cash, you will have the upper hand in the negotiations.

He who cares least wins in the negotiation game. As in all negotiations, it is wise to walk away when the deal is not going your way. Never let your own time deadlines or the opposition's time limits push you to give in to reach a settlement.

No matter how desperate your time situation, act as if you have all the time in the world. Once the opposite party knows you have a deadline, such as that you must leave by a certain time or that you must be at your new location by a definite date, they can delay the real negotiating until just before the deadline — when you will be most vulnerable.

If you are the buyer, don't let yourself or anyone else on your negotiation team fall in love with the property so that you have to buy it regardless. If you are the seller, develop a game plan so a prospective buyer can't back you up against a time deadline and take advantage of your vulnerable situation.

## PATIENCE

Paralleling the importance of time is patience: Foreclosure buyers must learn to exercise patience in all negotiations. By using patience, you will give the seller time to understand your viewpoint before he settles on the price. It takes time to understand the issues, weigh the risks, and determine one's expectations. Patience gives the seller and his family time to get used to the idea that what they wish for must be reconciled with the realities of what they can get. In a quick negotiation this is not possible. Patience therefore is a major component of negotiations.

Patience gives the buyer and seller a chance to find how best to benefit each other before a negotiation begins. It is not possible for either side to know beforehand the best way to resolve the problems, issues, and risks. New alternatives are discovered as information is brought to light. Both sides can benefit as a result of patient bargaining.

Patience works. This is what it can accomplish for you:

It divides the seller's family. The anxious members of the family tire quickly of waiting and begin to pressure the procrastinator.

It can lower the other party's expectations. If members of the other party are anxious and concerned about making a deal, they will lower their aspirations if you are patient and wait them out.

It leads to concession after concession. Patience and the fact that you don't need to deal can easily create doubt in the opposition's mind. To relieve that anxiety the opposition will make concessions in the hope of concluding the negotiations.

It forces a new look at priorities. The members of the other party know their own motivations better than you do, and your patience will cause them to review their alternatives, which in essence boil down to cash today or nothing at the Trustee's/Sheriff's Sale tomorrow.

It separates wishes from realities. Your patience will force the opposition to lower unrealistic expectations to consummate a real-world negotiation.

It brings new problems and issues to the surface. Maybe the opposition is under time pressure. Possibly it is the money that's important, or it is the terms. Maybe a balloon payment is due. Try to ferret out any new problems that patience itself or delay will cause.

It gets other people involved. The possibility that the deal won't close right away will increase anxiety and doubt among the opposition. Expect the opposition to bring more firepower to the table: different family members, co-workers, senior officers, each trying to draw the negotiations to a close.

It can cause a change in leadership from husband to wife. Your negotiation may have been with the less motivated member or the procrastinator of the family. The party who feels the most threatened may then step forward and make the concessions needed to complete the deal.

It allows third parties to mediate. Patience will create the opportunity of bringing in an independent third party to help the two sides resolve their differences.

## PLAN AHEAD

Do not go into a negotiation without listing every issue beforehand. Determine the price you will pay (this is your aspiration level) and the minimum and maximum initial price for each issue.

Do not be tempted to play it by ear. Nobody is smart enough to know all the answers unless he has thought about the issue beforehand. Never let an issue be discussed unless you are prepared for it. If you are unprepared to handle an issue when it is raised, ask for a recess to think it over or delay the decision until another day.

## START WITH THE EASY ISSUES

It is better to start talks with those issues that are easy to settle rather than with the highly controversial ones. Agreement on controversial issues is easier to reach if the issues are tied to other issues on which agreement was more easily reached. Among the easy issues you might include: When will they move to a new location? Who will be responsible for the house cleaning upon departure? Among the difficult issues are the questions of how much you will pay and when the selling party gets the money. In discussing issues of whatever kind, keep in mind:

- It is more effective to present both sides of the issue than only one side.
- When the pros and cons of an issue are being discussed, it is better to present the viewpoint you favor last.
- Listeners remember the beginning and end of a presentation better than they remember the middle.
- Listeners remember the end better than the beginning, particularly when they are unfamiliar with the arguments.
- Conclusions should be clearly reviewed; don't leave the seller unclear about what was decided.
- Repetition of a message will help the other party to understand the issues and accept them.

Questions and answers can be regarded as negotiations in their own right. Every question has the character of a demand. Every answer is a concession. Those who demand better answers in the right way are more likely to get them. Negotiators who have the guts to be skeptical and to demand evidence get more information.

## OFFERS AND DEMANDS

Don't set the initial demand to close as your final objective — leave some room for negotiation.

There is sufficient evidence to conclude that it pays to start low. Don't be shy about asking for everything you might want and more. Don't set your initial offer too close to your expected final objective. Leave some room to negotiate. Otherwise you will be too rigid, and the other party will not have the satisfaction of negotiating with you. If you stop negotiations too soon and make very few concessions of any kind, the other party will feel that you are not flexible and have little interest in consummation of the agreement. The negotiation must be win-win and satisfactory to both parties.

## DEADLOCK

Deadlock is one of the most important tactics in negotiations. Almost nothing tests the strength and resolve of an opponent more. Yet most people avoid deadlock. They are afraid of it. Alienation and deadlock have a traumatic effect on people. Having gone into a negotiation desiring agreement, we are left at impasse with a sense of failure. We tend to lose confidence and question our own judgment. Was there something different we could have said or done? Should we have accepted the last offer?

For you, the power of deadlock lies in your understanding what it does to both parties. It is a test of resolve and strength. The buyer and the seller become more flexible by deadlock. Both are more willing to compromise, especially if an escape in good faith is possible (thus saving face). If you are willing to reach a deadlock, you are in a position to get better results.

Indeed, one of the best reasons for making an offer a person can't accept is to focus on what he will accept. When people believe that no deal is likely, they talk candidly with one another. It is then that they often reveal their real motivation and goals. There is no good faith. So make him/her an offer he/she must refuse.

## KNOW WHAT YOU WANT

Chester Karrass, in his book *Give and Take* (New York: Thomas T. Crowell), said again and again: "People who had higher aspiration levels got high settlements. Those who expected less were willing to accept less." According to Karrass, an individual's level of aspiration represents his intended performance goal. It is a reflection of how much he wants. It is a standard he sets for himself. It is not a wish, but a firm intention to perform, and it involves his self-image: Failure to perform results in loss of self-respect. Karrass further explained that aspiration levels, risk taking, and success are related. In choosing goals, men are like gamblers laying a bet. They balance a need for success with its tangible and intangible rewards against the probability of failure and its possible costs. He went on to say: "People who know where they are going and why make better negotiators."

## THE BOTTOM LINE

The outcome of successful negotiation depends on the power you have and your skill at using your power. No rules specify what is fair and what is not fair. Negotiations usually determine the outcome of who gets paid the most.

Concentrate on your opponent's problems. They are your opportunities. Don't forget that each of you is at the negotiation because he believes he has something to gain by being there.

## CONCESSIONS

Never give a concession without obtaining one in return. A concession granted too easily does not contribute to the opponent's sense of satisfaction as much as one he struggles to obtain.

When the opponent makes a concession, don't feel guilty or shy about accepting it. Be matter-of-fact and resist the impulse to tell the opponent how wise he is to give the concession.

Don't make the first concession. Concessions that are easily made can serve to separate the parties rather than bring them together. Keep track of how many concessions you make. The final number is an important matter that can provide bargaining leverage. Keep a record.

Do not signal your concessions too clearly. Be careful of setting up predictable patterns. Each concession should point to a possible settlement. However, your opponent should not be confident that he can foresee where it will be made or whether it will be made.

Do not agree with an opponent who claims that an issue is beyond compromise.

DON'T WORRY IF THEY DON'T LIKE YOU. In the final phase of negotiations most men will not succeed in winning their objectives if they also try to be popular.

Say NO! You'll be amazed how the terms of your deal improve when you learn to say no! There were hundreds of bank failures in 1989 and 1990 in the USA. How many of the failures do you think were caused because the bankers said "NO" to those fantastic real estate loans?

If you are a buyer, be aware that the seller is constantly measuring you and closing in for the kill. Time is always the seller's enemy, not yours. The longer you take, the longer you have the use of your money and control over the terms of the deal, and the more likely the terms will improve.

Be able to walk away from the table without a deal. If you have to deal, then all the other side needs to do to win is outsit you. Deals don't get worse when you walk away from the table.

Remember: With a little effort a better deal can be found for both parties. Never fear to negotiate, no matter how great the differences are.

Some do's and don't's:

- Do not assume that you know what your opponent wants.
- Do not assume that your aspiration level is high enough. It is possible your demands are too modest.
- Never accept the first offer. First, your opponent is probably willing to make additional concessions. Second, your opponent will be left with the feeling that perhaps he was a bit foolish for starting at the wrong price.

- Don't be intimidated by the "last and final" offer.
- Don't be afraid to admit you have made an error in coming to an agreement.
- Do not make your own "last and final" offer until you have evaluated precisely how the statement will be made and how discussions will be continued if it is not accepted.
- Don't pick just any time to ask a question; wait for the right time.
- Don't interrupt if the other person is talking. Write your question down and wait.
- Don't think you are a Perry Mason. A negotiation is not a courtroom trial.
- Don't ask antagonistic questions unless you want to fight.
- Don't ask questions that cast doubt on the honesty of the other party. They won't make him honest. Don't talk; listen. Explain the benefits and the gains. Don't assume that the opponent knows what he has to gain from a settlement.
- Do write out your questions in advance. Few of us are bright enough to think on our feet.
- Do use every early contact as an opportunity to find facts. A telephone response questionnaire is a valuable asset for getting facts about the seller.
- Do ask questions like a "country boy," down-to-earth, not like a sophisticated negotiator. This attitude encourages more informative answers.
- Remain silent after you raise a question.
- Do ask some questions for which you already have the answers. It can help you gauge the credibility of the other man.
- Do have the courage to ask what may appear to be dumb questions.
- Do be persistent in following up your questions if the answer is evasive or inadequate.
- Do ask questions of the seller's wife, children, relatives, and neighbors. They'll give you better answers than the seller will.

## DUE DILIGENCE

You've negotiated a great deal and now it's time to prove to yourself that the deal is great and, more importantly, eliminate as much risk as possible. If this property has structural problems, i.e., termite damage, deteriorating foundation, or leaking roof, that could spell trouble for you, the buyer. If you've been fair but tough as a negotiator, you probably have agreed with the seller to purchase the property at a bargain price. Your negotiations will also determine who is responsible for the unknown damages, if any.

Sellers rarely know if they have structural problems. Should the property have a toxic waste problem or bad water in the well, or if it's sliding down the hill, these problems will become yours when the title changes from the seller to you, the new buyer. Do not take title until you have completed your due diligence.

In my seminar classes, I use the simple acronym TRAIT to teach the attendees the importance of the structural inspections and appraisal. TRAIT — Termite, Roof, Appraisal, Home Inspection, and Title report — doesn't cover all the bases, but it will give you a reminder and systematic procedure to follow to prevent risk and not expose your precious capital to the risks of the problem properties.

To this list you should add the specific reports required in your area of the country. For example, in rural areas a well water report would be extremely important. In other areas, a toxic waste report may be required, or a radon gas report. This list could become quite lengthy. The lesson is: Don't purchase the property until you have the reports and you know exactly what encumbrances are burdening the property. Remember, when you buy the property, you get whatever encumbrances are on the property. It's up to you to negotiate them off the property. No report, no purchase.

The author has written and uses purchase contracts that allow for deductions to be taken from the seller's equity/purchase price. These deductions are itemized when the professional reports (TRAIT) have been evaluated and a purchase decision has been concluded.

It works like this: If the seller agrees to sell the equity for let's say $15,000, then you, the buyer, will request and pay for the TRAIT reports. However, it will be the seller's responsibility to pay for any damages that the professional reports expose/reveal. For the purpose of our example, let's assume that the roof was water-tight and the home inspection showed no adverse problems but the termite/structural pest report showed $3,500 water damage in the bathrooms. The seller would then receive less than the $15,000 because this new-found damage is the seller's responsibility and would be deducted from the equity. Therefore, $15,000 less the $3,500 would net the seller $11,500.

Provided you state it in your contract, the same situation would apply if the seller advised you that $50,000 was owing on the first mortgage but when the lender sent the loan statement it revealed a balance due of $51,000. This overage would also be the seller's responsibility. You, as the buyer, have no way of knowing what these statements will reflect until you do a preliminary title report/abstract report and you write the lender/beneficiary and request the exact loan amount due.

The foreclosure buyer should be cautious with regard to how the seller is handled. First, be sure your contract advises the seller of his responsibility to pay for any unknown damages. Additionally, advise the seller that the final disbursement of monies will only take place after the mortgagee/lender has given written confirmation of the amounts due on the loans.

**FINAL DISBURSEMENT OF FUNDS**

**Example**
Does not relate to any specific case study

TO: Jesse R. Carranza

FROM: New Growth Financial

DATE: May 24, 1991

The following represents the breakdown of expenses which were deducted from the net due seller per the Equity Purchase Agreement dated 5-6-91:

AGREED UPON PURCHASE PRICE....................$ 15,000.00

Actual 1st loan amount.......................$ 51,000.00
Presumed 1st loan amount.....................$ 50,000.00
Difference.........< 1,000.00 >

Actual 2nd loan amount.......................$ 11,000.00
Presumed 2nd loan amount.....................$ 10,000.00
Difference.........< 1,000.00 >

Actual 3rd loan amount.......................$
Presumed 3rd loan amount.....................$
Difference.........<  >

TOTAL..............$

EXPENSES:
Termite repair.............................$ 3,500.00
Roof repair................................$
Pre-payment penalty........................$
Actual appraisal below amount of Equity Purchase Contract.............$
Miscellaneous
.................$

TOTAL..............$ 3,500.00

AGREED UPON PURCHASE PRICE....................$ 15,000.00

TOTAL OF DIFFERENCE IN LOAN AMOUNTS...........$< 2,000.00 >

LESS MONIES ADVANCED..........................$< 0 >

LESS EXPENSES.................................$< 3,500.00 >

AMOUNT DUE SELLER.....$ 9,500.00

# *America's Oldest Exterminating Service*

**HOME OFFICE: 626 POTRERO AVENUE • SAN FRANCISCO 94110 • (415) 647-2323**

**WESTERN DIVISION OFFICES**

| | |
|---|---|
| ALBUQUERQUE, NEW MEXICO—(505) 266-5888 | LOS ANGELES, CALIFORNIA—(800) 662-7673 |
| DENVER, COLORADO—(303) 534-0014 | PHOENIX, ARIZONA—(602) 242-2583 |
| LAS VEGAS, NEVADA—(702) 876-0780 | SACRAMENTO, CALIFORNIA—(916) 383-7673 |

*Consult Your Local Telephone Directory for Branch Office Nearest You*

**AUTHORIZATION AGREEMENT**

TO OUR CLIENT

The work outlined in this Termite Inspection Report will be performed promptly by our trained personnel using the "ACT" SYSTEM if you will sign ONE COPY OF THIS "AUTHORIZATION AGREEMENT" AND MAIL. No postage or addressing necessary.

ACT "SINCE 1860" — America's Oldest Exterminating Service assures you of top quality performance. If the recommendations outlined or the information given is not in accord with known data or with the desires and instructions of the one ordering the report, inform our inspector immediately.

PROPERTY ADDRESS 2422 Carolina St. - Vallejo

ACT EXTERMINATOR COMPANY is hereby authorized to perform the work as recommended in our STANDARD INSPECTION REPORT FORM dated 7-2-, 19 90.

Charges to perform the work are itemized below. Please note that there may be considerable savings if all work is authorized. Where required by ordinance or statute Client shall be responsible for providing or installing acceptable smoke detection devices.

Item #1b...$307.00 - 2a...$3,395.00 - 9a...$142.00 -

9b...$195.00 - TOTAL:...$4,039.00

Payment for work is due upon completion. Inspection fee may not be included and may be billed separately. Areas treated with WOOD PRESERVATIVE and/or SOIL TOXICANT will be retreated at no charge if reinfestation occurs within one year. This agreement covers only the work stipulated herein. If concealed damage is exposed during the performance of this work or if additional work is required by the City or County Building Inspector over and above what is recommended in our report, such work will not be performed under this agreement. A SUPPLEMENTARY REPORT will be issued and a SEPARATE QUOTATION for such work will be submitted.

A partial payment and/or progress payments may be required unless funds are held in an active Escrow account.

A late payment charge of 1½% per month may be charged to delinquent accounts, plus court costs and attorneys' fees in the event action for collection is required. Prices quoted are subject to acceptance within thirty (30) days.

Section 8513 of the California Structural Pest Control Act requires that all licensed termite operators submit this NOTICE TO OWNER prior to entering into a contract.

NOTICE TO OWNER

Under the California Mechanics Lien Law, any structural pest control operator who contracts to do work for you, any contractor, subcontractor, laborer, supplier or other person who helps to improve your property, but is not paid for his work or supplies, has the right to enforce a claim against your property. This means that after a court hearing, your property could be sold by a court officer and the proceeds of the sale used to satisfy the indebtedness. This can happen even if you have paid your structural pest control operator in full if the subcontractors, laborers or suppliers remain unpaid.

To preserve their right to file a claim or lien against your property, certain claimants such as subcontractors or material suppliers are required to provide you with a document entitled "Preliminary Notice." Prime contractors and laborers for wages do not have to provide this notice. Its purpose is to notify you of persons who might have the right to file a lien against your property if not paid.

TITLE INSURANCE CO. ADDRESS AND ESCROW NO. (IF APPLICABLE)

YOU, THE BUYER, MAY CANCEL THIS TRANSACTION AT ANY TIME PRIOR TO MIDNIGHT OF THE THIRD BUSINESS DAY AFTER THE DATE OF THIS TRANSACTION. SEE THE ATTACHED NOTICE OF CANCELLATION FORM FOR AN EXPLANATION OF THIS RIGHT.

Accepted by ______________________
Owner or Agent

Address ______________________

Date ______________________

FORM 2999 T (Rev 12/85)

*Offices Coast to Coast*

NO. 14476

**Termite Inspection Report**

**R**
**A**
**I**
**T**

*... Coast to Coast . . . . Serving America over 100 years*

**STANDARD STRUCTURAL PEST CONTROL INSPECTION REPORT** T 0180B (1)

**(WOOD-DESTROYING PESTS OR ORGANISMS)**

This is an inspection report only - not a Notice of Completion.

| ADDRESS OF PROPERTY INSPECTED / BLDG NO | STREET | CITY | DATE OF INSPECTION |
|---|---|---|---|
| 2422 | CAROLINA ST. | VALLEJO 94590 CO CODE 07 | 7/2/90 |

*America's Oldest Exterminating Service*
A SUBSIDIARY OF AMERICAN BUILDING MAINTENANCE INDUSTRIES
5650 IMHOFF DR., SUITE "E"
CONCORD, CA. 94520
(415) 685-0505

Affix stamp here on Board copy only

**A LICENSED PEST CONTROL OPERATOR IS AN EXPERT IN HIS FIELD. ANY QUESTIONS RELATIVE TO THIS REPORT SHOULD BE REFERRED TO HIM.**

FIRM LICENSE NO. PR 0293 | CO. REPORT NO. | STAMP NO. 3037020P

Inspection Ordered by (Name and Address) Jesse R. Caranza 2422 CAROLINA ST., VALLEJO 94590
Report Sent to (Name and Address) SAME
Owner's Name and Address SAME
Name and Address of a Party in Interest

Original Report [X] Supplemental Report [ ] Limited Report [ ] Reinspection Report [ ] No. of Pages: ____

| YES | CODE | SEE DIAGRAM BELOW | YES | CODE | SEE DIAGRAM BELOW | YES | CODE | SEE DIAGRAM BELOW | YES | CODE | SEE DIAGRAM BELOW |
|---|---|---|---|---|---|---|---|---|---|---|---|
| | S-Subterranean Termites | | | B-Beetles-Other Wood Pests | | | Z-Dampwood Termites | | X | EM-Excessive Moisture Condition | |
| | K-Dry Wood Termites | | | FG-Faulty Grade Levels | | | SL-Shower Leaks | | X | IA-Inaccessible Areas | |
| X | F-Fungus or Dry Rot | | | EC-Earth-wood Contacts | | | CD-Cellulose Debris | | X | FI-Further Inspection Recom. | |

1. SUBSTRUCTURE AREA (soil conditions, accessibility, etc.) 1
2. Was Stall Shower water tested? NONE. Did floor coverings indicate leaks? NO.
3. FOUNDATIONS (Type, Relation to Grade, etc.) NONE.
4. PORCHES . . . STEPS . . . PATIOS CONCRETE.
5. VENTILATION (Amount, Relation to Grade, etc.) NONE.
6. ABUTMENTS . . . Stucco walls, columns, arches, etc. NONE.
7. ATTIC SPACES (accessibility, insulation, etc.) 7
8. GARAGES (Type, accessibility, etc.) DETACHED, NOT INSPECTED.
9. OTHER 9

DIAGRAM AND EXPLANATION OF FINDINGS (This report is limited to structure or structures shown on diagram.)

General Description ONE STORY STUCCO, FURNISHED AND OCCUPIED.

Inspection Tag Posted (location) ELECTRIC PANEL.

Other Inspection Tags ____

The interior of furnished rooms; floors under covering; the interior of hollow walls; spaces between a floor and ceiling or soffit below; structural segments to which there is no access without defacing property or tearing out lumber, masonry, or finished work; and built-in cabinet work are inaccessible for inspection and are not included in this report unless specifically indicated. Building contents, furniture, on the premises, are similarly not removed and areas which they cover are considered inaccessible for inspection. It must be understood that infestation or infection by wood-destroying pests or organisms may exist in the above referred to inaccessible areas without outward manifestation of said infestation or infection. If further inspection of any area is desired, it will be performed upon authorization for which there may be an additional charge.

It is recommended that all items in this report be completed. ACT EXTERMINATOR COMPANY assumes no responsibility for infestations, infections, or damage resulting from any items not completed by this Company.
Prior to work being performed by any person or firm other than ACT EXTERMINATOR COMPANY, ACT should be contacted since we cannot be responsible, nor can we certify as to the presence or absence of infestations or infections where we have not re-inspected prior to the closing of any areas in which work or treatment will be or has been performed.
An additional charge will be made for each re-inspection performed where ACT has not done the work nor issued a completion notice for such work.

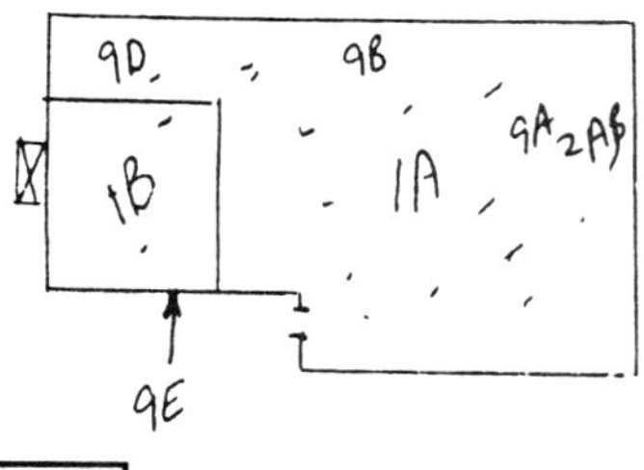


SUBSTRUCTURE AREA:

1A. AS THE STRUCTURE IS CONSTRUCTED OVER CONCRETE SLAB, WITH FINISHED WALLS AND FLOOR-COVERING, THERE IS NO WAY OF DETECTING INFEST-ATION CONCEALED BELOW. ROSE EXTERMINATOR COMPANY ACCEPTS NO RESPONSIBILITY FOR INFEST-ATIONS WHICH MAY ARISE IN THE FUTURE.

1B. PORTIONS OF STRUCTURE ARE INACCESSIBLE DUE TO RAISED FLOOR.

RECOMMENDATION: IF FURTHER INSPECTION IS DESIRED CUT ACCESS FOR FURTHER INSPECTION OF AREA BELOW.

STALL SHOWER:

2A. EXCESSIVE MOISTURE NOTED TO SHEETROCK OF HALL BATHROOM SHOWER OVER THE TUB.

RECOMMENDATION: REMOVE THE WALL COVERING, INSTILL WATERPROOF SHEETROCK AND NEW CERAMIC TILE OVER MASONRY BACKING. SHOULD DAMAGE

**Termite Inspection Report**
**R**
**A**
**I**
**T**

y WILLIAM PERRY License No. 15641 Signature

**YOU ARE ENTITLED TO OBTAIN COPIES OF ALL REPORTS AND COMPLETION NOTICES ON THIS PROPERTY FILED WITH THE BOARD DURING THE PRECEDING TWO YEARS UPON PAYMENT OF A $2.00 SEARCH FEE TO: STRUCTURAL PEST CONTROL BOARD, 1430 HOWE AVE., SACRAMENTO, CA 95825.**

T 0180 (2)

SECOND PAGE OF STANDARD INSPECTION REPORT ON THE PROPERTY LOCATED AT:

Address of Property Inspected: 2422 (Bldg. No.) CAROLINA ST. (Street) VALLEJO (City)

3037020P (Stamp No.) 7/2/90 (Date of Inspection)

2A. RECOMMENDATION CON'T: EXTEND INTO THE WALL STUDS, THE ADDITIONAL WORK WILL BE PERFORMED AT OWNER'S DIRECTION AND ADDITIONAL EXPENSE.

2B. TOILET NOTED LOOSE IN HALL BATHROOM.

RECOMMENDATION: OWNER TO CONTRACT PLUMBER FOR NECESSARY REPAIRS.

ATTIC:

7A. OWNER TO SIGN DAMAGE WAIVER IF INSPECTION OF ATTIC IS DESIRED.

OTHER:

9A. FUNGUS DAMAGE NOTED TO SHELF UNDER HALL BATHROOM VANITY.

RECOMMENDATION: REMOVE FUNGUS DAMAGE SHELF AND REPLACE WITH NEW.

9B. EXCESSIVE MOISTURE NOTED SHEETROCK UNDER KITCHEN SINK.

RECOMMENDATION: REMOVE SHEETROCK FOR FURTHER INSPECTION OF AREA BEHIND SHEETROCK. REPLACE SHEETROCK WITH NEW.

9C. EXCESSIVE MOISTURE NOTED SHEETROCK AROUND WINDOWS THIS IS COMMONLY DUE TO CONDENSATION.

RECOMMENDATION: OWNER TO KEEP AREAS UNDER OBSERVATION.

9D. LAUNDRY ROOM WAS INSPECTED AS POSSIBLE DUE TO HEAVY STORAGE.

RECOMMENDATION: IF FURTHER INSPECTION IS DESIRED OWNER TO REMOVE STORAGE.

9E. WINDOW NOTED BROKEN AT FRONT OF STRUCTURE WHICH MAY RESULT IN MOISTURE INTRUSION.

RECOMMENDATION: ONWER TO CONTRACT FOR REPLACEMENT OF WINDOW.

9F. MOISTURE STAINS NOTED TO ROOF EVES AROUND STRUCTURE.

RECOMMENDATION: WE RECOMMEND THE OWNER RETAIN THE SERVICES OF A QUALIFIED ROOFING CONTRACTOR TO EVALUATE THE PRESENT CONDITION OF ROOF AND MAKE ANY AND ALL NECESSARY REPAIRS.

9G. MISSING STUCCO AND STUCCO CRACKS NOTED TO EXTERIOR OF STRUCTURE.

RECOMMENDATION: OWNER TO SEAL AND MAINTAIN DURING NORMAL HOME MAINTENANCE.

NOTES:

A. SHOULD DAMAGE EXTEND INTO HIDDEN OR INACCESSIBLE AREAS DURING THE COURSE OF OUR REPAIRS, A SUPPLEMENTAL REPORT WILL BE ISSUED DESCRIBING OUR FINDINGS, RECOMMENDATIONS AND FURTHER COST.

B. THIS INSPECTION DOES NOT INCLUDE SURVEY OF THE APPLIANCE, HEATING, ELECTRICAL AND ROOF SYSTEMS. PERSONS DESIRING SUCH SHOULD CONSULT WITH THE PROPER TRADESMEN.

C. PRICES UPON REQUEST.

WP/DB

**Termite Inspection Report**

**R**
**A**
**I**
**T**

ROOF IMSPECTION AND REPORT #72490

NAPA VALLEY ROOFING & CONSTRUCTION

NAPA 253-9293

610 Trancas Street
Napa, CA 94558
CONTRACTOR'S LICENSE # 528492 • FREE ESTIMATES

VALLEJO 642-3780

| NAME | PHONE | DATE |
|---|---|---|
| JESSE CARRANZA | (415) 837-2106 | 7-24-90 |
| ADDRESS | JOB ADDRESS | |
| 785 FRONT ST. | 2422 CAROLINA ST | |
| CITY | CITY | |
| DANVILLE, CA. 94526 | VALLEJO, CA. | |

We propose to furnish all tools and equipment, all materials, and perform all labor necessary to complete the following:

AFTER A THOROUGH INSPECTION OF THE ROOFS AT THE ABOVE NAMED LOCATION, I HAVE FOUND TO BE IN THE FOLLOWING CONDITION:

1. DWELLING: FAIR CONDITION, PROBABLY 10-12 YEARS OLD. DETERIORATION NOTICED THROUGHOUT. PROBABLY SERVICABLE FOR TWO TO THREE MORE YEARS WITH REPAIR.

A. REPAIR; SEAL ALL PIPE/VeNT FLASHINGS, ETC. AS NECESSARY USING FLASHING COMPOUND AND NYLON WEBBING. COST OF $275.00

B. RE-ROOF; REMOVE HIP/RIDGE SHINGLES OVERLAY COMPOSITION SHINGLES, INSTALL NEW PIPE/VENT FLASHINGS, AS NECESSARY. TRIM WITH HIP/RIDGE. CLEAN UP HAUL DEBRIS. COST OF $2,500.00

2. GARADGE: POOR CONDITION. UNSERVICABLE. DETERIORATED BEYOND REPAIR.

A. INSTALL NEW ROOFING AS DESCRIBED ABOVE IN 1-B. COST OF $1,100.00

T
**Roof Inspection**
A **Report**
I
T

**We Propose** hereby to furnish material and labor — complete in accordance with above s

SIXTY FIVE DOLLARS dollars ($65.00)

Payment to be made as follows:

DUE AND PAYABLE

Terms: Accounts are due and payable within 30 days of completion. Past due acconts subject to late penalty plus finance charge of 1½% per month, unless other terms are endorsed by seller on sales contact, in which case I will pay strictly according to terms endorsed. I agree to pay any legal or court costs necessary to collect my account if it becomes past due and delinquent.

All material is guaranteed to be as specified. All work to be completed in a workmanlike manner according to standard practices. Any alteration or deviation from above specifications involving extra costs will be executed only upon written orders, and will become an extra charge over and above the estimate. All agreements contingent upon strikes, accidents or delays beyond our control. Owner to carry fire, tornado and other necessary insurance. Our workers are fully covered by Workmen's Compensation Insurance.

Authorized Signature [signature]

Note: This proposal may be withdrawn by us if not accepted within ______ days.

**Acceptance of Proposal** — The above prices, specifications and conditions are satisfactory and are hereby accepted. You are authorized to do the work as specified. Payment will be made as outlined above.

Date of Acceptance: ______

Signature ______

Signature ______

## INVOICE

**TRAIT Appraisal Report**

From:

RESIDENTIAL PROPERTY, INC.
1981 NORTH BROADWAY, SUITE 330
WALNUT CREEK, CA 94596

FILE NUMBER: RA7010C

INVOICE

To:

Attention: DIANE

NEW GROWTH FINANCIAL
185 FRONT STREET, STE. 207
DANVILLE, CA 94526

| Invoice Date | Appraisal Date | Appraiser | Client Case Number | Appraisal Office Tax ID Number | Appraisal Office Phone Number |
|---|---|---|---|---|---|
| 07/06/90 | 07/03/90 | JU | | 68-0030262 | 415-935-3444 |

PROPERTY INFORMATION

Purchaser/Borrower NEW GROWTH
Property Address 2422 CAROLINA STREET Unit
City VALLEJO Subdivision
County SOLANO State CA Zip 94591
Legal Description
Map Reference 134-E2

INVOICE INFORMATION

| | |
|---|---|
| Appraisal Fee Amount | $ 275.00 |
| Mail or Handling Fee | $ |
| Additional Charges 1 | $ |
| Additional Charges 2 | $ |
| Additional Charges 3 | $ |
| Sales Tax | $ |
| Total Amount of Invoice | $ 275.00 |

**Thank you for your business ! ! !**

| Invoice Date | Appraisal Date | Appraiser | File Number | Client Case Number | Client's Phone Number |
|---|---|---|---|---|---|
| 07/06/90 | 07/03/90 | JU | RA7010C | | 827-2106 |

From:

NEW GROWTH FINANCIAL
185 FRONT STREET, STE. 207
DANVILLE, CA 94526

AMOUNT DUE
$ 275.00

To:

Attention: ACCOUNTING DEPARTMENT

RESIDENTIAL PROPERTY, INC.
1981 NORTH BROADWAY, SUITE 330
WALNUT CREEK, CA 94596

AMOUNT ENCLOSED
$ ________

TERMS - Balance due upon receipt of invoice
Please return this portion with your payment. Thank you !

Valuation Section **UNIFORM RESIDENTIAL APPRAISAL REPORT** File No. RA7010C

Purpose of Appraisal is to estimate Market Value as defined in the Certification & Statement of Limiting Conditions.

**COST APPROACH**

BUILDING SKETCH (SHOW GROSS LIVING AREA ABOVE GRADE)
If for Freddie Mac or Fannie Mae, show only square foot calculations and cost approach comments in this space.

SEE ATTACHED SKETCH.

NO FUNCTIONAL OR EXTERNAL OBSOLESCENCE OBSERVED AT TIME OF INSPECTION.

LAND TO VALUE RATIO OF 30% TYPICAL FOR AREA.

LAND VALUE BY ABSTRACTION.

ESTIMATED REPRODUCTION COST-NEW-OF IMPROVEMENTS:

| | | |
|---|---|---|
| Dwelling 1455 Sq. Ft. @ $65.00 | = $ | 94,575 |
| Sq. Ft. @ $ | = | |
| Extras FIREPLACE | = | 3,000 |
| | = | |
| Special Energy Efficient Items | = | |
| Porches, Patios, etc. | = | 5,000 |
| Garage/Carport 667 Sq. Ft. @ $25.00 | = | 16,675 |
| Total Estimated Cost New | = $ | 119,250 |
| Less Depreciation: Physical 47,500 / Functional 0 / External 0 | = $ | 47,500 |
| Depreciated Value of Improvements | = $ | 71,750 |
| Site Imp. 'as is' (driveway, landscaping, etc.) | = $ | 10,000 |
| ESTIMATED SITE VALUE (If leasehold, show only leasehold value) | = $ | 35,000 |
| INDICATED VALUE BY COST APPROACH | = $ | 116,750 |

(Not Required by Freddie Mac and Fannie Mae)
Does property conform to applicable HUD/VA property standards? ☐ Yes ☐ No
If No, explain: N/A

Construction Warranty ☐ Yes ☒ No
Name of Warranty Program N/A
Warranty Coverage Expires N/A

**SALES COMPARISON ANALYSIS**

The undersigned has recited three recent sales of properties most similar and proximate to subject and has considered these in the market analysis. The description includes a dollar adjustment, reflecting market reaction to those items of significant variation between the subject and comparable properties. If a significant item in the comparable property is superior to, or more favorable than, the subject property, a minus (-) adjustment is made, thus reducing the indicated value of subject; if a significant item in the comparable is inferior to, or less favorable than, the subject property, a plus (+) adjustment is made, thus increasing the indicated value of the subject.

| ITEM | SUBJECT | COMPARABLE NO. 1 | | COMPARABLE NO. 2 | | COMPARABLE NO. 3 | |
|---|---|---|---|---|---|---|---|
| Address | 2422 CAROLINA ST | 625 SHELDON AVE VALLEJO, 135A2 | | 615 RUSSELL ST VALLEJO, 135A3 | | 33 BALBOA AVE VALLEJO, 135B3 | |
| Proximity to Subject | | 1 BLOCK NW | | 4 BLOCKS S | | 6 BLOCKS SE | |
| Sales Price | $VALUATION | | $ 110,000 | | $ 110,000 | | $ 122,000 |
| Price/Gross Liv. Area | $N/A | $86.48 | | $122.77 | | $87.14 | |
| Data Source | INSPECTION | MLS#201510/DOC#47432 | | MLS#200978/DOC#36367 | | MLS#292284/DOC#84461 | |
| VALUE ADJUSTMENTS | DESCRIPTION | DESCRIPTION | +(-)$ Adjustment | DESCRIPTION | +(-)$ Adjustment | DESCRIPTION | +(-)$ Adjustment |
| Sales or Financing Concessions | | CONVENTIONAL NO CONCESS. | | CONVENTIONAL NO CONCESS. | | 90% CONV NO CONCESS. | |
| Date of Sale/Time | 6/90 | 6/90 COE | | 5/90 COE | | 11/89 COE | |
| Location | RES ST | NR COMML | +6000 | RES ST | | RES ST | |
| Site/View | 6534/NONE | 5000/NONE | | 5000/NONE | | 9147/NONE | -2000 |
| Design and Appeal | CONV/AVG | CONV/AVG | | CONV/AVG | | CONV/AVG | |
| Quality of Construction | AVERAGE | AVERAGE | | AVERAGE | | AVERAGE | |
| Age | A-35, E-30 | A-40, E-25 | | A-46, E-30 | | A-35, E-25 | |
| Condition | AVERAGE | GOOD | -6000 | GOOD | -6000 | GOOD | -6000 |
| Above Grade Room Count (Total / Bdrms / Baths) | 5 / 3 / 1 | 6 / 3 / 1.5 | -1000 | 4 / 2 / 1 | | 6 / 3 / 2 | -1500 |
| Gross Living Area | 1455 Sq. Ft. | 1272 Sq. Ft. | +3500 | 896 Sq. Ft. | +11000 | 1400 Sq. Ft. | |
| Basement & Finished Rooms Below Grade | NONE | NONE | | NONE | | NONE | |
| Functional Utility | AVERAGE | AVERAGE | | AVERAGE | | AVERAGE | |
| Heating/Cooling | FAU/NONE | FAU/NONE | | FLR/NONE | | WALL/NONE | |
| Garage/Carport | 2 DETACHED | 1 ATTACHED | +1500 | 1 ATTACHED | +1500 | 1 ATTACHED | +1500 |
| Porches, Patio, Pools, etc. | PATIO | PATIO | | PATIO | | PATIO | |
| Special Energy Efficient Items | NONE NOTED | NONE KNOWN | | NONE KNOWN | | NONE KNOWN | |
| Fireplace(s) | 1 FIREPLACE | 1 FIREPLACE | | NO FIREPLACE | +1500 | NO FIREPLACE | +1500 |
| Other (e.g. kitchen equip., remodeling) | RECENT KIT CAB/LR PNT | NONE | SEE COND ADJ | NONE | SEE COND ADJ | NONE | SEE COND ADJ |
| Net Adj. (total) | | ☒ + ☐ - | $ +4000 | ☒ + ☐ - | $ +8000 | ☐ + ☒ - | $ -6500 |
| Indicated Value of Subject | | | $ 114,000 | | $ 118,000 | | $ 115,500 |

Comments on Sales Comparison: SEE ATTACHED ADDENDUM.

INDICATED VALUE BY SALES COMPARISON APPROACH $ 115,000
INDICATED VALUE BY INCOME APPROACH (If Applicable) Estimated Market Rent $N/A /Mo. x Gross Rent Multiplier N/A = $ N/A

R E

This appraisal is made ☒ 'as is' ☐ subject to the repairs, alterations, inspections or conditions listed below ☐ completion per plans and specifications.
Comments and Conditions of Appraisal: ALL SALES ARE CLOSED. NO CONDITIONS.

**T**
**R**
**Appraisal**
**I Report**
**T**

[R]econciliation: VALUE IS BASED ON THE COST APPROACH AND THE SALES COMPARISON ANALYSIS WITH THE [GREA]TER EMPHASIS ON THE LATTER.

[This ap]praisal is based upon the above requirements, the certification, contingent and limiting conditions, and Market Value definition that are stated in [...] FmHA, HUD &/or VA instructions.
[Fr]eddie Mac Form 439 (Rev. 7/86)/Fannie Mae Form 1004B (Rev. 7/86) filed with client JULY 3 19 90 ☒ attached.
[I] ESTIMATE THE MARKET VALUE, AS DEFINED, OF THE SUBJECT PROPERTY AS OF JULY 3 19 90 to be $ 115,000
[I] certify: that to the best of my (our) knowledge and belief the facts and data used herein are true and correct; that I (we) personally inspected the subject [propert]y, both inside and out, and have made an exterior inspection of all comparable sales cited in this report; and that I (we) have no undisclosed interest, present [or pros]pective therein.

[Apprais]er(s) SIGNATURE Review Appraiser SIGNATURE ☐ Did ☐ Did Not Inspect Property
NAME PAUL E. CHANDLER/MAI/J.HART (If applicable) NAME

Freddie Mac Form 70 10/86 (12 ch.) MCS, Richardson, TX (214) 699-7783 Fannie Mae Form 1004 10/86-1

Property Description & Analysis **UNIFORM RESIDENTIAL APPRAISAL REPORT** File No. RA7010C

**SUBJECT**

Property Address 2422 CAROLINA STREET — Census Tract 2503
City VALLEJO — County SOLANO — State CA — Zip Code 94590
Legal Description APN: 0071-033-07, LOT 43, SPRINGS MANOR 3
Owner/Occupant OWNER — Map Reference 135A3
Sale Price $ VALUATION — Date of Sale N/A
Loan charges/concessions to be paid by seller $ N/A
R.E. Taxes $ SEE PRELIM — Tax Year 89/90 — HOA $/Mo. N/A
Lender/Client NEW GROWTH FINANCIAL

PROPERTY RIGHTS APPRAISED: [X] Fee Simple; [ ] Leasehold; [ ] Condominium (HUD/VA); [ ] De Minimis PUD

LENDER DISCRETIONARY USE: Sale Price $ VALUATION; Date N/A; Mortgage Amount $; Mortgage Type; Discount Points and Other Concessions; Paid by Seller $; Source

**NEIGHBORHOOD**

| | | | | |
|---|---|---|---|---|
| LOCATION | [ ] Urban | [X] Suburban | [ ] Rural |
| BUILT UP | [X] Over 75% | [ ] 25-75% | [ ] Under 25% |
| GROWTH RATE | [ ] Rapid | [X] Stable | [ ] Slow |
| PROPERTY VALUES | [ ] Increasing | [X] Stable | [ ] Declining |
| DEMAND/SUPPLY | [ ] Shortage | [X] In Balance | [ ] Over Supply |
| MARKETING TIME | [X] Under 3 Mos. | [ ] 3-6 Mos. | [ ] Over 6 Mos. |

PRESENT LAND USE %: Single Family 70; 2-4 Family 5; Multi-family; Commercial 25; Industrial; Vacant
LAND USE CHANGE: Not Likely [X]; Likely [ ]; In process [ ]; To: N/A
PREDOMINANT OCCUPANCY: Owner [X]; Tenant [ ]; Vacant (0-5%) [X]; Vacant (over 5%) [ ]
SINGLE FAMILY HOUSING: Price $ (000) / Age (yrs): 90 Low 30; 135 High 50; Predominant 115 - 40

| NEIGHBORHOOD ANALYSIS | Good | Avg. | Fair | Poor |
|---|---|---|---|---|
| Employment Stability | | X | | |
| Convenience to Employment | | X | | |
| Convenience to Shopping | | X | | |
| Convenience to Schools | | X | | |
| Adequacy of Public Transportation | | X | | |
| Recreation Facilities | | X | | |
| Adequacy of Utilities | | X | | |
| Property Compatibility | X | | | |
| Protection from Detrimental Cond. | | X | | |
| Police & Fire Protection | | X | | |
| General Appearance of Properties | X | | | |
| Appeal to Market | X | | | |

Note: Race or the racial composition of the neighborhood are not considered reliable appraisal factors.

COMMENTS: THE SUBJECT IS LOCATED IN A NEIGHBORHOOD OF AVERAGE QUALITY SINGLE FAMILY HOMES SHOWING AN AVERAGE LEVEL OF MAINTENANCE. THE NEIGHBORHOOD IS BORDERED ON THE NORTH BY A COMMERCIAL STRIP, (LOCATED ALONG SPRINGS ROAD). FREEWAY ACCESS (INTERSTATE 80) IS LOCATED APPROXIMATELY 3 BLOCKS WEST FOR COMMUTE ACCESS.

**SITE**

Dimensions SEE ATTACHED PLAT MAP
Site Area 6534 SQUARE FEET — Corner Lot YES
Zoning Classification LDR-LOW DENSITY RES. — Zoning Compliance YES
HIGHEST & BEST USE: Present Use YES — Other Use N/A

| UTILITIES | Public | Other |
|---|---|---|
| Electricity | X | |
| Gas | X | |
| Water | X | |
| Sanitary Sewer | X | |
| Storm Sewer | X | |

| SITE IMPROVEMENTS | Type | Public | Private |
|---|---|---|---|
| Street | ASPHALT | X | |
| Curb/Gutter | CONCRETE | X | |
| Sidewalk | CONCRETE | X | |
| Street Lights | VAPOR | X | |
| Alley | NONE | | |

Topography LEVEL; Size AVERAGE FOR AREA; Shape IRREGULAR; Drainage APPEARS ADEQUATE; View NONE; Landscaping AVERAGE; Driveway CONCRETE; Apparent Easements NONE NOTED; FEMA Flood Hazard Yes* ZN C No X; FEMA* Map/Zone 060374 0010C2/22/83

COMMENTS (Apparent adverse easements, encroachments, special assessments, slide areas, etc.): DURING THE PHYSICAL INSPECTION OF THE SUBJECT PROPERTY, NO ADVERSE CONDITIONS WERE NOTED ON SITE. SEE PRELIMINARY TITLE REPORT FOR ANY ADVERSE CONDITIONS OF PUBLIC RECORD. PRELIM. WAS NOT REVIEWED AS PART OF THIS APPRAISAL.

**IMPROVEMENTS**

GENERAL DESCRIPTION: Units 1; Stories 1; Type (Det./Att.) DETACHED; Design (Style) CONV; Existing YES; Proposed NO; Under Construction NO; Age (Yrs.) +-35; Effective Age (Yrs.) 30
EXTERIOR DESCRIPTION: Foundation CONCRETE; Exterior Walls STUCCO; Roof Surface COMP. SHGL; Gutters & Dwnspts. GALV.STEEL; Window Type MET. SLIDE; Storm Sash NO; Screens METAL; Manufactured House NO
FOUNDATION: Slab YES; Crawl Space NO; Basement NONE; Sump Pump NONE; Dampness NONE NOTED; Settlement NONE NOTED; Infestation NONE NOTED
BASEMENT: Area Sq. Ft. NONE; % Finished N/A; Ceiling N/A; Walls N/A; Floor N/A; Outside Entry N/A
INSULATION: Roof [ ]; Ceiling UNK [X]; Walls UNK [X]; Floor [ ]; None [ ]; Adequacy AVG. [X]; Energy Efficient Items: NONE OBSERVED

**ROOM LIST**

| ROOMS | Foyer | Living | Dining | Kitchen | Den | Family Rm. | Rec. Rm. | Bedrooms | # Baths | Laundry | Other | Area Sq. Ft. |
|---|---|---|---|---|---|---|---|---|---|---|---|---|
| Basement | | | | | | | | | | | | NONE |
| Level 1 | X | 1 | AREA | 1 | | | | 3 | 1 | X | | 1455 |
| Level 2 | | | | | | | | | | | | |

Finished area above grade contains: 5 Rooms; 3 Bedroom(s); 1 Bath(s); 1455 Square Feet of Gross Living Area

**INTERIOR**

SURFACES (Materials/Condition): Floors CPT/VNL/TL/AVG; Walls DRYWALL/AVG; Trim/Finish WOOD/AVG; Bath Floor VINYL/AVG; Bath Wainscot NONE/*SEE ADD.; Doors WOOD/GD; Fireplace(s) BRICK #1
HEATING: Type FAU; Fuel GAS; Condition AVG.; Adequacy AVG.
COOLING: Central; Other NONE; Condition; Adequacy AVG.
KITCHEN EQUIP.: Refrigerator [ ]; Range/Oven [X]; Disposal [ ]; Dishwasher [X]; Fan/Hood [X]; Compactor [ ]; Washer/Dryer [ ]; Microwave [ ]; Intercom [ ]
ATTIC: None [ ]; Stairs [ ]; Drop Stair [ ]; Scuttle [X]; Floor [ ]; Heated [ ]; Finished [ ]; UNFIN. [X]

| IMPROVEMENT ANALYSIS | Good | Avg. | Fair | Poor |
|---|---|---|---|---|
| Quality of Construction | | X | | |
| Condition of Improvements | | X | | |
| Room Sizes/Layout | | X | | |
| Closets and Storage | | X | | |
| Energy Efficiency | | X | | |
| Plumbing-Adequacy & Condition | | X | | |
| Electrical-Adequacy & Condition | | X | | |
| Kitchen Cabinets-Adequacy & Cond. | | X | | |
| Compatibility to Neighborhood | X | | | |
| Appeal & Marketability | X | | | |

Estimated Remaining Economic Life; Estimated Remaining Physical Life

**AUTOS**

CAR STORAGE: Garage [X]; Carport [ ]; None [ ]; No. Cars 2; Condition AVG.; Attached [ ]; Detached [X]; Built-in [ ]; Adequate [X]; Inadequate [ ]; Electric Door [ ]; House Entry [ ]; Outside Entry [X]; Bsment Entry [ ]

**COMMENTS**

Additional features: THE SUBJECT PROPERTY'S ORIGINAL 2 CAR GARAGE (+-475'), WAS CONVERTED SEVERAL Y AGO INTO AN EXPANDED LIVING ROOM. WORK IS OF SIM. QUALITY & FUNCTION WITH INTERIOR ACCES CARPET FLR COVERING & ADEQUATE HEAT. NO PERMIT INFO. WAS AVAILABLE. INCLUDED IN RM CT & S

Depreciation (Physical, functional and external inadequacies, repairs needed, modernization, etc.): DURING THE INSPECTION OF THE SUBJEC PROPERTY, NO SIGNS OF FUNCTIONAL OR EXTERNAL INADEQUACIES WERE OBSERVED.
SEE ATTACHED ADDENDUM

General market conditions and prevalence and impact in subject/market area regarding loan discounts, interest buydowns and concessions: THE SUBJEC NEIGHBORHOOD HAS BOTH GOVERNMENT AND CONVENTIONAL FINANCING, THEREFORE SELLER'S CONCESSIC EXIST, HOWEVER THEY DO NOT APPEAR TO AFFECT MARKET VALUE. THE SUBJECT HAS NOT TRANSFERRED WITHIN THE LAST TWELVE MONTHS ACCORDING TO REDI.

Freddie Mac Form 70 10/86 (12 ch.) — MCS, Richardson, Texas (214) 699-7783 — Fannie Mae Form 1004 10/86-1

**TRAIT Appraisal Report**

# APPRAISAL ADDENDUM

BORROWER: Valuation  MAP REFERENCE: 135A3

ADDRESS: 2422 Carolina Street

CITY: Vallejo  STATE: CA  ZIP: 94590

LENDER: New Growth Mortgage

APPRAISERS: Paul E. Chandler & Julie Hart

## COMMENTS ON SUBJECT PROPERTY

The subject property has the following updates: living room was painted approximately 3 years ago; kitchen was updated approximately 4 years ago with new cabinets, vinyl floor covering and butcher block countertops.

The appraiser noted the following items of deferred maintenance which are reflected in its overall average condition rating: exterior trim paint is chipped and peeling and the exterior paint appears worn; living room carpeting is worn and not properly stretched, causing an uneven surface; there is currently no wainscoting for the bathroom shower/bathtub. The exposed drywall is currently covered with heavy plastic; some of the closet doors are missing; and the composition shingle roof appears slightly worn, however, the appraiser noted no signs of interior water damage.

## COMMENTS ON SALES COMPARISON

Comparable number four is a currently pending sale in the subject's neighborhood and was used for its proximity, similar room/bedroom count, age, square footage, garage conversion and time of sale. Adjusted sales price is based on the list price, however, per the listing agent, the sales price is within 1% of the list price. Estimated close of escrow is in two weeks.

Comparable number one front across the street to commercial buildings and is located approximately 100' south of the commercial strip along Springs Road, buffered by +-one single family home. This location is considered to be substantially inferior to the subject's and as such was given a $6000 location adjustment.

Comparable number three has a substantially larger lot than the subject and was adjusted $2000. (Approximately 76 cents per square foot).

All of the four comparables used are in superior condition to the subject, and therefore each was adjusted $6000.

Comparable number one has 1/2 bath more than the subject, and comparable number three has one full bath more. Comparable number one was adjusted $1000 and number three was adjusted $1500.

Comparable number one and two have less square footage than the subject, with comparable number two also having one less bedroom. Each comparable was given a square footage adjustment based on approximately $20 square foot, with comparable number one being adjusted $3500 and comparable number two $11000.

Comparables one, two and three all have one less garage than the subject, and each was adjusted $1500. Comparable number four has no garage parking, (due to its having been converted), and was adjusted $3000.

Comparables two, three and four were each adjusted $1500 for lack of a fireplace.

Comparable number four has a newly remodeled kitchen, new carpet floor covering, and new interior and exterior paint and was given an adjustment of $3000.

The comparables selected were considered to be the best available at the time of the appraisal and they support the value indication of the subject.

All comparables given equal consideration.

PAUL E. CHANDLER, MAI  DATE 7-3-90

JULIE HART  DATE 7-3-90

**T**
**R**
**A**ppraisal
**I** Report
**T**

2422 CAROLINA ST

VALLEJO, CA

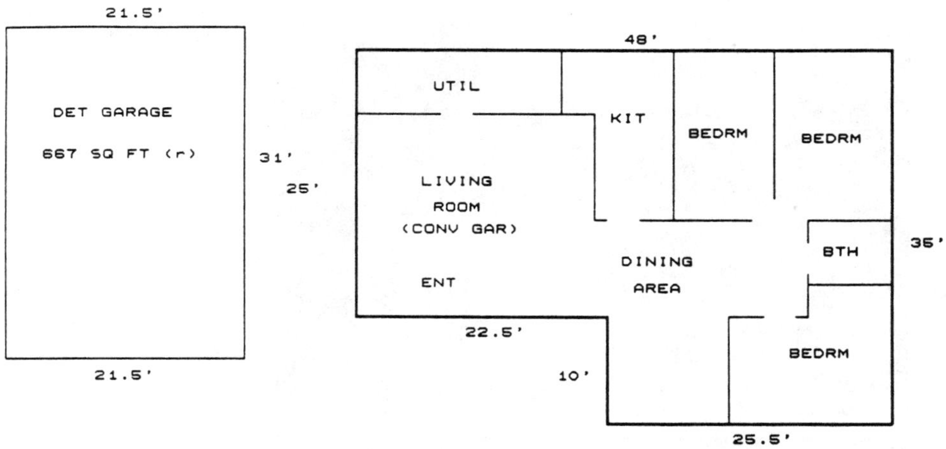


| Measurements | | | Total |
|---|---|---|---|
| 25.5' x | 35.0' | = | 892.5' |
| 22.5' x | 25.0' | = | 562.5' |
| First Level: | | | 1,455.0' |

| | |
|---|---|
| First Level: | 1,455.0' |
| Total area: | 1,455.0' |

Scale: 1" = 12'

T
R
Appraisal
I Report
T

## PHOTOGRAPH ADDENDUM

| | | |
|---|---|---|
| BORROWER: Valuation<br>ADDRESS: 2422 Carolina Street<br>CITY: Vallejo<br>LENDER: New Growth Financial | STATE: CA | ZIP: 94590 |

FRONT OF SUBJECT PROPERTY

REAR OF SUBJECT PROPERTY

STREET SCENE

PROPERTY SCIENCES

## COMPARABLE SALES

BORROWER: Valuation
ADDRESS: 2422 Carolina Street
CITY: Vallejo STATE: CA ZIP: 94590
LENDER: New Growth Financial

**COMPARABLE SALE #1**
625 SHELDON AVE.

**COMPARABLE SALE #2**
615 RUSSELL STREET

**COMPARABLE SALE #3**
33 BALBOA AVE.

**PROPERTY SCIENCES**

(415) 685-9220

**RESIDENTIAL INSPECTION SERVICE**
**1647 Willow Pass Road, Suite 290 Concord, CA 94520**

*2422 Carolina Street, Vallejo, CA.*

***This Confidential Report Was Prepared For:***

*New Growth Financial*

***IMPORTANT NOTICE TO THIRD PARTIES***
***OR OTHER PURCHASERS OF THIS PROPERTY:***

***RECEIPT OF THIS REPORT BY ANY PURCHASERS OF THIS PROPERTY (other than the above listed party(s) IS NOT AUTHORIZED BY DIABLO RESIDENTIAL INSPECTION SERVICE. DIABLO RESIDENTIAL INSPECTION SERVICE STRONGLY ADVISES AGAINST ANY RELIANCE ON THIS REPORT. WE RECOMMEND THAT YOU RETAIN A QUALIFIED PROFESSIONAL INSPECTOR TO PROVIDE YOU WITH YOUR OWN INSPECTION AND REPORT ON THIS PROPERTY.***

**T**
**R**
**A**
**Inspection Report**
**T**

# Residential Inspection Service

1647 Willow Pass Road, Suite 290 • Concord, CA 94520 • (415) 685-9220

**THIS CONTRACT LIMITS OUR LIABILITY...PLEASE READ CAREFULLY.**

Address 2422 Carolina Street, Vallejo, Ca. REPORT # ____________

Client New Growth Financial/Diane Swenson (representative)

I (client) hereby request a limited visual inspection of the structure at the above address to be conducted by RESIDENTIAL INSP. SERVICE ~~for my sole use~~ and benefit. I ~~warrant~~ that I will read the following agreement carefully. I understand that I am bound by all the terms of this contract.

**Initial Here** DS ____________

## SCOPE OF INSPECTION

Inspector will perform a limited **visual** home inspection to identify the general features and major deficiencies of the property.

Any area which is not exposed to view, is concealed, or is inaccessible because of soil, walls, floors, carpets, ceilings, furnishing, or any other thing is not included in this inspection. The inspection does not include any destructive testing or dismantling. Client agrees to assume all the risk for all conditions which are concealed from view at the time of the inspection. This is not a home warranty, guarantee, insurance policy or substitute for real estate transfer disclosures which may be required by federal, state or municipal statutes.

Whether or not they are concealed, the following ***ARE OUTSIDE THE SCOPE OF THIS INSPECTION:***

Building code or zoning ordinance violations; geological stability or soils condition; structural stability or engineering analysis; termites, pests or dry rot; asbestos, radon, formaldehyde, or other environmental hazards; building value appraisal; cost estimates; condition of detached buildings or pools (unless included for an additional fee); specific components noted as being excluded on the individual system inspection forms; private water or private sewage systems or any component thereof; swimming pools, spas, hot tubs (other than equipment and visible plumbing systems), saunas, steam baths, or fixtures and equipment; radio-controlled devices, automatic gates; elevators, lifts or dumbwaiters; thermostatic and time clock controls; water softener systems, solar systems, heat exchangers, freestanding appliances, or other personal property.

Your inspector is a home inspection generalist and is not a licensed engineer or expert in every craft. If your inspector recommends consulting other specialized experts, client must do so at client's expense.

I have read and agree to the above Scope of Inspection.

**Initial Here** DS ____________

**USE BY OTHERS:** Client promises inspectors that client has requested this inspection for client's own use only and will not disclose any part of the inspection report to any other person with these exceptions ONLY: one copy may be provided to the current seller(s) of the property for their use as part of my transaction only, and one copy may be provided to the real estate agent representing client for use in client's transaction only. Upon client's request a copy of the report may also be provided to a bank or other lender for use in client's transaction only.

**ATTORNEY'S FEES:** The prevailing party in any dispute arising out of this agreement, the inspection, or report(s) shall be awarded all attorney's fees, arbitrator and other costs.

## LIMITATION ON LIABILITY

**INSPECTOR'S LIABILITY FOR MISTAKES OR OMISSIONS IN THIS INSPECTION AND REPORT IS LIMITED TO A REFUND OF THE FEE PAID FOR THIS INSPECTION AND REPORT.** THE LIABILITY OF INSPECTOR'S PRINCIPALS, AGENTS, AND EMPLOYEES IS ALSO LIMITED TO THE FEE PAID. THIS LIMITATION APPLIES TO ANYONE WHO IS DAMAGED OR HAS TO PAY EXPE[...] BECAUSE OF MISTAKES OR OMISSI[...] TION AND REPORT. THIS LIABILITY [...] ING ON CLIENT AND CLIENT'[...] PRINCIPALS, ASSIGNS AND ANYONE [...] ERWISE CLAIM THROUGH CLIENT. [...] RISK OF ALL LOSSES GREATER THAN [...] INSPECTION. CLIENT AGREES TO A[...] REFUND OF THE FEE AS FULL SETT[...] ALL CLAIMS WHICH MAY EVER [...] INSPECTION.

T
R
A
**Inspection Report**
T

LIMITED INSPECTION [...]

CLIENT UNDERSTANDS THAT IF CLIENT WANTS AN INSPECTION WITHOUT A LIMIT ON LIABILITY TO A REFUND OF THE FEE PAID FOR THE INSPECTION, CLIENT MAY PAY AN ADDITIONAL FEE TO RECEIVE A REPORT WITHOUT THE LIMITATION.

Initial one of the two below:

DS ______ I do NOT agree ______ ______ I agree to pay an additional fee equal to four times the Inspection Fee listed above (minimum $1000) to receive a report without the above limitation on liability to the fee paid for this inspection.

ADDITIONAL INSPECTION FEE $ 1,350.00

## DISPUTE RESOLUTION

**ARBITRATION:** Any dispute concerning the interpretation of this agreement or arising from this inspection and report, except one for inspection fee payment, shall be resolved informally between the parties or by arbitration conducted in accordance with the rules of the American Arbitration Association except that the parties shall select an arbitrator who is familiar with the home inspection industry. The arbitrator shall conduct summary judgment motions and enforce full discovery rights as a court would as provided in civil proceeding by state code.

## PERMITS

DS ______ I do NOT agree ______ ______ I do agree to pay an additional fee of $ 200.00 for inspector to research and provide all building permits that appear on the municipal records for the above property.

**I have read, understand and agree to all the terms and conditions.**

Signed: Diane Swenson / New Growth Financial Dated: 7/3/90

Signed: ____________ Dated: ____________



1

# KEY TO THE MATRIX INSPECTION REPORT

The Matrix Outline Report lists the systems and components inspected by this company. Items not found in this report are considered beyond the scope of this inspection and should not be considered inspected at this time. Items found in **serviceable condition** are defined as capable of being used. Some serviceable items **may, however, show wear and tear.** Other conditions are checked, if applicable, in the body of the report. Please read the entire report for all items checked.

**Note:** This report contains technical information that may not be readily understandable to the lay person. Therefore, a verbal consultation with the inspector is a mandatory part of this inspection report. If you choose not to consult with the inspector, this inspection company cannot be held liable for your understanding or misunderstanding of this report's contents. **If you were not present during this inspection please call the office to arrange for your verbal consultation.**

☐ Client On Site ■ Client Not Present ☐ Client Did Not Attend Full Inspection

* Items that have an (*) Asterisk next to them.
The (*) Asterisk means this item or component warrants additional attention.

① Items that have a (①) Circled Number next to them.
The Circled Numbers are defined as follows:

① Recommended evaluation by a qualified licensed structural engineer/geologist **PRIOR TO CLOSE OF ESCROW.**
② Recommended evaluation and repairs as needed by a qualified licensed contractor **or** specialty tradesman dealing with that specific item or system **PRIOR TO CLOSE OF ESCROW.**
③ This inspection service does not probe surfaces; please refer to a qualified termite report for further information **PRIOR TO CLOSE OF ESCROW.**
④ Recommend evaluation by laboratory to determine presence of Asbestos **PRIOR TO CLOSE OF ESCROW.**

**T**
**R**
**A**
**Inspection Report**
**T**

ᵊ special "NOTES" in each section of the report for further information concerning the inspection.

→ Please Initial ________________ .

ᵊrstand the Key to the Matrix Inspection Report.

ᵊNot Present → Client's Initials ________________ .

Representative/Agent Initials ________________ .

**IMPORTANT NOTICE TO THIRD PARTIES OR OTHER PURCHASERS: RECEIPT OF THIS REPORT BY ANY PURCHASERS OF THIS PROPERTY (OTHER THAN THE ABOVE LISTED PARTY[S] IS NOT AUTHORIZED BY THE INSPECTOR. THE INSPECTOR STRONGLY ADVISES AGAINST ANY RELIANCE ON THIS REPORT. WE RECOMMEND THAT YOU RETAIN A QUALIFIED PROFESSIONAL INSPECTOR TO PROVIDE YOU WITH YOUR OWN INSPECTION AND REPORT ON THIS PROPERTY.**

**WEATHER CONDITIONS:** ■ Dry ☐ Wet

**HOUSE INFORMATION:** 2422 Carolina St., Vallejo, Ca.

| | |
|---|---|
| Approximate Year Built | Additions |
| Approximate Age of Roof | Stated by |

**SECTIONS INCLUDED ARE:**

| | |
|---|---|
| Section 1 Grounds | Section 2 Exterior/Foundation |
| Section 3 Roof | Section 4 Plumbing |
| Section 5 Heating | Section 6 Electrical/Air Conditioning |
| Section 7 Interior | Section 8 Garage |
| Section 9 Kitchen & Appliances | Section 10 Bathrooms |
| ~~Section 11 Pool & Spa~~ | |

Client: New Growth Financial (Diane Swenson - representative)
Date of inspection: July 5, 1990



FORM AK 112889

2

**SECTION I** GROUNDS **ADDRESS** 2422 Carolina St. 7/5/90

KEY: ◇ SIGNIFIES TYPE ○ SIGNIFIES GENERAL CONDITION □ SIGNIFIES SPECIFIC COMMENTARY

• SIGNIFIES ITEMS THAT WARRANT ATTENTION/REPAIR ①, ②, ③, ④ SEE KEY PAGE FOR SPECIFIC RECOMMENDATIONS

**DRIVEWAY** ◇ Asphalt ◆ Concrete ◇ Gravel ◇ Other

○ Appears Serviceable ○ Needs Repair•

■ Cracks Noted: ■ Typical □ Excessive• □ Surface Raised/Settled•

□ Erosion to Asphalt Noted• □ Sealant Suggested•

Comments:

**SIDEWALKS** ◆ Concrete ◇ Brick ◇ Paver/Tile ◇ Other

○ Appears Serviceable ○ Repair Suggested•

■ Cracks Noted: ■ Typical □ Excessive• □ Surface Raised/Settled•

Comments:

**LANDSCAPE**

○ Maintained ○ Maintenance Suggested•

■ Suggest Trimming Trees/Vines away from Structure• IN CONTACT WITH ROOF SURFACE AT FRONT

□ Trees Planted Close to Structure — Removal May Be Needed•

NOTE: Low voltage lighting systems are not a part of this inspection

**SPRINKLERS** N/A.

○ Appear Serviceable ○ Repairs Suggested•

□ Valve Leaks Noted• □ Broken Line/Heads• □ Anti-Siphon Valves Suggested•

□ Suggest Adjusting Spray Pattern away from Structures, Fences, Sidewalks, etc.•

□ Automatic Timers Not Tested — Valves Operated Manually• □ System Not Tested•

NOTE: Underground pipes cannot be judged for breaks or possible root intrusions. Association-maintained systems are not tested

**RETAINING WALLS** N/A. ◇ Concrete Block ◇ Stucco ◇ Other

○ Appear Serviceable ○ Damage/Movement Noted•

□ Movement/Cracks: □ Typical □ Excessive ③

Comments:

**GRADING** ◆ Flat Site ◇ Gentle Hill ◇ Steep Slope ◇ Stairstepped Pad

● Drainage of Site/Slope of Soil at Foundation Appears Serviceable ○ Correction Needed•

□ Suggest Pitching Slope of Soil away from Foundation•

□ Suggest Lowering Soil Below Stucco Screed•

■ See Termite Report for Recommendations on Earth-to-Wood Contact ③

□ Yard Drains Noted, Not Tested — Underground Pipes Cannot Be Judged.•

NOTE: This inspection does not include geological conditions or site stability information. For information concerning these c… or soils engineer should be consulted.

**PATIO** ◆ Concrete ◇ Brick ◇ Paver/Tile ◇ Other

● Appears Serviceable ○ Repair Suggested•

■ Cracks Noted: ■ Typical □ Excessive• ■ Settlement Noted•

□ Weatherproof Receptacles Suggested• □ Improper Wiring Noted•

□ Carpet Covers Patio — Could Not Inspect. Suggest Removal and Further Evaluation•

Comments:

**DECKS** N/A. ◇ Wood ◇ Concrete ◇ Waterproofed Coating ◇ Other

○ Appears Serviceable ○ Repair Suggested•

□ Cracked Membrane ② □ Deteriorated ② □ Rot Noted ③ □ Deck on Grade — Unable to Inspect•

□ Carpet Covers — Unable to Inspect• □ Handrails: □ Appear Serviceable □ Loose/Need Repair•

□ Space Between Intermediate Rails Appears Too Wide — Upgrade Suggested•

Comments:

**PATIO COVER** N/A.

○ Appears Serviceable ○ Suggest Repair/Securing•

□ Moisture/Damage Noted at Base of Posts ③

**EXTERIOR STAIRS** N/A.

○ Appear Serviceable ○ Repair Suggested•

□ Space Between Intermediate Rails Appears Too Wide — Upgrade Suggested•

□ Improper Rise/Run Noted• □ Handrails Loose/Improper•

Comments:

**FENCES & GATES** ◆ Wood ◆ Chain Link ◇ Wrought Iron ◇ Stucco ◇ Other

● Appear Serviceable ○ Repair Suggested•

■ Loose/Rotted Posts• □ Broken/Missing Boards• □ Loose/Missing Block•

□ Foliage Covers ____% — Unable to Fully Inspect• □ Gate Needs Adjustment/Rebuilding•

□ Cracks Noted □ Typical □ Excessive• □ Suggest Raising Height @ Pool/Spa Area•

□ Rusting Noted at Wrought Iron — Repair Suggested•

Comments: HARDWARE Pulled LOOSE AT FRONT WALK -



3

FORM AK 112889

**T**
**R**
**A**
**Inspection Report**
**T**

**SECTION II** EXTERIOR/FOUNDATION

**ADDRESS** 2422 Carolina St. 7/5/90

**KEY:** ◇ SIGNIFIES TYPE ○ SIGNIFIES GENERAL CONDITION □ SIGNIFIES SPECIFIC COMMENTARY

• SIGNIFIES ITEMS THAT WARRANT ATTENTION/REPAIR ①, ②, ③, ④ SEE KEY PAGE FOR SPECIFIC RECOMMENDATIONS

**WALLS** ◆Stucco ◇Wood Siding ◇Brick ◇Shingles ◇Other

○ Appear Serviceable ● Need Repair*
□ Cracks Noted: ■ Typical □ Excessive ② ■ Patch ~~Cracks~~/Openings* □ Damaged Siding*
□ Sloughing (Moisture Damage) Noted* □ Paint/Finish Needed* □ Wall Flashings: □ Appear Intact □ Damage/Defects Noted ②

Comments: STUCCO NOT SEALED AT KITCHEN SLIDING GLASS DOOR. ALSO HOLES NEED TO BE PATCHED

**TRIM** ◇Wood ◇Metal ◇Other

○ Appears Serviceable ○ Damage Noted*
■ Paint/Finish Needed* ● Moisture Stains/Damage Noted under Eaves ② ①
□ Loose Boards* □ Improper Flashing*

Comments: TRIM NOT FINISHED AT L.R. DOOR.

**CHIMNEY** ◇Brick ◇Metal ◆Stucco ◇Concrete ◇Other

● Appears Serviceable ○ Needs Repair*
□ Cracks or Separations Noted/Sealant Needed at Wall Flashing* □ Settlement Noted ②
■ Spark Arrestor: □ Noted ■ None Provided/Recommended*
□ Suggest Patching Cracks in Chimney Cap* □ Loose Brick ② □ Deteriorated Mortar ②

Comments:

**SLAB ON GRADE**

□ Slab not fully visible due to carpet and floor covering — no readily visible problem noted today.
■ Slab not fully visible due to carpet and floor covering — recommend further evaluation by removal of floor covering due to:
□ Cracks Noted* ●Uneven Areas in Flooring*
□ Visible ■ Partially Visible* □ Not Visible*
...ical □ Excessive ① IN AREAS VIEWED

**T**
**R**
**A**
**Inspection Report**
**T**

...ence some degree of cracking due to shrinkage in the drying process. In most instances floor coverings prevent recognition ...t the most severe cases. The inspector will, at additional cost, reinspect, provided the client removes floor covering and ... from damage caused by this process.

...N/F ◇Continuous Concrete ◇Pier/Post ◇Concrete Block ◇Brick ① ◇Other

○ Damage/Deterioration Noted* □ Earth-to-Wood Contact ②
□ Partial □ Inaccessible due to: □ Locked/No Access Opening* □ Ground Too Wet* □ Restricted Headroom* □ Pests*
...pears Serviceable □ Damaged/Missing* □ Foundation Bolts: □ Yes □ No ①
... □ Minor □ Excessive ① □ Deterioration: □ Minor □ Excessive ①
□ Efflorescence: □ Minor □ Excessive ① □ Moisture Noted* □ Debris Noted* □ Vents: □ Intact □ Blocked □ None ②

Comments:

**SUPPLY LINES** N/A

○ Appear Serviceable ○ Damage/Deterioration Noted*
□ Corrosion Noted: □ Minor □ Moderate* □ Excessive ② □ Leaks Noted ② □ Lack Support*

**WASTE LINES** N/A

○ Appear Serviceable ○ Damage/Deterioration Noted* ○ Not Fully Visible*
□ Corrosion Noted: □ Minor □ Moderate* □ Excessive ② □ Leaks Noted ② □ No Fall ②

**DUCTING** N/A

○ Appears Serviceable ○ Damage/Deterioration Noted*
□ Asbestos-like Material Noted ④ □ Dented ② □ Crushed ② □ Separations ②
□ Deteriorated Wrapping* □ Unable to Fully Inspect*

**ELECTRICAL** N/A

○ Appears Serviceable ○ Damage/Defects Noted* □ Wiring Lying on the Ground*
□ Open J Boxes* □ Unsecured Wiring* □ Improper Wiring ② □ Midline Splices ② □ Deteriorated Wiring ② □ Abandoned Wiring*

**BASEMENT** N/A

◇Full ◇Partial ◇None ◇Access from:
◇Post and Beam ◇Block ◇Poured Concrete ◇Brick ① ◇Earth ①

○ Appears Serviceable ○ Damage/Deterioration Noted*
□ Cracks: □ Minor □ Excessive ① □ Deterioration: □ Minor □ Excessive ①
□ Efflorescence □ Minor □ Excessive ② □ Debris Noted* □ Unable to Fully Inspect*

Comments:

**SUMP PUMP** N/A

○ Appears Serviceable ○ Damage/Deterioration Noted ②

Location: □ Noted — Not Tested* □ Suggested*

**NOTE:** The inspector is unable to test basement drains or sump pumps



4

FORM AK 112889

**SECTION III** ROOF

**ADDRESS** 2422 Carolina St. 7/5/90

KEY: ◇ SIGNIFIES TYPE ○ SIGNIFIES GENERAL CONDITION ☐ SIGNIFIES SPECIFIC COMMENTARY

• SIGNIFIES ITEMS THAT WARRANT ATTENTION/REPAIR ①, ②, ③, ④ SEE KEY PAGE FOR SPECIFIC RECOMMENDATIONS

■ Access Typical ☐ Unable to Fully Access Due to Height/Pitch/Weather

◆ Gable (*garage*) ◆ Hip ◇ Flat/Low Slope ◇ Mansard ◇ Parapet ◇ Other ______

**TYPE** *House Garage* ◆ Composition Shingles ◇ Wood Shake ◇ Wood Shingle ◇ Other ______

○ **Appears Serviceable/Within Useful Life**

● ***TYPICAL MAINTENANCE RECOMMENDED.*** This usually consists of repair/replacement of damaged/missing ridge and other shakes/shingles. This maintenance should help insure the watertightness of the building and be performed on a regular basis.•

■ General condition appears serviceable with signs of weathering and aging — regular maintenance and inspections are advised.•

☐ Few/Many Damaged or Missing Shakes/Shingles Needing Repair/Replacement ②

■ Weathering• ☐ Aging• ☐ Cracking• ☐ Felt Showing ② ☐ Holes/Openings ②

☐ Loose/Damaged/Missing Ridge ② ☐ Excessive Damage/Deterioration ②

☐ Roof Appears to Be at/Nearing the End of Its Useful Life ②

☐ Roof Material Appears to Be Improperly Installed ②

*PROTECTIVE GRANULAR COATING IS MISSING ON SOME SHINGLES.*

**TYPE** *N/A* ◇ Tile ◇ Concrete ◇ Clay ◇ Other ______

○ **Appears Serviceable/Within Useful Life**

☐ Cracked Tiles ② ☐ Missing Tiles ② ☐ Excessive Damage ② ☐ Loose Tile ②

☐ Displaced Tiles ② ☐ Broken Tiles ② ☐ Damaged/Missing Ridge ②

☐ Roof Material Appears to Be Improperly Installed ② ☐ Unable to Fully View Entire Roof•

**NOTE:** Roofs of this material are not walked to avoid causing damage. They are visually inspected with binoculars. Inspection is limited.

**TYPE** *N/A* ◇ Rock/Built Up ◇ Rolled Composition ◇ Other ______

○ **Appears Serviceable/Within Useful Life**

☐ ***TYPICAL MAINTENANCE RECOMMENDED.*** This usually consists of covering exposed/bare areas with additional aggregate material. Repair of open seams, cracks in flashings, deteriorated roof coverings, etc.•

☐ Excessive Damage/Deterioration Noted to Roof ② ☐ Roof Material Appears to Be Improperly Installed ②

☐ Blistering• ☐ Alligatoring• ☐ Deteriorated Paper ② ☐ Open Seams ② ☐ Exposed Nails•

☐ Evidence of Ponding/Poor Drainage Noted•

☐ Roof Appears to Be Nearing/at End of Useful Life ②

**COMMENTS (All Types)**

*HOUSE ROOF HAS A FEW AREAS THAT IS SHOW. & WILL NEED ONGOING MAINTENANCE- GARAGE ROOF IS IN BAD CONDITION - NEEDS TO BE*

**NOTE:** The foregoing is an opinion of the general quality and condition of the roofing material. The inspector cannot, an opinion or warranty as to whether the roof leaks or may be subject to future leakage. This report is issued in considerati disclaimer.

T
R
A
C
T
**Inspection Report**

**EXPOSED FLASHINGS** ◆ Metal ◇ Composition ◇ Other ______

○ **Appear Serviceable** ○ Damage Noted• *MOST FLASHINGS CAN NOT BE SEEN DUE TO BUILT UP LAYERS OF ROOF*

☐ *Separation(s)* Noted at: ☐ Chimney• ☐ Drip Edge• ☐ Vent Pipes• ☐ Other

☐ *Vent Caps:* ■ Serviceable ☐ Repairs Needed• ☐ Missing Caps•

☐ Damaged Flashing Noted• ☐ Improper Flashing Noted at

☐ *Skylights:* ☐ Appear Serviceable ☐ Damage/Defects Noted ②

*MASTIC USED IN SEVERAL AREAS SHOULD BE MAINTAINED IN SEALED CONDITION*

**GUTTERS & DOWNSPOUTS** ◆ Full ◇ Partial ◇ None Installed

○ **Appear Serviceable** ● Damage/Defects Noted•

■ Rusting Noted• ☐ Filled with Debris• ■ Damaged Downspouts• ☐ Loose•

☐ Recommend installing gutters and downspouts to help with site drainage• ■ Route Downspouts away from Building•

☐ *Scuppers installed with secondary drain:* ☐ Yes ☐ No•

**NOTE:** Gutters are not water tested for leakage

**Comments:** *DOWN SPOUTS LOOSE OR MISSING AT SEVERAL LOCATIONS.*

**ATTIC** ◇ Full ◆ Partial ◇ Truss ◇ Conventional Frame

☐ Accessible ☐ No Access ☐ Access Too Small

● **Appears Serviceable** ○ Damage/Defects Noted•

☐ *Ventilation:* ☐ Provided ■ Limited/~~None~~•

☐ *Insulation:* ■ Noted ☐ None•

☐ *Piping/Service Ducting:* ☐ Serviceable ☐ Disconnected/Damaged•

☐ Open Splices in Wiring/J Boxes Missing Covers ② ☐ Wiring Not Visible•

☐ *Stains Noted:* ☐ Minor• ☐ Excessive ②

☐ Sagging/Broken Framing ②

☐ The inspector is unable to determine if water stains are indicative of an active leak.

**NOTE:** Determining the presence of asbestos or other hazardous materials is beyond the scope of this inspection

**Comments:** *ACCESS TO GARAGE CONVERSION AREA ONLY. REMAINDER OF ATTIC NOT VIEWED.*



5

FORM AK 112889

# SECTION IV PLUMBING

**ADDRESS** 2422 Carolina St. 7/5/90

**KEY:** ◇ SIGNIFIES TYPE ○ SIGNIFIES GENERAL CONDITION ☐ SIGNIFIES SPECIFIC COMMENTARY

• SIGNIFIES ITEMS THAT WARRANT ATTENTION/REPAIR ①, ②, ③, ④ SEE KEY PAGE FOR SPECIFIC RECOMMENDATIONS

## MAIN LINE

◇ Copper ◆ Galvanized ◇ PVC (Check Elect. Ground) ◇ Other

☐ Size: 3/4" ☐ Pressure: 65 PSI @ 11 AM/PM

● Appears Serviceable ○ Damage/Defects Noted•

☐ Main Valve: ■ Operational ☐ Non-Operational ②

☐ Leaks Noted ②

☐ Pressure above 80 PSI — Suggest Adjustment/Repair/Installation of Regulator ②

☐ Handle Broken/Missing• ☐ Valve at Meter Only ☐ Excessive Corrosion at Valve•

Comments: CONDITION OF BURIED GALVANIZED PIPE CAN NOT BE ACCESSED. GALVANIZED PIPE IS KNOWN TO CORRODE INTERNALLY. THE PIPING IS OLD AND MAY HAVE HIDDEN DEFECTS.

## SUPPLY LINES

◆ Copper ◇ Galvanized ◇ PVC• ◇ Unable to Fully Determine• ◇ Other

● Appear Serviceable ○ Damage/Defects Noted•

☐ Corrosion Noted: ☐ Minor• ☐ Excessive ②

☐ Leaks Noted ② ☐ Loose Pipes• ☐ Water Hammer in Pipes Noted ②

☐ Copper/Galvanized Contact Noted — Suggest Correction ②

☐ Volume Restriction Noted: ☐ Minor• ☐ Excessive ②

☐ System Appears to Be Nearing/at the End of Its Useful Life ②

Comments:

## WASTE LINES

◆ Cast Iron ◆ Galvanized ◇ ABS ◇ Other

○ Appears Serviceable ○ Damage/Defects Noted• ☐ Lines Not Fully Visible•

☐ Rust/Corrosion Noted• ■ Leaks Noted ② ☐ Water Softener Installed/Not Inspected•

☐ Not Fully Visible• ☐ Fall May Be Insufficient for Adequate Drainage ②

... Serviceable ☐ Vents Damaged/Terminate Improperly ②

...vice, septic systems and all underground pipes are not a part of this inspection. Determining future drainage performance is

...S NOTED UNDER KITCHEN SINK. SEE TERMITE ... FOR EVALUATION OF DAMAGE

...ared Serviceable ☐ Some Inoperative ② ☐ Leaks Noted ② ☐ Missing/Broken Handles•

**T R A Inspection Report T**

## GAS SYSTEM

◇ Meter Location RIGHT SIDE NEAR FRONT ◇ LPG Tank Location

System Appears Serviceable ○ Damage/Defects Noted•

☐ Lines Corrosion Proofed Where Visible ☐ Lines Not Corrosion Proofed• HAVE PGE CHECK.

■ Improper Pipe Noted at: COPPER TUBING USE AT WATER HEATER ② ☐ Pipe Not 6" Above Ground ②

☐ No Shutoff Valve Provided at: ②

☐ Gas System Not On at Inspection — Suggest Gas Company Light and Test All Gas Appliances•

**NOTE:** Pipe condition is viewed above ground — underground piping cannot be judged. Pipes inside walls cannot be judged and the inspector does not perform tests for gas leaks or pipe sizing.

Comments: BASE OF METER AND PIPING COULD NOT BE VIEWED DUE TO THE PRESENCE OF CACTUS

## WATER HEATER

◆ Gas ◇ Electric ◇ Solar ◇ Other ◇ Capacity(s) 30 GAL

Location(s): ◇ Garage ◇ Utility Room ◇ Hall Closet ◇ Other LAUNDRY ROOM

Appear(s) Serviceable ○ Damage/Defects Noted

☐ Leaks Noted ② ☐ Rust Flakes Noted• ☐ Corrosion•

☐ Pressure Relief Valve Noted/Not Tested ☐ None Noted (Suggested)•

■ Recommend Extending Discharge Line from TPR Valve to Safe Location•

☐ Thermal Blanket: ☐ Installed ■ Not Installed

☐ Suggest 18" Platform for Unit(s)• ☐ Seismic Straps: ☐ Provided ■ Recommended•

☐ Combustion Air: ☐ Available ☐ Blocked/None Provided ②

☐ Vent Flue: ■ Intact ☐ Damaged/Disconnected ②

☐ Water Shutoff Valve: ■ Installed ☐ Missing/Broken ② BUT NEEDS TO BE ALIGNED TO TOP OF DRAFT DIVERTER.

■ Recommend Catch Pan Under Unit with Exterior Routed Drain Line•

☐ Improper Venting Noted ② ☐ Horizontal/Negative Fall on Vent Line ②

☐ Enclosure Serviceable ☐ Door Missing/Damaged• ■ Improper Firewall ②

**NOTE:** Estimate of remaining life is not a part of this inspection. Solar systems are not a part of this inspection.

Comments: GAS SUPPLY SHOULD NOT BE RUN IN COPPER TUBING



FORM AK 112889

6

**SECTION V** HEATING **ADDRESS** 2422 Carolina St. 7/5/90

KEY: ◇ SIGNIFIES TYPE ○ SIGNIFIES GENERAL CONDITION □ SIGNIFIES SPECIFIC COMMENTARY
• SIGNIFIES ITEMS THAT WARRANT ATTENTION/REPAIR 1, 2, 3, 4 SEE KEY PAGE FOR SPECIFIC RECOMMENDATIONS

**DESCRIPTION OF SYSTEM(S)**

Location of Unit #1 ◇ Garage ◇ Attic ◆ Hall Closet ◇ Other ____
Location of Unit #2 ◇ Garage ◇ Attic ◇ Hall Closet ◇ Other ____
Location of Unit #3 ◇ Garage ◇ Attic ◇ Hall Closet ◇ Other ____

NOTE: If heater/furnace is located in a bedroom, we recommend evaluation by a qualified heating contractor for sizing

Type of Heating Unit #1 ◆ Forced Air ◇ Gravity ◇ Floor ◇ Wall ◇ Radiant ◇ Other ____
Type of Heating Unit #2 ◇ Forced Air ◇ Gravity ◇ Floor ◇ Wall ◇ Radiant ◇ Other ____
Type of Heating Unit #3 ◇ Forced Air ◇ Gravity ◇ Floor ◇ Wall ◇ Radiant ◇ Other ____
Fuel Type Unit #1 ◆ Natural Gas ◇ Electric ◇ Propane ◇ Oil ◇ Other ____
Fuel Type Unit #2 ◇ Natural Gas ◇ Electric ◇ Propane ◇ Oil ◇ Other ____
Fuel Type Unit #3 ◇ Natural Gas ◇ Electric ◇ Propane ◇ Oil ◇ Other ____
Approximate BTU's ◇ Unit #1 ____ ◇ N/A ◇ Unit #2 ____ ◇ N/A ◇ Unit #3 ____ ◇ N/A

**CONDITION OF SYSTEM(S)**

● System(s) Appear(s) Operational □ Unit # ____ Damage/Defects Noted•
□ Unit # ____ Did Not Respond to Normal Controls 2 □ Unit # ____ Pilot Not Lit•
□ Unable to Inspect/No Utilities• □ Unit # ____ Electric Ignition Malfunction•

NOTE: Inspector does not light pilots. If pilots are "Off," a full inspection is not possible. It is suggested that heating systems be activated and fully inspected **PRIOR TO CLOSE OF ESCROW.**

**Venting**

● Appears Serviceable □ Not Applicable □ Unit # ____ Damage/Deterioration Noted 2
□ Unit # ____ Backventing Noted 2 □ Unit # ____ Soot Noted in Vent Chamber 2
□ Unit # ____ Inadequate Pipe Clearance 2 □ Unit # ____ Improper Vent Rise 2
□ Unit # ____ Improper Materials in Vent 2 □ Unit # ____ Unable to Fully Inspect Vent•
□ Unit # ____ Is Unvented 2

**Combustion Air**

○ Appears Serviceable □ Not Applicable □ Unit # ____ Inadequate 2
□ Unit # ____ Vents Blocked 2 □ Unit # ____ Vents Missing 2
■ Unit # 1 ____ Combustion and Return Air Sources Are Too Close or Mixing 2 SEE BELOW
□ Unit # ____ Recommend Sealing Platform at Heater Base/Holes in Platform 2

**Air Plenum**

● Appears Serviceable □ Unit # ____ Damage/Deterioration Noted• □ Not Applicable
□ Unit # ____ Air Leaks Noted/Suggest Sealing• ■ Unit # 1 ____ Asbestos-like Mater

**T**
**R**
**A**
**Inspection Report**
**T**

**Air Filters**

● Appear Serviceable Missing/Damaged• □ Unit # ____ Suggest Cleaning/Changing Filter•

NOTE: Electronic air cleaners and de-humidifiers are beyond the scope of this inspection

**Burners**

● Burner Flame(s) Appear(s) Typical Unit # ____ Unusual Flame Pattern Noted 2
□ Unit # ____ Rust Flakes Noted in Burn Chamber 2
□ Unit # ____ Soot/Charring Noted in Burn Chamber 2 □ Closed System/Unable to Inspect•

NOTE: THE INSPECTOR IS NOT EQUIPPED TO INSPECT FURNACE HEAT EXCHANGERS FOR EVIDENCE OF CRACKS OR HOLES, AS THIS CAN ONLY BE DONE BY DISMANTLING THE UNIT. THIS IS BEYOND THE SCOPE OF THIS INSPECTION. SOME FURNACES ARE DESIGNED IN SUCH A WAY THAT INSPECTION IS ALMOST IMPOSSIBLE.

**Ducts/Air Supply**

● Appear Serviceable Damage/Deterioration Noted•
□ Disconnected Ducts Noted 2 □ Crushed Ducts Noted 2 □ Low Air Volume Noted 2
■ Asbestos-like Material Noted 4 □ Damaged/Missing Register(s) Noted•

NOTE: Asbestos materials have been commonly used in heating systems. Determining the presence of asbestos can **ONLY** be performed by laboratory testing and is beyond the scope of this inspection.

**Normal Controls**

● Appear Serviceable Damage/Defects Noted•
□ Thermostat Broken/Loose• □ Suggest Moving Thermostat to a More Central Location•
□ Controls/Gauges Need Repair/Replacement 2 □ Switch Is Missing/Broken 2

**General Suggestions**

● Suggest Cleaning/Servicing Blower Motor, Pilot, Vent System, Burners• □ Leakage Noted at Boiler/Radiator/Pipe Fittings 2
□ Heater Makes Unusual Noise During Operation. Suggest Further Evaluation 2
□ Uneven Heat Distribution Noted. Suggest Further Evaluation 2 □ Unable to Locate Registers in All Rooms•

**General Notes**

DOOR TO BLOWER COMPARTMENT IS WARPED, Household AIR IS MIXING WITH COMBUSTION SUPPLY AIR. ALSO COMBUSTION SUPPLY AIR Should BE DRAWN FROM ATTIC BY INSTALLING SUPPLY DUCT PIPE DOWN TO WITHIN 1 FOOT OF CLOSET FLOOR, ALSO HAVE PGE



PERFORM FREE SAFETY INSPECTION PRIOR TO CLOSE OF ESCROW

**SECTION VI** ELECTRICAL/ AIR CONDITIONING **ADDRESS** 2422 Carolina St. 7/5/90

KEY: ◇ SIGNIFIES TYPE ○ SIGNIFIES GENERAL CONDITION ☐ SIGNIFIES SPECIFIC COMMENTARY

• SIGNIFIES ITEMS THAT WARRANT ATTENTION/REPAIR ①, ②, ③, ④ SEE KEY PAGE FOR SPECIFIC RECOMMENDATIONS

**SERVICE**

◆ Overhead ◇ Underground ◇ # of Lines ______
◇ 110V* ◇ 220V ◇ Breakers ◇ Fuses

Appears Serviceable ■ ~~Damage~~/Defects Noted*
☐ Loose/Damaged Connections at Masthead ② ■ Frayed Conductors ②
☐ Conductors Too Close to Ground ② ☐ Conductors Through Trees*

**Main Panel**

◇ Location EXTER / AT BACK # of 110 Circuits 6 # of 220 Circuits —
Appears Serviceable Damage/Defects Noted* (See Main & Sub Panel Notes Section Below)
60 ? Amps ■ Cannot Determine/No Main Breaker ☐ More Than Six Breakers with no Main Shutoff ②

NOTE: Six or fewer breakers usually do not require a main breaker

**Conductors**

◇ Power Cable: ◇ Copper ◆ Aluminum ◇ Cannot Determine
◇ Branch Cable: ◆ Copper ◆ ~~Aluminum (220V OK)~~ ◇ Cannot Determine

**Sub Panel**

◇ Location ______ # of 110 Circuits ______ # of 220 Circuits ______
◇ Location ______ # of 110 Circuits ______ # of 220 Circuits ______

**Main & Sub Panel Notes** GROUND WIRE VIEWED IN PANEL, FIELD TERMINATION NOT SEEN.

■ Grounding System Present Circuit and Wire Sizing Correct so Far As Visible Improper Wiring Noted
☐ Loose Clamp at Water Line or Ground Rod* ☐ No Observable Grounding System Noted ②
☐ Two Wires Connected to One Breaker Where Only One Should Be ② ☐ Sizing Correct So Far as Visible
☐ Overfusing at Main Panel (Fuse or Breaker Size Appear Too Large for Wire Size ②
☐ Overfusing at Sub Panel (Fuse or Breaker Size Appear Too Large for Wire Size) ②
☐ Aluminum Wiring at the General 110 Circuits Noted. Recommend That All Aluminum Wiring Connections Be Checked by a Qualified, Licensed Electrician Familiar with Aluminum Wiring ②
* ■ Electrical System Appears Outdated by Today's Standards — Upgrade Should Be Considered ②
■ ~~Missing~~ Deadfront Cover(s)* ☐ Missing 220 Volt Coupler(s)

**Comments:**

SCREWS MISSING FROM DEAD FRONT COVER. COVER CAN FALL OUT ... ENERGIZED PARTS IN PANEL.

**T**
**R**
**A**
**Inspection Report**
**T**

...s and Outlets Tested Appears to Be Serviceable
...e at: *
... Outlets Did Not Appear to Be Properly Grounded ②
...l at: ②
...e at: ②
...t(s) Noted at: ②
... Prevent Testing of All Outlets and Switches* ☐ Missing/Damaged Cover Plates Noted*
...d at: ② ☐ Garage ☐ Attic ☐ Crawlspace ☐ Kitchen ☐ Exterior ☐ Other
... Wiring Be Properly Protected at: ②
... ② ☐ Garage ☐ Attic ☐ Crawlspace ☐ Kitchen ☐ Exterior ☐ Other
☐ Junction Box Missing Cover at: * ☐ Garage ☐ Attic ☐ Crawlspace ☐ Kitchen ☐ Exterior ☐ Other
☐ Extension Cords Used Over 6' Long — Recommend Permanent Wiring to Fixtures at: ②

**Comments:**

ACCESS to RECEPTACLES IS VERY LIMITED.

**Air Conditioning** N/A

**Type**

◇ Central ◇ Window Mount ◇ Wall Mount ◇ Electric ◇ Gas* (Not Inspected)
Appears Operational Damaged/Defects Noted* No Power — Unable to Test*
☐ Air Temperature Below 65° — Unable to Test System at This Time*
☐ Unit Makes Unusual Noise During Operation — Recommend Further Evaluation ②
☐ Damage/Deterioration Noted ② ☐ Recommend Clearing Foliage from Unit* ☐ Recommend Servicing System and Checking Freon Level*

**Power**

◇ 110 Volt ◇ 220 Volt ◇ Electrical Disconnect Present
☐ No Disconnect Provided — Recommend Providing Shutoff Capability at Unit ②
☐ Proper Grounding Not Provided at Unit — Recommend Correction ②

**Condensate**

Condensate Line Installed
☐ Cannot Locate Termination Point* ☐ Line Disconnected/Damaged/Leaking ②

**Freon Lines**

Insulation Installed On-lines Insulation Damaged/Deteriorated* ☐ Lines Appear Damaged ②

NOTE: The inspector does not perform pressure tests on coolant systems; therefore no representation is made regarding coolant charge or line integrity. Subjective judgement of system capacity is not a part of the inspection.

**Comments:**



FORM AK 112889

8

**SECTION VII** INTERIOR **ADDRESS** 2422 Carolina St. 7/5/90

KEY: ◇ SIGNIFIES TYPE ○ SIGNIFIES GENERAL CONDITION ☐ SIGNIFIES SPECIFIC COMMENTARY

• SIGNIFIES ITEMS THAT WARRANT ATTENTION/REPAIR ①, ②, ③, ④ SEE KEY PAGE FOR SPECIFIC RECOMMENDATIONS

**DOORS (Entry)**

● Appear Serviceable ○ Damaged* ☐ See Remarks ■ Weather Stripping Intact ☐ Needs Repair* ☐ Recommended*
■ Deadbolts Operational ☐ Non-operational* ☐ None ☐ Doorbell Operational ☐ Non-operational* ■ None

Comments:

**DOORS (Interior)**

● Appear Serviceable ☐ Need Adjustment* ☐ Damaged at:*
☐ Hardware Operational ☐ Not Operational at:* ☐ Door(s) Rub at Jamb*

Comments: SEVERAL DOORS BLOCKED BY PERSONAL BELONGINGS

**DOORS (Exterior)**

◆ Sliding Glass ◇ French ◇ Other
○ Appear Serviceable ☐ Need Adjustment* ☐ Damaged at:*
■ Tempered Glass ☐ Not Tempered (Caution)* ☐ Unable to Determine
■ Latching Hardware Operational ☐ Not Operational* ☐ Screens Intact ☐ Damaged* AND MISSING ■ None Provided
☐ Tracks Intact ☐ Deteriorated*

Comments: SLIDING GLASS DOOR CAN NOT BE LOCKED OR LATCHED.

**WINDOWS**

◆ Aluminum ◇ Wood ◇ Steel ◇ Dual Pane
◇ Sliding ◆ Casement ◇ Double Hung ◇ Louver
■ Sample Tested Appeared Operational ☐ Non-operational at:*
☐ Broken Sash Cords* ☐ Some Difficult to Operate*
☐ Caulking/Glazing Compound ■ Deteriorated* ■ Few ☐ Many ☐ Cracked/Broken Glass Noted at:* L.R. & F.R.
■ Screens Installed ■ Few/Many Missing* ☐ Few/Many Damaged*

Comments: NON-TEMPORED GLASS IN PICTURE WINDOWS.

**INTERIOR WALLS**

◇ Drywall ◇ Plaster ◇ Paneling ◇ Wallpaper
● Cracks Noted: Typical Overall ☐ Excessive at: ②
☐ General Condition Serviceable ☐ Need Repairs*
☐ Furnishings Prevent Full Inspection — Do a Careful Check on Your Final Walkthrough*

Comments: HOLES UNDER KITCHEN SINK. - BEHIND STOVE

**NOTE:** The condition of walls behind wallpaper, paneling and furnishings cannot be judged

**T**
**R**
**A**
**Inspection Report**
**T**

**CEILINGS**

◆ Drywall ◇ Acoustic Spray ◇ Open Beam ◇ Plaster
○ General Condition Serviceable ☐ Damaged at:*
☐ Stains Noted at:*
■ Cracks Noted: Typical Overall ☐ Excessive at:*

Comments:

**NOTE:** Determining whether acoustic sprayed ceilings contain asbestos is beyond the scope of this inspection. For more information please contact the American Lung Association or an asbestos specialist.

**FLOORS**

◆ Carpet ◆ Vinyl ◇ Wood ◇ Tile ◇ Other
○ General Condition Serviceable ○ Damage/Deterioration Noted
☐ Cracked Tiles Noted at:* ☐ Wood Damaged at:*
☐ Vinyl Damaged at:* KITCHEN, BATH, HALL ■ Carpet Stained/Damaged at:*
☐ Furnishings Prevent Full Inspection — Do a Careful Check on Your Final Walkthrough*

Comments:

**NOTE:** General condition of floors only is included — determining odors is not included!

**FIREPLACE**

◇ Location(s) #1 F.R. #2 #3
◇ Mason Built ◇ Prefabricated ◇ Freestanding
☐ Mortar Joints Intact ☐ Deteriorated* ☐ Cracked/Loose Fire Bricks ②
☐ Damper Operational ■ Non-operational* ☐ None ☐ Gas Operational ☐ Inoperative ② ☐ Capped — No Test ☐ None
☐ Inappropriate Materials Used in Gas ② ☐ Gas Valve Found in Firebox ② ■ Recommend Cleaning Chimney Flue ②

Comments: HAS GAS LOG INSTALLED, GAS NOT CONNECTED. DAMPER FROZE OPEN.

**SMOKE/FIRE DETECTOR**

■ None Found* ☐ Indicator Light On ☐ Couldn't Test/No Test Button*
☐ Responded to Test Button ☐ Did Not Respond to Test Button* ☐ Suggest Additional Detectors in Appropriate Locations*

Comments:

**INTERIOR SPECIAL FEATURES** N/A

○ Ceiling Fan(s) Operational ☐ Non-Operational* ☐ Needs Balancing* ☐ Central Vacuum Installed But Not a Part of This Inspection*
☐ Intercom System Installed But Not a Part of This Inspection* ☐ Security System Installed But Not a Part of This Inspection*
☐ Interior Stairs Serviceable ☐ Suggested Improvement* ☐ Stair Handrail Secure ☐ Loose Railing Noted* ☐ No Rail Provided*
**Wet Bar:** ☐ Faucet Operational ☐ Leaks Noted*
**Counter:** ○ Appears Serviceable ☐ Damage/Deterioration Noted*
☐ Plumbing Under Sink Serviceable ☐ Leaks Noted* ☐ Improper Piping ②

Comments:



FORM AK 112889

9

**SECTION VIII** GARAGE

**ADDRESS** 2422 Carolina St. 7/5/90

**KEY:** ◇ SIGNIFIES TYPE ◯ SIGNIFIES GENERAL CONDITION ☐ SIGNIFIES SPECIFIC COMMENTARY

• SIGNIFIES ITEMS THAT WARRANT ATTENTION/REPAIR ①, ②, ③, ④ SEE KEY PAGE FOR SPECIFIC RECOMMENDATIONS

◇ Attached ◇ Detached ◇ Number of Cars ________

**ROOF**

Appears Serviceable ■ Damage/Defects Noted• NEEDS REPLACING

☐ Same As House ☐ Other ________ ☐ See Roof Section•

**Comments:** ________

**FLOOR**

Appears Serviceable ☐ Cracks Noted: ☐ Typical ☐ Excessive ②

■ Floor Is Not Fully Visible Due to:• CARPET, STORED BELONGINGS AND

**Comments:** DISABLED AUTO

**FIRE WALL** N/A

Appears Serviceable ☐ Needs Repair: Holes/Damage Noted to Wall Covering•

**Comments:** ________

**VENTILATION**

☐ Open ■ Screens Missing/~~Damaged~~• ☐ Blocked• ☐ None Provided

**Comments:** SCREENS SHOULD BE ADDED TO PREVENT PEST ENTRY

**DOOR ENTERING LIVING SPACE** N/A ◇ Solid ◇ Hollow Core (Non-fire Rated)• ◇ Other ________

☐ Pet Door Interrupts Integrity of Fire Door ② ☐ Door Does Not Latch•

☐ Self-closer Operational ☐ Non-operational• ☐ Lacks Self-closer•

**Comments:** ________

**PASSAGE DOOR TO EXTERIOR**

■ ~~Damaged~~/Delaminated• ☐ Needs Adjustment•

☐ Door Rubs at Jamb• ☐ Not Tested/Blocked/Locked•

T
R
A
**Inspection Report**
T

■ Damage Noted: ☐ Minor ☐ Excessive ②

☐ Door Warped• ☐ Door Needs Adjustment•

■ Not Safety-type Springs• ☐ Broken Springs Noted ②

Locked — Could Not Test•

TOP PITCHED FORWARD DID NOT ATTEMPT TO OPEN

**[OPEN]ER** N/A

Appears Operational ☐ Non-operational• ☐ Disconnected• ☐ None

☐ No Separate Electrical Receptacle for Opener ②

**Comments:** ________

**ELECTRICAL**

■ Appears Serviceable ☐ Not Visible

☐ Improper Wiring Noted ② ☐ Extension Cords Over 6'• ☐ Exposed Romex•

☐ Open Splices ② ☐ Junction Boxes Missing Covers•

**Outlets:** Appear Serviceable ☐ Open "U" Ground ② ☐ Two-prong ☐ Reversed Polarity• ☐ Some Inaccessible• ☐ Some Inoperative ②

**Comments:** ________

**MISCELLANEOUS**

☐ Moisture Stains Noted on Garage Ceiling•

■ Occupants' Belongings Block View of Entire Garage — Unable to Fully Inspect•

**Comments:** ________

**NOTE:** Determining the rating of firewalls is beyond the scope of this inspection

**LAUNDRY ROOM** ◇ Garage ◆ Service Area ◇ Other ________

● Plumbing (Water & Waste) Serviceable ☐ Leaks Noted• ☐ See Remarks

Elecrical Outlet Grounded ■ Not Grounded•

220 Service Operational ☐ Inoperative• ☐ None ☐ Could Not Test•

● Gas Provided ☐ Not Provided ☐ Capped ☐ Unable to View Gas Valve•

● Dryer Venting Provided ☐ Not Provided• ■ See Remarks• DOES NOT GO THROUGH WALL.

Laundry Sink Serviceable ■ None Provided

Plumbing Below Sink Serviceable ☐ Leaks Noted• ☐ Damage/Deterioration Noted• ☐ Improper Piping ②

Faucet Operational ☐ Leaking Noted•

**Comments:** ________

**NOTE:** Washing machines and dryers are not tested or moved during this inspection — condition of walls or flooring under cannot be judged. The inspector does not test washing machine drains or supply valves. Water supply valves if turned may be subject to leaking.



FORM AK 112889

10

**SECTION IX** KITCHEN & APPLIANCES — **ADDRESS** 2422 Carolina St. 7/5/90

KEY: ◇ SIGNIFIES TYPE ○ SIGNIFIES GENERAL CONDITION ☐ SIGNIFIES SPECIFIC COMMENTARY

• SIGNIFIES ITEMS THAT WARRANT ATTENTION/REPAIR ①, ②, ③, ④ SEE KEY PAGE FOR SPECIFIC RECOMMENDATIONS

**KITCHEN (General)**

Counters ◇ Tile ◆ Formica ◇ Other

● Appear Serviceable ☐ Minor Wear/Cracked• ☐ Missing Grout/Caulking•

● Cabinets Appear Serviceable ☐ Moderate/Heavy Wear• ☐ Damaged•

Window/Hardware Appears Serviceable ☐ Non-operational• ☐ None

Flooring ◇ Ceramic Tile ◆ Vinyl/Linoleum ◇ Wood ◇ Carpet

Appears Serviceable ■ Damaged: ■ Minor ☐ Excessive•

Lighting Appears Serviceable ☐ Non-operational/Flickering• ☐ Damaged Light Panel

Outlets ● Appear Serviceable ☐ Damage/Defects Noted• - COVER MISSING BEHIND REFG.

☐ Reverse Polarity 2 ☐ Inoperative 2 ☐ Open "U" Ground

Comments: SLIDING GLASS DOOR HWD. MISSING (CAN NOT LATCH OR LOCK)

**RANGE/COOKTOP**

# of Ovens 1 ◇ Gas ◇ Electric ◇ Combination

◇ Self-Cleaning ◇ Continuous Clean ◇ Electric Ignition

● Appears Serviceable ☐ Non-operational 2 ☐ No Test (Power/Gas Off)•

☐ Microwave Serviceable ☐ Non-operational 2 ■ Not Tested•

☐ Separate Cooktop Serviceable ■ Burner Did Not Operate 2

■ Oven Door Serviceable ☐ Damage Noted•

☐ Door Gasket Serviceable ☐ Not Applicable ☐ Damaged Gasket Noted•

■ Gas Shutoff Valve in Place ☐ Not Visible ☐ Not Provided 2

☐ Fan/Hood Operational ■ Non-operational 2 ☐ Filter Missing/Blocked•

Comments: OVEN DID NOT COME ON, RIGHT REAR BURNER DID NOT COME ON

NOTE: Self- and continuous cleaning operations are not tested during this inspection. The inspector does not test clocks, timing devices, lights, thermostat, calibration, or move appliances.

**DISHWASHER** N/A

Appears Serviceable ☐ Non-Operational ② ☐ No Test (Power/Water Off)

☐ Air Gap Device Present ☐ Recommend Installing Air Gap Device•

☐ Leaking Noted at Air Gap Device (Possible Blocked Drain Line)•

☐ Door Seals Appear Serviceable ☐ Deteriorated• ☐ Leaking Noted 2

☐ Condition (Door, Liner, Racks) Serviceable ☐ Rusting Noted at:•

☐ Soap Dish Inoperative• ☐ Washer Arm Appears Frozen 2

Comments:

NOTE: Determining full operability of drying cycle is beyond the scope of this inspection

T
R
A
Inspection Report
T

**GARBAGE DISPOSAL** N/A

Appears Serviceable ☐ Non-operational 2

☐ Blades Appear to Be Frozen/Missing 2 ☐ Unit Makes Unusual Noise•

☐ Splash Guard Serviceable ☐ Deteriorated/Missing•

Wiring Appears Serviceable ☐ No Ground Noted 2 ☐ Unable to Determine•

Comments:

**KITCHEN SINKS**

Appear Serviceable ☐ Minor Wear ☐ Heavy Wear/Chipped•

Faucet Serviceable ■ Leaking Noted•

☐ Plumbing Under Sink Serviceable ■ Leaking Noted• ☐ Improper Piping 2

☐ Recommend Sealing at Sink to Counter Connection ☐ Restricted View Below Sink•

Comments: SEE TERMITE REPORT FOR DAMAGE EVALUATION.

**KITCHEN SPECIAL FEATURES**

Trash Compactor Appears Serviceable ☐ Non-operational 2

☐ Water Purifier Installed But Is Not a Part of This Inspection•

☐ Instant Hot Water Maker Installed But Is Not a Part of This Inspection•

Built-in Blender Appears Serviceable ☐ Non-operational 2

☐ Ice-maker Line Installed ☐ Not Tested•

☐ Walk-in Pantry

Comments:

NOTE: Refrigerators are not part of this inspection



FORM AK 112889

11

**SECTION X** BATHROOMS **ADDRESS** 2422 Carolina St. 7/5/90

• SIGNIFIES ITEMS THAT WARRANT ATTENTION/REPAIR ①, ②, ③, ④ SEE KEY PAGE FOR SPECIFIC RECOMMENDATIONS

Locations: Bath #1 *Hall* Bath #2 ______ Bath #3 ______

**TOILET** #1 ● Appears Serviceable #2 ◯ Appears Serviceable #3 ◯ Appears Serviceable

| | #1 | #2 | #3 | | #1 | #2 | #3 |
|---|---|---|---|---|---|---|---|
| ☐ Toilet tank is loose at bath* | ☐ | ☐ | ☐ | ☐ Toilet is loose at base at bath* | ☐ | ☐ | ☐ |
| ☐ Suggest new wax seal at bath ② | ☐ | ☐ | ☐ | ☐ Cracked tank noted at bath* | ☐ | ☐ | ☐ |
| ■ Water runs continually in tank at* | ■ | ☐ | ☐ | ☐ Cracked bowl/base at bath* | ☐ | ☐ | ☐ |
| ☐ Does not flush properly at* | ☐ | ☐ | ☐ | ☐ Moisture detected around toilet ② | ☐ | ☐ | ☐ |

Comments:

**SINK** #1 ◯ Appears Serviceable #2 ◯ Appears Serviceable #3 ◯ Appears Serviceable

| | #1 | #2 | #3 | | #1 | #2 | #3 |
|---|---|---|---|---|---|---|---|
| ■ Sink ~~cracked~~/damaged at bath* | ■ | ☐ | ☐ | ☐ Corrosion/damage noted underside of sink* | ☐ | ☐ | ☐ |

**Faucet** *SEE COMMENTS* #1 ◯ Appears Serviceable #2 ◯ Appears Serviceable #3 ◯ Appears Serviceable

| | #1 | #2 | #3 | | #1 | #2 | #3 |
|---|---|---|---|---|---|---|---|
| ☐ Sink faucet leaks at bath* | ☐ | ☐ | ☐ | ☐ Corrosion/damage noted at sink faucet* | ☐ | ☐ | ☐ |
| ☐ Low water volume noted at ② | ☐ | ☐ | ☐ | ☐ Corrosion noted on supply valves below sink* | ☐ | ☐ | ☐ |

**Drain** #1 ◯ Appears Serviceable #2 ◯ Appears Serviceable #3 ◯ Appears Serviceable

| | #1 | #2 | #3 | | #1 | #2 | #3 |
|---|---|---|---|---|---|---|---|
| ☐ Slow draining noted at bath* | ☐ | ☐ | ☐ | ☐ Sink drain stopper did not operate at bath* | ☐ | ☐ | ☐ |
| ☐ Rust/corrosion on drain line at bath* | ☐ | ☐ | ☐ | ☐ Improper drain trap noted at bath ② | ☐ | ☐ | ☐ |
| ☐ Leaking noted at drain line at bath ② | ☐ | ☐ | ☐ | | | | |

**Counter & Cabinet** #1 ● Appears Serviceable #2 ◯ Appears Serviceable #3 ◯ Appears Serviceable

| | #1 | #2 | #3 | | #1 | #2 | #3 |
|---|---|---|---|---|---|---|---|
| ☐ Damage/deterioration noted to counter* | ☐ | ☐ | ☐ | ☐ Damage/deterioration noted to cabinet* | ☐ | ☐ | ☐ |
| ☐ Grout/caulking suggested at counter* | ☐ | ☐ | ☐ | ☐ Moisture damage noted below sink at bath* | ☐ | ☐ | ☐ |

Comments: *HANDLES ARE MISSING FROM SINK FAUCET. SINK WAS NOT USE OR INSPECTED*

**ELECTRICAL** #1 ● Appears Serviceable #2 ◯ Appears Serviceable #3 ◯ Appears Serviceable

| | #1 | #2 | #3 | | #1 | #2 | #3 |
|---|---|---|---|---|---|---|---|
| ☐ Outlet did not operate at bath ② | ☐ | ☐ | ☐ | ☐ Open U ground noted on outlet at bath* | ☐ | ☐ | ☐ |
| ☐ "G.F.C.I." protection did not respond ② | ☐ | ☐ | ☐ | ☐ "G.F.C.I." protection suggested at bath* | ☐ | ☐ | ☐ |
| ☐ Outlet is loose/broken at bath ② | ☐ | ☐ | ☐ | ☐ Hot-neutral reversed on outlet at ② | ☐ | ☐ | ☐ |
| ☐ No outlet found in bath* | ☐ | ☐ | ☐ | ☐ Outlet/switch too close to tub/shower at bath* | ☐ | ☐ | ☐ |
| ☐ Light did not operate at bath* | ☐ | ☐ | ☐ | ☐ Unable to determine light operation at* | ☐ | ☐ | ☐ |

G.F.C.I. protection is for safety in wet areas — older homes will commonly not be equipped with this device

*...MEND ADDING GFCI PROTECTION*

**T**
**R**
**A**
**Inspection Report**
**T**

... ● Appears Serviceable #2 ◯ Appears Serviceable #3 ◯ Appears Serviceable

| | #1 | #2 | #3 | | #1 | #2 | #3 |
|---|---|---|---|---|---|---|---|
| ...ate at bath* | ☐ | ☐ | ☐ | ☐ Exhaust fan makes an unusual noise at bath* | ☐ | ☐ | ☐ |
| ...on noted at bath* | ☐ | ☐ | ☐ | ☐ Recommend installing an exhaust fan at bath* | ☐ | ☐ | ☐ |
| ...al at bath* | ☐ | ☐ | ☐ | ☐ Broken/damaged window noted at bath* | ☐ | ☐ | ☐ |

**HEATER** #1 Appears Serviceable #2 Appears Serviceable #3 ◯ Appears Serviceable

| | #1 | #2 | #3 | | #1 | #2 | #3 |
|---|---|---|---|---|---|---|---|
| ☐ Heater did not operate at bath ② | ☐ | ☐ | ☐ | ☐ No heater/heat source provided at bath* | ☐ | ☐ | ☐ |

Comments: *HEAT SOURCE IS FROM FORCED AIR FURNACE ACTING AS A SPACE HEATER (NO REGISTERS EXCEPT AT HALL)*

**TUB** #1 ● Appears Serviceable #2 Appears Serviceable #3 ◯ Appears Serviceable

| | #1 | #2 | #3 | | #1 | #2 | #3 |
|---|---|---|---|---|---|---|---|
| ☐ Damage/deterioration noted to tub* | ☐ | ☐ | ☐ | ■ Moisture damage noted to wall/~~floor~~ by tub ③ | ■ | ☐ | ☐ |

**Faucet** #1 ● Appears Serviceable #2 Appears Serviceable #3 Appears Serviceable

| | #1 | #2 | #3 | | #1 | #2 | #3 |
|---|---|---|---|---|---|---|---|
| ☐ Leaking noted at faucet handles at bath ② | ☐ | ☐ | ☐ | ☐ Constant dripping at tub spout at bath ② | ☐ | ☐ | ☐ |
| ☐ Corrosion/damage noted at faucet* | ☐ | ☐ | ☐ | ☐ Low water volume noted at bath ② | ☐ | ☐ | ☐ |

**Drain** #1 ● Appears Serviceable #2 Appears Serviceable #3 Appears Serviceable

| | #1 | #2 | #3 | | #1 | #2 | #3 |
|---|---|---|---|---|---|---|---|
| ☐ Slow draining noted at bathtub* | ☐ | ☐ | ☐ | ☐ Drain stopper is not operational at bathtub* | ☐ | ☐ | ☐ |

Comments: *WALLS AROUND TUB ARE IN VERY POOR CONDITION, SEE TERMITE REPORT FOR EVALUATION ALSO DID NOT OPERATE SHOWER BECAUSE OF WALLS*

**SHOWER** #1 Appears Serviceable *NOT INSPECTED* #2 Appears Serviceable #3 Appears Serviceable

| | #1 | #2 | #3 | | #1 | #2 | #3 |
|---|---|---|---|---|---|---|---|
| ☐ Damage/deterioration noted to shower walls* | ☐ | ☐ | ☐ | ☐ Cracked/broken tiles noted at bath* | ☐ | ☐ | ☐ |
| ☐ Grout/caulking needed at shower walls* | ☐ | ☐ | ☐ | ☐ Caulking needed at tub to floor at bath* | ☐ | ☐ | ☐ |
| ☐ Moisture damage noted to wall/floor at ③ | ☐ | ☐ | ☐ | ☐ Grout/caulking needed at shower pan at bath* | ☐ | ☐ | ☐ |
| ☐ Slow draining noted at shower at bath* | ☐ | ☐ | ☐ | ☐ Low water volume noted at shower head in bath ② | ☐ | ☐ | ☐ |
| ☐ Leaking noted at water valve(s) at bath ② | ☐ | ☐ | ☐ | ☐ Shower diverter not operational at bath ② | ☐ | ☐ | ☐ |
| ☐ Leaking/dripping noted at shower head* | ☐ | ☐ | ☐ | ☐ Corrosion noted at shower fixtures at bath* | ☐ | ☐ | ☐ |

**Enclosure** #1 Appears Serviceable #2 Appears Serviceable #3 ◯ Appears Serviceable

| | #1 | #2 | #3 | | #1 | #2 | #3 |
|---|---|---|---|---|---|---|---|
| ☐ Glass does not appear to be tempered at bath* | ☐ | ☐ | ☐ | ☐ Unable to determine if glass is tempered at bath* | ☐ | ☐ | ☐ |
| ☐ Broken glass/enclosure at bath* | ☐ | ☐ | ☐ | ☐ Doors are difficult to operate at bath* | ☐ | ☐ | ☐ |
| ☐ Caulking needed at doors/enclosure at bath* | ☐ | ☐ | ☐ | ☐ Corrosion/damage noted at enclosure at bath* | ☐ | ☐ | ☐ |

**NOTE:** Determining whether shower pans are watertight is beyond the scope of this inspection. Recommend referring to termite report for information concerning the water testing of the shower pan/base

Comments:



12

FORM AK 112889

**GENERAL NOTES**

**ADDRESS** 2422 Carolina St. 7/5/90

ROOFING SURFACE: HOUSE WILL NEED ONGOING MAINTENANCE. GARAGE NEEDS REPLACEMENT.

PLUMBING: CONDITION OF GALVANIZED PIPE (UNDERGROUND SERVICE) IS UNKNOWN, INTERIOR PIPING (WHERE EXPOSED) APPEARS TO BE COPPER. NO SIGNIFICANT PROBLEMS VIEWED

CONDITION AND APPROVAL OF COPPER TUBING AS GAS SUPPLY PIPE SHOULD BE CHECKED.

ACTIVE LEAK NOTED IN DRAIN UNDER SINK.

SLIDING GLASS DOOR CAN NOT BE LATCHED OR LOCKED.

MOST DOORS WERE ~~NOT~~ INACCESSABLE FOR INSPECTION DUE TO STORED BELONGINGS AS WERE MOST 110 VOLT RECEPTACLES.

ELECTRICAL SERVICE AND PANEL IS ANEQUATED BY TODAYS STANDARDS, RECOMMEND UPGRADING

PG&E SHOULD INSPECT WATER HEATER FURNACE PRIOR TO CLOSE OF ESCROW

FURNACE BLOWER COMPARTMENT DOOR N... REPAIR AND COMBUSTION AIR SUPPLY BE CHANGED

WATER STAINS AND DETERIORATION IN ROOF OVER HANG AREA (COULD BE FROM AN OLD ROOF LEAK)

WINDOWS ARE CRACKED OR BROKEN IN THE LIVING ROOM AND FAMILY ROOM. THESE WINDOWS ARE NOT SAFETY GLASS.

GARAGE HAS BEEN CONVERTED TO FAMILY ROOM — (VERY, VERY LIKELY NOT TO PERMIT OR BY LICENSED (CONTRACTOR)

DRYER VENT TERMINATES INSIDE WALL (SHORT OF HOLE TO EXERIOR) SHOULD BE EXTENDED

OTHER PROBLEMS NOTED IN FOLLOWING PAGES READ THE ENTIRE REPORT.

THIS IS NOT A SUMMRY PAGE.



**T R A I T Inspection Report**

# Title Company

PRELIMINARY REPORT

- [x] 100 CEMENT HILL ROAD FAIRFIELD, CALIFORNIA 94533 · TELEPHONE (707) 429-2211
- [ ] 1241 ALAMO DR., SUITE 2 VACAVILLE, CALIFORNIA 95687 · TELEPHONE (707) 448-8431
- [ ] 1422 SPRINGS ROAD, SUITE A VALLEJO, CALIFORNIA 94590 · TELEPHONE (707) 554-0990
- [ ] 1015 1ST STREET BENICIA, CALIFORNIA 94510 · TELEPHONE (707) 745-4140

ME

FIRST UPDATE

NOW WITH 2 YEAR SHORT TERM RATE

ESCROW
5920 STONERIDGE MALL RD.
PLEASANTON, CA

ATTENTION: RICK

Your No. 21499 RJ
Our No. 403418 RM
Escrow Officer RAMA
Purchaser—
Property Address 2422 CAROLINA ST. VALLEJO

Dated as of AUGUST 17 1990 at 7:30 A.M.

T
R
A
I
T itle Report (Preliminary)

In response to the above referenced application for a policy of title insurance,

# Title Company

In response to the above referenced application for a policy of title insurance, COMPANY hereby reports that it is prepared to issue, or cause to be issued, as or Policies of Title Insurance describing the land and the estate or interest therein hereinafter set forth, insuring against loss which may be sustained by reason of any defect, lien or encumbrance not shown or referred to as an Exception in Schedule B or not excluded from coverage pursuant to the printed Schedules, Conditions and Stipulations of said Policy forms.

The printed Exceptions and Exclusions from the coverage of said Policy or Policies are set forth in the attached list. Copies of the Policy forms should be read. They are available from the office which issued this report.

THIS REPORT, (AND ANY SUPPLEMENTS OR AMENDMENTS HERETO) IS ISSUED SOLELY FOR THE PURPOSE OF FACILITATING THE ISSUANCE OF A POLICY OF TITLE INSURANCE AND NO LIABILITY IS ASSUMED HEREBY. IF IT IS DESIRED THAT LIABILITY BE ASSUMED PRIOR TO THE ISSUANCE OF A POLICY OF TITLE INSURANCE, A BINDER OR COMMITMENT SHOULD BE REQUESTED.

The form of policy of title insurance contemplated by this report is:

1. California Land Title Association Standard Coverage Policy [x]
2. American Land Title Association Owner's Policy Form B [ ]
3. American Land Title Association Residential Title Insurance Policy [ ]
4. American Land Title Association Loan Policy [ ]

Title Officer ____________

# TITLE COMPANY

# NOTICE

Section 12413.1 of the California Insurance Code became effective on January 1, 1990. This new law requires that any title insurance company, underwritten title company or controlled escrow company handling funds in an escrow or subescrow capacity must have all cash, checks and drafts representing disbursements to be made by it deposited into its escrow depository bank account before recording your transaction. It further states that the checks, etc. must be deposited and drafts actually collected before disbursement can occur.

The new law has added a three-tier structure for determining when the funds deposited can be disbursed, and to avoid any delay necessitated by this new law please consider the following:

1. SAME DAY AVAILABILITY

   A. Cash - provided deposited into escrow depository prior to close of escrow
   B. Electronic transfer (wired funds)

2. NEXT DAY AVAILABILITY (After date of deposit into escrow depository)

   A. Cashier's checks
   B. Certified checks
   C. Teller's checks

3. SEVEN DAY AVAILABILITY (After date of deposit into escrow depository)

   A. Personal checks
   B. Mortgage Company or Mortgage Banker Checks
   C. All other types of checks

4. AVOID USING DRAFTS

If you have any questions about the effect of the new law on your escrow please contact your local Title Company Office.

FORM 1030 (REV. 1/90)

403418
657

SCHEDULE A

THE ESTATE OR THE INTEREST IN THE LAND DESCRIBED OR REFERRED TO IN THIS SCHEDULE COVERED BY THIS REPORT IS:

A FEE

TITLE TO SAID ESTATE OR INTEREST AT THE DATE HEREOF IS VESTED IN:

JESSE & MARIA CARRANZA,
HUSBAND AND WIFE, AS JOINT TENANTS

ALL THAT CERTAIN REAL PROPERTY SITUATED IN THE COUNTY OF SOLANO, CITY OF VALLEJO, STATE OF CALIFORNIA AND MORE PARTICULARLY DESCRIBED AS FOLLOWS:

LOT 43, SPRING MANOR, UNIT 3, FILED ON SEPTEMBER 20, 1951 IN BOOK 12 OF MAPS, PAGE 20, SOLANO COUNTY RECORDS.

APN 71-033-070

403418
657

SCHEDULE B

AT THE DATE HEREOF EXCEPTIONS TO COVERAGE IN ADDITION TO THE PRINTED EXCEPTIONS AND EXCLUSIONS CONTAINED IN SAID POLICY FORM WOULD BE AS FOLLOWS:

1. PROPERTY TAXES, INCLUDING ANY ASSESSMENTS COLLECTED WITH TAXES, TO BE LEVIED FOR THE FISCAL YEAR 1990-1991 ARE A LIEN NOT YET PAYABLE.

2. THE LIEN OF SUPPLEMENT TAXES, IF ANY, ASSESSED PURSUANT TO THE PROVISIONS OF CHAPTER 3.5 (COMMENCING WITH SECTION 75) OF THE REVENUE AND TAXATION CODE, OF THE STATE OF CALIFORNIA.

3. THE HEREIN DESCRIBED PROPERTY LIES WITHIN THE BOUNDS OF THE VALLEJO SANITATION AND FLOOD CONTROL DISTRICT AND IS THEREFORE SUBJECT TO ALL THEIR TAXES AND ASSESSMENTS THEREOF. SAID TAXES ARE PAYABLE AND COLLECTED WITH THE CITY AND COUNTY TAXES.

4. MUNICIPAL AND ANY UNPAID CHARGES FOR THE CITY OF VALLEJO, IF ANY. FOR AMOUNTS DUE PLEASE CONTACT THE FOLLOWING:

   VALLEJO GARBAGE: (707) 552-3110
   WEED ABATEMENT: (707) 648-4565
   V.S.F.C.D.: (707) 644-8949 EXT. 224

5. AN EASEMENT FOR THE PURPOSES SHOWN BELOW AND RIGHTS INCIDENTAL THERETO AS SHOWN OR AS OFFERED FOR DEDICATION ON THE RECORDED MAP SHOWN BELOW
   MAP OF: SPRINGS MANOR UNIT 3
   RECORDED: IN BOOK 12 OF MAPS, PAGE 20
   EASEMENT PURPOSE: PUBLIC UTILITIES
   AFFECTS: WESTERLY 10 FEET OF THE PREMISES

6. COVENANTS, CONDITIONS AND RESTRICTIONS (DELETING THEREFROM ANY RESTRICTIONS BASED ON RACE, COLOR OR CREED) AS SET FORTH IN THE DOCUMENT
   RECORDED: SEPTEMBER 20, 1971, AS INSTRUMENT NO. 11753, PAGE 595, SOLANO COUNTY RECORDS

   SAID COVENANTS, CONDITIONS AND RESTRICTIONS PROVIDE THAT A VIOLATION THEREOF SHALL NOT DEFEAT THE LIEN OF ANY MORTGAGE OR DEED OF TRUST MADE IN GOOD FAITH AND FOR VALUE.

7. A HOMESTEAD DECLARATION
   EXECUTED BY: JESSE & MARIA CARRANZA
   DATED: FEBRUARY 17, 1987
   RECORDED: FEBRUARY 18, 1987, AS INSTRUMENT NO. 11787, PAGE 21272, BOOK 1987, SOLANO COUNTY RECORDS

403418
657

8. A DEED OF TRUST TO SECURE AN INDEBTEDNESS IN THE AMOUNT SHOWN BELOW, AND ANY OTHER OBLIGATIONS SECURED THEREBY

AMOUNT: $67,500.00
DATED: JANUARY 4, 1989
TRUSTOR: JESSE R. CARRANZA & MARIA T. CARRANCA , HUSBAND AND WIFE, AS JOINT TENANTS
TRUSTEE: GREEN AND CO., INC, A CALIFORNIA CORPORATION
BENEFICIARY: GREEN AND CO., INC., A CALIFORNIA CORPORATION
RECORDED: JANUARY 12, 1989, AS INSTRUMENT NO. 2430, BOOK 1989, SOLANO COUNTY RECORDS

ACCORDING TO THE PUBLIC RECORDS, INFORMATION ON THE ABOVE LOAN MAY BE AVAILABLE BY CONTACTING THE BENEFICIARY

AT: REEN AND CO., INC.
ADDRESS: 561 REDWOOD HIGHWAY, SUITE 224
MILL VALLEY, CA 94941

AN ASSIGNMENT OF THE BENEFICIAL INTEREST UNDER SAID DEED OF TRUST WHICH NAMES

AS ASSIGNEES: G. L. LANCASTER , TRUSTEE UNDER THE WILLS OF W.F. GOHEEN DTD 9/27/66, AS TO AN UNDIVIDED 19.5/67.5TH INTEREST; REEN MORTGAGE FUND I, A CALIFORNIA LIMITED PARTNERSHIP, AS TO AN UNDIVIDED 20/67.5TH INTEREST; JERRAD R. WONG & THERESA E. WONG , HUSBAND AND WIFE, AS JOINT TENANTS, AS TO AN UNDIVIDED 28/67.5TH INTEREST
RECORDED: MARCH 3, 1989, AS INSTRUMENT NO. 12947, BOOK 1989, SOLANO COUNTY RECORDS

A SUBSTITUTION OF TRUSTEE UNDER SAID DEED OF TRUST WHICH NAMES AS THE SUBSTITUTED TRUSTEE, THE FOLLOWING

TRUSTEE: STANDARD TRUST DEED SERVICE COMPANY
RECORDED: JUNE 22, 1990, AS INSTRUMENT NO. 48988, BOOK 1990, SOLANO COUNTY RECORDS

TAX INFORMATION:

PROPERTY TAXES FOR THE FISCAL YEAR SHOWN BELOW ARE PAID. FOR PRORATION PURPOSES THE AMOUNTS FOR FISCAL YEAR 1989-1990 ARE:

ASSESSMENT NO: 71-033-070
CODE AREA: 7000
TAX RATE: $1.073000
LAND: $ 22,523.00
IMPROVEMENTS: $ 45,046.00
PERSONAL PROPERTY: $ 0.00
EXEMPTION: $ 0.00
1ST INSTALLMENT: $ 441.00
2ND INSTALLMENT: $ 441.00

THE HEREIN DESCRIBED PROPERTY LIES WITHIN THE BOUNDS OF THE UNPAID GARBAGE DISTRICT AND IS THEREFORE SUBJECT TO ALL THEIR TAXES AND ASSESSMENTS THEREOF. SAID TAXES ARE PAYABLE AND COLLECTED WITH THE CITY TAXES.

403418
657

NOTE:

THE ONLY CONVEYANCES AFFECTING SAID LAND, WHICH RECORDED WITHIN TWENTY-FOUR (24) MONTHS OF THE DATE OF THIS REPORT, ARE AS FOLLOWS:

DOCUMENT: INDIVIDUAL GRANT DEED

GRANTOR: JESSE R. CARRANZA & MARIA T. CARRANZA, , DANIEL L. & THERESA E. MONDRAGON , JOINT TENANCY

GRANTEE: JESSE R. CARRANZA & MARIA T. CARRANZA , HUSBAND AND WIFE, AS JOINT TENANTS

RECORDED: JANUARY 12, 1989, AS INSTRUMENT NO. 2429, BOOK 1989, SOLANO COUNTY RECORDS

NOTE:

THE CHARGE FOR A POLICY OF TITLE INSURANCE, WHEN ISSUED THROUGH THIS TITLE ORDER, WILL BE BASED ON THE SHORT-TERM RATE.

NOTE:

ANY CONVEYANCE OF THE LAND DESCRIBED HEREIN SHALL BE SUBJECT TO CITY OF VALLEJO DOCUMENTARY TRANSFER TAX OF $2.20 PER $1,000.00 BASED ON THE FULL VALUE SALES PRICE IN ADDITION TO ANY OTHER APPLICABLE TRANSFER TAX.

NOTE:

THIS REPORT IS SUBJECT TO A MINIMUM CANCELLATION CHARGE OF $250.00 AS REQUIRED BY SECTION 12404 OF INSURANCE CODE AND RULE 2 OF BULLETIN NO. NS - 35E.

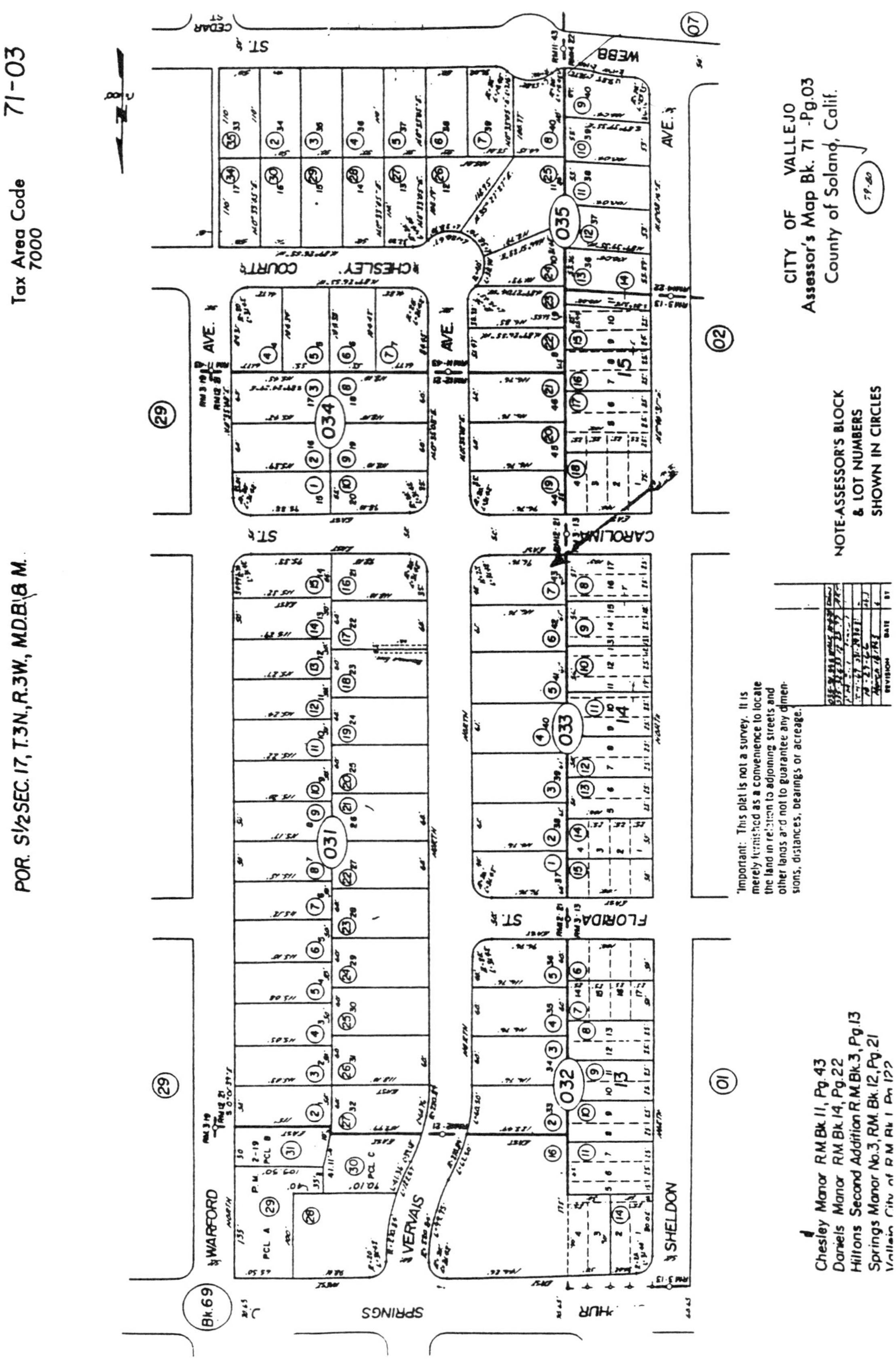

Tax Area Code 7000
71-03
POR. S1/2 SEC. 17, T.3N., R.3W., M.D.B.&M.
CITY OF VALLEJO
Assessor's Map Bk. 71 -Pg.03
County of Solano, Calif.
NOTE-ASSESSOR'S BLOCK & LOT NUMBERS SHOWN IN CIRCLES
Important: This plat is not a survey. It is merely furnished as a convenience to locate the land in relation to adjoining streets and other lands and not to guarantee any dimensions, distances, bearings or acreage.
Chesley Manor R.M.Bk. 11, Pg. 43
Daniels Manor R.M.Bk. 14, Pg. 22
Hiltons Second Addition R.M.Bk.3, Pg.13
Springs Manor No.3, R.M. Bk. 12, Pg. 21
CEDAR ST
WEBB AVE.
CHESLEY COURT
CAROLINA ST.
FLORIDA ST.
SPRINGS
WARFORD AVE.
VERVAIS
SHELDON
Bk. 69

# LIST OF PRINTED EXCEPTIONS AND EXCLUSIONS

## 1. CALIFORNIA LAND TITLE ASSOCIATION STANDARD COVERAGE POLICY - 1973

### SCHEDULE B

This policy does not insure against loss or damage, nor against costs, attorneys' fees or expenses, any or all of which arise by reason of the following:

Part I

1. Taxes or assessments which are not shown as existing liens by the records of any taxing authority that levies taxes or assessments on real property or by the public records.

Proceedings by a public agency which may result in taxes or assessments, or notices of such proceedings, whether or not shown by the records of such agency or by the public records.

2. Any facts, rights, interests or claims which are not shown by the public records but which could be ascertained by an inspection of the land or by making inquiry of persons in possession theeof.

3. Easements, liens or encumbrances, or claims thereof, which are not shown by the public records.

4. Discrepancies, conflicts in boundary lines, shortage in area, encroachments, or any other facts which a correct survey would disclose, and which are not shown by the public records.

5. (a) Unpatented mining claims; (b) reservations or exceptions in patents or in Acts authorizing the issuance thereof; (c) water rights, claims or title to water.

6. Any right, title, interest, estate or easement in land beyond the lines of the area specifically described or referred to in Schedule A, or in abutting streets, roads, avenues, alleys, lanes, ways or waterways, but nothing in this paragraph shall modify or limit the extent to which the ordinary right of an abutting owner for access to a physically open street or highway is insured by this policy.

7. Any law, ordinance or governmental regulation (including but not limited to building and zoning ordinances) restricting or regulating or prohibiting the occupancy, use or enjoyment of the land, or regulating the character, dimensions, or location of any improvement now or hereafter erected on the land, or prohibiting a separation in ownership or a reduction in the dimensions or area of the land, or the effect of any violation of any such law, ordinance or governmental regulation.

8. Rights of eminent domain or governmental rights of police power unless notice of the exercise of such rights appears in the public records.

9. Defects, liens, encumbrances, adverse claims, or other matters (a) created, suffered, assumed or agreed to by the insured claimant; (b) not shown by the public records and not otherwise excluded from coverage but known to the insured claimant either at Date of Policy or at the date such claimant acquired an estate or interest insured by this policy or acquired the insured mortgage and not disclosed in writing by the insured claimant to the Company prior to the date such insured claimant became an insured hereunder; (c) resulting in no loss or damage to the insured claimant; (d) attaching or created subsequent to Date of Policy; or (e) resulting in loss or damage which would not have been sustained if the insured claimant had been a purchaser or encumbrancer for value without knowledge.

---

## 2. AMERICAN LAND TITLE ASSOCIATION OWNER'S POLICY FORM B - 1970 (AMENDED 10-17-70)

### SCHEDULE OF EXCLUSIONS FROM COVERAGE

1. Any law, ordinance or governmental regulation (including but not limited to building and zoning ordinances) restricting or regulating or prohibiting the occupancy, use or enjoyment of the land, or regulating the character, dimensions or location of any improvement now or hereafter erected on the land, or prohibiting a separation in ownership or a reduction in the dimensions of area of the land, or the effect of any violation of any such law, ordinance or governmental regulation.
2. Rights of eminent domain or governmental rights of police power unless notice of the exercise of such rights appears in the public records at Date of Policy.
3. Defects, liens, encumbrances, adverse Claims, or other matters (a) created, suffered, assumed or agreed to by the insured claimant; (b) not known to the Company and not shown by the public records but known to the insured claimant either at Date of Policy or at the date such claimant acquired an estate or interest by this policy and not disclosed in writing by the insured claimant to the Company prior to the date such insured claimant became an insured hereunder; (c) resulting in no loss or damage to the insured claimant; (d) attaching or created subsequent to Date of Policy; (e) resulting in loss or damage which would not have been sustained if the insured claimant had paid value for the estate or interest insured by this policy.

(List of Printed Exceptions and Exclusions Continued on Reverse Side)

Chapter 7

# Curing the Defaulted Loans

## *How to Avoid the Most Expensive Mistake of Your Life*

### BRINGING THE LOAN CURRENT

It is important to bring the loans current, that is, to pay the unpaid installments (and any penalties) to cure the default as soon as possible. How you do it is a matter of tactics. To cure the default as quickly as possible, I suggest you make payments by using cashier's checks (see page 194).

By bringing the loans current you stop the foreclosure clock. However, if you plan to hold the property to rehabilitate or sell, it will be important to get the payment books. In the frenzy of completing the purchase and satisfying the sellers' needs, you may overlook the payment books, or, as happens in many cases, the seller has given up on the future and just thrown them away. Request that the seller sign a letter asking for new payment books. You may need to do some research to find the addresses of specific lenders because many savings and loans have numerous branches. If your lender happens to be a private party, you may have to get the address from the seller.

Most loans written today include a clause that enables the lender to accelerate the loan if the property is "alienated" (that is, if title is transferred). In effect, the lender can invoke such a clause to require the immediate payment of the balance of the loan if the property is transferred to a new owner or leased for any extended period of time. Usually, a few thousand dollars needed to make the delinquent loan payments is a reasonable cost of doing business; repayment of the entire loan is not.

If the lender does become aware that title has been transferred, the question arises, can or will the lender accelerate the loan? Federal law gives the lender the right to accelerate or make the entire loan balance due and payable upon the alienation or conveyance of title. In the practical world of doing business from day to day, this rarely if ever occurs. Lenders are generally happy just to be receiving payments on time. Loans that have fallen into default usually end up in special departments of the institutions: these have such names as the Foreclosure Department, Foreclosure Section, Trustee Productions, Sheriff's Sale, and Bankruptcy Departments. These departments all have their own little empires. Their primary function is to get the loan payments, and they rarely worry about accelerating the loans and requesting the full balance.

What are your alternatives? You could approach the lender prior to the purchase and request an assumption agreement. Or you could inform the lender that you will bring the loan current if you are given a written notice that the loan will not be accelerated.

You will need to decide if you want to assume the loans, to just make payments, or to bargain with the lenders. The simple procedure used in the example was to make payments, fix up the property, and sell it to a new purchaser, who then paid off both loans.

Expect the lenders to learn what is going on and to be aware of the rights they have under the law. However, because the defaulting loan is often transferred to a different department, it could be months before you get any correspondence from the lender.

### A Place to Live

Curing the loan default and paying the back taxes will save the property you have bought from foreclosure and free it of the defaulted lien notice. You have also solved the seller's long-term problems. But until the seller is out of the house, both seller and buyer have a short-term problem. You need possession, and the seller needs money. Many sellers in foreclosure have little or no money. They don't have enough to pay the first and last month's rent on a new dwelling. If you don't get them out, you'll never get possession. If, after you have deducted the costs of the termite and roof repairs and other liens, you see that you still have money due to the seller, you should consider assisting the seller in finding a new home. However, be cautious about how you spend these funds. Your only guarantee that the seller will indeed leave is to refrain from making the final payment until after the property has been vacated. *Don't violate this rule.*

Once again, it's a matter of solving problems. For both parties, the solution in this case is to have the seller find a new home. For the seller this is difficult because prospective landlords will request a complete credit application and expect the prospective tenant to pay for the credit report. When a seller is in default the credit report is likely to be a mess of everything from late payments to liens on the house, to abstracts or judgments from department stores. This is an extremely embarrassing and humiliating experience for the seller, and may cause him to reconsider the transaction with you and attempt to cancel your contract.

Help the seller out of trouble. Instruct the seller to find a place to live and tell him that you will guarantee the rent. Have the landlord call you to confirm the arrangement. Landlords like to have rent, and you want the property. So pay the rent in advance for the defaulting seller. This too, becomes an expense and is deducted from the price paid for the equity. A cashier's check assures the new landlord that the funds are available at the bank.

Keeping with our approach of using only professionals for our series of reports of termite inspections, roof inspections, and so forth, it is suggested that you notarize your payment of the seller's rent. That document will then become part of your settlement documents and not be subject to further inquiry.

## SETTLE WITH THE OWNER

The final procedure in the purchase of distressed property is to settle with the owner. The contract clearly stated that you would deduct the costs of repairs, taxes, and other expenses. Draw up a detailed bill of the expenses, making sure that your statement of account is as simple as possible. When you have completed your final walk-through and have determined that no additional damage has been incurred, and that the owners have removed all of their personal belongings, present the seller with the final statement and a cashier's check for the balance due, if any.

## REVIEW

- Find out who to pay. Who is the mortgagee or lender?
- Review the Notice of Default. Check the legal description. Is it the correct property?
- If the Notice of Trustee Sale has been issued, review it along with the legal description. The beneficiary or mortgagee, mortgagor, or attorney that filed the documents are the key to preventing the Trustee's/Sheriff's Sale. In the majority of cases, they want the money to cure/reinstate the loan and do not want to foreclose.
- Correspond with the lenders or their representatives.
- The lender will rarely give information to outsiders about the loans. Therefore, you should have the seller sign the letters and then use your own name and address as shown in the letters.
- Review the response from the lender.
- Send a letter to the lender to cure/reinstate the delinquent loan, accompanied by a cashier's check from the bank. Request that the lender direct a notice of rescission to your office after the check is tendered.

The process will be similar in the judicial states, but the documentation will have different nomenclature. The Default Notice will probably be listed as a complaint from the bank's attorney (plaintiff) against the homeowner (defendant). The sequence of paying the lender will remain the same as above. First, request the lender (mortgagee) advise you what is owed and then pay him with a bank check if you and the seller agree that the amount the lender claims is correct.

05 01
02/20/90

RE: 30 DAY FINAL NOTICE

| | |
|---|---|
| PAYMENT DUE JAN 1, 1990 | 2,631.28 |
| PAYMENT DUE FEB 1, 1990 | 2,631.28 |
| LATE CHARGES | 315.76 |
| TOTAL DUE | 5,578.32 |

LOAN NUMBER 359-008455

MAILING ADDRESS:

GUY GABBY
132 Corral Circle
San Ramon, CA 94583

**Warning Letter from the Lender**

DEAR CUSTOMER:

PRIOR TO BEGINNING FORECLOSURE, WE ARE REQUIRED UNDER THE TERMS OF YOUR LOAN TO NOTIFY YOU OF YOUR DEFAULT.

1. YOUR LOAN IS IN DEFAULT. THE AMOUNT NEEDED TO BRING YOUR LOAN CURRENT AND PREVENT FORECLOSURE IS SHOWN ABOVE. IT INCLUDES ALL PREVIOUSLY DUE AND UNPAID LATE CHARGES.

2. THIS AMOUNT PLUS THE PAYMENT BECOMING DUE NEXT MONTH MUST ALL BE PAID WITHIN THIRTY (30) DAYS OF THE DATE OF THIS NOTICE.

3. FAILURE TO MAKE FULL PAYMENT WILL RESULT IN ACCELERATION OF THE TOTAL LOAN AMOUNT AND THE COMMENCEMENT OF FORECLOSURE PROCEEDINGS. YOU ARE INFORMED THAT YOU HAVE THE RIGHT TO REINSTATE THE LOAN AFTER ACCELERATION AND THE RIGHT TO ASSERT IN THE FORECLOSURE PROCEEDING THE NON-EXISTENCE OF A DEFAULT OR ANY OTHER DEFENSE YOU MAY HAVE TO ACCELERATION AND FORECLOSURE. (SUCH RIGHT OF REINSTATEMENT IS SET FORTH IN THE MORTGAGE WHICH YOU EXECUTED, AND YOU ARE DIRECTED TO THAT INSTRUMENT FOR THE COMPLETE DETAILS OF SUCH RIGHT.)

4. WE ARE HEREBY GIVING YOU NOTICE THAT WE MAY MAKE OR CAUSE TO BE MADE REASONABLE ENTRIES UPON AND INSPECTIONS OF YOUR PROPERTY. WE WILL ATTEMPT TO CONTACT YOU BEFORE WE MAKE SUCH ENTRY. HOWEVER, IF THE PROPERTY IS DETERMINED TO BE VACANT OR ABANDONED, WE WILL TAKE STEPS NECESSARY TO PROTECT THE PROPERTY AGAINST VANDALISM OR OTHER TYPES OF DAMAGES, SUCH AS EXPOSURE TO THE ELEMENTS.

5. ALL FORECLOSURE COSTS AND EXPENSES INCURRED WILL BE YOUR RESPONSIBILITY TO PAY.

IF YOU HAVE A SINCERE DESIRE TO RETAIN YOUR PROPERTY AND WANT TO MINIMIZE YOUR COSTS TO REINSTATE YOUR LOAN, YOU MUST CALL US IMMEDIATELY.

LOAN SERVICE DEPARTMENT
1-800-635-5553

**CAL-WESTERN FORECLOSURE SERVICES**

August 04, 1989

Guy Gabby
132 Corral Circle
San Ramon, CA 94583

**Lender advising the homeowner of the impending Notice of Default**

Trustee's Sale No. 202361

Pursuant to the requirements contained in section 2924B of the Civil Code of the state of California, we enclose a copy of Notice of Default and Election to Sell under Deed of Trust with the recording date shown thereon in an envelope and with postage prepaid.

You will please observe that said Notice of Default and Election to Sell under Deed of Trust was recorded on 7/31/89 and that this notice was mailed within the required statutory time limit.

Unless you notify us at the address on the attached notice within 30 days after receiving this notice that you dispute the validity of the debt or any portion thereof, we will assume this debt is valid. If you notice that you dispute this debt, we will obtain a verification of the debt from the lender and mail you a copy.

If you make a request to us in writing within 30 days after receiving this notice, we will provide you with the name and address of the original creditor.

Sincerely,

Freddye Mays
Trustee's Sale Officer

Enclosure

RECORDING REQUESTED BY

WHEN RECORDED MAIL TO

CAL-WESTERN RECONVEYANCE CORPORATION

P.O. Box 9006
7863 La Mesa Blvd., 2nd Floor
La Mesa, California 92041-9006

(619) 466-9910
TRUSTEE'S SALE NO. 202361
LOAN NO. 51-839890

WE CERTIFY THIS TO BE A TRUE AND CORRECT COPY OF THE DOCUMENT RECORDED 7-31-89
INSTRUMENT 89143211
COUNTY CONTRA COSTA
CAL WESTERN RECONVEYANCE CORP
BY: Freddye M

SPACE AB

**Notice of Default**

## IMPORTANT NOTICE

IF YOUR PROPERTY IS IN FORECLOSURE BECAUSE YOU ARE BEHIND IN YOUR PAYMENTS, IT MAY BE SOLD WITHOUT ANY COURT ACTION, and you may have legal right to bring your account in good standing by paying all of your past due payments plus permitted costs and expenses within the time permitted by law for reinstatement of your account, which is normally five business days prior to the date set for the sale of your property. No sale date may be set until three months from the date this notice of default may be recorded (which date of recordation appears on this notice).

This amount is 5,144.68 as of JULY 25, 1989, and will increase until your account becomes current. You may not have to pay the entire unpaid portion of your account, even though full payment was demanded, but you must pay the amount stated above.

However, you and your beneficiary or mortgagee may mutually agree in writing prior to the time the notice of sale is posted (which may not be earlier than the end of the three-month period stated above) to, among other things, (1) provide additional time in which to cure the default by transfer of the property or otherwise; (2) establish a schedule of payments in order to cure your default; or both (1) and (2).

Following the expiration of the time period referred to in the first paragraph of this notice, unless the obligation being foreclosed upon or a separate written agreement between you and your creditor permits a longer period, you have only the legal right to stop the sale of your property by paying the entire amount demanded by your creditor.

To find out the amount you must pay, or to arrange for payment to stop the foreclosure, or if your property is in foreclosure for any other reason, contact: IMPERIAL SAVINGS ASSOCIATION
c/o CAL-WESTERN RECONVEYANCE CORPORATION, 7863 LA MESA BLVD., 2ND FLOOR, LA MESA, CA 92041
Attention: Freddye Mays (619) 466-9910

If you have any questions, you should contact a lawyer or the government agency which may have insured your loan.

Notwithstanding the fact that your property is in foreclosure, you may offer your property for sale, provided the sale is concluded prior to the conclusion of the foreclosure. Remember, YOU MAY LOSE LEGAL RIGHTS IF YOU DO NOT TAKE PROMPT ACTION.

## NOTICE OF DEFAULT AND ELECTION TO SELL UNDER DEED OF TRUST

NOTICE IS HEREBY GIVEN: Cal-Western Reconveyance Corporation, A California Corporation is Trustee under a deed of trust dated JULY 25, 1988 executed by GUY GABBY, A MARRIED MAN AS HIS SOLE SEPARATE PROPERTY as trustor, to secure certain obligations in favor of FINANCIAL CENTER MORTGAGE and assigned of record to IMPERIAL SAVINGS ASSOCIATION as beneficiary, recorded as document 88-129963 on JULY 29, 1988 in Book 14484 page 515 official records in the office of the County Recorder of CONTRA COSTA County, California, describing land therein as:

LOT 11, AS SHOWN ON THE MAPOF SUBDIVISION 5324, FILED APRIL 15, 1980 , MAP BOOK 236, PAGE 43, CONTRA COSTA COUNTY RECORDS, MORE PARTICULARLY DESCRIBED IN SAID DEED OF TRUST.

said obligations including a promissory note for the principal sum of $277,875.00 that a breach of, and default in, the obligations for which such Deed of Trust is security has occurred in that payment has not been made of:

Failure to pay monthly installments of interest & principal due JUNE 1, 1989 and subsequent installments due thereafter; plus late fees; together with any sums advanced by beneficiary under the terms and conditions of said deed of trust, and delinquent taxes, assessments, attorney's fees and insurance premiums if any.

That by reason thereof the present beneficiary under such Deed of Trust has deposited with said Trustee such Deed of Trust and all documents evidencing obligations secured thereby and has declared and does hereby declare all sums secured thereby immediately due and payable and has elected and does hereby elect to cause the trust property to be sold to satisfy the obligations secured thereby.

Dated: July 26, 1989

CAL-WESTERN RECONVEYANCE CORPORATION

by: Freddye Mays, Trsutee's Sale Officer

# *New Growth Financial*

*"The Distressed Property Experts"*

*(415) 837-2106 Fax #743-0926*

**Request for Loan Status (Beneficiary Statement)**

Cal-Western Reconveyance Corp.
7863 La Mesa Boulevard
Second Floor
La Mesa, CA 92044

Loan No.: Gabby
132 Corral Circle, San Ramon, CA

Gentlemen:

I am thinking of selling my house and in order to evaluate my future acceptance of an offer, I would appreciate sending me the following information:

1. What type of loan? (FHA, VA conventional, other) __________
2. Current interest rate? __________
3. Current monthly principal & interest payment? __________
4. Existing loan balance? __________
5. Can this loan be assumed? __________
   What are your assumption requirements? __________
   What are your assumption fees, if any? __________
6. Is there a prepayment penalty? __________
   How much? __________
7. Is there an impound account? __________

Thank you for your cooperation in this matter. Your early attention will be greatly appreciated.

Sincerely,

Guy Gabby
P.O. Box 5000, #412
Danville, CA 94526

*Our mailing address is: P.O. Box 5000, #412, Danville, Ca. 94526*
*Our offices are located at 185 Front Street, Suite 207 in Danville, California just behind the First Interstate Bank and only steps from Father Nature's Famous Restaurant.* ©

*New Growth Financial*

*"The Distressed Property Experts"*

*(415) 837-2106 Fax #743-0926*

**Seller's Authorization for lender to give loan status information to buyer**

October 10, 1989

Cal-Western Reconveyance Corp.
7863 La Mesa Boulevard
Second Floor
La Mesa, CA 92044

Loan No.: Gabby
132 Corral Circle, San Ramon, CA

Gentlemen:

I am aware that my loan is in default and I am working to take care of this situation. I would appreciate it if you would provide all necessary information concerning my loan with you to New Growth Financial, their agents or their assigns including, but not limited to, Ted Thomas and Diane Swenson.

Sincerely,

Guy Gabby

cal.western

*Our mailing address is: P.O. Box 5000, #412, Danville, Ca. 94526*
*Our offices are located at 185 Front Street, Suite 207 in Danville, California just behind the First Interstate Bank and only steps from Father Nature's Famous Restaurant.* ©

CAL-WESTERN
FORECLOSURE
SERVICES

**Response from lender requesting the loan status**

Reinstatement Breakdown

December 06, 1989

TS No. 202361
Loan No. 359008455
Lender: IMPERIAL SAVINGS ASSOCIATION

| | | | |
|---|---|---|---|
| Installment Due | 6/01/89 @ | $2,426.74 X 3 = | $7,280.22 |
| Payment Change | 9/01/89 @ | $2,631.28 X 4 = | $10,525.12 |
| Total Late Charges | | | $1,002.60 |
| Foreclosure Fees and Costs | | | $3,462.46 |
| | | TOTAL | $22,270.40 |

Note: Please send all future payments and correspondence to your lender.

7863 La Mesa Boulevard, 2nd Floor, P.O. Box 9006, La Mesa, California 92044-9006 (619) 466-9910

RECORDING REQUESTED BY

AND WHEN RECORDED MAIL TO

Trustee Sale No. 202361

CAL-WESTERN RECONVEYANCE CORPORATION
7863 La Mesa Blvd., 2nd Floor
P.O. Box 9006
La Mesa, California 92044

SPACE ABOVE THIS LINE FOR RECORDER'S USE

LOAN NO. 51-839890 **NOTICE OF TRUSTEE'S SA**

**Trustee's Sale Only 21 Days from this Notice to the Auction**

IMPORTANT NOTICE TO PROPERTY O'

YOU ARE IN DEFAULT UNDER A DEED OF TRUST, DATED JULY 2.. , UNLESS YOU TAKE ACTION TO PROTECT YOUR PROPERTY, IT MAY BE SOLD AT A PUBLIC SALE. IF YOU NEED AN EXPLANATION OF THE NATURE OF THE PROCEEDING AGAINST YOU, YOU SHOULD CONTACT A LAWYER.

On DECEMBER 5, 1989 , at 10:00 A.M. ,
CAL-WESTERN RECONVEYANCE CORP., a California corporation
as duly appointed trustee under and pursuant to Deed of Trust
recorded JULY 29, 1988 , as inst. No. 88-129963 , in book 14484
page 515 of Official Records in the office of the County Recorders of
CONTRA COS' County, State of California.
executed by GUY GABBY, A MARRIED MAN AS HIS SOLE SEPARATE PROPERTY

WILL SELL AT PUBLIC AUCTION TO HIGHEST BIDDER FOR CASH, CASHIER'S CHECK DRAWN ON A STATE OR NATIONAL BANK, A CHECK DRAWN BY A STATE OR FEDERAL CREDIT UNION, OR A CHECK DRAWN BY A STATE OR FEDERAL SAVINGS AND LOAN ASSOCIATION, SAVINGS ASSOCIATION, OR SAVINGS BANK SPECIFIED IN SECTION 5102 OF THE FINANCIAL CODE AND AUTHORIZED TO DO BUSINESS IN THIS STATE WILL BE HELD

At the main entrance to the City Hall, 1666 North Main
Street, Walnut Creek, California

all right, title and interest conveyed to and now held by it under said Deed of Trust in the property situated in said County and State described as:
LOT 11, AS SHOWN ON THE MAPOF SUBDIVISION 5324, FILED
APRIL 15, 1980 , MAP BOOK 236, PAGE 43, CONTRA COSTA
COUNTY RECORDS, MORE PARTICULARLY DESCRIBED IN EXHIBIT "A"
ATTACHED HERETO AND MADE A PART HEREOF.

The street address and other common designation, if any, of the real property described above is purported to be:
132 Corral Circle
San Ramon, California 94583

The undersigned Trustee disclaims any liability for any incorrectness of the street address and other common designation, if any, shown herein.

Said sale will be made, but without convenant or warranty, express or implied, regarding title, possession, or encumbrances, including fees, charges and expenses of the Trustee and of the trusts created by said Deed of Trust, to pay the remaining principal sums of the note(s) secured by said Deed of Trust to wit: $ 276542.76 with interest thereon from 5/01/89 @ 9.950 % per annum as provided in said note(s) plus cost and any advances with interest.
ESTIMATED OPENING BID $ 298084.91
The beneficiary under said Deed of Trust heretofore executed and delivered to the undersigned a written Dec.. ration of Default and Demand for S.. ..d a written Notice of Default and Election to Se' The undersigned caused said Notice of Default and Elect... ..ell to be recorded in the county where the real property is located

CAL-WES... RECONVEYANCE CORPORATION
7863 L... ..sa Blvd., 2nd Floor
P.O. B.. 9006
La Mesa, California 92044
XXXXXXXXXXXX (619) ~~466-3506~~ 466-9910
XXXXXXXXXXXX

Date: November 01, 1989

By [signature]
Authorized Signature
Fredd... ..a, Trustee's Sale Officer

Trustee No. 202361

EXHIBIT "A"

Lot 11, as shown on the Map of Subdivision 5324, filed April 15, 1980, Map Book 236, Page 43, Contra Costa County Records.

EXCEPTING THEREFROM:

All oil, gas, casinghead gas, asphaltum and other hydrocarbons and all chemical gas, now or hereafter found, situated or located in all or any part or portion of the lands described herein lying more than five hundred feet (500') below the surface thereof, together with the right to slant drill for and remove all or any of said oil, gas, casinghead gas, asphaltum and other hydrocarbons and chemical gas lying below a depth of more than five hundred feet (500') below the surface thereof; but without any rights whatsoever to enter upon the surface of said land or upon any part of said lands within five hundred feet (500') vertical distance below the surface thereof, as reserved in the Deed executed by Dame' Construction Co., Inc., a corporation, recorded July 27, 1981, in Book 10422, Page 133, Official Records.

**This Will Be Delivered with the Notice of Trustee's Sale**

# *New Growth Financial*

*"The Distressed Property Experts"*

*(415) 837-2106 Fax #743-0926*

**Buyer's payment to cure loan default**

December 4, 1989

Cal-Western Reconveyance Corp.
7863 La Mesa Blvd.
Second Floor
La Mesa, CA 92044

Attention: Freddye Mays

RE: T.S. #202361

Dear Ms. Mays:

Enclosed is our Cashier's check to reinstate loan number 359-008455 in the name of Guy Gabby. Also, please send a copy of the Notice of Rescission.

Thank-you for all your help.

Sincerely,

Diane Swenson
Administrative Assistant

ds
encls.

PURCHASER'S RECEIPT
BANK OF WALNUT CREEK
3130 CROW CANYON PLACE
SAN RAMON, CA 94583

REMITTER

Nº 02351

New Growth Financial

Debember 4, 89 90-3801/1211

DRAWN TO THE ORDER OF Cal-Western Reconveyance Corp.- - - - - - - - - - - - $ 22,385.40

22385dols40cts

CUSTOMER'S MEMO:

CASHIER'S CHECK

FOR Cure loan on 132 Corral Cir.

*Our mailing address is: P.O. Box 5000, #412, Danville, Ca. 94526*
*Our offices are located at 185 Front Street, Suite 207 in Danville, California just behind the First Interstate Bank and only steps from Father Nature's Famous Restaurant.* ©

RECORDING REQUESTED BY

AND WHEN RECORDED MAIL TO

Name
Street Address
City & State

Cal-Western Reconveyance Corp.
7863 La Mesa Blvd., 2nd Floor
P. O. Box 9006
La Mesa, California 92041
TRUST NO. 202361

Space above This Line For Recorder's Use

LOAN NO. 359008455

F

T.O.#

# NOTICE OF RESCISSION

OF NOTICE OF DEFAULT AND ELECTION TO SELL UNDER DEED OF TRUST

**Whereas,** the undersigned, as Trustee under that certain **Deed of Trust** hereinafter described heretofore delivered to said Trustee: and **Whereas,** Notice was heretofore given by the undersigned, as such Trustee, of breach of the obligations for which said Deed of Trust is security and of election to cause to be sold the property therein described, which Notice was recorded on JULY 31, 1989 in the Recorder's office of CONTRA COSTA County, California, as File 89 143211 in book XXXXXXX page XXXXXXXXXXX of Official Records;

**Now, Therefore, Notice is Hereby Given** that the undersigned, as such Trustee, does hereby rescind, cancel and withdraw said Notice of Default and Election to Sell under Deed of Trust; it being understood, however, that this rescission shall not in any manner be construed as waiving or affecting any breach or default — past; present or future — under said Deed of Trust, or as impairing any right or remedy thereunder, but is, and shall be deemed to be, only an election; without prejudice, not to cause a sale to be made pursuant to said Notice, and shall in nowise jeopardize or impair any right, remedy or privilege secured to the Beneficiary and/or the Trustee, under said Deed of Trust, nor modify nor alter in any respect any of the terms, covenants, conditions or obligations thereof, and said Deed of Trust and all obligations secured thereby are hereby reinstated and shall be and remain in force and effect the same as if said Notice of Default had not been made and given. Said Deed of Trust above referred to was executed by

GUY GABBY, A MARRIED MAN AS HIS SOLE SEPARATE PROPERTY

Trustor, CAL-WESTERN RECONVEYANCE CORPORATION, a California corporation, as duly appointed Trustee, and recorded as instrument 88-129963 on JULY 29, 1988 in book 14484 page 515 of Official Records and covering the following described property in CONTRA COSTA County, California.

LOT 11, AS SHOWN ON THE MAP OF SUBDIVISION 5324, FILED APRIL 15, 1980 , MAP BOOK 236, PAGE 43, CONTRA COSTA COUNTY RECORDS, MORE COMPLETELY DESCRIBED IN EXHIBIT "A" ATTACHED HERETO AND MADE A PART HEREOF.

**Notice of Rescission**

Dated December 06, 1989

CAL-WESTERN RECONVEYANCE CORPORATION

By: Freddye Mays
Freddye Mays, Trustee Sale Officer

Chapter 8

# Demystifying Escrow/ Settlement and Fattening Your Bank Account

## *Find Out Who Handles the Procedures in Your State*

### SETTLEMENT/ESCROW

What is meant by the term *escrow*? In some parts of the country, the escrow process is called title closing or settlement. You probably have plenty of questions about this mysterious procedure. Lots of real estate investors have heard about deeds going into escrow, but there is always the question: Does anything ever come out of escrow?

Buying or selling a home usually involves the transfer of large sums of money. This money and the related documents are usually handled by an escrow agent, who is an independent third party. Until the transaction is completed, this third party holds the money and the documents and upon specific instructions (usually written) he or she disburses the money and supervises the exchange of documents.

The escrow agent will have received funds and documents necessary to comply with the instructions, completed or obtained any special forms such as grant deeds, quitclaim deeds, promissory notes, and so on, and in due course will deliver those documents to the appropriate parties. The escrow holder, or company, impartially carries out the written instructions given by the parties involved in the transactions and must be provided with the information necessary to complete the transaction. An example of escrow instructions appears at the end of this chapter, beginning on page 211.

**Common Questions**

Let's learn what is necessary to manage the escrow/settlement process effectively. The ten most common questions are:

1. What information is needed to open escrow?
2. Is it important that you pay the seller or should the escrow agent pay the seller?
3. What does the escrow agent do with the funds you deposit into escrow?
4. What papers do you (not the seller) need to sign?
5. Who will prepare the papers and how long will that take?
6. What about new loans?
7. What about the loans in place?
8. What is title insurance and should I get it?
9. What problems should I anticipate in escrow?
10. Who makes the decision on when to close or complete the escrow?

**Impartial Third Party**

In the normal world of real estate, escrow/settlement involves an impartial third party (the escrow agent) whom buyers and sellers employ to handle the funds and documents and thus to minimize risk. The escrow agent is not a party to the transaction, but is instead obligated to safeguard the interests of both parties who are affected by the outcome of the transaction.

To open an escrow, you simply take your documents and all your instructions regarding the transaction to an impartial third party, most likely an escrow or title company. In your state that may be an abstract company or a real estate attorney. This third party has the responsibility of handling all details necessary for the property to change ownership.

Ultimately, when all of the details of paying lenders, computing taxes, exchanging documents, and dispensing monies to the appropriate parties at the correct time have been taken care of, the transaction is completed or, in some states, "escrow is closed" or "settlement" has been completed.

In the world of foreclosure purchasing, all of the same details are completed by escrow agents, but instructions differ from those in the normal escrow transaction. Loans are usually cured/made healthy and brought current by the foreclosure buyer, and the loans on the property are usually acknowledged and then taken "subject to" their remaining term and balance. The escrow officer will require instructions to that effect.

### Pay-off Statement

Otherwise, the escrow officer would request a demand or pay-off statement from the lenders and a statement of loan condition, that is, principal balance, interest rate, term, prepayment penalty, assumability, etc. Demand documents normally require payment of the loan balance in full. Normal real estate buyers purchase the property, request new loans from the bank, and then pay off old loans or encumbrances. Not so with foreclosure buyers.

Foreclosure buyers attempt to cure or bring current the existing loans and therefore must advise the escrow officer of their intentions. Expect to review with the escrow officer your contract of purchase (equity purchase contract). The contract will outline the intentions of both the buyers and sellers and will clarify them for the escrow officer.

The escrow officer's concerns are many. For example: Are the parties competent to carry out this contract? Is there a valid consideration? Is there a property involved? And finally, is there a mutual agreement as to terms and conditions?

In reality, escrow provides a clearing house for all funds, documents, and contracts between the parties. In most escrows the conditions and agreements (escrow instructions) must be met before the property changes hands.

### Advance Notice

Foreclosure buyers will receive a grant deed or a warrantee deed title to the property before the escrow closes. In California, this is immediately after the five-day right of rescission as specified in the Civil Code. This is an unusual step and most escrow officers have not handled the situation in that manner.Therefore, it is imperative that you advise the escrow company in advance of your normal operating procedures and allow their attorney to review and approve your contract.

Following the system flow chart, the next step after the foreclosure seller grant deeds the property to you or your company is to perform your "due diligence." This requires TRAIT:

Termite

Roof

Appraisal

Inspection of Home

Title Report (Preliminary)

Assuming these reports are to your liking, an escrow could be opened (and the grant deed or warrantee deed and other papers and documents included). Once again, the escrow officer acts as an impartial third party to the transaction. Therefore, it is your responsibility to advise the agent of your requirements in written form (escrow instructions).

### Escrow Officers Normally Expect To:

1. Order a Preliminary Title Report.
2. Secure pay-off demands on loans (we don't want pay-off demands ordered — we take "subject to").

3. Request reconveyance.
4. Secure loan documents from lenders.
5. Obtain documents (release) to clear outstanding liens.
6. Issue receipts for deposits and other funds.
7. Prorate taxes and interest.
8. Prepare buyer and seller statements.
9. Obtain title insurance.
10. Record the necessary documents to effect the transfer of the property.

## WHAT INSTRUCTIONS WILL YOU NEED TO OPEN AN ESCROW?

You'll need to provide the escrow company with the following information:

1. Purchase price, property description, and address.
2. Seller's name, address, and telephone number.
3. Buyer's name, address, and telephone number.
4. Termite report, roof report, house inspections, preliminary title, and appraisal.
5. Monies to pay loans and cure defaulting loans, if you don't do that yourself.
6. Financing information, if any. Generally speaking, foreclosure buyers will bring loans current and then take the property "subject to" the existing loans.
7. Closing date (completion date).
8. Tax bill information.

## WHAT IS A TITLE SEARCH?

The title search is a search of the county records regarding a specific piece of property. The search reveals any defects in the title, in addition to the encumbrances and liens of record. It will also show the property's tax status, current or delinquent.

The results of a title search are compiled into what most people refer to as a Preliminary Title Report. It could be called a Commitment of Title in your state, or an Encumbrance Report. No matter what it is called, it reflects the conditions under which the title company is willing to issue a policy of title insurance.

When the title search is performed, the examiner searches for:

1. The exact legal description.
2. The estate or interest in the property.

3. The vesting of the estate or interest (how much is owned).
4. The exceptions (lien encumbrances, defects affecting the particular interests). (Who are the owners?)
5. Assessor's Parcel Number.
6. Delinquent taxes, assessment bonds, or tax liens.

There are other things you should investigate that affect title to real property, things that do not normally appear in the property records at the recorder's office — for example, zoning restrictions, leases that might not be recorded, riparian (water) rights, adverse possession claims and mechanic's liens.

## WHAT ARE THE CC&RS?

Covenants, conditions, and restrictions, or CC&Rs, are limitations placed on the land that restrict or limit its use. They are normally included in the deed and will specifically outline what uses are prevented or prohibited on the land. They are created in the deed clauses and special agreements or in the general plan affecting the subdivision.

## WHAT IS AN EASEMENT?

An easement is a right granted by a property owner to another person allowing that person the use of land for certain purposes, or it may be a property right reserved by the former grantor. Easements are common for telephone cables, access roads, powerlines, or pipelines.

## WHAT ARE LIENS AND ENCUMBRANCES?

Encumbrances include anything that limits or burdens the title. Mineral, timber, and water rights held by the seller or a third party can qualify. Easements and restrictions or covenants in the deed that limit use are all encumbrances.

Liens are another kind of encumbrance. Liens are usually a result of the owner using the property as security for a long-term mortgage or trust deed. The owner pledges (hypothecates) the property to the mortgage to insure payment of a debt. The mortgagee has the right to sell the property in the event the homeowner (borrower) fails to pay the debt. The claim (lien) against the property makes transferring the title or selling the property difficult without first either paying the debt or buying the property "subject to" the debt.

## POINTERS THAT WILL HELP YOU CLOSE ESCROW FASTER

Do communicate with your escrow company and specifically with the escrow officer. Discuss all the terms of the contract and the transaction at the outset and then keep him or her advised of any subsequent changes or modifications.

Do read the Preliminary Title Report as soon as it arrives and discuss any questions you may have with the escrow or title officer. (Remember, this could be an attorney in your state.) Before you discuss the Preliminary Title Report with your clients, be sure you have reviewed it with the escrow officer or attorney.

Do advise the escrow officer that you are gathering the termite report, roof report, home inspection, and appraisal. If your escrow instructions require these reports be completed prior to settlement, advise the escrow officer when you will deliver them.

Do read and re-read the escrow instructions carefully in advance, word for word! Ask questions of your escrow officer if you are not entirely satisfied with your understanding on every point in the instructions.

Do check the prorations. It is your responsibility to know who pays the fees, taxes, and insurance. The escrow officer is not perfect; it is up to you to know and approve the numbers. You must understand the formula for prorations, the county customs, due dates, delinquency dates, credits, debits, and impounds so you can give your clients the answers easily if they request them. If you don't understand the transactions, ask questions until you do.

Do use the glossary at the end of this book and learn the meaning of the terms which appear in documents or instructions — for example, *alienations, acceleration, assume, subject to, demand beneficiary, mortgage, mortgagor, mortgagee, lis pendens, due on sale*. Your clear understanding of these terms will enable you to give correct explanations to your clients.

Do familiarize yourself with what's normal in your community/county/area with regard to costs to the buyer and costs to the seller. Discuss these with the seller/buyer prior to the closing so that they will know what to expect. This is particularly important if you do not have it in your written contract. The suggested procedure is to have all costs clearly outlined and agreed to in your written contract. There are significant differences between counties in some states. Know the mores and customs in your particular area. Unexpected costs can be a real jolt at closing time. Explanations take a lot of time, and sometimes there is even a delay in the closing because the buyer/seller is simply unprepared and does not have the amount required.

Do recognize that there are limitations as to what the escrow holder will do and will not do. The escrow officer is required to be an independent third party.

*What documents should I expect the escrow holder to require?*

- Loan documents
- Tax statements
- Fire and hazard insurance policies
- Title insurance policy
- Any document pertaining to the financing of the sale
- Requests from outsiders requiring payment

*For whom does the escrow holder work ?*

The escrow holder serves as a neutral stakeholder and the link between the principal parties, the seller and the buyer.

*What should I expect the escrow holder to do?*

Ask to be sure, but you can usually expect the escrow holder to:

- Prepare the escrow instructions.
- Request a preliminary title search to determine the condition of the present title, outstanding loans, tax liens, judgments.
- Request a beneficiary's statement if the debt is to be taken over by the new buyer.
- Comply with the lenders' requests in the matters of, for instance, late fees and prepayment penalties.
- Prepare the deed and other documents.
- Prorate taxes, interest, insurance, and rents.
- Secure releases on other encumbrances.
- Record the deed and any other documents as requested in the written escrow instructions.
- Request title insurance.
- Close the escrow when all the documents of the buyer and the seller have been completed.
- Distribute the funds as authorized by the written escrow instructions.

## WHAT ARE THE CLOSING COSTS?

A rule of thumb is that closing costs will be approximately 10%. This figure usually consists of:

- Real estate commissions
- Loan fees
- Escrow charge
- Title insurance premium
- Termite inspection payments
- Roof inspection payments

Understanding these costs is important so that you are prepared and aren't surprised on the settlement day.

## SOLVING THE MYSTERY OF ESCROW AND TITLE PROCEDURES

As a property buyer you need to be aware that others may have rights in the property. If the owner has contracted for debt and the property has been pledged (hypothecated) as collateral for the debt, the creditors are in effect part-owners of the property until the debt has been paid. The lien rights apply to the holders of the mortgage, holders of any leasehold rights, mining and air rights, unpaid taxes, lawsuits pending against the owner, bankruptcy proceedings, or other liens (claims) such as mechanic's liens. (As an example of the last item, you may find that the owner had a new roof installed but failed to pay the contractor's bill. The roofer may file a mechanic's lien in the hope that, when the property is sold, he will get some of the proceeds. All those who hold such claims are, in a limited way, part-owners. They cannot ordinarily be deprived of their interest except by having the claim settled or extinguished (cancelled). The property may be sold without their knowledge, but the claim is still good until satisfied. As a new owner you may know nothing about such part-owners, but you are still subject to their claims on your property.

## A GRANT DEED DOES NOT GIVE CLEAR TITLE

"Aha," you say, "but I have the grant deed. For an example of a grant deed, see page 218. Doesn't that give me a clear title?" Not at all! A deed is merely an instrument (in the form of a piece of paper) whereby a seller transfers his or her right of ownership, whatever it may be, to you. It is not proof that the person described as the seller is actually the owner. It does not do away with claims or rights others may have in the property. Nor can you determine from the deed what rights, liens, or claims may be outstanding against your title. In order for you, the new owner, to determine the status of the title, you must research the county records and determine the status of the liens and encumbrances. Among the hidden risks that may be discovered in a title search, one could include:

- The marital status of the owner
- The existence of undisclosed heirs
- The owner's mental incompetence or status as a minor
- Instances of fraud and forgery
- Defective deeds
- Confusions due to similar or identical names
- Errors in the records

## PITFALLS: UNDISCLOSED LIENS AND ENCUMBRANCES

Wise buyers always research title or purchase a Preliminary Title Report. Property owners have a tendency to forget liens that might have been filed by creditors or even unpaid secured or third trust deeds. If you are buying a property at a Trustee's/Sheriff's Sale, you must identify positively and establish the seniority of the trust deed/mortgage that is foreclosing. For example, if the trust deed/mortgage that is foreclosing is for $25,000, and the Trustee/Sheriff sells the property to you for $25,500, you will own the property for $25,500 assuming that there was no deed of trust/mortgage in a senior or prior position (one that was recorded at an earlier date). If you purchased a property at a Trustee's/Sheriff's Sale and a loan (deed of trust/mortgage) was recorded before the deed of trust/mortgage that you purchased was recorded, that deed of trust/mortgage will become your obligation. You will own the property. However, you will own it for the $25,500 you paid the Trustee plus the amount of the senior obligation. In other words, if you purchase property at a Trustee's/Sheriff's Sale for $25,500 cash and a subsequent title report or records search shows a senior lien in the amount of $50,000, you own the property for $50,000 plus $25,500, or $75,500; as the new owner, you are obliged to pay the senior lien.

## HOW TO FIND THE LIENS AND ENCUMBRANCES

Many owners do not know (some merely refrain from telling you) what is owed against the property, so you must determine what is owed.

So how do you find out? Let's revisit the three letter word, ASK. Keep on asking and you'll discover more than you ever dreamed about the property you are purchasing. To determine what is owed against any property:

- First, ASK the homeowner.
- Second, ASK the lender, if you know who it is.
- Third, ASK the Trustee.
- Fourth, ASK the title company to provide a Preliminary Title Report. Assuming that the title company will insure the property you are purchasing from an owner, your risk of undisclosed liens will be eliminated. However, the wise foreclosure buyer will spend time with the county records researching the liens and encumbrances, thereby assuring himself that he is buying exactly what he thinks he is buying.
- Fifth, ASK a broker to look in the MLS book.

## TITLE INSURANCE

Although title insurance is one of the larger closing costs in a transaction, many buyers view it as just another payment in acquiring their home. Yet if a problem arises with the property's title before or after the buyers take possession, it suddenly becomes important. It's vital that you understand title insurance.

Title insurance companies check for liens, claims, or encumbrances on a particular property before the title changes hands (is transferred). Title insurance is the business of eliminating risks before they occur. Most insurance pays you after you have had a loss or a disaster. Title insurers try to eliminate risk before they take the risk. Other insurers take risk and then research the actuarial tables and quote a premium. The coverage provided by the title company is designed to uncover any potential risks before they take on the insurance. To do so, title insurers maintain what they call title plants or banks, which house millions of pieces of information, some dating back many generations. These title banks are duplications of the county records in many ways. A property's background is checked to be sure that the deed or other document was properly transferred in the past sales. The title company also searches public records for deeds, court judgments, assessments, tax notices, easements, and other encroachments and many other documents pertaining to the title. The documents are usually referred to as instruments. Any instrument that is in the file could possible cloud the title, and that's exactly why one performs a title search and why you need title insurance to protect you in the event a document contains information that was unknown to you or the title company.

### Lien Removed

For example, a title search may disclose a lien securing repayment for a debt by a seller's creditor. If title is transferred and the lien isn't eliminated/removed, then the uninsured buyer is responsible for the debt. Another example might include neighbors who claim that their property is accessible only over the property you own or are prepared to purchase, so they have an easement on that part of the property. Unpaid taxes and judgments are easily forgotten by sellers, and if you buy the property you get what the seller has to sell — keep in mind that tax liens and judgments against the seller appear on the title report.

In most states, lenders won't agree to fund a mortgage or deed of trust without being protected by title insurance. Buyer's title insurance safeguards the buyer's interest in the property. In addition to paying for the title insurer's records search, the one-time premium protects the buyer from title problems that may arise later but were undetected during the title search. If buyers are required to defend a claim to title in court, the title insurer is normally obligated to pay the legal expenses. The buyer's title insurance policy is usually written for the amount of the property's purchase price.

Buyers may believe they don't have to purchase title insurance in states where real estate attorneys assume responsibility for title searches. Not so: Title insurance is still necessary because attorneys who do the title examinations are liable for only their own negligence, for example, errors in the public records, forged documents, and deed and mortgage releases.

Just because a property has recently been transferred does not mean that title insurance is unnecessary. A lot can happen in a few months: the seller could have a tax lien for income taxes or take out a second mortgage, go through a divorce, or file for bankruptcy. Possibly the state is in the process of claiming the property to build a freeway.

The rule is: *When in doubt, search the title, and always buy a title insurance policy to protect your interests.*

## WHAT TO DO DURING THE ESCROW PERIOD

- **Make a List of All the Repairs You Will Need Outside Bids for.**
  (Use Form found in this book).

- **Start Searching for Reputable Workers.**

You may already know a good painter, carpet layer, landscaper, etc. If not, ask friends or neighbors who have recently has work done to their homes to recommend people that did quality work at a reasonable price. Look for a "Handyman Service Guide" section in your local newspaper. This is not as good a source as people who have been recommended (same goes for the phone book), but if you have not been given any recommendations, then you have little choice. Ask for references and addresses of past jobs. Then go with your instincts.

- **Start Scheduling Appointments to Receive Bids.**

Schedule two or more workers at a time. This will cut down on how many times you will need to get the keys for the listing agent.

- **Get All Bids in Writing.**

Ask the bidders to give you an accurate estimate with a **"not to exceed"** clause. Also receive from him / her a definite start date and finish date. Stress how reliability is of the utmost importance.

- **Be Cautious When You Order in Advance.**

Confident that the sale will go through, then I would suggest that you place orders for the following as you can:

- ✔ Custom Made Drapes (10 weeks to make. ?? cheaper and less customized)
- ✔ Plants and Landscaping Materials
- ✔ Brick or Stones
- ✔ Appliances and Fixtures
- ✔ Shutters and Blinds

Notes: ______________________________________________

______________________________________________

______________________________________________

______________________________________________

______________________________________________

______________________________________________

______________________________________________

## *ESCROW PROCEDURES — FIND YOUR STATE*

| STATE | HANDLES CLOSING | CONVEYANCE |
|---|---|---|
| Alabama | Attorney | Warranty Deed |
| Alaska | Title Company/Private Escrow | Warranty Deed |
| Arizona | Title Company/Title Agents | Warranty Deed |
| Arkansas | Title Company/Attorney | Warranty Deed |
| California | Title Company/Escrow Company | Grant Deed |
| Colorado | Title Company/Brokers/Attorney | Warranty Deed |
| Connecticut | Attorney | Warranty Deed |
| Delaware | Attorney Special | Warranty Deed |
| District of Columbia | TitleCompany/Attorney | Warranty Deed |
| Florida | Title Company/Attorney | Warranty Deed |
| Georgia | Attorney | Warranty Deed |
| Hawaii | Attorney | Warranty Deed |
| Idaho | Escrow Company | Warranty Deed |
| Illinois | Title Company/Lender/Real Estate Agents/Attorney | Warranty Deed |
| Indiana | Title Company/Lender/Real Estate Agents/Attorneys | Warranty Deed |
| Iowa | Attorney/Real Estate Agent | Warranty Deed |
| Kansas | Title Company/Lender/Real Estate Agent/Attorney | Warranty Deed |
| Kentucky | Attorney | Grant Deed or Bargain & Sale Deed |
| Louisiana | Attorney/Corporate Title Agents | Warranty Deed |
| Maine | Attorney | Warranty or Quit Claim Deed |
| Maryland | Attorney | Grand Deed or Bargain & Sale Deed |
| Massachusetts | Attorney | Warranty or Quit Claim Deed |
| Michigan | Title Company/Lender/Real Estate Agent/Attorney | Warranty Deed |
| Mississippi | Attorney/Broker | Warranty Deed |
| Missouri | Title Company/Lender/Real Estate Agent/Attorney | Warranty Deed |
| Montana | Escrow Company | Warranty Deed |

## ESCROW PROCEDURES — FIND YOUR STATE

| STATE | HANDLES CLOSING | CONVEYANCE |
|---|---|---|
| Nebraska | Title Company/Lender/Real Estate Agent/Attorney | Warranty Deed |
| Nevada | Escrow Company | Grand Deed or Bargain & Sale Deed |
| New Hampshire | Attorney | Warranty or Quit Claim Deed |
| New Jersey | Attorney/Title Agent | Bargain & Sale Deed |
| New Mexico | Escrow Company | Warranty or Quit Claim Deed |
| New York | Attorney | Bargain & Sale Deed |
| North Carolina | Attorney/Lender | Warranty Deed |
| North Dakota | Attorney/Lender | Warranty Deed |
| Ohio | Title Company | Warranty Deed |
| Oklahoma | Title Company/Lender/Real Estate Agent/Attorney | Warranty Deed |
| Oregon | Escrow Company | Warranty or Bargain & Sale Deed or Land Contracts are common |
| Pennsylvania | Title Company/Real Estate Agent/Approved Attorney | Special/General Warranty Deed |
| Rhode Island | Attorney/Bank/Title Company | Warranty or Quit Claim Deed |
| South Carolina | Attorney | Warranty Deed |
| South Dakota | Title Company/Lender/Real Estate Agent/Attorney | Warranty Deed |
| Tennessee | Title Company/Attorney/A Party to the Contract/Lender Representative/ Outside Attorney | Warranty Deed |
| Texas | Title Company | Warranty Deed |
| Utah | Lender 60%/Escrow and Title Company the remainder | Warranty Deed |
| Vermont | Attorney | Warranty or Quit Claim Deed |
| Washington | Title Company/Escrow Company/ Lender/Attorney | Warranty Deed |
| West Virginia | Attorney | Warranty or Bargain & Sale Deed |
| Wisconsin | Title Company/Escrow Company/ Lender/Attorney | Warranty Deed |
| Wyoming | Real Estate Agent | Warranty Deed |

## ESCROW VS. TITLE INSURANCE

# Independent Escrow Co.

96001 Stoneridge Mall Rd.
Suite 120
Pleasanton, California

415 463.9600

# vs. Title Insurance Co.

# What are the Differences?

**INDEPENDENT ESCROW COMPANIES**

1 Types of Escrows:
- Loans
- Resale
- Tract
- New Construction Funding
- VA, FHA, Cal-Vet
- Exchange
- Sale of Notes (secured & unsecured)
- Manufactured Housing (mobile home)
- Business opportunity/Bulk Sale
- Liquor Licence
- Foreclosures

2 Negotiable Fees

3 Regulated by Commissioners of Corporations

4 Greater Specialization & Expertise in all

5 Faster Turnaround Time for Most Escrows

**TITLE INSURANCE COMPANIES**

1 Types of Escrows:
- Loans
- Resale
- Tract
- New Construction Funding
- VA, FHA, Cal-Vet
- Exchange
- Sale of Notes

2 Rigidly Structured Fees

3 Regulated by Insurance Commissioners

# SETTLEMENT / ESCROW

BUYER/BORROWER
ESCROW INSTRUCTIONS

TO: TITLE COMPANY
1390 Willow Pass Road, Suite 190, Concord, California 94520
Telephone No.: (415) 827-2008 FAX No.: (415) 689-1060

Escrow No. 56310 -JJ Escrow Officer Date August 22, 1989
Property Address: 1250 Carrison Street, Berkeley, California

ENCLOSED ARE THE FOLLOWING: Grant Deed, Addendums to instructions, read and approved statement of condition, preliminary title report, etc.

which you are instructed to use when you can obtain a CLTA OWNERS BINDER form policy of title insurance containing the insuring clauses, exceptions, exclusions, provisions and stipulations customarily contained in the printed provisions of such form with liability not less than $ 110,000.00 describing the land in the City of Berkeley County of Alameda and described in the Preliminary Report dated July 27, 1989

showing the FEE TITLE

in said land vested in:

Sandy Saylor

Subject to:

County and/or City taxes paid to July 1, 1989. Covenants, conditions, restrictions, rights of way, easements and reservations of record. Specifically, items No. 1,2,3,4 in the Preliminary Title Report dated July 27, 1989 and additional exception Exhibit "A"

Existing Deed of Trust in favor of Homeowners Mortgage and existing Deed of Trust in favor of Aetna Finance Company.

****************************************************************************

SEE ATTACHED SUBJECT TO CONTINUED

You are to prorate as of NA the following NONE

You are instructed to make deductions, adjustments and disbursements in accordance with the statement attached hereto and made a part hereof. Estimated amounts may be adjusted dependent upon date of close of escrow.

NOTICE: THE GENERAL PROVISIONS OF THIS ESCROW ARE PRINTED ON THE ATTACHMENT MADE A PART HEREOF. BUYER ACKNOWLEDGES THAT THE LIMITED AGENCY OF THE ESCROW AND THE RIGHTS OF THE PARTIES HERETO SHALL BE CONSTRUED IN ACCORDANCE THEREWITH.

If the escrow is not in condition to close by September 8, 1989, and demand or cancellation is received by you from any principal to this escrow after said date, you shall act in accordance with the General Provisions attached hereto and made a part hereof. If no demand for cancellation is made, you will proceed to close this escrow when the principals have complied with the escrow instructions.

Received____________________ Time________

TITLE COMPANY

____________________________

____________________ Date Signed: ________________

NEW GROWTH FINANCIAL, a California corporation
BY: ________________
TED THOMAS, Vice President

ADDRESS:
P. O. Box 217
Alameda, California 94501

Phone No: (415)837-2106

## SETTLEMENT / ESCROW

ESCROW INSTRUCTIONS - SUBJECT TO (continued)

TO: TITLE COMPANY

Escrow No.: 56310 - JJ
Date: August 22, 1989

Parties to this transaction understand that as a result of the passage of Insurance Code Section 12413, et seq. (SB 1550), the closing of this transaction will be delayed if any of the parties to this escrow, including, but not limited to the Buyer's/Borrower's lender, should present checks or other items which are not drawn on, or are not payable by a California financial institution, or drafts which are drawn on any financial institution regardless of its location. Escrow Holder is prohibited from disbursing funds for a minimum of eight (8) business days and a maximum of ten (10) business days from the date of delivery and the deposit by Escrow Holder of such checks, drafts or other items or until notification that the funds have been collected by the Escrow Holder's bank.

Escrow Holder is hereby instructed to deposit all items referred to herein immediately upon receipt of same, and record all documents in this transaction only upon Escrow Holder's compliance with California Insurance Code as stated above.

**Escrow company will hold the check for 10 days**

**************************************************************************

We understand that the current taxes may be increased pursuant to a revaluation by the assessor's office as follows:

"Escrow holder shall not be concerned with, or liable for payment, adjustment or proration of, Supplemental Taxes assessed pursuant to Chapter 498, Statutes of 1983, State of California, unless specifically reflected on the Tax Assessor's rolls. All assessments not shown on the tax rolls are to be adjusted outside of escrow. The title policy will contain an exception for the lien of any assessment of Supplemental Taxes assessed pursuant to Chapter 498, Statutes of 1983."

FURTHER, TITLE COMPANY MAY REQUIRE BUYER TO TAKE TITLE SUBJECT TO THE POSSIBLE LIEN OF SUPPLEMENTAL TAXES INCURRED BY SELLER. UNLESS SAID SUPPLEMENTAL TAXES ARE SPECIFICALLY REFLECTED ON THE TAX ASSESSOR'S ROLLS, CHICAGO TITLE COMPANY IS NOT TO BE LIABLE OR REPSONSIBLE FOR THE PAYMENT, ADJUSTMENT OR PRORATION OF THESE SUPPLEMENTAL TAXES, AS THEY ARE TO BE HANDLED OUTSIDE OF ESCROW BY THE PARTIES AS THEY MAY DEEM NECESSARY.

**Supplemental taxes will be due**

**************************************************************************

ALL PARTIES TO THIS ESCROW ACKNOWLEDGE THAT TITLE DOES NOT PROVIDE LEGAL ADVICE, NOR HAS IT MADE ANY INVESTIGATION, REPRESENTATION OR ASSURANCES WHATSOEVER REGARDING THE COMPLIANCE OF THIS TRANSACTION WITH ANY TAX, SECURITIES, OR OTHER LAWS OF THE UNITED STATES OR THE STATE IN WHICH THE TRANSACTION IS CONSUMMATED.

**No legal advice**

ESCROW RECOMMENDS THAT THE PARTIES OBTAIN INDEPENDENT LEGAL COUNSEL AS TO TAX, SECURITIES, OR OTHER LEGAL ASPECTS OF THIS TRANSACTION.

**************************************************************************

NEW GROWTH FINANCIAL, a California corporation, Assignee

BY: ____________________
TED THOMAS, Vice President

____________________
Buyer

(Page 2)

## SETTLEMENT / ESCROW

ESCROW INSTRUCTIONS - SUBJECT TO (continued)

TO: TITLE COMPANY

Escrow No.: 56310 - JJ
Date: August 22, 1989

I/We, the undersigned, hereby agree to waive termite inspection on the a mentioned property and hold Title Company harmless and without a liability in closing said escrow without termite inspection.

**No termite inspection**

*****************************************************************************

Enclosed herewith is a preliminary change of ownership report which effective July 1, 1985 is required to be COMPLETED, SIGNED AND RETURNED by the buyers of all properties located in the County of Contra Costa.

This form must accompany all deeds transferring ownership on properties in the County of Contra Costa or a fine of $20.00 will be levied against the buyer in the recording fees.

PLEASE RETURN THE COMPLETED FORM TO THE ATTENTION OF THE UNDERSIGNED SO AS NOT TO CAUSE DELAY AT CLOSING OR ADDITIONAL FEES TO BUYER.

*****************************************************************************

NEW GROWTH FINANCIAL, a California corporation, Assignee

BY ______________________
TED THOMAS, Vice President

______________________
Buyer

# SETTLEMENT / ESCROW

ESCROW INSTRUCTIONS - SUBJECT TO (continued)

TO: TITLE COMPANY

Escrow No.: 56310 - JJ
Date: August 22, 1989

IMPORTANT NOTICE TO NEW PROPERTY OWNERS

SUBJECT: AVOIDING PROPERTY TAX PENALTIES

Your Tax Collector's experience has shown that many tax delinquencies occur during the first year of property ownership. As a new property owner you should be aware of the following:

A) Tax bills are prepared and assessed against the owner as a lien on the property as of March 1st. The bills are mailed by the Tax Collector on or immediately prior to November 1st of each year. If your deed was recorded after March 1st, the bill will be mailed to the prior owner. If for any reason a property owner does not receive a tax bill for each parcel of property in which he has an interest by the 15th of November he should contact the Tax Collector's office. An exception to this would be arrangements made for an agent or lender to receive and pay a tax bill on the property owner's behalf.

B) The fiscal year for which taxes are levied is July 1st through June 30th. Taxes become a lien as of 12:01 A.M. March 1st preceeding the fiscal year.

C) THE FIRST installment is due and payable in the Tax Collector's office on November 1st and delinquent after 5:00 P.M. December 10th. A 10% penalty attaches thereafter.

D) THE SECOND installment is due and payable in the Tax Collector's office on February 1st and delinquent after 5:00 P.M. April 10th. A 10% penalty attaches thereafter. Also a $10.00 redemption charge is due when the second installment becomes delinquent.

E) If a delinquent date falls on Saturday, Sunday or legal holiday, the time of delinquency is 5:00 P.M. on the next business day.

F) The taxpayer, at his discretion, may pay both installments on or before December 10th. No additional bill is sent for the second installment. The second installment cannot be paid unless the first installment has been paid.

G) It is the property owner's responsibility to obtain and pay this bill. Non-receipt of a tax bill does not relieve the imposition of penalties after the delinquent date. The Tax Collector has no discretion regarding penalties.

WE SUGGEST THAT YOU READ YOUR TITLE REPORT AND/OR ESCROW PAPERS CAREFULLY TO ASCERTAIN WHICH TAXES WERE PAID IN CLOSING, AND WHICH TAXES YOU WILL BE CALLED UPON TO PAY. TO AVOID UNNECESSARY PENALTIES DUE TO THE FACT THAT YOU DID NOT RECEIVE YOUR BILL, YOU SHOULD WRITE TO: ALFRED P. LOMELI, CONTRA COSTA TAX COLLECTOR, P. O. BOX 631, MARTINEZ, CALIFORNIA 94553, AND GIVE HIM YOUR NAME, MAILING ADDRESS, AND YOUR TAX BILL NUMBER (PARCEL NO.) AND REQUEST THAT THE BILL BE MAILED IN YOUR CARE. IN THE EVENT THAT YOU ARE IN DOUBT ABOUT THE AMOUNT OR THE STATUS OF YOUR TAXES, CALL THE TAX COLLECTOR'S OFFICE AT (415) 646-4122.

We also want you to be aware that recent legislation will allow the County to reassess the property and levy increased taxes effective on the date of transfer of title to a new owner.

Escrow holder shall not be concerned with, or liable for payment, adjustment, or proration of Supplemental Taxes assessed pursuant to Chapter 498, Statutes of 1983, State of California, unless specifically reflected on the Tax Assessor's rolls.

NEW GROWTH FINANCIAL, a California corporation, Assignee

BY: ______________________ ______________________
TED THOMAS, Vice President Buyer

(Page 4)

# SETTLEMENT / ESCROW

ESCROW INSTRUCTIONS - SUBJECT TO (continued)

TO: TITLE COMPANY

Escrow No.: 56310 - JJ
Date: August 22, 1989

A. MEMORANDUM OF AGREEMENT

The undersigned hereby instructs you NOT to order a Beneficiary's Sta
Home Owners Federal/Knutson Mortgage concerning the Deed of Trust de
encumberance exception No. 3 of preliminary title report dated July 2

BUYER(S) AND SELLER(S) have entered into an agreement outside escrow, agreement in no way alters or amends this escrow except as you are hereinafter instructed, to the effect that Buyer will acquire title encumbered by the Deed of Trust dated January 6, 1984, executed by husband and wife in favor of Home Owners Mortgage Corporation, beneficiary, recorded January 27, 1984, Instrument No. 84-017637, Official records of Alameda County, California. That Buyer has agreed to pay the loan secured thereby current, if required. Buyer further agrees to pay the loan secured hereby as the installments fall due, that in consummating this transaction Buyer has elected not to enter into an agreement with the Beneficiary therein to assume said loan.

Buyer and Seller have agreed that the unpaid principal balance of said loan is $71,803.13. You are hereby authorized and directed to close the escrow based upon this representation and statement. No further BENEFICIARY'S STATEMENT is required and no liability will be assumed by Title Insurance Company.

B. UNDERSTANDINGS OF THE PARTIES AND INDEMNITY

BUYER and SELLER, each, are aware that the transaction to be consummated in this escrow may result in the beneficiary herein before mentioned accelerating, or attempting to accelerate, the maturity of this loan. Both Buyer and Seller, and each of them, together and individually (jointly and severally) relieve you of ANY liability regarding said Deed of Trust and Note secured thereby, including, but not limited to any alienation, acceleration, or "Due on Sale" clauses or any provisions contained therein for "Balloon" payments or permitting the interest rate or installments due to fluctuate, or ANY of the terms thereof, and severally, do and agree to hold you harmless for, and indemnify you against, and agree to defend you against any claim whatsoever arising therefrom and any attorneys fees, expenses or costs incident thereto.

**************************************************************************

NEW GROWTH FINANCIAL, a California corporation, Assignee

BY: ______________________
TED THOMAS, Vice President

______________________
Buyer

(Page 5)

**Agreement that the escrow officer will not order a beneficiary statement (loan status report)**

**Disclosure: Possible acceleration**

## SETTLEMENT / ESCROW

ESCROW INSTRUCTIONS - SUBJECT TO (continued)

TO: TITLE COMPANY

Escrow No.: 56310 - JJ
Date: August 22, 1989

**Disclosure: Unconscionable advantage law in California — buyer and seller acknowledgement**

We, the undersigned, being the sellers of the property commonly known as:125 Carrison Street, Berkeley, California and more particularly described in Title Company preliminary title report No.319310 dated July 27, 19[illegible] are aware of the fact that the property being sold is currently in foreclosu[illegible]. We are further aware that Section 11700 of the Business and Professions Code of the State of California, adresses the subject of unconscionable advantage relating to Sellers of property in foreclosure. You are hereby advised that no such advantage is being taken evidenced by the fact that fair market value is being paid for said property.

Date:________________

Seller

Seller

STATE OF CALIFORNIA )
)
COUNTY OF __________

On this ____ day of _________, in the year 1989, before me, the undersigned, a Notary Public in and for said County and State, personally appeared personally known to me or proved to me on the basis of satisfactory evidence to be the persons whose names are subscribed to the within instrument and acknowledged that they executed the same.

____________________________
Signature of Notary

******************************************************************************

We, the undersigned, being the buyers of the property known as: 1250 Carrison Street, Berkeley, California and more particularly described in Title Company preliminary title report No. 319310 dated July 27, 1989 are aware of the fact that the property being sold is currently in foreclosure. We are further aware that Section 11700 of the Business and Professions Code of the State of California, addresses the subject of unconscionable advantage relating to the Buyers of property in foreclosure. You are hereby advised that no such advantage is being taken.

Date Aug 22 1989

NEW GROWTH FINANCIAL, a California corporation, Assignee

BY
TED THOMAS, Vice President

**Disclosure information required by law. Check your state's regulations**

STATE OF CALIFORNIA )
)
COUNTY OF CONTRA COSTA )

On this the _____ day of __________ 1989 before me, the undersigned, a Notary Public in and for said County and State, personally appeared Ted Thomas, personally known to me or proved to me on the basis of satisfactory evidence to be the Vice President, of the corporation that executed the within Instrument, personally known to me or proved to me on the basis of satisfactory evidence to be the persons who executed the within Instrument on behalf of the corporation therein named, and acknowledged to me that such corporation executed the within instrument pursuant to its by-laws or a resolution of its board of directors.

__________________________
Notary signature

(Page 7)

# SETTLEMENT / ESCROW

## TITLE COMPANY

ESTIMATED BUYER'S/BORROWER'S SETTLEMENT STATEMENT

PAGE: 1

ESCROW NUMBER: 000056310 - JJ

CLOSING DATE: / /

BUYER: Andy Ash

SELLER: Carl and Carol Carr

PROPERTY: 1250 Carrison Street, Berkeley, California

| | CHARGE BUYER | CREDIT BUYER |
|---|---|---|
| Sales Price | $ 110,000.00 | $ |
| Assumed Loan With Home Owners Federal/Knutson Mortgage Loan Balance | | 70,014.32 |
| Assumed Loan With ITT CONSUMER FINANCIAL CORPORATION Loan Balance | | 28,856.61 |
| Binder | 687.50 | |
| Document Preparation | 100.00 | |
| Escrow Fees | 315.00 | |
| Extra Work Charges | 300.00 | |
| Recording Fees (EST) | 20.00 | |
| Transfer Tax (2) | 2,200.00 | |
| Transfer Tax (2) | 24.20 | |
| PAID OUTSIDE OF ESCROW | | 11,129.07 |
| Funds Due From Buyer At Closing | | 3,646.70 |
| TOTALS | $ 113,646.70 | $ 113,646.70 |

**Typical closing statement**

NEW GROWTH FINANCIAL, a California corporation

BY: ______________________

TED THOMAS, Vice President

## SETTLEMENT / ESCROW

RECORDING REQUESTED BY
TITLE COMPA'
AND WHEN RECORDED MAIL THIS DEED . ,, UNLESS OTHER-
WISE SHOWN BELOW, MAIL TAX STATEMENTS TO:

NAME Sandy Savlor
ADDRESS P. O. Box 217
Alameda, California 94501

Title Order No. 56310 - Escrow No. 56310 - JJ

SPACE ABOVE THIS LINE FOR RECORDER'S USE

319310

### CORPORATION GRANT DEED

Typical Grant Deed

The undersigned declares that the documentary transfer tax is 12.10 and is

☐ computed on the full value of the interest or property conveyed, or is

☒ computed on the full value less the value of liens or encumbrances remaining thereon at the time of sale.

The undersigned declares that the city/county transfer tax is 1,100.00

The land, tenements or realty is located in ☐ unincorporated area ☒ city of Berkeley

FOR A VALUABLE CONSIDERATION, receipt of which is hereby acknowledged,
NEW GROWTH FINANCIAL

a corporation organized under the laws of the State of California
hereby GRANT(S) to

SANDY SAYLOR

the following described real property in the City of Berkeley
County of Alameda , state of California:
LOT 6, IN BLOCK LETTERED "D", AS SAID LOT AND BLOCK ARE SHOWN ON THAT CERTAIN MAP ENTITLED "HEDEMARK AND BRANDOFF'S SUBDIVISION OF LOTS 1 TO 6 INCLUSIVE, AND 25 TO 29 INCLUSIVE, IN BLOCK "C" AND LOTS 14, 15 AND 17 TO 20 INCLUSIVE, IN BLOCK "D" OF THE CARRISON TRACT, BERKELEY, MARCH 1907", FILED APRIL 2, 1907, IN THE OFFICE OF THE COUNTY RECORDER OF ALAMEDA COUNTY.

ASSESSOR'S PARCEL NO. 053-1626-046

Dated August 22, 1989

NEW GROWTH FINANCIAL

BY: [signature]
TED THOMAS, Vice President

BY: __________

STATE OF CALIFORNIA
COUNTY OF } SS.

On this the ________ day of ________ 19__ before me, the undersigned, a Notary Public in and for said County and State, personally appeared __________, personally known to me or proved to me on the basis of satisfactory evidence to be the ________ President, and __________ personally known to me or proved to me on the basis of satisfactory evidence to be ________ Secretary of the corporation that executed the within instrument, personally known to me or proved to me on the basis of satisfactory evidence to be the persons who executed the within instrument on behalf of the corporation therein named, and acknowledged to me that such corporation executed the within instrument pursuant to its by-laws or a resolution of its board of directors.

__________
Signature of Notary

FOR NOTARY SEAL OR STAMP

Assessor's Parcel No. ________

MAIL TAX STATEMENTS TO PARTY SHOWN ON FOLLOWING LINE: IF NO PARTY SO SHOWN, MAIL AS DIRECTED ABOVE

Name Street Address City & State

# SETTLEMENT / ESCROW

A. U.S. DEPARTMENT OF HOUSING AND URBAN DEVELOPMENT
**DISCLOSURE/SETTLEMENT STATEMENT**

HUD #

B. TYPE OF LOAN

1. ☐ FHA 2. ☐ FMHA 3. ☒ CONV. UNINS.
4. ☐ VA 5. ☐ CONV. INS.

6. FILE NUMBER: 30020017ca
7. LOAN NUMBER: 40049-9
8. MORTG. INS. CASE NO.

If the Truth-in-Lending Act applies to this transaction, a Truth-in-Lending statement is attached as page 3 of this form.

C. NOTE: This form is furnished to give you a statement of actual settlement costs. Amounts paid to and by the settlement agent are shown. Items marked "(p.o.c.)" were paid outside the closing; they are shown here for informational purposes and are not included in the totals.

| D. NAME OF BORROWER: | E. NAME OF SELLER: |
|---|---|
| 315 SAN JOAQUIN AVE.<br>ANTIOCH, CA 94509 | NEW GROWTH FINANCIAL<br>185 FRONT STREET #207<br>DANVILLE, CA 94526 |

| F. NAME OF LENDER: | G. PROPERTY LOCATION: |
|---|---|
| MEDALLION MORTGAGE CO.<br>4180 TREAT BLVD.<br>CONCORD, CA. 94521 | 315 SAN JOAQUIN AVE.<br>ANTIOCH, CA. 94509 |

| H. SETTLEMENT AGENT: | PLACE OF SETTLEMENT: | I. SETTLEMENT DATE: |
|---|---|---|
| Benevest Escrow Company | 5920 Stoneridge Mall Road<br>Pleasanton, CA 94566 | 12/11/89 |

| J. SUMMARY OF BORROWER'S TRANSACTION | | K. SUMMARY OF SELLER'S TRANSACTION | |
|---|---|---|---|
| 100. GROSS AMOUNT DUE FROM BORROWER: | | 400. GROSS AMOUNT DUE TO SELLER: | |
| 101. Contract sales price | | 401. Contract sales price | 97,000.00 |
| 102. Personal property | | 402. Personal property | |
| 103. Settlement charges to borrower (LINE 1400) | | 403. | |
| 104. | | 404. | |
| 105. | | 405. | |
| 106. | | 406. | |
| 107. | | 407. | |
| 108. | | 408. | |
| 109. | | 409. | |
| 110. | | 410. | |
| 111. | | 411. | |
| 112. | | 412. | |
| *Adjustments for items paid by seller in advance* | | *Adjustments for items paid by seller in advance* | |
| 113. County taxes | | 413. County taxes 12/11/89 to 01/01/90 | 38.60 |
| 114. | | 414. | |
| 115. | | 415. | |
| 116. | | 416. | |
| 117. | | 417. | |
| 118. | | 418. | |
| 119. | | 419. | |
| **120. GROSS AMOUNT DUE FROM BORROWER** | | **420. GROSS AMOUNT DUE TO SELLER** | 97,038.60 |
| 200. AMOUNTS PAID BY OR IN BEHALF OF BORROWER | | 500. REDUCTIONS IN AMOUNT DUE SELLER | |
| 201. Deposit or earnest money | | 501. Payoff of 1st mortgage loan | 45,947.63 |
| 202. Principal amount of new loan(s) | | 502. Payoff of 2nd mortgage loan | 24,516.30 |
| 203. Existing loan(s) taken subject to | | 503. Settlement charges to seller (LINE 1400) | 3,070.70 |
| 204. | | 504. Existing loan(s) taken subject to | |
| 205. | | 505. Paid Outside of Escrow | 4,000.00 |
| 206. | | 506. HOME WARRANTY | 295.00 |
| 207. | | 507. | |
| 208. | | 508. | |
| 209. | | 509. | |
| 210. | | 510. | |
| 211. | | 511. | |
| 212. | | 512. | |
| *Credits to borrower for items unpaid by seller* | | *Credits to borrower for items unpaid by seller* | |
| 213. County taxes | | 513. County taxes | |
| 214. | | 514. | |
| 215. | | 515. | |
| 216. | | 516. | |
| 217. | | 517. | |
| 218. | | 518. | |
| 219. | | 519. | |
| 220. TOTAL AMOUNT PAID BY OR IN BEHALF OF BORROWER | | 520. TOTAL REDUCTIONS IN AMOUNT DUE SELLER | 77,829.63 |
| **300. CASH AT SETTLEMENT REQUIRED FROM OR PAYABLE TO BORROWER** | | **600. CASH TO SELLER FROM SETTLEMENT** | |
| 301. Gross amount due from borrower (line 120) | | 601. Gross amount due to seller (line 420) | 97,038.60 |
| 302. Less amounts paid by or in behalf of borrower (line 220) | | 602. Less total reductions in amount due to seller (line 520) | 77,829.63 |
| 303. CASH REQUIRED FROM BORROWER / CASH TO BORROWER | | 603. CASH REQUIRED FROM SELLER / CASH TO SELLER | 19,208.97 |

UB (11/86) -2B

## SETTLEMENT / ESCROW

| L. SETTLEMENT CHARGES | PAID FROM BORROWER'S FUNDS | PAID FROM SELLER'S FUNDS |
|---|---|---|
| 700. SALES/BROKER'S COMMISSION Based on price $97,000.00 | | |
| 701. Total commission paid by seller. Division of commission as follows: | | |
| 702. $2,910.00 to BETTER HOMES REALTY | | |
| 703. $ to | | |
| 704. | | 2,910.00 |
| 800. ITEMS PAYABLE IN CONNECTION WITH LOAN. | | |
| 801. | | |
| 802. | | |
| 803. | | |
| 804. | | |
| 805. | | |
| 806. | | |
| 807. | | |
| 808. | | |
| 809. | | |
| 810. | | |
| 811. | | |
| 812. | | |
| 813. | | |
| 814. | | |
| 815. | | |
| 816. | | |
| 817. | | |
| 818. | | |
| 819. | | |
| 820. | | |
| 821. | | |
| 900. ITEMS REQUIRED BY LENDER TO BE PAID IN ADVANCE. | | |
| 901. Interest from | | |
| 902. Mortgage insurance premium for mo. to | | |
| 903. Hazard insurance premium for 1 yrs. to | | |
| 904. | | |
| 1000. RESERVES DEPOSITED WITH LENDER FOR: | | |
| 1001. | | |
| 1002. | | |
| 1003. | | |
| 1004. | | |
| 1005. | | |
| 1100. TITLE CHARGES: | | |
| 1101. Settlement or closing fee to | | |
| 1102. Messenger Fee | | 30.00 |
| 1103. | | |
| 1104. | | |
| 1105. | | |
| 1106. | | |
| 1107. | | |
| 1108. | | |
| 1109. | | |
| 1110. | | |
| 1111. | | |
| 1112. Title insurance to NORTH AMERICAN TITLE CO. | | |
| (includes above items No.: | | |
| 1113. Lender's coverage $ 77,600.00 | | |
| 1114. Owner's coverage $ 97,000.00 | | |
| 1115. | | |
| 1116. | | |
| 1117. | | |
| 1118. | | |
| 1119. | | |
| 1120. | | |
| 1121. | | |
| 1200. GOVERNMENT RECORDING AND TRANSFER CHARGES | | |
| 1201. Recording fees: Deed $ 5.00 ; Mortgage $ 11.00 Releases $ 24.00 | | 24.00 |
| 1202. State tax/stamps: Deed $ ; Mortgage $ | | 106.70 |
| 1203. | | |
| 1204. | | |
| 1300. ADDITIONAL SETTLEMENT CHARGES | | |
| 1301. | | |
| 1302. | | |
| 1303. | | |
| 1304. | | |
| 1305. | | |
| 1400. TOTAL SETTLEMENT CHARGES *(entered on lines 103 and 503, Sections J and K)* | | 3,070.70 |

UB (11/86) -2A

## SETTLEMENT / ESCROW

**Benevest**
Escrow Company

COPY

5920 Stoneridge Mall Road, Pleasanton, CA 94566 (415) 463-8360

ESCROW INSTRUCTIONS

LAURA McRAE
Escrow Officer

Date: August 29, 1989
Escrow No.: 30019316CA

| | | |
|---|---|---|
| Paid outside of escrow | $ | 2,000.00 |
| Encumbrance of record (approximately) (1st & 2nd Deeds of Trust) | $ | 62,637.52 |
| TOTAL CONSIDERATION | $ | 64,637.52 |

all of which you are authorized to use provided on or before October 15, 1989, you can obtain a Policy of Title Insurance in the usual form, containing the exceptions customarily used at this date with liability limited to $64,637.52, insuring title to said property to be in the condition hereinbefore called for, but are not to be held responsible for liens that may attach after recording the documents called for herein, and you obtain a Deed, which when recorded will convey title to NEW GROWTH FINANCIAL, A CALIFORNIA CORPORATION

the record title to the following described property, situated in the County of ALAMEDA, State of California and described as follows:
Legal description attached hereto and made a part hereof.

Property Address: 2120 E 17TH STREET, OAKLAND, CA

COPY

SUBJECT TO:

1. All 1989-90 General and special county and city taxes, including any special district levies payments of which are included therein and collected therewith, for the current fiscal year, not delinquent, including taxes for the ensuing year, if any, a lien but not yet payable.
2. Conditions, restrictions, reservations, covenants, rights, rights of way, easements and the exception of minerals, oil, gas, water, carbons and hydro-carbon substances in, on or under said land, now of record, and in deed to file, if any, affecting the use and occupancy of said property.

C. IT IS UNDERSTOOD AND AGREED HEREIN THAT THE BUYER IS PURCHASING PROPERTY SUBJECT TO THE FIRST TRUST DEED LOAN MENTIONED ABOVE, AND WILL NOT BE ASSUMING SAID LOAN. BUYER AND SELLER HEREIN INSTRUCT AND AUTHORIZE ESCROW HOLDER TO CLOSE ESCROW WITHOUT OBTAINING THE APPROVAL OF THE LENDER AND BOTH BUYER AND SELLER HEREIN AGREE TO RELEASE BENEVEST ESCROW COMPANY AND TO HOLD SAID COMPANY HARMLESS OF ALL LIABILITY AND/OR RESPONSIBILITY IN CONNECTION WITH NOT OBTAINING SAID LENDERS APPROVAL AND FROM ANY LIABILITY AND/OR RESPONSIBILITY THAT MIGHT OCCUR IN THE FUTURE IN CONNECTION WITH SAME.

*Buyer not assuming the loan*

ADDITIONAL INSTRUCTIONS CONTINUED ON PAGE TWO

I will pay, on demand, regardless of the consummation of this escrow, all charges incurred by you for me, including fee for preparing instruments I execute, recording charges and your customary buyer's escrow fee.

Signature Ed Thomas
NEW GROWTH FINANCIAL
Address 185 FRONT STREET, #207, DANVILLE, CA 94526

I agree to sell the above described property for the amount and on the terms set forth above and you will use said money to place the title in the condition above required by paying any liens now against said property. I agree to pay your charges for your documents, recording, escrow and title charges.
You are authorized to attach transfer stamps to the deed in the amount required.

Signature Dennis Dork — Signature Dolly Dork
Dennis Dork — Dolly Dork
Address P.O. BOX 1971, CLEARLAKE, CA 95422

COPY

## SETTLEMENT / ESCROW

Benevest
Escrow Company

Escrow No. 30019316CA

Page 2

It is understood and agreed herein that the buyer is purchasing property SUBJECT TO the Second Trust Deed loan mentioned above, and will NOT be assuming said loan. Buyer and Seller herein instruct and authorize Escrow Holder to close escrow without obtaining the approval of SECOND LENDER and both Buyer and Seller herein agree to release Benevest Escrow Company and to hold said company harmless of all liability and/or responsibility in connection with not obtaining said lenders approval and from any liability and/or responsibility that might occur in the future in connection with same.

Signature Ted Thomas
NEW GROWTH FINANCIAL

Signature Dennis Dork
Dennis Dork

Signature Dolly Dork
Dolly Dork

**Buyer purchasing subject to: no assumption and no lender approval**

# SETTLEMENT / ESCROW

Benevest
Escrow Company

5920 Stoneridge Mall Road, Pleasanton, CA 94566 (415) 463-8360

BUYERS AND/OR BORROWERS INSTRUCTIONS

To: Benevest Escrow Company

Date: August 29, 1989 Escrow Officer: LAURA McRAE Escrow No.: 30019316CA
PROPERTY ADDRESS: 2120 E 17TH STREET, OAKLAND, CA HUD # N

I/We now hand you: (X) Balance due, as indicated below, in the form of cash/cashier's check
( ) Note and Trust Deed in favor of ______
( ) ______

All of which you may deliver and/or record when you obtain for my/our account a Deed to the real property described in your preliminary title report no. T193823 dated August 29, 1989, a copy of which I/we have read and hereby approve.
And when you can issue your CLTA Form Title Insurance Policy (and ALTA Policy if required by Buyer's Lender) with liability in the amount of $ 64,637.52, as indicated below, on the real property described in said report showing title vested in:
NEW GROWTH FINANCIAL, A CALIFORNIA CORPORATION

SUBJECT TO: County and/or City taxes not delinquent; covenants, conditions, restrictions, rights of way, easements and reservations of record:
(X) Preliminary report items numbered 1, 2, 3, 4, & 5
( ) Trust Deed to record in favor of ______
( ) ______

PRORATE AS OF close of escrow
( ) Taxes (based on latest available tax bill)
( ) Prepaid fire insurance premium
( ) Interest on existing loan
( ) Rents (based on statement provided by Seller)
( ) ______

You are authorized to make deductions, adjustments and disbursements in accordance with the following statement. Estimated amounts may be adjusted dependent upon date of close of escrow.

| ESTIMATED STATEMENT | DEBITS | CREDITS |
|---|---|---|
| PURCHASE PRICE | 64,637.52 | |
| Paid outside of Escrow | | 2,000.00 |
| CITY TRANSFER TAX | 614.06 | |
| CITY OF OAKLAND | 180.00 | |
| 1ST DEED OF TRUST(APPROX P.B.) | | 58,197.36 |
| 2ND DEED OF TRUST(APPROX. P.B.) | | 4,440.16 |
| Title Policy: NORTH AMERICAN TITLE COMPANY | 506.00 | |
| Revenue Stamps (on Deed) | 2.20 | |
| Recording | 50.00 | |
| Escrow Fee: Benevest Escrow Company | 350.00 | |
| Drawing Documents - Deed, Notes, etc. | 25.00 | |
| BALANCE DUE THIS COMPANY | | 1,727.26 |
| TOTALS | 66,364.78 | 66,364.78 |

The GENERAL PROVISIONS attached and made a part of these instructions and are by reference thereto incorporated herein and made a part hereof and have been read and are approved by the undersigned.

Any amendments of or supplements to any instructions affecting this escrow must be in writing. I will hand you any funds and instruments required to complete this escrow. All documents, balances and statements due the undersigned are to be mailed to the address shown below.

SIGNATURE NEW GROWTH FINANCIAL ADDRESS TELEPHONE

SIGNATURE CITY STATE ZIP

**Authorization not to order the beneficiary statement**

# SETTLEMENT / ESCROW

**ESCROW INSTRUCTIONS**

To: BENEVEST ESCROW COMPANY

Escrow No. 30019316CA

Date

5920 STONERIDGE MALL ROAD, #105
PLEASANTON, CA 94566

The undersigned hereby instruct you NOT to order a Beneficiary statement from Midfirst Savings & Loan concerning exception # 4 of preliminary report dated 8/29/89 .

We hereby reprsent and guarantee that the unpaid balance of the Note and Deed of Trust held by the above named party is $ 58,197.36 that the interest thereon has been paid to *** at the rate of *** % per annum and buyer is to take title subject to all terms and conditions contained therein.

...by instructed and authorized to close this escrow based ...presentation and statement. No further statement is requi... beneficiary themselves and approval of the beneficiary ... title to the subject property is NOT required to close

***NO INFORMATION HAS BEEN PROVIDED OR REQUIRED BY THE UNDERSIGNED PARTIES

Dennis Dork

Dolly Dork
(Seller)

BUYERS HEREIN ARE AWARE THAT THE FIRST NOTE AND DEED OF TRUST IS IN DEFAULT AT THIS TIME. ESCROW IS NOT RESPONSIBLE FOR ANY AMOUNTS DUE TO CURE SAID DEFAULT.

Initial______ ________

The aforesaid is hereby approved and the beneficiary statement is expressly waived. The undersigned is aware of the fact that the above mentioned Deed of Trust contains a clause which provides that in the event of sale or transfer of this property without approval of the beneficiary, the beneficiary may declare said Note due and payable, or in lieu thereof may charge an assumption fee and/or increased rate of interest.

You are hereby authorized and directed to proceed with the closing of this escrow. The undersigned holds Continental Land Title harmless from any responsibility or liability in this matter. If any litigation results from the action of any party to this escrow which litigation involves BENEVEST ESCROW COMPANY by reason of thier closing this escrow pursuant to the instructions contained therein, the prevvailing party is entitled to recover reasonable attorney fees and costs.

You are further instructed that if any payments made to the above beneficiary through this escrow are subsequently returned to you by them, you are authorized to return said funds to the undersigned. The buyer assumes all responsibility of notification to the lender of change of ownership and fire insurance coverage.

NEW GROWTH FINANCIAL, a California Corporation

(Buyer)

**Beneficiary statement may declare the note due and payable or charge an assumption fee**

Commonwealth of Pennsylvania
County of ss:

On this, the 20th day of June, 198[9], before me, a Notary Public for the Commonwealth of Pennsylvania, residing in the

the undersigned Officer,

personally appeared Stiff

known to me (satisfactorily proven) to be the person whose name is (are) subscribed to the within instrument, and acknowledged that he executed the same for the purposes therein contained.

I hereunto set my hand and official seal.

My Commission Expires:

NOTARIAL SEAL
FLORENCE LUCIANI, NOTARY PUBLIC
NORRISTOWN, MONTGOMERY COUNTY
MY COMMISSION EXPIRES MAY 10, 1990

Notary Public

**Typical Deed for Pennsylvania**

Record and Return to: TLC Title Insurance Company
1 Penn Square West, Suite 1301
30 South 15th Street, Phil.,PA 19102

Title No.: 00-11-22-33

Deed

Steve Stiff
and
Stella Stiff

-TO-

Max Marcus

Premises: 1511 Willow Street
Borough of Mt. Lebanon
Allegheny County, PA

John C. Clark Co., I

752-S

JUN 20 1990

Joan Smith

Recorder

The address of the above-named Grantee is Pittsburgh PA

On behalf of the Grantee

Fee Simple Deed No. 752-S

Printed for and Sold by John C. Clark Co., 1326 Walnut St., Phila.

**This Indenture** Made the 29th day of June in the year of our Lord one thousand nine hundred and eighty-nine (1989)

**Between** Steve and Stella Stiff

(hereinafter called the Grant

**Typical Deed for Pennsylvania**

Max Marcus

(hereinafter called the Grantee ), of the other part.

**Witnesseth** That the said Grantors, —————————————— for and in consideration of the sum of Forty-five Thousand Dollars ($ 45,000 ) lawful money of the United States of America, unto ---them----- well and truly paid by the said Grantee , at or before the sealing and delivery hereof, the receipt whereof is hereby acknowledged, —————— granted, bargained and sold, released and confirmed, and by these presents ———— grant, bargain and sell, release and confirm unto the said Grantee, her———heirs and assigns, in fee;

ALL THAT CERTAIN message and lot of land, Situate in the Borough of Mt. Lebanon County of Alleghany and State of Pennsylvania, being known as No. 1511 Willow Street, bounded and described as follows, to wit:

BEGINNING at a point on the Northwest side of Willow Street, at the distance of 151.17 feet Northeastwardly from the Northeast side of Freedley Street, a corner of this and other land now or late of Lloyd F. Kershner, known as 1509 Willow Street; thence Northwestwardly along said land of the said Kershner, the line passing through the middle of the partition wall dividing the house erected on this lot from that on the adjoining lot 119.92 feet to a point on the Southeast side of Bringhurst Alley; thence along the said side of said alley Northeastwardly 14.66 feet to a point of other land of said Kershner, known as No. 1513 Willow Street; thence Southeastwardly (omitted in prior deed) along said other land of said Kershner, the line passing through the middle of the partition wall dividing the house erected on this lot from that on the adjoining lot 119.92 feet to a point on the Northwest side of Willow Street aforesaid; thence along the said side of said Willow Street Southwestwardly 14.66 feet to the first mentioned point and place of BEGINNING.

Parcel No.: 1234-5678-9-10

BEING the same premises which Max Marcus by Deed dated March 16, 1983 and recorded March 18, 1983 in the Office for the Recorder of Deeds, in and for the County of Alleghany, Pennsylvania, in Deed Book 4703, page 1966, granted and conveyed unto Steve Stiff and Stella Stiff , husband and wife, in fee.

917

**Together** with all and singular the building and ——————————————— improvements, ways, streets, alleys, driveways, passages, waters, water-courses, rights, liberties, privileges, hereditaments and appurtenances, whatsoever unto the hereby granted premises belonging, or in any wise appertaining, and the reversions and remainders, rents, issues, and profits thereof; and all the estate, right, title, interest, property, claim and demand whatsoever of

them, ———————————— the said grantors, as well at law as in equity, of, in, and to the same.

**To have and to hold** the said lot or piece of ground described with the messuage or tenement thereon erected, ——————————— hereditaments and premises hereby granted, or mentioned and intended so to be, with the appurtenances, unto the said Grantee, her heirs, ——— heirs and assigns, to and for the only proper use and behoof of the said Grantee, her heirs, — heirs and assigns forever.

COMMONWEALTH OF PENNSYLVANIA DEPARTMENT OF REVENUE REALTY TRANSFER TAX JUN21 83 $450.00

| REALTY TRANS. TAX PAID |
|---|
| STATE 450.00 |
| LOCAL 450.00 |
| PER SB |

**And** the said Grantors, for themselves and their ———————————— heirs, executors and administrators do ———— covenant, promise and agree, to and with the said Grantee, her ——— heirs and assigns, by these presents, that they the said Grantors and their ——— heirs, all and singular the hereditaments and premises hereby granted or mentioned and intended so to be, with the appurtenances, unto the said Grantee, her ——— heirs and assigns, against them —— the said Grantors and their heirs, and against all and every person and persons whomsoever lawfully claiming or to claim the same or any part thereof, by, from or under him, her, them, ———— or any of them, shall and will by these presents, ————————————

———————————— WARRANT and forever DEFEND.

**In Witness Whereof,** the party of the first part has ———————— hereunto set their ——— hands and seals. Dated the day and year first above written.

**Typical Deed for Pennsylvania**

**Sealed and Delivered**
IN THE PRESENCE OF US:

Steve Stiff (SEAL)

Stella Stiff (SEAL)

917

GENERAL WARRANTY DEED, Statutory Form No. 22-S VOL 1685 PAGE 690 (Reprinted 9/88) apco Registered in U.S. Patent and Trademark Office anderson publishing co. cincinnati, ohio 45201

01721 General Warranty Deed*

Billy & Bea Borax, of Harris County,
for valuable consideration paid, grant(s) with general warranty covenants, to
Alan and Anne Ale, whose tax-mailing address is
17 Sumter St. Ridgewood, Ohio
the following REAL PROPERTY: Situated in the County of Harris in the State
of Ohio and in the City of Middlesex

Situated in the County of Butler in the State of Ohio and in the City of Middlesex

Being West 1/2 of Lot 896 as recorded in the Plat Records of Harris County Ohio.

**Typical Warranty Deed for Ohio**

RECEIVED FOR RECORD
JOYCE B. THA... RECORDER

90 JAN 16 PM 2:33
RECORD Deed
FEE 10-

TRANSFERRED
DATE 1-16-90
CONVEYANCE # 0379
FEE $ 33.00
EXEMPT
has complied with Section 319.202 of the Revised Code

Prior Instrument Reference: Volume Page of the Deed Records of
County, Ohio. Billy & Bea Borax
Grantor, releases all rights of dower therein. Witness their hand(s) this 4th day
of January, 19 90
Signed and acknowledged in presence of:

Tommi Tomme — Billy Borax
[signature] — Bea Borax

State of Ohio County of Warren ss.
BE IT REMEMBERED, That on this 4th day of January, 19 90, before me,
the subscriber, a Notary Public in and for said state, personally came,
Billy & Bea Borax the Grantor(s) in the
foregoing deed, and acknowledged the signing thereof to be their voluntary act and deed.
IN TESTIMONY THEREOF, I have hereunto subscribed my name and affixed my Official seal
on the day and year last aforesaid.

JEFFERY E. RICHARDS
Notary Public, State of Ohio
My Commission Has No Expiration Date
Section 147.03 ...

This instrument was prepared by

(1) Name of Grantor(s) and marital status.
(2) Description of land or interest therein, and encumbrances, reservations, and exceptions, taxes and assessments, if any.
(3) Delete whichever does not apply.
(4) Execution in accordance with Chapter 5301 Ohio Revised Code.

Auditor's and Recorder's Stamps

*See Sections 5302.05 and 5302.06 Ohio Revised Code.

Chapter 9

# Fixer-Uppers: The Big Money

*Tips from the Experts*

## MOTIVATED BUYERS/SELLERS

Creative selling or creative buying requires cooperative buyers and sellers. Foreclosures fall into this category on a regular basis. A property may need an injection of new monies and/or sweat equity, and the owner cannot or will not make the commitment necessary. This is especially the case when absentee owners are involved or when the owner does not have an interest in the property. A neglected property can be a considerable headache to such a landlord/property owner. He may be reluctant to invest in the property, yet if he doesn't, the property may continue to deteriorate to the point where the owner may not be able to control it effectively. This can create a favorable opportunity for you to solve the owner's foreclosure problem by using creative financing.

The point is that the foreclosure fixer-upper may create an unusually favorable atmosphere for a win-win negotiation. Further, many fixer-uppers are properties that have existing mortgages. These mortgages are more than likely carrying mortgage rates below market rates prevailing for new properties. An important advantage to the foreclosure fixer-upper is that the field is virtually wide open. Not that many buyers want to get involved with a property that needs work. These buyers want properties that have already been fixed.

Perhaps the most overlooked advantage of the foreclosure fixer-upper is its attraction for the first-time home buyer. The fixer-upper may be the last available entrance point for most people who simply want to stop renting and gain their fair share of the home-buying market. The fixer offers hope. The prices of such properties are usually below market if you are buying from the foreclosure seller. Sweat equity can be maximized under this situation. Mortgages may be affordable and assumable. At times, federal, state, and local governments as well as private mortgage companies have huge inventories of neglected and handyman properties.

## CAUTION

The foreclosure and fixer-upper approach can offer tremendous opportunities but requires caution on the reader's behalf: BUYER BEWARE. There are risks involved with this type of real estate. Most of these properties are sold "as is" at the Trustee's/Sheriff's Sale auction, and there can be serious hidden problems with the property, leaving the new owner with some unpleasant surprises if he hasn't done his due diligence — so follow the magic formula of TRAIT.

## DO YOU HAVE THE MONEY?

The foreclosure fixer offers a significant price reduction compared with current marketplace values for individuals who are willing to do the work.

Most renovations must be paid in cash, at least for materials and usually for contractors to do those jobs the handyman can't do himself. Some sort of method for funding the renovation will thus have to be worked out, and this may prove to be an obstacle to the purchase. Government loans, a few of which have been outlined in this text, can help.

## YOU AND THE CONTRACTOR

When you have talked with several contractors, you will have a better understanding of what precisely needs to be done. You will begin to get a more technical feel for the project — in fact, you will probably find it quite exciting to learn all about the projects. Listen for the contractor's ideas on ways to cut costs without hurting the project as a whole. It is very important to deal with a contractor who will allow you to get the most mileage for your dollars.

## CHOOSING THE CONTRACTOR

Keep in mind that this is the age of specialization: Don't hire a roof company to do the termite repairs, and don't hire a handyman to do a complete rehabilitation. They may be cheap, but you also will need to exercise full-time supervision and much more.

Many foreclosure buyers have found it quite effective to use companies named "Mr. Small and Son" or a similar designation. This shows that the company has probably been around for a while and that the father is passing his trade on to his sons. You will often find pride of workmanship in companies such as this. However, check the company's references and study its guarantees in any case. In some cities there is an organization called the Building Industry Association (BIA) that lists all of its members in good standing. It is helpful to know if the company has an awareness of the importance of the consumer. Also check the Better Business Bureau to find if there have been any complaints against the contractor. You may find that the contractor has many complaints against him, in which case you will want to exercise caution. However, don't let a couple of complaints scare you off. After all, no one will be able to please all of the people all of the time. I suggest you ask the contractor about the complaint, as he might not be aware of it. If he is, have him explain the situation to your satisfaction. Your objective in doing so is to open up a communication link with the contractor, allowing you to evaluate how he communicates the problem to you and how he goes about resolving similar problems.

By observing the contractor's demeanor, you can get an idea of the quality of his work. If he is neat and clean, friendly and courteous, that should be an indicator of the quality of his work, as well as how you will work together. Watch out for a contractor who asks for large amounts of money up front before he starts. If a contractor tells you he hasn't the money or credit to even start work...plan on trouble.

### Out in the Open

When dealing with contractors, you should get all your ideas out into the open. Take your time, remembering to be concise. Share any notes, articles, or pictures you may have, as well as your personal thoughts on the project. Be sure to give each contractor the same information so that you will get the same bid from each of them. While you are going over the project with the contractor, use the time to determine what type of workman he is by how well he listens to what you have to say, and whether he helps you along in your descriptions of the work that needs to be completed. Pay attention. For instance, does he listen well, or does he interrupt a lot? This will tell you whether he will follow your instructions in the future. It is important that the contractor follow the building codes. Be aware, however, that in many instances a contractor will use codes as an excuse for not doing what you want.

### Fixers

After you have discussed with the contractor the details of the project, it is time to look into the important financial area. At this point ask whether he is giving you an estimate or an itemized bid. These represent two different methods of figuring the bid price for your project, and there is a big difference between them. In an estimate, the contractor makes an approximate bid based only on an educated guess. This is most often the type of bid you hear of in disputes because the total price you pay can be several hundreds of thousands of dollars greater than the estimate. An itemized bid, however, is an exact bid detailing and itemizing all material costs, labor charges, taxes, and permits. Such a bid shows more exactly what the total price will be. I strongly suggest requesting an itemized bid to save yourself from unanticipated expenses.

### Check Them Out

When it's time to make a decision on whom to use, ask yourself the following: Are you going to do the job yourself? Think about the meetings that you had with the contractors. Did they meet your expectations? How did you feel when you first met? Did they listen? Did you receive an estimate or an itemized bid? Don't make your decision until you check the contractors' references and see work that was performed by him/her.

### References

When you talk to a contractor's references, ask the following questions:

- Would you hire the firm to work for you in the future? Why?
- Did they finish the work? If so, was it done on time?
- Was she well organized, neat, and clean?
- Has he worked for you before? Why?
- How close was his estimate? Did you agree to go over the budget? Why?
- How close was he to his original bid?
- Are you related in any way to this firm or any one that is a stakeholder?

### The Low Bidder

When a person needs work badly, WATCH OUT!! A willingness to bid far below what a job is worth often indicates poor job quality or use of substandard materials. When comparing contractors, don't let price be the only deciding factor. Save what you can, but I suggest you watch out for the lowest bidder unless you've worked together in the past or his references check out squeaky clean and you have seen the results of his work.

## BEFORE-AND-AFTER DOCUMENTATION

If you have a video camera, take good pictures before you start to document what you have done. Get every possible angle inside and outside the house. This record will be extremely helpful when you prepare to sell. And it will provide a good track record with prospective investors for future foreclosure projects. Pictures and snapshots can be displayed in your office. Conversations with potential partners, bankers, and outside investors will turn to your handiwork.

Don't forget about the mechanic's liens. Workers/vendors who assist you in your renovation have the right to place a mechanic's lien against your property.

Don't forget about insurance. If a worker is injured while working for you, you are responsible. If you haven't investigated the worker's compensation laws in your state, you had best get some advice from an insurance professional or your attorney as soon as possible.

Remember: In the real world of foreclosure buying and selling, everything takes twice as long and costs twice as much as originally estimated.

## GUIDELINES FOR SUCCESSFUL RENOVATIONS AND REPAIRS

### Sell It at a Profit Before You Buy

You must sell. And you must be certain you can sell at a profit even before you buy. That seems simple but most folks forget it. People often ignore a basic law of economics: You have to sell things in order to buy things, or you go bankrupt. Everyone claims it's easy to find foreclosure bargains in your market, especially with today's low interest rates and lots of banks and S&Ls with tons of problems. Well, a property is only a bargain if you can sell it and make a profit.

Even before you buy, you must answer four specific questions to ensure your profit when you sell.

1. What will people pay for this property?
2. How many people will want to buy it?
3. How will you convince others to buy your property rather than the one down the street?
4. What's the selling cost?

Keep in mind that you must create an image that sells the product! Do what buyers want done, not what your tastes dictate.

### Start with the Outside

First impressions are what counts!! Your project must have curb appeal. Brokers will tell you that most buyers of real estate have made up their minds before they get out of the car. Take a moment and pretend you are this buyer, the new owner with plenty of money and no desire to buy a deal...how will your house look to this buyer?

You don't want to sell to people like yourself who steal the property. You must entice that ready, willing, and able owner buyer-to-buyer, and he probably has other thoughts and ideas about buying. What will make your property special in his mind?

As an investor, you already know that you want to find properties just like this — ones that need work and lots of TLC. It's different when you sell. You must know your potential market. What will they pay? Will you need special financing? Maybe a lease option? If it's ugly, will anyone other than yourself want it?

### It's a Business

Remember: This is a business venture. Don't be a perfectionist. The details are important but don't delay or let insignificant items that are costly cut into your profits. Do enough to justify your asking price, but don't overdo it with special carpets, drapes, or paint. If the buyer can find something wrong, he will. PLAN FOR IT!! When he complains about some insignificant item, respond with "If I fix that crack in the window will you buy the house today?"

### Some Do's and Not-to-Do's

Replace scratched door knobs and cabinet handles. Remove the window screens and have a professional clean the windows every other week till the house is sold. Garage door openers are popular; if the property doesn't have one, have one installed. Do paint the outside for good curb appeal. Do paint inside; it not only freshens the house up but disguises old problems. Carpet is cheap. Think about putting thick padding under an inexpensive carpet. The padding will give the floor an expensive feeling. Don't overdo it with lot of upgrades. Most people like it neat and clean. It's difficult for them to judge the cost.

- Do paint the garage inside and the floor. This will give a "taken care of" perception to the new owner. Note that the garage must be empty at all times. Do patch the broken asphalt and concrete in the driveways.
- Do install new linoleum on the kitchen floor.
- Do replace the counter tops.
- Do paint the inside of all cabinets and kitchen cupboards. That includes bathrooms and all closets.
- Do replace faucets in the bathrooms and kitchens; it will give the house a well-maintained feeling.
- Do keep the lawns green and trimmed. Hedges and bushes that are cut and trimmed weekly will impress the most seasoned buyers. Everyone likes it clean and neat. Most folks don't live that way but they still like to see it that way.
- Do check with the city and determine if a building permit is required.
- Don't get emotionally involved with the project.
- Don't use the house to store your equipment or extra fix-it supplies. Cleanliness is Godliness to the prospective buyer. Your equipment will give the impression that you are not finished or not ready to move on.

## FOR A FINISHED LOOK

### Bathroom

- Get new toilet seats.
- Install new tile.
- Install new light fixtures.
- Install new shower doors and curtains.
- If necessary, install new or modern sinks with vanities.
- Install new towel racks and toilet paper holders.

### Family Room

- Paint the walls.
- Install new doors and new hardware and paint the old doors.

- Clean the fireplace and install new screen.
- Install new carpet.

**Kitchen**

- Install new counter tops and cabinets, or refinish the old ones.
- Install new fixtures.
- Install new towel racks.
- Install new appliances or clean old ones.
- Paint the walls.
- Install new linoleum.
- Install blinds in the windows.

**Bedrooms**

- Install new carpet or clean the old to look like new.
- Paint ceilings.
- Use light colors throughout.
- Avoid patterned wallpaper.
- Use mirrors to give an illusion of space and to reflect light.
- Open up small rooms with skylights.
- Open all drapes; light will make the rooms look bigger.
- Use blinds on all windows.

## FOURTEEN CRITICAL QUESTIONS

Before signing a partnership or joint venture agreement, make sure you know the answers to the following questions.

1. Who pays the monthly payments, taxes and insurance?
2. Who is on title and why in that manner?
3. Who qualifies the mortgage?
4. Who picks the lender; which lender is suitable?
5. How much is and who advances the down payment?
6. Who pays the closing costs, points, fees, and reports?
7. Who gets what percentage of the appreciation, if any?

8. What are the joint venture partner's rights and recourse if payments are not made?
9. What are the responsibilities of each joint venture entity?
10. How do we exit the contract prior to maturity?
11. Will the contract stand on its own?
12. What is expected of the manager?
13. Who performs major/minor repairs?
14. What about rights of survivorship if someone dies or is incapacitated?

## *Who to Call for "How To" Information...*

## TIPS FROM THE EXPERTS

# What You Should Know Before You Hire a Contractor

### CHECK THE CONTRACTOR'S LICENSE

Is the contractor properly licensed? In California, any job that costs $300 or more for material and labor must be performed by a contractor who holds a current, valid license from the Contractors State License Board in the specialty for which he or she is contracting.

Ask to see the contractor's pocket license and some additional form of identification. The name on the pocket license should be the same as the name of the contractor or the business name under which the contractor is working.

***It is illegal for a contractor to use another contractor's license just as it is for someone to use another's drivers license.***

When you establish that the contractor's or company's name matches what appears on the pocket license issued by the Contractors State License Board, then call the Board and ask if the license is valid. Phone numbers for local offices of the Board are listed at the end of this booklet.

Finally if the contractor is operating with a valid license, you may also want to find out whether the person you are considering working with is a member of a professional or trade association that has a code of ethics or standards for their trade. Find out if the members of the association have pledged to arbitrate disputes. You may want to contact the local chapter of the association to see wether it will act as an intermediary in case of disputes or arrange for an impartial arbitrator. ***Arbitration is voluntary.*** If you want an arbitration clause in your contract, make sure the contractor you are considering will agree to arbitrate any disputes that arise out of contract.

### MAKE SURE THE CONTRACTOR HAS WORKER'S COMPENSATION AND LIABILITY INSURANCE COVERAGE

Ask the contractor if the company is insured against claims covering workers' compensation, property damage, and personal liability in case of accidents. Ask to see a copy of the certificate of insurance or ask for the name of the contractor's insurance carrier and agency to verify that the contractor has this insurance. In California, workers compensation insurance coverage for contractors is required by law.

This is important for you as a home owner because if a worker is injured while working on your property and the contractor does not have insurance, you are the one who is going to have to pick up the bill for an in-

## TIPS FROM THE EXPERTS

jured workers' injuries and rehabilitation, if necessary. Don't let your homeowner's insurance policy become your contractor's liability coverage.

You may also wish to check the contractor out with your local building department, trade association or union, local consumer protection agency, consumer fraud unit in your city or district attorney's office, and the Better Business Bureau. Call these organizations to see if they have information about the contractor you are considering. Ask how long the company has been in business and find out if there are any complaints about the firm or other relevant file information.

### LICENSING

It bears repeating that any contractor performing a job which the total cost of the project including labor and materials is more than $300., the contractor must be licensed by the Contractor State License Board. Licensed contractors are subject to laws designed to protect the consumer.

Unlicensed contractors are a danger to your financial affairs because they expose you to significant financial harm in the event of injury or property damage. Unlicensed contractors usually do not have adequate boning or insurance.

Although an unlicensed contractor may give you a low bid, the risk of possible financial and legal consequences you may face probably outweigh any benefits a lower bid may seem to offer.

Please note: A licensed number appearing on a bid or contract does not necessarily mean the license is valid. Before you sign anything, call the Contractors State License Board, (CSLB) office in your area to make sure the contractor is properly licensed in the class for which work is to be performed and the license is in good standing. You should also ask about the contractor's disclosable complaints history and any prior legal actions that may have been taken against the contractor. Complaint history information is available form the CSLB Northern or Southern Regional Complaint Disclosure telephone numbers. The Northern number is (916) 366-5332. The Southern number is (213) 921-0910.

The information in this section was gathered from numerous sources including but not limited to the Department of Consumer Affairs and California Licensing Board.

## SOME THINGS TO CONSIDER

### Do:

- ❑ 1. Plan your project carefully
- ❑ 2. Shop around before hiring a contractor.
- ❑ 3. Get at least three written bids on your project.
- ❑ 4. Provide contractors from whom you request bids with accurate plans for drawings that will enable them to determine the scope of the work and the costs.
- ❑ 5. Check with the Contractors State License Board to see if a contractor is properly licensed.
- ❑ 6. Check out contractors with your local building department, trade associations or unions, consumer protection agency, and the Better Business Bureau.
- ❑ 7. Look at work the contractor has completed.
- ❑ 8. Ask your contractor to furnish a completion or contract bond.
- ❑ 9. Consult with more than one lending institution regarding the type of loan to obtain.
- ❑ 10. Ask your lender to recommend a funding control company.
- ❑ 11. Make sure your contract provided for a retention.
- ❑ 12. Make sure everything you and your contractor have agreed to is included in your contract.
- ❑ 13. Ask your contractor about inconveniences that may occur and plan accordingly.
- ❑ 14. Keep a job file.
- ❑ 15. Make sure you receive lien releases from subcontractors and material suppliers.
- ❑ 16. Make frequent inspections of the work, including a final walk-through.
- ❑ 17. Consult an attorney if a mechanic's lien is filed against your property.
- ❑ 18. Try first to negotiate with the contractor if problems or disagreements occur.

*This information is compiled by the Contractors State License Board*

## SOME THINGS TO CONSIDER

### Be sure your contract includes:

- ☐ 1. The name, address, and license number of the contractor, and the name and registration number of any salesperson who solicited or negotiated the contract.
- ☐ 2. The approximate dates (not number of working days) when the work will begin and be substantially completed.
- ☐ 3. A description of the work to be done, a description of the materials and equipment to be used or installed, and the price for the work.
- ☐ 4. A schedule of payments showing the amount of each payment in dollars and cents.
- ☐ 5. If the payment schedule contained in the contract provides for a downpayment, such downpayment shall not exceed $1,000 or 10 percent of the contract price, excluding finance charges, which ever is less. If the contract provides for the contractor to furnish performance and payment bonds, lien and completion bonds, a bond equivalent, or funding control, this limitation of downpayment does not apply.
- ☐ 6. A Notice To Owner regarding the state lien laws, and the right and responsibilities of an owner of property.
- ☐ 7. A description of what constitutes substantial commencement of work.
- ☐ 8. A notice that the failure of the contractor, without lawful excuse, to substantially commence work within 20 days from the approximate date specified in the contract when work is to begin is a violation of the Contractors License Law.

### Do Not:

1. Hire an unlicensed contractor
2. Hire a contractor without first shopping around
3. Act as an owner/builder unless you are very experienced in construction
4. Sign anything until you completely understand it and agree to the terms.
5. Make agreements with subcontractors or workers without consulting the prime contractor.
6. Ever pay cash, without proper receipt.
7. Make a downpayment without checking with your lender or the Contractors State License Board to make sure it does not exceed the legal limit.
8. Let your payments get ahead of the contractor's completed work.
9. Hesitate to ask questions of the contractor.
10. Make final payment until you are satisfied with the job.

## TIPS FROM THE EXPERTS

# GETTING UP ON ROOFS

Often the end result of using an unlicensed roofer is a bad roofing job or the wrong approach to the problem. This is worse than no job at all, and may end up costing you *more* in the long run.

Another reason to avoid this type of operator: if he does not pay the suppliers whose materials are used on your project, you may find a lien placed on your property even though you have paid for the work. This means you may end up paying for the same materials twice.

All in all, most home and building owners have found that using unlicensed, uninsured roofers is not worth the risk.

### HOW TO SELECT A PROFESSIONAL.

Because an informed customer is a good customer, find out as much as you can about the contractor you are considering.

Call the Bay Area Counties Roofing Industry Promotion Fund offices for contractor referrals.

Once you've contacted these contractors, ask those that bid on your job for the following:

- ❑ Evidence of his State contractor's license and license number.
- ❑ A written proposal that outlines what work is to be done, the amount that is to be charged, and the terms of the guarantee given.
- ❑ Proof of liability insurance, which protects you against personal injury to you or others and against damage to your property or the property of others while the contractor is working on your job.
- ❑ Proof of workers' compensation insurance, which protects the contractor's employees while working on your job.
- ❑ A list of customer references.

Check the customer references. Be sure the contractor has performed as promised.

If you have any doubts, call the Better Business Bureau or the Contractors' State License Board. You will find out quickly if there have been a number of unresolved complaints about the contractor.

Be careful not to base your selection on price alone. A low bid is *not* necessarily the best bargain.

### GUARANTEES.

The standard guarantee on roofing or reroofing that is recognized by the Associated Roofing Contractors of the Bay Area Counties, Inc. is three years. This assures that your roof's satisfactory performance will be proven through several weather cycles. Unlicensed operators who offer longer guarantees may not be around long enough to back them up. Remember: a guarantee is only as good as the contractor.

### SEASONAL ADVANTAGES.

If you have your roof done in the spring or summer, you will find better availability and faster service. The licensed contractor is able to schedule your job when he is not busy with emergency repairs created by bad weather. What's more, roof removal and reroofing projects are more effectively completed during dry weather.

### ABOUT RIPF.

The Bay Area Counties Roofing Industry Promotion Fund represents a concerned group of locally-based professional roofing contractors. They are dedicated to keeping industry standards high and to making it easy for you to locate a professional. They will help you in any way possible with your new roofing or maintenance and repair needs.

### THE ADVANTAGES OF USING A PROFESSIONAL ROOFING CONTRACTOR.

The most important part of maintaining your roof is to get the job done right the first time. This is

## TIPS FROM THE EXPERTS

where a licensed, insured roofing contractor comes in. He is the pro — someone who will deliver an effective, long-lasting roof and stand behind his work.

A licensed roofing contractor has a wide range of capabilities. He will work on decks and building foundations as well as roofs — wherever waterproofing is needed. He knows all types of roofing and can recommend the best application for your particular need. He will quote a fair price before he starts to work and will use only skilled craftsmen.

Whether they operate large or small businesses, professional roofing contractors all have the following traits in common. Professional roofing contractors are:

**Licensed.** The State of California has adopted standards for licensing roofing contractors. Only those who meet the standards by testing qualify for a state license.

**Well-established.** A professional roofing contractor will have a permanent place of business, a telephone number, a tax identification number and, where appropriate, a business license.

**Experienced and knowledgeable.** Roofing skills cannot be learned overnight. A professional roofing contractor is familiar with all kinds of roofs — asphalt and gravel, wood shingle and shake, composition shingle, tile and slate, as well as various kinds of specialty products.

**Insured, and committed to safety.** There are inherent dangers to applying a roof. The contractor who carries *both* workers' compensation insurance and liability insurance has protected you in the event of damage to your property and injury to his workers while work is being performed on your property.

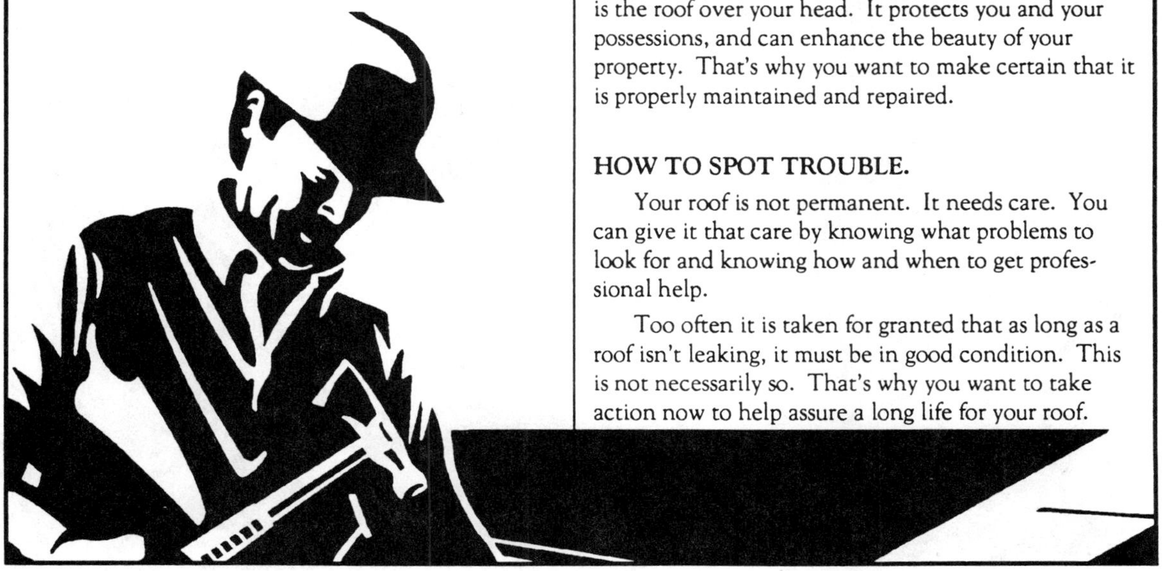

### BEWARE OF UNLICENSED ROOFERS.

Not all roofing contractors are professional, and too many home and building owners have paid dearly for using amateurs.

This type of operator is unlicensed, uninsured, and probably lacking in experience. He may use high pressure or scare tactics, and "bonus offers" to get your business.

If you do use an unlicensed, uninsured firm or individual, don't be mislead into believing that your homeowner's or personal liability policy necessarily protects you. In many cases, you may be liable for suit.

A large number of home and building owners have been dragged into litigation involving uninsured contractors. If an employee of an unlicensed, uninsured contractor is injured on your home or building, you may be responsible for his injuries or disabilities. In addition, you probably have no protection in the event damage is done to your property or the property of others by the roofer during the course of the work.

The most important part of your home or building is the roof over your head. It protects you and your possessions, and can enhance the beauty of your property. That's why you want to make certain that it is properly maintained and repaired.

### HOW TO SPOT TROUBLE.

Your roof is not permanent. It needs care. You can give it that care by knowing what problems to look for and knowing how and when to get professional help.

Too often it is taken for granted that as long as a roof isn't leaking, it must be in good condition. This is not necessarily so. That's why you want to take action now to help assure a long life for your roof.

## TIPS FROM THE EXPERTS

The best way for you to minimize roof repair bills is to prevent damage *before* it occurs. This means periodic inspections, either from the ground or on a ladder. Look for danger signs like:
1. Missing or cracked shingles. 2. Debris on the roof. 3. Clogged gutters and drains. 4. Curled shingles or other fatigued roofing materials. Indoors you'll want to check for leaks or damp areas and stains on ceilings.

Generally speaking, a newer roof should be inspected annually while a roof that is eight to ten years old or older should be inspected more often. If you are unable to safely make an inspection yourself, have a roofing contractor do it for you. The cost is reasonable, and it could prevent later unnecessary repairs.

### ROOFING REPAIRS

If your roof is relatively new and has developed only a minor leak, normally it can be easily corrected.

Shingles that are damaged or have blown away can be replaced, and leaks around flashings can be repaired.

If there is any damage done to the roof by storms, hail, flying debris, or by other tradesmen working on your completed roof, you should notify your roofing contractor immediately.

Remember that roof damage, if neglected, will only get worse. A neglected roof can cause damage to other possessions — possibly even structural damage to your home or building.

### WHEN TO REROOF.

If your roof is beyond repair or repair costs are excessive, reroofing is the best solution.

Most cities and counties in the Bay Area have adopted reroofing codes to define specific requirements necessary to reroof a structure. All competent roofing contractors are familiar with and comply with these codes.

When reroofing, the condition of the roof structure and its supports should be inspected for damage and repaired as needed. Hidden damage or dry rot not discernible at the time of the inspection may result in additional cost to the owner.

### ADDING INSULATION.

During a reroofing job, you have a unique opportunity to add insulating material. Because most of your heat loss occurs through the roof, adding this insulation will save you money on your energy bills.

If you need more information, call the Roofing Industry Promotion Fund offices today at (415) 635-8800.

### A FINAL REMINDER.

Make sure that you use a licensed, insured roofing contractor. This is your best assurance of getting a quality roof.

The information in this section was gathered from numerous sources including but not limited to the Department of Consumer Affairs and California Licensing Board.

John T. Banister,
Executive Secretary
8301 Edgewater Drive
Oakland, CA 94621
(415) 635-8800

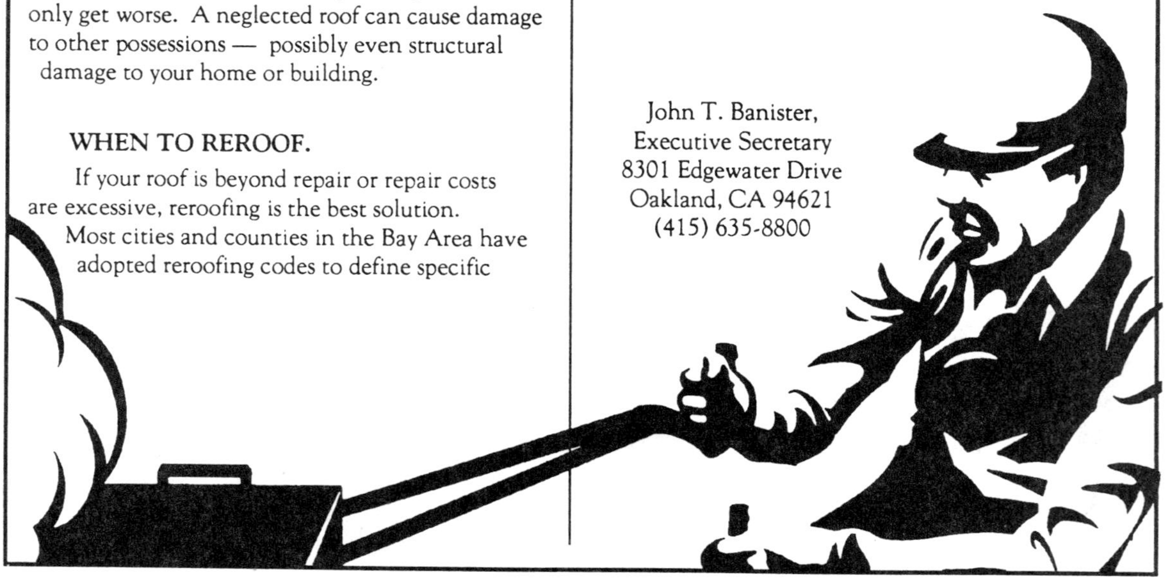

## TIPS FROM THE EXPERTS

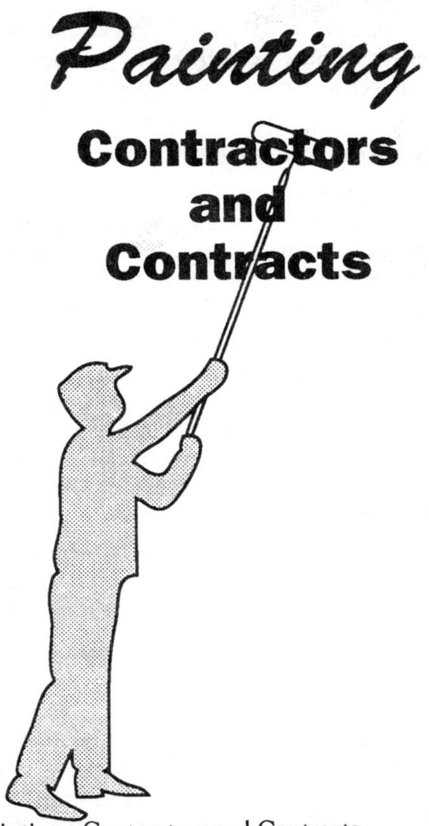


### Painting - Contractors and Contracts

Sooner or later most people decide its time to hire someone to paint their house, an apartment building they own, or a city block of business offices. Regardless of the size of the painting project you're contemplating, its success may well depend on some careful planning and the hiring of a state licensed painting and decorating contractor.

### WHY A LICENSED CONTRACTOR?

State law requires anyone who contracts to do painting work to be licensed by the Contractor State License Board, if the total price of the job will be $200 or more. Licensed contractors are regulated by laws designed to protect the public.

Unlicensed contractors typically are not bonded, and do not have liability or workers compensation insurance. If you hire an unlicensed contractor you may be financially responsible if injuries, fire or other property damage occur.

### PLANNING/PREPARATION

Although your painting project may not seem complicated, producing a finished job that looks good and will last requires skill and a knowledge of painting products and techniques. You should ask any contractor you consider hiring for advice on types and brands of paint, and any surface preparation which will be needed to extend the life of the job.

You should be aware that generally, for a quality job:

**INTERIOR SURFACES**, such as kitchen and bathroom walls, which will be painted with enamel should be washed prior to painting. If flat-wall paint will be used, any obvious dirt, grease or crayon marks should be removed. Wood trim should be sanded and, if not stained, painted with a gloss or semi-gloss enamel. Appropriate types of wallpaper and the surface preparation needed differ greatly. With a suitable *written* guarantee, you should take your contractor's advice.

**EXTERIOR** surfaces may or may not need to be washed - ask your contractor. As a general rule, any heavy accumulations of dirt should be removed. Loose or flaking paint should be removed by scraping or sanding or both, and the surface sealed or primed prior to the finish application of stain or paint.

You should discuss any possible inconvenience your painting project will create with your contractor. For instance, the furniture may have to be moved, you may have to leave your house, nearby shrubs or other landscaping may need to be covered, and vehicles may have to be moved. Be sure to make the necessary arrangements before the work is begun to prevent problems.

### BONDING

A painting contractor is required to have a license bond posted with the Contractors State License Board. However, this bond does not insure that your job will be completed. It is a good idea to ask your contractor to provide you with a "payment and performance" bond that covers the full price of your job. Although nothing can totally ensure you job will in fact be completed, a payment and performance bond provides a financial guarantee against mechanic's liens, which could be filed against your property by subcontractors or material suppliers should your contractor fail to pay them. A payment and performance bond also provides a source of funds for completing the job in the event your contractor does not do so. The bond should be for the full amount of your job,

## TIPS FROM THE EXPERTS

as the bonding company is only liable up to the amount of the bond.

A payment and performance bond will usually add 1 to 5 percent to the total contract price, but it can be well worth the cost, particularly on larger projects.

A contractor must be financially solvent and have a proven track record to obtain a payment and performance bond. A contractor who is new to the business or who has a small operation may have difficulty in obtaining such a bond.

If your contractor is unable to provide you with a payment and performance bond, or if you wish to use an additional method of security, you might consider using a joint control company. A joint control company is an escrow company that specializes in construction. Instead of paying the contractor directly, you pay the joint control company which in turn pays the contractor, subcontractor(s), material suppliers, etc. A good company will inspect the project before making payments, and provide a guarantee against valid mechanic's liens.

### CHOOSING YOUR CONTRACTOR

One of the best ways to select a contractor is through recommendations from people who have recently had painting work done. Other sources of referrals are painting contractor associations and painting industry funds. But, regardless of recommendations, before hiring a contractor you should:

- Ask for the contractor's state license number and call the Contractors State License Board to verify that it is issued for painting, is currently renewed, and is in good standing.
- Request a list of similar jobs the contractor has completed recently in the area. Look at the work and talk to the owners if possible.
- Ask if the contractor has liability and workers compensation insurance and request certificates of insurance.

### BIDS

It is a good idea to obtain more than one bid so that the prices and work offered can be compared. Request bids in writing. Remember that the lowest price may not always be the best. The contractor may have made a mistake, or may not have included all the work quoted by competitors. Be certain that each bid lists all the preparatory and finish work that the contractor has suggested, as well as the type and brand of paint.

### PAYMENT ARRANGEMENTS

You should be wary of a contractor who asks for payment prior to beginning the job. Most painting contractors do not require a down payment; full payment is usually requested on completion of the job, or in installments if the job will take a period of weeks.

If a contractor does ask for a down payment, remember that on home improvement projects (including painting) the legal limit which may be asked is 10 percent of the full price of the job (excluding finance charges) or $1,000, whichever is less. *Be certain that any down payment or schedule of installment payments is specified in exact dollars and cents in your contract.

* If your contractor provides a payment and performance bond covering your total job, or a joint control company approved by the Registrar of Contractors is used, this limitation on the down payment does not apply.

### YOUR CONTRACT

The law requires that contracts for home improvement jobs over $500 must be in writing. But even if your job is for less than this amount, you should INSIST ON A WRITTEN CONTRACT FOR YOUR OWN PROTECTION. A contract should contain:

- The name, address, license number and telephone number of your contractor, and the registration number of any salesperson involved.
- Payment arrangements and the total price of the job.
- A complete description of the work to be done, materials to be used (including all preparatory and finish work and the brand, type and color of paint).
- Approximate dates when work will begin and be completed.
- A statement that the contractor will do any necessary cleanup and removal of debris after the job is completed.
- A "Notice to Owner" explaining the state's mechanic's lien laws, and the ways to protect yourself and your property.
- A statement that the contractor will furnish a payment and performance bond or joint control com-

## TIPS FROM THE EXPERTS

pany, if this has been agreed upon.

- Any guarantees made verbally on the work to be done or the materials to be used.

After the contract is signed, any changes you and the contractor agree to make in the work or the materials to be used must be in writing. The written change order must also include any additions or reductions in the total job price.

If you have carefully planned the job, and selected a licensed painting and decorating contractor, the job should proceed without any major problems.

### IF PROBLEMS OCCUR

Sometimes, in spite of all the precautions taken, problems will occur. If this happens, first contact your contractor. Usually problems can be worked out and corrections will be made willingly. If not, file a written complaint with the Contractors State License Board. The Board's staff assists consumers with questions about contractors and will investigate all valid complaints.

### CONTRACTORS BOARD OFFICES
### NORTHERN CALIFORNIA

1-800-321-2752

Headquarters Office 916-366-5153
3132 Bradshaw Road
P.O. Box 26000, Sacramento 95826

San Francisco District 415-469-6200
301 Junipero Serra Blvd., #206, 94127

Oakland District 415-464-0964
1700 Broadway, 95612

San Jose District 408-277-1244
State Building, 3rd Floor, #319
100 Paseo De San Antonio, 95113

Sacramento District 916-445-3458
7171 Bowling Drive, Suite 410, 95823

Redding District 916-225-2640
429 Redcliff Drive, Suite 140, 96002

Fresno District 209-445-5281
3374 East Shields Ave., Room E-17, 93726

### SOUTHERN CALIFORNIA

Inglewood District 213-412-6395
One Manchester Blvd.
Suite 400, City Hall, 90301

El Monte District 213-620-4476
11001 E. Valley Mall, Room 303, 91731

Van Nuys District 818-901-5168
6150 Van Nuys Blvd., Suite 300, 91401

Ventura District 805-654-4515
2590 E. Main Street, Room 102, 93003

Long Beach District 213-590-5331
Cal Vet State Office Bldg.
245 W. Broadway, #145, 90802

Santa Ana District 714-558-4086
28 Civic Center Place, Room 690, 92701

San Bernardino District 714-383-4265
357 W. 2nd Street, Suite 2, 92401

San Diego District 619-237-7417
1350 Front Street, Room 5000, 92101

The information in this section was gathered from numerous sources including but not limited to the Department of Consumer Affairs and California Licensing Board.

Chapter 10

# You Own It: Let's Sell It and Make a Bundle

## *The Keys to the Vault*

### HELP YOURSELF

If you decide to use a broker to sell the property, try to help the broker as much as possible. Do not wait for a buyer. If you can't advertise your property, you will sit on it for a long time and use up all your profits in taxes and house payments. Selling real estate is easy if you price the property correctly and let the world know that it is available. The broker needs your help and support. If the broker won't advertise the property regularly, then you must change the broker's contract to require it or you must advertise it yourself.

Let the neighbors know about your sale. Hold an open house. Make up fliers with the broker's name on them and pay a high-school student to put one on each door for at least one mile around the house you want to sell. (Do not put the fliers in mailboxes. Mailboxes are for mail and the post office will reprimand you.)

The brokerage community will be helpful, and you should work closely with all real estate brokers. The brokers and agents are your friends, and they can show you many short cuts to the final sale. But don't wait for the brokers; your responsibility is to make money for yourself and your investors. If you advertise aggressively, distribute fliers, and conduct open houses and parties for the neighborhood, you will be successful. Exclusive listings by the brokerage community may require that they do all the promotion and advertising. If that is the case, don't sign the contract. Sales, promotion, and advertising will find you your clients. I'm not suggesting that you alienate the brokerage community, but I am suggesting that you conduct the sale, and that includes the advertisement, promotion, open houses, and the contacting of local charities and fraternal organizations.

Pricing is the key to selling. Don't be too greedy. Know your competition. Don't try for top dollar. You may get it eventually, but you will spend a lot in carrying costs to get it.

## DEFINE THE MARKET

Price is always important when it comes to sales. But even more important than price is knowledge of the market. The people who live in the country club side of town rarely, if ever, buy fixer-upper or foreclosure houses. Young eager beavers, real estate agents, opportunity seekers, and trade workers all know that the way to make bucks fast is through sweat equity.

Advertise and appeal to the people who are looking for this type of property. If you put your ad in the bridge club newsletter you are wasting money and effort. ASK! Find out where the fixer-upper people look to find values.

Look at your competition. Your price can be higher than theirs — if you have more to offer. Before you advertise, determine for yourself the best points of your property: Is it price? Is it location? Is it a bargain? Is the financing special? Is it the best? Is it the last of the model?

The answers to these questions will help you to define your USP (Unique Selling Proposition) or your USA (Unique Selling Attraction). Without these attributes, you'll have a tough time selling and competing in the market. Be different and your house will sell quickly. If you don't have a bargain or if you fixed it up yourself and want top dollar, write your ad to appeal to white-collar workers who play golf and tennis all weekend long.

## HOW DO YOU SELL IT?

In selling a house, keep three things in mind:

1. Know your buyers.
2. Make your advertising count.
3. Price the house to sell.

### Knowing the Buyer

Ask yourself: Who will find this house appealing? Why would they buy this home? Where would they look for a bargain? Is this a bargain? If so, can we prove it?

### Advertising to Effect

Determine which newspaper bargain hunters read and advertise — often this means local newspapers and penny-savers. Write an ad that appeals to the buyer looking for a fixer-upper.

Young couples and bargain hunters are the most logical prospects for fixer-upper houses. The young couples understand that they can make profits by using so-called sweat equity. For those few who are willing to clean up and fix up the problems of others, properties that are in disrepair provide the place to start. Almost everyone has a relative, a friend or acquaintance who purchased a house, fixed it up, and sold it for a large profit. If you are a seller, the question is: Who will purchase your property? It will rarely be a wealthy investor. Instead, it will almost always be a person who can work with his hands and has saved enough money for that first down payment. This same skillful person is willing to accept a house that is less than perfect just to get started in the world of real estate and home ownership.

Make up a flier to be delivered in the vicinity each Friday or Saturday before your open house. Fliers work. These fliers and newspaper ads brought more than thirty-five people to the first open house. Expect to distribute fliers on three or four Fridays and Saturdays. After all, most people have already planned the weekend by the time your first flier arrives. Repetition will pay off. Neighbors and their friends and relatives will buy your house, fixed up or not. So distribute numerous fliers. If, at each of your open house functions, you take names and addresses of interested buyers looking for fixer-uppers, you will soon have a list of hundreds of interested buyers to whom you can send announcements of your next foreclosure bargain. If you are selling your own properties, you will save money on brokerage commissions.

### Multiple Listing Service

Put the property on the Multiple Listing Service if you are a broker or plan to hire a broker. The brokers don't expect you to pay full commission if you are paying for advertising and doing most of the work, but they have clients that they worked hard to get. Don't chase them away by telling them "No commission." Offer them one-third but settle for one-half of what is a normal or customary commission for your section of the country. If you do bargain, be sure not to alienate the brokerage community. The brokers and agents are in business to help you, but they also want to get paid. Don't you?

## CLASSIFIED ADVERTISING

Ask yourself —

- Does this advertisement make a claim that is important to the reader?
- Is it believable?
- Does it give the information the reader needs for making a buying decision?
- Does it project the desired image?
- Does it gain the intended reader's attention and create interest in the proposition?

Remember, you must advertise constantly. Peoples' memories are very short and unless you advertise consistently, they will forget you.

### Classified Ads

Before you write, analyze your proposition. Why should people want to inquire about your proposition? How will they benefit by what you are offering? Make a list of all the reasons why a prospect should inquire. Success or failure depends upon analysis of the advantages in your proposition and the way you present them.

### Four Basic Appeals

Self-interest is the strongest force in human nature, so your ads must offer benefits. You need to offer your customers something they want.

1. What people want to gain: money, health, popularity, security, leisure, time, pride of accomplishment, advancement, enjoyment, self-confidence, personal prestige.
2. What people want to save: time, money, work, discomfort, worry, doubts, risk, personal embarrassment.
3. What people want to do: business for themselves, self-expression, resist domination, dominate others, satisfy curiosities, admire beauty, collect things, win affection, improve themselves.
4. What people want to be: successful, social, up-to-date, creative, admired, first, beautiful, proud, influential, efficient, recognized, important.

Whatever commodity it is that you are offering, tie it in with the intangibles that people really want. They'll see your commodity as a way of getting what they are looking for.

### Make Your Ad Understandable

Don't let your readers wonder what you are offering. Be specific. Explain what your product or service will do for them. Don't play guessing games. Tell them what you have for sale, what it will do for them, how much it will cost, and where they can contact you.

Use simple, everyday language. Appeal to the masses, not only to the highly educated. Make your ads easy to read and to understand. Your readers may hesitate to answer your ads because they suspect you might have omitted something or because they have no assurance that you will deliver what you advertise. Don't exaggerate; don't make it sound too good to be true.

Not all of these pointers will apply directly to the business of dealing in foreclosure properties, but I included them to reinforce the basic idea: Find something that someone wants and offer it in such a way that people have confidence in you as a person and in your business.

Here are twelve proven ways to win confidence:

1. Offer free samples — nothing is more convincing.
2. Ship on approval — free examination inspires confidence.

3. Offer mailing aids — make it easy for your readers to respond.
4. Accept trade-ins — create confidence in your product.
5. Guarantee satisfaction — disarm your readers.
6. Show that you are a member of a trade or professional society — a recognized standing inspires confidence.
7. Mention how long you have been in the business — you will add prestige to your company.
8. Welcome visitors — face-to-face contact builds good will.
9. Make payments refundable — give your readers an escape clause.
10. Stress that no salesman will call — you will kill a major objection immediately.
11. Do not ask for immediate payment — the words "send no money" are very reassuring.
12. Notarize your documents — notarization convinces your readers of your honesty and respect for fair dealing.

### Writing your Ads

Creating a classified ad is like sending an invitation to a party. Before mailing an invitation, you must decide on the guest list. The same is true in classified advertising. Before you write an ad, you must first know who your target is going to be.

Remember your ad will be competing with hundreds of other ads. First, you must catch the reader's eye. To make your ad stand out among the rest, place your opening line in caps, followed by an exclamation mark. You can make your ads come alive by using emotional appeals and by creating "word pictures" that benefit the buyer.

According to Mary Ellen Randall, author of *Real Estate Advertising Made Easy*, a well-written ad will have three objectives: Educate by providing basic facts (location, style, number of bedrooms), stimulate (the reader wants more information), and motivate the reader to call. *Real Estate Advertising Made Easy* was designed to guide the reader through a step-by-step process in developing a successful marketing strategy for each listing. The book helps the reader to position himself and his product and to focus on marketing principles as they apply to real estate. *Real Estate Advertising Made Easy* was designed to bridge the gap between theory and practical knowledge. This book is available from Plan It, 159 Pathon Place, Williamsburg, NY 14221.

Another helpful text is *Classified Secrets*. This book takes the reader through the entire process of writing classified ads. The reader will gain an understanding of the reasoning behind effective ads by learning to analyze the parts of an ad and the functions of each. The book also presents a highly detailed examination of the features, benefits, and potential targets for hundreds of residential property types and situations. Similar methods can be applied to nonresidential properties as well. An extensive chapter on investment properties shows you how to apply your knowledge of classified ad writing to get the attention of investors. This book is available from Longman Financial Services Publishing, 520 N. Dearborn Street, Chicago, IL 60610.

### GET TESTIMONIALS

Testimonials and guarantees are probably the most important attributes of a good sales presentation. Customers who sell their property need reassurance that they will be treated fairly and equitably. You can considerably reduce the skepticism that your clients will have by effective use of testimonials. Carefully read any testimonials you get in the mail. Note that if they are convincing, you will find yourself considering the product. Ask your sellers if they are happy with your service. If they are, get them to write a convincing testimonial. Be sure you obtain a release to use the testimonial in your promotions or direct mail. If your seller is prepared to tell you on a piece of paper what problem it was that you solved and how efficiently you solved it, new prospective clients will find the testimonials believable. If you take care of your clients and treat them as you would like to be treated, you will succeed.

### ESTABLISH A BOOK OF BUYERS

The book of buyers is a list of people who have responded to previous foreclosure advertisements (newspapers) and people who have heard from friends, neighbors, or investors that make a business of buying distressed property. The individuals usually telephone me and explain what they want, knowing that information is extremely important. I do not need to sell those clients property. It's just a matter of solving the client's problem. All buyers — of cars, houses, or appliances — are skeptical. The buyers of this book are skeptical. Instead of selling something to them, I provide a solution to their problem. That is why I provide down-to-earth, valuable information from a practitioner — information that solves their problems.

The purchaser of your foreclosure real estate wants a good deal — that is, a property that is priced below market — in order to make money. Bargain hunters do not know the process of locating, contacting, negotiating, performing due diligence and reducing risk, buying down second loans, rehabilitating, newspaper advertising, direct mail response, selling, contracts, and going through escrow. Your buyer only wants you to solve his problem by finding a property that is below market value.

#### How to Start a Book of Buyers

The first step is to save the name, address, and telephone number of everyone who calls you or talks to you about foreclosure. Soon you will have more buyers than you can handle. Keep the names on a list. Once your list has more than ten names on it, ask the big question: "Would you like to be called first if the deal has more than $20,000 in potential profit?" Keep in mind that you will be performing all the risk-reducing due diligence reports. The reports will tell you your potential profit.

I've learned that even though a person may give me $5,000 to be in the book of buyers list, having attended a seminar, read a book, or heard from a friend that this is a fast-bucks business with quick profits and no work, he or she does not necessarily buy. Foreclosure buyers who want to make money and who are really sincere about buying foreclosures will give you money in advance to be on this preferred buyers list. Take advantage of this source of funds and active buyers. This system only works if you do. Yes, you'll make good money — $100,000 a year or more — but many people who say they want to and put up the money will in fact drop out when it comes time to do the work. That is just the way life is. My policy is to give the clients' money back after they have been exposed to four properties. The buyers who are serious will buy in that period of time; the others will not. Sending the money back is much easier than letting the buyers' anxiety build up. Once they become nervous, they'll start to telephone you to talk about how worried they are. Be easy on yourself. Just send the money back.

References:

Creps, Dennis, *How to Make Your Advertising Profitable*, (602/297-0607).

Kennedy, Steve, and Johnson, Deborah, *2001 Winning Ads for Real Estate,* Carlsbad Industries, Yorba Linda, CA 92686.

Pivor, William and Bradley, *Classified Secrets*, Longman Financial Services Publishing, 520 N. Dearborn Street, Chicago, IL 60610.

Randall, Mary Ellen, *Real Estate Advertising Made Easy,* 159 Pathon Place, Williamsburg, NY 14221.

## OPEN HOUSE FLYER

# Rental
# Open House

### Special Offer to
### Mills College Faculty

Bring this dollar bill to our Open House
and if your serial number matches the
one posted in the house, you are the lucky
winner of a crisp $50.00 bill!

LOCATION:
**3214 Wyman Street, Oakland**

DATE:

TIME:
**2:00 to 4:00 p.m.**

**Walk to work!** This freshly decorated rental
home has three bedrooms and one bath
upstairs and a separate one bedroom/
one bath with kitchenette downstairs.

HOMES FOR SALE

# Foreclosure / REO

3 Bed., 2 Bath Needs Work.........

Paint – In & Out
Carpet Clean-up

2707 Sugar Plum Drive, San Jose

Real Market Value...$235,000-240,000

**Your Cost $196,000**

Great fixer-Upper for the Right Person

Call...

*New Growth Financial*

**(415) 837-2106**

HOMES FOR SALE

# Foreclosure
# Foreclosure

## BARGAIN FIXER

BERKELEY...............1404 Harmon St. Clean
2 bedroom, 1 bath

**$147,000.**

SAN LEANDRO.........1792 Willow Ave. Appraised at
6 bedroom, 4 bath $266,000

**$231,000.**

SUNNYVALE.........660 Toyon Avenue Fixer
3 bedroom, 2 bath

**$232,000.**

DAMAR SEZ GRID IS $345,000.
Next door is for sale at $300,000.

*New Growth Financial*

**(415) 837-2106**

TYPICAL HOMES FOR SALE FLYER

# Ugly Duckling

Zero Down Payment

Fixer in Pleasant Hill

Needs Paint - Landscaping

It's A Mess!!

4 Bedromm

2 Bath

**$220,000 owner will carry!**

330 Kathleen Drive

Drive By Then Call...

*New Growth Financial*

**(415) 837-2106**

TYPICAL HOMES FOR SALE FLYER

# $5,000
# Moves You In!

$5,000 Down -Lease Option

Cute 3 bedroom, 2 bath. $1,250/month includes $312/month credit towards $165,000. base price for 3 years, then seller finances with no more down!

Buy like rent!

Realistic credit qualifying. Vacant.

2318 Saxon Street - Martinez

*New Growth Financial*

**(415) 837-2106**

## TYPICAL "FOR SALE" ADS

**FORECLOSURE GOLD MINE**

YOU'LL MAKE A BUNDLE
NICE NEIGHBORHOOD.
COMPS OF $400,000+
LAST APPRAISAL $390,000
3 + 2 NEEDS WORK — AS IS
$320,000

**NEW GROWTH FINANCIAL**
**(415) 837-2106**

---

**★★VALLEJO★★**
4 bdrms, 3 full baths, 2 mstr suites, walk to schools & parks. $159,000. Call Bkr 707-428-1771

**600-Other Counties Homes for Sale**

CLEARLAKE Almost nu Altra Modern, 3 bdrm 2 ba, 1600 sqft. 100x100 lot. $89,000. (707)995-9348

FREE....
Weekly list of properties FOR SALE "By Owner" Prices, addresses, etc.

Help-U-Sell
Brentwood 634-7653
Discovery Bay 516-0700
Manteca (209)239-6651
Tracy (209)835-6800
W.Stockton (209)474-2996

MODESTO nice & neat 3bdrm 2ba, $110,995 2817 Japonica Way. 209-673-6256

★★★★★★★★
SAN JOSE

FORECLOSURE /REO

2707 Sugar Plum Dr.
SAN JOSE

3 bdrms, 2 baths. Needs paint, carpets & clean-up. $196,000.

NEW GROWTH FINANCIAL
(415),837-2106
★★★★★★★★

---

**AFFORDABLES!**

**OPEN SUNDAY 1-4**
**VICTORIAN!**
**2512 13th Avenue**
**HOME AND INCOME**

Immaculate/vacant 3 br, dr, laundry, storage, nice yard lower 2 br, large basement for? OWNER WILL CARRY FIRST for qualified buyers. Asking $285,000.
Roy Barker-eves: 549-3758

**OPEN SUNDAY 1-4**
**2506 13th Avenue**
**WORK AT HOME?**

Unusual and flexible floor plan for the work-at-home or extended family could be 3 brs w/3 baths/level entry, skylight, 2 kitchens, basement. OWNER WILL CARRY FIRST For qualified buyers. Asking $215,000. Roy Barker-eves: 549-3758

**EMERYVILLE**

Large Scale 2 br, dr, fp, laundry, yard. Asking $135,000. Try minimum down. Mickey

**NORTH OAKLAND**

Restored Victorian 1 bedroom, full basement, nice yard, dead-end street, termite cleared. Asking $115,000. Try minimum down. Mickey

**NORTH OAKLAND**

2 BR. FRPL PLUS OFFICE.
$155,000. TRY MIN DWN PYMT. LARRY

**NORTH OAKLAND**

4BR 3BA. QUIET STREET.
$155,000. LOW DWNPYMNT. LARRY

**PANO VIEW - OAKLAND**

4BR 2BA. MOTIVATED SELLER.
$179,000. LOW DOWNPYMNT. LARRY

*Central Realty Service*

658-2177

## TYPICAL "FOR SALE" ADS

**$7000 MOVES YOU IN**

$7000 down lease/option. Cute 3 br. 2 ba. $1650 mo. incl. $100 mo. credit towards $229K base price. 3 yrs. then seller finances with no down! Buy like rent, realistic credit qualifying. VACANT. 2707 Sugarplum Dr.

New Growth Financial
415 837-2106

**RENT TO OWN!**

**$5000 DOWN**
**LEASE OPTION**

CUTE 3 BDRM. 2 BATH
$1250/MO. INCLUDES:
$312/MO. CREDIT TOWARDS
$165,000 BASE PRICE
THREE YEARS THEN
SELLER FINANCES
WITH NO MORE DOWN!
BUY LIKE RENT!
REALISTIC CREDIT QUALIFYING.
VACANT

**2318 SAXON ST.**
**MARTINEZ**

New Growth Financial
(415) 837-2106

**$5000**
**MOVES YOU IN!**

- **$5000 Down**
- **Lease Option**

***Cute 3 Bdrm, 2 Bath***

$1250./Month includes $100/month credit towards $165,000 base price. Three years then seller finances with ***NO MORE DOWN!***

- BUY LIKE RENT
- Realistic Credit Qualifying
- VACANT

2318 Saxon St., • MARTINEZ

*New Growth Financial*

(415) **837-2106**

No Tool Box Is Required
It's Ready To Be Lived In!

*Quiet Neighborhood*

This eye-pleasing home is blessed with upgraded kitchen & bathrooms.

3 Bedrooms - 2 Baths 2318 Saxon St., Martinez

$165,000

Instantly appealing inside and out. Immediate possession. Special financing. Drive by, then call . . .

NEW GROWTH FINANCIAL
(415) 837-2106

**5% DOWN PAYMENT**
**3 BEDROOM - 2 BATH**

— WHITE GLOVE RESTORATION —
ALL THE WORK HAS BEEN DONE
SPICK & SPAN - LOOKS BETTER THAN NEW!
UPGRADED KITCHEN AND BATHROOMS
$165,000
• Drive by, then call. 2318 Saxon Street, Martinez •

**CALL US AT (415) 837-2106 FOR**
DETAILS ON OWNING THIS HOME
**NEW GROWTH FINANCIAL**

## ADDING UP THE COSTS OF REFINANCING

Borrowers should not only shop around for the lowest interest rate when refinancing, but also look at a host of additional closing costs:

**Loan origination fee —** A fee lenders charge of 1 point to 1.5 points (each point is 1 percent of the loan amount due up front). Each eighth of a percent added to the interest rate will lower the fee by 3/8 to 3/4 of a point.

**Appraisal fee** — property value is determined for a minimum of $250 which can range upward depending upon the size and value of the home. For example, $600,000 homes and above can cost $400 to $1,000.

**Escrow fees —** A firm that holds funds in escrow until a transaction is completed typically charges a base amount of $200 to $300 plus $1.50 per $1,000 of loan amount.

**Processing or funding fee** — $200 to $400 charged by lender to close the deal.

**Title insurance fee** — Title report and insurance policy, which guarantees ownership of property can cost between $550 and $2,400, depending upon the loan amount.

**Home inspection fee** — If the appraisal shows the property has a problem, then an inspection may be needed to certify it is not in poor condition. For instance, a termite inspection can cost between $35 to $75. But this does not include corrective work.

**Tax service contract** — A one-time fee of $60 to $85, depending upon the size of the loan, which is paid to a firm that notifies the lender if your property taxes are delinquent and if you do not pay taxes during the term of the new loan.

**Recording fees** — A $15 to $30 charge for recording the transaction at the county Hall of Records.

**Sub-escrow fee** — Charged by every title company for handling any payouts or recordings which can cost $75 to $100 above the title insurance fee.

**Loan documentation fee** — Lenders can charge a separate fee of $50 to $150 for preparing loan documents.

**Demand and reconveyance fees** — The cost to pay off any existing trust deeds, loans, which generally runs $90 to $125 per loan.

**Wire transfer fee** — Banks fund many loans by wiring money to the title insurance company so that the money can be immediately credited for a fee of $75 to $85.

**Delivery fees** — It can cost $25 to $50 to deliver documents between escrow companies and lender during the loan approval process.

**Residential mortgage credit report fee**— Credit check of loan applicant required by lender costs between $45 and $50.

## TYPICAL MORTGAGE BROKER FLYER

**CSF CAL-STATE FUNDING**
*Real Estate Finance Specialists*

### Offered at: $90,000

**Financing Examples:**

| | 10% Down Payment | 20% Down Payment |
|---|---|---|
| Loan Amount | $81,500 | $72,000 |
| Down Payment | $9,000 | $18,000 |
| 30 yr. fixed @ 9.250% | $666 | $592 |
| 30 yr. due in 5 fixed @ 8.5% | $622 | $553 |
| 1 yr. adjustable @ 7.85% | $587 | $522 |

* On less than 20% down loans, private mortgage insurance may be required.

**Corporate:**
1700 S. El Camino Real, Suite 407
San Mateo, Ca 94402
(415) 574-5746

5 Crow Canyon Ct., Suite 100
San Ramon, CA 94583
(415) 838-5988

39159 Paseo Padre Parkway, Suite 204
Fremont, CA 94538
(415) 791-1217

## TYPICAL MORTGAGE BROKER FLYER

**CAL-STATE FUNDING**
*Real Estate Finance Specialists*

**Offered at: $125,000**

**Financing Examples:**

| | 10% Down Payment | 20% Down Payment |
|---|---|---|
| Loan Amount | $112,500 | $100,000 |
| Down Payment | $12,500 | $25,000 |
| | | |
| 30 yr. fixed @ 9.250% | $926 | $823 |
| 30 yr. due in 5 fixed @ 8.5% | $865 | $769 |
| 1 yr. adjustable @ 7.85% | $816 | $725 |

* On less than 20% down loans, private mortgage insurance may be required.

**Corporate:**
1700 S. El Camino Real, Suite 407
San Mateo, Ca 94402
(415) 574-5746

5 Crow Canyon Ct., Suite 100
San Ramon, CA 94583
(415) 838-5988

39159 Paseo Padre Parkway, Suite 204
Fremont, CA 94538
(415) 791-1217

## BEFORE YOU SELL CHECK LIST

| Items To Be Completed | Date I Will Complete It By |
|---|---|
| Home is in excellent repair/looks good | ______________ |
| Have a realistic sale price | ______________ |
| Have five financing programs done | ______________ |
| Have a Mortgage Banker to my home | ______________ |
| Prepare my notebook with information | ______________ |
| Purchase my front yard sign | ______________ |
| Contact my home warranty agent | ______________ |
| Prepare my flyer | ______________ |
| Have flyers printed | ______________ |
| Prepare my advertising budget | ______________ |
| Prepare my advertisement | ______________ |
| Establish the dates they will first run | ______________ |
| Contact the title or abstract company | ______________ |
| The date I will become more flexible if my house has not sold as quickly as I want | ______________ |
| The date I "MUST" move on | ______________ |

## PREPARE FOR THE SALE

### Interior Walk-Thru

| | | Yes | No |
|---|---|---|---|
| 1. | All cobwebs cleaned? | | |
| 2. | All light fixtures cleaned? | | |
| 3. | Oven cleaned? | | |
| 4. | Drip pans on stove cleaned? | | |
| 5. | Sink sanitized? | | |
| 6. | Under the sink organized? | | |
| 7. | Linen closet organized? | | |
| 8. | Coat closet organized? | | |
| 9. | Toilet bowl flush installed? | | |
| 10. | All mildew killed? | | |
| 11. | Fixtures spotless with shine? | | |
| 12. | Inside windows cleaned? | | |
| 13. | All drapes and curtains cleaned? | | |
| 14. | Refrigerator door car polished? | | |
| 15. | Washer and dryer car polished? | | |

### Exterior Inspection

| | | Yes | No | When | Comments |
|---|---|---|---|---|---|
| 1. | Curb clearly marked? | | | | |
| 2. | Lawn Green? | | | | |
| 3. | Shrubs and trees pruned? | | | | |
| 4. | Exterior bugs sprayed? | | | | |
| 5. | Eaves freshly painted? | | | | |
| 6. | Side yard debris stacked? | | | | |
| 7. | All animals leavings cleaned? | | | | |
| 8. | Shrubs cleared from heating unit? | | | | |
| 9. | Garage cleaned, items put away? | | | | |
| 10. | Front door cleaned? | | | | |
| 11. | Outside windows cleaned? | | | | |
| 12. | Childrens toys put away? | | | | |

## GUIDELINE OF EXPENSES

**Estimated Sales & Fix Up Costs**

| | |
|---|---|
| • Paint Exterior | $1,500. - 2,500. |
| • Yard Work | 500. - 2,000. |
| • Repair Garage | 500. |
| • Paint Interior | 1,000. |
| • Wall to Wall Carpets | 2,000. |
| • Replace Drapes | 700. |
| • Patch Holes | 300. |
| • New Linoleum | 900. |
| • Fix Windows | 300. |
| • Replace Electrical Equipment | 100. |
| • Miscellaneous | 500. |
| ESTIMATED REPAIRS COSTS | $9,200. - 11,700. |

**Estimated Cost of Sale** (based on a $100,000 sale)

| | |
|---|---|
| • Real Estate Broker Commission (6%) | $6,000. |
| • Points For a New Loan (2%) | 2,000. |
| • Policy of Title Insurance | 450. |
| • Escrow Fees | 500. |
| • One Year Home Warranty | 325. |
| • Loan Application Fee | 425. |
| • Transfer Tax & Misc. Fees | 350. |
| TOTAL | $10,500. |
| • Termite Report & Repairs | 3,5000. |
| • Other Misc. Repairs | 9,2000. |
| TOTAL | $12,700. |
| TOTAL SALE COSTS | $23,200. |

Carrying cost for 3 months - $3,000.

| | |
|---|---|
| • Sale Price | $100,000. |
| • Loans | (60,000) |
| • Selling Costs | (23,000) |
| • Carrying Costs | (3,000) |
| • Equity | $13,800. |

**Don't forget to include the following monthly costs when calculating you potential profits:**

• Mortgage Payments • Homeowners Association Dues
• Taxes and Insurance • Utilities • Yard Maintenance
• Pool & Spa Maintenance • Advertising Costs

Chapter 11

# Where the Money Is

## *Sources of Funding and How to Tap Them*

### PERSISTENCE AND PLANNING

For any business, the bottom line never varies: Those who become successful had planned for it. They did their homework thoroughly, with diligence and a high degree of motivation. Success is achieved through persistence and planning. Those who are aware of these facts and who are willing to take the trouble will succeed. In this chapter you will learn:

How to build a long-term relationship with your banker:

- To structure your loan applications so that they get attention
- To reduce the banker's risk
- To work out a business plan

How to raise money from ZERO, using:

- Hidden assets
- Credit sources

- Non-bank borrowing
- Vendors

How to manage the purchase and resale of distressed property as a successful small business.

The reasons banks turn down loan applications are varied and numerous. Lack of patience is one of the most common faults of new businesspeople. Sooner or later, if you decide to do business in the foreclosed property market, you will need the services of a bank because that is where the money is. Banks are in business to lend money, but they always want their money back, with interest. Building a good relationship with a bank will take time. Don't assume that you can walk into the bank, shake a few hands, and then be on your way with a briefcase full of money.

Believe me, it doesn't happen that way. It doesn't even make sense. Would you, as a trained businessperson, lend money quickly to an unknown person or entity? Never! You would spend time getting to know the person and the business and find out what the money was going to be used for.

What you are going to do is to educate your banker and make him or her your friend. But for now let's get back to this matter of patience. The bank does want your business, but it wants it on terms that will enable it to make money, not lose it. Your job is to educate your banker and build his confidence that you know what you are doing, and to demonstrate how you will pay the bank back.

Remember that you are trying to cultivate a long-term relationship. You plan to purchase more than one distressed property, don't you? If yours is a one-shot deal, the banker probably won't waste time with you. After all, he only has so much time and he understands that building this relationship will take time and lots of effort on his part. The time you take to educate the loan officer is time he spends being educated. The bank expects its loan officers to make productive, profitable loans with the minimum amount of risk, in a short time, and efficiently. Patience is a virtue that is respected by the loan officers. If you have patience, you are demonstrating your ability to plan for a long-term relationship.

Lack of patience usually indicates that you have a crisis pending. Remember: Bankers love to lend you money when you don't need it. By demonstrating your patience you indicate your confidence in yourself and your business proposal. Thinking for the short term, lack of planning, lack of knowledge, and lack of confidence in yourself will kill any deal. Slow down and do your homework. You must know what you want the money for; how much you will want — to the penny; how much you will be needing as a reserve — to the dollar; how long the money will be out of the bank; how you will pay the bank its interest and principal; and when and from what source you will pay. Be prepared. One of the most common errors committed by people new to business is to visit the bank to request a loan, but without a business plan.

## TEN REASONS TO TURN DOWN A LOAN

When bankers review loan applications, they are looking for elements in the deal that will give them security — the assurance that the money they lend will be returned to them at a profit and within a reasonable time. They turn down loans when they have doubts. Reasons for rejecting loan applications vary from bank to bank, but they are likely to include the following. If the prospective borrower has:

- Inadequate collateral
- Little management experience
- Little business experience
- No other sources of repayment except the purposes for which the loan is being sought
- No track record
- A poor credit rating
- Insufficient income
- Too much debt (referred to as "being overleveraged")
- Little information about the project
- Too speculative a purpose for requiring the money

A smart borrower will review this list and, if possible, make sure that each of these concerns of the loan officer is addressed within his business or personal loan request.

## BE PREPARED — AND BEAT THE COMPETITION

Look at things from the banker's perspective. First review in depth, that is, really study the reasons why loans are turned down and find any that could apply to you. If you prepare an answer for the banker that will eliminate his concerns, you are miles ahead of your competition. Don't forget that you are not selling your deal at this point. You are solving, yes, solving the banker's problems and answering his questions. He wants to lend the money — that's what he is in business for. The key to the vault is in resolving his apprehensions and anxieties. Be prepared.

Build up your banker's confidence by demonstrating your planning ability and your overall business acumen. This preparation will raise you to the rank of good customer, but it won't be accomplished without patience and planning on your part.

Obtaining and maintaining a good relationship with a bank is a major rung in the ladder to success. Without the banker, your success and progress towards financial independence will be slowed considerably. The long-term relationship will develop only if you are honest and reliable. Your credibility will be demonstrated each time you perform as you agreed to in your loan contract.

Now, having convinced you of the need for preparation, I will give you some idea of where to start. Remember the five questions the banker will ask, no matter who wants the loan. He will ask:

- What is the purpose of the loan?
- How much money do you want?
- How long do you want the money for?
- How are you going to repay?
- If the deal does not work out as planned, where will you get the money to repay?

Make sure that you can answer these questions in detail.

### No Risk for the Banker

Remember, bankers want to lend you the money. However, they like to lend money with the least amount of risk. If you can show more than one method of repayment, the banker will know you understand the problem. Eliminate the bank's risk as much as possible. For example, you plan to borrow to buy the house, fix it up, and sell it again. If the market is slow and you can't sell to repay the bank, what will you do? If you don't know, it is best to figure out a solution before you apply for the loan. Again, preparation is the key to the vault. It is a simple formula. Make the banker's work less risky, and you build friendships and credibility.

### Financial Projections

When it comes to financial projections, be aware that they will be estimates only, but make sure they are credible estimates. Is it possible for you to explain in narrative form what the projections mean and what is meant by each item?

Don't balloon the values of properties, automobiles, and other assets. Include appraisals, if available. Pictures, diagrams, and maps are helpful. Prices taken from the Multiple Listing Service of comparable properties will enhance your credibility and allow the banker to compare your project with similar real estate values.

The section on financial data will show what funds are needed from banks, investors, and yourself. It should show how you intend to raise the money and how you intend to use it — and how you plan to pay it back. Keep in mind that lenders and investors will have different objectives and that their objectives will be different again from yours.

### Don't Forget Your Exit Plan

Do you have an exit plan? How will you cash out of this business? How will you cash out of each property? Will you become a lender? Is the plan agreed to by everyone? How will you sell the business?

### Conflicts

Even the most optimistic plans will have some drawbacks. Positives and negatives must be confronted head on. Don't discount the caution flags, and don't ignore the red flags. It is easier to confront them in the plan and make allowances for them than to be completely surprised later.

### Emphasis

The importance of the market research is second to no other part of the business plan. If there is no market, you have no business. Describe your market and why you will be successful within that market. Show hard evidence of your market knowledge, state clearly who will buy your real estate and why. Describe in detail how you will locate and then sell your distressed property purchases.

## BORROW YOUR WAY TO WEALTH

To build a real estate empire starting from zero is difficult but not impossible. It requires that you become resourceful, very flexible, and creative. Don't spend all your earnings on consumer goodies, cars, travel, eating out. Save those hard-earned dollars to build a real estate empire. If you spend only on essentials you soon will have a cash hoard to get you started or to help you to continue to grow financially. Real estate that appreciates is like money in the bank: It continues to grow and produce profits year after year.

### Partnerships

If you have little or no money available to purchase your next property, then you will need to think about partnerships, joint ventures, and properties that do not require a down payment. Let's think things through together. The following paragraphs contain a few suggestions that you may find helpful.

Start making a list of people you know who might need some extra income from an investment that they don't have to work at. How about a fifty-fifty partnership? You could purchase a distressed property with their money. Your experience and labor could contribute the other half of the investment.

How about forming a small group of investors, a syndicate? Assuming you need $5,000 to buy a property before the Trustee's Sale, could you find ten friends, relatives or co-workers each prepared to put up $500? I don't suggest that you put them all on the deed as co-owners. This could create a cumbersome situation when you sell. Consider instead an informal written agreement or a partnership agreement. They put up the money; you do the work. On their behalf you purchase, manage, fix up, and sell the property. Both sides of the partnership benefit.

### Need Down Payment?

Most property purchases need down payments. You have no money for the down payment? Do you own life insurance? Most whole life policies allow you to borrow against them. The interest rate on such loans is normally substantially below market rates. Check your policy. You will be surprised at how cheap it is to borrow.

If borrowing is impractical, remember that term insurance is cheap. You can probably cash in your old whole life policy and purchase good term insurance for a much smaller annual payment. You will then have a lump sum in cash to buy and rehabilitate one or more distressed properties, or you can advertise for the cash you need. Place the advertisement in your local newspaper under Money Wanted. Don't be surprised if the newspaper asks you to pay in advance. In my own experience an advertisement run under the Money Wanted category had to be paid for in advance, even though I ran the same advertisement under one of the newspaper's real estate categories and was not expected to provide advance payment.

To succeed with an advertisement for money, you need a Unique Selling Proposition (USP). You need to offer, for example, a short term, or a high yield, or some security for the money partner. After all, who are you? That is the question you must answer before the investor calls. Plan your presentation, otherwise you will ramble. Give information on the facts and benefits for the investor right away. Be sure your incentives are adequate to attract people who have the money. Everyone can get between 5% and 7% interest in any bank. You must offer 25% or even 50% to attract good investors.

### Credit Cards

Some very creative investors in real estate actually use the cash provisions of their credit cards to start building their wealth. The rate of interest on the borrowed money is high but certainly no higher than the rate you would pay a joint-venture partner.

### Good Job, Good Credit

Many small finance companies will lend you money if you have a good job and your credit rating is good. If you have a short-term real estate deal such as a foreclosure or pre-Trustee's Sale purchase, the transaction will probably have more than enough actual return to pay the high interest of a finance company loan and still leave you with substantial profits and your credit rating enhanced. If your credit rating is less than desirable, even disastrous, you had better start looking for a co-signer for the note. Sometimes small finance companies will take the co-signer's property as security or collateral.

### What About Your Boss?

Many employers will advance funds for education, new cars or trucks, sometimes even down payments for the first home. Your employer might be prepared to provide the down payment and take title to the house while you do the work. You would then split the profits. As an added incentive, the employer might receive all the tax benefits.

### Credit Unions

Does your firm have a credit union? Does a member of your family work for a firm that has a credit union? This could be a great source of cash. Credit unions sometimes request payment on the loan be deducted from your paycheck, so keep that in mind. Credit unions may lend money to you and your new-found partner if you both have existing savings accounts, which will provide the needed security.

### Hypothecation

You need also to be aware that most lenders require some sort of security and will accept hypothecated securities. By hypothecation you are pledging assets but are not required to deliver to the lender either title to those assets or the assets themselves. Thus, you might have the ability to pledge your car, your tools, your other property, or even your skills (barter).

### Home Improvement Loan Insurance (Title I)

There are a number of other sources of money, especially for fixing up property for resale. Uncle Sam, for one, has various loan programs that will advance money for property rehabilitation. The Department of Housing and Urban Development (HUD) allows credit unions and other qualified lenders to make home improvement loans from their own funds and, in exchange for a premium, insures the lender against a possible loss.

These loans may be used for any improvements that make the home more livable and useful. They cannot be used for luxury items or to pay for work already done. The Housing and Community

Development Act of 1974 provided that the loans may also be used to finance improvements to conserve energy or to install solar energy systems.

The loan may be for up to $17,500, may bear interest up to no set limit, and must be paid back within fifteen years. Lenders determine eligibility for and process these loans, generally as unsecured personal loans. Loans in excess of $2,500, excluding finance charges, must be secured with a lien (a mortgage or deed of trust) against the improved property. Loans in excess of $17,500 excluding finance charges require prior approval from HUD. Loan limits are applied only to one particular improved property. Individual borrowers are not subject to the limits.

### Eligibility Requirements

1. Borrower(s) must have at least a one-third interest in the improved property and must hold:

   a) a fee title

   b) a life estate

   c) either a) or b) above, subject to a mortgage, deed of trust, etc., and hold an installment land contract or a lease that has a fixed term expiring note less than six months after the maturity of the note (unless the improvement is a built-in kitchen or carpeting, which require a ninety-nine-year renewable lease)
2. Borrower(s) must have a satisfactory credit rating.
3. Borrower(s) must have enough income to repay the loan over its term.
4. To the lender's knowledge, the borrower must not be past due more than fifteen days on any obligation owing to or insured by the federal government.

### FHA Title I

The advantages of the FHA Title I Home Improvement Loan programs are numerous. First of all it is easy to qualify, and that can be important if you are starting out with no money. Even the requirement that you own the home is fairly easily met. You could own as a partnership, or as a joint tenant, or as a tenant-in-common. The amount loaned can be up to 120% of the purchase price of the house. This loan will give you the money to fix up the property and make it saleable. Often the loan may be regarded as free money from the government because you yourself don't have to pay it back. Title I loans are usually fully assumable by the purchasing party. Most purchasers are happy to assume this loan because it means they will be required to provide a smaller down payment in the transaction.

### Promissory Notes

Sellers of distressed property need cash, but they might be prepared to take a promissory note with either monthly or even weekly payments. This type of financing would give you the time to fix up and re-sell the property.

### What About Those Vendors?

If you plan to use the same vendors for the paint, carpeting, appliances, etc., or the same carpenters, roofers, and so on, they may lend you money in return for the business and a good return on their money.

### You Might Expect

Whenever you borrow money, you should be aware that you will be expected to meet certain conditions:

- That you will need a co-signer
- That you will need parents, friends, and acquaintances to help
- That you will pay higher-than-market interest rates
- That your monthly payments will be higher
- That your loan terms will be shorter
- That you may be required to share your profits with the lender
- That you will need to establish a win-win-win attitude — first the seller wins, then the investor wins, and finally you win.

## MANAGING A SMALL BUSINESS

This book is not based on some esoteric theory. It is based on proven methods. The information has been tested and is working today. The examples are taken from actual transactions. If you apply the rules and procedures given here, you will consistently make money buying and selling foreclosure and distressed property.

It won't be easy...are you motivated? I'm not advocating a get-rich-overnight scheme. There's really no such thing in business. I am writing about building a respectable, enduring business in foreclosure and distressed property that is based on sound and innovative business practice. What I am writing is a guide to success. Allow books and skilled people to help you and you'll be surprised how well you will do.

### Magic

Success is not magic. Here are some of the reasons that made a success of small businesses and some hints about managing growth. To be successful in a small business, you must wear many hats and perform numerous duties. You must be first of all an entrepreneur, then a technician, and, finally, a manager. Although it is sometimes difficult, you must know your competition and your field of expertise inside out.

To stay ahead, constantly evaluate your business so that you can incorporate innovative ideas; take the time to know your market thoroughly and be familiar with the products it values. For example, everyone wants fixer-uppers. If you know your market, you won't be purchasing the wrong property at a Trustee's Sale. Homes in country club areas might be nice, but can you sell them easily?

Understand your weaknesses and your strengths and those of your products. Take pride in your business — after all, it's an extension of you. Provide your customers with the products they want. Be sensitive, know their needs, be aware of how to reach them, and, most important, what will convince them to buy your properties.

Advertising is a must, but test each ad. Is it pulling in the calls? If not, drop that ad and write a new one. An ad that is met with silence is not offering your customers what they are looking for. You need an ad that will serve the customer.

### Managing Your Time

Be willing to work day and night, but don't do it all yourself. Prepare your helpers to handle the routine or day-to-day work. If necessary, hire a consultant to help you tap the full resources of your business. Staff is the nucleus of your business. They face the customer, so select them carefully. Every one of your employees is a different individual. Each has a different personality. Expect to treat each one differently.

Keep up with what is happening around you. Read at least one newspaper daily and know and be familiar with the financial pages. Keep up-to-date so that you understand the big picture.

The way to become an expert is to read. First of all, set aside time every day to read and prepare yourself for the future. If you can find only twenty minutes every day, you will have made available more than two hours a week, approximately ten hours every month. In ten hours you can easily read at least two books on real estate, finance, sales, home inspections, banking, and all the related subjects that will make you an expert. The average person reads five books each year; most read fewer. You will be way ahead of your competition if you spend twenty minutes a day reading about your business. By the time you have read 120 books about real estate and distressed properties, the world will consider you an expert! All it takes is twenty minutes per day/ two books a month, and in five years you will be teaching the classes. In ten years, with that twenty-minute-a-day investment, you'll have 240 books under your belt.

### Creating Market Plan: Some Ideas

Effective and detailed business plans are sometimes difficult to produce. But putting in the effort to develop a written business plan will force you to clarify your thinking. The business plan will be your blueprint to success. Keep it flexible, so that you can adjust to market changes. Be aware that high interest rates mean more foreclosures; low interest rates mean that defaults will probably be refinanced and that the properties will not appear at Trustee's Sales tomorrow. Adapt to changing circumstances. Working capital will be the critical issue. Line up investors when you have spare time. Plan your cash flow.

### Define Your Business

Define your product or products. Will you be a specialist in buying the real estate owned by the banks or institutions (REOs), or do you see yourself as the auction specialist, buying at Trustee's Sales? Possibly your strength lies in dealing with the homeowner before the Trustee's Sale and purchasing the property in the default period.

Define the geographical area in which you will specialize — or are you prepared to work all over the United States? Describe your competition. Name names. Describe how the competition works. Describe how you are different from the competition. Describe the way you will promote your properties.

### Define Your Customers

- Who are your customers?
- Who needs the kinds of property you intend to deal with?
- Give details of income, sex, age, etc.
- Describe their patterns or habits. Where do they go, what do they do, what do they read?
- What do they buy from you?
- What is it that they value and that you can supply?

### Define Your Advertising

How will you communicate? How do your customers find you? Decide whether you will use direct marketing, newspapers, fliers, or other means of advertising your business. What works? What doesn't? What does it cost? What about different methods? How do you test the market? What can you improve in the future?

## WHERE CAN YOU GET HELP FOR A SMALL BUSINESS?

The Small Business Administration (SBA) sponsors SCORE, the Service Corps of Retired Executives. This organization was established in 1964 as a volunteer program staffed by retired business men and women. These volunteers offer their skills, knowledge, and experience without cost to the owners and managers of small businesses who experience management difficulties and to people who have never been in business and want to start a business. In the United States there are over 250 chapters of SCORE, and a membership of more than 12,000 executives.

SCORE chapters sponsor and conduct business workshops and seminars for the small business community. The members share their diverse business backgrounds and skills in such areas as management, retailing, wholesaling, accounting, marketing, manufacturing, sales promotions, and advertising. What they offer is free counseling.

## STAYING OUT OF TROUBLE

Purchasing real property can be a risky proposition. Most new investors in foreclosure property have little experience with purchasing, repairing, and selling real property. Take advantage of the hundreds of experts who are available to assist you with the purchase: brokers, attorneys, relatives, friends, and so on. There are experts who will help you with your inspections and repairs, or you can do them yourself to save money. The big questions are always: What work needs to be completed? What will it cost? Home inspection companies will perform detailed surveys to familiarize you with the good and bad features of what you are buying. Termite and roof companies will provide formal reports within days to allow you to make up your mind about the condition of your prospective purchase. Develop reliable sources of information and your property purchases will be less eventful and you won't be confronted with surprising extra costs. If a property has hidden defects — if the foundation is deteriorating, if the house is infested by termites, or if the floor is damaged and leaking — you need to know beforehand. If you are aware of the problems you can deduct the cost of such repairs from the purchase price.

## CONCLUSION

With this book in hand, you too can succeed in locating, buying, and selling distressed properties. But you must be willing to open your mind to new ideas and prepare thoroughly. With the proper competitive attitude and a willingness to understand that the road to success is not always smooth, you will find that persistent effort will carry you to your destination.

# WHERE TO FIND THE MONEY

## CAPITAL AVAILABLE

ARBITRAGE - SELF-LIQUIDATING, revolutionary financing wave of future millions available. No repayment, no collateral, no credit. We know what's, where's, how's, on receiving money. Complete details: $5.00. Financial Enrichment, P.O. Box 178, Dept. ENT#2, Chazy, NY 12921.

LOANS & VENTURE CAPITAL available. Reputable firm. Free consultation. $75K minimum. DataMerge, Inc.: 1-(800) 228-1372.

TURN YOUR INVOICES INTO immediate cash. Cash within 24 hours. Bank-to-bank transfers. We assume the credit risk. Call Jeff Farkas for further information. Toll free number: 1-(800) 241-CASH. Advantage Funding Corp.

MORTGAGES PURCHASED. NET QUOTES! Brokers welcome. Continental Mortgage: 1-(800) 288-5807, Extension 1051.

CAPITAL AVAILABLE. COMMERCIAL R.E., business loans, secured, unsecured. Call: (203) 790-4268.

CAPITAL AVAILABLE FOR ALL VIABLE, commercial projects. Brokers welcome. Minimum $500K. (516) 427-8600.

## FINANCIAL

CASH GRANTS AVAILABLE from foundations! Never repay! 401 sources/application instructions, $3.00. Fundsearch, Box 19107-KR, Washington, DC 20036.

DEBTS? BILLS PILING UP? Bad credit's no problem. We'll help! Licensed/bonded. Applications accepted $500-$50,000. Not a loan company. UAC, Dept. E, P.O. Box 26295, Birmingham, AL 35226, or call: 1-(800) 326-8284.

FEDERAL LOANS for small businesses now available. (800) 777-6342 for free details.

UNSECURED LOANS BY MAIL. Get $500 - $25,000 regardless of credit history. Easy payback plan. Send for free application. Commonwealth Financial Services, 940 Royal Street, Suite 257-E, New Orleans, LA 70116.

LOANS $5,000 - $100,000. UNSECURED, no collateral or equity required. Apply today! (717) 558-8177.

BORROW ANY AMOUNT. Quickly, on signature/secured immediately. Apply now! (404) 879-5514.

$5,000 CASH AVAILABLE to start/expand your business. Guaranteed. Free revealing details. Write: American Business Club, 301-AN Plymouth Drive, Dalton, GA 30721-9983.

## VENTURE CAPITAL

JUMBO LOANS $250K and up. Commerical start-ups, working capital, expansion, accounts receivable, mergers and acquisitions. Self-liquidating loans also. (813) 328-3317, 24 hours. It takes money to make money.

GENESIS COMPUTER SERVICES, INC. We search the country finding venture capital sources for you. (800) 444-5690.

VENTURE CAPITAL SOURCE HOTLINE. Over 2,500 sources. Minimum $50,000 for businesses only. (619) 456-9527.

VENTURE CAPITAL SOURCES! Any amount, no finders fees, no contracts! (914) 528-0536.

## WHERE TO FIND THE MONEY

**460**
**MONEY LOANED**

NEED CREDIT REPAIR?
* Free Initial Consultation...
* Fourth Year in Business
* Negatives Deleted - Legally
* 5000 Satisfied Clients
* Bonded, Guaranteed Service
* Mortgage Readiness Program

**MICHAEL JAY**
**& COMPANY**
THE CREDIT REPAIR PEOPLE
595 MARKET ST., SUITE 2500
* 415/986-3132 *

THE FINANCIAL SOLUTIONS
Bad Credit OK
Personal Loans to $35,000
Business Loans to $500,000
Debt Consolidations
Mastercard Available
Full Service Financial Programs
1-800-487-5402

*SIGNATURE CASH LOANS*
Bad Credit, No Credit
No Problem. Our Money Sources Has Funding Immediately. Must Be Employed and Need Money Now! Recieve in Days, Pay Monthly. Call Today for Info. (213) 882-8191
BDM Money Source

RECEIVABLE FINANCING
Cash Now For Your Invoices In 24-48 Hours!! Money Management Since 1980. (415) 982-7730

* VENTURE CAPITAL *
Start-ups, expansion, acquisitions, REAL ESTATE. $750K min. No front fees.
Loan originator/private lender.
California funding. 619-441-2970

**$ CASH FAST $**
NO QUALIFYING!
★APPLY BY PHONE★
☆1 HOUR APPROVAL☆
1st, 2nd & 3rd Trust Deeds
√Credit Problems OK
√Employment Problems OK
√Foreclosure OK
√Bankruptcy OK
ALSO BUY Or LEND On TD's
PURCHASE/REFINANCE!
LOW FIXED/ARM RATES
Gary 24 Hours 7 Days
(714) 569-1515

COMPLETE CREDIT REPAIR
STARTING AT
$99.95
CREDIT CARDS & LOANS
CREDIT CONSULTANTS INC.
If past credit problems are keeping your from having a car, boat, house or credit cards;
WE CAN HELP!!
CALL NOW
714-489-0865
Fast, Professional Results.

$2500- $10,000+
Guaranteed if employed
1-800-472-1021, 9am-9pm. EST

**INSTANT** Relief. Major debt consolidation. Up to $30K guaranteed. Open 7 days. 800-283-0036

**LOANS:** Bill Consolidation. Auto. Low Int. Bad Credit OK. No Coll. $2K-$50K. CFS. 213-798-3004

**LOANS-LOANS-LOANS**
$2500-$1 mil. Business/pers /unsecured. 1-800-759-1201

**$20,000 CASH LOANS**
Even with credit problems. 8am-10pm. 1-800-456-4007.

**CASH PROBLEMS?** We can help! All loans available, immediate relief. 1-800-338-8549

**FAST** & Simple Real Estate loans Private funds. No job, poor credit, foreclosure OK 239-8500

**FINANCIALLY** tight? Refinance constr/comml. RE loans. Bad credit OK. Paul. 332-LOAN

LOANS
PERSONAL LOANS!
CAR - BOAT - HOME
Bankruptcy - Foreclosures
Call (415) 491-4432

MONEY MONEY MONEY
IMMEDIATE HELP! Debt consolidations & personal loans to $20K. Everyone considered. Call now, 1-800-543-6634

**BILLION $ OPPORTUNITY.** $5M capital needed for production & distribution of transformational seminar, movie & video. Baron. 415-944-7784

FINANCIAL PROBLEMS?
We can help! Debt consolidation for all major credit cards or personal loans up to $20,000. 1-800-325-7024, 7 DAYS

HAVE BAD CREDIT?
Free office consult. with credit law expert. We clear bad credit legally & help get M/C, Visa, with no sec. deposit. 521-1306

**$5,000 LOANS-$72.46/MO.**
**$10,000 LOANS-$143.47/MO.**
Special high risk lenders.
VISA/MC/VISA GOLD-
$19.95 Call 1-900-535-8535

CONSOLIDATION LOANS
To $25,000. Bad Credit OK! Real People. Real help. Bankruptcy OK (513) 521-7300

GET OUT FROM UNDER!!!
We Can Help
$1000-$20,000 debt consolidation /personal loans. 1-800-932-8788

**MONEY TO LOAN**
Business or personal. EZ to qualify. SASE for application. PO Box 254, Tye TX 79563

**SIGNATURE LOANS.** Business or personal venture. Easy to qualify. SASE for application. P.O. Box 254, Tye TX 79563.

$ CAPITAL NETWORK
$25K & up for business/comm'l. & venture capital. 252-5933

## WHERE TO FIND THE MONEY

**Money to Loan 54**

$0

$5000 TO $$$$$$$

Pac-West Mortgage

* Direct Lender
* No Middleman Fees
* Conventional & Non-conventional programs
* Bank Turn Downs
* Bankruptcy OK
* No Application Fee
* Good Credit
* Poor Credit
* Multi-Family to 20 Units
* Commercial Loans
* Cash Back on Rentals
* We Buy Contracts
* & TRUST DEEDS
* DEBT CONSOLIDATION
* 1st MORTGAGES

WE MAKE THE DECISIONS

WE LEND THE MONEY

CALL

222-0217

**Money to Loan 54**

$0-$5,000,000
ARM @ 7.95%
For Consolidation or Any Worthwhile Purpose
Cash Back On Rentals
Prime West Mortgage Inc
624-0762 or 1-800-852-9572

---

$10,000 - $500,000 AVAILABLE on real prop, private funds; good rates, fast svc. APFC, 246-4204

---

8.875% FIXED
APR 9.125% (Residential Only)
Many programs. No app fees. Free estimates. Also Comm'l, Construction-Perm. Various lines of credit.
Consolidated Mortgage 635-5446
Bend 383-3766
Hood River 386-2258

---

ABLE TO FUND CASH BACK
★ REFINANCE ★
★Any Real Estate-Any Reason
★Commercial or Residential
★No Upfront Fees
★2nd Mortgages OK
★Bad Credit OK
Please call 1-800-878-7150 or 206-742-7150 Linnwood, WA

---

BEST RATES & TERMS!
FIXED RATE 9.50% APR
PURCHASE OR REFI
Credit lines, 2nd mtgs, construction rollover loans, hard to place loans, mobile home financing. Investors: cash back on rentals.
FIRST PACIFIC MORTGAGE CO.
Open Mon thru Sat 8-5
Call for appt. 24-hrs a day
654-7369 or 241-3829

---

CASH To Finance Your Property Or Contract. 223-9066

---

MONEY for comm'l, investment, home construction loan. Fixed & ARM equipmnt leasing 246-2474

---

TOUCHSTONE MORTGAGE
• Purchases • Refinance
• Hard To Place Loans
• Private Money Available
CALL US! 288-0848

---

UNLIMITED CAPITAL, Available for business purposes. $250,000 up. 645-5494 - Trans Comm Inc.

---

VENTURE CAPITAL SOURCES
Start-up to leverage buy-outs
$50,000 - $10,000,000
Wise Investments, 1-678-2624

**Money to Loan 54**

Turned Down For A
MORTGAGE?
Maybe We Can Help
Free Consultation
Unusual Loans Welcome
THE LOAN RANGERS
620-7272

**Contracts, Mortgages 57**

$

CASH
We Pay Top Dollars
FOR
- MORTGAGES -
- TRUST DEEDS -
- CONTRACTS -
IN THE BUSINESS OF SERVING OREGON SINCE 196?
CALL ?25-1212
5100 SW Macadam, Suite 300
Portland, Oregon 97201
THE MORTGAGE EXCHANGE, INC.

$

---

?-18% EARNINGS on well-secured short-term, interest only TD's. APFC, 246-4204.

---

2-DAY SERVICE
We will beat any qualified quote!
AMERICAN EQUITIES INC.
239-1561

## WHERE TO FIND THE MONEY

### 461 MONEY WANTED

**MULTI MILLIONARE** wants to borrow up to $500,000 at 10% interest from pvt source. Loan secured by prime SF prop. Phone 524-1177 anytime

**REAL** Estate Loan Wanted on Oceanfront Ranch Home plus 7 bldgs nr Half Moon Bay Golf Course. Huge equity. Amount/terms negotiable. 726-4725

### 101 REAL ESTATE LOANS

AAA
Homeowner Loans
30 YR. FIXED OR
ADJUSTABLE RATE LOANS
FIRSTS & SECONDS
POOR CREDIT
FORECLOSURES
BANKRUPTCY
USUALLY NOT A PROBLEM
IF YOU'VE BEEN
TURNED DOWN
BY ANY LENDER
CALL
SUPERIOR HOME LOANS
HAYWARD 889-1900
DUBLIN 828-3952
LIC. REAL ESTATE BROKER
HELPING HOMEOWNERS
FOR 25 YEARS
88-582

CALL TODAY
CASH TOMORROW!

I BUY & MAKE & LOAN
on 1st, 2nd, 3rd & 4th TDs!
Local or Out of Town-State!
(Some ates.)
SAN FRANCISCO
LENDING
108 Caledonia #1
Sausalito
Principal/Broker (89-3)
800-688-LEND
415-332-8929

### 700 Real Estate Information & Announcements

**EQUITY SHARING**

Do you want to invest in Real Estate but don't want tenant problems or negative cash flow? Security Pacific Real Estate, Jim Burckard, 938-9200; 672-5424.

**HOME INSPECTIONS**

When you buy or sell. Comprehensive property evaluation. Bay Area Home Inspections, prof. cert. #1028. Call 827-1499.

WHY RENT?: Antioch/Pittsburg, let me guide you thru the buying process. Sandy, R.E. Broker, Better Homes Realty, 779-0453 or 427-4964.

**FOR SALE BY OWNER SEMINAR**
BOOKS AND ALL FORMS, $25.
CALL 838-9700 FOR INFO.

ALL FORECLOSURES: 4 months before auction + auctions, REO's sent to you daily! 754-7039.

### 461 MONEY WANTED

**63 ALMOND FARMERS** seek outside capitol for expansion. Future looks great. Contact Jim Barstow 209-667-4855

**LOAN BROKERS**, We seek funds for commercial 1st deeds of trust, high commission. Inquire FAX 415-433-9024

**NEED** $32,500. 1st D of T in Vallejo. 50% LTV or $51,800 1st D of T in Pittsburg. 70% LTV, Earn 15%. PIMC, 415-937-4610.

**CONSISTENT HIGH YIELDS** Earn 12% to 25% APR. interest on your money. 1-800-776-9806

**INVESTORS** needed for new start-up environmental lab. 415- 454-3464

**$50,000**, 15%, 68% L.T.V., 2nd. $92,500, 14%, 69% L.T.V., 2nd. Call Brad 391-3610

**ATTENTION** Investors. RE returns, excess of 20%. 573-8741

**DISC.** $15K. $50K 2nd. ARM 9, 10, 12%. 10 yr. 10U. 805-397-4750

**$30K** note, discounted 2nd TD, 14% int., 70% LTV, 838-5899

### 103 REAL ESTATE INVESTMENTS/ JOINT VENTURES

**ESTABLISHED**, profitable Napa Valley Winery seeks capital for vineyard acquisition, growth and expansion of facilities. Would welcome equity or joint venture. box 7051 c/o SF Newspapers, PO Box 7228, SF 94120.

**FORCLOSURE** LISTS & Trustee Sales. Placer, Nev & El Dorado Ctys, Grass Vly to Placerville incl Lake Tahoe. 916-663-4724

**$500K** NOTE for sale, 2nd on estate in Woodside, 4 mos left. 19% yield. Brkr. 800-848-4460

**25** yr old Japanese co. seeks U.S Acquisitions. $5 million & up. Mr. Hakita, 921-6941

**RISKLESS** R.E. Venture. $100K needed. Len: 415- 658-5934

### 701 Investment Property

NEW East Bay single family homes for sale. National firm will triple net lease homes for sales models. Minimum investment $100,000. 1031 Exchange will be considered. Call John Johnson PULTE HOME CORPORATION
**(415) 460-0100**

$180,000-$200,000 EQUITY in San Ramon home & $200,000 avail. Would like to trade for 8-10 units in Concord/Antioch area. Prins. only. Send proposal to: P.O. Box 1377, Oakland, CA 94604, Attn: Cliff.

**Equity Preservation Inc.**
Exchange Accommodator
Intermediary
674-1031; (800) 544-1031

RICHMOND
5 Unit apt. building fully leased. Units recently refurbished near BART. $225,000. Agt.
TLC Property Mgmt. 456-4800

**$10K DOWN**
Walnut Creek duplex, 3 bedroom, 2 bath. Agt. 672-9476.

BENICIA, 16 Units. Good cond. good rents, $1.1M. Kathleen, Olson Realty, (707) 745-3602

CONCORD 4-Plex. All 2 bdrm., excellent location, $255,000. Dome Realty, 676-5495.

### 102 REAL ESTATE SERVICES

**BUYERS...** Now is the time to invest in Real Estate. For market knowledge & excel. service, call your exclusive agent: Carl Meiswinkel, 979-5708.

**DON'T** sell your property for less than it's worth. Talk to a real estate fix-up consultant. Call our 24 hour information line. Haywood Marketing 985-7449.

**GOVERNMENT** HOMES. Delinquent tax property. Repossessions. Call (1) 805-962-8000 Ext. Q-8779 for current repo list.

**FORECLOSURE** acquisition specialist prof brokerage svcs, all prices & locations. 883-5200

**NOE** VALLEY & SUNSET homes wanted by my cash buyers. Ira Blatt, Bkr 989-2063 24 hrs

**PACIFISIA** REALTY rents your vacant apts. to qualified tenants. 4829 Geary 668-4355.

**QUICK** Cash for trust deeds & property. Far East & local investor. Cal East, Chen 467-9500

1,000's OF FORECLOSURES; daily investor list. 415-754-7039

### 105 REAL ESTATE WANTED

**JAPANESE INVESTORS** will pay CASH for your home, condo, apts, comm'l, indus, land for golf crs. SF, Penin or Bay Area. GOODIN RLTY (415) 697-4080
Associated With
NAKAMATA RLTY, Tokyo Japan

**URGENTLY** need SF 2-3BR home to $350,000 nr Parochial school. Good down payment. Mr. Kish, Agt. 415/282-8685.

**1-2** acre heavy industrial prop. Reas. priced. Prefer Martinez/Pittsburg. 213-921-1431 days

**GENERAL** Contractor seeks financial partners for fixer uprs, S.F. area. 771-6532; 673-2925

I pay cash for your property - any condition. Al Baldini, 587-6707, for confidential appraisal. Agt.

**QUICK CASH** For Your Property
Foreign & Local Investors
LEE Prop & Inv. Rltrs 346-7201

**CASH.** Any cond, Quick closing. John Finnegan 878-9440 x260

**CONTRACTOR** seeks partner for fixer upr in SF 954-4228; 861-6621

# MONEY WANTED

## 461 MONEY WANTED

**CAPITAL NEEDED!** Great Opportunity! Public healthcare company needs $300,000 equity to requalify for Nasdaq listing. Tremendous upside opportunity. Series principals only, 702-733-8805, Mr. Goldsmith.

**$165,000** sought by new California corporation to finance initial production of patented consumer products. Equity available in exchange for funding of first cycle of business. Huge potential. 415-681-7490

EXCEPTIONAL SITUATION
Smart remote control light ($20) Expd MBA sks funding 454-7733

**$25K** -$100K+ for leasing co., fully secured/insured, priv. parties only. 415-838-1609

**NEED** $580,000. 1st loan on Market St. Bldg. Willing to pay very good rate. 777-4615

**CO SIGNER** nd for $5000 personal loan. $700 to co signer 589-4932

**DISCOUNTED** alot $250K 2nd 15% int. 70% LTV. 638-5899

**$65k** 2nd for 55K, 16% pre-paid, 66% LTV. P.A. home. 326-0455

**1ST TD**, $83,500. Yield 15%, 12mos. 28% LTV. Bkr. 332-8802

**$130K** 1st TD, 15 1/2% int. only, 2yrs. 50% LTV, land. 945-9770

EXCELLENT INVESTMENT OPPTY
NNN Lease
7%, 11 years remaining on lease with 5 year option to extend. Principals only. TRICO REALTY, Tom or Michelle, 714-751-4420

## 105 REAL ESTATE WANTED

**JAPANESE** INVESTORS will pay CASH for your home, condo, apts, comm'l, indus, land for golf crs. SF, Penin or Bay Area. GOODIN RLTY (415) 697-4080 Associated With NAKAMATA RLTY, Tokyo Japan

**WANT** TO BUY a meeting hall or preferably a Church for 100 people in Burlingame or Millbrae area. Price negotiable. CALL 415- 342-4120

**3-** 10ACS. for agricultural purposes. Existing residence pref'd. Utilities. 707-584-3975

I pay cash for your property - any condition. Al Baldini, 587-6707, for confidential appraisal. Agt.

**QUICK CASH** For Your Property Foreign & Local Investors LEE Prop & Inv, Rltrs 346-7201

**CASH!** Any Cond., Quick Closing! J.F. FINNEGAN, 878-9440 x260

**CASH** I Buy Homes. I make a firm ofr within 48hrs 415-929-1355

I BUY HOUSES if seller will take mo. pmts for equity. 759-9846

## Business Opptys Wanted 324

Looking to buy estab. vending route. Video games, min. 20 machines, PP to PP. 538-1534

RESTAURANT or Deli Chef w/catering business nds loc. Irvine or So. County. 589-1239

## Inventions & Patents 333

Product Develop. • Mktg • Distribution • Royalties MarketMED Inc. 544-1474

## Investment Opportunity 341

★ INVESTORS NEEDED ★
Join Us, we are buying and selling REO's (bank repos) in So Cal. We are buying houses at 50% to 70% of mkt value. We need cash & fin statements. Up to 100% return in 6 mo. Inv & profits secured by RE. Capital Investment Co 714-567-4700

## Money Wanted 357

Investor/Partner for well established Embroidery Mfg/ custom apparel retailer. Expansion, debt payoff & new equipment needed. 248-2780 ask for Ed

Investors $5K/30K/100K/300K/ 1.8M. Fastest growing ntwrk co, hi tech prod, no risk, highest return. Sun 10am, 3200 S. Bristol #750 C.M (@ Anton).

Needed private investor or lender. $15/$20K built out new apparel store has $55K own invested. 818/913-8609

Want to borrow money against insurance co. stocks. Will pay 15-18% interest. 714-879-8193 or 714-699-7932

$100K to $150K dollar wanted on $375K fountain Vlly home. xlnt credit and LTV 968-0254

2nd TD on Anaheim home, $80K equity. Weak credit. Call 213/590-8978

Forming partnership to buy & flip distress RE grt return w/ min invest. Bkr 213-943-5355

## Money To Loan 361

CASH NOW!
1st, 2nd, 3rd T.D.
No Qual Equity Loans
3-5 Day Funding
- Telephone approvals
- Credit, income, probs ok
- Foreclose, BK ok
- Subject to equity verif.

Lowest Fixed ARM Rates
714-373-0807
213-598-1393
Commercial Mortgage

INVESTOR PARTNER
Start up bus opportunity in multi-billion $ consumer product/service industry. Ownership + equity int. 10xROI, 3-5 yrs. + qtrly Div. Need $750k NOW! Serious Principals Only PP (714) 841-5530 John

## ADVERTISING RESULTS

Publication & Date ______________________

Position ______________________

Cost ______________________

Number of People Who Responded ______________________

Number of People Who Looked ______________________

Comments of Those Who Looked ______________________

______________________

Was Property Sold / Rented / Optioned ______________________

Write a Reaction to the Ad ______________________

______________________

______________________

______________________

______________________

---

Publication & Date ______________________

Position ______________________

Cost ______________________

Number of People Who Responded ______________________

Number of People Who Looked ______________________

Comments of Those Who Looked ______________________

______________________

Was Property Sold / Rented / Optioned ______________________

Write a Reaction to the Ad ______________________

______________________

______________________

______________________

______________________

# The Real Estate Underground

## *Little-Known REOs, IRS Tax Sales, and Local County Tax Sales*

*Chapter* 12

***R**eal* Estate Owned (REO) is the real estate formally used as collateral for loans that have foreclosed. The ownership of the property itself has reverted to the bank, insurance company, or individual lender. In this chapter you will learn:

- How REO sales take place
- How to buy from the banks
- Who holds the REOs
- Where the best deals are
- How to buy at IRS sales
- How to buy at state tax sales
- The details of the judicial foreclosure sale process

## THE PROCESS OF SELLING REOS

REOs have advantages and disadvantages for the foreclosure buyers. The big advantage in buying REOs from the bank is that the lender has the ability to restructure the loan with favorable terms, lower interest rates, and long payment schedules. It is also possible to negotiate low down payments of approximately 5% to 10%, and bargain for a waiver of points and fees. There is a good possibility that the lender will even offer a discounted purchase price. But none of these advantages is guaranteed. The disadvantage is that if no member of the public bids at the Trustee's/Sheriff's Sale, the lender may have lent too much on the property or the property might be losing value for some other reason.

### Defaulting Loan

The foreclosure action is a result of a borrower's defaulting on a loan that was secured by real estate. Usually, a lender has lent money to the owner of a property and the property is used as security to assure the lender that the loan will be repaid. If the lender does not receive payments as promised and agreed, the lender has the authority, given when the borrower signs the trust deed or mortgage, to foreclose under the contract. In California, the buyer signs a deed of trust and a promissory note. In other states the relevant document may be called a mortgage and promissory note.

### Trustee

The deed of trust (mortgage) contains a provision that requires the beneficiary (the lender) to deliver the note and deed of trust to an independent third party called a Trustee. The Trustee holds the deed of trust and note until it is paid in full. If the property owner does not pay as agreed, the beneficiary (lender) will advise the Trustee (the third party) to sell the property to the highest bidder at a Trustee's Sale and then repay the loan with the proceeds from the sale. The Trustee will advertise the property for sale in a legal newspaper and possibly in other papers of general circulation. Notices of Trustee's/Sheriff's Sales are also posted on bulletin boards in county and public buildings.

If the Trustee announces the auction (Trustee's Sale) to sell the property and no one shows up to make a competitive bid, the lender automatically bids for the property at the minimum price that the announcement advertised as the sale price. In common terms that is referred to as "the lender bids in." The astute buyer contacts the lender after the sale and starts negotiations. If the lender is foreclosing on a property with more equity than the mortgage value, for example, a \$100,000 mortgage and a \$200,000 sale value, the foreclosure buyer should expect very little cooperation from the lenders. The lender knows that this type of sale will attract a crowd to the Trustee's/Sheriff's Sale. In other circumstances the lender will be motivated to sell the property. However, being motivated does not mean that the lender will give you the property. The bank officer you talk with will be obligated to sell for the highest price possible. After all, he works for the bank, and stockholders really frown on his giving money away.

### Rich Stockholders

Expect no favors and don't believe everything you read in the newspapers about financial institutions going broke and just crying to rid themselves of REOs. They do indeed have too many

REOs, but the mandate of the institutions is to make the stockholders rich — not you. If you approach the lender with a win-win attitude, you'll open the door. REOs can be a gold mine, but like all mining, will take some effort and time. Remember: Bank officers are being evaluated by their superiors every day, not to mention by the bank board and the FDIC. In the negotiations you therefore become a real opponent. Don't become obnoxious. Work at building rapport and a long-term relationship will develop. And keep in mind the negotiation techniques discussed in Chapter 6.

## WHO HOLDS REOS?

Almost anyone who lends money and secures it with real estate could end up with an REO. Banks, savings and loan institutions, and insurance companies have most of the property in this category. However, let's not forget the federal government: Federal Housing Authority (FHA) and Veterans Administration (VA) foreclosures are not unusual. Together the VA and HUD/FHA foreclose on more than 40,000 homes and apartment properties each year. Even individuals who sell their property can end up with REOs when the new buyers neglect to pay. To find REOs, look in the local and legal newspapers for the announcements of Trustee's/Sheriff's Sales and subscribe to a commercial service that provides information on defaults. Contact the note holders, local and regional banks, savings and loan associations, personal property lenders (such as Morris Plan and Beneficial Finance Corporation), real estate brokers who specialize in REOs, over-extended builders and developers, private owners, and credit unions.

None of these lenders is in the real estate business. Their business is in the lending of money, and every property that finds its way back to them as an REO is a mark of an unsuccessful deal. Therefore, these lenders are motivated sellers. Motivated sellers are what you need to make a success of the distressed property business. If the seller is not motivated, your chance of getting a good deal is reduced significantly.

## BUYING FROM BANKS

Banks and savings and loan associations have special rules about the disposition (sale) of REOs. For example, they almost always get an appraisal; they usually ask a broker or professional contractor to estimate the fix-up costs, and they usually attempt to sell the property themselves or to deal with a local broker.

If you plan to purchase from the bank or institution, you must know the value of the property before you contact the bank for an appointment. It is wise also to attend the sale to find out what price the institution paid to get the property back. With these two pieces of information you will know what you can pay and what openings there are for bargaining and negotiation. Sellers will always listen to proposals that either make their position better or eliminate risk of future loss.

### "Mr. Big"

If your initial telephone call does not reach the correct person at the bank, you will end up frustrated because the business of REOs and foreclosure is usually one of the least advertised, least-known departments in the bank. Be sure you get the proper department and then talk to Mr. Big.

Even if you do get the right department, your initial telephone call may be surprising; you may be told that the bank has no REOs. Of course, you've already been to the Trustee's/Sheriff's

Sale and know that it does. The answer may be prompted by one of two reasons. The REO department may not have had the property turned over to it as yet, or if you are telephoning out of the blue, the bank will not know that you are not a stockholder checking to see if it has made any bad loans. Banks and savings and loan associations tend to be pretty closed about REOs – justifiably, since REOs depress their earnings. What you must do, having discovered the property identity, is to visit the institution yourself and talk to Mr. Big in the REO department. Your subsequent telephone discussions will be more candid.

Write all of the sources discussed in the previous section and tell them of your interest in purchasing REOs. A few weeks later follow up with another letter. Send a series of at least three. Then begin to call on the REO departments regularly. Request meetings with the REO officer or officers and tell them what you can do for them. That is what they want to know, because REOs generally create a lot of extra work for their reluctant owners and, as noted, are frequently an embarrassment.

**Brokers/Government**

Telephone the real estate brokers and discuss your purchase intentions. Then visit the brokers and the government offices. Tell them again of your interest and desire to purchase. Local brokers usually have an inside track about how much activity is taking place in the local market. Take advantage of this information and do not overbid the property. Many local brokers have lists of foreclosed properties distributed by government agencies such as FHA/HUD and the Farmer's Home Administration, and these lists are updated regularly. With a simple request to the government agency you can receive these listings directly.

## CAUTION

REO buyers are usually a little too anxious and show very little patience. They are fooled into thinking that theirs is the only deal in town at such a low price. Be patient and very cautious. Foreclosures, REOs, tax sales, and the whole business of distressed real estate is very profitable, but if you buy the wrong house in the wrong location or one with structural or other problems, you won't profit. Keep in mind that the "as is" clause means just that; as the government contract reads: "it is your problem once you own it."

The author has seen properties purchased from the banks and savings and loan associations that did not meet local building codes. Local laws require that deficiencies be repaired and the property upgraded to standard before it may be occupied. If you are unable to rehabilitate the property because of high costs or building restrictions, you will have a problem. It is very important you ascertain the costs of repairs and research local building codes and ordinances before you buy.

## THE BEST DEALS IN REOS

Unusual properties can be very profitable for the REO investor. From time to time, the Small Business Administration (SBA) will have a foreclosure. Such properties were originally used as security for loans to start businesses. Should the business fail, the SBA will have an REO (foreclosed home) on its hands. The properties may be located in better than average areas, so pursue this source and stay on the mailing list.

For investors who are knowledgeable about farming operations, Farmer's Home Administration has many foreclosures and REOs. Find the local FHA office in the telephone book and call to request that your name be entered on the mailing list. These properties are special in that the new buyer must know either how to sell the property quickly or how to produce revenue to meet the mortgage payment. There is a tremendous amount of agricultural and forest land available to buyers of distressed property, but it is no business for a neophyte.

The best deals in the REO market can be expected on properties that are foreclosed upon by out-of-state investors. Many property owners find themselves unable to collect mortgage payments owed to them after they have moved to another state to retire or to work. These sellers are eager to sell their property or to lease it. It is difficult for the out-of-state owner to look after such an asset from a distance, and the property usually deteriorates rapidly.

Many alert REO investors make good deals quickly in their market. The out-of-state investor or owner may also be less knowledgeable about values or may just need the steady income that a new investor can provide. An additional benefit is the financing that sellers can provide. By financing the REO, the seller can assure the new buyer a quick deal with little competition.

## IRS-FORCED SALES: BIG BUCKS FOR THE SAVVY INVESTOR

One profitable strategy for buying bargain properties is to purchase distressed or foreclosure property from the IRS. The property isn't necessarily distressed or damaged—however, the owner usually is. Distressed owners have liens filed against them and their assets (homes) and until these obligations are paid, they can in many cases be foreclosed upon. The statutes of the different states also apply, so you must research the rules for your state.

### Powerful IRS

Who can foreclose or repossess property, you might ask? The IRS is a federal agency and has been granted a great deal of power. If a taxpayer does not pay taxes when due, the IRS will assess the delinquent tax and make a request for payment. If the taxpayer fails or refuses to pay, the IRS will then place liens on the personal and real property. The IRS will file (record) a Notice of Federal Tax Lien with the county recorder. This document will be recorded against all the assets of the individual or the corporation in the county where the real property is located.

After the lien has been recorded against the property, the IRS can seize and sell the property. The IRS will give the homeowner notice of the lien and also a notice of intent to seize. At this point, things get sticky for the homeowner/delinquent taxpayer. The revenue officer has great powers granted by the federal government to take many actions. The revenue officer will determine a quick sale price for the property. This may or may not produce enough revenue to completely clear the debt to the IRS.

### "As Is"

When the sale takes place, the IRS will sell the property subject to the existing liens and mortgages that have priority to its attachment. The bidder at the auction should keep in mind that they are purchasing a property "as is" and subject to the liens that were recorded prior to the IRS Notice of Federal Tax Lien.

The IRS office or revenue agent is not required to advertise the sale of the property in any specific manner. This is different from the situation that applies with Sheriff's Sales and Trustee's Sales of real estate. Therefore, a relatively small group of investors follows the IRS sales. This lack of publicity opens a window of opportunity for those who develop the knowledge of the sales process and the methods to track the sales.

The question in most investors' minds is: How do I locate these forced distressed sales? The answer lies in the Internal Revenue Code, which requires that a notice of sale be published at least once in a newspaper of general circulation published in the county where the property is located. If there is no newspaper of general circulation, the revenue officer is required to post notice at the post office and at least two other places. This notice must be posted at least ten days before the sale. How do you find which paper is the paper of general circulation? That's a good question. If you live in a major metropolitan area, expect there to be numerous papers, perhaps as many as ten. The local library is a good place to research the newspapers. I suggest that you check with the local IRS office: ask if they have a bidder's list or a hot line (telephone recording) to advise potential buyers of the availability of pending forced sales. At the same time ask which newspaper they prefer to utilize for their advertising or announcements.

One owner lost his home when he failed to pay delinquent taxes by the time and date specified on a notice mailed to him. Another homeowner waited until the last day of his notice, the day of the sale. He was at the tax office at 12:00 noon, but was two hours late for the sale, which took place at 10:00 A.M.

## COUNTY TAX SALES — GENERAL INFORMATION

The date and time of sales usually differ from one county to another within a state. While auction hours usually are scheduled during the course of the business day, many sales are completed before noon. As a buyer you should expect many of the owners to pay their delinquent taxes between the time of the last published listing and the day of the sale. An up-to-date auction list of parcels for sale is published on a regular basis. Generally, the list of parcels being auctioned that day is provided a few hours prior to the sale. If you intend to bid, you should find this list well worth the price you may have to pay for it, although it is often free.

For most sales for delinquent taxes, the notice requires the auction to take place at the front door of the courthouse. Usually, however, the sales are actually held in an auditorium or an office inside the courthouse.

## WHAT INFORMATION DO YOU NEED?

The answer is simple: You need the same information that is common to lawyers, sheriffs, county clerks, and tax collectors. This information is not a mystery, nor is it intentionally withheld from the public, but it is something most people are unaware of. This information is available to the public every working day in the public records.

It is paramount that property owners, bidders, and purchasers both search the county records and ask the county staff members to obtain information about the sale. You can bid effectively only if you know whether there is a redemption period or not, how and when a tax deed is acquired, whether the property is burdened by liens or has other legal problems. The answers to all these questions are in the public records of the county where the sale is conducted.

## REDEMPTION RIGHTS AND OTHER REGULATIONS

In states that have redemption periods, tax sales are not an outright sale of the real property. They may instead take the form of a sale of the lien for the unpaid taxes and charges. A little research will tell you whether this is the case in your state. In addition, many states protect the owner's rights when the owner is serving in the armed forces.

Regulations may vary from state to state and among counties in states. For example, some states keep the excess amount of the bids. Others pass this money on to the seller or delinquent taxpayer. Laws are constantly being amended in state legislatures and other bodies. Plan on taking the time to get to know the laws in your particular state.

Lenders at auctions are high bidders the majority of the time. The cash requirements at the sale/auctions make the sale out of bounds for all but the most serious investors and bargain hunters.

### How to Find REOs

There are many ways to track down lender-owned REOs. Here are a few:

The Yellow Pages: Call every mortgage lender. Keep in mind that they won't tell you they have an inventory of foreclosure properties. Mail to lenders. Your state banking or savings and loan office will have the addresses. Be prepared to do numerous mailings in a short period of time to prove you are a serious investor/buyer.

Visit bank branches in your community and find the person who handles either foreclosures or repossessed property.

Follow the property after the Trustee's/Sheriff's Sale. Many of the properties will be owned by out-of-state lenders. This could be a benefit to you in your negotiations.

CNB COLORADO NATIONAL BANK OF DENVER

February 1, 1991

Mr. Ted Thomas
Box 5000, Suite 412
Dauville, CA 94521

RE: Real Estate Owned
Property Information Report As of December 31, 1990

Dear Mr. Thomas:

Do you know someone who may be interested in 296.5 acres of land in the Del Camino area of Weld County which is zoned for mixed-use development? CROSSROADS DEL CAMINO has excellent access, good visibility, all utilities, favorable zoning, and terrific mountain views.

The above-referenced property is just a sample of the many Real Estate Owned properties offered by Colorado National Bankshares, Inc. in the enclosed Property Information Report. Please utilize . this confidential information for your purposes only.

Please feel free to call us if you have questions regarding any of the properties listed in the report. Colorado National Bankshares, Inc. welcomes any inquiries you may have regarding the listed properties.

We would like to extend to you our best wishes for a prosperous New Year!

Sincerely,

Leo H. Connell, Jr.
(303 892-4272)

James E. Obst
(303 899-4325)
OREO Administrators

LHC/JEB/pb
Enclosure

Seventeenth Street at Champa
Denver, Colorado 80202
(303) 893-1862

Mailing Address:
P.O. Box 5168
Denver, CO 80217

COLORADO NATIONAL BANKSHARES, INC.
REAL ESTATE OWNED
PROPERTY INFORMATION REPORT
AS OF 12-31-90

| Type | Property Location | List Price | Comments and Description | Property Number | Contact |
|---|---|---|---|---|---|
| Com I | Commercial office building, I-70 & Kipling, Denver, CO | 1,950,000 | 44,869 Sq Ft GLA multi-tenant office building built in 1983. Occupancy is approximately 75%. | 01-104 | Denver, Jim Obst, 899-4325 |
| Com U | 13th & Speer, Denver, CO | 1,780,240 | Part of triangular parcel of ground bordered by 13th, 14th, Speer and Fox streets. Located near the proposed convention center. Approx. 63,590 sq. ft. zoned B8. | 01-007 | Denver, Leo Connell, 892-4272 |
| Com U | Hunter's Hill, Littleton, CO | 1,400,000 | 7.14+ Acres located at the northwest corner of South Yosemite Street and East Dry Creek Road. Property is zoned for retail/restaurant development. | 01-067 | Denver, Leo Connell, 892-4272 |
| Com U | Between Ohio & Kentucky Ave. Glendale, CO | 1,250,000 | Unimproved office/apartment, 5.39 acres planned site development district in City of Glendale. | 01-048 | Denver, Leo Connell, 892-4272 |
| Mul U | Old Mill, Littleton, CO | 1,000,000 | 15.4+ acre tract of land, Homestead in the Willows, filing #17. Property is zoned for multi-family residential development. | 01-062 | Denver, Leo Connell, 892-4272 |
| Com U | Arapahoe & Holly, Littleton, CO | 790,000 | 3.9+ acres located at the Southeast corner or East Arapahoe Road and South Holly Street. Zoned for retail and restaurant development. Under contract. | 01-066 | Denver, Leo Connell, 892-4272 |
| Com I | 2601 Blake St., Denver, CO | 750,000 | Combination of 2 multi story buildings, 22,545 sq. ft. office/showroom. | 01-081 | Denver, Leo Connell, 892-4272 |

CNB COLORADO NATIONAL BANK OF DENVER

Prepared by: OREO Administrators
Leo H. Connell, Jr. (303) 892-4272
James E. Obst (303) 899-4325

**FDIC**
Federal Deposit Insurance Corporation
P.O. Box 7549, Newport Beach, California 92658-7549•(714) 975-7213•OUTSIDE CALIFORNIA ONLY 1-800-327-FDIC

April 16, 1991

Dear Investor:

Thank you for your interest in the Federal Deposit Insurance Corporation Western Regional Marketing Packet. The Marketing Packet is updated bimonthly and offers a brief property description, listing price, and who to contact for more information.

Future mailings will include information regarding specific properties and/or special sales events. It is our intent to furnish you, the investor, with information about properties suitable to your investment needs.

The FDIC sells real estate in "as is" condition, and makes no warranties, either written or implied. Normally, the buyer makes his/her own arrangements for any financing necessary to complete the purchase.

Some of our properties are marketed by exclusive listing with real estate brokers, and any inquiries about these should be directed to the broker. For further information regarding properties not listed with a broker, please call the FDIC Real Estate Marketing Center at (800) 388-4607.

Please complete the enclosed form and return it to us if you would like to receive the next updated marketing packet. Your name will be removed from our list unless you respond using the attached form. Please type or print legibly on the enclosed form.

Sincerly,

Edward Kato
Department Head
Real Estate Owned/Marketing

EK:syl

Enclosures

/syl
a:invstmt-ltr

**The following pages include excerpts of the actual document.**

**For example:**

Arizona 6 of 66 properties are shown
California 6 of 80 properties are shown
Colorado 7 of 28 properties are shown
Hawaii all properties are shown
Idaho all properties are shown
Montana 6 properties are shown
Nevada 7 of 9 properties are shown
New Mexico 6 of 67 properties are shown
Oregon 5 of 42 properties are shown
Texas 6 of 15 properties are shown
Utah 5 of 63 properties are shown
Washington 5 of 7 properties are shown
Wyoming all properties are shown

**FDIC REAL ESTATE DEPARTMENT**
**Toll Free: 1-800-388-4607**
**LISTING OF REO PROPERTIES**

**APRIL 1991**

**ARIZONA**
**BY CITY**

| Bank/Asset # | Address / Property Description | Type Property |
|---|---|---|
| **APACHE JUNCTION** | | |
| 4105/000134001 | S/E Corner of Deleware Dr. & Round-Up St.<br>10 acre parcel in Apache Junction. Multi family Resid.(CR-5)<br>Listed w/Prudential R.E./Paul Rizza/602-730-5200. | LAND<br>**$225,000** |
| **COCHISE COUNTY** | | |
| 5986/451214001 | West of Hwy. 90, Huachuca City, Cochise County, AZ<br>Vacant land, approx. 74 acres. | LAND<br>**$40,700** |
| **GILA BEND** | | |
| 4232/000191001 | Rural Route 796, Gila Bend, AZ<br>5 single family residential lots. | 5 LOTS/SFR<br>**$99,000** |
| **GILBERT** | | |
| 4105/000124001 | 6 & 7 Palo Verde Rd., Gilbert AZ<br>comm. strip shopping center Palo Verde Rd. & Gilbert Rd.<br>20,200 sq. ft. of space. | COMM. SHOPPING CENTER<br>**$660,000** |
| 5986/351002001 | 33 Riata, "The Groves", Gilbert, AZ<br>Semi-custom 3,000 sq. ft. luxury home on 1/3 acre. 4 oversized bdrms and 3 baths, custom pool. Listed w/Prudential Arizona/Candyce Hopwood/602-954-6888 | SFR<br>**$189,000** |
| **GLENDALE** | | |
| 4105/000118001 | Glendale, Lamar & 55th Ave., Glendale<br>4 M-1 lots approx. 7,000 sq. ft. each, located between Glendale Ave. & Lamar Rd. Ready for construction. | M-1 LOTS<br>**$55,000** |

This List is intended to provide interested parties with preliminary information only. FDIC makes no representations or warranties as to the accuracy or completeness of the information. FDIC reserves the right to withdraw any property from this List at any time and without notice. Prices are subject to change, and any offer to purchase an asset is subject to approval by the appropriate Credit Review Committee.

FDIC Real Estate Department
Toll Free: 1-800-388-4607
LISTING OF REO PROPERTIES

APRIL 1991

CALIFORNIA
BY CITY

| Bank/Asset # | Address<br>Property Description |
|---|---|
| **ADELANTO** | |
| 7577/000014001 | 12063 - 12075 Crippen Ave., Adelanto, CA 6 UNIT<br>3 bldgs., 4 units - 2 bedroom, 1 bath & 2 units - 1 bedroom, 1 bath. **$162,000** |
| **ARMONA** | |
| 7541/000071001 | Hume & Oak, Armona, CA RAW LAND<br>13 acres, zoned AL, Light Agricultural and one homesite. If interested, send letter of intent. **$63,800** |
| 7541/000072001 | Intersection of 14th Ave. & Ada St., Armona, CA RAW LAND<br>Partially competed subdivision. 32 parcels in various stages of development. DO NOT DISTURB EXISTING OCCUPANTS. If interested, send letter of intent. **$648,000** |
| 7541/000073001 | 14th Ave. & Oak, Armona, CA RAW LAND<br>12 acres, zoned R-16. If interested, send letter of intent. **$68,200** |
| **BAKERSFIELD** | |
| 7566/000004001 | SWC Morning Drive & Pioneer, Bakersfield, CA APARTMENTS<br>Morning Drive Apts., 112 Unit apartment complex. 70% completed, with 1.49 acres comml land. **$1,500,000** |
| 7541/000025001 | 4300 Stine Rd., Bakersfield, CA COMMERCIAL<br>Presidio West. 8 Office buildings, 70,572 sq. ft. 100% vacant. **$2,124,000** |

**FDIC REAL ESTATE DEPARTMENT**
**Toll Free Number: 1-800-388-4607**
**LISTING OF REO PROPERTIES**

**APRIL 1991**

**COLORADO**

| Bank/Asset # | Address<br>Property Description | | |
|---|---|---|---|
| **ARAPAHOE** | | | |
| 7576/000226001 | So. Side East Drycreek Rd & So. Arapahoe County, CO<br>48 vacant lots located in the Spring Creek St. Foxridge Planned developm. 5.4 acres. | LOTS | $166,650 |
| **ARVADA** | | | |
| 7576/000239001 | 4935 Allison St., Arvada, CO<br>45,920 rentable sq. ft. | WAREHOUSE | $1,000,000 |
| 7576/000208001 | 4941 Allison St., Arvada, CO<br>45,920 rentable sq. ft. | WAREHOUSE | $1,000,000 |
| 7576/000215001 | 5930 W. 56th Ave., Arvada, CO (IN ESCROW)<br>35,000 gross rentable sq. ft. | WAREHOUSE | $440,000 |
| 7576/000219001 | A. 8041 W. I-70, Arvada, CO<br>35,378 gross rentable sq. ft. | WAREHOUSE | |
| 7576/000222001 | B. 8141 W. I-70, Arvada, CO<br>35,378 Gross rentable sq. ft.<br>A & B to be sold together. | WAREHOUSE | $1,355,750 |
| 7576/000237001 | 6333 E. 38th Ave., Arvada, CO<br>Vacant 38,080 rentable sq. ft. warehouse. Contact Pat Zamberletti/Mathis Asset Mgr/303-295-1133 | WAREHOUSE | $380,000 |

This List is intended to provide interested parties with preliminary information only. FDIC makes no representations or warranties as to the accuracy or completeness of the information. FDIC reserves the right to withdraw any property from this List at any time and without notice. Prices are subject to change, and any offer to purchase an asset is subject to approval by the appropriate Credit Review Committee.

FDIC REAL ESTATE DEPARTMENT
Toll Free Number: 1-800-388-4607
LISTING OF REO PROPERTIES

APRIL 1991

HAWAII

| Bank/Asset # | Address<br>Property Description | | |
|---|---|---|---|
| **HILO** | | | |
| 7516/000059001 | 24 Pukihea St., #210, Hilo, HI<br>1 bedroom condo, 484 sq. ft.<br>Sealed Bid. | CONDO<br>**$28,000** | |

This List is intended to provide interested parties with preliminary information only. FDIC makes no representations or warranties as to the accuracy or completeness of the information. FDIC reserves the right to withdraw any property from this List at any time and without notice. Prices are subject to change, and any offer to purchase an asset is subject to approval by the appropriate Credit Review Committee.

**FDIC REAL ESTATE DEPARTMENT**
**Toll Free Number: 1-800-388-4607**
**LISTING OF REO PROPERTIES**

**APRIL 1991**

**IDAHO**
**BY CITY**

| Bank/Asset # | Address / Property Description |
|---|---|
| **BINGHAM COUNTY** | |
| 2558/005743001 | Sections 3 & 4. Top 2S. Rge 37 EBM — CROPLAND<br>162 acres cropland. " Wolverine Road."<br>(IN ESCROW) Listed w/Higgins Realty/Phil Young/208-785-1294.<br>**$166,100** |

This List is intended to provide interested parties with preliminary information only. FDIC makes no representations or warranties as to the accuracy or completeness of the information. FDIC reserves the right to withdraw any property from this List at any time and without notice. Prices are subject to change, and any offer to purchase an asset is subject to approval by the appropriate Credit Review Committee.

**FDIC REAL ESTATE DEPARTMENT**
**Toll Free Number: 1-800-388-4607**
**LISTING OF REO PROPERTIES**

**APRIL 1991**

**MONTANA**
**BY CITY**

| Bank/Asset # | Address<br>Property Description | |
|---|---|---|
| **BILLINGS** | | |
| 7521/000302001 | 1130 Carise Rd., Billings, MT<br>Versatile commercial building.<br>Retail space downstairs, 2 apts. upstairs. | COM'L BLDG.<br>**$85,250** |
| 7521/000299001 | 803 Carise St., Billings, Mt.<br>134 storage units ranging in size from 25 to 600 sq. ft.<br>Listed w/Chuck Platt/406-656-9944. | MINI-STORAGE<br>**$110,000** |
| 7521/000300001 | 924 Highway 87 East, Billings, MT<br>Metal commercial building on 2 acres. Hwy 87 frontage. | COM'L BLDG.<br>**$110,000** |
| **COOPER VALLEY** | | |
| 2766/300535001 | Cooper Valley Estates, MT<br>9.7 acres midway between Helena & Great Falls. Could be hunters base camp. Listed w/Frank Rubis/406-453-3288. | LAND<br>**$9,000** |
| **FROMBERG** | | |
| 3487/000548011 | Former Bank Building situated on Lots 1-6 of Block 2 Oiginal plat, Fromberg, MT<br>Fromberg is located 45 miles SW of Billings. The structure is 3,685 sq. ft. of Class C construction. Improvements are in excellent shape. Could be used for many different purposes. | BANK BLDG.<br>**$64,900** |
| **HUNGRY HORSE** | | |
| 7521/000006001 | 215 First Ave, Hungry Horse, MT<br>Com'l Bldg. Incomplete construction. Listed w/Pete Putizer 406-892-2177. | COM'L BLDG.<br>**$20,000** |

This List is intended to provide interested parties with preliminary information only. FDIC makes no representations or warranties as to the accuracy or completeness of the information. FDIC reserves the right to withdraw any property from this List at any time and without notice. Prices are subject to change, and any offer to purchase an asset is subject to approval by the appropriate Credit Review Committee.

**FDIC Real Estate Department**
**Toll Free: 1-800-388-4607**
**LISTING OF REO PROPERTIES**

**APRIL 1991**

**NEVADA**

| Bank/Asset # | Address<br>Property Description |
|---|---|
| **GARDNERVILLE** | |
| 7559/000002001 | 1488 Douglas, Gardnerville, NV — 4-PLEX<br>2 bedrooms, 960 sq. ft. each, close to town.<br>**$225,000** |
| **LAS VEGAS** | |
| 7554/000016001 | 1701 Katie Ave. #96,99,87, Las Vegas, NV — 3 CONDOS<br>2 bd/2 bth, 970 Sq. Ft. each. Can be purchased seperately.<br>#87 Listed w/Circle Realty/Vicky England/702-870-0224.<br>**$207,000** |
| 7554/000055001 | 1424 Smokey Glen Cir., Las Vegas, NV — 3-SFR's<br>1 - 3 bd/2 bth, 1,301 Sq. Ft. 2 - 3 bd/2 bth, 1,576 sq. ft. each. Can be purchased seperately. Listed w/American Group Realtor/Carl Unger/702-595-5000.<br>**$251,900** |
| 7576/000015001 | 4600 W. Sirius, Las Vegas, NV. — APTS.<br>Cameron Park Apartments, 316 units. Built in 1981.<br>98% occupancy.<br>**$10,400,000** |
| 7554/000051001 | 5054-5090 Kell Ln, Las Vegas, NV. — APT/LAND<br>"Lone Palm Apartments", 40 unit & vacant land.<br>Near Nellis, AFB.<br>**$1,750,000** |
| **MINDEN** | |
| 7559/000004001 | 1590 Fourth St., Minden, NV — HIST. COML BLDG.<br>1920's bank bldg. partially refurbished. Approx. 5700 sq. ft.<br>On historical register. Covenant recorded on file.<br>**$264,000** |
| **RENO** | |
| 7525/000008001 | 12 Miles No of Reno Stead Airport, Reno, NV — 114 VACANT LOTS<br>The lots vary in size from 1.66 acres to a majority of the lots with approx. 40 acres.<br>**$1,900,000** |

This List is intended to provide interested parties with preliminary information only. FDIC makes no representations or warranties as to the accuracy or completeness of the information. FDIC reserves the right to withdraw any property from this List at any time and without notice. Prices are subject to change, and any offer to purchase an asset is subject to approval by the appropriate Credit Review Committee.

FDIC REAL ESTATE DEPARTMENT
Toll Free: 1-800-388-4607
LISTING OF REO PROPERTIES

APRIL 1991

NEW MEXICO
BY CITY

| Bank/Asset # | Address<br>Property Description | Type Property |
|---|---|---|
| **ALBUQUERQUE** | | |
| 2578/001551002 | 901-4th St. Albuquerque, N.M.<br>Parcel of land consisting of approx. 17,750 sq. ft. improved with a small gas station, & located in the central business (redevelopment) area. Zoned SV-2C. Gas tank removed. (IN ESCROW)<br>**$49,000** | GAS STATION (Non) (Operating) |
| 2578/001553002 | Paradise Hills Blvd. & Lyons Blvd., Northwest Albuquerue, N.M.<br>Unimproved 9.7 acres zoned C-1 for commercial use. Property listed with Coldwell Banker. Contact Mike Schiffer @505-242-9999.<br>**$755,000** | COMM. LAND |
| 2578/909321001 | Lot D, Blk 8, Enchanted Mesa Addition, Albuquerque, NM<br>6.864 sq. ft. of commercially zoned land. 139.94 x 50.06 x 134.3 site has visibility access. Parcel best suited for commercial/retail use.<br>**$37,000** | LAND |
| 2578/909323001 | 10405 Comanche N.E. Albuquerque, NM<br>Retail building consisting of approximately 2,600 sq. ft. on a 22,317 sq. ft. site. Building was converted to a child care center. (IN ESCROW)<br>**$121,000** | Commercial |
| 2578/909334001 | 105 General Arnold Way, Albuquerque, NM<br>4 plexe apartment building. 2 bedroom, 2 bath each unit. Listed w/Camco R.E./505-292-2021.<br>**$95,700** | |
| 2578/909335001 | 109 General Arnold Way, Albuquerque, NM<br>4 Plex apartment building, 2 bedroom,2 bath each unit. Listed w/Camco R.E./505-292-2021.<br>**$95,700** | |

This List is intended to provide interested parties with preliminary information only. FDIC makes no representations or warranties as to the accuracy or completeness of the information. FDIC reserves the right to withdraw any property from this List at any time and without notice. Prices are subject to change, and any offer to purchase an asset is subject to approval by the appropriate Credit Review Committee.

**FDIC REAL ESTATE DEPARTMENT**
**Toll Free Number: 1-800-388-4607**
**LISTING OF REO PROPERTIES**

**APRIL 1991**

**OREGON**
**BY CITY**

| Bank/Asset # | Address / Property Description |
|---|---|
| **ALBANY** | |
| 7554/000001001 | 631 Elm St., Albany, OR — 2 OFFICE CONDOS<br>2 medical office condominium units. Listed w/Jackson Cooper & Assoc./503-754-6320. **$157,500** |
| **BROOKS** | |
| 7554/000054001 | 6896 Waconda Rd, Brooks, OR (IN ESCROW) — SFR/10 ACRES<br>SFR on 10 acres, residential tract & part time farm. Split level w/attached 2 car gar., general purpose building 40'X 100', shop building 24'X40' & metal grain bin 24' in dia. 18' high, small stream crosses property. 3 level home, 6 bed, 2 bath, two 1/2 baths, 3,086 sq. ft. Listed w/ Coldwell Banker/Ross Rhoten/503-585-8050. **$160,000** |
| **CLACKAMAS COUNTY** | |
| 3468/005744001 | 1 mile N. of Colton, Tax lot 604, Map 4-3E, Sect. 33<br>24.06 acres, timberland w/possiblity of one SFR built w/ approval of management plan. **$39,700** |
| **CORVALLIS** | |
| 7525/000001001 | 815 NW Ninth St., Corvallis, OR — RETAIL<br>Avery Square - 76,768 sq. ft. retail center. Built in 1984. 25% occupied. Listed w/Jackson Cooper & Assoc. & Pac West Real Estate/503-574-6320 or 503-686-8246. **$2,300,000** |
| 7565/000006001 | NW Corner 9th and Garfield, Corvallis, OR — LAND<br>Ashcreek - 1.63 acres of partially improved land. Listed w/ Jackson Cooper & Assoc/503-754-6320 **$350,000** |

This List is intended to provide interested parties with preliminary information only. FDIC makes no representations or warranties as to the accuracy or completeness of the information. FDIC reserves the right to withdraw any property from this List at any time and without notice. Prices are subject to change, and any offer to purchase an asset is subject to approval by the appropriate Credit Review Committee.

**FDIC REAL ESTATE DEPARTMENT**
**Toll Free Number: 1-800-388-4607**
**LISTING OF REO PROPERTIES**

**APRIL 1991**

**TEXAS**

| Bank/Asset # | Address<br>Property Description |
|---|---|
| **AUSTIN** | |
| 7541/000024001 | 9811 Bee Cave Rd., Austin, TX LAND<br>Bee Caves - 4.59 acres of land, zoned limited office.<br>Listed w/REMAX/Tom Turner/912-794-9292. **$150,000** |
| **BEDFORD** | |
| 7553/000002001 | 380 Ft. North of Hwy 183, Bedford, TX LAND<br>Approx. 6 acres near Hwy 183. Zoned light & heavy com'l.<br>Listed w/Lee Schmitt/214-987-9167. **$154,000** |
| **CORPUS CHRISTI** | |
| 7578/000015001 | 853 Quetzal St., Corpus Christi, TX APTS<br>4 unit apartment complex. Listed w/REMAX/David Wallace/<br>512-994-1089 **$53,900** |
| 7578/000016001 | 857 Quetzal St., Corpus Christi, TX APTS<br>4 unit apartment complex. Listed w/REMAX/David Wallace/<br>512-994-1089 **$53,900** |
| 7578/000090001 | 849 Quetzal St., Corpus Christi, TX APTS.<br>4 unit apartment complex. Listed w/REMAX/David Wallace/<br>512-994-1089 **$54,900** |
| 7578/000096001 | 909 Quetzal St., Corpus Chrisit, TX APTS<br>4 unit apartment complex. Listed w/REMAX/David Wallace/<br>512-994-1089 **$50,000** |

This List is intended to provide interested parties with preliminary information only. FDIC makes no representations or warranties as to the accuracy or completeness of the information. FDIC reserves the right to withdraw any property from this List at any time and without notice. Prices are subject to change, and any offer to purchase an asset is subject to approval by the appropriate Credit Review Committee.

**FDIC Real Estate Department**
**Toll Free: 1-800-388-4607**
**LISTING OF REO PROPERTIES**

**APRIL 1991**

**UTAH**
**BY CITY**

| Bank/Asset # | Address<br>Property Description | Type Property |
|---|---|---|
| **BOUNTIFUL** | | |
| 3950/100086011 | South of Canyon Creek Dr.<br>25 acres zoned R-1. AP#01-017-0011 | LAND<br>**$85,000** |
| 3950/100016011 | 1270 Canyon Creek Dr., Bountiful, UT<br>1.74 acres vacant land. AP#01-017-0019. | LAND<br>**$15,000** |
| **BRIANHEAD** | | |
| 3950/100009011 | North Loop Rd., Brianhead, UT (IN ESCROW)<br>Part of Sec. 2, - .92 Acre of land.<br>AP# A-1150-0011. Listed w/Coldwell Banker/Sue Southwick/<br>801-586-9411. | VACANT LAND<br>**$19,000** |
| **CLINTON** | | |
| 7516/000070001 | 1268 West 1750 North, Clinton, UT IN ESCROW<br>4 bedroom, 2 bath, 1801 sq. ft. SFR. 2 car garage, forced air heat, swamp cooler, fireplace, thermo windows. 12 yrs. old. | SFR<br>**$81,000** |
| **DRAPER** | | |
| 3950/100022011 | 263 West 14700 South, Draper, -Equestrian Center<br>This is a 79-stall horsebarn situated on 2+ acres of land.<br>Listed w/Craig Boyer/801-776-4134. | LAND & BARN<br>**$209,900** |

This List is intended to provide interested parties with preliminary information only. FDIC makes no representations or warranties as to the accuracy or completeness of the information. FDIC reserves the right to withdraw any property from this List at any time and without notice. Prices are subject to change, and any offer to purchase an asset is subject to approval by the appropriate Credit Review Committee.

**FDIC REAL ESTATE DEPARTMENT**
**Toll Free Number: 1-800-388-4607**
**LISTING OF REO PROPERTIES**

**APRIL 1991**

**WASHINGTON**
**BY CITY**

| Bank/Asset # | Address<br>Property Description | |
|---|---|---|
| **BREWSTER** | | |
| 3468/005014001 | Apple Valley Bargain Barn, Brewster, WA<br>6,750 sq. ft. of com'l bldg. on 10 acres of land. Building has 2 story front portion housing offices & retail space, while the back is an open shop area. Listed w/Town & Country/ Jim Asmussen/509-826-4725. | COML BLDG.<br>**$123,000** |
| **LONGVIEW** | | |
| 7565/000016001 | Columbia Heights Rd.<br>20.51 acres residential land. | LAND<br>**$675,000** |
| **OKANAGON** | | |
| 3468/005017001 | 1617 2nd NE., Okanagon, WA.<br>Comm. Bldg. Leased to 1 comm. tenants/gross $400 mo. Listed w/C-21/Norma Shrove/509-826-2011 | COM'L BLDG.<br>**$102,500** |
| 3468/004959011 | 2080 Elmway, Okanogan, WA<br>Lot is 1.1 acre corner on Elmway (U.S. 101) and John St., formerly a mobile home sales lot. | LOT<br>**$39,000** |
| **OLYMPIA** | | |
| 7565/000037001 | 1818 Evergreen Park Dr., Olympia, WA<br>Five detached 3 story buildings. 72/1 bedroom. 21 studios 16/2 bedroom. 2/3bedroom. 12/4 bedroom units, built 1972. 77,787 Sq.Ft., 3.06 acres. Proj: $451,820 EGI, $205,870 NDI. | APARTMENTS<br>**$2,200,000** |

This List is intended to provide interested parties with preliminary information only. FDIC makes no representations or warranties as to the accuracy or completeness of the information. FDIC reserves the right to withdraw any property from this List at any time and without notice. Prices are subject to change, and any offer to purchase an asset is subject to approval by the appropriate Credit Review Committee.

Real Estate Department
Toll Free: 1-800-388-4607

LISTING OF REO PROPERTIES

APRIL 1991
WYOMING

| Bank/Asset # | Address<br>Property Description | | |
|---|---|---|---|
| **EVANSTON** | | | |
| 3950/100072011 | Aspen Grove Townhouses, Evanston, WY.<br>4 acres of raw land. Zoned com'l. All utilities available to site. | 4 ACRES | **$6,600** |

This List is intended to provide interested parties with preliminary information only. FDIC makes no representations or warranties as to the accuracy or completeness of the information. FDIC reserves the right to withdraw any property from this List at any time and without notice. Prices are subject to change, and any offer to purchase an asset is subject to approval by the appropriate Credit Review Committee.

**Date:** April 30, 1991

**Federal Deposit Insurance Corporation**
**P.O. Box 7549**
**Newport Beach, CA 92658-7549**

**ATTN: Real Estate Marketing**

**If you wish to continue receiving the marketing packet and for any changes in mailing address, please complete the information requested below.**

**PLEASE PRINT CLEARLY TO GUARANTEE MAILING**

**( ) Check here if change of address**

**NAME** Ted Thomas

**FIRM** NEW GROWTH FINANCIAL

**ADDRESS** P. O. Box 5000 #412

**CITY** Danville, CA 94526

**TELEPHONE #** (415) 837-2106

**If we can be further assistance, feel free to contact the Marketing Department at (800) 388-4607.**

**Thank you for your interest.**

# FEDERAL DEPOSIT INSURANCE CORPORATION CONSOLIDATED OFFICE PHONE NUMBERS

## DALLAS REGION

Oklahoma and Texas.

| | |
|---|---|
| Oklahoma City, OK, Consolidated Office | (405) 842-7441 |
| Midland, TX, Consolidated Office | (915) 685-6909 |
| Addison, TX, Consolidated Office | (214) 239-3317 |
| Houston, TX, Consolidated Office | (713) 270-6565 |
| San Antonio, TX, Consolidated Office | (512) 737-3100 |
| Dallas, TX, Consolidated Office | (214) 701-2402 |

## CHICAGO REGION

Arkansas, Illinois, Iowa, Kansas, Louisiana, Minnesota, Missouri, Nebraska, North Dakota, South Dakota, and Wisconsin.

| | |
|---|---|
| O'Hare, IL, Consolidated Office | (708) 671-8800 |
| Bossier City, LA, Consolidated Office | (318) 742-3290 |

## NEW YORK REGION

Alabama, Connecticut, Delaware, District of Columbia, Florida, Georgia, Indiana, Kentucky, Maine, Maryland, Massachusetts, Michigan, Mississippi, North Carolina, New Hampshire, New Jersey, New York, Ohio, Pennsylvania, Puerto Rico, Rhode Island, South Carolina, Tennessee, Vermont, Virginia, West Virginia and the Virgin Islands.

| | |
|---|---|
| Knoxville, TN, Consolidated Office | (615) 544-4500 |
| Orlando, FL, Consolidated Office | (407) 273-2230 |
| South Brunswick, NJ, Consolidated Office | (201) 422-9000 |
| Atlanta, GA, Consolidated Office | (404) 880-3120 |

## SAN FRANCISCO REGION

Alaska, Arizona, California, Colorado, Guam, Hawaii, Idaho, Montana, Nevada, New Mexico, Oregon, Utah, Washington and Wyoming.

| | |
|---|---|
| Irvine, CA, Consolidated Office | (714) 975-3200 |
| Denver, CO, Consolidated Office | (303) 296-4703 |
| Anchorage, AK, Consolidated Office | (907) 786-6362 |

Financial Services of America

Call Toll Free 1-800-736-5263

| LISTING | ADDRESS | CITY | STATE | PRICE | LENDER | CONTACT | PHONE | COMMENTS | DATE |
|---|---|---|---|---|---|---|---|---|---|
| 9585712 | 3700 NORTH MAIN STREET #7 | FALL RIVER | MA | 48500 | CROSSLAND SAVINGS | C21-HQ | 800 321-2579 | CONDO | 01/18/91 |
| 9585605 | 3700 NORTH MAIN STREET #9 | FALL RIVER | MA | 51500 | CROSSLAND SAVINGS | C21-HQ | 800 321-2579 | CONDO | 01/18/91 |
| | 4800 WESTHAVEN | FORT WORTH | TX | N/A | CROSSLAND SAVINGS | JAY JENKINS | 817 625-9974 | SFR | 10/30/90 |
| 9381419 | 536 GLEN EAGLE DRIVE WEST | FRIENDWOOD | TX | 83000 | CROSSLAND SAVINGS | PAT SHOLLAR | 800 392-4497 | SFR | 01/28/91 |
| 7204 | 3300 BL & HWY 441 | GAINESVILLE | FL | 290000 | CROSSLAND SAVINGS | GARY JOHNSON | 813 745-3482 | SFR | 10/30/90 |
| 8539678 | 3905 SW 26TH TERRACE | GAINESVILLE | FL | N/A | CROSSLAND SAVINGS | LEE HORNE | 801 321-7912 | 4-PLEX | 03/12/91 |
| 6512 | 3915 SW 26TH TERRACE | GAINESVILLE | FL | N/A | CROSSLAND SAVINGS | LEE HORNE | 801 321-7912 | SFA | 03/12/91 |
| 8538720 | 7717 SW 95TH LANE | GAINESVILLE | FL | 60000 | CROSSLAND SAVINGS | GARY JOHNSON | 904 373-4279 | SFR | 03/12/91 |
| | NW 23RD TERRACE & NW 62ND | GAINESVILLE | FL | 100000 | CROSSLAND SAVINGS | GARY JOHNSON | 813 745-3482 | SFR | 10/30/90 |
| | US 441 & NW 23RD TERRACE | GAINESVILLE | FL | 80000 | CROSSLAND SAVINGS | GARY JOHNSON | 813 745-3482 | SFR | 10/30/90 |
| 6924 | WEST RIVER SALES | GALESVILLE | MD | N/A | CROSSLAND SAVINGS | LEE HORNE | 801 321-7912 | SLIPS | 03/12/91 |
| | 5114 SHOREGATE | GARLAND | TX | N/A | CROSSLAND SAVINGS | REO DEPT | 813 745-3482 | SFR | 10/30/90 |
| | 5417 WES PARADISE LANE | GLENDALE | AZ | 110000 | CROSSLAND SAVINGS | DON LEWIS | 801 350-9601 | SFR | 01/14/91 |
| 6294 | 522 AVENUE "J" EAST | GRAND PRAIRIE | TX | 24000 | CROSSLAND SAVINGS | LETA HOWELL | 212 262-1800 | CONDO | 01/28/91 |
| 0190199 | 3 DOHNE COURT | GREENLAWN | NY | N/A | CROSSLAND SAVINGS | DOREEN HOLY | 800 638-7669 | SFA | 03/12/91 |
| | S-132 MARIMERS INN | HILTON HEAD | SC | N/A | CROSSLAND SAVINGS | TOM RHOADS | 803 785-8811 | SF | 10/30/90 |
| | 3801 EAST BAY DR #104 | HOLMES BEACH | FL | 75900 | CROSSLAND SAVINGS | RICHARD KESTIN | 813 747-2045 | CONDO | 10/30/90 |
| 8432031 | 11503 SURBURBAN DRIVE | HOUSTON | TX | 11000 | CROSSLAND SAVINGS | ERA BELTWAY PROPERTI | 713 495-1300 | DUPLEX | 01/28/91 |
| 6393 | 401 BRIARCLIFF | HOUSTON | TX | N/A | CROSSLAND SAVINGS | BARBARA DAMIEO | 713 890-7777 | SFD | 01/28/91 |
| 0211292 | 1304 GULF BOULEVARD #302 | INDIAN ROCKS | FL | N/A | CROSSLAND SAVINGS | LEE HORNE | 801 321-7912 | | 03/12/91 |
| 0193854 | 20019 GULF BLVD #1 | INDIAN SHORES | FL | 98500 | CROSSLAND SAVINGS | JOHN SEE | 813 596-8181 | CONDO | 10/30/90 |
| 6253 | 4262 CUESTA | IRVING | TX | 41900 | CROSSLAND SAVINGS | SHIRLEY WALKER | 214 258-8001 | SFA | 01/28/91 |
| 1178339 | 658 WINDCREST | KELLER | TX | N/A | CROSSLAND SAVINGS | LEE HORNE | 801 321-7912 | | 01/28/91 |
| | 318 SPRING BRANCH LANE | KENNEDALE | TX | 29000 | CROSSLAND SAVINGS | PAUL KRANTZ | 813 745-3482 | SFR | 10/30/90 |
| 0342618 | 2804 CORNELL COVE | LAGO VISTA | TX | N/A | CROSSLAND SAVINGS | DON LEWIS | 801 350-9601 | | 03/12/91 |
| 0176693 | 12760 INDIAN ROCKS 1105 | LARGO | FL | N/A | CROSSLAND SAVINGS | LEE HORNE | 801 321-7912 | | 03/12/91 |
| 1117910 | 9255 MOHAWK STREET | LAS VEGAS | NV | N/A | CROSSLAND SAVINGS | DON LEWIS | 801 350-9601 | | 01/28/91 |
| 0354746 | 6 VIA SPES NOSTRA | LEE CANYON | NV | 185000 | CROSSLAND SAVINGS | DON LEWIS | 801 350-9601 | | 01/28/91 |
| 8900004 | 627 EAST 111TH PLACE | LOS ANGELES | CA | N/A | CROSSLAND SAVINGS | CARMEN TORRES | 213 585-1744 | | 03/12/91 |
| 6952 | 6952 BEAVERLETT | MATHEW | VA | N/A | CROSSLAND SAVINGS | LEE HORNE | 801 321-7912 | LAND | 01/28/91 |
| | 8350 GREENBORO DR #1-312 | MCLEAN | VA | 220000 | CROSSLAND SAVINGS | EVA TSOMOANAS | 703 971-3315 | MULTI | 10/30/90 |
| 1256419 | 148 SOUTH 54TH STREET | MESA | AZ | N/A | CROSSLAND SAVINGS | LEE HORNE | 801 321-7912 | | 03/12/91 |
| 1259219 | 160 SOUTH 54TH STREET | MESA | AZ | N/A | CROSSLAND SAVINGS | LEE HORNE | 801 321-7912 | | 03/12/91 |
| 1259209 | 202 SOUTH 54TH STREET | MESA | AZ | N/A | CROSSLAND SAVINGS | LEE HORNE | 801 321-7912 | | 03/12/91 |
| 0001693 | 3029 EAST CICERO STREET | MESA | AZ | N/A | CROSSLAND SAVINGS | DON LEWIS | 801 350-9601 | | 03/12/91 |
| 8305831 | 3817 EAST MINTON PLACE | MESA | AZ | N/A | CROSSLAND SAVINGS | DON LEWIS | 801 350-9601 | | 03/12/91 |
| 1256409 | 5346 EAST ARBOR CIRCLE | MESA | AZ | N/A | CROSSLAND SAVINGS | LEE HORNE | 801 321-7912 | | 03/12/91 |
| | 623 W GUADALUPE #228 | MESA | AZ | N/A | CROSSLAND SAVINGS | BARB LOFITS | 602-263-9696 | CONDO | 10/30/90 |
| 3173980 | 2437 RED RIVER STREET | MESQUITE | TX | N/A | CROSSLAND SAVINGS | ROBIN WILLIAMS | 214 270-4411 | | 01/28/91 |
| 0628016 | 129 WEST 86TH STREET #1 | NEW YORK | NY | N/A | CROSSLAND SAVINGS | JAMES ROMAN | 212 475-4200 | | 01/28/91 |
| 0621359 | 140 WEST 69TH STREET | NEW YORK | NY | 125000 | CROSSLAND SAVINGS | SHEILA VOGEL | 212 744-3516 | CO-OP | 01/28/91 |
| 0622753 | 167 PERRY STREET #2G | NEW YORK | NY | N/A | CROSSLAND SAVINGS | DON LEWIS | 801 350-9601 | | 01/28/91 |
| 0732438 | 77 BLEEKER STREET #104N | NEW YORK | NY | N/A | CROSSLAND SAVINGS | JAMES DOMAN | 212 475-4200 | | 01/28/91 |
| | 77 BLEEKER STREET #726 | NEW YORK | NY | N/A | CROSSLAND SAVINGS | REO DEPT | 813 745-3482 | CONDO | 10/30/90 |
| 2341611 | 10457 BIRKENHEAD ROAD | OKLAHOMA CITY | OK | N/A | CROSSLAND SAVINGS | MARILYN PYROR | 800 558-2211 | | 01/28/91 |
| | 60 DAVIS CUP DRIVE #104 | PAGOSA SPRINGS | CO | 35000 | CROSSLAND SAVINGS | MARIETTA ARENDEL | 813 758-1156 | CONDO | 10/30/90 |
| | LONE PINE #106 | PAGOSA SPRINGS | CO | 49900 | CROSSLAND SAVINGS | RANDY FEHRENBACHER | 303 731-2262 | CONDO | 10/30/90 |
| | LONE PINE #107B | PAGOSA SPRINGS | CO | 35000 | CROSSLAND SAVINGS | RANDY FEHRENBACHER | 303 731-2262 | CONDO | 10/30/90 |
| | LONE PINE #108 | PAGOSA SPRINGS | CO | 49000 | CROSSLAND SAVINGS | RANDY FEHRENBACHER | 303 731-2262 | CONDO | 10/30/90 |
| | LONE PINE #109B | PAGOSA SPRINGS | CO | 49900 | CROSSLAND SAVINGS | RANDY FEHRENBACHER | 303 731-2262 | CONDO | 10/30/90 |
| 5044408 | 48 PRICE STREET | PATCHOGUE | NY | N/A | CROSSLAND SAVINGS | DON LEWIS | 801 350-9601 | | 01/28/91 |
| 1085281 | 1449 EAST BASELINE ROAD | PHOENIX | AZ | N/A | CROSSLAND SAVINGS | STEVE WILKINS | 602 831-1010 | RSDTL | 01/14/91 |
| | 2141 EAST RANCHO DRIVE | PHOENIX | AZ | 270000 | CROSSLAND SAVINGS | BOB WHITE | 602 953-4000 | SFR | 10/30/90 |
| 3015519 | 1613 GLENWICK DRIVE | PLANO | TX | N/A | CROSSLAND SAVINGS | TOM VOOSEN | 214 248-3409 | | 01/28/91 |

The

# Real Estate Exchange Reporter

*Staying on Top of the Commercial Real Estate and REO Market*

**Editor: Terry Struthers**
**736 7th Street Boulder, Colorado 80302**

**Published by DataSource RE, Inc.**
**Phone: (303) 444-9194 FAX: (303) 447-2520**

February 27, 1991

Dear Ted,

DataSource RE, Inc. maintains a list of over 40,000 investment foreclosed properties nationwide. This includes about 20,000 Resolution Trust Corporation properties. The other 20,000 comes from approximately 4,000 financial institutions across the US.

We track all real estate with the exception of individual single family residences. Over 1/4 of the properties are in the state of Texas. The other states with large REO inventories are Florida, Louisiana, Oklahoma, Colorado and Arizona. The fastest growing lists are the states in the northeast. The midwest has weathered the current real estate storm the best.

The average price of a property on our database is about $1,000,000. There many apartments from 2 units to 600 units, office buildings, retail centers, land and many other bargains out there.

We believe that with the current real estate situation, land is a long term and riskier investment. On the other end of the safety spectrum are large apartment structures. These tend to lead a market out of a slump. The danger is getting in too late. That time has passed for many markets that were in the heart of the REO belt of the late 1980's.

Our newsletter tracks these trends in the foreclosed real estate inventory across the country. We sort through the data geographically and by property type and summarize what is happening with prices, sales, inventory level and make-up of the inventory. In addition we track the government institutions which control foreclosed real estate such as the Resolution Trust Corporation (RTC), FDIC, Freddie Mac, SBA, etc.

Currently, the government is in control of much of the investment real estate. I'm afraid the report card so far on the ability of these institutions (especially the RTC) to sell real estate is not too encouraging. A survey of our subscribers found that most were frustrated with their attempts to purchase properties. In fact, a vast majority said they would never go back to the RTC to purchase properties again. The rate of sales reflects this attitude. A study we did found that RTC properties were selling at 1/3 the rate of other foreclosed commercial real estate.

The good news is that there is value in the properties held by Uncle Sam and, with some persistence and the willingness to learn the government's new rules of the game, buyers can get to those properties. We have spoken to several investors who have said they have been successful in purchasing multiple properties once they have the system figured out. Another sign of hope is the announcement by the RTC that they plan to put much of the sales effort back into the public sector.

In any case, whether the property is in government hands or from banks, life insurance companies, savings and loans, or where ever, we are the nations most complete source of REO properties. I would remind you that we do not cover individual single family homes, townhome/condos or lots. Our focus is the investor market.

The following page exhibits how we display our information in the printed version and what data is included in the floppy diskette database for each property.

Sincerely,

Terry Struthers, President

# Real Estate Exchange Database by DataSource RE, Inc.

## TREND WATCH

**Inventory Analysis**
The numbers in () are results from 3 months ago.

### ALASKA
**Total # of Properties- 361**
REO-354 RTC-7
**Value of Priced Properties - $41.3 Million**
(226 properties averaging $182 thousand/ppty)
**Top 3 categories**
1) Commercial buildings - $13.6 Million
2) Bulk Residential Land - $8.2 Million
3) Commercial Land - $3.4 Million
**Top Cities/Metro Areas**
Anchorage - $25.1 Million
**Largest Non-RTC Properties**
$2.5 million - 36,468 sq. ft. commercial bldg in Anchorage
$2.1 million - 36,351 sq. ft. retail bldg. in Anchorage

### ARIZONA
**Total # of Properties - 1,281 (1,257)**
REO-445 RTC-836
**Value of Priced Properties - $1.42 Billion ($1.36 Bill.)**
(1,054 properties averaging $1.35 Million/ppty)
**Top 3 categories**
1) Bulk Residential Land - $350.9 Million (1)
2) Commercial Land - $304.2 Million (2)
3) Apartments - $165.0 Million (3)
**Top Cities/Metro Areas**
Phoenix - $1.2 Billion ($1.0 Bill.)
Tucson - $131.6 Million ($255.0 Mill.)
**Largest Non-RTC Properties**
$27.0 Million - 47,558 sq. ft. office bldg in Phoenix (New)
$22.4 Million - 1,427 acres of residential land in Scottsdale
$17.0 Million - 256,043 sq. ft. retail bldg. in Phoenix (New)

### CALIFORNIA
**Total # of Properties - 633 (623)**
REO-131 RTC-502
**Value of Priced Properties - $604.0 Million ($518.1 Mill.)**
(368 properties averaging $1.64 Million/ppty)
**Top 3 categories**
1) Office Bldgs - $126.7 Million (1)
2) Apartment Bldgs - $57.2 Million (-)
3) Retail Bldgs - $47.4 Million (-)
**Top Cities/Metro Areas**
Los Angeles Metro - $232.3 Million ($220.0 Mill.)
Bay Area - $88.0 Million ($60.0 Mill.)
**Largest Non-RTC Properties**
$25.0 Million - 331,000 sq. ft. office bldg in San Mateo
$24.9 Million - 85,749 sq. ft. Mixed commercial in San Francisco
$17.5 Million - 146,044 sq. ft. office bldg in Santa Ana

### COLORADO
**Total # of Properties - 1,783 (1,747)**
REO-1,125 RTC-658
**Value of Priced Properties - $1.07 Billion ($1.04 Bill.)**
(1,283 properties averaging $834 thousand/ppty)
**Top 3 categories**
1) Commercial Land - $181.1 Million (1)
2) Office Bldgs - $162.3 Million (3)
3) Apartment Bldgs - $143.8 Million (-)
**Top Cities/Metro Areas**
Denver Metro-$582.9 Million ($551.9 Mill.)
Colorado Springs - $251.8 Million ($144.1 Mill.)
**Largest Non-RTC Properties**
$15.0 Million - 864 acres of residential land in Colo. Springs
$15.0 Million - 124,551 sq. ft. office bldg. in Denver
$15.0 Million - 318 unit Apartment bldg in Westminster

### FLORIDA
**Total # of Properties - 1,785**
REO-983 RTC-802
**Value of Priced Properties - $1.42 Billion ($1.14 Bill.)**
(1,362 properties averaging $1.04 Million/ppty)
**Top 3 categories**
1) Retail Bldgs - $277.9 Million (2)
2) Apartment Bldgs - $216.3 Million (1)
3) Residential land - $174.1 Million (-)
**Top Cities/Metro Areas**
Miami Metro-$310.1 Million ($166.0 Mill.)
Tampa/St. Pete - $248.1 Million ($176.3 Mill.)
**Largest Non-RTC Properties**
$16.5 Million - 600 unit apartment bldg. in Orlando
$16.5 Million - 449 unit Condos in Miami (Price Drop)
$16.0 Million - 23,959 sq. ft. retail bldg in Miami area

### HAWAII
**Total # of Properties - 1**
REO-1 RTC-0
$2.5 million for 6.8 acres of commercial land in Kailua Kona

### IDAHO
**Total # of Properties - 34**
REO-31 RTC-3
**Value of Priced Properties - $12.3 Million**
(28 properties averaging $439 thousand/ppty)
**Top categories**
1) Commercial land - $8.6 Million
**Largest Non-RTC Properties**
$6.0 Million - 3.17 acres commercial land in Coeur d' Alene

### LOUISIANA
**Total # of Properties - 2,660 (2,561)**
REO-1,387 RTC-1,273
**Value of Priced Properties - $406.4 Million ($379.0 Mill.)**
(1,362 properties averaging $178 thousand/ppty)
**Top 3 categories**
1) Apartment bldgs - $103.0 Million (1)
2) Residential land - $50.0 Million (2)
3) Office bldgs - $42.7 Million (3)
**Top Cities/Metro Areas**
New Orleans Metro-$173.2 Million ($167.2 Mill.)
Baton Rouge - $78.2 Million ($62.6 Mill.)
**Largest Non-RTC Properties**
$6.8 Million - 528 unit apartment bldg. in New Orleans
$4.66 Million - 196 unit Hotel in New Orleans area (New)
$3.9 Million - 304 unit apartment bldg in New Orleans

Please call us at 1-800-477-9194 or 303-444-9194 if you have further questions.

## MONTANA
Total # of Properties - 26
REO-23 RTC-3

## NEW MEXICO
**Total # of Properties - 280 (275)**
REO-93 RTC-187
**Value of Priced Properties - $165.3 Million ($156.4 Mill.)**
(238 properties averaging $695 thousand/ppty)
**Top 3 categories**
1) Residential land - $38.0 Million (1)
2) Office bldgs - $37.0 Million (2)
3) Apartment bldgs - $38.8 Million (3)
**Top Cities/Metro Areas**
Albuquerque - $113.5 Million ($104.3 Mill.)
**Largest Non-RTC Properties**
$9.3 Million - 158,782 sq. ft. retail bldg in Albuquerque
$7.0 Million - 40,000 sq. ft. office bldg in Santa Fe
$6.9 Million - 200 unit apartment bldg in Albuquerque

## NEVADA
**Total # of Properties - 92 (92)**
REO-43 RTC-49
**Value of Priced Properties - $83.6 Million ($74.9 Mill.)**
(62 properties averaging $1.34 Million/ppty)
**Top 3 categories**
1) Apartment bldgs - $30.2 Million (1)
2) Retail bldgs - $13.2 Million (2)
3) Twmhm/Condo bldgs - $5.4 Million (-)
**Top Cities/Metro Areas**
Las Vegas - $49.0 Million ($37.5 Mill.)
Reno - $15.9 Million ($15.5 Mill.)
**Largest Non-RTC Properties**
$9.8 Million - 316 unit apartment bldg in Las Vegas
$6.9 Million - 230 unit apartment bldg in Sparks

## OKLAHOMA
**Total # of Properties - 1,052 (919)**
REO-559 RTC-493
**Value of Priced Properties - $232.6 Million ($226.3 Mill.)**
(917 properties averaging $247 thousand/ppty)
**Top 3 categories**
1) Commercial land - $43.2 Million (2)
2) Apartment bldgs - $35.2 Million (3)
3) Office bldgs - $27.0 Million (-)
**Top Cities/Metro Areas**
Oklahoma City - $82.7 Million ($70.1 Mill.)
Tulsa - $63.0 Million ($85.4 Mill.)
**Largest Non-RTC Properties**
$8.0 Million - 67.3 acres of commercial land in Tulsa
$7.8 Million - 352 unit apartment bldg in Tulsa

## OREGON
**Total # of Properties - 101**
REO-61 RTC-40
**Value of Priced Properties - $18.7 Million**
(47 properties averaging $398 thousand/ppty)
**Top 3 categories**
1) Residential land - $5.9 Million
2) Office bldgs - $3.4 Million
3) Industrial land - $1.6 Million
**Top Cities/Metro Areas**
Portland - $5.4 Million
**Largest Non-RTC Properties**
$1.6 Million - 47.1 acres of industrial land in Portland
$1.5 Million - 352 unit nursing home in Portland

## TEXAS
**Total # of Properties - 10,510 (9,584)**
REO-5,096 RTC-5,414
**Value of Priced Properties - $7.1 Billion ($6.7 Bill.)**
(7,340 properties averaging $967 thousand/ppty)
**Top 3 categories**
1) Commercial land - $1.46 Billion (1)
2) Apartment blgs - $1.34 Billion (2)
3) Office bldgs - $1.04 Billion (3)
**Top Cities/Metro Areas**
Dallas/Ft. Worth - $2.28 Billion ($2.12 Bill.)
Houston - $1.12 Billion ($1.13 Bill.)
San Antonio - $.74 Billion ($.72 Bill.)
Austin - $.72 Billion ($.72 Bill.)
**Largest Non-RTC Properties**
$55.6 Million - 1.4 million sq. ft. of office space in Dallas
$40.0 Million - 321,488 sq. ft. office in Addison
$35.0 Million - 1,285 acres of commercial land in Carrollton

## UTAH
**Total # of Properties - 605**
REO-305 RTC-300
**Value of Priced Properties - $117.6 Million**
(374 properties averaging $314 thousand/ppty)
**Top 3 categories**
1) Commercial land - $21.6 Million
2) Residential land - $21.6 Million
3) Resort land - $15.0 Million
**Top Cities/Metro Areas**
Salt Lake City - $27.8 Million
**Largest Non-RTC Properties**
$15.0 Million - resort land Park City
$6.4 Million - 5,306 acres agricultural land in Summit County

# COUNTY OF SACRAMENTO
## TREASURER-TAX COLLECTOR
## COUNTY CLERK-RECORDER

John Dark
TREASURER-TAX COLLECTOR
COUNTY CLERK-RECORDER

George L. Thacher
ASSISTANT TREASURER
Willie H. Ross
ASSISTANT TAX COLLECTOR
Craig A. Kramer
ASSISTANT COUNTY CLERK-RECORDER
Christopher J. Ailman
CHIEF INVESTMENT OFFICER

January 30, 1991

New Growth Financial
P.O. Box 5000, #412
Danville, CA 94526

Dear Mr. Thomas:

In response to your inquiry, property in Sacramento County that have five or more years delinquent taxes are offered for sale at public auction in January of each year. Bids are accepted verbally and the opening bid is not less than twenty five percent of the fair market value of the property. Payment for property purchased at the sale must be made in full immediately after the sale in the form of cash, cashier's check, money order or traveler's check.

A list of properties subject to sale and other information pertaining to the current sale is available in this office the first week of November each year. No mailing list is maintained for request of this information. The first week in January a copy of the final publication of tax-defaulted properties subject to sale at public auction are mailed to parties who have inquired about the auction and live outside the County of Sacramento. I have enclosed a general information sheet for your information.

If you have further questions about the Sacramento County tax-defaulted land auction, please contact the deputy listed below at the letterhead address or phone (961) 440-6621.

Very truly yours,

WILLIE H. ROSS
Assistant Tax Collector

BY: Ellen Tubbs
Deputy

700 H Street, Room 1710 Post Office Box 1703 Sacramento, CA 95812-1703 (916) 440-6744

## IMPORTANT INFORMATION ON REAL PROPERTY

## SOLD AT PUBLIC AUCTION

### INSPECTION OF PROPERTY

**CAUTION - INVESTIGATE BEFORE YOU BID - PHYSICAL INSPECTION OF THE PROPERTY IS STRONGLY RECOMMENDED.** Do not attempt to purchase property at the auction unless an investigation has been made as to the exact location, desirability, and usefulness of the property. Parcels are sold on an 'AS IS' basis and the County in no way assumes any responsibility implied or otherwise, that the properties are in compliance with zoning ordinances and conform to building codes and permits. An investigation may reveal that the property is in a street or alley, in a flood control channel or landlocked. The structure that may be shown on the tax sale list may no longer exist at the time of the auction and a lien may have been or will be placed on the property for the removal of the structure. Regardless of its recorded description, the size, shape, or other characteristics may render the property useless.

Should a parcel have a mobile home, the sale is for the real property only and does not include the mobile home. Mobile homes are considered personal property, unless they are on a permanent foundation.

Vacant (unimproved) land (which accounts for most property offered at our tax sale) may not have an address, therefore, the approximate geographic location can be determined through the use of the County Assessor's Plat Maps. Exact boundary lines of property can only be determined by a survey of the property, initiated at the purchaser's expense. Parcel maps are available for inspection and/or purchase prior to the tax sale in the Assessor's Office, 700 "H" Street, Room 1650, Sacramento, CA 95814.

To determine what use can be made of the property, consult the Zoning Department of the City if the parcel is located within the city limits or Zoning Information for the County Planning Department if the parcel is located in the unincorporated areas of the County. The County Recorder's Office records may show information regarding recorded easements on a property.

### BIDDING PROCESS

**Anyone who wishes to bid on property offered for sale MUST FIRST REGISTER AND BE ASSIGNED A BID CARD before the auction begins.** Please return the bid card to the registration table when leaving the sale.

The property will be offered in item number order. All sales are final and must be paid for immediately, unless the successful bidder wishes to continue bidding for other properties. **Should the successful bidder make a mistake and bid on the wrong property, the sale will remain final.**

No bid will be accepted for less than the minimum price as defined by Revenue and Taxation Code Section 3698.5. State law dictates that the minimum bid for a public auction tax sale parcel shall be no less than 25% of the County Assessor's fair market value, as determined within one year prior to the date of the tax sale. However, a minimum bid for a parcel can be set at a greater amount to ensure collection of the amount of delinquent taxes, penalties and costs thereon.

This is an oral public auction requiring verbal bids on the properties. Bidding will be in increments of $100.00 until the parcel is sold to the highest bidder. Higher increments are acceptable should the bidders wish to expedite the sale.

A purchase agreement is required to be signed by the successful bidder following the sale of each item offered. Payment in full of the amount bid, plus documentary stamp tax prescribed by County ordinance, is required to be paid at the time of the sale. **All sales will be for cash in lawful money of the United States, certified check, cashier's check, or travelers check.** No credit transactions are accepted. **PERSONAL CHECKS WILL NOT BE ACCEPTED.** All checks should be made payable to the purchaser and endorsed over to the Sacramento County Treasurer-Tax Collector in payment of a successful purchase. This will allow the purchaser to negotiate those checks not used. **Bidders should have proper funds on hand at the time the sale begins. No opportunity will be given for any successful bidder to leave the sale and go to the bank.** No cash refunds, other than for cash payments, will be made at the time of sale. All refunds for payments made by certified funds will be issued by County warrant within sixty (60) days following the date of sale.

Any property for which no bid is received at the time it is first offered, will be reoffered at the end of the sale.

## TAX DEED

All successful bidders must complete a deed information sheet for each parcel. Since the information you provide on the deed information sheet is used to complete the recorded tax deed, it is of the utmost importance that it is correct and complete. Receipts of payment showing all deeding information will be mailed to the purchaser within seven days after the sale. These receipts should be checked carefully for any errors in deeding information so that the purchaser may notify the Treasurer-Tax Collector of corrections before the recording of the tax deeds. Approximately four weeks after the date of purchase, a tax deed will be recorded by the Treasurer-Tax Collector. After recordation, the deeds will be returned to the respective purchasers by the County Recorder. **Should title to the property you purchased be recorded incorrectly due to your failure to provide the correct information, IT WILL BE YOUR RESPONSIBILITY TO CORRECT THE TITLE.**

Example of styles of vesting:

John Doe and Mary Doe, husband and wife as joint tenants
John Doe and Mary Doe, husband and wife as community property
Mary Doe, a married woman, as her sole and separate property
John Doe, a single man, as his sole and separate property
John Doe, a single man, as to a 1/2 undivided interest and
Mary Doe, a single woman, as to a 1/2 undivided interest

## TITLE INSURANCE

Title companies **MAY NOT** issue their policy of title insurance on a notice of power to sell tax-defaulted property for one year, **unless** a quiet title action has been successfully pursued in the courts, or in lieu thereof, quit claim deeds are acquired from the former owner and every lien holder.

## INCUMBRANCES

Pursuant to Section 3712 of the Revenue and Taxation Code, tax deeds convey title to the purchaser free of all prior incumbrances of any kind **EXCEPT:**

A) Any lien for installments of special assessments, which installments will become payable upon the secured roll after the time of sale.

B) The lien for taxes or assessments or other rights of any taxing agency which does not consent to the sale under this chapter.

C) Liens for special assessments levied upon the property conveyed which were, at the time of the sale under this chapter, not included in the amount necessary to redeem the tax-defaulted property, and, where a taxing agency which collects its own taxes has consented to the sale under this chapter, not included in the amount required to redeem from sale to the taxing agency.

D) Easements constituting servitude upon or burdens to the property; water rights, the record title to which is held separately from the title to the property; and restrictions of record.

E) Unaccepted, recorded, irrevocable offers of dedication of the property to the public or a public entity for a purpose, and recorded options of any taxing agency to purchase the property or any interest therein for a public purpose.

F) Unpaid assessments under the Improvement Bond Act of 1915 (Division 10 [commencing with Section 8500] of the Streets and Highway Code) which are not satisfied as a result of the sale proceeds being applied pursuant to Chapter 1.3 (commencing with Section 4671) of Part 8.

G) Effective July 1, 1989, any Federal Internal Revenue Service Liens pursuant to provisions of Federal Law, may not be discharged by the sale, even though the Tax Collector has provided proper notice to the Internal Revenue Service before that date.

Pursuant to Section 3725 of the California Revenue and Taxation Code, a proceeding based on alleged invalidity or irregularity of any proceeding instituted under this chapter can only be commenced within one year after the date of execution of the Tax Collector's deed. Therefore, purchasers may find it prudent to delay any improvement on the property for this one year period.

As a convenience, some bond information is provided, but its accuracy is not guaranteed. If property is encumbered with foreclosed or unforeclosed street bonds, irrigation assessments, income tax liens, etc., a notice of power to sell tax-defaulted property may or may not discharge these obligations. A notice of power to sell tax-defaulted property will not abolish easements constituting servitudes upon or burdens to the property.

**ALL SALES ARE FINAL, UNLESS,** the County Board of Supervisors rules them invalid. If the sale is ruled invalid, all of the purchase price will be refunded.

Any additional information concerning this sale, can be obtained by contacting the Sacramento County Treasurer-Tax Collector, Tax-Defaulted Land Unit at (916) 440-6621.

CONTRA COSTA COUNTY TAX COLLECTOR'S OFFICE
ALFRED P. LOMELI, TREASURER-TAX COLLECTOR
1991 PUBLIC AUCTION INFORMATION SHEET

The 1991 Public Auction of tax-defaulted property in Contra Costa County will be held:

WEDNESDAY, FEBRUARY 27, 1991 10:00 a.m.

Room 107, McBrien Administration Building, 651 Pine Street, Martinez, CA

*************************************************************************************

THE TAX COLLECTOR'S OFFICE RESERVES THE RIGHT TO WITHDRAW ANY PARCEL FROM THE AUCTION LIST.

Redemptions on parcels on the list must be made by the close of business on the last business day PRIOR to the date the sale begins. Redemptions by mail must also be received on the last business day prior to the date the sale begins.

MINIMUM BID is one half (½) of Fair Market Value. However, minimum bid on a parcel can be set at a greater amount to assure collection of the amount of tax and penalties.

Parcel ownership CAN NOT be obtained by paying off the back taxes.

To bid at the Auction, a Certified Check, for $100.00 should be received by the Tax Collector's Office at least two weeks prior to the date of the sale, AND NOT LATER than the close of business on the last business day prior to the date of the sale. Checks should be made payable to either "Alfred P. Lomeli," or "Contra Costa County Tax Collector." If mailed, it should be sent to Tax Collector, P.O. Box 631, Martinez, CA 94553, Attention: Redemption.

The check can be applied toward the purchase price. If you are not a successful bidder, your deposit will be returned within fifteen days.

Purchases of property at the Auction must also pay a Documentary Transfer Tax on the amount of the bid. The tax is based on the rate of $ .55 for each $500.00 or fractional part of each $500.00 when the bid exceeds $100.00. The following example shows amounts required.

| Amount of Bid | Increase It By Another: | Necessary Transfer Tax |
|---|---|---|
| $ 0.00 to 100.00 | $.00 | $ .00 |
| 100.01 to 500.00 | .55 | .55 |
| 500.01 to 1,000.00 | .55 | 1.10 |
| 1,000.01 to 1,500.00 | .55 | 1.65 |
| 1,500.01 to 2,000.00 etc | .55 etc. | 2.20 etc. |

Puchasers of property within the City of Richmond must also pay a Richmond City Transfer Tax in addition to the Documentary Transfer Tax. The rate is $7.00 per $1,000.00 of the purchase price. For example:

| Amount of Bid | Richmond Transfer Tax |
|---|---|
| $ 0.00 to 1,000.00 | $ 7.00 |
| 1,000.01 to 2,000.00 | 14.00 |

Property purchased at the Auction must be PAID FOR IN FULL at the Auction. Cash and personal checks will be accepted. If the purchase price is $50,000.00 or greater, a credit transaction will be accepted. The purchaser must deposit $5,000.00 or ten percent (10%) of the purchase price, whichever is greater. The transaction MUST be completed within 90 days.

Map books of the parcels are available for public inspection at the Tax Collector's Office. Copies may be bought at the Assessor's Office: 834 Court St., Martinez, M-F, 8-12 & 1-4.

For further information contact the Redemption Department of the Tax Collector's Office:
Room 100, 625 Court St., Martinez, CA, M-F 8-5, (415) 646-4122
Mailing Address: Tax Collector, P.O. Box 631, Martinez, CA 94553, Attn: Redemption

(SEE REVERSE SIDE)

| ITEM | PARCEL NO. | ASSESSEE | SITE | CITY/AREA | MINIMUM BID |
|---|---|---|---|---|---|
| PUBLIC AUCTION SALE | | | | | |
| 2. | 159-060-038 | David & Patricia Kavert | 4075 Folsom Ct | Concord | 147,500 |
| 3. | 430-260-014 | Wayne & Evelyn Eng | N. Rancho Pl | Pinole | 61,000 |
| 4. | 430-260-021 | Wayne & Evelyn Eng | N. Rancho Pl | Pinole | 62,000 |
| 5. | 430-260-027 | Wayne & Evelyn Eng | N. Rancho Pl | Pinole | 60,000 |
| 6. | 513-162-004 | Ethel Dotson | 396 South St | Richmond | 8,000 |
| 7. | 529-180-011 | Advance Mortgage Corp | 2213 Burbeck Ave | Richmond | 45,000 |
| 8. | 534-072-017 | Patricia Williams | 709 Pennsylvania Ave | Richmond | 3,300 |
| 9. | 538-161-014 | L.C. & Louise Campbell | 225 MacDonald Ave | Richmond | 22,500 |
| 10. | 538-310-003 | Mark Jr. & Jettie Mae Lowe | 418 Bissell Ave | Richmond | 8,000 |
| 11. | 538-360-009 | Frank Torres, Ronald Williams | 26 2nd St | Richmond | 7,000 |
| 12. | 550-171-025 formerly 550-171-011 | Frederick Ross | S. 3rd St | Richmond | 1,750 |
| 13. | 561-151-016 | Buelah Mae Mason | 233 Willard Ave | Richmond | 3,000 |
| 14. | 561-152-012 | M.E. & Peggy Richards | Vernon Ave | Richmond | 7,000 |
| 16. | 218-420-004 | E Thomas Eck III, Tre | San Ramon Valley Blvd | San Ramon | 75,000 |
| ~~17.~~ | ~~148-440-017~~ | ~~Robert Hooker~~ | ~~1346 Las Juntas~~ Way # D | ~~Unincorp~~ | 77,500 |
| 18. | 409-021-020 | Theodore Stills | Vernon Ave | Unincorp | 2,000 |
| 20. | 409-060-026 | Alma Electric Co | 1628 1st St | Unincorp | 3,500 |
| 21. | 409-131-013 | James & Corina Ray | 1733 7th St | Unincorp | 2,000 |
| 22. | 409-240-019 | Lola Robinson | 3rd St | Unincorp | 2,600 |
| 23. | 409-262-007 | Nathaniel & Mary Evans | 1926 4th St | Unincorp | 4,400 |
| 24. | 416-102-009 | Marion & Rosemary Mc Craw | 2716 Road 20 | Unincorp | 7,500 |

Additional Information:

If title is requested to be vested in other than the actual purchaser, a notarized letter stating the manner in which title shall be vested must be submitted.

Department of the Treasury / Internal Revenue Service

# Notice of Public Auction Sale

Under the authority in Internal Revenue Code section 6331, the property described below has been seized for nonpayment of internal revenue taxes due from

John R. Doe 440 OLD HWY 4; ANTIOCH, CA 94509

The property will be sold at public auction as provided by Internal Revenue Code section 6335 and related regulations.

**Date of Sale:** THURSDAY MAY 9, 1991

**Time of Sale:** 10:00 am - pm

**Place of Sale:** 2850 SHADELANDS DRIVE; WALNUT CREEK, CA 94598

**Title Offered:** Only the right, title, and interest of John R. Doe in and to the property will be offered for sale. If requested, the Internal Revenue Service will furnish information about possible encumbrances, which may be useful in determining the value of the interest being sold (See the back of this form for further details.)

**Description of Property:** The following described real property in the City of Antioch, County of Contra Costa, State of California: A portion of the Northeast one quarter of Section 25, Township 2 North, Range 1 East, Mount Diablo Base and Meridian, more particularyly described as follows:

A parcel bounded on the East by a public road whose Western boundary intersects the section line on the North boundary of Section 25, Township 2 North, Range 1 East, at a point 615 feet, more or less, West of the Northeast corner of Section 25, the Western boundary of said public road extending therefrom in a direction that is approximately South $2^{\circ}$ 48' East, said parcel being more particularly described as follows:

Beginning at a point on the Western boundary of a public road described above which point bears South $2^{\circ}$ 48' East 8.20 feet from the intersection of said road boundary with a fence line marking the North line of Section 25, forming the line between lands of Fitzpatrick and Uren, thence from said point of beginning, South $2^{\circ}$ 48' East, 100 feet; thence South $89^{\circ}$ 57 West, 185.8 feet; thence North $2^{\circ}$ 48' West 100 feet; North $89^{\circ}$ 57' East 185.9 feet to the point of beginning.

CONTINUED ON PAGE 2

**Property may be Inspected at:** 200, 206 / 206A San Joaquin Avenue, Antioch, CA 94509
( DRIVE BY ONLY )

**Payment Terms:**

- [ ] Full payment required on acceptance of highest bid
- [X] Deferred payment as follows: 20% at time of sale, balance in full no later that 12 o'clock noon Friday May 17, 1991

**Form of Payment:** All payments must be by cash, certified check, cashier's or treasurer's check or by a United States postal, bank, express, or telegraph money order. Make check or money order payable to the Internal Revenue Service.

| Signature | Name and Title *(Typed)* | Date |
|---|---|---|
| Jeanne Kurtz | Jeanne Kurtz Revenue Officer | 04-22-91 |
| Address for information About the Sale: 2850 Shadelands Drive; Walnut Creek, CA 94598 | | Phone: 946-0894 |

Form **2434** (Rev. 3-84)

**Nature of Title**

The right, title, and interest of the taxpayer (named on the front of this form) in and to the property is offered for sale *subject to any prior valid outstanding mortgages, encumbrances, or other liens in favor of third parties against the taxpayer that are superior to the lien of the United States.* All property is offered for sale "where is" and "as is" and without recourse against the United States. No guaranty or warranty, express or implied, is made as to the validity of the title, quality, quantity, weight, size, or condition of any of the property, or its fitness for any use or purpose. No claim will be considered for allowance or adjustment or for rescission of the sale based on failure of the property to conform with any expressed or implied representation.

**Redemption Rights**

The rights of redemption, as specified in Internal Revenue Code section 6337, are quoted as follows:

***Sec. 6337. Redemption of Property.***

***(a) Before Sale.***— Any person whose property has been levied upon shall have the right to pay the amount due, together with the expenses of the proceeding, if any, to the Secretary at any time prior to the sale thereof, and upon such payment the Secretary shall restore such property to him, and all further proceedings in connection with the levy on such property shall cease from the time of such payment.

***(b) Redemption of Real Estate After Sale.***

(1) Period.—The owners of any real property sold as provided in section 6335, their heirs, executors, or administrators, or any person having any interest therein, or a lien thereon, or any person in their behalf, shall be permitted to redeem the property sold, or any particular tract of such property at any time within 180 days after the sale thereof.

(2) Price.—Such property or tract of property shall be permitted to be redeemed upon payment to the purchaser, or in case he cannot be found in the county in which the property to be redeemed is situated, then to the Secretary, for the use of the purchaser, his heirs, or assigns, the amount paid by such purchaser and interest thereon at the rate of 20 percent per annum.

**Effect of Junior Encumbrances**

***Sec. 6339(c). Effect of Junior Encumbrances.***

A certificate of sale of personal property given or a deed to real property executed pursuant to section 6338 shall discharge such property from all liens, encumbrances, and titles over which the lien of the United States with respect to which the levy was made had priority.

Jeanne Kurtz, Revenue Officer
**Internal Revenue Service**
2850 Shadelands Drive

Walnut Creek, CA 94596

Official Business
Penalty for Private Use, $300

OAKLAND, CA
PM
1987

U.S. MAIL

Postage and Fees Paid
Department of the Treasury
554

Thomas
Bx 5000 #412
Danville, CA 94526

• U.S.GPO:1987-0-181-457/62367

Form **2434** (Rev. 3-84)

ATTACHMENT TO NOTICE OF PUBLIC AUCTION SALE

John R. Doe

Description of Property Continued:

EXCEPTING THEREFROM:

That portion thereof conveyed to State of California by deed recorded February 20, 1967 in Book 5309 of Official Records, page 244.

Assessors Parcel No. 071-050-036

Site Address: 2764 Lone Tree Way
Antioch, CA 94509

Commonly known as: 200 San Joaquin Ave, 206/206A San Joaquin Ave
Antioch, CA 94509 Antioch, CA 94509

| FORM 2434-B (Rev. Sept. 1985) | Department of the Treasury – Internal Revenue Service<br>**Notice of Encumbrances Against or Interests in Property Offered for Sale** |
|---|---|

As of this date, the following are the encumbrances against or interests in the property (as described in the Notice of Public Auction or Notice of Sealed Bid Sale) that was seized for nonpayment of Internal Revenue taxes due from: John R. Doe

Some of these encumbrances or interests may be superior to the lien of the United States.

| Type of Encumbrance or Interest | Amount of Encumbrance or Interest | Date of Instrument Creating Encumbrance or Interest | Date and Place Recorded | Name and Address of Party Holding Encumbrance or Interest | Date of Information |
|---|---|---|---|---|---|
| Deed of Trust | $ 43,056.86 | 11-10-82 | 11-16-82<br>Contra Costa Co.<br>Recorders Office<br>Martinez, CA 94553 | East Bay Mortgage Inc.<br>250 Juana Avenue<br>Suite 210<br>San Leandro, CA 94577 | 04-24-91 |
| Deed of Trust | 123,462.60 | 09-19-89 | 09-27-89<br>Contra Costa Co.<br>Recorders Office<br>Martinez, CA 94553 | East Bay Mortgage Inc.<br>250 Juana Avenue<br>Suite 210<br>San Leandro, CA 94577 | 04-24-91 |
| Notice of Federal Tax Lien | 44,226.19 | 02-05-90 | 02-08-90<br>Contra Costa Co.<br>Recorders Office<br>Martinez, CA 94553 | Internal Revenue Service | 04-24-91 |
| Notice of Federal Tax Lien | 20,492.84 | 02-05-90 | 02-08-90<br>Contra Costa Co<br>Recorders Office<br>Martinez, CA 94553 | Internal Revenue Service | 04-24-91 |
| Deed Of Trust | 8,845.84 | 05-03-90 | 05-11-90<br>Contra Costa Co<br>Recorders Office<br>Martinez, CA 94553 | Founders Title Company<br>3000 Clayton Road<br>Concord, CA 94519 | 04-29-91 |
| Notice of Federal Tax | 3,818.09 | 11-29-90 | 12-10-90<br>Contra Costa Co<br>Recorders Office<br>Martinez, CA 94553 | Internal Revenue Service. | 04-24-91 |

**NOTE:** The Internal Revenue Service does not warrant the correctness or completeness of the above information, and provides the information solely to help the prospective bidders determine the value of the interest being sold. Bidders should, therefore, verify for themselves the validity, priority, and amount of encumbrances against the property offered for sale. Each party listed above was mailed a notice of sale on or before 04-29-91 (date).

| Signature | Name and Title (typed) | Date |
|---|---|---|
| *Jeanne Kurtz* | Jeanne Kurtz Revenue Officer | 04-29-91 |

Form 2434-B (Rev. 9-85)

FORM 2434-B
(Rev. Sept. 1985)

Department of the Treasury – Internal Revenue Service

**Notice of Encumbrances Against or Interests in Property Offered for Sale**

## Authority and Effect of Sale

Pursuant to authority contained in sections 6331 and 6335 of the Internal Revenue Code and the regulations thereunder, and by virtue of a levy issued by authority of the District Director of Internal Revenue, the right, title, and interest [in the property described in the notice of sale] of the taxpayer [whose name appears on the reverse side of this document] will be sold.

Such interest is offered ***subject*** to any prior outstanding mortgages, encumbrances, or other liens in favor of third parties, which are valid against the taxpayer and are superior to the lien of the United States. The reverse of this document provides information regarding possible encumbrances or interests which may be useful in determining the value of the interest being sold. All interests of record were mailed a notice of sale.

The property will be sold "as is" and "where is" and without recourse against the United States. The Government makes no guaranty or warranty, expressed or implied, as to the validity of the title, quality, quantity, weight, size, or condition of the property, or its fitness for any use or purpose. No claim will be considered for allowance or adjustment or for rescission of the sale based upon failure of the property to conform with any representation, expressed or implied.

Notice of sale has been given in accordance with legal requirements. If the property is offered by more than one method, all bids will be considered tentative until the highest bid has been determined. The property will be sold to the highest bidder, and the sale will be final upon acceptance of the highest bid in accordance with the terms of the sale.

Payment must be made by cash, certified check, cashier's or treasurer's check or by a United States Postal, bank, express, or telegraph money order. All checks or money orders must be made payable to the Internal Revenue Service. A certificate of sale will be delivered to the successful bidder as soon as possible upon receipt of full payment of the purchase price.

Section 6339(c) of the Code states that a certificate of sale of personal property given or a deed to real property executed pursuant to section 6338 will discharge that property from all liens, encumbrances, and titles which are junior to the federal tax lien by virtue of which the levy was made. If real property is involved, section 6337 of the Code provides that the taxpayer, his or her heirs, executors, or administrators, or any person having an interest therein, or lien thereon, or any person in behalf of the taxpayer may redeem real property within 180 days from the date of its sale by the Internal Revenue Service. The redemption price to be paid to the successful bidder is the successful bid price plus 20 percent per year interest from the date of payment by the successful bidder to the date of redemption. If the property is not redeemed within the 180-day period, the District Director shall, upon receipt of the certificate of sale, issue a deed to the purchaser, or his assignee.

☆ U.S. Government Printing Office: 1986—491-451/54249

Form **668(Y)**
(Rev. January 1989)

Department of the Treasury - Internal Revenue Service

# Notice of Federal Tax Lien Under Internal Revenue Laws

| District | Serial Number | *For Optional Use by Recording Office* |
|---|---|---|
| | 53421 | |

**As provided by sections 6321, 6322, and 6323 of the Internal Revenue Code, notice is given that taxes (including interest and penalties) have been assessed against the following-named taxpayer. Demand for payment of this liability has been made, but it remains unpaid. Therefore, there is a lien in favor of the United States on all property and rights to property belonging to this taxpayer for the amount of these taxes, and additional penalties, interest, and costs that may accrue.**

COPY OF [illegible]
MAR 25 1991

Name of Taxpayer
John Doe

Residence
Main Street, Harris, Calif.

**IMPORTANT RELEASE INFORMATION:** With respect to each assessment listed below, unless notice of lien is refiled by the date given in column (e), this notice shall, on the day following such date, operate as a certificate of release as defined in IRC 6325(a).

| Kind of Tax *(a)* | Tax Period Ended *(b)* | Identifying Number *(c)* | Date of Assessment *(d)* | Last Day for Refiling *(e)* | Unpaid Balance of Assessment *(f)* |
|---|---|---|---|---|---|
| 10 | | 123456 | 11/05/90 | 12/05/[illegible] | $35,000 |

Place of Filing
Sacramento

**Total** **$** $35,000

This notice was prepared and signed at Mary Smith, on this,

the [illegible] day of [illegible], 19____.

Signature [signature] | Title [illegible]

(**NOTE:** Certificate of officer authorized by law to take acknowledgments is not essential to the validity of Notice of Federal Tax lien Rev. Rul. 71-466, 1971 - 2 C.B. 409)

Form **668(Y)** (Rev. 1-89)

Part 3 - Taxpayer's Copy

INSTRUCTIONS ON HOW TO APPLY FOR

# Certificate of Discharge of Property From Federal Tax Lien

Department of the Treasury **Internal Revenue Service**

Publication 783 (Rev. 1-84)

**Submit your typewritten application and all accompanying documents in triplicate to:**

District Director of Internal Revenue
(Address to District in which the property is located)
Attention of : Chief, Special Procedures Staff
Given Date of Application

## Information required on application

Please give the name and address of the person applying, under section 6325 ( )( )( ) of the Internal Revenue Code, for a certificate of discharge. Give the name and address of the taxpayer, and describe the property as follows:

1. Give a detailed description, including the location of the property for which you are requesting the certificate of discharge. If real property is involved, give the description as contained in the title or deed to the property, and the complete address (street, city, state). If the certificate is requested under section 6325 (b)(1), also give a description of all the taxpayer's property remaining subject to the lien.

2. Show how, and when the taxpayer has been, or will be, divested of all rights, title and interest in and to the property for which a certificate of discharge is requested.

3. Attache a copy of each notice of Federal tax lien, or furnish the following information as it appears on each filed notice of Federal tax lien:
- the name of the Internal Revenue District;
- The name and address of the taxpayer against whom the notice was filed
- The date and place the notice was filed

4. List the encumbrances (or attach a copy of the instrument that created each encumbrance) on the property which you believe have priority over Federal tax lien. For each encumbrance show:
- The name and address of the holder;
- A description of the encumbrance;
- The date of the agreement;
- The date and place of the recording, if any;
- The amount due as of the date of the application, if known (show costs and accrued interest separately);
- Your family relationship, if any to the taxpayer and to the holder of any other encumbrances on the property.

5. Itemize all proposed or actual costs, commissions and expenses of any transfer or sale of the property.

6. Furnish information to establish the value of the property for which you are applying for a certificate of discharge. In every case furnish an estimate of the fair market value of the property which will remain subject to the lien, In addition,
- If private sale - Submit written appraisals by two disinterested people qualified to appraise the property, and a brief statement of each appraiser's qualifications.
- If public sale (auction) already held - Give the date and place the sale was held, and the amount for which the property was sold.
- If public sale (auction) to be held - Give the proposed date and place of the sale , and include a statement that the United States will be paid in its proper priority from the proceeds of the sale.

7. Give any other information that might in your opinion, have bearing upon the application.

8. Furnish any other specific information the District Director requests.

9. If you are submitting the application under the provisions of section 6325(b)(3), dealing with the substitution of proceeds of sale, attach a copy of the proposed agreement containing the following:
- Name and address of proposed escrow agent:
- Caption, type of account, name and address of depositary for the account;
- Conditions under which the escrow fund is to be held;
- Conditions under which payment will be made from escrow, including the limitation for negotiated settlement of claims against the fund;
- Estimated cost of escrow;
- Name and address of any other party you and the District Director determine to be a party to the escrow agreement;
- Your signature, and those of the escrow agent, District Director and any other party to the escrow agreement;
- Any other specific information the District Director requests.

10. Give a daytime telephone number where you may be reached.

11. Give the name, address and telephone number of your attorney or other representative, if any.

12. Make the following declaration over your signature and title: "Under penalties of perjury, I declare that I have examined this application, including any accompanying schedules, exhibits, affidavits, and statements, and to the best of my knowledge and belief it is true, correct, and complete.

## ADDITIONAL INFORMATION

**Please follow the instructions in this publication when applying for a Certificate of Discharge of Property From Federal Tax Lien.**

The District DIrector has the authority to issue a certificate of discharge of a lien that is filed on any part of a taxpayer's property subject to the lien.The following sections and provisions of the Internal Revenue Code Apply:

Section 6325(b)(1), if it is determined that the property remaining subject to the lien has a fair market value of at least double the sum of the amount of the unsatisfied tax liability and the amount of all other liens and encumbrances having priority over the Government's lien.

Section 6325(b)(2)(A), if there is paid in partial satisfaction of the liability secured by the lien an amount determined to be not less than the value of the interest of the United States in the property to be discharged.

Section 6325(b)(2)(B), if it is determined that the interest of the United States in the property to be discharged has no value.

Section 6325(b)(3), if the property subject to the lien is sold and, under an agreement with the Internal Revenue Service, the proceeds from the sale are to be held as a fund subject to the liens and claims of the United States in the same manner, and with the same priority, as the liens and claims on the discharged property.

1. No payment is required for the issuance of a certificate under section 6325(b)(2)(B) of the Code. Payment is required for certificates issued under section 6325(b)(2)(A). Do not send the payment with your application, however. The District Director will notify you after determining the amount due.

2. The District Director will have your application investigated to determine whether is issue the certificate, and will let you know the outcome.

3. A certificate of discharge under section 6325(b)(2)(A) will be issued upon receipt of the amount determined to be the interest of the United States in the subject property under Federal tax lien. Make remittances in cash, or by a certified, cashier's, or treasurer's check drawn on any bank or trust company incorporated under laws of the United States, or by any State, or possession of the United States, or by order. (If you pay by uncertified personal check, issuance of certificate of discharge will be delayed until the bank honors the check.

4. If application is made under section 6325 (b)(2)(A) or 6325 (b)(2)(B) because a mortgage foreclosure is contemplated, there will be a determination of the amount required for discharge or determination of the amount required for discharge or a determination that the Federal tax lien interest in the property is valueless.

Within 30 days from the date of the application, the applicant will receive a written conditional commitment for a certificate of discharge. When the foreclosure proceeding has been concluded, a certificate of discharge will be issued in accordance with the terms of the commitment letter.

5. If applications made under the provisions of section 6325(b)(3), the District Director has the authority to approve an escrow agent selected by the applicant. Any reasonable expenses incurred in connection with the sale of the property, the holding of the fund, or the distribution of the fund shall be paid by the applicant or from the proceeds of the sale before satisfaction of any claims and liens. Submit a copy of the proposed escrow agreement as part of the application.

Chapter 13

# Sheriff's and Trustee's Sales

## *The Remarkable Secret of the Hottest Investment of the Past Five Years*

**HOW TO BUY AT AUCTION**

In this chapter you will learn:

- The advantages and disadvantages of buying at a Trustee's/Sheriff's Sale
- Who is qualified to buy
- How to read Notices of Default (NODs) and Notices of Trustee's Sale
- How to analyze the numbers before the sale to ensure that you make a big profit

You will also learn:

- The requirements of a Judicial Sale proceeding
- The principles of bankruptcy law and how it affects distressed property

The best-known market for distressed property is the Trustee's/Sheriff's Sale, which is held at the end of the foreclosure period when the defaulting owner has been unable to cure the default. The property is auctioned, and if no one bids on it, it reverts to the lender. Rarely are there enough proceeds remaining from the bidding for the hapless owner to collect.

A *Judicial Sale / Sheriff's Sale* is held for similar reasons (nonpayment of a loan), but because it is a judicial procedure, it requires the participation of the court, and is more cumbersome, expensive, and time-consuming.

Had the defaulting owner declared bankruptcy (also a legal procedure) and then still not been able to cure the default, the property could be sold for the benefit of the creditors at a *Sheriff's Sale*. Once again, the effect on the owner is probably the same: The owner receives little if any of the proceeds.

## JUDICIAL SALES

Judicial foreclosure differs from a foreclosure under a deed of trust in that a court process is involved and different instruments (documents) are signed by the borrower/mortgagors and the lender/mortgagee.

Some states use mortgages as the security instruments to secure a loan on residential property. The mortgage is simply a document signed by a borrower who hypothecates (pledges) his property as security. In the event of default or nonpayment, the lender will file suit in court requesting permission to sell the property to recover the debt. If the lender's suit prevails, the court will authorize the lender to evict the borrower, reclaim and ultimately sell the property, and finally recover the funds loaned. This process is called a judicial foreclosure. The process is cumbersome because it requires attorneys and court dates with their associated delays and extra costs. It could take a lender as long as one year to collect its principal.

### Nonjudicial Foreclosure

In comparison, the deed of trust system is much simpler because it is a matter of established law and so does not require a court to adjudicate. Therefore, the system is referred to as a nonjudicial foreclosure. For example, when a homeowner signs a deed of trust, he is called the trustor and the party loaning the funds is called the beneficiary. Up to this point, the relationship is similar to that between a mortgagee (lender) and a mortgagor (borrower). However, under the deed of trust system, the trustor (homeowner) pledges (hypothecates) his home as security and gives a Trustee, who is an independent third party, the right to sell the home at auction in the event of default or nonpayment. The beneficiary is required only to advise the Trustee of lack of payment or default. The Trustee will then issue an NOD (Notice of Default), and the remaining process, a matter of law, is pretty much automatic and does not get jammed up in the court system.

## SHERIFF'S/JUDICIAL SALES: ADVANTAGES AND DISADVANTAGES

The Trustee's/Sheriff's Sale is the auction process everyone has read about. Sales are conducted in the highly populated counties almost daily. If the property has a value above the loan amount outstanding, this is a great opportunity. The sales are listed in the legal newspapers (see page 347) and posted at the county courthouse and other public places. Check your state and county for the exact publication requirements.

Buying at this juncture has some advantages. One is that the Foreclosure Consultants Law does not apply; another is that you receive a deed from the Trustee, a trustee deed. In your state, this might be a sheriff's deed or a certificate of title. The disadvantage is that the property is not accessible before the auction. In most instances, you are unable to check the roof, hire a termite inspector, or evaluate the structure or the foundation. Bid accordingly, or you'll pay the price later.

Page 350 shows a *Notice of Default*, the legal document that alerted the owner and the public that the lender has begun the foreclosure proceeding, which, in fact, begins on the date on which the NOD is recorded. It lists the owner's indebtedness to date. But be aware that the sum of money mentioned in the default notice refers only to the particular deed of trust/mortgage on which the lender has elected to foreclose, and this amount may well be only part of what is owed on the property. You must determine what other debt the property is carrying before you can calculate its probable worth to you.

Page 353 shows a *Notice of Trustee's Sale*, which is published about a month before the scheduled sale. Check your state and county for the exact publication requirements. Again, the indebtedness to date is noted, but again, that is only as much as has accumulated on the foreclosing deed of trust/mortgage.

The Trustee's/Sheriff's Sale is very businesslike, and no emotions are involved. If other bidders are competing, learn from them. Grade yourself and judge your knowledge of values and your overall understanding of the market. Compare yourself with the competition. Don't let other professional bidders intimidate you. They will be worrying about you as much as you are worrying about them. Do your homework, know the resale value of the property you are bidding on, and don't get excited. Set a maximum bid and stop when the crier (auctioneer) reaches that amount. It is okay to lose the deal; I can assure you there will be more distressed property available.

Rarely will you find first-time buyers bidding at a Trustee's/Sheriff's Sale. It would be unusual to see an amateur who does not understand real estate values and the associated liabilities of buying and bidding at such a sale. That isn't to say that the sale is closed to the public; it's not. From time to time, an amateur will buy at the sale and drive the price higher than a professional like yourself (after reading this book) would consider reasonable. The amateur will get stung by paying too much. Don't worry about him. He won't be back until he has recovered his loss.

## WHO'S MOTIVATED

The major reason for bidding at the Trustee's/Sheriff's Sale is that the profit potential is very high. Foreclosure sales are outside the regular real estate market, so no laws of supply and demand prevail. Real estate brokers do not represent the sellers or the buyers in this market; even the sellers do not represent themselves. No one is trying to get the best possible price for the property. Real estate brokers and agents are not pushing for commissions and trying to drive prices up. The bidders at the Trustee's/Sheriff's Sale are other foreclosure buyers, all of whom are trying to buy for as little as possible.

The competitive bidding process of any auction is difficult to predict. You can be assured that, if the real estate market is hot (high demand) and homes are selling fast (in less than thirty days), you'll find a lot of bidders at Trustee's/Sheriff's Sales. If the property is a bargain, which is what we are looking for, you should expect competition from other bargain hunters. If they are professionals, they will know values and not raise their bids above the point at which they can make a profit.

You should make a step-by-step analysis of your costs before you buy at a Sheriff's/Trustee's Sale.

## WHAT ABOUT THE REDEMPTION PERIOD?

*Redemption* (the right to buy back the property even after it has been auctioned) applies after the public auction in some states. However, for REOs and VA and HUD property the redemption period will already have expired. You should review the status of judicial and nonjudicial auctions in all the states in which you want to purchase property (see pages 356–57).

The rules governing the redemption period are different from state to state and for different types (residential/farm) property. First determine the rules for your state and then learn the exceptions to the rules, if any. It is possible to purchase at the auction (which may be called a Sheriff's Sale in your state) and find that the homeowner who loses the property at the sale has as long as a year in which to redeem the property. This is a business risk that you must evaluate prior to bidding at the auction sale. From a practical standpoint you must consider the fact that the party redeeming the property will be required to pay cash plus an interest rate of return on your investment. This requirement tends to reduce the likelihood of most redemptions.

In other states, such as California, the sale is final and the homeowner (trustor) has no right of redemption. However, procedures vary from state to state, so check the codes and statutes for your state.

## BANKRUPTCY

Bankruptcy law and probate law are complicated, and the details are really beyond the scope of this book, but a brief outline will suffice as an introduction. A person or business may file for bankruptcy in any federal bankruptcy court, and in doing so must report all assets and liabilities as well as income. Immediately upon receipt of the bankruptcy filing, an automatic stay goes into effect, stopping all creditors from enforcing collection actions and usually preventing lawsuits until the stay is lifted. Thus, bankruptcy temporarily stops the foreclosure process, and any property involved may not be sold until the bankruptcy court lifts the stay.

The federal bankruptcy code is administered by courts and the Trustees, and the federal system in most cases takes precedence over the state court system. The sections of the Bankruptcy Code that buyers of distressed property should concern themselves will include Chapter 7, which results in a liquidation of debt, and the more commonly used Chapters 11 and 13, which enable corporations and individuals, respectively, to attempt to reorganize and pay off the debt.

### Chapter 7

Chapter 7 is commonly used when an individual or a business has liabilities that exceed assets and there is little possibility that the debtor will be able to pay the debts even if the payments are postponed to a future date. The estate (the assets) are assigned to a trustee in bankruptcy, who will sell them. The proceeds are then distributed to the creditors on a pro rata basis. Taxes are always paid first, unless a court order prevents their payment. Then wages are paid, and, finally, unsecured liens. The holders of secured liens, for example, real estate loans, must look to their security (the property itself) for a return of their investment.

### Chapter 11

Chapter 11 consists of that section of the code that applies to the reorganization of businesses. If a business is attempting to continue to function, the management requires relief from creditors in order to operate at all. The business will file for a Chapter 11 (reorganization) bankruptcy. Creditors may or may not appoint a creditors' committee. A committee, if formed, has the responsibility to assist the court and management with the reorganization of the debtor's commitment, including the reduction of wage and labor costs and release from union contracts. The Chapter 11 bankruptcy several years ago of Continental Airlines provides a good example. The company abrogated its union contracts, was therefore able to reduce labor costs significantly, and so survived. If successful, Chapter 11 companies will pay creditors over a period of time. If not, the creditors' committee and management will develop a plan to liquidate the assets and distribute the proceeds to the creditors.

### Chapter 13

Chapter 13 is for individuals who hope to work out a repayment program. Individuals can find themselves in various difficulties, such as those caused by a death in the family, divorce, medical expenses, and loss of work for extended periods. Bills accumulate rapidly after such setbacks. If the individual is employed steadily, but needs time to make payments to creditors, a repayment plan is permitted under Chapter 13 protection. The bankruptcy court will, as in all bankruptcies, require reports of progress and will issue guidance. The bankrupt individual must be capable of paying current debts on secured loans in addition to paying the agreed (possibly compromised) debts on past due bills. If the bankrupt individual is still unable to meet his or her commitments, the court will require that the assets be liquidated and the proceeds be divided among the creditors.

### Some Cautions for Foreclosure Buyers

If you plan to buy before the Trustee's or Sheriff's Sale or at the sale itself, find out if the seller is in bankruptcy. If the homeowner has filed for protection under Chapter 13 of the Bankruptcy Code, and many of them have, you as a pre-foreclosure buyer cannot purchase the home without court approval. The sellers don't always realize this fact, or possibly they may forget to mention it to you. This oversight can waste your time and money because the work that you do and any money you pay the seller will disappear; the court will more than likely rule that the creditors have first rights on the debtor's equity in the home anyway. As always, use the three-letter word — *ask* the seller about bankruptcy.

If the property is in bankruptcy, the lender will request from the court a relief of stay in order to sell the property at an auction sale. Lenders usually plead that their equity is in jeopardy and that the security is marginal or deteriorating. If the court approves, and it usually does, the lender will receive permission to foreclose and sell at a Trustee's/Sheriff's Sale. If the lender is granted a relief of stay by the court, the only alternative for the trustor/homeowner is to pay cash for the loan delinquency (which is unrealistic if one is in bankruptcy) or allow the sale to proceed and accept the associated loss of equity, if equity is available.

### Can Bankruptcy Cause Trouble after the Trustee's Sale?

Be aware that the bankruptcy laws are federal, not state, laws. If the real estate has been sold prior to a Trustee's or Sheriff's Sale under a state law, the sale can be set aside under the federal Bankruptcy Code if, in the court's opinion, the property was sold for substantially less than its fair market value or if some other unreasonable action occurred. Creditors can petition the court to make such a ruling if they suspect unfairness or think they can increase the settlement from the ultimate distribution of funds.

But don't pass up property that comes on the market as a probable bankruptcy sale. The potential to make a lot of money is there for that motivated person who is willing to learn about the gray or unknown areas of the law.

*The speed of the leader is the speed of the pack.*

— Dr. Derek Newton

## TRUSTEE'S/SHERIFF'S SALES

The rules governing Trustee's/Sheriff's Sales differ from state to state, so it is imperative that you review the rules with your local sheriff and attorney. For example, in some states if you bid and win, then change your mind after placing a deposit, you can forfeit your deposit and be held liable.

In some states cash is needed the day of the auction, and the amount varies from 10% to 100% of the sale price.

In your search for bargain purchases, I suggest you attend at least four or five actual auctions (Sheriff's/Trustee's Sales). There are several reasons for attending an actual auction:

1. You have plenty of cash and want a bargain property, and you don't have time to follow all the other methods in this book.
2. The current debt owned on the property is too high, and if it were purchased before the auction there wouldn't be any profit potential. For example, the first and second loan amount to more than the property is worth. After the auction, the second is extinguished.
3. The seller won't sell before the auction. This doesn't make sense, but it happens every day.
4. The seller has disappeared and can't be located.

### Opportunities

Auctions present opportunities, but also plenty of traps. That's why you should attend numerous auctions before making a bid and then only after thorough research. Here are some of the things you can expect.

1. The auction is relatively quick — sometimes only two or three minutes and it's over. Don't be late or you'll miss your chance to bid.

2. Many more people will attend than bid. Expect to see small groups, but most of them will be spectators. Expect the auctioneer to verify everyone's qualifications before the auction. Most auctioneers will request identification and a certified check or cash up to the amount you intend to bid. Without verification, you don't know who you are bidding against, and whether he or she is qualified to raise the price and cause you to bid higher than you had planned.
3. Bidding may start at a strange level — therefore, you should know what is owed so there won't be any surprises. The bid could be for a second mortgage above a first. Know what you are buying!!! Don't bid up a second mortgage without knowing exactly what is due on the first. Don't forget about taxes and other liens that may have a superior position to the lien that you are bidding on. Research the title and the encumbrances, or don't be a player. You could end up bankrupt by taking on more debt than you can handle.
4. If you are the high bidder on a second, you can take over the first loan. If the bank is the high bidder on the second loan, it can substitute you as the new owner at a later date. Go to the sale and make a deal with the bank later, and you won't need to use all your cash.

Expect one of three events to occur at the Trustee's/Sheriff's Sale:

1. The sale is postponed, and this happens more often than not.
2. The bank is high bidder and gets the property back. In the all-cash states the bank gets the property as much as 95% of the time. In the states that don't require all cash, the bank still gets the property up to 75% of the time.
3. A private investor/purchaser like yourself is the high bidder and ends up with a bargain purchase. After the sale it's OK to make a deal with this person because they may be willing to give you a bargain just to turn the profit quickly. Think about that; could you do the same with other bidders?

## PROBLEMS

If the homeowner is still in the house and you're the successful bidder at the Trustee's/Sheriff's Sale it will be your responsibility to remove the occupant. The legal process to remove the occupant physically from a house you acquire at a Trustee's/Sheriff's Sale can take months. Meanwhile, you are responsible from the date of the sale for principal, interest, taxes, and insurance payments.

The law is written to protect tenants, even deadbeats who don't pay their debts. The judge most likely doesn't own any rentals, and is not and never has been a landlord. The judge assumes you are a slumlord, and that you are evil and gouging poor people for rent so you can get wealthy. A good research book regarding evictions is *The Landlord Law Book*, by Nolo Press, Berkeley, California.

## WHAT TO DO BEFORE ATTENDING A TRUSTEE'S/SHERIFF'S SALE

Verify before attending the auction:

- That the sale/auction has not been postponed.
- The bank's or lender's bidding instructions to the auctioneer. Bankers sometimes will take their loss on the property at the sale. If that's the case, don't bid above the price they will get for it. You can probably buy the property after the sale for less than the minimum sale price to the public.
- The cash deposit requirements.
- The cash required and when it is due.
- The type of payment required — for example, cashier's check, certified check, or money order.

Don't make the check payable to an institution, make it payable to yourself. Then you can endorse it over to the auctioneer. Otherwise, you may not be able to cash the checks or put them back in your account since they are made payable to an outsider.

In summary, obtain your local foreclosure procedures and bidding instructions from your sheriff's office or clerk of the court. Your county may or may not provide written procedures. In the rare case where they do not, you'll need to research the rules or have an attorney review them with you.

### Success Steps Before the Trustee's/Sheriff's Sales

Determine market value using comps, comparables, appraisals, computer sources, DAMAR and DATAQUICK, title company property profiles, and drive-bys.

Establish your maximum bid and stick with it. Some bidders get caught up in the excitement and forget the objective is not to win the bidding but to get a good deal.

Last-minute cancellations occur quite frequently. Telephone on the day of the auction to verify the time, place, and minimum bid. The auctions are frequently cancelled or postponed because the sellers file for bankruptcy to prevent or delay the sale. Another reason for postponement could be that an investor such as yourself has put up the money to stop the foreclosure.

At the auction, qualify the other bidders. Only qualified bidders with certified funds are supposed to bid. If the auctioneer doesn't qualify the bidders you could be bidding against yourself because the other party does not have any money.

Determine your cash needs. Will you need all the cash or will it only require a deposit? How much of a deposit? When will you have to come up with the remaining balance? Hours? Days? Weeks? This is all very important information. If you default, will you lose your deposit? Upon re-auction can you be held responsible for any deficiencies between your original bid and the new bid?

What are your intentions for the property? To fix it up, then sell it in the retail market? Or a quick turnaround? Fast bucks or the last bucks?

### To the Lender

What will you do if the property is auctioned at the sale to the lender? You could write a letter and tell them you observed the Trustee's/Sheriff's Sale and you want an appointment to discuss the possible purchase of the property. At this point, the property is an REO, and will end up on a new person's desk. He won't even know that he was the high bidder, since the paperwork will take days or maybe weeks to reach him or her. You might end up talking to a realtor at this point, or possibly the institutional lender will have a staff member handle the situation. In either case you want to make an offer, and you already probably know more about the property in question than the lender does.

## JUDICIAL FORECLOSURE

As noted earlier in this chapter, the foreclosure laws in each state are complicated. In most states, a variety of foreclosure methods are available to a lender. Real estate law firms are the experts in the liquidation laws and will provide the specific information regarding the statutes in your state.

Readers should understand the concepts of power of sale foreclosure and a judicial foreclosure and, in a few states, the strict methods of foreclosure. The various methods are dictated by the state laws. The method of foreclosure is further dictated by the language of the security instrument.

### Power of Sale Foreclosure

This is the most common method of foreclosure. It is used primarily in the western and southern states. The law in these states allows the borrower to waive the right to a court proceeding in the event of a default. This waiver or provision is included in the language of the security instrument (loan document). The instrument's language must specify the notice period and terms under which the foreclosure sale may occur. Each state's statutes provide for a minimum period of notice to prevent abuses by lenders.

In most power of sale states, the common security instrument (loan document) is a deed of trust/trust deed. The trust deed is a three-party instrument. The parties involved include the Trustor (borrower), the Trustee (independent third party), and the beneficiary (lender). The Trustee holds title to the property for the benefit of the Trustor/borrower. This right to hold title is granted to the Trustee in the language of the trust deed. The Trustee also holds the title to the property for the benefit of the beneficiary. Again, this is outlined in the language of the trust deed. The Trustee's only legal rights are to act as a fiduciary and to execute the responsibility that is granted in the trust deed instrument.

If the Trustor/borrower defaults, the trustee is given the right (is empowered) to serve notice in the required manner to the Trustor. This is usually accomplished at the request of the lender (beneficiary). The Trustee must act as a fiduciary, that is, person of trust, and act only within the confines of specific state statutes.

Assuming default by the Trustor/borrower, the Trustee is empowered to serve the notice of default. Again, this action is usually at the request of the lender and was authorized by the Trustor in signing the trust deed at the time of the initial borrowing. The notice is in a legal form which is published in the newspaper. The state statutes specify the exact details of publication and notice to the public. Following the specific notice periods and publication, the property may be sold at a public auction.

Power of sale foreclosure is in most cases faster and less expensive than other methods of foreclosure, although there are cases in which a lender may want to foreclose via the judicial method. Your attorney can advise you. An example of a judicial foreclosure would be if a deficiency judgment is desirable and not obtainable under the power of sale method.

### Judicial Foreclosure

The judicial foreclosure is the second most common method of foreclosure. The judicial foreclosure proceeding takes place in the county where the property is located. The process takes place in the courtroom or other place designated by the judge.

Judicial foreclosure states use a mortgage, which is a two-party instrument. The parties involved are the mortgagee/lender and the mortgagor/borrower.

The judicial action is different from state to state, and is specified in the state's statutes. The following similarities are common to most states that use the judicial foreclosure process. The reader should be aware that this simplified analysis has been compiled for instructional purposes. Many states will require more steps to complete the foreclosure process.

### Step 1: *Filing of the Complaint*

This is the initial step. The complaint is filed in the county in which the property is located and names all parties that may have an interest in the property. The attorney will usually file a lis pendens at the same time that the complaint is filed. The filing of the lis pendens will put the world on notice of the litigation. The complaint will describe the nature of the default and parties involved.

When the complaint is filed, a summons is placed with the sheriff or processor for service upon all the named defendants (homeowner). The homeowner will have a specified time depending on state law to answer the complaint.

### Step 2: *Entry of Decree of Judgment*

This is the next step in the legal process. The complaint will set a time and place where the parties will come together before a judge to present their arguments. In most cases, the mortgagor (homeowner) will not appear and will be defaulted. If that is the case, the court will grant the mortgagee lender a judgment, which will join (merge) the terms of the note into the judgment and cut off the mortgagor's right to reinstate the note by paying the delinquent payments. The judgment will set the total debt, including all fees, principal, interest, and allowable advances. The judgment will also order the property sold at auction in the event that the total debt is not paid.

### Step 3: *Notice of the Foreclosure Sale*

This step will let the public know that the property is going to be sold at auction. The announcement of the foreclosure sale will be given in a manner prescribed by state law. This will alert all possible bidders of the pending sale so that the highest possible price can be obtained through competitive bidding. This is fine in theory, but in the real world often only the lender will tender a bid.

### Step 4: *The Foreclosure Sale*

The sale is held following the required notice period if the judgment amount is not paid. The sale is held at a public auction under the direction of the court. The lender is allowed to bid up the established debt without additional payment. The successful bidder will become the owner of the property, upon payment subject to redemption rights of the mortgagor if any.

### Redemption Period

In some states the law allows the mortgagor to recover the property — that is, redeem the property by paying the bid amount, plus interest, to the successful bidder during a period after the foreclosure sale. Redemption periods are usually allowed in agricultural states and may be extended by state law. Possession rights of the property during the redemption period vary. Review your state law for the correct timing.

### Strict Foreclosure

Vermont and Connecticut have laws that allow the use of a strict foreclosure. In this type of foreclosure, there is no actual sale of the property at an auction, as in trust deed states. The court provides the homeowner with protection for a limited period of time. Then the creditors are given what is called a law day to bid for the property. All lien holders are given time to bid on the property and cure the loan. If none of the lien holders bids successfully and pays the first mortgage holder his back payments and fees due, the property goes to the holder of the first mortgage. This process can take many months during which payments and penalties will accrue.

Distressed property buyers should be aware that this type of foreclosure allows the alert buyer an opportunity to mail letters and contact the seller over a long period of time offering to purchase his interest.

## *DISCLAIMER*

**The above summary is incomplete, and the reader should be aware that this is a simplified analysis compiled for instructional purposes. Many states will require additional steps and procedures. Your legal counsel is your best adviser in these matters.**

# JUDICIAL PROCESS - COURT ACTION

## JUDICIAL FORECLOSURE PROCESS

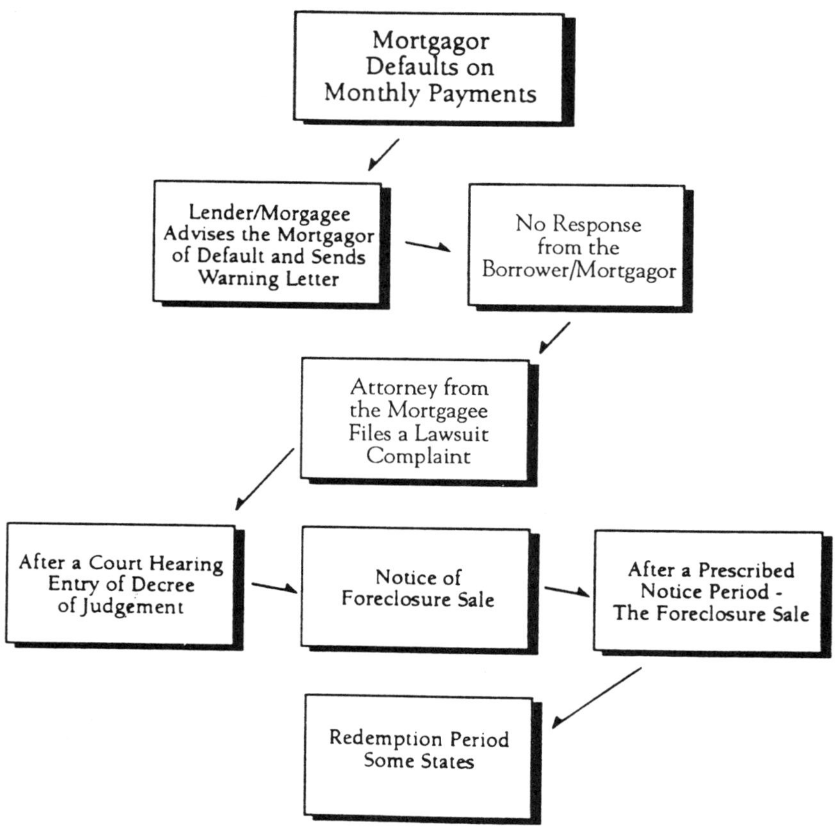

## SHERIFF'S NOTICE OF AUCTION

# SHERIFF'S SALE

By virtue of a Writ of Execution No. 85-07430, issued out of the Court of Common Pleas of Montgomery County, Pa., to me directed will be sold at Public Sale on

# Wednesday, Feb. 20, 1991

at 1:00 O'clock P.M., Prevailing time, in Court Room "A" at the Court House, in the Borough of Norristown, said County the following described Real Estate:

ALL THAT CERTAIN one-half double brick house and lot of land situate in the Borough of Pottstown, in the County of Montgomery and State aforesaid, bounded and described as follows, in accordance with a survey thereof made by Ralph E. Shaner, Engineer, Pottstown, Pa. on June 24, 1912 as follows:

BEGINNING at a point on the Southwesterly side of Evans Street in line of land formerly of Irvin S. Bitting, now of Harry Wilson, said point marking the center line of the partition wall of the house hereon erected and the house erected on the premises of Harry Wilson; thence extending South 63° 28' East through the middle of said partition wall 60 feet 3 inches to an angle point; thence continuing by said land South 58° 33' East 62 feet 6 inches to a point on the Northwesterly side of 10 feet wide alley; thence extending along said side of said alley North 27° 9' East 20 feet to a point in line of land of William S. Shaner; thence extending along said land North 58° 13' West 59 feet 2 inches to an angle point; thence continuing by said land North 63° 28' West 68 feet 2 inches to a point on the Southeasterly side of Evans Street aforesaid; thence extending along the said side of Evans Street South 15° 5' West 20 feet 5 inches to the place of BEGINNING.

PARCEL No. 16-00-07508-00-9.

LOCATION of Property: 230 N. Evans Street, Pottstown, Pa. 19464.

THE IMPROVEMENTS THEREON ARE:

## Single Family Residential Dwelling

SEIZED AND TAKEN IN execution as the property of

Larry J. Hine and Karen L. Hine; Real Debt $39,489.85 and to be sold by

FRANK P. LALLEY, Sheriff

DOWN MONEY: A deposit of ten (10%) percent of the Price Bid or One Thousand ($1,000.00) Dollars, which ever amount is greater, shall be required to be paid in cash or by certified check to the Sheriff as down money on each property purchased.

SHERIFF'S OFFICE, NORRISTOWN, PA.

TO ALL PARTIES IN INTEREST AND CLAIMANTS:

Notice is hereby given that a schedule of distribution will be filed by the Sheriff on March 20, 1991, and distribution will be made in accordance with the schedule unless exceptions are filed hereto within ten (10) days thereafter.

## TRUSTEE/TRUSTOR RELATIONSHIP

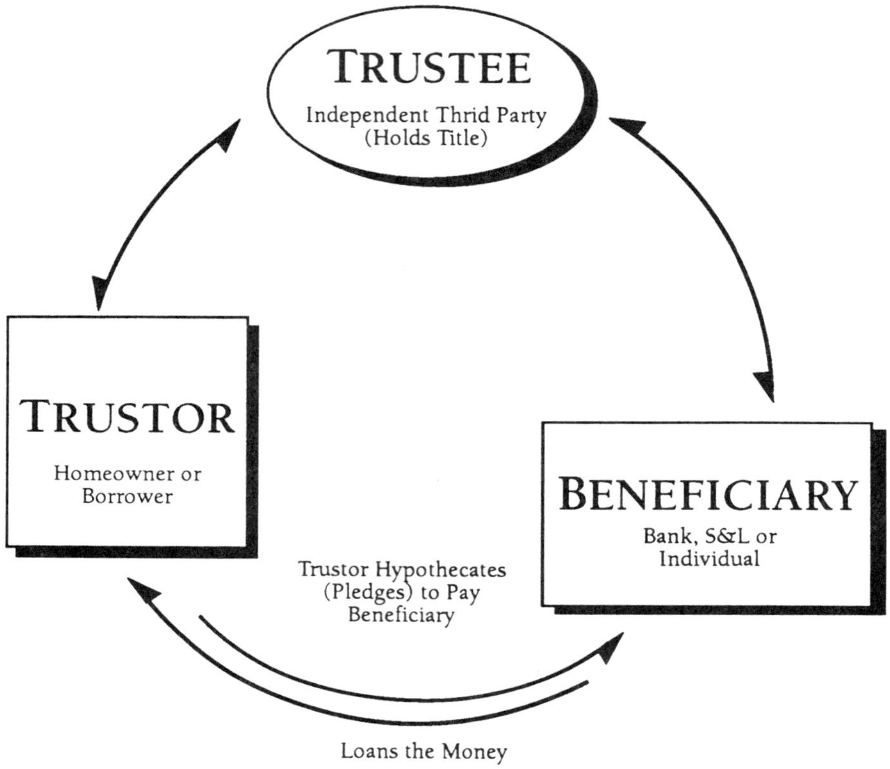

### Default Time Period in California

| Notice of Default Issued | 1/1 | ◀ 3 Months ▶<br>Loan Reinstatement Period | 4/1 | 21 DAY<br>Advertising Period<br>"Full Balance Due" | Trustee's Sale Auction |
|---|---|---|---|---|---|

# SHERIFF'S SALE–RULES OF THE ROAD

## MONTGOMERY COUNTY

### 1991 DATES FOR SHERIFF SALES ON REAL ESTATES

| DATE OF SALE | LAST DAY TO FILE | DATE OF SALE | LAST DAY TO FILE |
|---|---|---|---|
| (1) January 16, 1991 | December 3, 1990 | (7) July 17, 1991 | June 3, 1991 |
| (2) February 20, 1991 | January 7, 1991 | (8) August 21, 1991 | July 8, 1991 |
| (3) March 20, 1991 | February 4, 1991 | (9) September 18, 1991 | August 5, 1991 |
| (4) April 17, 1991 | March 4, 1991 | (10) October 23, 1991 | September 9, 1991 |
| (5) May 22, 1991 | April 8, 1991 | (11) November 27, 1991 | October 14, 1991 |
| (6) June 19, 1991 | May 6, 1991 | (12) December 18, 1991 | November 4, 1991 |

**SUPPLEMENT**

**Montgomery County Law Reporter**

Vol. 126 NORRISTOWN, PA., January 10, 1991 No. 8

JANUARY 16, 1991

CONDITIONS OF SALE

The down money, as advertised, must be paid to the Sheriff immediately after the property is knocked down to the highest bidder; otherwise the property may be immediately put up again for sale. A second bid accompanied by the required down money may be registered in writing with the Sheriff immediately after the property is knocked down to the highest bidder. Down money must be paid in cash or by certified check except in the case of members of the Montgomery Bar whose personal or endorsed checks will be accepted.

The balance of the purchase money together with the cost of preparing the deed poll and such other costs as are by law imposed upon the purchaser must be paid in cash or by certified check to the Sheriff within ten (10) days of the sale without any further demand. In default thereof the Sheriff may settle with the second bidder who has made the required deposit, upon receipt of the highest sum bid and the aforesaid costs less both deposits already made, within ten (10) days after the first bidder's failure to settle. In case no second bid be registered or no settlement made, the property may be sold again at the risk of the defaulting bidder, and in case of any deficiency on such resale he shall make good the same to any person injured thereby even though the down money required to be paid at the later sale shall have been increased by any charge in the conditions of the sale.

The deposit or down money paid by any bidder who fails to comply with the above conditions shall be forfeited and applied on the purchase by any second bidder or, if the property is resold, to cost or any liens or equitable claims thereon discharged thereby but not satisfied out of the proceeds thereof including the right of the real owner to have the highest bid first made realized.

The Sheriff shall not be liable for loss or damage to the premises sold resulting from any cause whatsoever, and makes no representation or warranty regarding the condition of the premises.

If the Sheriff's grantee is to be other than the record purchaser, a written assignment must be filed or such fact certified by the attorney on the writ when he is the purchaser.

**To all parties in interest and claimants:**

Notice is hereby given that schedules of distribution will be filed by the Sheriff on February 19, 1991, and distribution will be made in accordance with the schedules unless exceptions are filed thereto within ten (10) days thereafter.

By virtue of various writs issued out of the Court of Common Pleas of Montgomery County, Pa., to me directed will be sold at Public Sale on WEDNESDAY, January 16, 1991, at 1:00 o'clock P.M., prevailing time in courtroom "A" at the Court House, Swede and Airy Streets, in the Borough of Norristown, said County, the following described real estate:

**1.** 66-6588

ALL THAT CERTAIN Lot of ground, situate in the **Twp. of East Norriton.**

Seized and taken in execution as the property of **Richard A. and Theresa C. Gennone** at the suit of Continental Bank and Trust Co. Debt: $24,298.48.

**William Kinkead,** Attorney

**2.** 82-11613

ALL THAT CERTAIN Lot of ground with the buildings, Situate in **Cheltenham Twp.**

Seized and taken in execution as the property of **Barry L. Axler and Leslie C. Axler,** his wife at the suit of Continental Bank. Debt: $49,769.31

**James W. Hennessey,** Attorney

**3.** 82-17549

ALL THAT CERTAIN lot of ground with the buildings, Situate in the **Twp. of Upper Dublin.**

Seized and taken in execution as the property of **Paul S. Lipschutz and Barbara Lipschutz and U.S.A.,** at the suit of Continental Bank. Debt: $83,098.46.

**James W. Hennessey,** Attorney

**4.** 83-1525

ALL THOSE TWO CERTAIN lots with the buildings, Situate in the said **Twp. of Abington.**

Seized and taken in execution as the property of **Rose A. Lucas** at the suit of Federal National Mortgage Assoc. Debt: $14,497.20.

**Michael Meehan,** Attorney

## SHERIFF'S SALE–RULES OF THE ROAD

**42.** 90-14928
PREMISES "A"
ALL THAT CERTAIN lot of ground with the buildings Situate in **Whitemarsh Twp.**
ALL THAT CERTAIN lot of land situate in the **Twp. of Whitemarsh.**
PREMISES "B"
ALL THAT CERTAIN tract of land situate in the **Twp. of Whitemarsh**
#1-ALL THAT CERTAIN lot of ground with the buildings situate in the **Twp. of Whitemarsh.**
#2-ALL THAT CERTAIN lot of ground situate in the **Twp. of Whitemarsh.**
#3-ALL THAT CERTAIN lot of ground with the buildings situate in the **Twp. of Whitemarsh.**
Seized and taken in execution as the property of **James Zerby, John and Mary Dinan and Redcor Properties, Inc.** at the suit of The Bryn Mawr Trust Company. Debt: $867,423.49.
**Craig H. Fox,** Attorney

**43.** 90-15141
ALL THAT CERTAIN messuage and lot of ground known as No. 512 Norma Lane, Situate in the **Borough of Norristown.**
Seized and taken in execution as the property of **Frank Cardo** at the suit of Household Realty Corporation. Debt: $16,206.26.
**Bernard Pollick,** Attorney

**44.** 90-15715
ALL THAT CERTAIN lot of ground, with the buildings, being Lot No. 17 on a Certain Plan of Lots made for Francis Houston and Ellen Josephine Houston, his wife, and Edward J. Houston, Situate in the **Twp. of Lower Gwynedd.**
Seized and taken in execution as the property of **William Clayton and Thelma Clayton,** at the suit of Beneficial Savings Bank. Debt: $42,170.13.
**Richard J. Hodgson,** Attorney

**45.** 90-16149
ALL THAT CERTAIN lot of ground with the buildings, situate in **Cheltenham Twp.**
Seized and taken in execution as the property of **Nettie Lee Morris and Herbert A. Morris** at the suit of The Travelers Mortgage Services. Debt: $121,350.45.
**Barbara A. Fein,** Attorney

**46.** 90-16295
ALL THAT CERTAIN lot of ground, Situate in **Lower Merion Twp.**
Seized and taken in execution as the property of **Michael A. Mullock and Andrea E. Mullock** at the suit of Liberty Savings Bank. Debt: $218,222.
**Jill E. Jachera,** Attorney

**47.** 90-16424
ALL THAT CERTAIN lot of land, situate in the **Borough of Conshohocken.**
Seized and taken in execution as the property of **Robert Sickerott and Dawn Sickerott** at the suit of Wells Fargo Credit Corporation. Debt: $97,462.77.
**Barbara A. Fein,** Attorney

**48.** 90-17704
ALL THAT CERTAIN piece of ground situate in **Upper Dublin Twp.**
Seized and taken in execution as the property of **Fort Washington Realty Properties Partnership** at the suit of Provident Mutual Life Insurance Company of Philadelphia. Debt: $3,463,670.85.
**John F. Dougherty, Jr.,** Attorney

**49.** 90-17784
ALL THOSE TWO (2) CERTAIN lots or piece of land, being Lots Nos. 12 and 13, Block "I", on revised plan of lots of Saybrooke Park, Section No. 2, recorded in Deed Book No. 1447, page 600, situate in the Seventh Ward of the **Borough of Pottstown.**
ALSO ALL THAT CERTAIN lot or piece of ground, known and designated as the Northeasterly half of Lot 14, Block I, Section 2, on Plan of Saybrooke Park, revised April 1942 and recorded in Deed Book 1447, page 601, situate in the **Borough of Pottstown.**
Seized and taken in execution as the property of **Nelson Burnett and Susan Burnett** at the suit of Philadelphia National Bank. Debt: $97,286.92.
**Francis M. Correll, Jr.,** Attorney

**50.** 90-18497
ALL THAT CERTAIN lot of ground, with the buildings Situate in the **Twp. of Perkiomen.**
Seized and taken in execution as the property of **Paul J. Sedowsky and Barbara Sedowsky** at the suit of Coreast Savings Bank, FSB. Debt: 68,314.57.
**Frank Federman,** Attorney

**51.** 90-18687
ALL THAT CERTAIN messuage and tract of land situate in the **Borough of Norristown.**
Seized and taken in execution as the property of **John F. Prisco** at the suit of Cenlar Federal Savings Bank. Debt: $46,519.54.
**Barbara A. Fein,** Attorney

**52.** 90-18802
ALL THOSE THREE CERTAIN lots of ground situate in **Upper Dublin Twp.**
Seized and taken in execution as the property of **Lillian English and Russell J. Ellis** at the suit of Metmore Financial, Inc. Debt: $68,887.28.
**Frank Federman,** Attorney

**53.** 90-19361
ALL THAT CERTAIN messuage and lot of land, Situate in the **Borough of Norristown.**

## SHERIFF'S SALE–RULES OF THE ROAD

Seized and taken in execution as the property of **Ferrol C. Walker** at the suit of Maryland National Bank. Debt: $47,025.40

**Frank Federman,** Attorney

**54.** 90-19971

ALL THAT CERTAIN Lot of ground, with the buildings, Situate in the **Twp. of Springfield.**

Seized and taken in execution as the property of **D. Edward Wiser** at the suit of Chestnut Hill National Bank. Debt: $160,567.48.

**David E. Stern,** Attorney

### DEFENDANTS — List No.



### LOCALITIES

#### Townships



#### Boroughs

RECORDING REQUESTED BY

AND WHEN RECORDED MAIL TO

CALIFORNIA TRUST DEEDS, INC.
125 12th Street Suite #111
Oakland, Ca. 94607

(415) 444-2682

T.S. No. 5072

COPY OF DOCUMENT RECORDED
MAR - 9 1990 90-067071
HAS NOT BEEN COMPARED WITH ORIGINAL
ALAMEDA COUNTY RECORDER

SPACE ABOVE THIS LINE FOR RECORDER'S USE

# Notice of Default

## IMPORTANT NOTICE

**IF YOUR PROPERTY IS IN FORECLOSURE BECAUSE YOU ARE BEHIND IN YOUR PAYMENTS, IT MAY BE SOLD WITHOUT ANY COURT ACTION, and you may have the legal right to bring your account in good standing by paying all of your past due payments plus permitted costs and expenses within the time permitted by law for reinstatement of your account, which is normally five business days prior to the date set for the sale of your property. No sale date may be set until three months from the date this notice of default was recorded (which date of recordation appears on this notice).**

**This amount is $** 2,074.95 **as of** March 9, 1990**, and will increase until your account becomes current. You may not have to pay the entire unpaid portion of your account, even though full payment was demanded, but you must pay the amount stated above.**

**However, you and your beneficiary or mortgagee may mutually agree in writing prior to the time the notice of sale is posted (which may not be earlier than the end of the three-month period stated above) to, among other things, (1) provide additional time in which to cure the default by transfer of the property or otherwise; or (2) establish a schedule of payments in order to cure your default; or both (1) and (2).**

**Following the expiration of the time period referred to in the first paragraph of this notice, unless the obligation being foreclosed upon or a separate written agreement between you and your creditor permits a longer period, you have only the legal right to stop the sale of your property by paying the entire amount demanded by your creditor.**

**To find out the amount you must pay, or to arrange for payment to stop the foreclosure, or if your property is in foreclosure for any other reason, contact:** BARBARA GOODMAN, c/o California Trust Deeds, Inc., 125 - 12th Street, #111, Oakland, CA 94607 415/444-2682

(NAME OF BENEFICIARY OR MORTGAGEE) (MAILING ADDRESS) (TELEPHONE)

**If you have any questions, you should contact a lawyer or the government agency which may have insured your loan.**

**Notwithstanding the fact that your property is in foreclosure, you may offer your property for sale, provided the sale is concluded prior to the conclusion of the foreclosure. Remember, YOU MAY LOSE LEGAL RIGHTS IF YOU DO NOT TAKE PROMPT ACTION.**

---

The undersigned hereby gives notice of a breach of the obligation for which the following Deed of or transfer in trust was given:
Trustor: Mary Joel, also know as Mary Anne Joel a single woman
Trustee: PLACER TITLE COMPANY
Dated: 03/01/89 Recorded: 03/08/89 as Doc. No. 89-063487
in Book Page of Official Records of the County of ALAMEDA
State of California, and notice of intention to sell or cause the property subject to said deed of or transfer in trust to be sold to satisfy said obligation. All sums secured by said deed of trust have been and are declared by the beneficiary to be and are immediately due and payable, by reason of said breaches.

NATURE OF BREACH: Failure to pay installment of interest which became due 12/15/89,

## NOTICE OF TRUSTEE SALE

# SAN BERNARDINO COUNTY

# TRUSTEE SALES

**APPLE VALLEY, ( 367-B1 )**
**9445 YUCCA RD 92308**

T:SEC 21, T4N, R3W. SBBM B:00000 L:RESID U:
APN:0438-321-12 LAST SOLD: 12/14/89
BUILT: 1963 ZONING: LAND $: 25000
BR: 1 USE CODE: 0510 BLDG $: 90000
BA: 1.0 BLDG SIZE: 1570 ASSD $: 115000
UNITS: LOT SIZE: 1.25A
T/DEED#: 89-486216 DEFAULT#: 90-473756
LOAN DATE: 12/14/89 DEF REC: 11/30/90
LOAN AMT: 115000 DEL AMT: 9176
OTH LOAN: AS OF: 11/27/90

OLIVER,JAMES R
9445 YUCCA RD
APPLE VALLEY, 92308
TRUSTEE NO: 203210
LOAN NO: 2682701
CAL-WESTERN RECONVEYANCE CORP
7863 LA MESA BLVD, 2ND FL
LA MESA 92041
619-466-9910
BENEFICIARY: 619-466-9910
FIRST NATIONAL BANK
7863 LA MESA BLVD, 2ND FL
LA MESA 92041

SALE DATE:04/09/91 10:30AM PLACE:351 N ARROWHEAD AVE BID $: 129954
SALE #:91-84109 REC:03/12/91 SAN BERNARDINO

**CHINO**
**12951 BENSON AVE #131 91710**

T:11996 B: L: U:50
APN:1020-082-021 LAST SOLD: 12/17/87
BUILT: 1983 ZONING: LAND $: 24786
BR: 1 USE CODE: 530 BLDG $: 46104
BA: 1.5 BLDG SIZE: 960 ASSD $: 70890
UNITS: LOT SIZE: 960
T/DEED#: 88-378152 DEFAULT#: 90-470358
LOAN DATE: 11/08/88 DEF REC: 11/28/90
LOAN AMT: 67750 DEL AMT: 4473
OTH LOAN: AS OF: 11/27/90

ORTIZ, SARAESTHER
12951 S. BENSON AVE #131
CHINO 91710
TRUSTEE NO: 303154
LOAN NO: 151644-2
CAL-WESTERN REC. CORP.
7863 LA MESA BL., 2ND FLR
LA MESA 92041
619-466-9910
BENEFICIARY: 619-466-9910
WESTERN REC. CORP.
7863 LA MESA BL., 2ND FLR
LA MESA 92041

SALE DATE:04/05/91 10:30AM PLACE:351 N ARROWHEAD AVE BID $: 67255
SALE #:91-86322 REC:03/14/91 SAN BERNARDINO

**CHINO ( 291-B2 )**
**14929 SANDALWOOD LANE 91710**

T:7046 B: L:174 U:
APN:1025-411-18 LAST SOLD: 09/01/89
BUILT: 1964 ZONING: LAND $: 51400
BR: 3 USE CODE: 510 BLDG $: 95350
BA: 2 BLDG SIZE: 1247 ASSD $: 146750
UNITS: LOT SIZE: 92X107
T/DEED#: 89-389059 DEFAULT#: 90-462477
LOAN DATE: 10/16/89 DEF REC: 11/20/90
LOAN AMT: 10000 DEL AMT: 11119
OTH LOAN: AS OF: 11/16/90

GUERRA, CHRISTIAN PATRICK & MC
14929 SANDALWOOD LANE
CHINO 91710
TRUSTEE NO: T1011901176
LOAN NO:
TRUSTEE CORP.
P.O. BOX 9392
BREA 92622
714-671-1917
BENEFICIARY: 714-671-1917
PAMELA FROST & JAMIE RIVERA
P.O. BOX 9392
BREA 92622

SALE DATE:04/04/91 11:30AM PLACE:351 N ARROWHEAD AVE BID $: 12738
SALE #:91-87618 REC:03/14/91 SAN BERNARDINO

**CHINO ( 33-F1 )**
**6212 SERENE CT. 91710**

T:8830 B: L:17 U:
APN:1015-522-17 LAST SOLD: 08/01/86
BUILT: 1974 ZONING: LAND $: 26530
BR: 3 USE CODE: 510 BLDG $: 79060
BA: 2 BLDG SIZE: 1200 ASSD $: 105590
UNITS: LOT SIZE: 65X114
T/DEED#: 90-127351 DEFAULT#: 90-480650
LOAN DATE: 04/03/90 DEF REC: 12/06/90
LOAN AMT: 31311 DEL AMT: 3620
OTH LOAN: AS OF: 12/04/90

ESCOTO, FRANCISCO & MARIA L.
6212 SERENE CT.
CHINO 91710
TRUSTEE NO: 506904
LOAN NO: 6471304957
TRANSAMERICA TITLE INS. CO
P.O. BOX 359
SANTA ANA 92702
BENEFI
TRANSA
P.O.
CHINO

SALE DATE:04/11/91 02:30PM PLACE:351 N ARROWHEAD AVE
SALE #:91-86027 REC:03/13/91 SAN BERNARDINO

By Permission
"Daily Commerce"
Los Angeles, CA

## FORECLOSURE PROCESS/TRUSTEE SALE PROCEDURES

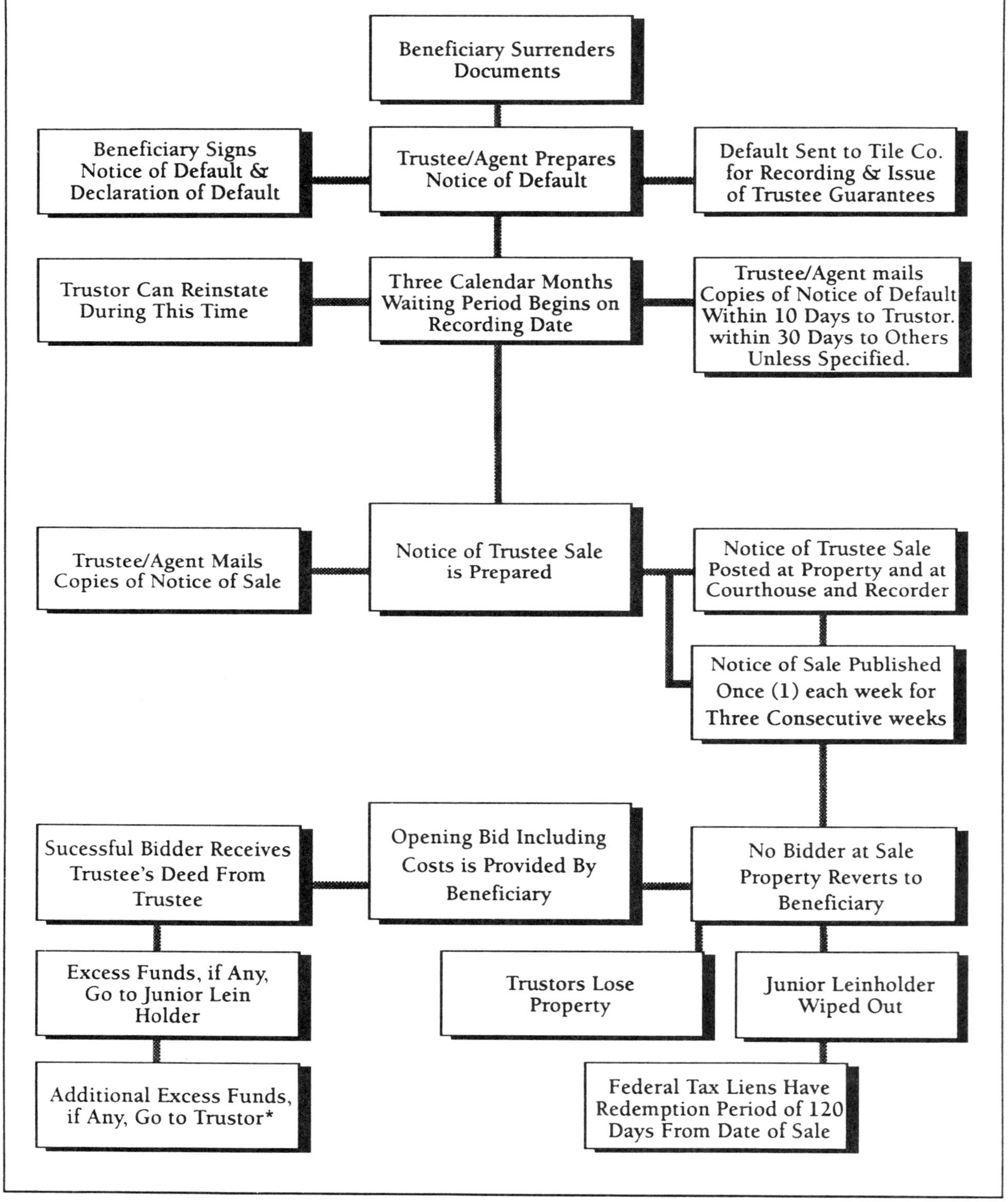

WHEN RECORDED MAIL TO:

CALIFORNIA LOAN SERVICING, INC,
39899 Balentine Drive, Suite 165
Newark, CA 94560
(415) 490-8835

# NOTICE OF TRUSTEE SALE

LN No.: ________

TS No.: 90-1602

## NOTICE

YOU ARE IN DEFAULT UNDER A DEED OF TRUST DATED SEPTEMBER 18, 1990 UNLESS YOU TAKE ACTION TO PROTECT YOUR PROPERTY, IT MAY BE SOLD AT A PUBLIC SALE. IF YOU NEED AN EXPLANATION OF THE NATURE OF THE PROCEEDING AGAINST YOU, YOU SHOULD CONTACT A LAWYER.

NOTICE is hereby given that on TUESDAY, the 9th /day of APRIL 19 91 at the hour of 10:00 A.M. at the MAIN STREET ENTRANCE TO THE CITY HALL, 1666 NORTH MAIN STREET,

in the City of WALNUT CREEK, County of CONTRA COSTA California. CALIFORNIA LOAN SERVICING, INC, a California corporation as Trustee, will sell at public auction to the highest bidder, for cash, in lawful money of the United States, all payble at the time of the sale, the following described real property, situated in the City of CONCORD County of CONTRA COSTA Sate of California, and described as follows:

PARCEL "C" AS SAID PARCEL IS SHOWN ON PARCEL MAP FILED JULY 3, 1973 IN BOOK 28 OF PARCEL MAPS, PAGE 44, CONTRA COSTA COUNTY RECORDS.

APN: 147-322-009

The Street address and other common designation, if any, of the real property described above is purported to be: 1675 DAVID AVENUE, CONCORD, CA.

The undersigned disclaims any liability for any incorrectness of the Street address or other common designation, if any, show herein.

Said sale will/be made, but without warranty, express or implied, regarding title, possession, or encumbrances, to pay the remaining principal sum of the note(s) secured by said Deed of Trust, with interest thereon, as provided in said note(s), advances, if any, under the terms of the Deed of Trust, fees, charges and expenses of the Trustee and of the trusts created by said Deed of Trust in the amount of approximately $ 132,143.25 pursuant to the power of sale conferred in that certain Deed of Trust Executed by CLINTON MATHIS WALKER AND JACQUELINE RUTH WALKER, HIS WIFE AS JOINT TENANTS as Trustors, to NORTHWESTERN TITLE COMPANY OF ALAMEDA COUNTY, a corporation, As Trustee, for the benefit and security of HERBERT R. MEYER, TRUSTEE MEYER FAMILY TRUST UTD 1/1/76

Dated, Sep. 18, 1990, and Recorded Oct. 01,1990 Instr. No. 90-205132 Book 16155 Page 802, Official Records of the County of CONTRA COSTA, Default was recorded DEC. 10,1990

CALIFORNIA LOAN SERVICING INC
39899 BALENTINE DRIVE, SUITE 165
NEWARK, CA 94560
(415) 490-8835
B. PERRY,

RECORDING REQUESTED BY

AND WHEN RECORDED MAIL TO:

Name New Growth Financial
Street Address c/o Ted Thomas
177 Front St., Ste. 207
City & State Danville, CA. 94526

MAIL TAX STATEMENTS TO

Name same as above
Street Address
City & State

CERTIFIED TO BE A TRUE COPY OF
OF DOCUMENT RECORDED 11-1-88
SERIES NO. 88-201531
OF OFFICIAL RECORDS
Chicago Title Insurance Co.
BY [signature]

SPACE ABOVE THIS LINE FOR RECORDER'S USE

Loan No.: 32228739 **Trustee's Deed Upon Sale** CFE/TF TS No. 54900

The undersigned grantor declares: under penalty of perjury

(1) The grantee herein ~~xxx~~ — was not the foreclosing beneficiary.
(2) The amount of the unpaid debt together with costs was ................ $ 200,336.42
(3) The amount paid by the grantee at the trustee sale was ................ $ 200,400.00
(4) The documentary transfer tax is ................................ $ 220.55
(5) Said property is in ( ) unincorporated area: ( x ) City of DANVILLE, and

**CAL FED ENTERPRISES**, a California corporation, (herein called Trustee), as the duly appointed Trustee under the Deed of Trust hereinafter described, does hereby grant and convey, but without warranty, express or implied, to

NEW GROWTH FINANCIAL

(herein called Grantee), all of its right, title and interest in and to that certain property situated in the city of DANVILLE County of CONTRA COSTA State of California, described as follows:

LOT 3, MAP OF SUBDIVISION 6199, FILED OCTOB ER 10, 1983, MAP BOOK 273, PAGE 19, CONTRA COSTA COUNTY RECORDS.

FOR COMPLETE LEGAL DESCRIPTION SEE EXHIBIT "A" ATTACHED HERETO AND MADE A PART HEREOF

TRUSTEE STATES THAT: This conveyance is made pursuant to the powers conferred upon Trustee by that certain Deed of Trust dated 12/14/84 and executed by JOHNNY A. KIPP

as trustor, and recorded 01/04/85 in Book -- Page -- Instrument No. 85-866, of Official Records of CONTRA COSTA County, California, and after fulfillment of the conditions specified in said Deed of Trust authorizing this conveyance.

Default occurred as set forth in a Notice of Default and Election to Sell which was recorded in the office of the Recorder of said County.

All requirements of law regarding the mailing, publication and personal delivery of copies of the Notice of Default and the posting and publication of copies of the Notice of Sale, without regard to whether a Request For Notice has been recorded, have been complied with.

Said property was sold by said Trustee at public auction on SEPTEMBER 30, 1988 at the place named in the Notice of Sale, in the County of CONTRA COSTA, California, in which the property is situated. Grantee, being the highest bidder at such sale, became the purchaser of said property and paid therefor to said Trustee the amount bid, being $ 200,400.00, in lawful money of the United States, or by the satisfaction, pro tanto, of the obligations then secured by said Deed of Trust.

**In Witness Whereof**, said **CAL FED ENTERPRISES**, a California Corporation, as Trustee, has this day caused its corporate name and seal to be hereunto affixed by its officer, thereunto duly authorized by resolution of its Board of Directors.

STATE OF CALIFORNIA
COUNTY OF LOS ANGELES } ss.

On October 04, 1988 before me, the undersigned, a Notary Public in and for said State,

CAL FED ENTERPRISES,
as Trustee aforesaid.

ORDER NO: 55814
Page 2

The land referred to in this report is situated in the State of California, County of Contra Costa and is described as follows:

UNINCORPORATED AREA

LOT 3, MAP OF SUBDIVISION 6199, FILED OCTOBER 10, 1983, MAP BOOK 273, PAGE 19, CONTRA COSTA COUNTY RECORDS.

EXCEPTING THEREFROM:

"ALL OIL, GAS, ASPHALTUM AND OTHER HYDROCARBONS AND ALL CHEMICAL GAS, NOW OR HEREAFTER FOUND, SITUATED OR LOCATED IN ALL OR ANY PART OR PORTION OOF THE LANDS DESCRIBED HEREIN LYING MORE THAN FIVE HUNDRED FEET (500') BELOW THE SURFACE THEREOF, TOGETHER WITH THE RIGHT TO SLANT DRILL FOR AND REMOVE ALL OR ANY OF SAID OIL, GAS, CASINGHEAD GAS, ASPHALTUM AND OTHER HYDROCARBONS AND CHEMICAL GAS LYING BELOW A DEPTH OF MORE THAN FIVE HUNDRED FEET (500') BELOW THE SURFACE THEREOF; BUT WITHOUT ANY RIGHTS WHATSOEVER TO ENTER UPON THE SURFACE OF SAID LAND OR UPON ANY PART OF SAID LANDS WITHIN FIVE HUNDRED FEET (500') VERTICAL DISTANCE BELOW THE SURFACE THEREOF."

AS RESERVED IN THE DEED FROM BLACKHAWK CORPORATION, RECORDED OCTOBER 18, 1983, IN BOOK 11489, PAGE 228, OFFICIAL RECORDS.

ASSESSOR'S PARCEL NO. 203-750-003

## FORECLOSURE KEY FACTORS CHART

| STATE ID | SECURITY INSTRUMENT | FORECLOSE METHOD | INITIAL ACTION | MONTHS TO COMPLETION | REDEMPTION PERIOD* | DEFICIENCY PROVISION |
|---|---|---|---|---|---|---|
| AL | Mortgage | Non-Judicial | Publication | 1 month | 12 months | Allowed |
| AK | Deed of Trust | Non-Judicial | Notice of Default | 3 months | None | Allowed[1] |
| AZ | Deed of Trust | Non-Judicial | Notice of Sale | 3 months | None | Allowed[2] |
| AR | Mortgage | Judicial[3] | Complaint | 4 months | None | Allowed |
| CA | Deed of Trust | Non-Judicial | Notice of Default | 4 months | None | Prohibited |
| CO | Deed of Trust | Non-Judicial | Notice of Election | 2 months | 75 days[4] | Allowed |
| CT | Mortgage | Strict[5] | Complaint | 5 months | None | Allowed |
| DE | Mortgage | Judicial | Complaint | 3 months | None | Allowed |
| DC | Deed of Trust | Non-Judicial | Notice of Default | 2 months | None | Allowed |
| FL | Mortgage | Judicial | Complaint | 5 months | None | Allowed |
| GA | Security Deed | Non-Judicial | Publication | 2 months | None | Allowed |
| HI | Mortgage | Non-Judicial[6] | Publication | 3 months | None | Allowed |
| ID | Trust Deed | Non-Judicial | Notice of Default | 5 months | None | Allowed |
| IL | Mortgage | Judicial | Complaint | 12 months | None[7] | Allowed |
| IN | Mortgage | Judicial | Complaint | 5 months | 3 months[8] | Allowed |
| IA | Mortgage | Judicial | Petition of F/C | 5 months | 6 months[9] | Allowed |
| KS | Mortgage | Judicial | Complaint | 4 months | 6-12 months[10] | Allowed |
| KY | Mortgage | Judicial | Complaint | 6 months | None[11] | Allowed |
| LA | Mortgage | Executory Process | Petition for Process | 2 months | None | Allowed |
| ME | Mortgage | Judicial | Complaint | 6 months | None[12] | Allowed |
| MD | Trust Deed | Non-Judicial | Notice | 2 months | None | Allowed |
| MA | Mortgage | Judicial[13] | Complaint | 3 months | None | Allowed |
| MI | Mortgage | Non-Judicial | Publication | 2 months | 6 months[14] | Allowed |
| MN | Mortgage | Non-Judicial | Publication | 2 months | 6 months[15] | Prohibited[16] |
| MS | Deed of Trust | Non-Judicial[17] | Publication | 2 month | None | Allowed |
| MO | Deed of Trust | Non-Judicial | Publication | 2 months | None | Allowed |
| MT | Trust Deed | Non-Judicial | Notice | 5 months | None | Prohibited[16] |
| NE | Mortgage[18] | Judicial[18] | Petition[18] | 5 months | None | Allowed |
| NV | Deed of Trust | Non-Judicial | Notice of Default | 4 months | None | Allowed |
| NH | Mortgage | Non-Judicial | Notice of Sale | 2 months | None | Allowed |
| NJ | Mortgage | Judicial | Complaint | 3 months | None | Allowed |
| NM | Mortgage | Judicial | Complaint | 4 months[19] | None[19] | Allowed |
| NY | Mortgage | Judicial | Complaint | 4 months | None | Allowed |
| NC | Deed of Trust | Non-Judicial | Notice of Hearing | 2 months | None | Allowed |
| ND | Mortgage | Judicial | Complaint | 3 months | 60 days[20] | Prohibited |
| OH | Mortgage | Judicial | Complaint | 5 months | None | Allowed |
| OK | Mortgage | Judicial[21] | Complaint | 4 months | None | Allowed |
| OR | Trust Deed | Non-Judicial | Notice of Default | 5 months | None | Allowed |
| PA | Mortgage | Judicial | Complaint | 5 months | None | Allowed |
| RI | Mortgage | Non-Judicial | Publication | 2 months | None | Allowed |
| SC | Mortgage | Judicial | Complaint | 6 months | None | Allowed |
| SD | Mortgage | Judicial | Complaint | 3 months | 180 days[22] | Allowed |
| TN | Deed of Trust | Non-Judicial | Publication | 2 months | None | Allowed |
| TX | Deed of Trust | Non-Judicial | Publication | 2 months | None | Allowed |
| UT | Deed of Trust | Non-Judicially | Notice of Default | 4 months | None | Allowed |
| VT | Mortgage | Judicial | Complaint | 7 months[23] | None | Allowed |
| VA | Deed of Trust | Non-Judicial | Publication | 2 months | None | Allowed |
| WA | Deed of Trust | Non-Judicial | Notice of Default | 4 months | None | Prohibited[24] |
| WV | Trust Deed | Non-Judicial | Publication | 2 months | None | Allowed |
| WI | Mortgage | Judicial | Complaint | Varies[25] | None | Allowed |
| WY | Mortgage | Non-Judicial | Publication | 2 months | 3 Months[26] | Allowed |

* Statutory redemption period following the foreclosure sale. *This period is in addition to foreclosure completion time.*

*Footnotes:*

1 Must foreclose judicially in order to preserve right to pursue recovery through a deficiency judgment.
2 Deficiency judgements not allowed on one or two family homes situated on less than 2.5 acres
3 If the mortgage contains authorizing language, or if a deed of trust is used, foreclosure may be by non-judicial process
4 The redemption period following the sale is 6 months if the property is used for agricultural purposes.
5 Judgment of Foreclosure by Sale may be ordered by the judge if the mortgagor has substantial equity in the property.
6 Many foreclosures in Hawaii are still foreclosed via the Judicial method.
7 Recent changes to Illinois law place the redemption period prior to the sale date
8 If the mortgage is dated prior to July 1, 1975, there is a six month redemption period
9 Iowa has substantial exceptions to the redemption periods for agricultural property and non owner occupied property
10 Length of redemption period following the sale depends on mortgagor's equity
11 Redemption period of 12 months follows the sale if the bid amount is less than 2/3 of the appraised value
12 If the mortgage is prior to 10/1/75 and silent on the the redemption period, a 1 year redemption period will exist
13 Massachusetts law also allows for alternate forms of foreclosure including Entry and Possession
14 Redemption period is increased to 12 months if property in excess of three acres and 33% equity. Vacant 3 months
15 The redemption period will be 12 months if the mortgage is dated prior to 7/1/67 or if agricultural property
16 A deficiency judgment may be pursued if foreclosure is conducted judicially
17 Foreclosure may also be conducted judically if a deficiency judgment is desired
18 Nebraska also allows for deeds of trust which can be foreclosed non-judicially if provided in the security instrument
19 Redemption period preceeds sale. Mortgages after 1965 have 1 month redeption. Prior to 1965 period is 3 months
20 Redemption period following sale for mortgages after 7/1/81 is the later of 6 months from complaint or 60 days from sale
21 Oklahoma Power of Sale provides for foreclosure by publication if power is granted in the security instrument
22 Redemption period is one year if limited language is not included in the security instrument
23 The redemption period preceeds the final action. If the mortgage is dated prior to 4/1/68, the redemption period is 12 months
24 A deficiency judgment may be awarded if the foreclosure is conducted judicially. Most VA guaranteed loans are judically foreclosed
25 Redemption period preceeds the sale. Length of redemption varies from 2 months to 12 months depending on themortgage and occupancy
26 Agricultural property will have a 12 month redemption period following the sale

Prepared by: Dennis A. Jankowski

# *EPILOGUE*

***I*** wish I could say that all of those who read this text will be successful. Some of you will persevere and succeed; others will decide it is too much work; still others will give up when confronted with the complexity of learning something new. I guarantee the systems and methods suggested in this book. I can't guarantee that you will implement them.

If your goal was entertainment and education only, I thank you for buying my book. If you sincerely need more help, telephone me — (510) 837-2106 — and I will advise you. From time to time I conduct results-guaranteed seminars. They are expensive — but results are what you pay for. You'll be able to measure your results by reviewing your bank balance and watching it increase.

# *APPENDIXES*

## Appendix A

# NEWSPAPER ADVERTISING

**HOW TO WRITE A NEWSPAPER AD THAT WILL BRING YOU SUCH AN AMAZING FLOOD OF SUPER-PROFITABLE FORECLOSURE OPPORTUNITIES THAT YOU CAN'T HANDLE THEM ALL!**


Nolan & Associates Advertising
(916) 723-3070

CONGRATULATIONS on your decision to learn Ted Thomas' secrets of buying and selling foreclosure properties.

I can personally verify that Ted's system works. I decided to test it for myself and as you can see by the title company check reproduced below, it is indeed a great way to make many thousands of extra dollars, without giving up your current source of income. Or, if you like, with a little effort it can become a full time business.

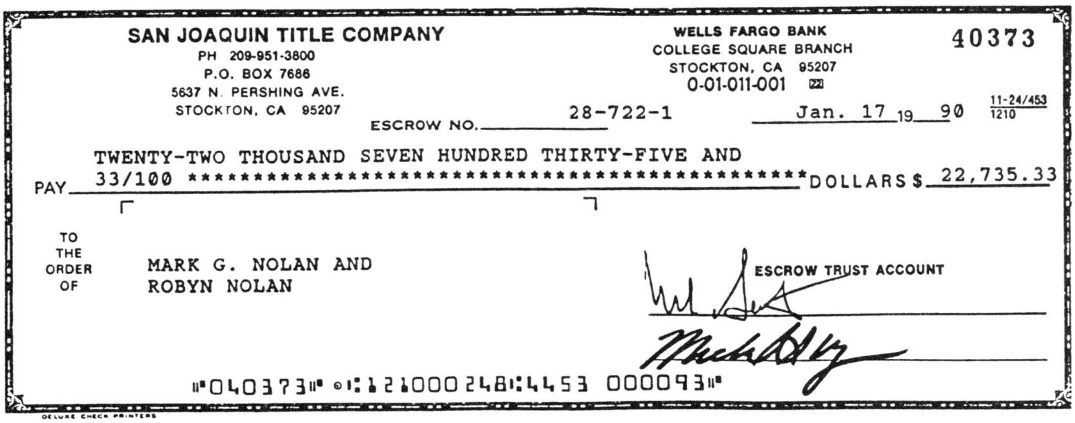
SAN JOAQUIN TITLE COMPANY
PH 209-951-3800
P.O. BOX 7686
5637 N. PERSHING AVE.
STOCKTON, CA 95207

WELLS FARGO BANK
COLLEGE SQUARE BRANCH
STOCKTON, CA 95207
0-01-011-001

40373

ESCROW NO. 28-722-1 Jan. 17 19 90 11-24/453 1210

PAY TWENTY-TWO THOUSAND SEVEN HUNDRED THIRTY-FIVE AND 33/100 ************************************************* DOLLARS $ 22,735.33

TO THE ORDER OF MARK G. NOLAN AND ROBYN NOLAN

ESCROW TRUST ACCOUNT

⑈040373⑈ ⑆121000248⑆4453 000093⑈

My name is Mark Nolan. I run an advertising agency that specializes in direct response and the results-getting ads I've created have helped my many clients sell everything from $1 books to millions of dollars worth of real estate. From high tech to home made and everything in-between. Financial offers, jewelry, cosmetics, magazines, diets and audio cassettes. All kinds of clothing, investments, foods, music, vitamins, lingerie, even a horse ranch. You name it, advertising I've written has sold it.

Now I want to tell you an advertising secret that will have your phone ringing off the hook with foreclosure opportunities.

Reprinted by permission

## Appendix A

# NEWSPAPER ADVERTISING

You may be wondering just how a person can buy and sell real estate properties with mail order techniques.

Sure, you've bought (and maybe sold) various items through mail order ads ... but real estate property?

Believe it!

Here is just one example of a large property that was sold by mailing out sales letters:

**THE LONDON BRIDGE!**

No kidding.

An English city engineer named Harold King wanted to sell the London Bridge because it was scheduled to be torn down.

He mailed out 2000 sales pieces at a cost of $1,230. The result? An American investor purchased the historic bridge at a price of $2,460,000. Not a bad return on a $1,230 investment, eh? That's about $2,000 back for every dollar invested.

This goes to show that real estate can and is being sold with mail order techniques -- plus some followup phone calls and in-person deal making of course.

### AND NOW, THE AMAZING STORY OF HOW A NEWSPAPER "ARTICLE" SENT TED'S DIRECT MAIL RESPONSE THROUGH THE ROOF!

Ted Thomas is not only one of the people in this world that I admire and respect, he is also a friend and a client of my advertising agency.

Some time ago, Ted came to me with a challenge.

He is a very talented advertising copywriter in his own right and he had written some "killer" sales letters that were helping him to cash in on the foreclosure property market.

His challenge was for me to improve the pulling power of the letters, if possible.

You can read some of Ted's actual letters in this manual. They are sent to people who are facing imminent foreclosure and each letter in the series is designed to do one thing, get them to call and give Ted an opportunity to buy their property.

Ted was already making a fortune from these letters and didn't need any help from anyone. However, one of the keys to Ted's success is that he's always working to improve his results.

## Appendix A

# *NEWSPAPER ADVERTISING*

Towards that goal, he challenged me to create an additional insert piece to mail along with his successful sales letters that would boost his response even higher.

We talked about creating a brochure or insert, but we wanted something that would give the mailing piece a big dose of added credibility to overcome doubts in the mind of the readers.

We finally decided to swipe an idea from Gary Halbert.

One of the rules of direct response marketing is that if you are going to copy someone's idea, only copy from the best!

Gary is known as "The Maven of Marketing, The Prince of Print, and The Hemingway of Headlines." He publishes a super-valuable newsletter in which he wrote the following:

"Think about what could be the best possible piece of luck you could have. Think about a reporter who heard a rumor about your product or service and decided to check it out. And then, he fell in love with it. In fact, he loved it so much, he went back to his typewriter and wrote a full-page rave article about what you are selling.

Wouldn't that be nice? Sure would. However, it is also un-likely that such a thing will happen. So . . .

**YOU BE THAT REPORTER!**

You write the rave 'article.' Just like a reporter would. And, at the end of the article, you perform a "public service" for your readers by telling them where and how to order."

(To subscribe contact: The Gary Halbert Letter, Suite 4, 5701 Overseas Hwy, Marathon, FL 33050, phone number (305) 743-5291.)

That's exactly what I did for Ted.

I wrote a "news article" where I acted as an editor and "interviewed" him on how he helps people who are facing foreclosure (what a guy). I urged anyone who finds themselves in that situation to contact Ted for help, pronto.

I'm going to teach you step-by-step how to write your own "news article" but first let me tell you where we ran this ad....

**NOWHERE!**

We didn't run the ad in the newspaper at all, we simply had a newspaper publisher print it up on newsprint so it looked like an actual news article torn out of the paper.

## Appendix A

# NEWSPAPER ADVERTISING

Next we folded up these pieces of newsprint and mailed them out to prospects along with a sales letter. Soon, Ted started getting even more phone calls and the people who called were telling him "I read about you in a newspaper story...."

Don't ya love it?

Another way to use this newspaper piece is to mail them out in a blank envelope and attach a post-it note to the article or scribble a note in handwriting on it that says something like "I thought this news might be helpful to you, best wishes." Sign it with only an initial, like "R" or "J" because everyone knows someone with a name that begins with one of those initials.

The idea is to give the impression that a concerned friend has torn out the story and sent it to your prospect. They rack their brain wondering who sent it and how they knew about their impending foreclosure.

This often works like crazy because it is very close to some of the best advertising action you can get...

**WORD OF MOUTH**

Be sure you mail the news piece in a blank envelope without your name or return address on it. And use a real stamp, not a postage meter imprint. How many average people have a postage meter in their home? Give the impression that some friend of theirs actually tore this out of the paper, put it in an envelope, stuck a stamp on it and dropped it in the mail.

Now, if you want to be totally authentic, you can go ahead and run the ad in a local newspaper and ask them to print up extra copies of that page, front and back, for your use.

This adds extra impact because the people who read this piece can see the name of the paper and the date right up there at the top of the page. They can even go to the library and look up that day's paper and see your smiling face right there on page 47 if they are that curious.

This does create two problems, however.

One problem is that you will have to cough up the cash to pay for running the ad in the newspaper.

The second problem is that you now have a dated mailing piece. You may find that after a while it becomes old news and the date actually works against you, not for you.

To circumvent these problems, do what Ted and I did. Print the ad smaller than a full size page and forget about running it in the paper just to get the masthead and the date at the top.

## Appendix A

# NEWSPAPER ARTICLE

## *New Growth Financial . . . A Company with a Heart*

# Unique Firm Helps Families When Foreclosure Threatens

DANVILLE, CA—If you, or someone you know happens to be one of the 5,000 or more families who face default and possible foreclosure each year in Contra Costa County, you know what a traumatic experience it can be.

To learn more about how people can successfully deal with their foreclosure problem, this reporter held the following interview with Ted Thomas, Vice President of New Growth Financial. Mr. Thomas specializes in rescuing families that find themselves in a foreclosure situation, and have too little money to pay off their debts.

Before I interviewed Ted Thomas I investigated his company, New Growth Financial, and conducted a thorough background check. I found that New Growth Financial is a member in good standing of the Better Business Bureau. The company also belongs to the Chamber of Commerce and serves on the Contra Costa Board of Realtors.

Through their good works, combined with giving free public seminars and publishing informative booklets on this subject, New Growth Financial has become known as the "Distressed Property Experts" in Contra Costa and Alameda Counties. (Later in this interview you'll receive information on how to attend their free seminar titled **How To Stop Foreclosure**, and also get a copy of their helpful reports, **18 Ways To Avoid Foreclosure**, and **Eye-Opening Facts About Foreclosure**).

To round-out my investigation, I collected the comments of people who have been rescued by New Growth Financial. People who were actually facing foreclosure and who turned to Ted Thomas' company for help and assistance. The stories I uncovered were as dramatic and heart-warming as any you'll see on prime time television. But these stories were *true*. These stories were about *real* people. . . people in our county. . . people like you and me. On that positive note I want to move right into the actual interview with New Growth Financial's Vice President, Mr. Ted Thomas.

**QUESTION: TED, EXACTLY WHAT CAUSES A FORECLOSURE?**

*ANSWER:* Well Mark, there are many contributing factors that can lead to foreclosure—illness, unemployment, divorce, unexpected expenses, accumulated debts—but the one immediate cause is usually failure to make the monthly payments on your home.

Some of the other reasons can include: Failure to pay taxes or protect your home with insurance. Even lack of upkeep or appearance can trigger a foreclosure action.

**QUESTION: SO PEOPLE GENERALLY HAVE AN IDEA THAT THEY MAY BE FACING FORECLOSURE SOON?**

*ANSWER:* Yes, a "*Notice of Default*" seldom comes as a surprise. You are seldom unaware of the fact that you have missed payments on your home . . and probably have lived in dread of the day when such a notice will arrive.

**QUESTION: WHAT STEPS CAN THE BANK TAKE AGAINST YOU?**

*ANSWER:* Even though you have an excellent excuse for missing the tardy payments, don't expect a sympathetic or understanding reaction from your "friendly" banker or other lender. He loaned you the money, and he wants it back.

However, give it a try. If he thinks you can handle future payments, sometimes the lender will try to work something out with you. *Usually not.*

**QUESTION: AT THIS POINT, I UNDERSTAND THAT YOU HAVE ONLY 111 DAYS TO ACT?**

*ANSWER:* Correct. Once you receive your "*Notice of Default*" you have three months to make *all* back payments, *plus* penalties, on your loan. If you do this before the deadline, your loan will be re-instated, and everything will go on as before.

If you *cannot* clear up your past-due payments within this three-month grace period, the lender will probably take the next step, a "*Notice of Trustee's Sale.*" This notice gives you 21 more days to save your home. A notice, announcing the auction of your home at Trustee sale will be published in a newspaper. If you can pay your *entire* loan off *in full* (the total 30-year loan—not just back payments), you have saved your home. If not, you had better start packing.

**HOW NEW GROWTH FINANCIAL HAS COME TO THE RESCUE FOR OTHER PEOPLE IN OUR COMMUNITY**

"Ted Thomas took the time to explain how his service worked," said Horst Ehler. "He did not pressure me, but let me make my own decision.

"Without help from New Growth Financial, it would have been very hard to find a place to live. But the money he gave me more than made up the deposit I needed to move into an apartment. Without that money, I don't know where I would have ended up.

If I come up against this problem again, Ted Thomas would be the first person I'd call. . . I highly recommend him."

□ □ □

Thomas Johnson writes, "Having endured such an experience (foreclosure), I would like to recommend that anyone else finding himself in similar circumstances contact Ted Thomas of New Growth Financial.

"Mr. Thomas not only correctly advised me of my options, but outlined a plan that helped me in resettling my family and regaining a measure of stability in our lives.

Mr. Thomas and his staff performed efficiently and with sensitivity to our problems at a time which that kind of professionalism and attitude was essential to me and my family."

□ □ □

"You won't be disappointed! I wasn't," says Geneva Stutsman. "I was able to sell my home to New Growth Financial just days before the Trustee sale."

Try to imagine the alternatives:

- Eviction
- No money to start over
- More bills

"These were the alternatives I faced. What do you have to lose? New Growth Financial paid me cash and I was able to stop my losses. When every dollar counts it's good to know that the cashier's check is good at any bank.

Find out for yourself. I know you'll agree they work quickly and quietly. I'm happy with the fair treatment I received."

□ □ □

John Stutsman writes, "Time was running out! We sold our home to New Growth Enterprises in less than one week and received more money than we bargained for.

"Now it's time for you to decide. You owe it to your family to salvage as many dollars as possible. New Growth Financial even allowed us to stay in our home weeks after the sale.

I know you will find them more than fair and they stand behind their claims. In other words, New Growth Financial performed as they said they would."

*Editor's Note: There are many more positive testimonials about New Growth Financial than we have space to print here. These will serve as an example of the consumer response to the company. — Mark Nolan, Ed.*

**FACING FORECLOSURE?**
It's Ted Thomas to your rescue!
Call **(415) 837-2106**

**QUESTION: WHAT SHOULD READERS OF THIS NEWSPAPER DO IF THEY, TOO FACE POSSIBLE FORECLOSURE?**

*ANSWER:* I suggest they call me. . . today. New Growth Financial is a unique company. We're in the business of rescuing families that find themselves in a foreclosure situation, and have too little money to pay off their debt. We're here to help.

Usually, the only way out at this point is to sell your home. However, realtors estimate it takes an average of 100 days to sell a home. You haven't got 100 days.

I'll meet with you and discuss your situation. If no alternative solution can be worked out, my company will offer you *cash* for your home—enough cash to pay off the mortgage and have some left over to make a fresh start.

We will take all of the hassle off your shoulders. We will contact the lender and tell him in no uncertain terms that he is to deal with our company from now on. We will put a stop to the harassment too. No more letters or middle-of-the night phone calls. You'll be saved the embarrassment, financial loss and credit problems that result from a Trustee's auction.

**QUESTION: WHAT KIND OF GUARANTEE DO YOU OFFER FOR YOUR SERVICES?**

*ANSWER:* If, in the meantime, you should get a better offer from another buyer than you can get from New Growth Financial, we will tear up our contract, and let you pocket the extra cash. We've built our business on reputation and trust. That's why we're members of the Better Business Bureau, Chamber of Commerce, and the Board of Realtors. That's also why we have so many testimonials and customer referrals. The client comes first!

A fascinating interview and a welcome relief for anyone who is in foreclosure now or fear they may face foreclosure in the near future. For those who want a free copy of New Growth Financial's reports and/or just want to talk over how they can help you, write or call Ted Thomas at New Growth Financial, 185 Front Street, Suite 207, Danville, CA 94526. There is no cost or obligation for this service. Call **(415) 837-2106.**

## Appendix A

# INFORMATION ON EDITORIAL ADS

### HERE ARE SOME TIPS ON HOW TO WRITE YOUR OWN EDITORIAL STYLE AD

Your "story" should have a beginning, a middle and and end. Just like any other story. It sounds obvious, but how many articles have you stopped reading half way through because they seemed to wander on aimlessly? Plenty. So think in three parts:

PART 1) Tell what the news is about and why it's important to the reader.

PART 2) Prove what you say, or give relevant facts to substantiate the story.

PART 3) End with a flourish. In our case, ask for action.

### THE MOST IMPORTANT PART OF YOUR AD IS THE HEADLINE

The headline is responsible for about 75% of the pulling power of your ad. If the headline doesn't get the reader's attention instantly they won't read past it and your ad never get's a chance to sell anything.

The key word here is attention.

There is an age-old, tried and true formula to remember when writing an ad and it's known as the AIDA formula.

**A** -- Get the reader's attention

**I** -- Arouse the reader's interest

**D** -- Stimulate the reader's desire

**A** -- Ask the reader to take action

The late, great Robert Collier, author of the classic The Robert Collier Letter Book offered this variation on the formula:

Attention

Interest

Description

Persuasion

## Appendix A

# INFORMATION ON EDITORIAL ADS

Proof

Close

Here are more tips for writing a good editorial-style ad.

* After your headline, your first paragraph is all important. It must arouse your reader's interest and make him settle in to read the entire story.

* Use subheadings to guide the reader's eye down the columns. A question and answer format is an easy way to accomplish this. (See Ted's ad) Put the questions in bold type.

* Use good old serif typestyles. Stay away from sanserif type. If you do use sanserif, use it only in the headline. All newspapers use Times Roman type or something similar. You want your ad to look like a real news story so use standard news type.

* Don't reverse type -- white type on black background. It's hard to read and it screams "This is an advertisement!"

* If you are confused about typesetting, find a newspaper that will set the story into type for you. That way you know it will look authentic. It will have been typeset on the same machine as the rest of the actual newspaper.

* Feature testimonials from happy customers if you have them. If not, join the Better Business Bureau and Chamber of Commerce so you can brag about being a member. It gives you added legitimacy and is a lends "proof" that you can be believed.

* Tell the whole story. The master, Claude Hopkins, wrote "The motto here is, 'The more you tell the more you sell.' And it has never failed to prove out so in any test we know." Amen. Many people will tell you that no one will read a whole page of writing. In the next breath they'll tell you about the 300 page book they just finished and how they "couldn't put it down!"

Claude Hopkins was the father of scientific advertising and wrote a book by that title. The book is so important that David Oglivy said "Nobody should be allowed to have anything to do with advertising until he has read this book (Scientific Advertising) seven times. It changed the course of my life."

Mine too. Get it. Read it. Read it again. And again.

Hopkins wrote an advertisement of five full pages filled with words for Schlitz beer. In just a few months, Schlitz shot up from fifth place in sales to number one.

The most words anyone has ever used in a single page was 6,450, in an ad for Merrill Lynch. It ran in the New York Times and produced 10,000 responses. From an ad without any coupon. (The offer was buried in the text near the end.)

## Appendix A

# INFORMATION ON EDITORIAL ADS

My hero, David Oglivy, is probably one of the greatest ad men alive today. In his amazing book Oglivy On Advertising he writes:

"There is no law which says advertisements have to look like advertisements. If you make them look like editorial pages, you will attract more readers. Roughly six times as many people read the average article as the average advertisement. Very few advertisements are read by more than one reader in twenty.

Next time you construct an ad, pretend you are an editor; you will get more readership.

If you abandon the conventional graphics of advertisements and adopt editorial graphics, your campaigns will become islands of good taste in an ocean of vulgarity."

If you don't own a copy of this book get one immediately and read it cover to cover at least three times. Once you do so you'll know more about effective advertising than the employees at most "creative" advertising agencies.

This editorial-look stragegy in advertising has been proven profitable over and over again. One famous example is a very successful ad run by Ben Suarez some time ago for his amazing book Seven Steps to Freedom. (Read Ben's book too, it's great!)

The ad looked exactly like a news story. The headline read

**OHIO MAN DISCOVERS THE SECRET OF**

**HOW TO ESCAPE THE AMERICAN RAT RACE**

The subheading was a killer too. It read, **"7 Simple Rules Net This Working Man Without Any Money or Experience $145,000 in First Year."**

The story was set in columns and started out with a byline:
**"By John Whitehead, Special Features Writer."**

There was a photo of the family with this caption underneath: "Swarez does his system in his motor home while his wife, Nancy, drives and his two daughters, Sharon and Michele, play and sight-see. That's the family's pet shetland sheepdog on a favorite perch."

To see a full copy of Ben Suarez's winning masterpiece of an ad, read the book How To Get Rich In Mail Order by Melvin Powers.

## Appendix B

# NEGOTIATING

### The Good Negotiator

The good negotiator, no matter what the business, has a number of clearly recognizable characteristics. The good negotiator:

- Is a careful planner who thinks out the problem before starting the negotiations and is sure of his or her facts.
- Can visualize the final outcome; is able to define, for himself or herself, what is expected of the deal.
- Recognizes the inherent conflict and uncertainty in any negotiating process; even good negotiators can't predict exactly how things will turn out.
- Sets high goals and is tenacious and persistent.
- Recognizes that personal issues will affect the outcome and make allowances for such issues.
- Has patience.

Essentially, the good negotiator is self-confident, well-informed, imaginative, tolerant, and not likely to be side-tracked.

All negotiations are contests, but they are not wars. Both sides need to be prepared to give as well as take, and the following twleve points might be considered rules of the game.

1. Leave yourself room to negotiate. If you are the seller, start high; if you are the buyer, begin low. Don't pick your figures out of the air. Have a justifiable reason for whatever price you ask. Do your homework. Use the facts, not fantasy. Find the hidden agendas. Get the seller's demands on the table; keeps yours hidden.
2. Don't hurry. Be patient. The seller needs time to get used to you and develop a trust in you. People do not make decisions easily. They need time to adjust to the difference between what they thought they could and what they will be getting by the time the transaction is closed.
3. Don't talk too much. When you are talking, you can't be listening to your opponent's responses. In addition, excessive talking may be interpreted as a sign of nervousness.
4. Always remember you are dealing with real money and real emotions. That means that is is not important that you always be popular. If you are afraid to say no, you are like most people. Be persistent. Say no again and again, if necessary. Your opponent will finally get the message.

**Appendix B**

## NEGOTIATING

5. Don't give away the candy store. Make your opponent work for every concession. People don't appreciate something they get for nothing. Conserve your concessions. Offer them later rather than sooner. The longer your opponent waits, the more the concessions will be appreciated.

6. If you make a concession quickly, you will raise your opponent's aspirations. Be alert to the size and frequency of your concessions. They should be getting smaller as your negotiations progress.

7. Keep records. Sometimes negotiations take days, or even weeks. Don't forget where you are and what you have already agreed to. Track your concessions and those of your opponent. Be alert for a pattern in them.

8. It's OK to change your mind. If you have not finalized the agreeement and you have given a concession you regret, withdraw it. It's the final signing of the agreement that makes the deal, not the numerous little concessions along the negotiating trail.

9. Always emphasize the possible loss of benefits and the fact that certain benefits will not be available if the agreement is not reached. Make your opponent aware that you are stretching your resources in making such a generous offer.

10. Tell a story. Discuss the situation of someone who got into difficulties because he or she passed up the opportunity for a settlement.

11. If you don't reach a decision, find out what is troubling your opponent and see what you can do to solve the problem. Don't be afraid to ask.

12. Give the sellers good reasons to settle; assure them that they are doing the right thing.

13. Say NO — you'll be amazed how the terms of your deal improve when you learn to say no! There were hundreds of banks failures in 1988 and 1989 in the USA. How many of the failures do you think were caused because the bankers said NO to those fantastic real estate loans?

    If you are a buyer, be aware that the seller is constantly measuring you and closing in for the kill. Time is always the seller's enemy, not yours. The longer you take, the longer you have the use of your money and control over the terms of the deal the more likely the terms will improve.

    Walk away from the table without a deal.

    If you have to deal, then all the other side needs to do to is to outwit you. Deals don't get worse when you walk away from the table.

**Appendix C**

# *RESEARCHING THE COUNTY RECORDS*

## The ABCs of Researching the Real Property Title

A few brief rules:

1. What is it you are trying to do?

   Your task in doing a title search is to identify all the encumbrances against a particular property and their order of priority.

2. What is an encumbrance? you ask.

   The answer is, anything owed against the property.

For Example:

- Taxes
- Assessments
- Liens
- Easements
- Mortgages
- Trust deeds
- Pending legal actions (lis pendens)
- Vendors claimes (liens)
- Encroachments (zoning, easements)
- Building restrictions

This list is not necessarily in order of priority.

3. Who's number 1 in terms of priority of encumbrances? that's the big question!

   Priority/seniority for the purposes of our discussion is who gets paid first, and who will be second and so forth, if a foreclosure action is activated.

4. According to Barry Adams in his book *Researching the Title of Real Property,* the order of priority is:

   A. Property taxes

   B. CC&Rs or conditions, covenants or restrictions of record. The CC&Rs pertain to how the land will be used. Zoning regulations (no high rises), preservation of minerals, residential use (no farms in the city).

   The following possible lien holders all have equal levels of priority: deeds of trust, mortgages, state and federal tax liens, abstracts of judgment (lis pendens), mechanic's and other involuntary liens. Among this list of potential liens, priority is determined by the date of recordation.

5. How is a lien or encumbrance removed from the records?

   Actually, all documents stay in the records but the lien is released or satisfied by the following methods:

## Appendix C

# RESEARCHING THE COUNTY RECORDS

| Encumbrance | Documents Used to Eliminate |
|---|---|
| Judgments | Satisfaction of judgment or release of lien |
| Deed of trust | Reconveyance deed or deed of reconveyance |
| Tax liens | Certificate of discharge of lien |
| Lien | Release of lien |

6. What do I need to know about the County Recorder's Office?

   First and most important to understand is how the documents are recorded and filed. Documents also are called or referred to as *instruments*. These instruments are recorded by the County Recorder and are assigned a specific number by the recorder. The documents are actually stamped in and out. The stamp is on the upper right corner with the date and time of day. The date and time establishpriority when documents are filed. Each document is assigned a specific or unique instrument/document number along with the book and page of where the document is recorded. This book and page number is what you need on the Grant Deed and becomes the information by which each of the documents can be located in the County Recorder's Office records. The documents or instruments could be recorded by a unique number system or could be recorded by the book and page number of indexing system. It depends on the particular county, its judge, the budget, and its priorities.

7. The most asked question is always: Why are documents recorded with the County Recorder?

   This is the recognized method of giving notice to all interested parties. A more formal document is recorded with the County Recorder's Office to impart *constructive notice* to the world that this document is officially on record. In lay terms, this means you must check the records at the Recorder's Office if you expect to be knowledgeable about real property and the encumbrances and liens which apply to real property.

8. Must all documents (liens and encumbrances) be filed at the County Recorder's Office?

   No. A document does not have to be recorded to be legal and binding.

**Appendix C**

# RESEARCHING THE COUNTY RECORDS

9. How will I protect myself from unrecorded liens or encumbrances?

   Unrecorded liens could be a problem! The only way to protect yourself from unrecorded liens or other documents is to buy title insurance through an attorney. The function of the title policy is to insure you if an unrecorded encumbrance is exposed after you take ownership of the property; then the title insurance company is liable for it rather than you. Simply stated, if an unrecorded lienholder makes a claim against you after you take ownership, it is the title insurance carrier's responsibility to defend your title and, if the claimant prevails, it is the title insurer's responsibility to pay the claim or satisfy the claimant.

## Appendix C

# A SECTION OF LAND — 640 ACRES

Quarter Sections and Subdivisions Thereof

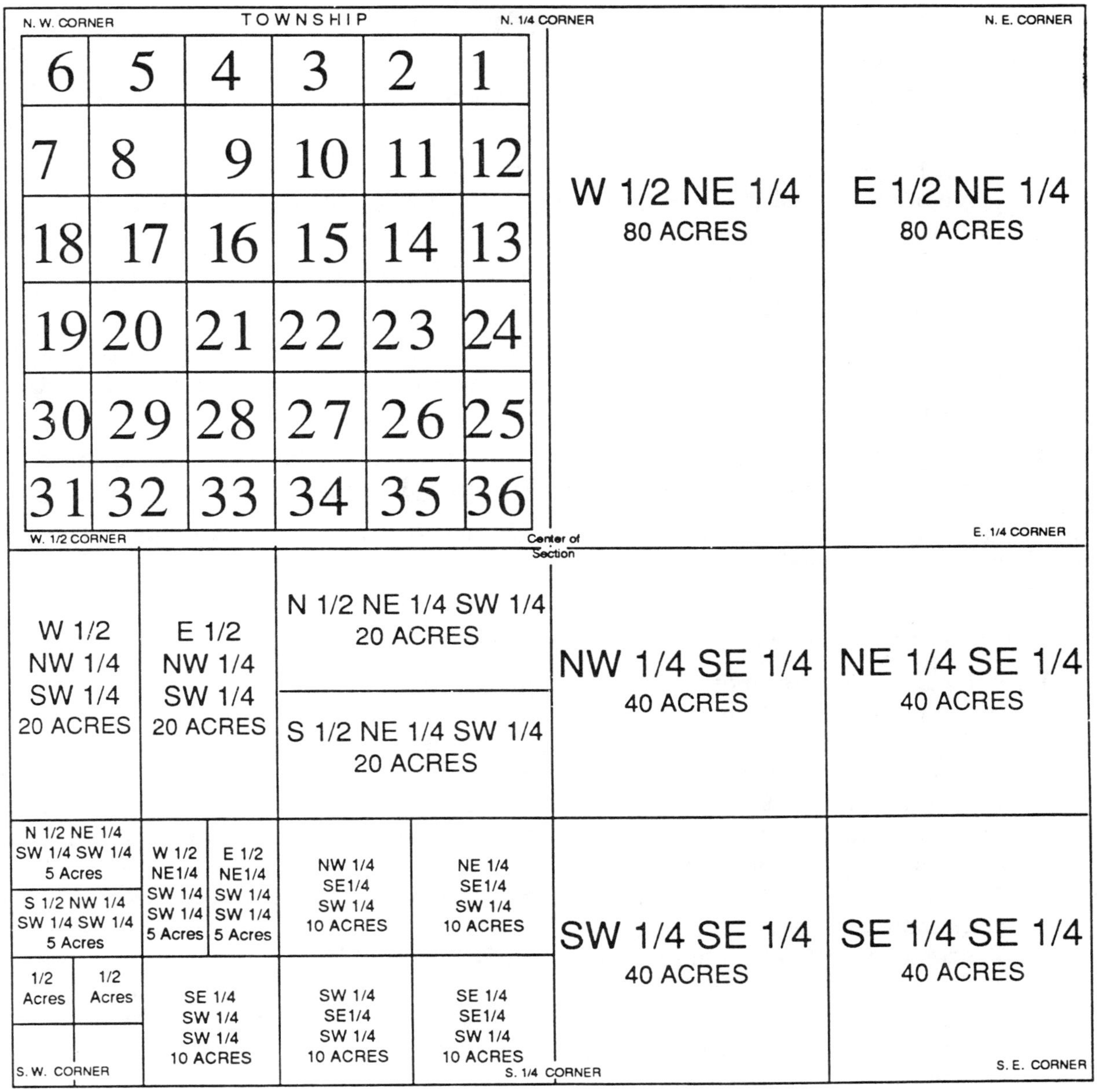

**Appendix D**

# MARKETING

### Four Basic Appeals

Do something beneficial for the reader. Self-interest is the strongest force in human nature, so your ads must offer benefits. You need to offer your customers something:

1. What people want to gain: money, health, popularity, security, leisure, time, pride of accomplishment, advancement, enjoyment, self-confidence, personal prestige.
2. What people want to save: time, money, work, discomfort, worry, doubts, risk, personal embarrassment.
3. What people want to do: business for themselves, self-expression, resist domination, dominate others, satisfy curiosity, admire beauty, collect things, win affection, improve themselves.
4. What people want to be: successful, social, up-to-date, creative, admired, first, beautiful, proud, influential, efficient, recognized, important.

Whatever commodity it is that you are offering, tie it in with the intangibles that people really want. They'll see your commodity as a way of getting what they are looking for.

Here are twelve proven ways to win confidence:

1. Offer free samples—nothing is more convincing.
2. Ship on approval—free examination inspires confidence.
3. Offer mailing aids—make it easy for your readers to respond.
4. Accept trade-ins—create confidence in your product.
5. Guarantee satisfaction—disarm your readers.
6. Show that you are a member of a trade or professional society—a recognized standing inspires confidence.
7. Mention how long you have been in the business—you will add prestige to your company.
8. Welcome visitors—face-to-face contact builds good will.
9. Make payments refundable—give your readers an escape clause.
10. Stress that no salesman will call—you will kill a major objection immediately.
11. Do not ask for immediate payment—the words "send no money" are very reassuring.
12. Notarize your documents—notarization convinces your readers of your honesty and respect for fair dealing.

## Appendix E

# TESTIMONIALS

Testimonials must be totally believable. Your goal is to convince the client to respond, and to do that you must prove you're okay to deal with.

Here's how! Use these ten effective techniques:

1. Don't write the testimonial. Have the client do so. It will sound real, and even if it has errors in grammar, that's okay because that's the way people are.
2. The client must say that your service worked. The first customer will still wonder if it was true. So, show a photo of the client in front of the house; that will help to authenticate the testimonial.
3. Use competitive market data. If you are a leader in your area of business, have the client cite how you beat your competition with better service, paid more money, did it faster and so on.
4. Do you belong to community organizations? Think about a letter from the Chamber of Commerce, your banker, the Lions Club, the Better Business Bureau, any professional organization that you are part of. The letterhead will authenticate you.
5. Are you an expert? Get someone else to say so. Include that in your mail piece.
6. Did you graduate from this course or read *Foreclosure Profits*? Then you are a member of the National Society of Foreclosure Professionals. Tell the client so.
7. When clients speak to you and your service in a favorable manner, ask them if you can quote them. The answer is usually yes. Write the comments down and have them sign it and get a release. Maintain a testimonial file.
8. Use articles about yourself that have been written in newspapers, professional journals, newsletters. If none have been written, write a news release about your new business and get it published. Then use copies of that newspaper piece in your letters as a testimonial.
9. Hold a free Stop Foreclosure Seminar for people in your community. Mail a seminar announcement to all the defaulting homeowners. After the seminar, ask the people what they learned about avoiding foreclosure. Write it down, ask them to sign it and give you a free referral. You taught them to solve their problem.
10. After you have successfully completed a foreclosure purchase and sale, write a short case history, three or four paragraphs, showing all the benefits to the person whose problem you solved. Have it notarized after it has been signed by the family you helped.

## Appendix E

# TESTIMONIALS

**Springwood Financial**

January 12, 1990

Mr. Ted Thomas
New Growth Financial
P.O. Box 5000, #412
Danville, CA 94526

Dear Ted:

I am responding to your November 8, 1989 letter. Enclosed is a letter which has proven results along with an insert I send with every letter.

I send to NODs only and send a series of 7 letters, one every 2 weeks, starting about one and one-half weeks after the NOD has been recorded at the county recorder's office. I send only to people in Santa Clara County. There are 40 to 50 new defaults in this county each week. I've been sending letters consistently since the middle of April, 1989. I send between 1200 and 1500 letters per month. As you know, this is a very competitive county and many other people are contacting homeowners in default. People I have met with who received my letters have estimated that they receive between 50 and 100 letters relating to their default. One homeowner told me he received 50 letters in a three-week period.

I get an average of 3 to 4 calls per week on all letters. I get about 1 call per week on this letter, which is the last letter I send. I have written 6 contracts. Two contracts were rescinded by the homeowner. I rescinded one contract. I purchased 3 houses. The third one is still on the market. The first two have been sold and escrow has closed. My net cash profit from those two houses after deducting all expenses except mailing expense was $56,000.

If you have any questions, give me a call. I'll be looking forward to receiving the book of foreclosure letters, and "Your Complete Guide To Foreclosure Profits."

Sincerely,

Scott Warner
President

50 Airport Parkway #146 · San Jose, Cal[illegible]rnia 95110 · Telephone (408) 437-7744

## Appendix E

# *TESTIMONIALS*

Please sign and date the release below. At the bottom please print or type how you would like your name to appear.

I hereby give Ted Thomas unconditional permission to use my name as specified below, my occupation, age and my letter to him, in whole or in part, for use in promotional materials.

Date: Feb 4, 1990

Signature

Signature

Name as you wish it to appear: SCOTT WARNER

## Appendix E

# TESTIMONIALS

**Springwood Financial**

# Who is Scott Warner?

### HE HAS MADE MONEY AS:

- Real Estate Broker
- Electronics Engineer
- Investment Counselor
- Property Manager
- Computer Consultant
- Financial Planner
- Real Estate Investor
- Management Consultant
- Office Leasing Agent
- Telecommunications Consultant
- Venture Fund Raiser
- Marketing Manager
- Real Estate Syndicator
- Business Owner

### HE HAS EARNED THE FOLLOWING:

- Masters Degree in Business
- Junior College Teaching Credential
- Sigma Alpha Epsilon
- Real Estate Broker
- Bachelor of Science
- Two U.S. Patents
- Masters of Science
- Eta Kappa Nu

### HE HAS LIVED IN:

- Dayton, Ohio
- Northbrook, Illinois
- Palo Alto, California
- Lafayette, Indiana
- Sunnyvale, California
- Columbus, Ohio
- Evanston, Illinois

### WHAT IS HE TRYING TO SELL?

His company helps homeowners in foreclosure to avoid having their homes sold at public auction. He works personally with homeowners to help them evaluate their alternatives. If appropriate, his company will purchase the homeowner's equity for cash or another money solution will be pursued.

### WHAT ARE OTHER PEOPLE SAYING?

Realtors and Title Companies are impressed with his organized procedures and reputation for integrity and customer service. Homeowners praise his caring attitude and his fair and rapid response to their financial problems.

50 Airport Parkway #146 · San Jose, California 95110 · Telephone (408) 437-7744

## Appendix E

# TESTIMONIALS

**Springwood Financial**

**IS YOUR FORECLOSURE PROBLEM SOLVED?**

Dear Homeowner,

I hope you've solved your problem. Truly. I hate to see people needlessly losing their homes at public auction. But it happens every week on the steps of the county courthouse right here in Santa Clara County. If your problem is solved, you may now gleefully throw this letter in the round file. But if you still have the foreclosure ax hanging over your head, listen up,

**IT'S JUST A FEW MORE DAYS BEFORE THE AX FALLS!**

Be honest with yourself for a minute. Do you really think the lender cares what happens to you? The lender wants his money - period. If you don't have it or you can't get it to pay him before the trustee sale, your house will be lost at the public sale and you could lose all your equity.

**ASK A PROFESSIONAL HOW TO SAVE YOUR EQUITY.**

Don't be afraid to seek professional help. Call me today at 408-437-7744. Ask for Scott. We will buy your equity for cash. The cash will be in your hands in ten days. Here's what I'll do when you call:

First, I'll ask you some questions about your property and answer any questions you may have.

Second, I will visit your home and make an agreement which is fair to you.

Third, I will call the lenders and tell them to deal with me and leave you alone. They like this because I tell them I have the cash to pay those past due payments.

And finally, I will hand you a cashier's check for your equity so you can solve your money problems and get a fresh start.

**I KNOW YOU ARE SKEPTICAL.**

Am I right? Of course I am. But you know what? You're never going to know if I can help unless you call. And time is running out. You only have a few more days. Call me now at 408-437-7744 and make me prove my claims, or drop in to my office if you're in

(Turn the page over)

50 Airport Parkway #146 · San Jose, California 95110 · Telephone (408) 437-7744

## Appendix E

# *TESTIMONIALS*

the area. We're at 50 Airport Parkway across from the Red Lion Inn near Highway 101 and North First Street. Our office hours are 9 AM to 5 PM Monday through Friday.

**THE CHOICE IS YOURS.**

1. Throw this letter away and miss the chance to get the cash you need to begin again.

2. Call me now and put an end to your money hassles.

3. Do nothing and let indecision rob you of the equity in your house. Please don't let this happen.

You have nothing to lose! Look at this ironclad guarantee:

```
***********************************************************
*                                                         *
*                  UNCONDITIONAL GUARANTEE                *
*                                                         *
*  If you are afraid someone will take advantage of you,  *
*  let me relieve you of that fear.  If you get a better  *
*  written offer, I will cancel our contract and you will *
*  have no obligation.  How could anything be more fair   *
*  than that.  Don't delay.  You could lose thousands of  *
*  dollars if your property is sold at public auction.    *
*                                                         *
***********************************************************
```

Make this the turning point in your life. Just reach for the telephone and dial 408-437-7744. Ask for Scott. I really do care. I really can help.

Sincerely,

Scott Warner

Scott Warner
President

P.S. When you do pick up the telephone and call me, rest assured you are under no obligation and you won't get the hard sell.

**THE CASH YOU NEED WILL BE IN YOUR HANDS IN TEN (10) DAYS.**

Just pick up the telephone and dial 408-437-7744. Ask for Scott.

Remember. If you take no action, your house will be sold at public auction and you will be evicted. That's the law. Make sure this doesn't happen to you.

## Appendix E

# TESTIMONIALS

**M MARLINE FINANCIAL**
917 E. Morada Pl. · Altadena, CA 91001 · (818) 797-7249

Ted Thomas
New Growth Financial
185 Front St., Suite 207
Danville, CA 94526

April 4, 1991

Dear Ted,

You know, it's amazing how time flies when you're having fun! An old cliche, but still very true. Ted, it's been eleven months since I took your course. That was April of 1990. And I would like to share with you my successes.

First of all, I'm still working at this new vocation of mine. Part time I'm putting in about 15-20 hours a week. However, because of how things are going, I'm about to hire an assistant.

Well Ted, so far I've closed three deals. Let me take a moment to tell you about them. The first deal resulted in my being able to "flip" the deal in seven weeks, and I made $8,800 dollars. The second deal turned out to be an instant lease, which I made $9,300 up front, and it has a repurchase option attached to it which will pay me an additional $5,000 or maybe up to as much as $20,000 later on. The third deal turned out to be an eleven week remodel project. Granted, a lot of time, however, I made $22,200 on that one.

Ted, I feel great about being able to accomplish these deals. However, I must remember to thank you wholeheartedly, because without the help that you've given me this wouldn't have been able to be accomplished. Ted, I appreciate you always being there when I needed you. Geez, I'd hate to be able to count the amount of times you and I have talked deals that didn't work, plus talk deals that have worked. In the last eleven months, I bet I've talked to you fifteen times. In all that time, you were open, receptive, guiding, and helpful. And most of all, Ted, the 'Win! Win! Win!' philosophy that you literally preach is the basis that gives me the confidence to succeed in the little amount of success I've had so far.

SUBSCRIBED AND SWORN TO BEFORE ME
THIS 4th DAY OF APRIL 1991
NOTARY PUBLIC

OFFICIAL SEAL
J. WEHMEYER
Notary Public—California
LOS ANGELES COUNTY
My Comm. Exp. July 1, 1991

With respect and gratitude,

Mike McCann

P.S. If anyone asks me "Mike, how in the world did you accomplish this?" I've got a two word answer to them: Ted Thomas. (Incidentally, Ted, I'm currently looking at two more deals.)

## Appendix E

# TESTIMONIALS

NEW DIMENSION MANAGEMENT
"DISTRESSED PROPERTY SPECIALIST"
(616) 364-9887

Mr. Ted Thomas
New Growth Financial
185 Front Street, Suite 207
Danville, CA 94526

March 27, 1991

Dear Ted:

Please forgive the delay in getting back to you. It was not intended, just worked out this way. I have enclosed the signed release for your use.

A couple of thoughts regarding our week with you, Mark Nolan and John Beck as well as the super people who made up the "Class of Feb. '91". In a nutshell, it was a tremendous experience, unlike any seminar or educational meeting type that I have ever attended. It was "hands on" all the way, including field training complete with an actual presentation (which resulted in a deal no less) which took place with the entire class present. Unbelievable! (Also 18 hour days. This I am not used to, but again not only worthwhile, but also most enjoyable). Anne Marie (who is really our resident seminar attender) had a great time and of course was equally impressed. She was a great help to me during the class and continues to be a great help now that we are back and have launched this new phase of our business.

We have only been in operation for about three weeks (which has been primarily a learning process) but, none the less we are off and running.

We mail weekly (have enclosed sample of our letters, #1, 2, and 3 and would welcome your comments) utilizing the Grand Rapids Legal News as a source of foreclosure prospects and a combination of County Mapping & Description and Register of Deeds Departments for correct names and addresses etc. We have developed a fairly good system for generating this information and getting our letters out (at least we are not totally crazy yet) which allows us to integrate this activity with the rest of our business.

While as yet, we don't have a closed deal to report, we have had a couple of opportunities. (We just could not make the "right" deal... one that was mutually beneficial or at least beneficial to us. But as you say "They are not all good deals out there". In this regard since we have far fewer opportunities than you and the others located in California, we must be very careful. (We only have about 12-14 Default Notices - Notice of Mortgage Sale, per week). Some of these are redeemed before the sale, thus the temptation is great to jump on anything that comes up during the 4-6 week pre-foreclosure period (4-6 weeks to sale from time Notice of Default appears in paper).

1

NEW DIMENSION MANAGEMENT • 4191 PLAINFIELD N.E., STE. 183 • GRAND RAPIDS, MI 49505

## Appendix E

# TESTIMONIALS

At any rate we feel we are going to be very successful with this and we simply must be somewhat patient.

As far as anyone out there who is thinking of taking your seminar, but can't get by the choking sensation caused by your fee, tell them to call me. I am not necessarily a skeptic, but I am a business person and I take a hard look at this kind of investment, especially when it's a seminar. (Also when I have to fly clear across the country to attend). I did some choking also, but not only did I determine that it sounded like a worthwhile investment (one that would return itself many many times over) I also insisted that my wife attend. To say the least, we both feel we got our money's worth and then some. From a business standpoint or from just a plain money making opportunity standpoint, I would highly recommend your program. With the Ted Thomas System, you can't lose.

In closing Ted, I would like to say it was a genuine pleasure meeting you and being with you during our seminar week. You proved to be not only the professional I expected, but also a true gentleman and one who I am proud to call a friend. Anne Marie sends her love.

Best Regards,

George J. O'Hara

Anne Marie O'Hara

GOH/mb

## Appendix E

# TESTIMONIALS

**RCMCC**
**MID-LIFE RESOURCE CENTER**

Suite 219
415 West Foothill Boulevard
Claremont, California 91711
714/624-3464

New Growth Financial
Ted Thomas, Vice President
185 Front Street
Danville, CA 94526

April 9, 1991

Dear Ted,

Your 5-day workshop on foreclosure investing has given me such incredible amount of knowledge and hands-on experience, that exactly two weeks after I completed the workshop I bought a foreclosure home here in Southern California. I also want to thank you for your spontaneous advice on how to handle escrow when I called you by phone then. That was a critical and reassuring step in helping me to complete my first transaction smoothly.

My interest in foreclosure investing got started early in 1990, when I began to receive increasing number of phone calls in my normal business hours from privately held corporate owners, seeking helps not only for their businesses, but for their homes as well. Many of their homes were facing foreclosures, as well as those of their key employees, due to business failures. It took me a whole year before I decided to learn about foreclosure investing. Here in Southern California, there is no shortage of foreclosure seminars. Unfortunately, most of them are the academic and seat-warmer types. Instead, what I was looking for is a hands-on, step-by-step, how-to seminar taught by someone doing it. That was when I received John Beck's announcement letter, just three days before the start of your February seminar. John used the exact words I had in mind. Naturally I picked up the phone, called John, and signed up.

Did I get what I wanted out of your workshop? You bet I did! I got more than that! It came about when you took our whole class on the fourth day of the workshop to Oakland, CA, negotiated a deal, and signed up to buy a property in foreclosure. That dealmaking process became the very role model through which I completed my first foreclosure transaction last month.

Again, thank you for the helps thus far. I also know that your experience-in-doing, John Beck's legal knowledge on real estate, and Mark Nolan's expertise on direct mail marketing are no more than a phone call away from me. Knowing such combined "knowledge, experience, and time" backing me, I can't possibly fail in creating "money" through foreclosure investing in the months ahead. Along the way, I hope to make a difference in helping individuals, families, and corporations in distress to move on with their lives.

With best regards,

Don M. Yee

... center of knowledge, experience, money & time ...

## Appendix E

# TESTIMONIALS

**Equisource Funding Corp.**
Investing in Mortgages Nationwide

February 24, 1991

New Growth Financial
Ted Thomas, Vice-President
185 Front Street
Danville, CA 94526

Dear Ted:

I can't believe how much I have learned from you over the last five days. There is no way I can fail now, except by ignoring the step by step process you have developed.

What a skeptic. I called John Beck. I called past students. I called you. Twice! I grilled every one of you. It took me three weeks to decide even with all the guarantees you offer.

What a difference. Now that the course is over, I firmly believe that, if I didn't crash and burn first, I would have labored a good year to attain the skill level you have given me in this class. Not to mention the thousands of dollars I would have spent on developing all the legal forms!

I have it all now. That huge binder with the whole process laid out step 1, step 2 step 3, ...... The audio tape of the whole course to listen to whenever I need refreshing. But most importantly, I have you, Mark Nolan and John Beck as near as my phone. I truly can't fail!! So who needs guarantees?

I'm looking forward to a long and profitable relationship. I very sincerely thank you, Mark and John. I now have every confidence that I can reach the goals and dreams I have set for myself and my family.

With Respect,

Joe Rash

PS: After I blabbered on and on about the course, my wife said it reminded her of the chinese proverb about teaching a man to fish and you feed him for a lifetime. So when I leave my office from now on, I think I'll hang up a "Gone Fishing" sign.

A Licensed Mortgage Loan Broker
P.O. Box 1507
Windsor, CA 95492
Toll Free: (800) 533-3587
Tel.: (707) 838-3587
Fax: (707) 838-3667

## Appendix E

# TESTIMONIALS

April 22, 1991

New Growth Financial
Mr. Ted Thomas, Vice President
185 Front Street
Danville, CA 94526

Dear Ted:

After purchasing two pre-foreclosure properties from you, I felt it was time to learn for myself - what's involved, how I might be able to find pre-foreclosures and purchase them too? So I decided that the best way to go about doing that was to go to the most knowledgeable person I know regarding pre-foreclosures - you!

I want you to know that this past week has been the most tremendous learning experience imaginable. I've learned so much in such a short period of time. The class size of eight was great, which I think contributed to the fact that I was receiving personal and individualized attention. I especially liked working with the class and the instructors; Mark Nolan was informing as well as entertaining. Thanks to his enthusiasm and sense of humor, the class was not long nor drawn out as with some courses being offered these days. John Beck gave me legal knowledge about pre-foreclosures which was most helpful, but I think the most exciting part of the entire program for me was getting to see you in action - negotiating with the sellers/homeowners. Being able to witness that part of the class was so invaluable. I feel confident that I will do well after finishing with this course.

There is no set amount that you could charge for the course that would be equal to what was taught. I know that I will re-coop that $5,000 and surpass that figure 3x's by following your system on pre-foreclosures.

Thank you Ted, for a course well done.

Sincerely,

Janice Levai

Janice Levai

P.S. My husband, Julius can't wait to sign up for your next course!

## Appendix F

## NEWSPAPER ARTICLES

The Inter-City Express

Established in 1909

Vol. 83, No. 160 • Oakland, Calif. • NORTHERN CALIFORNIA'S DAILY REAL ESTATE NEWSPAPER • 50¢ • Friday Evening, August 11, 1989

# Direct mail plan revives investor's fortune

Ted Thomas remembers the hardship he encountered when the Tax Reform Act in 1986 dramatically restricted real estate tax benefits. When his multi-million-dollar real estate empire collapsed because of the new tax laws, Thomas spiralled into bankruptcy. In financial distress, he was stripped of his company, his upscale Blackhawk home, his credit cards and his dignity. Friends fell by the wayside, and former associates' wives spat at his wife in the grocery store. Thomas compares his predicament to having AIDS or leprosy.

Thomas had it all. Then lost it.

So it's not surprising to detect a note of empathy in his voice when Thomas talks about the plight of other people who have fallen into the foreclosure abyss, and how he has molded these devastating episodes into one of the best methods for investing in distressed properties.

"As a cross section of the world, these people aren't so bad," Thomas said. "They aren't criminals -- although other people treat them that way. They are people who have fallen on hard times for one reason or another. I can talk to people on their level because I've been through the ordeal myself."

Thomas, who is vice president of New Growth Financial, a Danville investor's collective, says the keys to his recent success in real estate investing are streamlined marketing and his ability to strike deals that benefit not only his company but also the people in default.

His approach is simple. Thomas uses several services to cultivate a list of owner names and addresses for defaulted properties. He then mails out a series of letters to the people on the list, telling them he wants to buy their property before it is auctioned off at a trustee's sale.

"The key to success is good marketing," Thomas said. "You can get in touch with people in different ways -- by knocking on their doors and by hanging messages on their doorknobs. But the best way to communicate with people is by mail."

When they read the information in Thomas' mailings, owners in default are led to face the reality of their situation. At this point, they often contact Thomas. He asks them to complete a questionnaire, decides if the property is worth buying and conducts an inspection of the property to help assess its true value. He then does his own title search to make sure there are no liens against the property; using a title company to do this search would take too long, he says.

If the deal still seems solid after the inspection, Thomas makes an offer. Walking away from properties that don't measure up is also part of the game he plays. Thomas encourages owners to whom he makes offers to grab deals that seem better than the ones he makes.

Pre-foreclosure investor Ted Thomas

"I have a policy that says 'if you find another deal, take it,' " Thomas said. "Sometimes people think they can get a better deal, but then they find themselves in a pickle later on."

Customers who walk away often come back later, he says. The alternative to accepting an offer like Thomas' can be far worse.

In California, notices of default are published in a newspaper of general circulation, such as The Inter-City Express.

*See* **THOMAS**, *page* **2**

# THOMAS

*Continued from page 1*

The owner in default has 90 days from the time the notice of default is published to "cure" the default. If the defaulted loan is not cured within this time, the property goes into foreclosure. The bank to which the payments have not been made then appoints a trustee to auction off the property for the amount owed on the loan. The holder of the loan, the person who has defaulted, generally gets nothing when the home is auctioned at trustee's sale.

Thomas' system of preventing the property from going into foreclosure by buying its equity from the owner is often more lucrative all around. This way, the owner receives some money for the property and has the resources to begin anew. Thomas then turns around and sells the property to a waiting purchaser, who has paid several thousand dollars to be put on Thomas' waiting list for the properties he acquires. People who buy such properties from Thomas are typically willing to fix up the properties, then sell them at a profit.

"This is a great way for young people to get into a house," Thomas said. "If they fix up a house, they can turn around and sell it for a good profit."

Thomas's approach of intervening early, before the property falls into the hands of the bank and trustee, creates a triple-win situation for the buyer, the seller and the bank. As a testament to his success, Thomas typically turns over many properties each month, with profits from the sales spilling into New Growth Financial's coffers, pleasing a group of long-term investors Thomas refuses to name.

Thomas warns, however, that the foreclosure business is not an easy road to riches.

"A lot of people who get into the foreclosure business think that they'll get rich quick," said Thomas. "The truth of the matter is that this business is a lot of hard work, and I like to stress that when I talk about foreclosures."

Originally from Boston, Thomas was not always an investor. When he first came to California after working as an airline pilot, he became an airborne traffic reporter for KCBS radio in San Francisco. He got into real estate when he started his own investment company. While running New Growth Financial, Thomas has been writing a soon-to-be-released book, "Your Complete Guide to Foreclosure."

## Appendix F

# NEWSPAPER ARTICLES

PUBLISHED SINCE 1893

Seattle Daily Journal of Commerce

Published Daily Except Sunday, © 1989 Seattle Daily Journal of Commerce | Second Class Postage paid at Seattle, Washington 98104 1482 Price 60 cents | Vol. 96, No. 167, Thursday, July 20, 1989

# Foreclosures offer good opportunities

BY REBECCA BUXTON
Journal staff reporter

To most people, reaping the profits from someone's unfortunate property foreclosure seems a sordid profession. But things are not always what they seem, as evidenced by the "Thomas System."

Ted Thomas is the founder of the "Thomas System," a step-by-step system of making profits by helping people avoid foreclosure.

Thomas, in association with the Jefferson Institute, a training center for entrepreneurship and investment education, is holding workshops in the Seattle area to promote his investment strategy.

During the workshop Thomas will cover such topics as "How to make a 100 per cent return with very little cash investment; How to price your property to sell; How to become a marketing genius and How to find a buyer for your 'fixer-upper' before you lift a hammer or paint brush."

According to Howard Ruff, chairman of the Jefferson Institute, "The 'Thomas System' is the ideal real estate program for our times because it doesn't depend on tax shelter benefits, it doesn't depend on appreciation, and it doesn't depend on income. It's a unique business opportunity and what's more, it meets a growing demand."

The basic idea of the system is to find a property scheduled for foreclosure, buy it from the owner, pay off the mortgage and then sell the property for a profit.

Over the past 18 years Thomas has bought, managed and sold more than $200 million worth of real estate. And he happens to know the trauma of foreclosure first hand.

In 1986 his combined personal and corporate assets were worth $178 million, he said. New tax laws, a negative cash flow and a lack of investors helped cause his business to go bankrupt.

Ted Thomas

"When my business went under, and I was faced with the foreclosure of my property, I realized there was no one there to help me," Thomas says.

In the two years since his bankruptcy, Thomas has built a successful new business by using the strategies he discovered the hard way.

"My system is a win, win, win situation," he says, because everybody involved benefits. The owner of the property gains at least enough to get back on his feet, the lender receives its money and the agent can earn an average of $5,000 per completed transaction.

While he admits that the basic idea of buying and selling foreclosure properties is not original, he believes his system is.

The step-by-step outline is what makes the system unique. The structure of the plan is rigid, but the techniques are flexible enough to fit individual circumstances.

> "My system is a win, win, win situation."

However, it is not a get-rich-quick scheme. The plan works as a marketing strategy that must be run like a business.

The ten simple steps can be employed full-or part-time. Seasoned real estate brokers, first-timers, retired people and students have learned how to search for and find the best foreclosure properties, advertise effectively and avoid unnecessary risks.

One feature of the system is what Thomas likes to call his "Guerilla Marketing Tactics." This marketing plan combines traditional and new marketing techniques to reach a target group of buyers.

Direct mail and flier distribution are commonly used advertising strategies. Another technique Thomas employs involves working with neighborhood groups such as church congregations. Thomas pays the group to get its members out to look at a house in the area. Then, waiting lists are established using the people who have shown an interest. "They may not want the house you have right now, but at least you know they're interested, and you can contact them the next time," Thomas adds.

Although the average person only works on the system part time, one or possibly two foreclosure transactions can be still be completed per month, he said.

Thomas recently finished a 500-page book entitled "Your Complete Guide to Foreclosure Profits," in which case studies of his own experiences are examined.

The book illustrates the substantial rise in foreclosures over the last decade. In 1980 the Veterans Administration reported 10,254 foreclosures nationwide. In 1988 the number had risen to 36,739. Housing and Urban Development reported 27,722 property foreclosures nationwide in 1983. By 1988 the number had increased by 300 per cent to 88,598.

With over 200 foreclosures per month in King County alone, Thomas says there are many good business opportunities.

Cities with dominant industries generally have the highest foreclosure rates, due to their changing economies. Houston and Dallas are now suffering almost 1,000 foreclosures per month, Thomas says, due to falling oil prices. When the American automobile industry suffered a recession in the early 1980s, foreclosures in Detroit skyrocketed.

The Seattle area has felt the same kind of sting. During the Boeing slump in the early 1970s, foreclosures in the northwest were high.

Because real estate is a cyclical market, there will always be foreclosure opportunities, Thomas explains.

"If an area needs housing, developers and cities generally tend to overbuild, in turn causing a housing surplus and indirectly causing more foreclosures," Thomas adds.

The short workshop is actually intended to be an introduction to an intensive three-day seminar planned in Seattle in August.

******

***The workshop will be held July 22 at 9:20 a.m. at the Red Lion Inn/SeaTac, 18740 Pacific Highway S., Seattle. The pre-registration cost is $19 and tickets at the door will cost $29. For more information and pre-registration call 1-800-627-6019.***

## Appendix G

# POWERFUL DIRECT MAIL THAT WORKS

John N. Beck II
2200 Central Avneue, Suite 203
Alameda, CA 94501
(415) 523-6115

This mail piece pulled
$200,000 worth
of business

Now YOU have the opportunity to obtain ALL the inside knowledge it takes to become a successful foreclosure investor!

**As a subscriber to the Distress Sales Report newsletter, I'm offering you one final opportunity to learn ALL you need to know to become a successful foreclosure investor. How? -- by simply lessoning to Ted Thomas!**

Who's **Ted Thomas**? He's a fellow Distress Sales Report newsletter subscriber – just like you. When he received his first issue of the Distress Sales Report and attended his first Subscriber Continuing Education Seminar, he knew almost NOTHING about foreclosures. Further he had financial problems; **he was in the middle of a very unpleasant bankruptcy!!**

NOW (some three years latter) he is quite possibly THE **most successful** pre-foreclosure investor in California!

Ted makes <u>at least</u> **two to five bargain deals per month!! Right here in California. Right now! Today!**

**And Ted makes money! BIG money!**

Many of his deals NET him more money than the average American family earns (working hard) in an entire year! [For instance, see the lead article in the **May 1988** issue of the Distress Sales Report (the first article I ever wrote about Ted) – Ted used his system to buy a pre-foreclosure super-bargain, then put the property up for sale as a for-sale-by-owner, sold the property with the escrow closing some six weeks later and netted out, after all expenses, in excess of $40,000.00!! And this was all done with an investment of less than $15,000.00 out-of-pocket!!]

On average Ted earns over $30,000.00 per month – for instance, during the first quarter of this year (**working his system <u>part time</u>**) he made **$100,400.00!**

After having observed Ted's continuing success at buying and selling foreclosures, I've concluded that he clearly has the special skills, abilities and knowledge that my subscribers – **that you** – <u>need</u> to also become a successful foreclosure investor. Therefore I contacted Ted to see if he would agree to give a seminar for my subscribers – **for you**. BUT not just another foreclosure seminar – or, for that matter, NOT just another Ted Thomas' foreclosure seminar. I insisted upon a special,

## Appendix G

# POWERFUL DIRECT MAIL THAT WORKS

intensive, no-holds-barred, all-questions-answered, NOTHING-HELD-BACK seminar on how he actually does it – in his offices, where he actually does it. And I insisted that the seminar be given while he's actually doing it!

[I didn't want another "academic" seminar: I think I already do a very good job providing academic information. I wanted a hands-on, step-by-step, how-to seminar taught by someone doing it. Doing it very successfully. Where he's doing it; when he's doing it. While he's doing. From the very first step through to the last step. Step-by-step. Academic information is (in my opinion) extremely valuable – BUT there is NO substitute for actually doing it (for on-the-job training, if you will) It's easy to talk about something, but (as we all know) doing it is another matter altogether.]

Further I insisted that the seminar group be small – small enough so that **everyone attending could get to know Ted personally**. And where he could get to know each and every attendee personally – get to know **you** personally.

Basically, to the fullest extent humanly possible, I wanted a seminar designed to create an environment which would produce financial SUCCESS for YOU and the other attendees.

**Ted agreed.** We held this special, intensive, no-holds-barred, all-questions-answered, NOTHING-HELD-BACK seminar during the week of July 23rd through the 27th. **It was a success!** So successful, that Ted agreed to hold one more during the week **starting Monday, October 8th** and continuing on through to Friday, October 12th.

I worked hard in setting up the first seminar. **Hard enough that I believe it was THE best foreclosure seminar ever given! AND I'm working even harder setting this next one up. So hard, in fact, that I know the next one will be even better!**

**Why?**

The **first reason**: I've already said this a number of times, but it bears saying again: "To my knowledge, **Ted is the most successful pre-foreclosure investor in California." And Ted will personally give this seminar.**

[Ted has learned valuable lessons. Lessons which have taken years (and thousands of dollars) to learn, but (once learned) have made him many tens of thousands of dollars (actually many hundreds of thousands of dollars). For instance, ask him to relate the details on how he just bought a $370,000 property having $425,000 worth of outstanding liens against it for just $250,000! He turned some $55,000 worth of "negative equity" into some $90,000 in potential profit. Magic? No, of course not! It's knowledge – BUT the right bit of knowledge used at the right time can produce "magical" results!]

The **second reason: Only ten people** will be allowed to attend. This will insure that you get **personal, in-depth, hands-on** training.

(Ted has done pre-foreclosure seminars for others like **Howard Ruff's Jefferson Institute** and **Mark O. Haroldsen's Millionaires In Training** programs, but these seminars have had an average attendance of around 60 people! With 60 people there's hardly enough time to learn everybody's name – much less provide the personal attention each of you needs to fully understand, appreciate and sucessfully operate Ted's lucrative system!)

## Appendix G

# POWERFUL DIRECT MAIL THAT WORKS

The **third reason**: You will work **personally** with Ted in **Ted's own office** – you will not just be told by Ted how he does it, but you will SEE, step-by-step, how he does it. You will **participate**, step-by-step, in the process – even to the point of going out on calls. Ted has agreed to share his office, small staff, computer programs, letter writing secrets, negotiating strategies – his ENTIRE mail order marketing system with you one on one. For five full days! (The Jefferson Institute and Millionaires In Training programs were four days. When I taught one of these with Ted, I found that four days just wasn't enough time to completely cover Ted's system. I insisted that this seminar be a full five days. Ted agreed.)

[Obviously this is invaluable! Any successful business involves a complete, self-contained system. Developing such a system – such a "turn-key" operation – on your own can take a tremendous amount of time, effort and energy – not to mention, money. Numerous false starts can be taken; numerous mistakes can be made. These false starts and other mistakes eat up valuable time, often require substantial effort and expend considerable energy. They can lead to (success stopping) frustration. And, unfortunately, failure! BUT this can be avoided! If you have a system and if you learn how to make that system produce for you! Ted has such a system: he will give it to you and he will personally show you how to make it produce for you.]

The **fourth reason** I believe this seminar will be the most valuable foreclosure seminar ever given: It's not going to be just another instructor "talking at you" – with Ted's assistance, **YOU ARE GOING TO TAKE ACTION!** Action to start making **you** money NOW!

The KEY to success with Ted's pre-foreclosure purchase system is developing effective mailing pieces – letters to home owners in foreclosure which get results! OUR GOAL FOR YOU: To develop at least five letters that will bring results!!

Ted will teach you a complete, effective, money-making pre-foreclosure purchase system. Then you and Ted (and Mark Nolan) will work together to develop mailing pieces which produce responses – letters with powerfully effective language and attention grabing layouts. The letter you take away will be "camera ready" – ready for you to immediately reproduce and send out!! You will be able to immediately start **working Ted's system** – working it with actual properties currently in foreclosure in the county you intend to invest. Working that system with the **sole object** of making **you money** as quickly as possible.

You are going to stop talking about it and actually start doing it! NOT take action after the seminar is over! You will start taking action **during** the seminar. With hands on assistance by Ted Thomas every step of the way. Step-by-step.

The **fifth reason**: **Mark G. Nolan** will participate for **one full day**. You ask: "Who's Mark Nolan?" He's Ted's Mail Order Marketing Specialist! Mark runs a California advertising agency that specializes in results-getting, direct response ads. He's helped clients sell everything from $1.00 books to millions of dollars worth of real estate. You name it; advertising he's written has sold it!

As Mark says of Ted: "He is a very talented advertising copywriter in his own right and he had written some 'killer' sales letters that were helping him to cash in on the foreclosure property market." But Ted **always** wants to IMPROVE the effectiveness of his marketing pieces. **An effective piece will make you thousands upon thousands of dollars!** And ineffective piece? Don't even bother to send it! Ted hired Mark (or as Mark states: "Challenged" him) to develop an even more effective piece – a piece with even greater pulling power. Mark met the "challenge" with a unique – and highly effective piece! THE MOST EFFECTIVE PIECE TED HAS USED TO DATE! Mark knows mail order marketing – and he will tell you what he knows.

## Appendix G

# POWERFUL DIRECT MAIL THAT WORKS

The **sixth reason**: You'll be provided **continuing support until you succeed.** You'll be provided with an extensive workbook with case studies of deals Ted has actually done – with ALL the documentation associated with those deals.

And you will receive an audio tape set of the entire seminar so that you can play it back over and over again (while you're commutting to and from your current job) until you completely understand everything covered at the seminar.

AND until you have **successfully** completed your first two purchases, **Ted Thomas** will be available to personally assist you in **EVERY aspect** of your personalized program. You will be able to call him at a special phone number from 4:00 to 6:00 p.m., Monday through Friday.

FURTHER, **Mark Nolan** will also be there to provide you with continuing support. As you already know, an effective marketing piece is the KEY to the successful execution of Ted's system. Developing effective, money-making pieces is absolutely critical! Both Ted and Mark will be there during the seminar to assist you in developing those pieces – and, after the seminar, they'll STILLto be there to provide you with the continuing support you will need. They will BOTH work with you UNTIL you have developed effective, money-making mailing pieces.

As I stated above, Mark is in the business of creating money-making mailing pieces; he charges $500.00 per page of copy! BUT you'll be able to mail or FAX your letters directly to Mark – and he'll review them, make suggestions and then return them to you. ALL for FREE! And he (like Ted) will be only a phone call away to assist you with your mail order marketing problems – and to discuss specifics with you on how to develop your own effective mailing pieces.

And still further, I (as a California attorney) will also be there to provide continuing support. At the seminar, you'll be provided ALL of the legal forms you need to work Ted's system. After the seminar, I will personally work with you to customize those forms to met your special needs. **(You will, in effect, have your own personal law office – at NO additional cost.)**

The **sixth reason**: **This seminar is guaranteed.** But Ted's guarantee is no ordinary guarantee! **I insisted upon that.**

> **Guarantee:** You MUST make at least $5,000.00 using Ted's System on your first two foreclosure transactions or he'll refund the difference up to the entire tuition. I wanted to make this guarantee such that you would have nothing to lose by trying!

Except, you say, you might not be able to make even one deal. If you're afraid you won't make even one deal, take a look at this next guarantee – a guarantee nobody BUT somebody who really knows how to make bargain deals – who actually, consistently, MAKES bargain deals – would ever dare to make.

> **Guarantee:** If you haven't make a deal within nine months of taking Ted's course and have followed the rules of the road which Ted will clearly explain, **Ted Thomas** will personally find one for you! Or he will allow you to joint venture with him in one of his bargain deals!

## Appendix G

# POWERFUL DIRECT MAIL THAT WORKS

**Will Ted really do that? Yes, he will!!**

**Can Ted really do it? Yes, he can! He already has!**

Just ask **Janice** and **Julius Levai** of San Francisco. They're long-time subscribers to my Distress Sales Report newsletter who both regularly attend my Subscriber Continuing Education Seminars. They learned of Ted and his system at those seminars. And they learned that when Ted is activily engaged full-time working his system, he makes more deals that he has time to personally close. Consequently he sells these excess deals to certain select investors – for a fraction of their value. Janice and Julius paid $5,000 to be placed on **Ted's Select Investor's List**. What happened? Let Janice tell you in her own words: "Both Julius and I would like to take this opportunity to thank you again for the super deal that we had purchased from you – a 2 bedroom, 2 bath condominium in Castro Valley. We purchased the condomimum for $85,000 and as of this evening we will be signing a contract for sale at $142,500." Did this make a difference in their lives? Janice's answer: "This has made a difference in our lives." Of course it did! Julius has a camera repair business and Janice manages and operates a postal and business services business. As Janice stated: "We wondered why we are continuing in our 9:00-5:00 jobs."

Or just ask **Jesse Carranza**, also of San Francisco. Jesse's retired. He's also a long time subscriber to the Distress Sales Report. He also learned of **Ted's Select Investor's List** from my seminars. Jesse also paid his $5,000.00 to get on that list. The results? They're spectacular!! During the last year Jesse (and his partners) have purchased nine properties from Ted. They've resold eight of those properties – making **close to $100,000** on those completed deals! (Note: Jesse will be attending this next seminar and will be available to answer any questions you might want to ask him.)

You can even ask **Mark Nolan**! As indicated earlier, Ted hired (or "challenged") Mark to produce a mailing piece even more effective than Ted's. To meet this challenge, Mark had to learn about Ted's system. In the process, he became very much impressed by it. So much so that he took a contract assignment from Ted. The results: Have him show you a copy of the $22,735.33 title insurance company check he received! (Even if you don't ask, Mark's going to show you a copy anyway!!)

And (for that matter) don't forget to ask me! On the first deal which my wife, Joyce, and I did off **Ted's Select Investor's List**, we netted $5,000.00 in less than three weeks. (For details on this deal, see the lead article in the **September 1988** issue of the **Distress Sales Report** entitled "**An Assignment of the Purchase Contract – The Ultimate No-Money-Down, Quick Turn Money-Maker.**")

(OR ASK **Mike Curia**, one of the ten subscribers who attended the first special, intensive, no-holds-barred, all-questions-answered, NOTHING-HELD-BACK Ted Thomas seminar. After completing that seminar, Mike took an assignment on a property which Ted has purchased earlier. He painted and otherwise renovated the property and, then, resold it – with the escrow due to close sometime before this next seminar! We'll have him attend and tell you how he did!!)

**Ted** finds them; those on **Ted's Select Investor's List** sell them – and reap substantial profits. Take Ted's seminar, work with Ted's system and if, within nine months, you haven't make a bargain pre-foreclosure deal, you're on **Ted's Select Investor's List** free of charge – **guaranteed!**

And the **seventh** (and last) **reason** I believe this seminar will be the most valuable foreclosure seminar ever given: I will **personally** be there during the **entire seminar** to see that

## Appendix G

# *POWERFUL DIRECT MAIL THAT WORKS*

Ted gives you everything that's promised. And to provide all the assistance I can to make this seminar everything I've stated it's going to be. Plus I (as a California attorney) will be there to help Ted provide you the continuing assistance you need **after** the seminar's over. That's my promise to you.

**How much is all this going to cost you?** Only $5,000.00. And I say "only" because this is the only pre-foreclosure seminar I know of where you will get this kind of value. PERIOD! Five thousand dollars to learn from the master a system which can make you thousands, even (as Ted does) tens of thousands of dollars each month. Month in and month out. Working full time or working part time. A system which, after you have acquired the knowledge to make it work, can cost less than a thousand dollars to start.

And (as I have said) has the potential to make **tens of thousands of dollars** – or (as with Ted himself) even **hundred's of thousands of dollars**! **That's got to be a bargain!**

**Remember:** This special, intensive, no-holds-barred, all-questions-answered, NOTHING-HELD-BACK, five day seminar will be given one more time – during the week starting **Monday, October 8th**.

**If you're interested in this (what may be a once-in-a-lifetime) opportunity, give me a call at (415) 523-1267 or my wife, Joyce, a call at (415) 523-6115.**

Sincerely yours,

John N. Beck II

P.S. Remember only ten subscribers will be allowed to attend. **Space has to be limited!** There is (in my opinion) no other way that you can learn to duplicate the extraordinary success which Ted has experienced. It MUST be personal! Reserve a space today. Don't be left out!

P.P.S. Are you tired? Tired of commutting to a job you don't like. Tired of having others tell you when to get up, when you can take a break, when you can eat lunch, when you can go home – even when you can take a vacation. Tired of paying your bills each month and having little left over to show for your efforts. Maybe not even enough to take a decent vacation. Here's what may be a once in a lifetime opportunity to start changing all that. Call me at (415) 523-1267 or Joyce at (415) 523-6115 and reserve a space.

P.P.P.S. Remember, Ted's system is an extraordinary business opportunity: After you have acquired the knowledge to make it work, his system can cost **less than one thousand dollars** to get started. The cost of the seminar can be billed to your Visa, MasterCard or American Express credit cards.

**Appendix H**

# RECOMMENDED READING

Allen, Robert G., *Creating Wealth,* Simon & Schuster
Beck, John, and Ron Starr, *Take This House Please,* 2 vols., John Beck Publishing
Bly, Robert W., *The Copywriter's Handbook,* Dodd, Mead
Burton, Phillip, and Scott Purvis, *Which Ad Pulled Best*, NCT Business Books
Caples, John, *How To Make Your Advertising Make Money,* Prentice-Hall
———, *Tested Advertising Methods*, Prentice-Hall
Cohen, William A., *Building a Mail Order Business*
Collier, Robert, *The Robert Collier Letter Book,* Prentice-Hall
Collins, Tom, and Stan Rapp, *Maxi-Marketing,* McGraw-Hill
Davidson, Jeffrey P., *Marketing on a Shoestring*
Elias, Stephen, *Make Your Own Contract*
Fisher, Roger, and William Guy, *Getting To Yes,* Penguin
Gadow, Sandy, *All About Escrow*
Garfield, Charles, *Peak Performance*
Gerber, Michael, *The E Myth,* Ballinger
Halbert, Gary C., *16 Amazing Secrets You Can Use To Sell Anything to Anyone without ever Meeting Them in Person*
Harper, Rose, *Mailing List Strategies*
Hodgson, Richard S., *Direct Mail and Mail Order Handbook*
Hopkins, Claude, *My Life in Advertising,* NCT Business Books
———, *Scientific Advertising*, NTC Business Books
Kabs, Jim, *Profitable Direct Marketing,* Crain
Karrass, Chester, *Give and Take,* Thomas Y. Crowell
———, *The Negotiation Game,* Thomas Y. Crowell
Kosel, Janice, *Bankruptcy — Do It Yourself*
———, *Chapter 13*
Lant, Jeffrey, *Money-Making Marketing,* JLA Publications
Levinson, Jay Conrad, *Guerilla Marketing,* Houghton Mifflin
———, *Guerilla Marketing Attack*
MacKay, Harry, *Swim with the Sharks,* William Morrow
Mancuso, Joseph, *How To Prepare and Present a Business Plan*
———, *How To Start, Finance, and Manage Your Own Business*
———, *How To Write a Winning Business Plan*
Maltz, Maxwell, *Psycho Cybernetics,* Wilshire
Ogilvy, David, *Confessions of an Advertising Man,* Atheneum
Porter, Michael, *Competitive Advantage,* The Free Press
———, *Competitive Strategy,* The Free Press
Powers, Melvin, *How To Get Rich in Mail Order,* Wilshire
Ries, Al, and Jack Trout, *Positioning,* McGraw-Hill
———, *Marketing Warfare*
Roman, Kenneth, and Jane Maas, *How To Advertise*
Ruff, Howard, *Making Money*

**Appendix H**

# RECOMMENDED READING

Schwab, Victor O., *How To Write a Good Advertisement,* Wilshire
Schwartz, Eugene M., *Breakthrough Advertising,* Boardroom Books
Simon, Julian, *How To Start and Operate a Mail Order Business,* McGraw-Hill
Stone, Bob, *Successful Direct Marketing Methods,* National Textbook
Tzu, Sun, *The Art of War,* Delacorte
Van Hoelscher, Russ, *Selling Information by Mail,* Profit Ideas

# GLOSSARY

## A

**Acceleration Clause:** Clause in trust deed or mortgage giving a lender the right to call all sums owing him to be immediately due and payable upon the happening of a certain event.

**Acceptance:** When the seller's or agent's principal agrees to the terms of the agreement of sale, approves the negotiation on the part of the agent, and acknowledges receipt of the deposit in subscribing to the agreement of sale, that act is termed the *acceptance*.

**Accrued Items of Expense:** Those incurred expenses that are not yet payable. The seller's accrued expenses are credited to the purchaser in the closing statement.

**Alienation:** The transferring of property from one person to another.

**Alienation Clause** (Acceleration Clause; Due on Sale Clause): A clause that states that upon sale or transfer of certain property, a loan is immediately due and payable.

**All-Inclusive Deed of Trust** (Wrap Around Contract): A form of deed of trust that, in addition to any other amounts actually financed, includes the amounts of any prior deeds of trust.

**Amortization:** The repayment of a debt in installments.

**Amortization mortgage:** A debt, of which the periodic repayments are used to reduce the principal outstanding as well as paying off the current interest charges.

**Apportionment:** The adjustment of the income, expenses, or carrying charges of real estate that are usually computed to the date of closing of title so that the seller pays all expenses to that date. The buyer assumes all expenses from the date on which the deed is conveyed to the buyer.

**Appraisal:** An estimate of a property's value made by an appraiser who is usually presumed to be an expert in this work.

**Appraisal by comparison:** An estimate of value made by comparing the sale prices of other similar properties.

**Appurtenance:** Something which is outside the property itself but belongs to the land and adds to its greater enjoyment, such as a right-of-way or a barn or a dwelling.

**Assessed valuation:** A valuation placed upon property by a public officer or a board as a basis for taxation.

**Assessment:** A charge against real estate made by a unit of government to cover a proportionate cost of an improvement such as a street or sewer.

**Assessor:** An official who has the responsibility of determining assessed valuation.

**Assessor's Parcel Number** (APN): A number assigned by the county tax assessor to identify a parcel of real property.

**Assignment:** The method or manner by which a right or contract is transferred from one person (the assignor) to another (the assignee).

**Assumption of mortgage:** Occurs when a person takes title to property and assumes liability for the payment of an existing note or bond secured by a mortgage against the property.

**Attest:** To witness to, either by observation or by signature.

## B

**Balloon payment:** A final installment payment, larger than previous installments that pays off a debt.

**Bankruptcy**: An action filed in a federal bankruptcy court that allows a creditor to reorganize or discharge credit obligations due to insolvency. A property owner may restrain foreclosure action by filing bankruptcy.

**Bearer:** Lender in whose hands the promissary note remains until it is paid in full.

**Beneficiary:** (1) One entitled to the benefit of a trust; (2) One who receives profit from an estate, the title of which is vested in a trustee; (3) The lender on a security of a note and deed of trust.

**Beneficiary's Statement** ("Benny Statement"): A written statement of the conditions and remaining balance of a loan secured by a deed of trust.

**Betterment:** A property improvement that increases the property's value.

**Bill of sale:** A document by which title to personal property is passed from seller to buyer.

## C

**Capital improvement:** Any permanent structure erected to extend the useful life and value of a property. (The replacement of a roof would be considered a capital improvement.)

**Chain of title:** A history of the conveyances and incumbrances affecting a title from the time the original patent was granted, or as far back as records are available.

**Chattel:** Personal property, such as household goods or fixtures.

**Chattel mortgage:** A mortgage on personal property.

**Client:** The one by whom a broker is employed (the principal) and by whom the broker will be compensated.

**Closing date:** The date upon which the buyer takes over the property.

**Cloud on the title:** An outstanding claim or encumbrance that, if valid, would affect or impair the owner's title.

**Collateral:** Additional security pledged for the payment of a debt.

**Color of title:** An apparent, invalid, title.

**Condemnation:** The acquisition of private property for public use, with fair compensation to the owner.

**Conditional sales contract:** A contract for the sale of property stating that, although delivery is to be made to the buyer, the title is to remain vested in the seller until the conditions of the contract have been fulfilled.

**Consideration:** Anything given as an inducement to enter into a contract, such as money or personal services. Any contract, lease, obligation, or mortgage may subsequently be modified without consideration provided that the change is made in writing and signed.

**Constructive notice:** Information that a person is assumed, by law, to have simply because it could be ascertained by proper diligence and enquiry, for example, information that is to be found in the public records.

**Conversion:** In terms of property, the exchange of personal or real property of one character or use for another.

**Conveyance:** The transfer of the title of land from one person to another.

**Correlation:** The final stage of the appraisal process in which the appraiser reviews the data and estimates the subject property's value.

**Covenants:** Agreements written into deeds and other instruments promising performance or nonperformance of certain acts, or stipulating certain uses or restrictions on the property.

**Current value:** The value at the time of an appraisal.

## D

**Debt Service:** Annual amount to be paid by a debtor for money borrowed.

**Deed:** An instrument in writing duly executed and delivered, that conveys title to real property.

**Deed of Reconveyance**: An instrument that releases and discharges a deed of trust.

**Deed restriction:** A restriction imposed in a deed to limit the use of the land. A deed might include clauses preventing the sale of liquor or defining the size, type, value, or placement of improvements.

**Deed of Trust** (Trust Deed): A deed given by the property owner to secure performance of an act (such as making payments on a loan). A deed of trust is a type of mortgage.

**Default:** Failure to fulfill a duty or promise, or to discharge an obligation; omission or failure to perform an act. In property foreclosure, usually the failure to pay loan installment repayments when they become due.

**Defeasance clause:** The clause in a mortgage that permits the mortgagor to redeem his or her property upon the payment of the obligations to the mortgagee.

**Deficiency judgment:** When the security for a loan is sold for less than the amount of the loan, the unpaid amount (the deficiency) is held by law (the judgment) to be the liability of the borrower unless the new owner has assumed the debt.

**Demand note:** A note that is payable on demand of the holder.

**Devise:** A gift of real estate made to the devisee in the will of the devisor.

**Distributee:** Person receiving or entitled to receive land as representative of the former owners.

**Documentary Transfer Tax:** A tax applicable to transfers of real property. Notice of payment is entered on the face of the deed or on a separate paper filed with the deed.

**Due on sale clause:** *See* Alienation clause.

## E

**Earnest money:** Down payment made by a purchaser of real estate as evidence of good faith.

**Easement:** A right that may be exercised by the public or individuals on, over, or through the property of others.

**Encroachment:** A building, part of a building, or obstruction that intrudes upon the property of another.

**Encumbrance:** *See* Incumbrance.

**Equity:** In real estate, the difference between the value of the property and the amount owed on it. Also call the owner's interest.

**Equity cushion:** The amount of equity required before a lender will make a loan.

**Equity loan:** Junior (subordinate) loan based on a percentage of the equity.

**Equity right of redemption:** A right of the owner to avert foreclosure by paying the debt, interest, and costs.

**Escrow:** A written agreement between two or more parties providing that certain instruments or property be entrusted to a third party to be delivered to a designated person upon the fulfillment or performance of some act or condition.

**Estate:** The degree, quantity, nature and extent of interest (ownership) that a person has in real property.

**Estoppel certificate:** An instrument executed by the mortgagor setting forth the status of and the balance due on the mortgage as of the date of the execution of the certificate.

**Eviction:** A legal proceeding by a landlord to recover possession of real property.

**Exclusive agency:** An agreement to employ one broker only. If the sale is made by any other broker both are entitled to commissions.

**Exclusive right to sell:** An agreement to give, for a specified period, only one broker the right to sell. If a sale during the term of the agreement is made by the owner or by any other broker, the broker holding the exclusive right is entitled to compensation.

**Extension agreement:** An agreement that extends the life of a mortgage.

### F

**FHA mortgage loan:** Mortgage loan insured by the Federal Housing Administration.

**Financing statement:** This is the instrument that is filed in order to give public notice of the security interest and thereby protect the interest of the secured parties in the collateral.

**First lien:** Debt recorded first against a property. *See also* First mortgage

**First mortgage:** Mortgage that has priority as a lien over all other mortgages. In cases of foreclosure, the first mortgage must be satisfied before other mortgages are paid off.

**Foreclosure:** A procedure whereby property pledged as security for a debt, is in the event of default in payments or terms, sold to pay the debt

**Front foot:** A measurement of property made for sale or valuation purposes by which each "front foot" on the street line extends the depth of the lot.

### G

**Grace period:** Additional time allowed to perform an act or make a payment before a default occurs.

**Grant:** A term used in deeds of conveyance of lands to indicate a transfer.

**Grant Deed:** A deed of conveyance that implys that the grantor (sellor) is granting an actual interest and has not previously granted such interest to anyone else.

**Grantee:** The party to whom the title to real property is conveyed.

**Grantor:** The person who conveys real estate by deed; the seller.

**Guardian's deed:** Issued to the person responsible for the estate of a minor or incompetent.

### H

**Habendum clause:** The "to have and to hold" clause that defines or limits the quantity of the estate granted in the deed.

**Hypothecate:** To use something as security without giving up possession of it.

### I

**Impound Account:** An account held by a lender that is used him or her to advance payments of certain expenses or charges (e.g., taxes and insurance) that are incidental to property ownership and that may protect the lender's security.

**Incumbrance:** Any right to or interest in property interfering with its use or transfer, or subjecting it to an obligation. In connection with foreclosure property, the most likely incumbrances are mortgages and claims for unpaid taxes.

***In rem*:** A legal proceeding taken against the property as distinguished from a proceeding taken against a person. Used in taking land for nonpayment of taxes, etc.

**Installments:** Parts of the same debt, payable at successive periods as agreed; payments made to reduce a mortgage.

**Instrument:** A written legal document.

**Involuntary lien:** A lien imposed against property without consent of the owner, e.g., taxes, special assessments.

**J**

**Jeopardy:** To have one's property or liberty subjected to a possibly adverse decree of a court or agency.

**Joint tenancy:** Ownership of property by two or more persons, each of whom has an undivided interest *(q.v.)* with the right of survivorship *(q.v.)*.

**Judicial Foreclosure:** A foreclosure action that is exectuted by the court.

**Junior mortgage:** A mortgage second or subsequent in lien (subordinate) to a previous mortgage.

**L**

**Land Sale Contract** (Contract of Sale): A document that may be used to sell real property that transfers ownership rights but does not actually transfer title.

**Lien:** A legal right or claim upon a specific property that attaches to the property until a debt is satisfied.

**Life estate:** The conveyance of title to property of the duration of the life of the grantee.

**Life tenant:** The holder of a life estate.

***Lis pendens*:** A legal document, filed in the office of the county clerk giving notice that an action or proceeding affecting the title to the property is pending in the courts .

**Listing:** An employment contract between principal and agent, authorizing the agent to perform services (usually the sale) for the principal involving the latter's property.

**Lot Book Report:** A report made by a title company that identifies any encumbrances recorded against a particular property. A lot book report does not identify liens recorded in the name of the owner that may affect property (e.g., abstract of judgement).

**M**

**Marketable title:** A title that the court considers to be so free from defect that it will enforce its acceptance by a purchaser.

**Mechanic's lien:** A claim made to secure the price of labor done upon and materials furnished for uncompensated improvement.

**Metes and bounds:** A term used in describing land by setting forth all the boundary lines together with their terminal points and angles.

**Mortgage:** An instrument in writing, duly executed and delivered, that creates a lien upon real estate as security for the payment of a specified debt, which is usually in the form of a bond.

**Mortgage commitment:** A formal indication, made by a lending institution, that it will grant a mortgage loan on property in a certain specified amount and on certain specified terms.

**Mortgage reduction certificate:** An instrument executed by the mortgagee (*q.v.*), setting forth the status of and the balance due on the mortgage as of the date of the execution of the instrument.

**Mortgagee:** The party who lends money and takes a mortgage to secure the payment.

**Mortgagor:** A person who borrows money and gives a mortgage on his or her property as security for the payment of the debt.

### N

**Notary public:** A person authorized to take acknowledgments to certain classes of documents, such as deeds, contracts, mortgages, and before whom affidavits may be sworn.

**Notice of default:** Letter sent to a defaulting party as a reminder of the default. It may state a grace period *(q.v.)* and the penalties for failing to cure the default.

**Notice of Rescission:** A document that is used to cancel a notice of default and declare that the default has been corrected.

### O

**Offest statement:** Statement by an owner of property or an owner of a lien against property setting forth the present status of the liens against said property.

**Open Mortgage:** A mortgage that has matured or is overdue and, therefore, is "open" to foreclosure at any time.

### P

**Party wall:** A wall built along the boundary between two properties.

**Performance bond:** A bond used to guarantee the specific completion of an endeavor in accordance with a contract.

**Plat Book:** A public record containing maps of land showing the division into streets, blocks, and lots and indicating the measurements of the individual parcels.

**Points:** Discount charges imposed by lenders to raise the yields on their loans.

**Power of Attorney:** A written instrument (document) duly signed and executed by an owner of property that authorizes an agent to act on behalf of the owner.

**Prepayment Clause:** A clause in a mortgage that gives a mortgagor (*q.v.*) the privilege of paying the morgage indebtedness before it becomes due.

**Proration:** Allocation of closing costs and credits to buyers and sellers.

**Purchase money mortgage:** A mortgage given by a grantee in part payment of the purchase price of real estate.

### Q

**Quiet title suit:** A suit in court to ascertain the legal rights of an owner to a certain parcel of real property.

**Quitclaim Deed:** A deed that conveys simply the grantor's rights or interest in real estate; generally considered inadequate except when interests are being passed from one spouse to the other.

### R

**Real Estate Owned:** Property acquired by a lender through foreclosure and held in inventory; commonly referred to as REO.

**Recording:** The act of writing or entering in a book of public record instruments affecting the title to real property.

**Recourse:** The right to claim against a prior owner of a property or note.

**Redemption:** The right of a mortgagor to redeem property by paying a debt before sale at foreclosure; the right of an owner to reclaim his or her property after it has been sold to settle claims for unpaid taxes.

**Release clause:** A clause included in a blanket mortgage that gives the owner of the property the privilege of paying off part of the debt, and thus freeing part of the property from the mortgage.

**Request for Notice of Default:** A document that under statutory provisions, allows certain interested parties to request and be entitled to notification of a default.

**Right of redemption:** *See* Equity Right of Redemption.

**Right of survivorship:** Right of the surviving joint owner to succeed to the interests of the deceased joint owner. This right is a distinguishing feature of a joint tenancy or tenancy by the entirety.

## S

**Sales contract:** A contract by which the buyer and seller agree to terms of sale.

**Satisfaction piece:** The receipt for a mortgage that has been paid off.

**Second Deed of Trust:** A Deed of Trust that is in a subordinate position to another Deed of Trust securing the same parcel.

**Second mortgage:** A mortgage made by a home buyer in addition to an existing first mortgage.

**Special Assessment:** An assessment made against a property to pay for a public improvement.

**Subdivision:** A tract of land divided into lots or plots.

**Subordination clause:** A clause in a mortgage that gives priority to a mortgage taken out at a later date.

**Survey:** The process by which a parcel of land is measured and its area ascertained; also the blueprint showing the measurements, boundaries, and area.

## T

**Tax sale:** Sale of property after a period of nonpayment of taxes.

**Tenancy in common:** An ownership of realty by two or more persons, each of whom has an undivided interest (*q.v.*), without the right of survivorship (*q.v.*).

**Tenancy by the entirety:** An estate that exists only between husband and wife with equal right of possession and enjoyment during their joint lives and with the right of survivorship.

**Tenancy at will:** A license to use or occupy lands and tenements at the will of the owner.

**Title:** Evidence of the ownership of land.

**Title Company:** Firm examining title to real estate and/or issuing title insurance.

**Title defect:** Unresolved claim against the ownership of property that prevents presentation of a marketable title. Such claims may arise from failure of the owner's spouse, or former part owner, to sign a deed, current liens against the property, or an interruption in the title records of a property.

**Title insurance:** A policy of insurance that protects the holder from any loss caused by defects in the title.

**Title Report:** Document indicating the current state of the title, such as easements, covenants, liens, and any other defects. The title report does not describe the chain of title.

**Title search:** An examination of the public records to determine the ownership and encumbrances affecting real property.

**Torrens Title:** A system provided by state law for the registration of land titles whereby the ownership and encumbrances can be readily ascertained from an inspection of the Register of Titles without the necessity of a search of public records.

**Trust Deed:** Conveyance of real estate to a third party to be held for the benefit of another. It is commonly used in some states in place of mortgages that conditionally convey title to the lender.

**Trustee:** One who holds legal title to property in trust for the benefit of another person and who is required to carry out specific duties with regard to the property, or who has been given power affecting the disposition of property for another's benefit.

**Trustee's Deed:** A Deed given by the trustees to the successful bidder at a trustee's sale. A Trustee's Deed may effectively remove subordinate liens.

**Trustee's Sale:** A nonjudicial action whereby a trustee may auction and sell property secured by a Deed of Trust subsequent to a default in the terms and conditions of the loan.

**Trustee's Sale Guarantee:** A title insurance policy for the benefit of the trustee handling a foreclosure action.

## U

**Undivided interest:** Ownership of real estate by joint tenants or tenants in common under the same title.

## V

**Valuation:** Estimated worth or price. The act of valuing by appraisal.

**Vendee's lien:** A lien against property under contract of sale to secure a deposit paid by a purchaser.

## W

**Warranty Deed:** A conveyance of land in which the grantor guarantees the title to the grantee.

**Without recourse:** Words used in endorsing a note or bill to denote that the future holder is not to look to the endorser in case of nonpayment.

**Wraparound Contract:** *See* All-inclusive Deed of Trust.

**Wraparound loan:** A new loan encompassing any existing loans.

# INDEX

## ORDER FORM FOR BOOK AND TAPES

Please send me the following items for *YOUR COMPLETE GUIDE TO FORECLOSURE PROFITS:* Actual case studies of transactions from A to Z; How to make $10,000 in seven weeks and $30,000 in 16 weeks; How to bid on HUD Repos; VA discounts bidding; Illustrations.

| | Quantity | Unit Price | Total |
|---|---|---|---|
| **Book —hard cover** | | **$95.00** | |
| **Tape Set — 12 hours** | | **$150.00** | |
| **Book and Tapes** | | **$200.00** | |
| | | Subtotal | |
| | | CA residents add 8-1/4% sales tax | |
| | | Shipping and Handling | **$5.00** |
| | | **TOTAL** | |

*Send this order with check for total to:*

**NEW GROWTH FINANCIAL**
P. O. Box 490
Danville, CA 94526-0490

**SHIP TO:**

Name______________________________

Address____________________________

City__________________State______Zip______

I understand that I may return these items for a full refund if not completely satisfied.

## ORDER FORM FOR BOOK AND TAPES

**P**lease send me the following items for *YOUR COMPLETE GUIDE TO FORECLOSURE PROFITS:* Actual case studies of transactions from A to Z; How to make $10,000 in seven weeks and $30,000 in 16 weeks; How to bid on HUD Repos; VA discounts bidding; Illustrations.

| | Quantity | Unit Price | Total |
|---|---|---|---|
| **Book —hard cover** | | **$95.00** | |
| **Tape Set — 12 hours** | | **$150.00** | |
| **Book and Tapes** | | **$200.00** | |
| | | Subtotal | |
| | | CA residents add 8-1/4% sales tax | |
| | | Shipping and Handling | **$5.00** |
| | | **TOTAL** | |

*Send this order with check for total to:*

**NEW GROWTH FINANCIAL**
P. O. Box 490
Danville, CA 94526-0490

**SHIP TO:**

Name______________________________

Address______________________________

City________________ State______ Zip______

I understand that I may return these items for a full refund if not completely satisfied.

FREE — BONUS — FREE — BONUS — FREE — BONUS — FREE — BONUS

*If you didn't purchase this book directly from the author and want to know more about escrow — or add another case study to your library of knowledge....*

***Clip this coupon and mail to:*** **NEW GROWTH FINANCIAL**
P. O. Box 490
Danville, CA 94526-0490

***Ship information to:***

**Name**____________________________

**Address** ____________________________

**City**____________________ **State**______ **Zip** ______

FREE — BONUS — FREE — BONUS — FREE — BONUS — FREE — BONUS

## ORDER FORM for FORECLOSURE GOLDMINING

**Yes** — Rush me *FORECLOSURE GOLDMINING, High Profit, Low Risk Real Estate for the 90'$.*

| | Quantity | Unit Price | Total |
|---|---|---|---|
| **Book — Perfectbound 432 pages** | | **$29.95** | |
| | | | |
| | | | |

*Send this order with check for total to:*

**NEW GROWTH FINANCIAL**
P. O. Box 490
Danville, CA 94526-0490

| | |
|---|---|
| Subtotal | |
| CA residents add 8-1/4% sales tax | |
| Shipping and Handling $5.00, $1.50 each additional book | |
| **TOTAL** | |

**SHIP TO:**

Name____________________________

Address____________________________

City____________________ State______ Zip______

I understand that I may return these items for a full refund if not completely satisfied.


## ORDER FORM for FORECLOSURE GOLDMINING

**Yes** — Rush me *FORECLOSURE GOLDMINING, High Profit, Low Risk Real Estate for the 90'$.*

| | Quantity | Unit Price | Total |
|---|---|---|---|
| **Book — Perfectbound 432 pages** | | **$29.95** | |
| | | | |
| | | | |

*Send this order with check for total to:*

**NEW GROWTH FINANCIAL**
P. O. Box 490
Danville, CA 94526-0490

| | |
|---|---|
| Subtotal | |
| CA residents add 8-1/4% sales tax | |
| Shipping and Handling $5.00, $1.50 each additional book | |
| **TOTAL** | |

**SHIP TO:**

Name____________________________

Address____________________________

City____________________ State______ Zip______

I understand that I may return these items for a full refund if not completely satisfied.